Luc Roubeux
7 juillet '97.
Montréal.

DATABASE
MANAGEMENT
AND DESIGN
▼

DATABASE MANAGEMENT AND DESIGN

▼

GARY W. HANSEN
Brigham Young University

JAMES V. HANSEN
Brigham Young University

SECOND EDITION

PRENTICE HALL
Upper Saddle River, New Jersey 07458

Library of Congress Cataloging-in-Publication Data

Hansen, Gary W. (Gary William)
    Database management and design / Gary W. Hansen, James V. Hansen.
  — 2nd ed.
      p.   cm.
    Includes bibliographical references and index.
    ISBN 0-13-308800-6 (hard cover)
    1. Database management.   2. Database design.   I. Hansen, James
  V. II. Title.
    QA76.9.D3H348   1996
    005.74—dc20
                                   95-34167
                                         CIP

ACQUISITIONS EDITOR: PJ Boardman
EDITORIAL ASSISTANT: Jane Avery
DESIGN DIRECTOR: Patricia Wosczyk
INTERIOR DESIGNERS: Lisa Delgado/Lorraine Castellano
COVER DESIGNER: Lorraine Castellano
COVER IMAGE: KYOTO a quilt created by Miriam Nathan-Roberts
MANUFACTURING BUYER: Paul Smolenski

 © 1996 by Prentice-Hall, Inc.
A Simon & Schuster Company
Upper Saddle River, New Jersey 07458

Printed in the United States of America

10 9 8 7 6 5 4 3 2 1

ISBN 0-13-308800-6

Prentice-Hall International (UK) Limited, *London*
Prentice-Hall of Australia Pty. Limited, *Sydney*
Prentice-Hall Canada Inc., *Toronto*
Prentice-Hall Hispanoamericana, S.A., *Mexico*
Prentice-Hall of India Private Limited, *New Delhi*
Prentice-Hall of Japan, Inc., *Tokyo*
Simon & Schuster Asia Pte. Ltd., *Singapore*
Editora Prentice-Hall do Brasil, Ltda., *Rio de Janeiro*

To our parents

William E. and Ellen N. Hansen

and

Heber L. and Myrtle J. Hansen

BRIEF CONTENTS

CONTENTS

Part Two

DATABASE DESIGN   83

Four

Five

Part Three

RELATIONAL DATABASE IMPLEMENTATION   173

Six

Part Four

MANAGING THE DATABASE ENVIRONMENT   361

Eleven

Twelve

Part Six
LEGACY DATABASE SYSTEMS   487

PREFACE

This book is intended to be used as a text in introductory database courses for information systems students at either the undergraduate or graduate level. As such, it may be easily integrated into a larger information systems curriculum that includes business programming, systems analysis, system design, data communications, etc.

The book provides comprehensive coverage of business database systems. It is organized around the database development life cycle which provides the framework for discussing conceptual and implementation design, database implementation, and the management environment. Throughout the book, we use conceptual data modeling, first as a basis for a thorough discussion of conceptual design, and then subsequently as a means for design implementation using the relational, hierarchical, and network models. We also include coverage of languages in all models, as well as client/server database implementations and knowledge-base systems. All of these topics are set in a framework of strategic and tactical management issues that include database planning, DBMS selection, database administration, security and integrity, and distributed databases.

▼ Distinguishing Features

▼ The book has a simple and straightforward topical organization that is based on the database development life cycle. This makes it easy for students to see how topics relate to each other and where the material being studied fits into an organization's overall system development activities. Early chapters introduce concepts of strategic data planning, data sharing, and three-level architecture, emphasizing the concept that the technical aspects of database systems are determined by genuine business information needs.

▼ We provide a thorough coverage of conceptual design in Chapter 4. This includes the traditional basic coverage of objects, relationships, and attributes as well as in-depth coverage of more powerful topics, such as aggregation.

▼ Conceptual data design forms the basis for our approach to database design in the relational (Chapters 5-6), network (Chapter 15), and hierarchical (Chapter 16) models. Because of the modular structure of the chapters, design in these models may also be taught without references to object-oriented modeling.

▼ Four business cases featuring a distribution company, a manufacturer, a construction company, and a consulting firm are continued throughout the book. We include dialogue that relates directly to realistic business database problems.

▼ We provide flexibility for the different approaches used by different instructors. The chapters are self-contained, allowing chapters to be selected for coverage as desired.

▼ The book includes thorough coverage of relational languages: SQL (Chapter 7), Query-by-Example (Chapter 8), and relational algebra and calculus (Chapter 6), as well as the standard languages for hierarchical and network databases. We also include new coverage relating to client/server DBMS's (Chapter 9). The SQL chapter includes extensive new coverage on the SQL-92 ANSI standard, and our chapter on QBE discusses general aspects of the language as well as its implementation in a particular commercial system. Throughout these chapters on language, our tutorial style presents many examples and gives detailed explanations of each language feature.

▼ New Material in This Edition

▼ This edition includes substantial coverage of client/server systems, including an entire chapter devoted to client/server DBMS's and application development environments. Specifically, we examine features of Oracle and SQL Server Database Management Systems and the PowerBuilder application development environment. We explore principles that these systems introduce that provide powerful additions to the theoretical basis found throughout the book.

▼ Our SQL chapter has been enhanced to include significant coverage of the SQL-92 standard. Those features relating to data definition language, foreign key and other constraint definition, new data types, and relational algebra operation implementation are explored in some detail.

▼ Chapter 2 provides the Bonhomie Case which was previously included as a supplement. This case makes it possible for the student to get immediate "hands-on" experience with a database system while obtaining background in the process of system development.

▼ Existing chapters have been reworked and enhanced. This has resulted, for example, in new material on physical implementation (dynamic hashing), distributed database systems (optimal file allocation), and an entirely new section on object-oriented database systems.

▼ Teaching and Learning Aids in the Text

▼ Each chapter begins with a scenario taken from the four continued cases. The scenario presents a realistic situation dealing directly with the chapter's material and highlighting the chapter's key topics. This scenario is immediately followed by a list of chapter objectives, stated as skills the student will acquire. The balance of each chapter includes numerous other examples based on these four continued cases as well as a number of other cases.

▼ A very large number of figures are included to illustrate database modeling, query solutions, and other topics. Our chapter on client/server systems includes illustrations taken directly from computer screens used to develop our examples. We use the second color to highlight important ideas in figures.

▼ The book has a large bibliography listing up-to-date research articles so that interested students may explore topics in depth.

▼ End-of-chapter materials are standardized. Each chapter includes a summary of the chapter's material. Additionally, materials for assignment include review questions which can be answered directly from the text; problems and exercises which stress and develop depth of understanding; and projects and professional issues for more advanced work.

▼ A margin glossary gives definitions of key terms in the margins of the text where they are available for easy reference. A comprehensive glossary is provided in the back of the book.

▼ A Note on Notation

Throughout the book, many examples are presented to illustrate concepts in data modeling, languages, and so forth. Compound data names are often used in these examples. Sometimes we use hyphens to join the parts of these compound names, and sometimes we use underscores. Our choice of connector (hyphen or underscore) is normally dictated by the prevailing use in industry. For example, the data names in the chapter on the network model use hyphens as required by the CODASYL standard, whereas the chapters on SQL and QBE use underscores.

The student implementing a particular project or case on a live system should determine which convention the system requires. A successful implementation of one of our examples may require converting hyphens to underscores or vice versa. In any case, the conversion is not difficult, and any comparison of our results with the student's should not cause confusion.

▼ To the Instructor

Our aim throughout the book is to provide material for both the beginning and advanced student, presented in a lucid manner. We have also addressed several different viewpoints. Thus, if you desire to present the subject from a management viewpoint or from a technical viewpoint you may select chapters as needed for your approach. If your interest is to emphasize database design or data manipulation languages, the book provides strong support in both of these areas. Finally, you may select chapters to follow a traditional approach to the subject, or you may embark on more advanced topics emphasizing current research directions. The following list of chapters in several areas can be used to tailor your course to your requirements.

Management Chapters
1, 2, 3, 11, 12, 13

Technical Chapters
2, 4, 5, 6, 7, 8, 9, 10, 14, 15, 16

Database Design Chapters
4, 6, 10, 15, 16

Language Chapters
6, 7, 8, 9, 14, 15, 16

Advanced Chapters...
4, 7, 9, 14

At Brigham Young University, we use the book in a two-semester sequence. The first semester focuses on database design and management, covering Chapters 1-6, 10, and selections from 11-16. The second semester focuses on database languages and decision support, covering Chapters 7, 8, 9, and portions of 11-16.

▼ Supplements

In order to aid professors using Database Design and Management, an *Instructor's Manual* has been prepared by the authors. The instructor's manual provides the instructor with teaching suggestions, suggested answers to all problems and exercises in the textbook, test questions, and overhead transparency masters for selected figures from the textbook. We are also providing case supplements, written by Jim Hansen, that provide tutorials in Microsoft *Access* and *Paradox for Windows*.

▼ Acknowledgments

A number of reviewers provided useful insights and suggestions that helped in preparing the final version of the book. They are: Kirk P. Arnett, Mississippi State University; David J. Auer, Western Washington University; Eli B. Cohen, Wichita State University; Orlando E. Katter, Jr., Wingate College; Rajeev Kaula, Southwest Missouri State University; Richard Kerns, East Carolina University; Constance A. Knapp, Pace University; Paul E. Laski, Northern Virginia Community College; Ronald Maestas, New Mexico Highlands University; Scott McIntyre, University of Colorado; Victor Meyers, Hawaii Pacific University; Stevan Mrdalj, Eastern Michigan University; William P. Wagner, Villanova University; and Ahmed Zaki, College of William and Mary.

1

DATABASES
AND THEIR CONTEXT

▼

I n Part I you will be introduced to databases and database systems. As we outline the historical and organizational context of databases, our discussion will focus on answers to the following questions:

What is a database and what is a database system?

How did database systems originate?

How are database systems developed?

How do organizations use and control databases?

Chapter 1 deals with the first two of these questions. In this chapter we review the historical development of database systems. We see how business needs have shaped the development of technology and how the information implicit in data has come to be regarded as a valuable corporate resource. Our discussion will conclude with a description of the four principal components of a database system: hardware, software, data, and people.

Chapter 2 addresses the next question. Here we examine a typical application and look at the step-by-step process of database system development. You will see how an actual database system can be implemented on a typical system. If you have access to a database management system, you will have the opportunity to develop table definitions and screens to implement this sample database.

Chapter 3 answers the last question by discussing database systems in their organizational context and by introducing and discussing the database development life cycle. We discuss the need for sharing data at all levels of an organization, describe the process of strategic data planning, and outline the role database administration personnel play in controlling and protecting the database. We also show that database design, although performed concurrently with system design, should be placed in a larger framework than the design of any one system. A well-conceived database will then become the foundation for many application systems.

C H A P T E R

DATABASE SYSTEMS AND THE EVOLUTION OF DATABASE TECHNOLOGY

Susan Broadbent, CEO, and Sanford Mallon, CIO (chief information officer), of International Product Distribution are verbally sparring over systems technology. Susan, seeing an opportunity for some fun, needles him: "You want us to convert to a client/server database system, Sandy? Is this another one of your harebrained schemes?" Sanford responded, "Harebrained? When have I ever made a proposal that wasn't conceived with brilliance and executed with intricate precision?"

"Well, let's see. When you came here, you took us from our manual system to a file-oriented system. Then came the database systems—network followed by relational. Now you want to go to a client/server platform. If those schemes were brilliantly conceived, why did they have to be changed every few years?"

Sanford laughed. Susan's smile told him she was well aware of the reasons for each change and of the significant benefits the company reaped each time. He replied, "It's been a long haul, hasn't it, keeping up with technology?"

"Yes. But you've been exceptional at staying abreast of developments and moving us to them when they would help our business the most. And to think that it all began so simply . . . ."

Susan Broadbent and Sanford Mallon are reflecting with satisfaction on several decades of business growth supported by data access technology. In this chapter, we review (1) the development of this technology as it affected and was affected by business needs and (2) the four major components of a modern database system—hardware, software, data, and people. After reading this chapter, you should be able to:

▼ Discuss the strengths and weaknesses of the early sequential and random access file systems.

▼ Explain how information has come to be regarded as a valuable resource in modern organizations.

▼ Describe the historical evolution of the hierarchical, network, and relational database systems and the business needs that led to their development.

▼ Explain how four components—hardware, software, data, and people—work together to form today's database systems.

▼ The Evolution of Database Technology

The sophistication of modern database technology is the result of a decades-long evolution in data processing and information management. Tugged on one side by the needs and demands of management, and restrained on the other by the limits of technology, data access technology has developed from the primitive methods of the fifties to the powerful, integrated systems of today.

Management's expectations have grown in parallel to the evolution of technology. The early data processing systems performed clerical tasks that reduced paper handling. More recent systems have expanded to production and management of information, which has come to be viewed as a vital company resource. Today the most important function of database systems is to provide the basis for corporate management information systems.

Implementation of technological change has been guided by genuine business needs. Management will only authorize a new computer system when it sees a clear benefit to offset the system's cost. And despite pitfalls and risks, benefits have been realized in many cases. Moreover, the end is not yet in sight and won't be for some time to come. New technology, such as object-oriented databases and client/server platforms, addresses new problems and will result in more powerful systems for the future.

The close relationship between database technology and business needs may be easier to understand if we take a closer look at the experience of International Product Distribution.

▼ Case: International Product Distribution

Susan Broadbent is founder, owner, and president of International Product Distribution (IPD), which sells over 3,500 products from more than 300 manufacturers in countries all over the world. IPD has headquarters in Chicago with international offices in Brussels, Buenos Aires, Lagos, New Delhi, Tokyo, and Sydney. More than 2,700 sales representatives work locally in over 100 countries, each of them reporting to a regional office. The company has annual revenue of about $500 million and profit of about $50 million.

After selling children's clothing for a single manufacturer to department stores in the Chicago area for a number of years, Susan decided she could increase her income significantly if she represented several manufacturers. Thus, she founded International Product Distribution. Her concept was simple: (1) Identify manufacturers in various countries whose products consistently exhibit a strong standard of quality. (2) Identify retail outlets that emphasize the sale of such products. (3) Establish strong business relationships with both manufacturers and retailers by providing the retailers with appropriate products from the manufacturers.

Initially, she had a small staff and dealt only with Chicago area retailers and midwestern manufacturers. Shortly, however, she was supplying products to merchants from St. Louis to Cleveland. Her first international sales were to stores in Toronto. After three years, IPD had representatives in Europe, and two years later in Tokyo. Offices in Buenos Aires, Sydney, Lagos, and New Delhi followed. Employees in each office included sales representatives and buyers. Purchased products were sold in the country of manufacture or could be exported for sale in another country. Figure 1.1 illustrates the relationship between IPD and its suppliers and retailer customers. As you can see, products flow from the manufacturer to an IPD warehouse and on to the retailer.

When the company was young, records of sales, product purchases, and inventory were kept by hand. By the end of the second year, however, business had grown to the extent that it was necessary to purchase a minicomputer to track this information and produce reports, billing statements, and payments, as shown in Figure 1.2. Sanford Mallon was hired to implement this file-oriented system and manage a staff of programmers, data entry operators, and operations personnel.

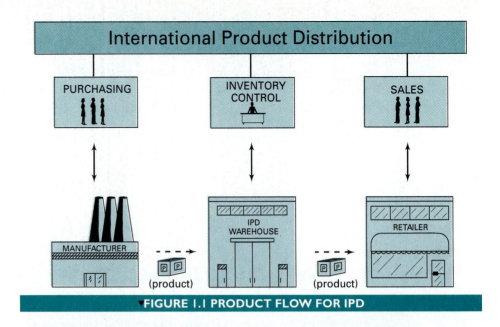

▼FIGURE 1.1 PRODUCT FLOW FOR IPD

▼FIGURE 1.2 DATA PROCESSING FLOW FOR IPD

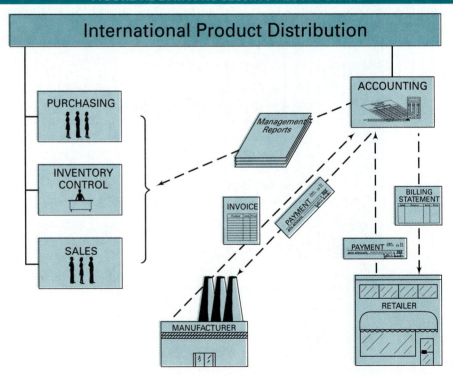

▼ File-Oriented Systems

Early business computer systems were used primarily for accounting functions: accounts receivable, accounts payable, payroll, and so on. These functions had to be carried out for a business to operate. Consequently, the cost of computer systems that could perform these functions was easy to justify. The manual effort required for payroll or accounts receivable, for example, was so great that an automated system that could replace the manual system would pay for itself in a short time.

Because these systems performed normal record-keeping functions, they were called **data processing systems.** Not surprisingly, the programmers and analysts who designed them followed their natural inclination to mimic the existing manual procedures in their programming. Thus, the computer files corresponded to paper files, and the records in the computer files contained information that an individual file folder in a manual system might contain.

Figure 1.3 shows some files and sample data from the original file-oriented system of International Product Distribution. Each table represents a file in the system. That is, we have a CUSTOMER file, a SALES-REPRESENTATIVE file, a PRODUCT file, and so on. Each row represents a record in the file. Thus, the PRODUCT file contains three records. Each of these records contains data about a different product. The individual data items or fields in the PRODUCT file are PROD-ID, PROD-DESC, MANUFACTR-ID, COST, and PRICE.

data processing system An automated system for processing the data for the records of an organization.

▼FIGURE 1.3 SAMPLE DATA FROM THE FILE-ORIENTED SYSTEM AT IPD

CUSTOMER

CUST-ID	CUST-NAME	ADDRESS	COUNTRY	BEGINNING-BALANCE	MONTH-TO-DATE-PAYMENTS
100	Watabe Bros	Box 241, Tokyo	Japan	45,551	40,113
101	Maltzl	Salzburg	Austria	75,314	65,200
105	Jefferson	B 918, Chicago	USA	49,333	49,811
110	Gomez	Santiago	Chile	27,400	28,414

SALES-REPRESENTATIVE

SALREP-ID	SALREP-NAME	MANAGER-ID	OFFICE	COMM-%
10	Rodney Jones	27	Chicago	10
14	Masaji Matsu	44	Tokyo	11
23	Francois Moire	35	Brussels	9
37	Elena Hermana	12	B.A.	13
39	Goro Azuma	44	Tokyo	10

PRODUCT

PROD-ID	PROD-DESC	MANUFACTR-ID	COST	PRICE
1035	Sweater	210	11.25	22.00
2241	Table Lamp	317	22.25	33.25
2518	Brass Sculpture	253	13.60	21.20

SALE

DATE	CUST-ID	SALREP-ID	PROD-ID	QTY	TOTAL-PRICE
02/08	100	14	2241	200	6650.00
02/12	101	23	2518	300	6360.00
02/12	101	23	1035	150	3300.00
02/19	100	39	2518	200	4240.00
02/22	101	23	1035	200	4400.00
02/25	105	10	2241	100	3325.00
02/25	110	37	2518	150	3180.00

MANUFACTURER

MANUFACTR-ID	MANUFACTR-NAME	ADDRESS	COUNTRY
210	Kiwi Klothes	Aukland	New Zealand
253	Brass Works	Lagos	Nigeria
317	Llana Llamps	Lima	Peru

Inadequate Data Manipulation Capabilities.   Indexed sequential files allowed applications to access a particular record by a key, such as a Product ID. For example, if we knew the Product ID for table lamps, we could directly access the product's record within the PRODUCT file. This was adequate so long as we only wanted a single record.

However, suppose we wanted a set of related records. We might be interested, for example, in identifying all sales to IPD's customer Maltzl. Perhaps we need to know the total number of sales, or the average price, or which products are being purchased and from which manufacturers. Such information would be difficult, if not impossible, to obtain from a file system because file systems are unable to provide strong connections between data in different files. Database systems were specifically developed to make the interrelating of data in different files much easier.

Excessive programming effort.   A new application program often required an entirely new set of file definitions. Even though an existing file may contain some of the data needed, the application often required a number of other data items. As a result, the programmer had to recode definitions of needed data items from the existing file as well as definitions of all new data items. Thus, in file-oriented systems, there was a heavy interdependence between programs and data.

Even more important, data manipulation in file-oriented languages such as COBOL was difficult for complex applications. This meant that both the initial and the maintenance programming efforts for management information applications were significant.

Databases provide a separation between program and data, so that programs can be somewhat independent of the details of data definition. By providing access to a pool of shared data and by supporting powerful data manipulation languages, database systems eliminate a large amount of initial and maintenance programming.

▼ Database Systems

Database systems overcome these limitations of file-oriented systems. By supporting an integrated, centralized data structure, database systems eliminate problems with data redundancy and data control. A centralized database is available throughout the company and if, for example, a customer's name must be changed, the change is available to all users. Data are controlled via a data dictionary/directory (DD/D) system, which is itself controlled by a group of company employees known as database administrators (DBAs). New data access methods greatly simplify the process of relating data elements, which in turn enhances data manipulation. All of these features of database systems simplify the programming effort and reduce program maintenance.

data model A conceptual method of structuring data.

At present we are in the midst of a decades-long effort to develop increasingly powerful database management systems. This process has seen the evolutionary development of systems based on three principal **data models,** or conceptual methods of structuring data. These three data models are the hierarchical, the network, and the relational. In the next two sections, we outline the historical development of database systems based on these three models.

Hierarchical and Network Model Systems

Indexed sequential files solved the problem of directly accessing a single record within a file. For example, take another look at Figure 1.3. If we had the first sale record shown in the SALE file but wanted to know the name and address of the customer involved in the sale, we could simply use the Customer ID (100) to look up the customer's record in the CUSTOMER file. This tells us that the customer who made the order was Watabe Bros.

Now suppose that we want to reverse the process. Instead of wanting to know the customer involved in a sale, we want to know all the sales to a given customer. We start with the Watabe Bros. customer record, and now we want all their sale records. We cannot do this directly in a file system. It was for such applications that database systems were originally developed.

The first database systems, introduced in the mid-sixties, were based on the **hierarchical model,** which assumes all data relationships can be structured as hierarchies. To illustrate this we modify our database of Figure 1.3 slightly. Now instead of sales which contain only a single product, we have invoices which in turn have invoice lines. Each customer has multiple invoices, and each invoice has multiple lines. Each line records the sale of a single product. Figure 1.8 gives some examples. The INVOICE and INVOICE LINE files replace the SALE file from Figure 1.3.

Figure 1.9 illustrates how we can make a hierarchy showing the relationships between customers, invoices, and invoice lines. A customer is thought to "own" invoices, which in turn "own" invoice lines. In a hierarchical database system, these three files would be tied together by physical pointers, or data fields added to the individual records. A **pointer** is a physical address which identifies where a record can be found on disk. Each customer record would contain a pointer to the first invoice record for that customer record. The invoice records would in turn contain pointers to other invoice records and to invoice line records. Thus, the system would easily be able to retrieve all the invoices and invoice lines that apply to a given customer.

hierarchical model A data model that assumes all data relationships can be structured as hierarchies.

pointer A physical address which identifies where a record can be found on disk.

▼FIGURE 1.8 IPD FILES HAVING A HIERARCHICAL RELATIONSHIP

```
CUSTOMER
```

CUST-ID	CUST-NAME	ADDRESS	COUNTRY	BEGINNING-BALANCE	MONTH-TO-DATE-PAYMENTS
100	Watabe Bros	Box 241, Tokyo	Japan	45,551	40,113
101	Maltzl	Salzburg	Austria	75,314	65,200
105	Jefferson	B 918, Chicago	USA	49,333	49,811
110	Gomez	Santiago	Chile	27,400	28,414

```
INVOICE
```

INVOICE-#	DATE	CUST-ID	SALREP-ID
1012	02/10	100	39
1015	02/14	110	37
1020	02/20	100	14

```
INVOICE LINE
```

INVOICE-#	LINE-#	PROD-ID	QTY	TOTAL-PRICE
1012	01	1035	100	2200.00
1012	02	2241	200	6650.00
1012	03	2518	300	6360.00
1015	01	1035	150	3300.00
1015	02	2518	200	4240.00
1020	01	2241	100	3325.00
1020	02	2518	150	3180.00

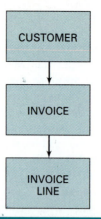

Suppose we are interested in adding information about customers to our hierarchical database. For example, since our customers are department store companies, we may want to keep a list of stores for each customer. In that case, we would expand the diagram of Figure 1.9 to look like that of Figure 1.10. CUSTOMER is still related to INVOICE, which is related to INVOICE LINE. CUSTOMER is also related, however, to STORE and STORE is related to CONTACT. By CONTACT, we mean a buyer to whom we would sell merchandise for a particular store. We see from this diagram that CUSTOMER is at the top of a hierarchy from which a large amount of information can be derived.

These figures show the kind of interfile relationships that are easily implemented in the hierarchical model. It became apparent very quickly, however, that this model had some significant limitations, since not all relationships could be expressed easily in a hierarchical framework. For example, to take the present case a step further, it is obvious that we are not only interested in the relationship between customers and invoices; we are also interested in the relationship between sales representatives and invoices. That is, we want to know all the invoices that a particular sales representative has produced so that we can issue commission statements. This new relationship is shown in Figure 1.11.

**▼FIGURE 1.10 A HIERARCHICAL MODEL OF THE RELATIONSHIP
BETWEEN CUSTOMER, INVOICE, AND STORE**

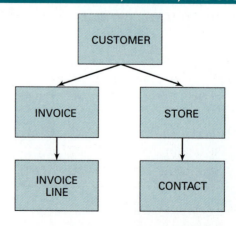

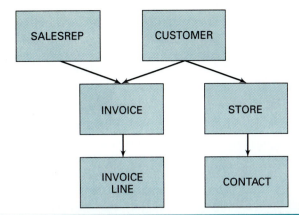

▼ FIGURE 1.11 A NETWORK MODEL OF THE RELATIONSHIP
BETWEEN SALES REP, CUSTOMER, AND INVOICE

child An "owned" record in a hierarchical relationship.

parent An "owner" record in a hierarchical relationship.

network A data relationship in which a record can be owned by records from more than one file.

This diagram is not a hierarchy, however. In a hierarchy, a **child** can have only one **parent.** In Figure 1.10, INVOICE is a child and CUSTOMER is its parent. In Figure 1.11, though, INVOICE has two parents—SALESREP and CUSTOMER. We call diagrams like these **networks.** Because of the obvious need to handle such relationships, in the late sixties *network* database systems were developed. Like hierarchical database systems, network database systems used physical pointers to tie records in different files together.

The dominant hierarchical DBMS is IBM's IMS, developed in the mid-sixties. In the late sixties and early seventies, a number of network DBMSs were developed and successfully marketed, and this data model was eventually standardized as the CODASYL model. We will discuss both of these data models and their data definition and manipulation capabilities at length in later chapters.

Relational Database Systems

The use of physical pointers was at once a strength and a weakness of the hierarchical and the network database systems. The pointers were a strength because they allowed the quick retrieval of data having predetermined relationships. The weakness was that these relationships had to be determined *before* the system was put into operation. Data based on other relationships were difficult, if not impossible, to retrieve. As users became more familiar with database systems and their power to manipulate data, they quickly found these limitations unacceptable, as this encounter at IPD shows.

"Cordelia, we are getting quite frustrated with the number of management questions our database system cannot answer easily. When you and Sandy convinced us that we should convert to a network database system, you claimed that we would be able to answer most questions that we would be likely to ask."

Susan Broadbent, IPD CEO, and Dick Greenberg, IPD sales manager, are talking to IPD's database administrator (DBA), Cordelia Molini, about the shortcomings of their current network database management system. This is not a new complaint.

With each new system, IPD management finds as they begin to ask "What if . . ." questions that the system does less than they would like. Although the network system has served them well for several years, they are now reaching the point where more and more of the information they need is difficult to obtain. Cordelia is well aware of these frustrations.

"Well, perhaps we should have said many *questions you would be likely to ask. With experience, we have found that there is a very broad variety of questions users want to ask." Cordelia continues: "The problem we face is that the network system depends on* physical *pointers to tie data in different files together. If you ask a question that does not naturally follow those pointers, we can't answer the question without a significant amount of programming. Now tell me, can you give me a better idea of the types of questions you need answers to?"*

Dick replies immediately. "We want to answer all kinds of questions, Cordelia. We really can't characterize them by type because that would be too limiting. Ideally, we would like to be able to ask any question we want, and if the answer is in the data, the system will give us the answer."

"From what you say, it sounds like we need to seriously consider moving to a relational database system. Physical pointers aren't used in a relational system. Data can be related if a logical *connection exists, so we don't have to worry about defining which relationships are most likely to be used by the system."*

Susan asks, "Does that mean, for example, that Dick can ask whether products made in Ghana are selling well in Korea? Or how well a sales representative in Rio is doing selling electronic equipment from Amsterdam?"

"Yes. Both those questions are easy to answer in a relational system. Besides, you will find you will not have to work through a programmer nearly as often. Managers who are willing to learn a relatively simple data manipulation language can answer more of their own questions by accessing the system directly. What do you think, Susan?"

"It sounds like something that deserves further investigation. If the technology is sound, we should think seriously about moving to it. Why don't you look into it and put together a proposal?"

In 1970, E. F. Codd published a revolutionary paper (Codd, 1970) that strongly challenged the conventional wisdom of the database "establishment." Codd argued that data should be related through natural, logical relationships inherent in the data rather than through physical pointers. That is, people should be able to combine data from different sources, if the logical information needed to make the combination was present in the data. This opened up an entirely new vista for management information systems, since database queries need no longer be limited by the relationships indicated by physical pointers.

To illustrate the shortcomings of database systems that rely on physical pointers, consider Figure 1.12. Here we have shown that CUSTOMER, INVOICE, and INVOICE LINE are connected by physical pointers. MANUFACTURER and PRODUCT are also connected. The broken line between INVOICE LINE and PRODUCT indicates that these two are *logically* related, since every invoice line refers to a specific

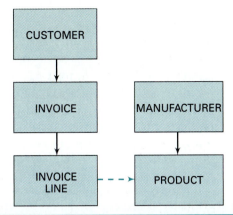

product. Suppose, however, that PRODUCT has *not* been connected to INVOICE LINE by a physical pointer. How can the following management report be obtained?

For each customer, identify the manufacturers whose products the customer has ordered.

This requires navigating from CUSTOMER through INVOICE and INVOICE LINE, over to PRODUCT, and then up to MANUFACTURER. But since the physical connection between INVOICE LINE and PRODUCT does not exist in the database, this navigation cannot be done through the normal database facilities. Instead, old-fashioned and cumbersome file processing techniques must be used to obtain the requested information. This would necessitate a considerable amount of complex programming. In contrast to this, database systems that support the retrieval of data based on *logical* relationships would easily solve such problems.

In his paper, Codd proposed a simple data model in which all data would be represented in tables made up of rows and columns. These tables were given the mathematical name *relations,* and from this the model was named the relational model. Codd also proposed two languages for manipulating data in tables: relational algebra and relational calculus (to be discussed in Chapter 6). Both these languages support data manipulation on the basis of logical characteristics rather than the physical pointers used in the hierarchical and network models.

By handling data on a conceptual rather than a physical basis, Codd introduced another revolutionary innovation. In relational database systems, entire files of data can be processed with single statements. By contrast, traditional systems require data to be processed one record at a time. Codd's approach enormously improves the conceptual efficiency of database programming.

The logical manipulation of data also makes feasible the creation of query languages more accessible to the nontechnical user. Although it is quite difficult to create a language which can be used by *all* people, regardless of their previous computer experience, relational query languages make the accessing of databases realistic for a much larger group of users than was previously possible.

The publication of Codd's papers in the early seventies set off a flurry of activity in both the research and commercial system development communities as they worked to bring out a relational database management system. The result was the release of relational systems during the last half of the seventies supporting such languages as Structured Query Language (SQL), Query Language (Quel), and Query-by-Example (QBE). As the personal computer became popular during the eighties, relational systems that ran on microcomputers also became available. In 1986 SQL was adopted as the ANSI standard for relational database languages. This standard was updated in 1989 and 1992. We discuss aspects of SQL-92 in Chapter 7.

All these developments have greatly advanced the state of the art in database management systems and increased the availability of information in corporate databases. The relational approach has proven to be quite fruitful. Moreover, continuing research promises to provide increasingly powerful capabilities as we acquire a more complete understanding of user needs with respect to database systems.

Today relational systems are considered the standard in up-to-date commercial data processing operations. Of course, file-oriented systems, as well as hierarchical and network database systems, are still plentiful and, for a number of applications, the most cost-effective solution. However, the clear trend for some time has been for companies to convert to relational systems whenever feasible.

It would be wrong to assume that the relational database systems now available represent the last word in DBMS development, though. The relational systems of today are still evolving and in significant respects changing their underlying nature to allow users to address more complex problems. From our point of view, one of the most significant of these changes is occurring in the area of object-oriented databases. In Chapter 4 we will discuss a conceptual data model that has important features used in object-oriented databases. An additional development of substantial importance is the emergence of the client/server platform as the basis for computing and database access in an organization. We give an overview of this concept in the next section.

Figure 1.13 shows a timeline describing the historical development of the data access methods we have discussed. Table 1.1 provides a feature comparison of the various data access methods.

▼TABLE 1.1 FEATURE COMPARISON OF DATA ACCESS METHODS

Data Access Method	Features
Sequential Files	All records in a file must be processed in sequence
Random Access Files	Supports direct access to a specific record Difficult to access multiple records related to a single record
Hierarchical Database	Supports access to multiple records related to a single record Restricted to hierarchical data relationships Dependent on predefined, physical pointers
Network Database	Supports hierarchical and nonhierarchical network data relationships Dependent on predefined, physical pointers
Relational Database	Supports all logical data relationships Logical data access, independent of physical implementation techniques

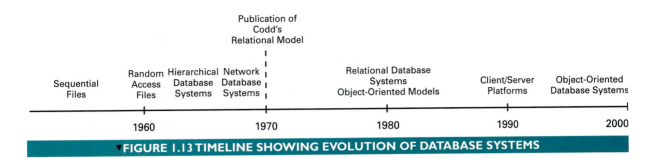

▼ FIGURE 1.13 TIMELINE SHOWING EVOLUTION OF DATABASE SYSTEMS

▼ Current Directions—Client/Server Platforms

"All right, Sandy, explain to me why you think converting to a client/server platform would help us? What is client/server anyway?"

Susan and Sanford are continuing the technology discussion we found them in as the chapter began. IPD has progressed through file and database systems and is now considering the next step. Naturally, before they make a move they want to know where they're going and whether it will be cost-effective.

"A client/server platform *is usually a local area network—a LAN—to which a number of desktop computers are attached and which contains a special computer we call a* server. *The desktop computers are* clients, *which ask the server for a variety of services."*

"For example?"

"The server might send them programs like word processors or spreadsheets, or it might execute database queries and send them the results. The basic idea is that each machine does what it does best. The server retrieves and updates data, the client does special computations and presents data to the end user."

"Will it be cheaper?"

"Not necessarily."

"Then what advantages does it offer?"

"Our systems will be much more powerful and easier to use. Every end user will have a Graphical User Interface to work with. Besides that, the systems will have many additional functions since there is a computer on every desk. We'll also be able to increase capacity more easily and inexpensively by just adding machines incrementally. And we'll be in a more flexible position to take advantage of new hardware and software."

"Sounds good so far. Put together a group to study the advantages and risks. If their report is favorable, we can go ahead."

The introduction of the IBM PC in 1981 established the desktop workstation as a standard in the office. Word processing, spreadsheet, and other software alone justified the use of these machines. It was only natural, moreover, for them to be

client/server platform
A local area network consisting of client computers which receive services from a server computer.

database server A program running on server hardware to provide database services to client machines.

Graphical User Interface (GUI) Screens and functions that provide a graphical means for an end user to access a computer system.

open systems The concept of connecting a variety of computer hardware and software to work in concert to achieve user goals.

interoperability The state of multiple heterogeneous systems communicating and contributing to completion of a common task.

tied together to allow users to communicate via electronic mail and to access common resources like printers and disks. Initially servers were set up to control printing and file access. These were *print servers* and *file servers*. For example, the file server responding to a client request for a specific file would send the entire file over the network to the client machine (Figure 1.14). Today, however, most servers are **database servers**—programs which run on server hardware and provide database services to client machines (Figure 1.15). Thus, a client may be running an application program and need to execute a query of a database. To do this it sends a request for data to the database server, which in turn carries out the query and returns the resulting data to the client. The application program may also send data to the server with a request to update the database. The server would carry out this update.

The power of the client/server platform lies in the division-of-labor concept. The client is the front-end machine that interfaces directly with the user. It handles the **Graphical User Interface (GUI)** and does computations and other programming of interest to the end user. The server is the back-end machine and handles those parts of the job which are common to many clients—such as database access and update.

Conceptually, client/server platforms are part of the **open systems** concept, under which all manner of computers, operating systems, network protocols, and other software and hardware can be interconnected and work in concert to achieve user goals. In practice, however, the problems of getting such a variety of operating systems, network protocols, database systems, and so on working together can be extremely challenging. The goal of open systems is to achieve **interoperability,**

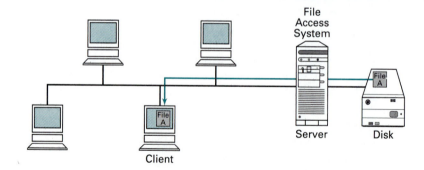

▼**FIGURE 1.14 RETRIEVING AN ENTIRE FILE FROM A FILE SERVER**

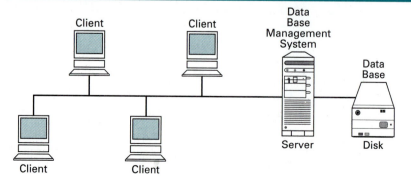

▼**FIGURE 1.15 CLIENTS INTERACTING WITH A DATABASE SERVER**

which is the state of two or more heterogeneous systems communicating and each contributing some portion of work to a common task.

In a sense, client/server computing is the culmination of an early vision of distributed computing power together with the data control and access inherent in a centralized computer. Visionaries asserted the imminence of distributed computing for over two decades, but it hasn't really become a reality until recently. Although many difficult interoperability problems remain to be solved, the prospects for ever increasing computing power and database access at the end-user level have never been more encouraging.

▼ Database Systems: Hardware, Software, Data, People

So far, we have discussed database systems and their capabilities in general terms. Now it is time to take a closer look at the components that make up such a system. A database system is more than just data or data in combination with database management software. A *complete* database system in an organization consists of four components: hardware, software, data, and people.

Hardware

The *hardware* is the set of physical devices on which a database resides. It consists of one or more computers, disk drives, CRT terminals, printers, tape drives, connecting cables, and other auxiliary and connecting hardware.

The computers, used for processing the data in the database, may be mainframe, mini-computers, or personal computers. In the example given previously, IPD initially began processing with a minicomputer and then later upgraded to a mainframe computer. Mainframe and minicomputers have traditionally been used on a stand-alone basis to support multiple users accessing a common database. Personal computers are often used with stand-alone databases controlled and accessed by a single user. However, they can also be connected in a client/server network, providing multiple users access to a common database stored on disk drives and controlled by a server computer. The server itself may be a more powerful desktop computer, a minicomputer, a mainframe, or a powerful multiprocessor computer. Figure 1.16 illustrates a variety of hardware configurations.

Disk drives are the main storage mechanism for databases and are essential since they allow random access, without which database processing would be impossible. Desktop computers, CRT terminals, and printers are used for entering and retrieving information from the database. Tape drives provide rapid and inexpensive backup of data residing on the disk drives.

The success of database systems has been heavily dependent on advances in hardware technology. A very large amount of main memory and disk storage is required to maintain and control the huge quantity of data stored in a database. In addition, high-speed computers, networks, and peripherals are necessary to execute the large number of data accesses required to retrieve information in an acceptable amount of time in an environment with a large number of users. Fortunately, computer hardware has become increasingly powerful and significantly less expensive during the years of database technology development. This has made possible the widespread use of database systems.

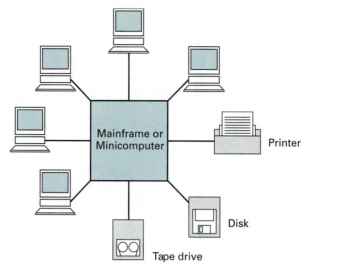

(a) Mainframe or minicomputer
supporting access through
multiple terminals

(b) Personal computer
used with a stand-
alone database

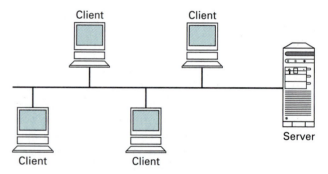

(c) Desktop computers connected in a
client/server network, all accessing a
database stored on a server computer.

▼FIGURE 1.16 THREE POSSIBLE HARDWARE CONFIGURATIONS
FOR DATABASE SYSTEMS

Software

A database system includes two types of software:

▼ General-purpose database management software, usually called the
database management system (DBMS).

▼ Application software that uses DBMS facilities to manipulate the database to achieve a specific business function, such as issuing statements or analyzing sales trends.

Application software is generally written by company employees to solve a
specific company problem. It may be written in a standard programming language,
such as COBOL or C, or it may be written in a language (commonly called a fourth-
generation language) supplied with the database management system. Application

software uses the facilities of the DBMS to access and manipulate data in the database, providing reports or documents needed for the information and processing needs of the company.

The *database management system* (DBMS) is systems software, similar to an operating system or a compiler, that provides a number of services to end users, programmers, and others (Figure 1.17). As its name implies, the DBMS exists to facilitate the management of a database. To this end a DBMS typically provides most of the following services:

▼ A centralized data definition and data control facility known as a data dictionary/directory (DD/D) or catalog

▼ Data security and integrity mechanisms

▼ Concurrent data access for multiple users

▼ User-oriented data query, manipulation, and reporting capabilities

▼ Programmer-oriented application system development capabilities

Data Dictionary/Directory (DD/D). A data dictionary/directory subsystem keeps track of the definitions of all the data items in the database. This includes elementary-level data items (fields), group and record-level data structures, and files or relational tables. Not only does the DD/D maintain this information, but it keeps track of relationships that exist between various data structures. Additionally, it maintains the indexes that are used to access data quickly. It also keeps track of screen and report format definitions that may be used by various application programs.

▼FIGURE 1.17 COMPONENTS OF A DATABASE MANAGEMENT SYSTEM

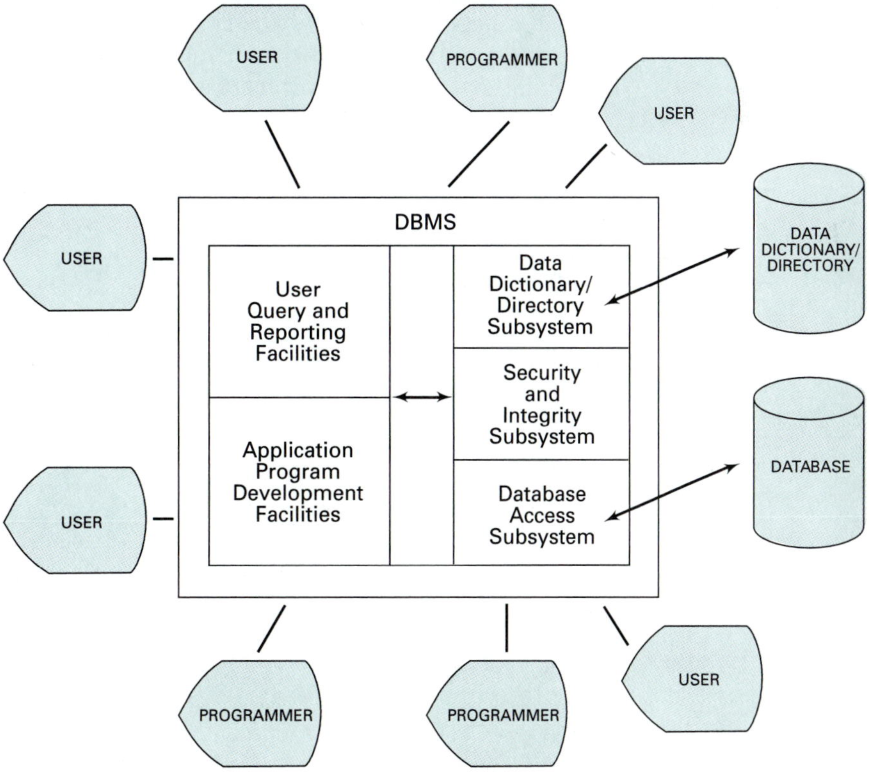

metadata Data in the data dictionary which describe the database.

data view A definition of a restricted portion of the database; also called a view.

The data dictionary can be viewed as being a part of the database itself. Thus, the database is *self-describing,* since it contains information describing its own structure. The information in the data dictionary is called **metadata,** or "data about data." The metadata are available for query and manipulation, just as other data in the database.

Data security and integrity mechanisms. The database is a valuable resource needing protection. The DBMS provides database security by limiting access to the database to authorized personnel. Authorized users will generally be restricted as to the particular data they can access and whether they can update it. Such access is often controlled by passwords and by **data views,** which are definitions of restricted portions of the database, as illustrated in Figure 1.18. The integrity and consistency of the database are protected via constraints on values that data items can have and by backup and recovery capabilities provided within the DBMS. Data constraint definitions are maintained in the data dictionary. Backup and recovery are supported by software that automatically logs changes to the database and provides for a means of recovering the current state of the database in case of system failure.

Concurrent data access for multiple users. One of the chief functions of the DBMS is to support the access, retrieval, and update of data in the database. The DBMS provides the physical mechanisms allowing multiple users to access a variety of related data quickly and efficiently. This support extends to users in remote locations who must access the database through a telecommunications system. The DBMS facilities provide interface with telecommunications systems so that requests for data and the resulting responses will be properly routed.

The centralization of data in a database increases the probability that two or more users will want to access the same data concurrently. If the DBMS allowed this, the two users would certainly affect each other's work and could damage it. Thus, it is important that the DBMS protect the data being accessed by one user from simultaneous update by another user. To do this, the DBMS uses sophisticated locking mechanisms to protect the data currently being updated by a user, while at

▼FIGURE 1.18 USER VIEWS OF A DATABASE

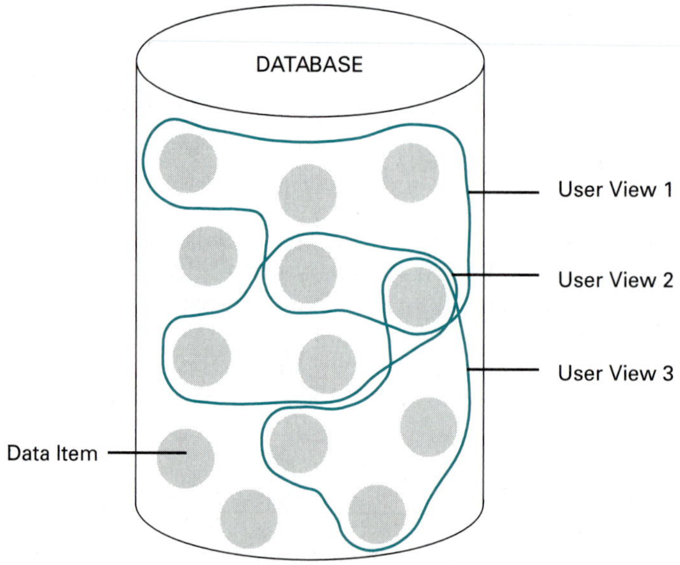

the same time providing concurrent database access and acceptable system response time to other users.

User-oriented data query and reporting.   One of the most valuable aspects of a DBMS is its provision of user-oriented data manipulation tools. These easy-to-use query languages allow users to formulate queries and request one-time reports directly from the database. This relieves the company's programming staff of the burden of formulating these queries or writing special-purpose application software.

Associated with query languages are report generators. Often the query language will contain facilities to format the results of queries as reports. The formulated query itself can be saved for use later and its result can be produced as a regular report. When this is the case, the query language can be viewed as a report generator. In addition, report generators may also be provided which have more powerful reporting facilities than those available in the query language.

Application development facilities.   Besides making it easier for the user to access the database for information, the DBMS commonly provides significant assistance to the application programmer as well. Such tools as screen, menu, and report generators; application generators; compilers; and data and view definition facilities are standard. More important, modern database systems provide language components that are much more powerful than those of traditional languages, making the programming process itself considerably more efficient.

Data

Clearly, no database system can exist without data, the basic facts upon which a company's processing and information needs are founded. The important factor to consider here, however, is that the data of which a database is constituted must be carefully and logically structured. Business functions must be analyzed, data elements and relationships must be identified and precisely defined, and these definitions must be accurately recorded in the data dictionary. Data can then be collected and entered into the database according to the defined structure. A database built in harmony with these procedures can be a powerful resource for providing the organization with timely information.

People

users People who need information from the database to carry out their primary business responsibility.

The IPD case identified two different *types* of people concerned with the database. Susan Broadbent and Dick Greenberg are **users,** people who need information from the database to carry out their primary business responsibility, which itself is in some other functional area. Sanford Mallon and Cordelia Molini, by contrast, are **practitioners,** people whose primary business responsibility is to design and maintain the database system and its associated application software for the benefit of the users. Examples of people in each of these categories may be as follows:

practitioners People responsible for the database system and its associated application software.

Users: Executives, managers, staff, clerical personnel
Practitioners: Database administrators, analysts, programmers, database and system designers, information systems managers

procedure Written instructions describing the steps needed to accomplish a given task in a system.

The **procedures** people use to accomplish their goals in the system constitute an important aspect of this component. Virtually no system completely automates a user task. Manual procedures must be developed to provide a smooth interface between the users of the system and the system itself. An example of such a procedure would be the audit control by which the users determine that the total amount deposited in the bank on a given day agrees with the total amount of cash received for that day as shown in the system. There are normally many such procedures in a system, and the success of the system often depends as much on the skill with which such procedures are developed to mesh with the system functions as it does on the structure of the system itself.

Relationship of the Four System Components

Figure 1.19 summarizes the relationship among the four components of a database system. *Practitioners* (analysts and database designers) in consultation with *users* identify *data* needs and design database structures to accommodate these needs. The database structures are then specified to the *DBMS* through the data dictionary. *Users* enter *data* into the system by following specified *procedures*. The entered data are maintained on *hardware* media such as disks and tapes. *Application programs* that access the *database* are written by practitioners and users to be run on *computers*. These programs utilize the command language of the DBMS and make use of the information contained in the data dictionary. These programs generate information, which can be used by executives and managers to make business decisions. Application programs may also generate billing statements and other documents used by the customers of the business. Thus, it can be seen that in a properly designed and functioning system all four components—hardware, software, data, and people—fit together in a single system to accomplish the goals of the organization.

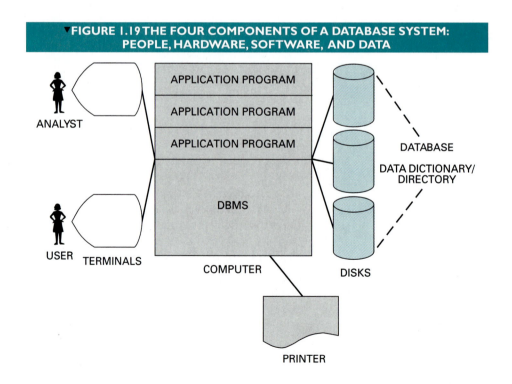

▼FIGURE 1.19 THE FOUR COMPONENTS OF A DATABASE SYSTEM: PEOPLE, HARDWARE, SOFTWARE, AND DATA

Summary

In this chapter, we have reviewed the development of database technology, starting with the early file access methods and proceeding through the principal approaches to database processing. We have also identified and discussed the four main components of a database system: hardware, software, data, and people.

In the early years of data processing, during the fifties and early sixties, sequential file processing was the rule. All data resided on sequential files, which required the processing of complete files by application programs. During the sixties, as direct access disk storage became widely available, random access file processing became feasible and popular. This file access method allowed the direct access of specific data from a file.

As computer data processing systems became ever more important, businesses began to recognize that information was a corporate resource of considerable value. More and more they perceived that the data to answer numerous business questions were available in their data processing files. As a consequence they began to push for management information systems that would use the power of the computer to produce information from corporate data. This initiated the demand for database systems which would more effectively manage data access and manipulation.

In the mid-sixties, the first database systems, based on a hierarchical structuring of data, were introduced. These systems provided for the retrieval of multiple records associated with a single record of another file. Shortly after, network database systems were developed which supported significantly more complex relationships between records of different files. Both the hierarchical and network database models required the use of predefined physical pointers for linking related records.

In 1970, E. F. Codd's paper on the relational data model revolutionized the thinking of the database industry. Codd's approach called for the access and manipulation of data solely in terms of its logical characteristics. During the seventies and eighties, a number of relational database systems were developed, and at present they dominate the commercial marketplace.

In recent years with the proliferation of inexpensive personal computers in the workplace, networking methods have been developed allowing users of these computers to share resources. A server computer on the network provides database access to these desktop workstations allowing an efficient and powerful division of labor: The server retrieves the data which the requesting client machine processes and displays for end-user manipulation. Client/server networks have developed a high degree of sophistication and are being found more and more commonly in business enterprises.

Conceptually, a database system in a large organization consists of hardware, software, data, and people. The hardware configuration is comprised of one or more computers, disk drives, terminals, printers, tape drives, network connections, and other physical devices. The software includes a database management system (DBMS) and application programs which use the DBMS to access and manipulate the database. The data, representing the recorded facts important to the organization, reside physically on disk but are logically structured in a way to make their access easy and efficient. People, both database system users and practitioners, work together to define the characteristics and structure of the database system and to create the application programs which will provide the information essential to the company's success.

Review Questions

1. Define each of the following terms in your own words:
  a. data processing system
  b. random access processing
  c. management information system
  d. database
  e. database system
  f. data model
  g. hierarchical model
  h. pointer
  i. network
  j. client/server platform
  k. open systems
  l. interoperability
  m. database management system
  n. data view
  o. procedure
  p. metadata

2. What are the important characteristics of sequential and random access file systems? What weaknesses of sequential file access do random access methods remedy?

3. Discuss the importance of information as an organizational resource. How have database systems helped to increase the value of information to organizations?

4. Compare and contrast the features of hierarchical, network, and relational database systems. What business needs led to the development of each of them?

5. List and briefly describe each of the four main components of a modern database system.

6. Describe each of these components of a database management system (DBMS):
  a. Data dictionary/directory (DD/D)
  b. Data security and integrity
  c. Concurrent data access for multiple users
  d. Data query, manipulation, and reporting
  e. Application system development facilities

7. List three examples of each of the following:
  a. Users
  b. Practitioners

8. Define each of the following:
  a. ISAM
  b. IMS
  c. DBA
  d. SQL
  e. Quel
  f. QBE

BONH
AN I
DATAB

Problems and Exercises

1. Match the following terms with their definitions:

__data	a. Computer program that performs a task of practical value
__key	b. Organized or summarized data
__information system	c. Isolated facts
__synonyms	d. People who need information from the database
__parent	e. People responsible for the database system
__users	f. Automated system that organizes data to produce information
__application program	g. Terms that mean the same thing
__homonym	h. "Owned" record in a hierarchical relationship
__child	i. "Owner" record in a hierarchical relationship
__information	j. Has different meanings in different contexts
__practitioners	k. Data fields that uniquely identify a record
__database server	l. Provides convenient means for end-user access to system
__Graphical User Interface	m. Provides database services to client machines

2. Define a key for each of the files in Figure 1.3.

3. Which of the following can be regarded as *data* and which as *information?*
  a. Marshall Dobry received more commission than any other sales representative this year.
  b. Marshall Dobry was born December 12, 1960.
  c. The western region produced over $500,000 in sales during each month of the last quarter.
  d. Product A235 is profitable.
  e. Product A235 is manufactured in Des Moines.

4. Organize the following files into a hierarchy for a bank's database: PAYMENT, SAVINGS ACCOUNT, DEPOSIT, CUSTOMER, LOAN ACCOUNT, WITHDRAWAL.

5. Organize the following files into a network for a shipping company's database: SHIPMENT, TRUCK, SENDER, PACKAGE, RECEIVER.

6. For problems 4 and 5, identify fields that may be found in each file. Identify key fields for each file.

7. Explain how uncontrolled concurrent processing in a database system could lead to damaged data in the following situations:
  a. Making flight reservations in an airline reservation system.
  b. Updating quantities of a product in an inventory control system.
  c. Updating a checking account balance in a bank.

Pro

1. Visi
gramn
tems.
discus
the va
have?
in the
serve

2. Ske
using

Assur

3. Re
quen
over
appr

Diane Bradbury was talking with her sister Karen. The previous weekend they had done the catering for a friend's wedding reception, and things had gone quite well. A number of compliments were received, and their friend was very pleased. Diane commented, "You know, Karen, we have often talked about starting a small business. Remember last year when we saw that lovely old home for sale, and we thought what a wonderful place it would be for a bed-and-breakfast venture. Well, of course, we didn't have the money to buy the house, but it seems we could start a catering business without a large investment—and I think we could be very good at it."

Karen replied, "I feel exactly the same way. I know we could do the catering work—but neither of us is experienced in keeping track of records, finances, and all the details of running a business. How would we handle those matters?"

"Don't worry," responded Diane. "My husband says that many small businesses are able to operate quite effectively with a microcomputer database system. It's some kind of software that makes record keeping convenient and information readily accessible. He says anyone can learn to use it."

The Bonhomie Catering case is an easy-to-follow scenario that informally introduces several of the database design concepts that are developed more extensively in later chapters.

This chapter helps you get a gentle overview of the database design and implementation process. This experience will provide motivation for later topics, as well as generating insights and questions as later material is studied.

After studying this chapter, you will

▼ Have gained an intuitive understanding of the role of a conceptual data model in developing a database system.

▼ Have a basic notion of how a data model is translated into an implementation model.

▼ Have a preliminary acquaintance with some common DBMS features.

▼ The Bonhomie Catering Case

Background

Bonhomie Catering was started by two sisters who were looking for a way to make some extra money at a job that interested them. Their homes on Bainbridge Island are a short ferry ride from downtown Seattle. For better or for worse, Bainbridge Island has developed rapidly as more and more people have been attracted to this beautiful, wooded island in Puget Sound—a location offering open space combined with easy access to the economic and cultural advantages of Seattle.

Along with the growth on Bainbridge Island has come opportunity for small business ventures. The island attracts a number of tourists, and specialty shops featuring art pieces, books, and local food have burgeoned. Entertainment has become an increasing part of community life on Bainbridge Island, particularly among the more affluent. Seeing an opportunity to try something on their own, Karen and Diane Bradbury decided to put their culinary skills to commercial use.

Both Karen and Diane were energetic and imaginative, in addition to being talented at food preparation. Moreover, they were both personable and well liked among their friends and neighbors on the island. Their business was launched through the help of a mutual friend who was the wife of the chair of the Music Department of a large university in the Seattle area. The Music Department was renowned and relied on patronage for supporting many of its programs. Consequently, the chair and his wife entertained groups of patrons often.

After successfully catering two events for the Music School, Karen and Diane were retained as the catering service for all subsequent events. With this coup in hand, they were able to acquire a number of additional clients—some of whom entertained regularly. The net result was more business than Karen and Diane could handle on their own, so additional help was acquired, and the name Bonhomie Catering was adopted.

Currently, Bonhomie Catering is owned by Diane and Karen Bradbury. There are three other employees: Peter Mancha, Dale Guber, and Jeff Hoops.

Business Operations

Bonhomie has several customers who request catering services on a regular basis. This business is interspersed with irregular customers and those trying the service for the first time. Diane or Karen develops estimates for each job as follows: The type of food, its preparation, and its service are first determined. The job is then priced on a per-serving basis. This amount is multiplied by the maximum number of expected guests. This information is recorded on a job estimate sheet and then entered into a microcomputer.

Employee Services

Twenty percent of the revenues from each job are earmarked for employee compensation. If more than one employee works a job, the 20 percent is divided among them. Employees are paid every two weeks. Diane and Karen are responsible for purchasing supplies and equipment. Diane keeps track of who works on each job and determines the amounts to be paid to each employee. Karen takes responsibility for paying all other bills.

Purchasing

All purchases are made on account with various vendors in the area. Karen usually pays bills within 30 days of billing unless there is a discount available for early payment.

Job Scheduling

Employees are assigned to each job according to skills and availability. On occasion, additional part-time help is required, but those needs are usually satisfied by drafting members from Diane and Karen's families. Diane usually makes job assignments at least one week in advance. When a job is completed, the supervisor (who could be Karen, Diane, or an employee) completes a job sheet listing the equipment used, who worked on the job, and their hours.

Promotion

Diane and Karen have been effective at selling catering services by personal contact. Also, many jobs have come by word of mouth from satisfied clients. Not leaving anything to chance, Diane and Karen have occasionally created flyers, which have been distributed to local shops that are frequented by potential clients. They have also placed advertisements in Bainbridge Island's daily newspaper.

Financial Status

Since Diane and Karen operate Bonhomie Catering out of their homes, they have little overhead. Some equipment was initially purchased, and they have what is needed for current levels of business. Most costs are expended for labor and food purchases. Profits are determined by subtracting wages and food costs from the revenue received for each job.

▼ Database Design and Implementation

Our purpose in this section is provide you with some insight concerning the steps needed to design a simple database for Bonhomie Catering. We will use the PARADOX FOR WINDOWS DBMS to illustrate some implementation features that are common to many DBMSs. Since we don't delve into the details of the PARADOX system, the presentation is somewhat generic and easily accessible to you.

A Description of the Sales/Cash Receipts Cycle

The first step in developing a database for Bonhomie is to create a conceptual data model of its business practices. We need the following entities to illustrate Bonhomie's sales/cash receipts cycle: CLIENT, PROJECT, EMPLOYEE, FOOD TYPE, and PAYMENT. In our data model we will represent these entities with boxes. For example, the PROJECT entity looks like this:

PROJECT

Figure 2.1 is a data model diagram that shows how the entities relate to each other.

What does Figure 2.1 say about Bonhomie's sales/cash receipts cycle? Look at the relationship between the PROJECT entity and the EMPLOYEE entity.

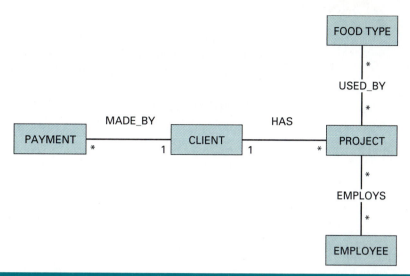

The line between entities means they are related. The "*" and "*" tell how they are related. The relationship between PROJECT and EMPLOYEE is read like this:

1. Each PROJECT can employ one or more (*) EMPLOYEEs.
2. Each EMPLOYEE can work on one or more (*) PROJECTs.

In other words, each employee can work on several projects, and each project can employ several employees.

Let's examine another relationship. Look at the relationship between the CLIENT entity and the PROJECT entity.

Again, the line between the two entities means they are related. The "1" and "*" tell how they are related. The relationship between CLIENT and PERSONNEL is read like this:

1. Each CLIENT can have one or more (*) PROJECTs.
2. Each PROJECT can have only one (1) CLIENT.

In other words, each catering project can be requested by only one client, but each client can request many catering projects.

In Figure 2.1 you can see two kinds of relationships. They are:

1. One-to-many (1 to *), shown in the CLIENT and PROJECT, and CLIENT and PAYMENT relationships.
2. Many-to-many (* to *), shown in the PROJECT and EMPLOYEE, and PROJECT and FOOD TYPE relationships.

There is also another kind of table relationship that we won't be using for the sales/cash receipts cycle. It is the one-to-one (1 to 1) relationship.

Now that we know what entities are involved and how they relate to each other, we are prepared to begin mapping our model to an implementation.

From Entities to Tables

A *table* can be thought of as an implementation of an entity from our model. In a table, data are arranged in fields and records (equivalently, columns and rows). For example, the CLIENT table might look something like this:

Name	Address	Phone
Chuck Brown	321 Schultzville Seattle, WA 92890	565-9980
Debbi Allen	15250 Riverside Lane Seattle, WA 98432	645-2322
Leroy Brown	52000 Basketball St. Seattle, WA 91130	685-4526
Al Franken	5230 Wesley Avenue Seattle, WA 93401	684-2388

Name, Address, and *Phone* are examples of fields. The *Name* field is a column that contains only names. A record is a row that contains a client's name, address, and phone number. As you can see, the CLIENT table contains four records, one for each client, and three fields, *Name, Address,* and *Phone.* The fields describe properties of the entities that are deemed important.

Now, let's define this table in a DBMS. We need to create five tables for Bonhomie. They are CLIENT, PROJECT, EMPLOYEE, FOOD TYPE, and PAYMENT. Let's start with the CLIENT table.

Creating a Table

Suppose that we wish to divide the address information into four fields: Street, City, State, and Zip Code. We then have a total of six fields: *Name, Street, City, State, Zip,* and *Phone.*

Now that we have selected the fields, let's design a corresponding table with the DBMS. Look at Figure 2.2. Here we observe typical requirements for designing a database table. We see field names (e.g., *Name, Street,* and so on), an indication of the data type that will be used in each field (here, "A" denotes alphanumeric), the size of each field, and an indication of which field is to function as the key (a field whose value is unique to each record).

We have created the structure of the CLIENT table, and it is now ready to receive data.

In similar fashion, we next create the other four tables as shown in Figure 2.3.

Data Model Diagram Revisited

In order to represent our data model faithfully, we must ensure that the tables relate to each other the way they should. Do you remember the three kinds of table relationships? They are repeated here for convenience:

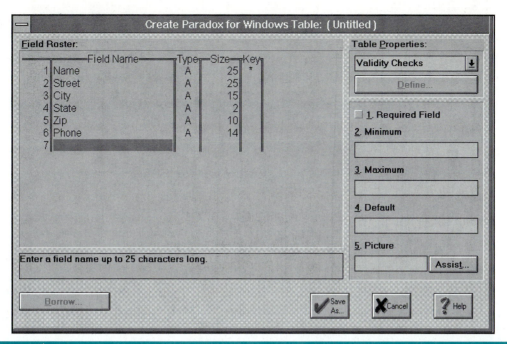

▼FIGURE 2.2

Field Name	Type	Size	Key
Proj#	N		*
Date	D		
#Guests	N		
Est. Cost	$		
Amt. Charged	$		

▼FIGURE 2.3(a) PROJECT TABLE

Field Name	Type	Size	Key
SS#	A	11	*
Name	A	25	

▼FIGURE 2.3(b) EMPLOYEE TABLE

▼FIGURE 2.3(c) FOODTYPE TABLE

Field Name	Type	Size	Key
Food Name	A	25	*

Field Name	Type	Size	Key
Proj#	N		*
Amt. Rec.	$		

1. One-to-one (1 to 1) doesn't exist in Bonhomie's model.

2. One-to-many (1 to *) shown in the MADE-BY and HAS relationships.

3. Many-to-many (* to *) shown in the USED-BY and EMPLOYS relationships.

To make sure these relationships are correctly represented in the tables we have made, we must follow certain rules for each table based on the particular relationship. Let's take a second look at our diagram.

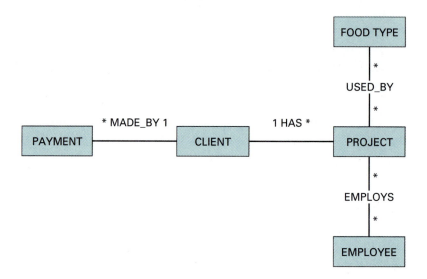

There are three table rules that govern table relationships.

Table Rule 1:
If two tables have a one-to-one (1 to 1) relationship, then the key field of one of the tables must be placed in the other table.

Since none of our relationships requires adherence to Table Rule 1, we move to

Table Rule 2:
If two tables have a one-to-many (1 to *) relationship, then the key field of the one (1) table must be placed in the many (*) table.

In the diagram, two relationships admit to Table Rule 2, the HAS and MADE-BY relationships.

To follow Table Rule 2 for the CLIENT and PAYMENT tables, we place *Name,* the key field of CLIENT, in the PAYMENT table after the *Proj#* field. Since *Name* is the key of the CLIENT table and is used to link the tables, it is known as a foreign key.

Next, we have

Table Rule 3:
If two tables have a many-to-many relationship (* to *), then a new table must be created that has the key fields of the two tables.

In the diagram, two relationships follow Table Rule 3, USED-BY and EMPLOYS. To satisfy our rule we must create two new tables. We first design the table that will link PROJECT and FOODTYPE. We will name this table USED_BY. It will have three fields: *Proj#* (first key), *Food Name* (second key), and *Qty*. Notice that our USED_BY table contains the key fields of both PROJECT and FOODTYPE.

Field Name	Type	Size	Key
Proj#	N		*
Food Name	A	25	*
Qty	N		

USED_BY TABLE

Now let's design the table that will link PROJECT and EMPLOYEE. We name the table EMPLOYS. It will have three fields: *Proj#* (first key), *SS#* (second key), and *Hrs*. Using the same steps, construct the EMPLOYS table.

Field Name	Type	Size	Key
Proj#	N		*
SS#	A	11	*
Hrs	N		

EMPLOYS TABLE

Notice how the data model diagram looks in its modified version (Figure 2.4), and that the new tables follow the applicable Table Rule 2.

Now all of the tables are designed and relate to each other correctly. By "relate to each other correctly," we mean that the tables relate in the way that accurately represents the information structure of Bonhomie Catering.

Setting Validity Checks

Since the best way to guarantee the storage of valid data is to prevent incorrect data from being entered in the first place, DBMSs typically allow you to impose restrictions (validity checks) for each field in your database tables.

The types of validity checks that are commonly provided include:

Required Field: Data must be entered in this field before the record can be saved.

Minimum: The smallest value this field will accept.

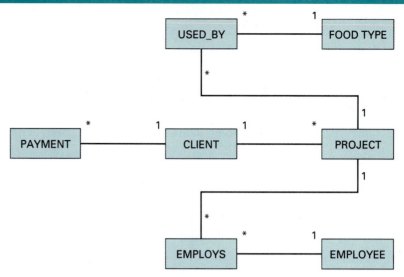

Maximum:	The largest value this field will accept.
Default:	The value that will be automatically placed in the field by PARADOX.
Picture:	A template of the valid data and format for the field.

With these checks you can make sure that zip codes, phone numbers, and social security numbers are entered in the correct format; that dollar figures are within a reasonable range; and that key fields always contain data. An example of adding validity checks to some of our tables is shown in Figure 2.5.

Field Name	Required Field	Minimum
Proj#	✔	
Est. Cost		0.00
Amt. Charged		0.00

▼FIGURE 2.5(a) PROJECT TABLE

Field Name	Required Field	Picture
SS#	✔	###-##-####

▼FIGURE 2.5(b) EMPLOYEE TABLE

Field Name	Required Field
Food Name	✔

FIGURE 2.5(c) FOODTYPE TABLE

Field Name	Required Field	Minimum
Proj#	✔	
Amt. Rec.		0.00

▼FIGURE 2.5(d) PAYMENT TABLE

Field Name	Required Field	Minimum	Maximum
Proj#	✔		
Food Name	✔		
Qty		0	999

▼FIGURE 2.5(e) USED_BY TABLE

Field Name	Required Field	Minimum	Picture
Proj#	✔		
SS#	✔		###-##-####
Hrs		0	

▼FIGURE 2.5(f) EMPLOYS TABLE

▼Additional DBMS Features

Data Entry Through Simple Forms

A form is a way to view or enter data into a table in a certain way—one record at a time. Forms belong to tables; that is, you can't design a form unless you have already created a table. Forms contain some or all of the fields that the related table has.

The reason we want to design forms is for data entry. When we start to put information into the tables, it helps to have forms that facilitate the data entry process. Although we could enter the data directly into the tables, using forms is often a faster, more effective, and accurate way to enter the data.

We have created tables to represent the sales/cash receipts cycle of Bonhomie. The forms that we consider are for the purpose of recording a sale, recording payment received, and recording other information that the sale involves.

The simplest example is a form that allows input to just one table. A catering project involves employee labor. When the project is completed, Bonhomie needs to know who worked on the project and how long he or she worked. To enter this information, we can create the **Work Form.** Note that this form inputs information into the EMPLOYS table, which contains three fields: *Proj#* (first key), *SS#* (second key), and *Hrs.*

An example is shown in Figure 2.6.

▼FIGURE 2.6

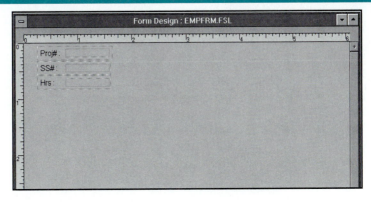

A Multi-Table Form: The Request Form

A multi-table form is an elegant way to enter data into several tables concurrently. We demonstrate with a multi-table **Request Form.** The Request Form is going to help us put a variety of sales information into our tables. When a client requests catering from Bonhomie, the information he or she gives to Bonhomie affects three of our tables: PROJECT, CLIENT, and USED_BY. Let's review how this works.

When a catering request is received, Bonhomie records certain information (a) and places it in specific tables (b):

1. (a) The catering project number
   (b) PROJECT, USED_BY

2. (a) The client's name
   (b) PROJECT, CLIENT

3. (a) The date of the catering, number of expected guests, estimated cost of the catering, and the amount charged the client
   (b) PROJECT

4. (a) The client's street, city, state, zip code, and phone number
   (b) CLIENT

5. (a) The types of food the client wants and the quantity of each to be provided
   (b) USED_BY

As you can see, information is going to three tables. By creating a multi-table form, we can send the right information to the desired table and field in one easy step. Without further detail, we show an example of the finished **Request Form** in Figure 2.7. Example data entered using forms are illustrated in Figure 2.8.

▼FIGURE 2.7

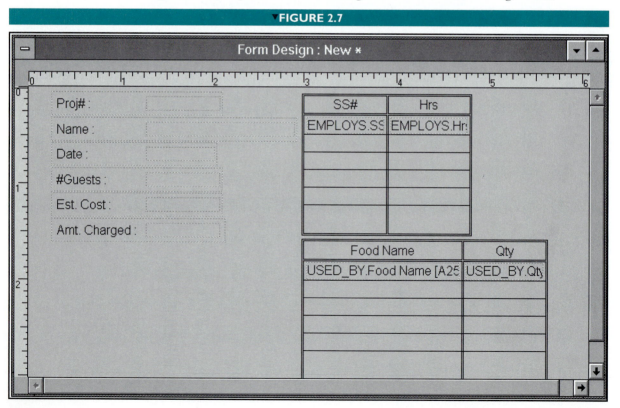

Name	Street	City	State	Zip	Phone
Baskerville, Eugene	120 Fir Lane	Redmond	WA	98204	123-4560
Jordan, Harry	14 Elm	Winslow	WA	98223	245-9366
Smith, Carrie	25 Alpine Dr.	Everett	WA	98882	546-4322

▼FIGURE 2.8(a) CLIENT TABLE

Proj#	Name	Date	#Guests	Est. Cost	Amt. Charged
1	Jordan, Harry	3/21/93	100	$600.00	$850.00
2	Smith, Carrie	4/15/93	50	$325.00	$425.00
3	Baskerville, Eugene	4/17/93	25	$275.00	$350.00
4	Smith, Carrie	5/1/93	35	$325.00	$560.00

▼FIGURE 2.8(b) PROJECT TABLE

▼FIGURE 2.8(c) USED_BY TABLE

Proj#	Food Name	Qty
1	chocolate mousse	125
1	root beer	75
1	sparkling punch	150
1	steak	100
2	7-Up	75
2	hamburger	75
2	jello	50
2	shortcake	50
3	beef kabobs	60
3	fruit plates	50
3	green salads	50
3	Sprite	60
4	asparagus	45
4	baked potato	60
4	cranberry juice	50
4	fruit flip	35
4	prime rib	40

▼ Obtaining Management Information from Our Database

Now that we have (1) defined the tables needed in our database, (2) defined the relationship between the tables (table diagram and data model), (3) created the tables, and (4) entered data into tables, we are now ready to use our database to obtain information to aid in the management of Bonhomie.

A query is simply a question which the information in a database can answer. The language we illustrate allows the user to ask questions of a database using visual templates instead of text commands, but both text and visual languages emanate from the same relational language theory. In any case, these matters will be clarified in later chapters.

Let's walk through a simple query.

Query 1. This query will provide us with a listing of all our clients' names along with the cities in which they live. We do the following:

1. Select **File** | **New** | **Query** from the main menu.

2. From the Select File dialog box, choose the table that will be involved in the query. Select CLIENT.DB and click **OK.** A blank query template will appear which contains all the fields from the CLIENT table.

3. Click the check boxes next to the *Name* and *City* fields. These fields have now been selected and will be the only ones that appear on the output. Your query window should look like the one in Figure 2.9(a).

4. Click the Query Run button, ⚡, from the Speedbar or press **F8**. This runs the query and gives you an answer table (Figure 2.9(b)).

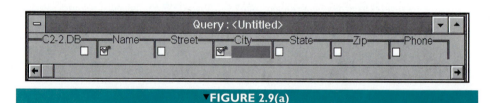

▼FIGURE 2.9(a)

▼FIGURE 2.9(b)

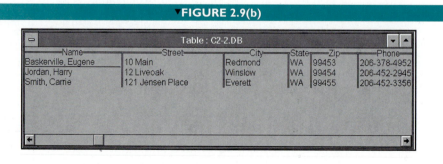

A large number of useful queries are just this easy.

Query 2.   Suppose we want a list of all catering jobs currently scheduled for the month of April 1993, the client names, and how many guests are expected to be at each event. We proceed as follows:

1. Select *File* | *New* | *Query* from the main menu.
2. Since this query involves information from the PROJECT table, select PROJECT.DB from the Select File dialog box and click **OK.** Again we see a blank query template, but this time it will be for the PROJECT table.
3. Click the check boxes next to the *Name, Date,* and *#Guests* fields.
4. Click on the *Date* field again and type "4/../93". The two periods indicate any valid day in April and thus any project date in April will appear in the answer table. The query will look like Figure 2.10(a).
5. Click the Query Run button, , or press **F8,** and the query result is shown in Figure 2.10(b).
6. Close both windows and decide if you are going to save the query or not. If you want the query saved, click **Yes** and enter a query name. Then click **OK.** If you don't want to save the query, click **No.**

Thus far our queries have involved only one table, yet we'll see that it is straightforward to link data from several different tables by using example elements. We will demonstrate this in our next query.

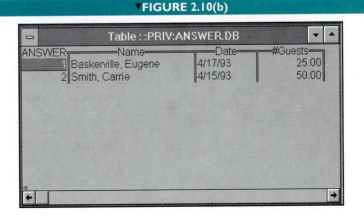

▾**FIGURE 2.10(a)**

▾**FIGURE 2.10(b)**

Query 3. This query asks for those foods and their quantities that were used on projects having more than 25 guests. Notice that foods and their quantities appear in the USED_BY table, but that the number of guests by project is in the PROJECT table. To accomplish a multi-table query, we do the following:

1. Select **File** | **New** | **Query** from the main menu.
2. Select PROJECT.DB and click **OK.** Don't worry, we will select the USED_BY table in another way. Once again the PROJECT table's blank query template will be visible.
3. Clicking the Add Table button on the Speedbar will bring up the Select File dialog box. Select the USED_BY table (USED_BY.DB) and click **OK.** Now a blank template for both queries can be seen.
4. Check the boxes next to the *#Guests, Food Name,* and *Qty* fields.
5. Click on the *#Guests* field and type ">25".

Now let's link the two tables. The obvious link for the tables is the *Proj#* field and to perform the link we click on the Join Tables button, which once again appears on the Speedbar. After clicking the Join Tables button, we click on the *Proj#* field in templates for both the PROJECT and USED_BY tables. PARADOX creates a unique example element and places the same one in both templates. The multi-table query can now be successfully completed.

6. Click the Join Tables button and then click the *Proj#* field in each of the table templates. A red EG01 will appear in both fields indicating that the link was successful. The query now should look like the one depicted in Figure 2.11(a).

7. Click the Query Run button, or press **F8.** Compare your answer table to the one in Figure 2.11(b).

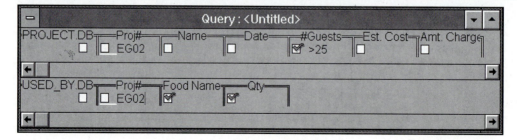

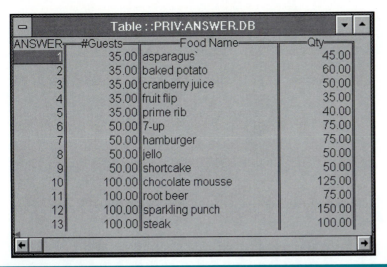

ANSWER	#Guests	Food Name	Qty
1	35.00	asparagus`	45.00
2	35.00	baked potato	60.00
3	35.00	cranberry juice	50.00
4	35.00	fruit flip	35.00
5	35.00	prime rib	40.00
6	50.00	7-up	75.00
7	50.00	hamburger	75.00
8	50.00	jello	50.00
9	50.00	shortcake	50.00
10	100.00	chocolate mousse	125.00
11	100.00	root beer	75.00
12	100.00	sparkling punch	150.00
13	100.00	steak	100.00

▼FIGURE 2.11(b)

Summary

In this chapter we have introduced elements of database design and implementation that will be pursued more rigorously in subsequent chapters. The application was realistic but simple enough so that we hope you have gained insight for the method. In addition, we have taken the application from design to implementation. The discourse on implementation illustrates the power of a DBMS without going into great detail.

Review Questions

1. Describe in your own words the difference between a table and a field.

2. How is a table represented in a diagram of an information system?

Problems and Exercises

1. Using a simple example of a business system, sketch a diagram similar to those used in the chapter. Identify all relationships between tables as one-one, one-many, or many-many.

2. Using the results of (1), create the related tables.

3. Using the results of (2), create appropriate data entry forms, and enter some sample data.

Projects and Professional Issues

1. If you are familiar with or have access to other DBMSs, use the example of this chapter to compare and contrast their methods of creating tables, entering data, and expressing queries.

2. Find a local business (or, alternatively, write a case) that will provide the basis for developing a small database application. Design and implement that application.

C H A P T E R

DATABASE SYSTEMS IN THE ORGANIZATION

▼

"As you can see, Susan, this strategic database plan outlines the path IPD informa-tion systems will take for the next five years. In five years, we will complete database system installations in all our offices."

Cordelia Molini, database administrator at International Product Distribution (IPD), is presenting a five-year database planning report to Susan Broadbent, IPD's CEO. IPD has just completed a strategic database planning project, for which Cordelia was the project leader.

Susan queries: "Did you address the problem of keeping our data secure in an in-ternational environment?"

"Yes, and we analyzed the associated costs and risks. We also considered the infor-mation needs of IPD's functional areas and different levels of management. As you review the report's details, you will see we have given proposed schedules for several database development projects as well as their estimated costs."

"This is excellent work. Your team is to be congratulated for giving us a database system framework that fits our business plan so well."

database A collection of interrelated, shared, and controlled data.

In this chapter, we focus on the organizational environment in which databases exist and how databases and their environment interrelate. Additionally, we examine the process of developing a specific data-base system. To facilitate our discussion, we add to our simple definition of a data-base: A **database** in an organization is a collection of interrelated, shared, and controlled data. After reading this chapter, you should be able to:

▼ Discuss data sharing in an organization between different functional areas, management levels, and geographical locations.

▼ Explain why and how strategic database planning is done in an orga-nization.

▼ Understand the control function of database administration.

▼ List and explain the risks and costs of database systems.

▼ Diagram and explain the standard foundation for database structure, the ANSI/SPARC three-level architecture.

▼ Describe the steps in the database development life cycle and their interrelationships.

The first four sections of the chapter deal with the management issues relating to organizational data sharing, strategic data planning, management control of data, and risks and costs of databases. The last half of the chapter is specifically con-cerned with management issues relating to the design and implementation of a database. Thus, we will discuss the questions of separating physical and logical data structure and of developing a database through a development cycle methodology.

▼ Data Sharing and Databases

*I*PD's database system went through several stages of evolution before it reached its current level of sophistication. To better understand why IPD decided to change to a database system, we look back several years to a conversation between Susan Broadbent and Sanford Mallon, IPD's chief information officer.

"Sandy, I think our company is becoming too compartmentalized. As the functional groups grow, they get more and more isolated. I don't think many groups care what the other groups are doing."

"I'm sorry to hear that, Susan, but what does that have to do with me?"

"Thanks a lot, pal! I can see the isolationist attitude has reached Information Systems, too. All right, I'll explain. Our groups produce management reports for themselves, but they don't share information with other groups. For example, Marketing gets all kinds of data about customer satisfaction and dissatisfaction with products. But Product Evaluation never sees it. Why can't we get our people to share information more effectively?"

"Actually," Sandy replied, "Product Evaluation has seen those marketing reports, but they say their format is confusing. We could write programs to get Evaluation the information they need, but Marketing won't let other groups access their data. They're afraid it'll get trashed or misused."

"You've talked before about converting to a database system. Would that help us solve this problem?"

"It certainly would. We'd be able to share data in a controlled way, so Evaluation could get what they need without hurting Marketing. Of course, we'd have to assure Marketing—and all the other functional areas—that if they give up some control, the database system will protect their data. In addition, I can show them that a good database system will offer many advantages."

"Sandy, that sounds good to me. If you present these ideas to the functional groups, I'm sure they'll agree."

Perhaps the most significant difference between a file-based system and a database system is that data are shared. This requires a major change in the thinking of users, who are accustomed to feeling they "own" the data resulting from their daily work activities. Data sharing also requires a major change in the way data are handled and managed within the organization. Part of this comes from the sheer amount of data that needs to be organized and integrated. To help you understand the challenge of using a database to share data, let's take a closer look at the nature of organizational data that need to be shared. We will consider three types of data sharing: (1) between functional units; (2) between management levels; and (3) between geographically dispersed locations.

Sharing Data Between Functional Units

The term *data sharing* suggests that people in different functional areas use a common pool of data, each for their own applications. Without data sharing, the marketing group may have their data files, the purchasing group theirs, the accounting group theirs, and so on (Figure 3.1(a)). Each group benefits only from its own data.

In contrast, the effect of combining data into a database is synergistic; that is, the combined data are more valuable than the sum of the data in separate files. Not only does each group continue to have access to its own data but, within reasonable limits of control, they have access to other data as well (Figure 3.1(b)). In this environment, the Marketing department, for example, is better off because it has access to data from Purchasing, especially product evaluations, which provide valuable input for marketing campaigns. In return, Product Evaluation gains access to Marketing's feedback about customer satisfaction. We call this concept of combining data for common use **data integration.**

data integration Combining data for common use.

Sharing Data Between Different Levels of Users

Different levels of users also need to share data. Three different levels of users are normally distinguished: operations, middle management, and executive. These levels correspond to the three different types of automated business systems that have evolved during the past three decades: **electronic data processing** (EDP), **management information systems** (MIS), and **decision support systems** (DSS). Sprague (Sprague and Watson, 1989, pp. 11–12) gives a description of them:

electronic data processing Computer automation of paperwork at the operational level of an organization.

EDP was first applied to the lower operational levels of the organization to automate the paperwork. Its basic characteristics include:

management information system Automated system focused on information for middle management.

▼   a focus on data, storage, processing, and flows at the operational level;

▼   efficient transaction processing; . . .

▼   summary reports for management. . . .

The MIS approach elevated the focus on information systems activities, with additional emphasis on integration and planning of the information systems function. In *practice,* the characteristics of MIS include:

decision support system Automated system providing strategic information to senior management.

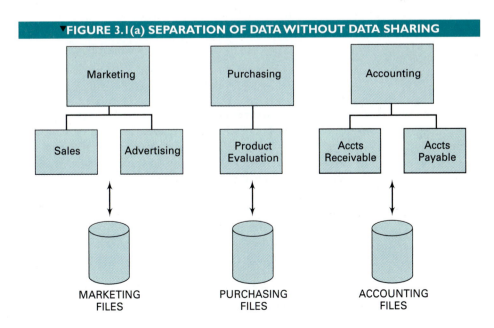

▼**FIGURE 3.1(a) SEPARATION OF DATA WITHOUT DATA SHARING**

Marketing — Sales, Advertising → MARKETING FILES

Purchasing — Product Evaluation → PURCHASING FILES

Accounting — Accts Receivable, Accts Payable → ACCOUNTING FILES

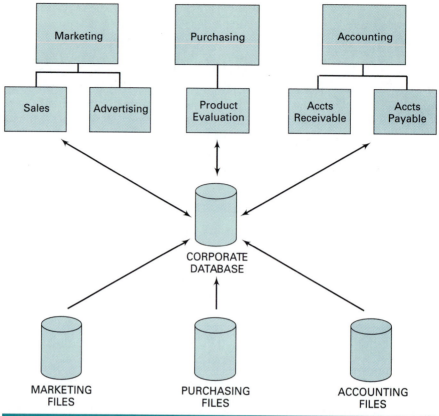

▼ an information focus, aimed at the middle managers . . .

▼ an integration of EDP jobs by business function, such as production MIS, marketing MIS, personnel MIS, etc.; and

▼ inquiry and report generation, usually with a database. . . .

[A] DSS is focused still higher in the organization with an emphasis on the following characteristics:

▼ decision focused, aimed at top managers and executive decision makers;

▼ emphasis on flexibility, adaptability, and quick response . . .

▼ support for the personal decision-making styles of individual managers.

The relationships of these systems to different management levels is illustrated in Figure 3.2. These levels of users and systems naturally require three different types of data. The user at the operational level needs data for transaction processing. This might include data for new accounts or changes to existing accounts, purchases, payments, and so on. This detailed data can then be summarized for the information needs at other higher levels. For example, the MIS level might utilize summaries to indicate which sales representatives were most, or least, productive. Executives at the highest level use decision support systems to discover long-term trends that apply to their own corporation as well as to identify the economic, social, and political environment in which they operate. The DSS helps them make decisions such as building a new factory, starting or dropping a product line, and so on. Thus, a DSS uses summary data from within the company as well as market, demographic, and other data from outside sources.

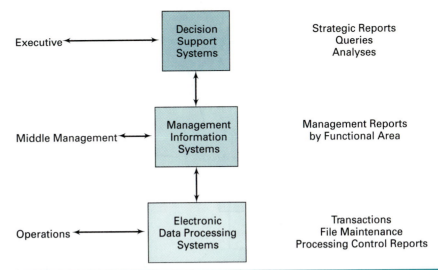

▼FIGURE 3.2 SYSTEMS CORRESPONDING TO DIFFERENT MANAGEMENT LEVELS

Sharing Data Between Different Locations

A company with several locations has important data distributed over a wide geographical area. Sharing these data is a significant problem. As IPD's branch offices grew, data interchange between home office and branches became increasingly inadequate, as illustrated in the following conversation.

*"**L**et me see if I understand what you mean, Dick. With offices spread over the globe, it's becoming more and more difficult to get timely reports."*

"That's right. By the time they send their data to Chicago and our people enter them into the system, it's already too late for us to make a good business decision. Moreover, the international offices want to use the data right there and not have to make extra copies of it."

"I think it's time for us to consider a distributed database system. It's possible with today's technology to keep data at the office where they originate, yet to access them from anywhere in the world via data lines. We can do queries in Sydney that use data in Brussels and Buenos Aires. It'll be sophisticated, but I think we can do it in a cost-effective manner."

centralized database
Database physically confined to a single location.

A **centralized database** is physically confined to a single location, controlled by a single computer (Figure 3.3). Most functions for which databases are created are accomplished more easily if the database is centralized. That is, it is easier to update, back up, query, and control access to a database if we know exactly where it is and what software controls it.

The size of the database and the computer on which it resides need not have any bearing on whether the database is centrally located. A small company with its database on a personal computer (PC) has a centralized database just as does a large company with many computers, but whose database is entirely controlled by a mainframe.

The project team should not strive for a detailed information model in this plan. Detailed models will be developed during subsequent database design projects. Instead, as James notes, the project team should identify stable elements in the organization's information structure—elements not likely to be altered with organizational changes. According to Martin, at the end of six months the information model is often thought to be 90 percent complete. This implies that most of the main elements have been identified, so the model will have value for strategic planning.

The Database Development Life Cycle (DDLC)

The strategic planning team may conclude the organization should have *several* databases rather than a single all-encompassing corporate database. Many companies come to this conclusion because their operations are so diverse. The task of implementing a single database for all their needs would be so risky and expensive the project itself might never succeed. For them, comprehensive databases in several well-defined areas are a better option. Of course, communication between these databases would now be difficult, but they view this as the lesser evil.

The strategic database plan recommends the number and kind of databases that should be developed, as illustrated in Figure 3.7. It also indicates a schedule for

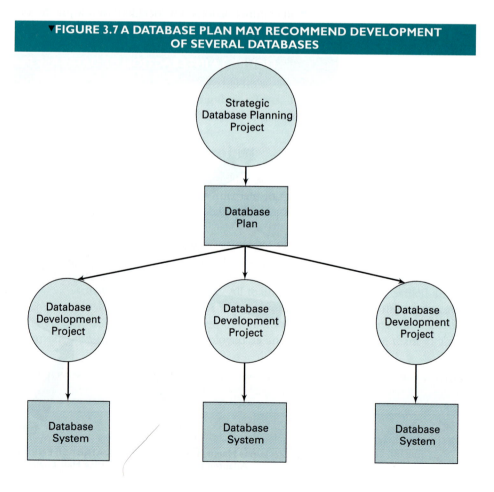

▼FIGURE 3.7 A DATABASE PLAN MAY RECOMMEND DEVELOPMENT OF SEVERAL DATABASES

distrib
systen
tem ma
system
conne
cation

these projects. After the plan receives final approval, the plans for designing and implementing specific databases can be carried out. The methodology for doing this is the database development life cycle.

database development life cycle (DDLC) A process for designing, implementing, and maintaining a database.

The **database development life cycle (DDLC)** includes information gathering to determine user data needs; database schema (logical structure) design to satisfy those needs; selection of a DBMS to support the use of the database; development of computer programs to utilize the database; and review of user information needs in context of the developed database.

Since this life cycle constitutes the major area of interest for this book, we will be studying it in detail in the last part of this chapter. Nearly all the remainder of the book is concerned with developing skills for carrying out the design and implementation steps of the life cycle.

▼ Databases and Management Control

database administration Personnel with responsibility for controlling and protecting the database.

As a company resource of significant value, the database requires control and protection. This responsibility is usually assigned to the **database administration (DBA).** The DBA should coordinate the design of the database, train users to access the database, guide the development and implementation of data security procedures, protect the integrity of data values, and make sure system performance is satisfactory.

In a small organization, one person carries out all these responsibilities. Often, however, these functions are assigned to a group of people. This is most likely in a large organization where the DBA responsibilities are divided among several people, managed by a chief administrator.

The functions of the DBA include:

▼ database design

▼ user training

▼ database security and integrity

▼ database system performance

Database Design

conceptual database design Identification of data elements, relationships, and constraints for a database.

value constraint A rule defining the permissible values for a specific data item.

physical database design Determination of storage devices, access methods, and indexes for using a database.

Conceptual database design consists primarily of defining the data elements to be included in the database, the relationships that exist between them, and the value constraints that apply. A **value constraint** is a rule defining the permissible values for a specific data item. **Physical database design** determines the physical structure of the database and includes such decisions as what access methods will be used to retrieve data, and what indexes will be built to improve the performance of the system.

To carry out conceptual database design, the DBA staff must include personnel who are expert in design concepts as well as skilled at working with user groups. The DBA designers work with users in various areas and design *portions* of the database. Such database portions are called **views** and are intended for use by the originating group. These views must then be integrated into a complete database **schema,** which defines the logical structure of the entire database. This process is illustrated in Figure 3.8.

The conceptual design process requires the resolution of conflicts between different user groups. For example, different groups may use the same term in con-

view A definition of a restricted portion of the database; also called a data view.

schema A definition of the logical structure of the entire database.

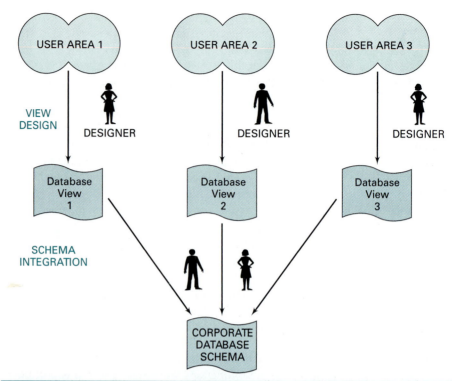

tradictory ways. Or groups may be jealous of their data and resist allowing others to access it, as illustrated by the conflict between IPD's marketing and product evaluation groups, discussed earlier in the chapter. Reasonable controls must be established that define which groups can access which data. The DBA must be able to negotiate resolutions to conflicts like these.

Technically oriented DBA staff members carry out the physical design, so they must know precisely how the DBMS handles data access and which access methods will be most efficient. Their goal is to optimize the total combination of hardware, software, and human resource costs. Ideally, they seek to minimize system response time within the constraints of hardware and software costs.

Initial database design and implementation must be followed by a continuous maintenance of the logical and physical structure of the database. Changes in business requirements, hardware and software capabilities, and processing volumes lead to the need for changes to both the logical and physical design of the database.

The DBA occupies a strategic position in the definition and enforcement of company data standards. Since database design is centrally controlled, the DBA can define standards for data naming; data formats; and screen, report, and file formats. This simplifies documentation and training requirements and provides for a more thorough systems integration within the company.

Database design decisions are documented in the data dictionary. The DBA controls the contents of the data dictionary and records there as metadata the names of data elements, files, screens, report forms, and the like. As we noted in Chapter 1, the metadata in the data dictionary can be queried and manipulated. However, their manipulation is very carefully controlled by the DBA, since the data in the data dictionary are vital to the proper functioning of the database system as a whole.

User Training

Many of the advantages resulting from data sharing can only be realized in practice if users understand how to use the DBMS facilities. The DBA is responsible for educating users in the structure of the database and in its access through the DBMS. This can be done in formal training sessions, by interacting with users to create database views, through user's manuals and periodic memos, and through company information centers.

information center
An area where users have facilities to do their own computing.

An **information center** is an area where users are provided with facilities to do their own computing. Auxiliary software packages for data manipulation may be provided, as well as training and simple programming services. The DBA provides staff for such centers to give users an outlet for answering questions and solving information processing problems, while relieving the information systems staff from the numerous "simple" requests that are a natural part of every organization's information needs.

Database Security and Integrity

The concept of combining an organization's data into one common pool accessible to all has both advantages and disadvantages. The obvious advantage of data sharing is offset by the disadvantage that data can be misused or damaged by users who do not have original responsibility and authority over the data. The DBA provides procedures and controls to prevent the abuse of data.

The DBA assigns ownership of the data in a database view to the originating group. The owning group may then grant access to the data in the view to other groups within the organization. This access may be restricted to portions of the data, to **retrieve only access,** or to access with update allowed. Information regarding access rights to data is maintained by the DBA in the data dictionary.

retrieve only access
Database access with no update allowed.

Access to the database is ultimately controlled by a password mechanism, whereby a user attempting access gives a system-validated password. The system allows the validated user only those access rights recorded in the data dictionary. The DBMS controls access as well as keeping statistical information about data accessed and entered by the user. The DBA is responsible for assigning passwords and controlling access privileges. By this means, the DBA greatly reduces the risk of one group's damaging another's data.

data integrity Accuracy and consistency of data values in the database.

Data integrity refers to the problem of maintaining the accuracy and consistency of data values. Security mechanisms, such as passwords and data views, protect data integrity. In addition, value constraints are maintained in the data dictionary. Unfortunately, value constraint definition and enforcement is a major area of weakness for current database management systems. We can identify many more constraints than we can define to the DBMS. Thus, it may be necessary for programs to be coded which will carry out constraint verification for new data being entered. Such programming may be reasonably assigned to the DBA staff.

Backup and recovery mechanisms supported by the DBMS preserve data in event of system failure. The DBA, however, must define procedures to recover lost data. Users must know what to do after a system crash to reenter all, and only, the data needed.

Database System Performance

A database system being simultaneously accessed by many users may respond very slowly at times because the physical problems associated with users competing for the same resources are not trivial. Thus, the DBA staff should include technically

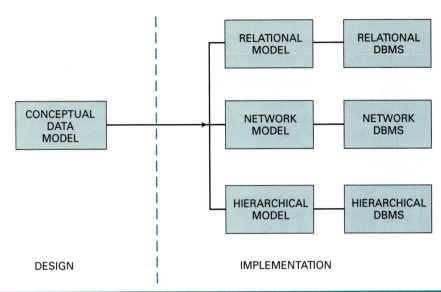

Database Design and the Traditional SDLC

system development life cycle (SDLC) A process for system development.

Systems analysis texts normally describe a system development procedure called the **system development life cycle (SDLC).** This procedure typically consists of steps such as feasibility study, requirements definition, system design, programming and testing, installation and training, and review and maintenance.

A natural question arises: How does database design fit into this outline? Meyer (1988) argues that to increase their effectiveness, system developers need to take a close look at the assumptions underlying the traditional SDLC. The SDLC emphasizes identifying business functions and developing application systems to perform those functions. Naturally, as Meyer notes, the SDLC methods are based on a **function-oriented approach.** That is, they view systems from the standpoint of the functions they perform rather than of the data they perform these functions on. Thus, structured analysis emphasizes dataflow diagrams, tracking the progress of data through a sequence of transformations, refining them through a series of levels. The same is true of structured design, which views a system as a single function successively decomposed into levels of subfunctions.

function-oriented approach Views a system from the perspective of the functions it should perform.

By concentrating on functions, these methods neglect data, and especially the *structure* of data, which functions manipulate. The result, says Meyer, is that these systems have short-term value at the expense of the long-term needs of the users. This happens because shortly after installation a system's functions become a subset of the functions users actually want. Almost immediately, the users see a large variety of additional services they want from the system. These needs cause problems for function-oriented systems, since their design may require major revision to accommodate additional functions.

data-oriented approach Focuses on the analysis of data used by the functions.

The **data-oriented approach,** by contrast, focuses on the analysis of data used by the functions. It has two advantages: (1) The data elements are a considerably more stable part of a system than are the functions. This is because a given set of data elements can be combined in a very large number of ways to give answers to various possible questions. If we view each possible question as a system function, it is easy to show that the set of possible functions will always be much larger than the number of data fields. (2) As we will see in Part II, the proper structuring of a database schema requires sophisticated analysis of classes of data items and their interrelationships. Once a logically sound database schema is built, any number of functional systems may be designed to take advantage of the schema's data. Without such a schema, however, the database may only be useful for a single application. Thus, the function-oriented approach is good for short-term system development but of less real value over the longer term.

We see then that by using the data-oriented approach, the data become the foundation on which a large variety of different functional systems can be built. Figure 3.11 expands the database plan of Figure 3.7, showing how it leads to one or more database systems, which in turn lead to multiple functional systems.

▼FIGURE 3.11 FUNCTIONAL SYSTEMS BASED ON DATABASE SYSTEMS

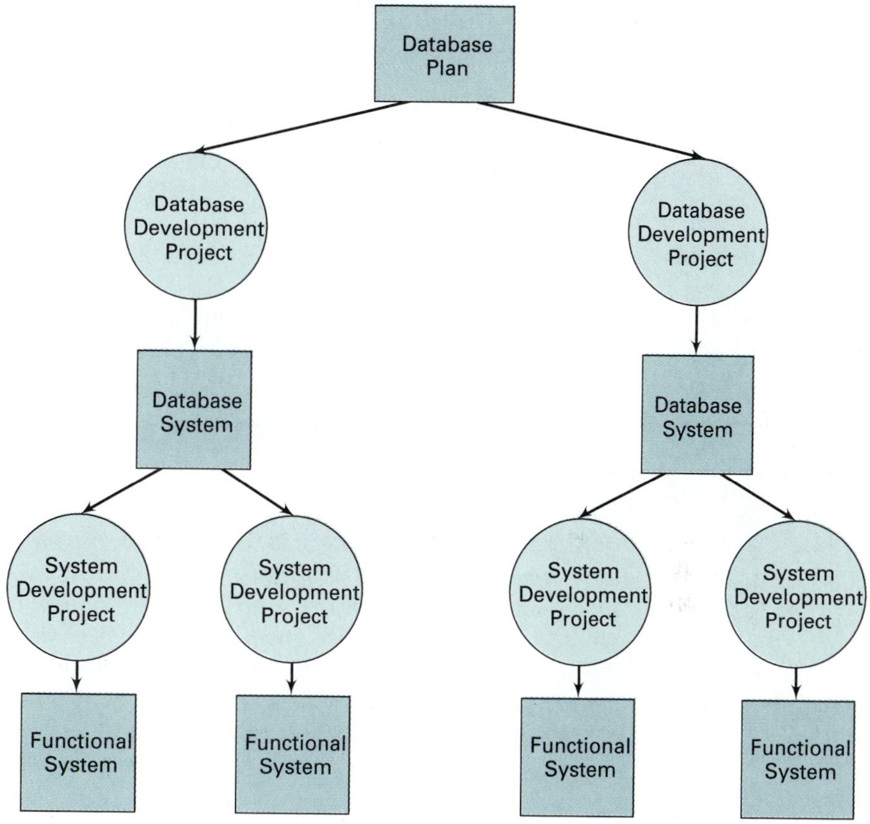

The Database Development Life Cycle (DDLC)

Figure 3.12 shows a database development life cycle (DDLC), which consists of six stages:

1. Preliminary planning
2. Feasibility study
3. Requirements definition
4. Conceptual design
5. Implementation
6. Database evaluation and maintenance

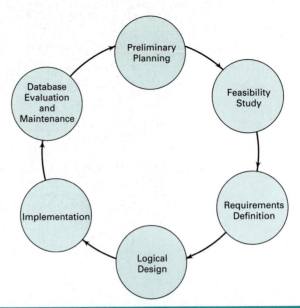

▼FIGURE 3.12 A DATABASE DEVELOPMENT LIFE CYCLE

As can be seen, this life cycle differs from the SDLC only in its emphasis: The DDLC is concerned with the development of a comprehensive *database* and the programs needed to process it. In the rest of this section, we describe the main tasks of each stage, using the experience of Zeus Corporation as an illustration.

Case: The Zeus Corporation

The Zeus Corporation started with a project completed while the Blue brothers were getting MBAs at a midwestern business school. The project focused on the creation of a company to manufacture and market running shoes. Both Bill and Steve Blue had been high school cross country runners and had continued to run after high school. As part of a business strategy course, they developed a plan to manufacture and distribute running shoes. As they thought through the details, their initial desire to simply satisfy course requirements grew. At this time, very few companies marketed genuine running shoes, and they felt the market would be receptive. When their instructor encouraged them, they decided to test their idea by creating the Zeus Corporation.

The brothers rented a garage and purchased basic equipment and an initial stock of materials. Their biggest initial challenge—getting running-shoe stores to accept a new and untried brand—was largely overcome by providing free shoes to a number of elite runners, who provided free media exposure and testimonials. After two meager years, the quality of their product began to pay off, and revenues doubled over the following two years and grew in subsequent years until annual revenues reached a level of about $50 million.

Zeus's information systems had basically evolved as the company grew, with new applications being developed as needs were identified. Two years ago, a consultant had helped the company establish a long-range business plan and a corresponding plan for management information systems (MIS). A central part of the MIS plan was the development of a corporate database system.

Preliminary Planning

preliminary planning
Planning for a database that occurs during the strategic database planning process.

Preliminary planning for a specific database system takes place during the strategic database planning project. After the database implementation project begins, the general information model produced during database planning is reviewed and enhanced if needed. During this process, the firm collects information to answer the following questions:

1. How many application programs are in use, and what functions do they perform?
2. What files are associated with each of these applications?
3. What new applications and files are under development?

This information can be used to establish relationships between current applications and to identify uses of application information. It also helps to identify future system requirements and to assess the economic benefits of a database system. It is documented in a generalized conceptual data model.

Feasibility Study

feasibility study Portion of the DDLC that determines technological, operational, and economic feasibility of database.

A **feasibility study** involves preparing a report on the following issues:

1. Technological feasibility. Is suitable technology available to support database development?
2. Operational feasibility. Does the company have personnel, budget, and internal expertise to make a database system successful?
3. Economic feasibility. Can benefits be identified? Will the desired system be cost-beneficial? Can costs and benefits be measured?

The Zeus feasibility study was done by an interdepartmental team comprised of a systems analyst, an engineer, a marketing specialist, a production supervisor, a financial analyst, and a database specialist. They were guided by a corporate MIS steering committe of high-level managers from each functional area. The steering committee approved each phase before the next phase was started. The focus of each phase was as follows:

technological feasibility Determination of hardware and software availability for database system.

1. The first phase was a **technological feasibility** study to determine if hardware and software were available to service their information needs. It included analysis of whether the capabilities and resources were already present in the company or whether they would have to be purchased, and whether training was needed. It turned out that all required hardware was already present at Zeus, although the DBMS would have to be acquired.

operational feasibility Determination of availability of expertise and personnel needed for the database system.

2. **Operational feasibility.** This included analysis of skill and labor requirements needed to implement the system. A preliminary assessment suggested that, although Zeus had competent, experienced programmers and analysts, a good deal of training would be required. The training needs encompassed users and some systems personnel. The DBA had previously been identified and trained from the ranks of systems personnel.

economic feasibility Cost-benefit study of proposed database system.

3. The **economic feasibility** study turned out to be challenging. The expected benefits of installing a database were difficult to quantify. This is a fairly typical ex-

perience. The project team addressed this challenge by seeking answers to these questions:

    a. How soon can benefits be expected?

    b. Is data sharing by user departments politically feasible?

    c. What risks are involved if a database system is implemented?

    d. What applications will be implemented, and what benefits are sought from those applications?

    e. What is the competition doing?

    f. How will the database system aid in accomplishing corporate long-range plans?

On the cost side, the simplest factors to measure were out-of-pocket costs for software, hardware, and programming. While these costs are not entirely subject to management control, it was felt the firm could enjoy cost savings by establishing standards before database software was installed, and by not installing a query language before there were sufficient data to warrant its effective use.

The project team also mentioned hidden costs associated with database implementation. These typically result from unforeseen changes in the way systems function. For example, it is easy to underestimate the time needed to integrate independent application systems. In addition, software changes may require unanticipated hardware upgrades to ensure adequate performance. Such changes quickly add to development costs.

The results of each feasibility examination were favorable, and the steering committee gave approval to move ahead with requirements definition.

Requirements Definition

requirements definition Determination of management and functional area information requirements.

Requirements definition involves defining the scope of the database, identifying management and functional area information requirements, and establishing hardware/software requirements. Information requirements are determined from questionnaire responses, interviews with managers and clerical users, and reports and forms currently being used. The general information model created during database planning is expanded to models for each functional area. These are the basis for the detailed database design to be carried out in the next stage. The results of this stage are described in the following four tasks.

Although not every firm will follow identical steps, there are some basic notions identified with successful requirements definition. At Zeus, the following tasks were completed:

1. The database system scope was defined by analyzing management's information requirements. The team also considered whether the database should be distributed or centralized and what teleprocessing facilities were required. A brief narrative was produced describing the scope of the system. It was decided that a centralized database encompassing most major functional areas would be developed.

2. User requirements at management and operational levels were documented with a generalized information model for each functional area, along with definitions of the application systems necessary to satisfy those requirements. The information models for each functional area were conceptual data models (discussed in Chapter 4). User requirements were also documented with narratives from user interviews, reports, and preprinted forms (Figure 3.13), and answers to a questionnaire (Figure 3.14).

Zeus Corporation

Boswick, TN

Purchase Order

Order No. 1848

Date 2/21/9X

Date Needed 3/15/9X	Vendor		Department Parts Inventory	Purchasing Agent T. Achilles
	Code	Name		
	215	Shoe Pieces, Inc.		

Part No.	Description	Quantity	Unit Price	Extended Price
4831	Laces	5000	.17	850.00
4922	Insoles	1000	2.30	2300.00
			Total	3150.00

▼FIGURE 3.13 A PREPRINTED PURCHASE ORDER FORM

▼FIGURE 3.14 A QUESTIONNAIRE TO BE USED DURING REQUIREMENTS DEFINITION

```
YOUR FUNCTION
Describe your area of responsibility. _____
What are your principal duties that require information from
computer applications? _____


USE OF INFORMATION
1. From what applications do you receive information? _____
2. How often is the information received? _____
3. What do you do with this information? _____
4. What security precautions must you take with respect to
   the information? _____
5. For what applications do you submit data? _____
6. Are there contemplated changes to any of your current activities
   involving any of the above information? Please describe
   briefly. _____
```

3. General hardware/software requirements were established along with the levels of performance to be supported. Considerations in this area included the number of users normally accessing the system, the number of transactions entering the system each day, and the amount of printing that would be required. This information was used to determine the size and type of computer and DBMS needed as well as the amount of disk space and printing support. A narrative report with figures showing the hardware and software configuration was produced.

4. A plan was drafted for a time-phased development of the system, including identification of initial applications. The guiding principles were: (1) The applications should be relatively small and noncritical to limit the impact of any problems in introducing a database; or (2) they should be for users very supportive of the database system development.

Conceptual Design

conceptual design
Creation of conceptual-level schema for database.

The **conceptual design** stage creates the conceptual schema for the database. Specifications are developed to the point where implementation can begin. During this stage, detailed models of user views are created and integrated into a conceptual data model recording all corporate data elements to be maintained in the database.

At Zeus, conceptual design focused on development of a model of the firm's reality. Development of the model was guided by information contained in policy and procedure manuals, as well as the guidelines and generalized models for the functional areas from requirements definition. Through in-depth interviews with users and careful examination of company forms, these models were enhanced. They were then integrated as part of conceptual design and became the basis for implementation.

The modeling task of the conceptual design step was a key component in the consultant's recommendation of the DDLC. At first, Steve Blue, Zeus's executive vice-president, was skeptical of this technique. He queried their consultant, Linda Kelly, very carefully:

*"**L**inda, what's wrong with the way we do things now?"*

"Your current methods are tied too closely to a file-oriented way of thinking, Steve. You've inherited this approach from the early days when technology left no choice but to design databases as files. But the fact is that problems are simply not structured this way. You need an approach that is much more natural. In other words, you need to move from a physically oriented approach to a logically oriented one. A conceptual design methodology will do that."

"Now wait a minute. As I understand it, a relational database system will move us from the physical to the logical orientation."

"A relational database will help primarily with data manipulation, not data structure. The relational model itself is still essentially file oriented, since relational tables are really just like files. The relational model is fine for working with relatively simple problems. But to do rigorous analysis of complex business problems, you need a more powerful methodology. That's why I recommend conceptual database design."

"What do you mean by conceptual?"

Linda explained, "The conceptual design methodology is also called semantic *modeling. Semantic* means *meaning. That is, we capture the* meaning *of* data and rela-

tionships in our modeling. In this design methodology, we think in terms of objects instead of files. Objects are things like sales representatives, products, managers, sales, and so forth. Even more important, we think in terms of named relationships between objects. For example, a manager manages a sales representative. Manager and sales representative are objects. Manages is a relationship between them. As problems become more complex, conceptual design helps us to think more clearly and to keep a large number of complex relationships straight in our minds. Without this methodology, our systems would become hopelessly confused."

"Well, I agree we need to handle more complex problems. Does this mean that we shouldn't get a relational database management system?"

"No, it doesn't. Think of conceptual modeling as a tool that creates clear designs that can readily be converted to high-quality relational models. You will have better systems, but they can still run on existing relational DBMS software."

"It sounds like you've got all the bases covered. Let's follow through with it."

First, as Zeus executed the DDLC, the conceptual design step consisted of creating detailed conceptual models of user views in different functional areas. These models together constituted the external level in the three-level architecture. Second, these user views were integrated into a single conceptual model giving the conceptual-level database schema. With this completed, they were ready for implementation.

Implementation

database implementation The steps required to change a conceptual design to a functioning database.

During **database implementation,** a DBMS is selected and acquired. Then the detailed conceptual model is converted to the implementation model of the DBMS, the data dictionary built, the database populated, application programs developed, and users trained (Figure 3.15).

At Zeus, implementation began with DBMS selection and acquisition. For several reasons, they chose a relational DBMS. The next step was mapping the firm's conceptual model to a relational implementation model using the procedures outlined in Chapter 5. The resulting table structures were then defined for the DBMS. This was done by using a data definition language (DDL) supplied with the DBMS to develop the data dictionary.

Building the data dictionary (DD) is a crucial step in implementation because the DD is a central repository for data structure definitions in the database. Because it contains information about access authority, security rules, and related controls, the DD acts as a control center for the system. It is used to enforce data standards and eliminate problems in coordinating data sharing among applications.

The next step was to populate the database by loading data from Zeus's files into the database. This was done through a data conversion program that used the data manipulation language (DML) supplied with the DBMS.

The team then surveyed user views and applications that would use the database. For some users, it was decided a special application program written by the programming staff would provide the simplest access to the database with the fewest security problems. This was most often true for clerks and other employees who recorded the firm's daily business. The team thought it best to train other users to use the data manipulation language to directly access the database.

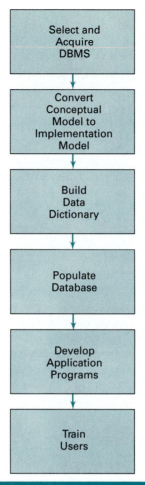

The final step was to develop procedures for using the database and to set up training sessions on these procedures and the other facilities of the system.

Evaluating and Enhancing the Database Schema

Evaluation involves interviewing users to determine if any data needs are unmet. Changes are made as needed. Over time the system is maintained via the introduction of enhancements and the addition of new programs and data elements, as business needs change and expand.

▼ Building Skills in Database Development

As Table 3.1 shows, most of this book is devoted to helping you develop skills in executing the database development life cycle. Thus, Part II covers database design. Chapters 4 and 5 describe the process and methodology of conceptual data modeling, which is essential to the successful construction of a logically sound database, showing how a conceptual model can be converted to a relational implementation model. Part III then focuses on relational database implementation. Chapters 6, 7, 8, and 9 intro-

▼ TABLE 3.1 COVERAGE OF THE DDLC

DDLC Step	Chapter
Preliminary Planning	3
Feasibility Study	3
Requirements Definition	3, 4
Conceptual Design	2, 3, 4, 9
Implementation:	
DBMS Selection	13
Conversion to Implementation Model	2, 5, 7, 8, 9, 15, 16
Physical Model	10
Data Dictionary Development	12
Application Program Development	2, 7, 8, 9, 15, 16
Management Control	11, 12

duce the relational languages, theoretical and applied, and discuss the facilities available in client/server systems. Chapter 10 concludes by explaining the physical model.

Part IV expands the topic of database implementation by discussing the management of the database environment. It deals with management topics such as database administration, security and integrity (Chapter 11), and distributed databases (Chapter 12) that were introduced in this chapter. DBMS selection is covered in Chapter 13. Part V contains one chapter to discuss the advanced topics of knowledge-base systems and object-oriented systems (Chapter 14). The final part, Part VI, covers the legacy database models, the network (Chapter 15) and the hierarchical (Chapter 16).

As you study this material, you will develop skills in database design and data manipulation that will be essential in a business database environment. You will also understand management issues that significantly affect many of the decisions made about database systems. The background material provided throughout the book will help you to understand the context of database systems in today's business world. By acquiring these skills, understanding the key management issues, and being familiar with the context of databases, you will be well equipped to function in the advanced environment of management information systems.

Summary

In this chapter, we have discussed the organizational context in which database systems function. In the first half of the chapter we saw that the concept of data sharing can be viewed from three perspectives—between different functional areas, between different levels of management, and between different geographical locations. We discussed the concept of strategic database planning and indicated how it lays the foundation for all database systems to be used in the organization. We then examined the database administration function, outlining this group's responsibility for: (1) the logical and physical design of the database; (2) training users in the structure of the database and in the procedures required for accessing and updating it; (3) protecting the database from misuse, inappropriate access, and inadvertent damage; and (4) assuring that the system as a whole performs at an acceptable level. Finally, we discussed some of the risks and costs of the database approach to an organization, including organizational conflicts over data sharing, potential failure of a database development project, database system failure and consequent database damage, increased overhead costs, and the need for sophisticated personnel for database development and operation.

The last half of the chapter was devoted to a discussion of database development. We explained the ANSI/SPARC three-level database architecture; we contrasted the function-oriented approach of the traditional system development life cycle (SDLC) with the data-oriented approach of the database development life cycle (DDLC); and we outlined the steps of the DDLC and described the activities included in each step.

Three-level architecture describes a database as consisting of the conceptual, external, and internal levels. The conceptual level is the logical schema which defines the entire database from the perspective of the organization. The external level consists of the various views by which the users throughout the organization understand, access, and update the database. The internal level is the physical definition of the database by which the DBMS controls and updates the database.

The traditional SDLC views systems from the standpoint of the functions they are to perform. Since data elements tend to be more stable than functions, we saw that the database structure should be developed prior to the development of functional systems. A properly developed database system will be the foundation on which many functional systems can be built.

The DDLC consists of six steps: preliminary planning, feasibility study, requirements definition, conceptual design, implementation, and database evaluation and maintenance. Preliminary planning takes place primarily during strategic database planning. Information from the database plan is reviewed and brought up to date as part of the DDLC. The feasibility study is carried out to determine technological, operational, and economic feasibility. Requirements definition determines the information requirements of management as well as those of the functional areas to be served by the database. Conceptual design results in a comprehensive conceptual data model, which gives a detailed logical schema for the entire database. During implementation, the DBMS is acquired, the conceptual design is converted to an implementation design, the data dictionary is built, the database is populated, application programs are developed, and the users are trained. After implementation, the database itself is evaluated to determine whether it is in fact meeting users' needs. Needed enhancements to improve database useability and to address changing business needs are carried out.

Review Questions

1. Define each of the following terms in your own words:
   a. database
   b. electronic data processing
   c. management information system
   d. centralized database
   e. database development life cycle
   f. database administration
   g. physical database design
   h. value constraint
   i. three-level architecture
   j. internal level
   k. preliminary planning
   l. technological feasibility

m. requirements definition

n. database implementation

2. Discuss the advantages and disadvantages of data sharing for each of the following:

a. Different functional areas

b. Different geographical locations

3. How can transaction-level data be used to support information needs at management and executive levels? What other kinds of information may be needed for strategic decision making?

4. Discuss the following aspects of the strategic database planning project:

a. Support of senior management

b. Project team composition

c. Length of project

d. Scope of project

e. Output of project

f. Relationship of project with database development life cycle

5. What is the responsibility of database administration with respect to:

a. Conceptual database design

b. The information center

c. Data integrity

d. Database system performance

6. List all the potential drawbacks you can think of associated with implementing and using a database system. Classify them according to whether they are risks or costs. Explain why you classify them in that way.

7. Explain the difference between the conceptual and external levels in the ANSI/SPARC three-level architecture.

8. Explain the meaning of the statement: "The database exists in reality only at the [ANSI/SPARC] internal level."

9. Discuss the differences between function-oriented system development and data-oriented system development. Why is data-oriented system development more likely to allow a broader range of functions?

10. List and briefly describe each of the six steps in the database development life cycle.

Problems and Exercises

1. Match the following terms with their definitions:

___decision support system

___retrieve only access

___database planning

___operational feasibility

___external level

___conceptual database design

___data integrity

a. Where users can find computing facilities

b. Restricted portion of the database

c. Multiple database systems connected by communication lines

d. Focuses on the analysis of data used by the functions

e. Creation of a conceptual-level schema

f. No update allowed

g. Strategic effort to determine long-term information needs

__*view*__	h. Combining data for common use
__*data integration*__	i. Identifies elements, relationships, and constraints
__*system development life cycle*__	j. Structural level defining the logical schema
__*function-oriented approach*__	
	k. Structural level defining user views
__*distributed database system*__	l. Accuracy and consistency of values
__*schema*__	m. Provides strategic information
__*information center*__	n. Defines logical structure of entire database
__*conceptual design*__	o. Cost-benefit study
__*data-oriented approach*__	p. A process for system development
__*conceptual level*__	q. Determines availability of expertise and personnel
__*feasibility study*__	r. Views a system from the perspective of the functions it should perform
__*economic feasibility*__	s. Determines technological, operational, and economic feasibility

2. IPD's functional areas include inventory, marketing, sales, purchasing, accounting, order processing, and product evaluation. Identify the functional areas that (1) need data or (2) could use data contained in each of the following documents. Explain in each case why they need the data or how they could use them.

    a. An order from a department store in Canada for 100 glass crystal vases.

    b. A report showing sales and returns of products for each sales representative in the Latin American region.

    c. A report showing changes in quantity on hand for each product over a three-month period.

    d. A report showing current quantity on hand for each product, together with average product cost and current price.

3. Classify the following types of information as to whether they are most significant at the operational, middle-management, or executive level:

    a. The population of Clark County is 500,000 and has doubled in each of the last two decades.

    b. The Smiths are two months past due on their account.

    c. Becky Daines got married and now her last name is Martinez.

    d. Galen has led the Eastern region in sales for seven months in a row.

    e. Wilson's check bounced again!

    f. The repair costs for that old equipment in the Charlesville factory have gone through the roof, new employees are impossible to find there, and transportation costs in and out of Charlesville are becoming exorbitant.

4. In a geographically distributed organization, which types of information would be needed centrally and which types locally?

    a. A country's payroll tax laws.

    b. A factory's total monthly payroll.

    c. A sales office's monthly sales figures by product line.

    d. A sales office's weekly sales figures by sales representative.

5. Discuss the following strategic database planning projects:

    a. The project team spent a full year interviewing at least one clerk from every processing unit in the company.

b. The project team carefully investigated the information needs of the home office but spent no time in the branch offices because they were only interested in high-level information.

6. Categorize each of the following into the database administration tasks of design, training, security/integrity, and performance:

   a. Showing Helen Blomquist how to construct a query to identify the average percentage of returns for each product.

   b. Reducing order entry response time to two seconds.

   c. Reissuing passwords for every system user.

   d. Directly relating every sale to the sales representative who made the sale.

7. Identify the potential difficulties in the following situations:

   a. A functional area is reluctant to allow other areas to access its data.

   b. Senior management initiates a database project without being fully convinced of its value.

   c. The computer controlling a centralized database goes down.

   d. An on-line system needs more rapid response time than the DBMS can provide.

   e. The only database administrator for a company in a small town suddenly leaves to work for a company in another state.

8. Identify the ANSI/SPARC levels for each of the following:

   a. An index giving the disk address of each record in a PERSONNEL file.

   b. A partial version of the PERSONNEL file containing only the name and address of each employee.

   c. A combination of sales transaction data and customer data which shows the product number of the product sold and the customer's number, name, and address but does not show the sales representative number.

   d. A file giving the disk address of an employee record together with the disk addresses of the records of all the employee's dependents.

   e. Data giving the names of all files and fields in the database together with definitions of interrelationships between fields in different files.

9. Identify information system functions that the following sets of data elements can be used to perform:

   a. For a department store: product number, regular price, sale price, cost, quantity sold, department, sales representative, commission rate, supervisor. (Example: Using regular price, sale price, and cost, profit at the regular price and profit at the sale price can be calculated.)

   b. For a consulting firm: consultant, consultant rank, hourly rate by rank, client, client type, hours a consultant worked for a particular client, date to which the hours billed apply, project type, project leader. (Example: Using consultant, rank, rate, hours worked, and dates, the total amount billed for a consultant's work for a client in a month can be calculated.)

10. In which step(s) in the DDLC would each of the following be performed?

    a. Obtaining a reasonable estimate of the operating cost of a database system.

    b. Determining the files used by the quarterly sales report.

    c. Determining whether the organization has people who are technically qualified to design and manage a database.

    d. Determining the major functions performed by the accounts payable system.

    e. Entering data into the database.

    f. Identifying the information needed by the manager of the purchasing department relative to the quality of service provided by vendors.

g. Determining changes needed to make the database more effective.

h. Specifying the complete conceptual structure of the database.

i. Writing and testing database application programs.

j. Determining which functions the database system will perform in each area.

k. Determining whether communications technology is powerful enough to make a worldwide distributed system practical.

11. Explain how the information concerning current applications and files that is gathered during preliminary planning can be used to help determine future information requirements.

12. List the preprinted forms that might be used by each of the following:

a. An insurance company

b. An electric company

c. A department store

d. A university

Projects and Professional Issues

1. Interview an executive in a large organization who recently conducted a strategic database planning study. Determine answers to the following questions:

a. What was the composition of the project team? How many members did it have and what were their professional backgrounds? Was a consultant engaged as a team advisor?

b. What was the nature of senior management's commitment to the project? Did they believe in its potential success or were they skeptical? What influence did their commitment have on the attitude of other employees?

c. What was the result of the project? Was a DBMS purchased? Was a new database designed and installed? How many functional areas and levels of management do the database and its application programs serve? Were distributed databases considered? What are the organization's database plans for the future?

2. Write a research paper on the difference between a *data administrator* and a *database administrator*. Determine whether most organizations make a distinction between the two in practice.

3. Write a research paper on a database implementation that failed. Try to determine why the project failed. What circumstances existed in this case that may not exist in other cases? What lessons can be drawn from the experience of the people in the project?

4. Write a research paper on the issues that led up to the ANSI/SPARC report on three-level architecture. Why did the committee recommend the levels it did? What was the historical context for its report? Were any issues left unresolved?

5. Examine the files and the functions of an installed application system. Discuss the system with some of its users to determine whether they would like the system to perform other functions. Identify which data items from the current system and which new data items would be required by the new functions.

6. Research the concept of the database development life cycle in current textbooks and trade periodicals. Try to identify versions of the DDLC that are different from the one given in this chapter. What do these versions have in common? Try to synthesize the various versions into a single, generic DDLC.

2

DATABASE DESIGN

▼

I n Part II, we deal with the problems of requirements definition, logical design, and implementation design in the database development life cycle. As you work through the material of this part, you will develop skills in requirements analysis, conceptual database design, normalization, and relational data model implementation.

In Chapter 4, you will be introduced to conceptual design and will see how the concepts of object relationships, attributes, and generalization and specialization can be used to create information models. We also apply these principles to design solutions of more complex problems. Sophisticated analysis and design techniques are discussed and applied to a number of practical examples from a wide variety of business situations.

Chapter 5 introduces the relational model and explains its significance in the history of database processing. It is the predominant model in today's business environment for implementation of new systems. The process of database normalization and conceptual model conversion are also defined and illustrated.

model A repr
of reality that
only selected

most of them irrelevant to the transaction. Thus, a model of Bookkeeping's view of the transaction will keep only those details Bookkeeping deems relevant.

Of course, some of the details regarded as irrelevant by one user may be very important to other users. Imagine, for example, that you are developing a database system for a fast-food restaurant. Weather conditions may be a significant aspect of the manager's reality, since a cold day may produce a far different mix of sales than a warm day. As a result, the manager may want to track these changes and order supplies accordingly. The number of people waiting in line may be another important aspect of the manager's reality, since the manager needs this information to schedule counter workers and minimize customer waiting. Thus, different users will have different models of reality.

A database incorporates a model of reality. The DBMS manages the database so that each user can record, access, and manipulate the data that constitute his or her model of reality. By manipulating data in a large variety of ways, users can derive the information needed to run an enterprise successfully. Thus, models are powerful tools for eliminating irrelevant details and understanding the reality of individual users.

Modeling reality is in many ways like solving a story problem. Both require you to sift through details to create a "correct" model of a portion of reality. This means you must associate, or **map**, elements in reality to elements in the model. If this mapping is done properly, then the model can be used to solve the problem. If not, the model cannot produce the correct solution. Many people find story problems difficult because they are not comfortable with the mapping process itself. In fact, Figure 4.1 may represent your own view of story problems. If so, we hope to help you become more comfortable with both modeling and mapping reality. We will begin with simple, basic modeling concepts and show how these can be used to build, step by step, a powerful solution to what may appear to be a complex problem. As you study the examples and work through the exercises and cases, you will develop substantial data modeling skills.

map To associate elements in one sphere with elements in another sphere.

▼ FIGURE 4.1 THE FAR SIDE

THE FAR SIDE   By GARY LARSON

Hell's library

Source: Copyright 1987 Universal Press Syndicate. Reprinted with permission. All rights reserved

◆ MODELS AT DIFFERENT LEVELS ◆

Although it may not be obvious, we are using the term *model* at three different levels in our discussion. These levels (not related to the three levels of ANSI/SPARC architecture) are illustrated in Figure 4.1S.

At the lowest level, we say that the current state of a particular database is a model of reality because it is a record of selected facts about reality that are currently true. For example, the database may record the fact: "Margaret Smith lives at 845 Puente Avenue." If Margaret's address changes, then the database state must change if it is to continue as an accurate model of reality.

At the next higher level, the schema, describing the structure of the database, is a model of a set of models (that is, it is a model of a set of database states). The schema models a huge range of database states by defining those characteristics that all of these states have in common. Thus, "Name" and "Address" are recorded in the schema as characteristics that apply to many different people and that change from time to time.

At the highest level, the database design methodology describes the constructs and rules that may be used in formulating a schema. Therefore, this level is also a model of a set of models (possible database schemas). A given design methodology, such as the conceptual data model or the relational model, is a model at this highest level and describes in general terms a potentially enormous set of schemas.

In summary then, we speak of the conceptual data model, which is a methodology for creating database schemas for particular application situations. These database schemas are themselves models that provide the logical structure to capture facts about a particular portion of reality. When these facts are captured and recorded in a computer database system, then the database itself is a model of the current state of reality. Each of the two upper levels of Figure 4.1S is a model of the level below it.

▼FIGURE 4.1 S THREE LEVELS OF MODELS

Model Level	Sample Model	Typical Construct
Design Methodology	Object-Oriented, Relational, etc.	Objects, Relationships Tables, Columns
	models a set of	
Database Schema	Database Schema	Person, Name, Address, Is-Employed-By
	models a set of	
Current State of Reality	Database	Margaret Smith 845 Puente Avenue

Conceptual Data Models

The data modeling methodology we will study and use in this chapter could be called an **object-oriented model** because it presumes a computer representation of real-world entities as "objects" having their own object identities and attributes and participating in relationships, rather than as records in traditional file-oriented systems. It is generally acknowledged that object-oriented representations more accurately reflect the logical essence of real-world applications than do record-based representations. For this reason, our methodology could also be called **semantic** because it provides a powerful means of mapping the *meanings* of things in reality to constructs in the model. Since the early seventies, a number of conceptual, semantic data models have been proposed. We will be using a generic modeling methodology, which has features common to most of these proposed models. For simplicity of reference throughout the book, we will call this model the *conceptual data model*.

In Chapter 2 we gave an introductory example which showed a simple conceptual data model. Now we are ready to define these ideas more precisely and, additionally, to introduce more powerful concepts, which will allow us to define even more sophisticated models.

◆ OBJECT-ORIENTED OR SEMANTIC MODELING? ◆

Object-oriented databases are the result of the convergence of two research disciplines: semantic data modeling and object-oriented languages. These disciplines developed independently but during the 1980s began to merge with important implications for database processing.

Semantic data modeling was originally developed for the purpose of increasing the effectiveness and accuracy of database design (Hull and King, 1987). Semantic modeling methods were found to be appropriate for many user problems and could be easily converted to record-based implementation models such as the hierarchical, network, and relational models. Abrial introduced the binary semantic data model in 1974, and this was followed during the next several years by Chen's entity-relationship model (Chen, 1976), the semantic data model (SDM) of Hammer and McLeod (1981), and the functional data model (Shipman, 1981). These and other data models, as well as extensions to these models, approached the problem of data modeling for purposes of database design from a variety of perspectives, yet they had in common the aim of providing a means to capture the *semantics* or the meaning of the application area being modeled. Chen's entity-relationship (E-R) model has been the most popular semantic model and is commonly found in books on conceptual data modeling and database design.

While those involved in semantic data modeling were primarily concerned with data structure, the developers of *object-oriented programming languages* were more interested in the behavior of data objects. That is, they were looking for ways of manipulating data that would focus on the data *and* the manipulation (query, computation, update) capabilities of the language. Data structure was a secondary concern.

The convergence of these two areas came when researchers began to apply concepts of object-oriented languages to semantic data structures. The result is the notion of an *object-oriented database.* In this merger of disciplines, the object-oriented terminology has tended to predominate, and so we speak of objects rather than entities, as we would if we were to use semantic terminology. In addition, object-oriented languages emphasize several concepts which were not found in Chen's original E-R model: object identity, object superset and subset hierarchy, and inheritance. We discuss all of these later. Thus, the methodology we use combines Chen's E-R model with concepts from object-oriented modeling. The E-R model forms the basis of our conceptual data model, and object-oriented modeling contributes several significant enhancements.

▼ Fundamentals

The principal elements of a conceptual data model are *objects* and *relationships.* Objects are often thought of as *nouns,* and relationships are regarded as *verbs.* Although additional constructs are provided in some conceptual data models, objects and relationships are powerful enough for the problems we will be considering.

Objects

Objects represent things that are important to users in the portion of reality we want to model. Examples of objects are people, automobiles, trees, dishwashers, houses, hammers, and books. These are concrete objects. Conceptual objects would be companies, skills, organizations, product designs, business transactions, and job classifications.

From the preceding, it may not be clear whether an object is a particular thing (an individual person, a particular automobile, a specific bank) or a *set* of things (all people, all automobiles, all banks). To avoid ambiguity, we will use the term **object set** to refer to a set of things of the same kind and **object instance** to refer to a single member (or element) of an object set. As Figure 4.2 shows, we will use rectangles to graphically represent object sets and points to represent instances. The name of an object set, given in all capital letters, is the singular version of the object. Thus, "PERSON" is the name of the object set representing people. A "person" (lowercase) is an instance of the object set PERSON. We write "person IN PERSON" to indicate that person is an instance of PERSON, or that the instance "person" is in the object set "PERSON."

object set A set of things of the same kind.

object instance A particular member of an object set.

▼**FIGURE 4.2 AN OBJECT SET AND AN OBJECT INSTANCE**

The object set name — PERSON — The object set

An object instance — • person

lexical object set An object set consisting of instances that can be printed.

abstract object set An object set consisting of instances that cannot be printed.

surrogate key A unique computer system identifier for an abstract object instance; it has no meaning outside the computer system.

Object sets are either **lexical** or **abstract**. Instances in lexical object sets can be printed, while the instances in abstract object sets cannot. Thus, for example, NAME would be a lexical object set, since the instances in NAME are names, which are strings of characters that can be printed. DATE, AMOUNT, and SOCIAL-SECURITY-NUMBER are other examples of lexical object sets, since dates, amounts, and social security numbers can also be printed.

PERSON, on the other hand, is abstract because a person cannot be printed. While it is true that a person can be *represented* by a lexical object such as a name or social security number, we nevertheless insist that a person is *not* a name or a social security number. For example, a person's name or social security number can change, but the person continues to be the same person. Therefore, to achieve a more accurate model of reality, we distinguish between abstract object sets and lexical object sets.

In a computer implementation of a conceptual model, a lexical object instance would be represented by a string of printable characters. An abstract object instance would be represented by an internal number which has no meaning outside the system. This internal number is sometimes called an *object identity*, or a **surrogate key**, meaning that it represents and uniquely identifies the real-world abstract object instance.

Suppose a person named Juanita Perez is in the PERSON object set. In an actual implementation of this object set, Juanita would be represented by some surrogate key, say "13948226." Her name (Juanita Perez), social security number, birthdate, height, weight, and other such information would be recorded as lexical data and would be associated in the database with the surrogate key representing her. Users would only see these lexical data. They would never see 13948226 in association with Juanita. But the system would use the surrogate in associating Juanita in all the possible numerous relationships that are part of the database.

Surrogate keys solve problems arising from traditional types of keys. For example, in many systems it is very difficult to change a key value. Social security number is often used as a key to uniquely access information about a person. What happens if the social security number is incorrect? Since this number has legal importance *outside* the database system, it *must* be corrected. But this could lead to a great many difficulties within the database, since there may be many references to that social security value. This problem is eliminated by using surrogate keys, since they are defined by the system and have no meaning outside the system. If Juanita Perez's social security number is incorrect, we merely change it. Nothing else in the database will be affected, since nothing else refers to the social security number. Instead, all references to Juanita Perez use the surrogate key.

Specialization and Generalization

specialization An object set that is a subset of another object set.

generalization An object set that is a superset of (or contains) another object set.

Some object sets are contained within other object sets. For example, MAN (the set of men) is contained within PERSON. This means that every man (every instance of the set MAN) is also a person (an instance of the set PERSON). Similarly, WOMAN is contained within PERSON. We say that MAN is a **specialization** of (or subset of) PERSON. We can represent this by writing MAN PERSON. PERSON, on the other hand, is a **generalization** or superset of MAN (and of WOMAN). We designate specialization/generalization graphically as shown in Figure 4.3(a). The U-shaped symbol indicates the direction of set containment. The top of the U "opens" to the larger or containing set. If we placed the sets side by side, the U would be on its side, pointing in the direction of PERSON. If PERSON were the bottom box, and MAN were the top box, the U would be upside down. We could also show MAN within

PERSON (Figure 4.3(b)). Since many object sets can be contained within a single set, this technique tends to cause crowded diagrams.

Suppose George is a man. Then George is also a person. This is shown graphically in Figure 4.4. Note that two points represent the same person. One point represents him as an instance in PERSON, and one point represents him as an instance in MAN. There is really only one instance. It is just shown as residing in two different object sets. The importance of this will be illustrated shortly.

▼**FIGURE 4.3 ALTERNATE REPRESENTATIONS OF SPECIALIZATION AND GENERALIZATION**

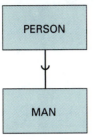

(a) The Specialization-Generalization Relationship

PERSON
MAN

(b) An Alternate Representation of Specialization

▼**FIGURE 4.4 TWO POINTS REPRESENTING THE SAME INSTANCE**

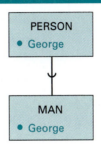

Relationships

relationship A linking between instances of two object sets.

A **relationship** links two object sets. Consider the object sets MARRIED MAN and MARRIED WOMAN. We can define the IS-MARRIED-TO relationship between these two sets by associating each married man with his wife (or, conversely, each married woman with her husband). The IS-MARRIED-TO relationship consists of a set of married couples, the husband coming from the MARRIED MAN object set and the wife coming from the MARRIED WOMAN object set. Graphically, we represent a relationship between two object sets by showing a line (with an optional embedded diamond) connecting the two sets (Figure 4.5(a)).

A relationship is itself an object set, consisting of pairs of instances taken from the two object sets it relates. That is, each instance of a relationship is a pair of instances from the two object sets. If

```
MARRIED MAN = {Adam, David, John}        and

MARRIED WOMAN = {Joan, Linda, Michelle}  and

Adam            is-married-to    Joan
David           is-married-to    Linda
John            is-married-to    Michelle
```

then

```
IS-MARRIED-TO =
    {(Adam, Joan), (David, Linda), (John, Michelle)}
```

The braces ({ }) here are used to indicate a set. Figure 4.5(b) shows this information graphically. We see then that the IS-MARRIED-TO relationship is itself an object set whose instances are married couples. An object set like IS-MARRIED-TO, which is derived from a relationship between other object sets, is called an **aggregate object set**.

Aggregate object sets can be given object set names and can participate in relationships, just as normal object sets. In Figure 4.5(c), the aggregate of IS-MARRIED-TO is named MARRIED-COUPLE, and it participates in several relationships. The HAS-ANNIVERSARY-DATE relationship connects a married cou-

FIGURE 4.5 REPRESENTATIONS OF A RELATIONSHIP

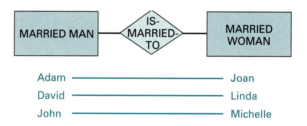

(a) The IS-MARRIED-TO Relationship

(b) Some Instances of IS-MARRIED-TO

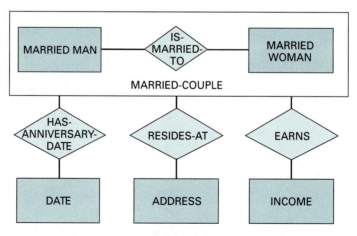

(c) The MARRIED-COUPLE Aggregate Object Set Participating in Relationships

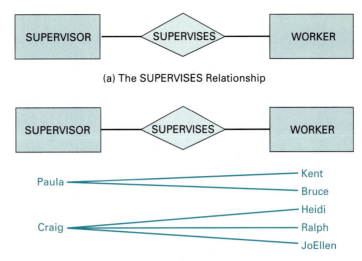

(a) The SUPERVISES Relationship

(b) Instances of the SUPERVISES Relationship

ple to their anniversary date; the RESIDES-AT relationship connects the couple to their address; and the EARNS relationship connects them to their total combined income.

As another example of a relationship, consider the two subsets of a company's employees, SUPERVISOR and WORKER. We define the instances of WORKER as employees who do not supervise other employees. The SUPERVISOR set consists of employees who supervise workers. The SUPERVISES relationship (note the verb) associates each supervisor with the workers he or she supervises (Figure 4.6(a)). Figure 4.6(b) illustrates instances that may be found in the SUPERVISES relationship.

Generalization/specialization represents a special type of relationship. Recall that in Figure 4.4 two different points represented the same person—George. The point in MAN representing George is related via this subset relationship to the point in PERSON representing George. In fact, every point in MAN is related to exactly one point in PERSON. Some points in PERSON, however, are related to points in WOMAN. Thus, every point in PERSON is related to either zero or one point in MAN. We can capture this type of information about relationships by adding cardinality to our diagrams.

Cardinality

cardinality The maximum number of instances of one object set related to a single instance of the other object set.

The **cardinality** of a relationship refers to the maximum number of instances in one object set that are related to a single instance in the other object set. For example, if we assume each married person has only one spouse, the cardinality of the IS-MARRIED-TO relationship is one in each direction (Figure 4.7).

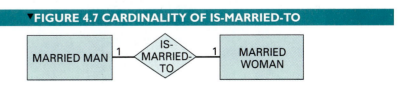

▼FIGURE 4.7 CARDINALITY OF IS-MARRIED-TO

Although we are normally interested only in maximum cardinality, it is sometimes useful to specify minimum cardinality. Suppose, for example, that we restate the IS-MARRIED-TO relationship so that it exists between the sets MAN and WOMAN (Figure 4.8(a)). Since many men and women are not married, the minimum cardinality is zero in both directions. We write "0,1" next to the WOMAN object set to indicate that any given man is married to between zero and one wives. Conversely, the 0,1 next to the MAN object set states that each woman is married to between zero and one husbands (Figures 4.8(b,c)).

Some relationships do not have a specific value for maximum cardinality. For example, a supervisor supervises at least one and possibly many workers. We indicate this cardinality as 1,*, where "1" indicates the minimum cardinality and "*" simply means "many." Conversely, if we assume that any given worker has one and only one supervisor, the cardinality in the other direction is 1,1 (Figure 4.9).

The cardinalities of the specialization or subset relationship are always the same. Every instance in the generalization set is related to zero or one instance in the specialization set, and every instance in the specialization set is related to exactly one instance in the generalization set (Figure 4.10).

Maximum cardinality is a much more important concept than minimum cardinality. To simplify our diagrams, therefore, we will only indicate minimum cardinal-

▼FIGURE 4.8 MINIMUM AND MAXIMUM CARDINALITIES

a.

b.

Any given man is married to 0 to 1 woman.

c.

Any given woman is married to 0 to 1 man.
(Relationship diagrams can be read from left to right or from right to left.)

▼FIGURE 4.9 CARDINALITY OF SUPERVISES

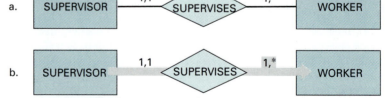

a.

b.

Any given supervisor supervises between 1 and many workers.

c.

Any given worker is supervised by exactly 1 supervisor.

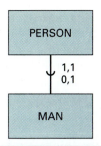

ity when it is needed. Except in the subset relationship (whose minimum cardinalities were discussed previously), omitted minimum cardinalities can be assumed to be zero.

A maximum cardinality of one in one direction of a relationship corresponds to the mathematical concept of a function, which sets up a one-to-one or many-to-one correspondence between two sets. Therefore, a relationship with a maximum cardinality of one in one direction is called **functional** in that direction. The supervisor/worker relationship in Figure 4.9 is functional from worker to supervisor. That is, if we know who the worker is, then we can uniquely determine his or her supervisor. This relationship is *not* functional in the other direction, since a supervisor has many workers.

If the maximum cardinalities in both directions of a relationship are one, we say the relationship is **one–one**. If the maximums are one in one direction and many in the other direction, we say the relationship is **one–many**. Finally, if the maximum cardinalities are many in both directions, we say the relationship is **many–many**. Table 4.1 summarizes the three basic relationship cardinalities.

Attributes

We have represented object sets as boxes and instances as points. This is very abstract. (What could have fewer features than a point?) We normally think of object instances as having a number of attributes that serve to distinguish them. For example, a person has a name, a birthdate, a social security number, height, weight, gender, eye color, hair color, a father, mother, and possibly a spouse. How do we represent these attributes?

functional relationship A relationship having a maximum cardinality of one in at least one direction.

one–one Relationship cardinalities of one in both directions.

one–many Relationship cardinalities of one in one direction and many in the other.

many–many Relationship cardinalities of many in both directions.

▼TABLE 4.1 THE THREE BASIC RELATIONSHIP CARDINALITIES

Cardinality	Notation	Examples
One–one	1:1 or 1-1	A husband has *one* wife. A wife has *one* husband. (The marriage relationship is one–one.)
One–many	1:* or 1-*	An employee is in *one* department. A department has *many* employees. (The employment relationship is one–many.)
Many–many	*:* or *-*	A student takes *many* courses. A course has *many* students. (The enrollment relationship is many–many.)

attribute Functional relationship from an object set to another set.

An **attribute** of an object is really just a functional relationship of that object's object set with another object set. Thus, two of the attributes listed previously are shown as relationships in Figure 4.11. We will find it convenient, however, to represent some attributes more simply, as shown in Figure 4.12. Note that the relationship name and the object name are, in a sense, combined into the name of the attribute (especially BIRTHDATE). We see, then, that writing attributes in this manner is merely a shorthand notation for writing relationships. Generally, this shorthand notation may be used whenever we do not intend to use the attribute as an object in yet another relationship.

In normal usage (which we will follow), attributes are *functional* relationships from the object set to the attribute. That is, the value of the attribute is uniquely determined for each object instance. For example, each person has exactly one birthdate and (in our database) one social security number. The maximum cardinality on the attribute side of these relationships is always one, and for this reason we will always omit attribute cardinalities from our diagrams. If a particular object instance has no value for one of its attributes, we say that that attribute has a **null** value for the object instance.

null attribute value An attribute value that does not exist for a specific object instance.

It is important to realize that attributes must be kept conceptually separate from the objects they describe. Recall from our earlier discussion that the values of attributes will frequently change while the objects associated with them remain the same. Thus, a person will change height, weight, name, and hair color but will remain the same person. This does not mean that all attributes do change values. In fact, we often try to identify attributes that do not change because they can be used as external keys.

key A value that can always be used to uniquely identify an object instance.

Keys. A **key** is a value which can always be used to uniquely identify an object instance. We previously mentioned surrogate keys, which would be used within a

▼FIGURE 4.11 ATTRIBUTES SHOWN AS RELATIONSHIPS

SOCIAL SECURITY NUMBER

DATE

1

HAS-SOCIAL SECURITY-NUMBER

1

WAS-BORN-ON

1

*

PERSON

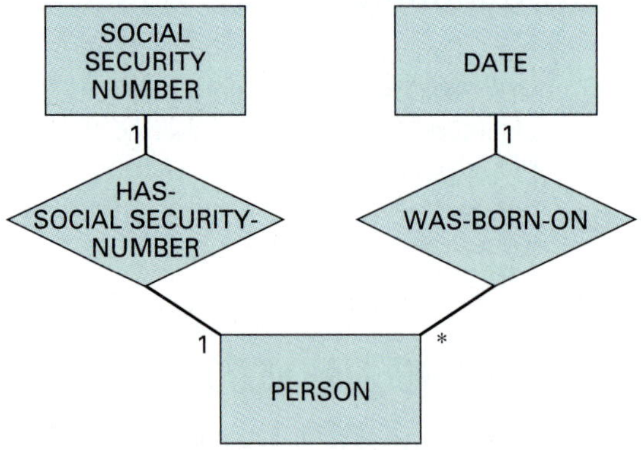

▼FIGURE 4.12 ATTRIBUTE NOTATION

SS# BIRTHDATE

PERSON

computer system to identify instances in abstract (nonlexical) object sets. PERSON, for example, is an abstract object set. In an implementation of a conceptual database, each person in the object set PERSON would have a surrogate key to identify that person within the database. But since the surrogate key cannot be used outside the system, database users need some other way of identifying instances of PERSON. This is accomplished through external keys.

An **external key** (also called an **identifier**) is a lexical attribute or set of lexical attributes whose values always identify a single object instance. A lexical attribute is an attribute formed using a lexical object set. Thus, external keys can be printed and read by users and serve as means by which specific object instances can be identified externally to the database system. We will usually refer to an external key as simply a key. In Figure 4.12, for example, SS# could be a key for PERSON if we assume each social security number corresponds to exactly one person. That is, the minimum and maximum cardinalities from SS# to PERSON are 1,1. Birthdate, on the other hand, could not be a key, since any given date is the birthdate for many different people.

Sometimes more than one attribute is needed to form a key. Suppose that PERSON in Figure 4.12 is being used in a genealogical database, which traces family trees. Because many of the people in PERSON died before social security numbers were introduced, we need something other than SS# for the key. Perhaps name, birthdate, and birthplace would be sufficient. If so, then the combination of these three attributes would form the key for PERSON. If not, then something additional may be needed. If necessary, we can always make up an identification number whose uniqueness can be enforced within the system. We denote an attribute as an external key by underlining the attribute name (Figure 4.12).

Not every object set needs to have a key. For example, in a database that records sales transactions, the user may be interested only in recording amount of sale and product sold. Obviously, many sales will have the same values for amount and product. It would be unreasonable to require the user to provide a unique key value for every sales transaction. Thus, the database would record only the information the user desires about each transaction, but it would still record separate instances for each transaction. Figure 4.13 shows two different sales attached to an amount of 5.95 and to product A237. The user will see two sales transactions but has no means of distinguishing between them and no interest in doing so. Thus, the absence of a key is of no consequence.

Specialization/Generalization and Attributes. If an object is a specialization of another object, then the specialization object **inherits** all of the attributes and rela-

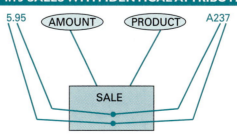

▼FIGURE 4.13 SALES WITH IDENTICAL ATTRIBUTE VALUES

tionships of the object it specializes. MARRIED PERSON, for example, is a specialization of PERSON. Thus, a married person has a name, social security number, address, and so on, just by virtue of being a person. The MARRIED PERSON object set inherits these attributes from the PERSON object set. In addition, the specialization object set can have attributes of its own. For example, SPOUSE would be an attribute of MARRIED PERSON, but not of PERSON. These concepts are illustrated in Figure 4.14.

Not only does a specialization inherit attributes, but it inherits all relationships. Figure 4.15 illustrates that PERSON is related to COMPANY via WORKS-FOR. MARRIED PERSON, being a specialization of PERSON, is also related to COMPANY via WORKS-FOR. Suppose John Doe is a married person working for XYZ Company. Then there is a point in MARRIED PERSON representing John Doe, a point in PERSON representing John Doe, and a point in COMPANY representing XYZ Company. John Doe in MARRIED PERSON is related to John Doe in PERSON, which is in turn related to XYZ Company. Consequently, John Doe in MARRIED PERSON is related to XYZ Company.

Inheritance of attributes and relationships is an important concept, since it allows us to define subsets of object sets which have attributes and relationships of their own but still retain all of the attributes and relationships of the superset. This makes it possible to model reality much more precisely than we could without the inheritance concept.

▼FIGURE 4.14 SPECIALIZATIONS INHERIT ATTRIBUTES

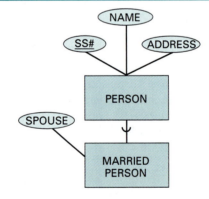

▼FIGURE 4.15 INHERITING RELATIONSHIPS

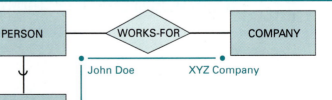

▼Examples

Let us try now to create conceptual data models for some real-world problems.

Example 1: The Bank Data Model

Our first example can be used to answer some of the questions posed at the beginning of the chapter. We are interested in creating a conceptual data model of the bank's business that will reflect the reality of Robert Goldthumb, President of Alchemical Bank and Trust (ABT).

The bank has checking accounts, savings accounts, and customers (Figure 4.16(a)). We establish appropriate relationships between these as shown in Figure 4.16(b). We are now in a position to answer these questions:

How many checking accounts do we have? How many savings accounts? How many customers?

The answers to these questions are obtained by merely counting the instances in each of the three object sets. With the appropriate software, Goldthumb could use his personal computer to ask these questions any time, or he could receive a periodic report.

Note how much more cleanly the database handles these questions than a traditional file-based system would. In a file-based system, without the interfile connections provided by a database, there may very well be just two files—one for the checking accounts and one for the savings accounts. In each of these files, customer information would be embedded in a number of fields (customer name, address, and so on). The third question—"How many customers"—would be difficult to answer, since we would have to extract all of the customer data from the two files, sort them, and throw out duplicates. In a database, however, these customer data can be maintained separately while still preserving the desired connections with account information.

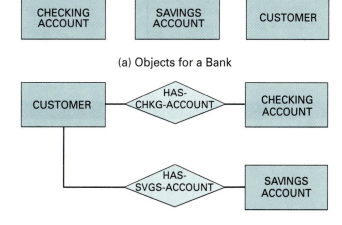

▼FIGURE 4.16 THE BANK DATA MODEL: BASIC OJBECTS AND RELATIONSHIPS

(a) Objects for a Bank

(b) Simple Relationships Between Bank Objects

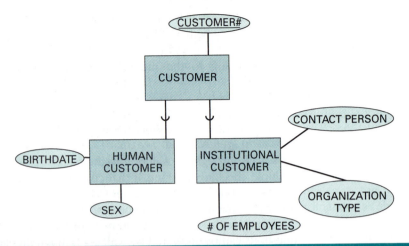

▼**FIGURE 4.20 ATTRIBUTES BY TYPE OF CUSTOMER**

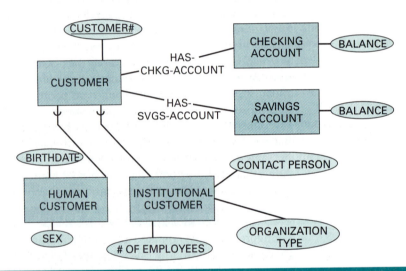

▼**FIGURE 4.21 ACCOUNTS FOR DIFFERENT CUSTOMER TYPES**

institutional customers. Within INSTITUTIONAL CUSTOMER, we can also distinguish using the ORGANIZATION TYPE attribute. For example, ORGANIZATION TYPE could possibly be Business, Nonprofit, Church, or Government Agency. To answer the second question, we start at HUMAN CUSTOMER and trace through CUSTOMER to CHECKING ACCOUNT via HAS-CHKG-ACCOUNT. We do this for each human customer and record the balance. When we're done, we compute the average balance for human customers. Then we follow the same procedure for INSTITUTIONAL CUSTOMER. Finally, to answer the question we compare the two averages.

Example 2: Stratton's Fruit Orchards

Vern Stratton, Maple Glen fruit grower, has been in the fruit business for 50 years. Before him, his father and grandfather owned his orchards, and he anticipates that at least some of his grandchildren will inherit them. Since the nineteenth century they've kept excellent records, which could constitute the basis for a comprehensive information system.

Vern is interested in the answers to questions like these:

How many varieties of peaches do we have in the Springtown orchard? How many trees die on average in the Lee's Valley orchard each year? What is the average age of my apple trees? How many plum trees have more than one variety on them?

Figure 4.22 gives a simple data model that can be used to obtain answers to these questions. The ORCHARD object set contains an instance for each orchard. The AREA attribute describes the orchard. Thus, AREA would have values such as Springtown, Lee's Valley, and so on. Each orchard is related to those trees (instances of TREE) that are in the orchard. Therefore, the instances of TREE stand for specific, physical trees rather than types of trees. Each tree was planted in a specific year and may or may not have died. If the tree has died, then YEAR DIED contains a value; otherwise, it is null.

Trees have species and species have varieties. For example, apple is a species and Jonathan and Red Delicious are varieties. Since branches can be grafted onto trees, a given species of tree might bear more than one variety. Thus, an apple tree that was originally Red Delicious could also bear Jonathan and Roman Beauty. Each tree has only one species, but it may have multiple varieties. Of course, there are many trees of each species and variety. Finally, each variety corresponds to only one species, although a species may have many varieties.

To answer the first question, we start with the ORCHARD object set. Using the AREA attribute, we identify the Springtown orchard. We then identify all the trees in that orchard by tracing to the TREE object set. From there we go to SPECIES, find "peach" and eliminate all those trees that are not peach trees. Now from TREE we trace all the Springtown peach trees to the VARIETY object set and identify all the varieties of peaches in the Springtown orchard.

Example 3: A Logic Problem Involving Mapping

You have probably seen logic problems in the games section of a newspaper or magazine. Usually such problems cannot be completely solved with the principles

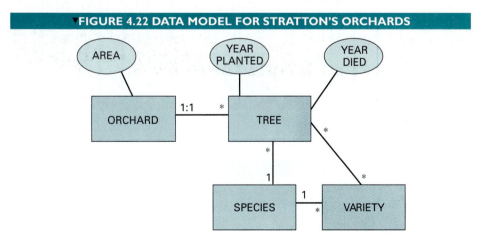

▼FIGURE 4.22 DATA MODEL FOR STRATTON'S ORCHARDS

of this chapter, but they can be simplified by defining objects and relationships appropriately. The following comes from Wylie (1957, p. 1):

In a certain bank, the positions of cashier, manager, and teller are held by Brown, Jones, and Smith, though not necessarily respectively.

The teller, who was an only child, earns the least.
Smith, who married Brown's sister, earns more than the manager.

What position does each man fill?

Figure 4.23 represents this problem graphically. We have four objects and corresponding relationships. Note that the minimum and maximum cardinalities for the relationship between POSITION and EMPLOYEE are 1,1 in both directions. When we make the assignments for this relationship, we will have the solution to the problem. We are trying to assign each employee to his position. We have listed the three positions and three employees next to their object sets. The clues tell us something about the employees' comparative earnings and how many brothers and sisters they have. This information is indicated on the diagram.

Figure 4.24 gives the solution to the problem. This was derived as follows: Since Smith earned the most, he could be neither the manager nor the teller. Therefore, Smith is the cashier. Brown has a sibling (his sister is married to Smith), so he's not the teller, who has no siblings. So Brown is the manager. Consequently, Jones must be the teller.

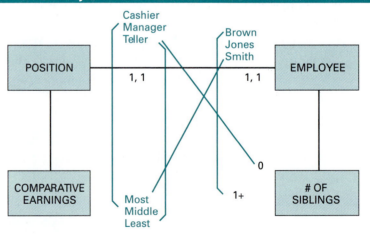

▼FIGURE 4.23 OBJECTS AND RELATIONSHIPS FOR BANK EMPLOYEES

▼FIGURE 4.24 SOLUTION TO BANK EMPLOYEES PROBLEM

▼ Building Conceptual Data Models from Existing Reports

The models we have been developing in this chapter are based on information implicit in the types of questions that *managers* would ask. Consequently, these models form the basis for *management information systems*. We are also interested, however, in models that could be used in the *data processing systems* which process the transactions that occur daily in most businesses. In this section, we examine two report forms that are used for transactions by many businesses and show how conceptual data models can be derived from these forms. These forms are used by Manwaring Consulting Services, a case study which we introduce now and which we will use in several future chapters to illustrate the steps in database design and implementation.

Case: Manwaring Consulting Services

*J*oan Manwaring, CPA, has operated Manwaring Consulting Services for the last ten years. Manwaring Consulting employs six consultants who perform consulting projects for Manwaring clients. Each project involves one or more consultants and may last several weeks or several months, depending on the scope of the project.

Estimates. *For each engagement taken, Joan must make a proposal for services. The proposal includes a scope, objective, task structure, and fee structure, among other things. The fees Joan charges can vary greatly among the different types of engagements. Fees are based on the benefits provided to the client, and the time and effort expended in completing the engagement. All information pertaining to the engagement is kept for future reference. Any adjustments made to the estimate are shown to the client and are recorded.*

Cash Receipts. *Although many of the smaller engagements are paid for in cash, most of the customers pay on account. Payment is due upon completion of the engagement, unless credit arrangements have been made. The credit accounts are ususably paid by the clients on time, but Joan sometimes has to send second notices to the client in order to collect payment.*

Cash Disbursements. *Although many supplies are charged directly to a specific engagement, some supplies and equipment are associated with multiple engagements or overhead. All supplies are bought on account.*

A Data Model for Purchases

Manwaring's purchase order form, used for ordering supplies, is shown in Figure 4.25. It includes the vendor's name and address, the date, order number, and vendor number. It also gives the vendor stock number, product, and price for each product. The total, including tax, is given at the bottom.

From this form, we can derive the following object sets: VENDOR, ORDER, PRODUCT. The attributes of these three sets as well as the relationships between

MANWARING CONSULTING
SERVICES
950 MAIN
EASTON, PA 11111

PURCHASE ORDER

Date	Order Number	Vendor Number
3/19	384	23

Stock #	Product Description	Price
3821	Box of #2 Pencils	4.00
4919	Box of Legal Pads	8.90
	Tax	.77
	Total	13.67

Vendor: Consolidated Office Supplies
                   414 S. Choctaw Drive
                   Flagship, PA 12345

▼**FIGURE 4.25 A PURCHASE ORDER FOR MANWARING CONSULTING SERVICES**

them are shown in Figure 4.26. Note the cardinalities of the relationships. The relationship between ORDER and VENDOR has one–many cardinality because each order is made from only *one* vendor, but a given vendor can receive *many* orders. The INCLUDES relationship between ORDER and PRODUCT is many–many because an order includes *many* products and a product can be found on *many* orders.

▼**FIGURE 4.26 THE INITIAL PURCHASE ORDER DATA MODEL**

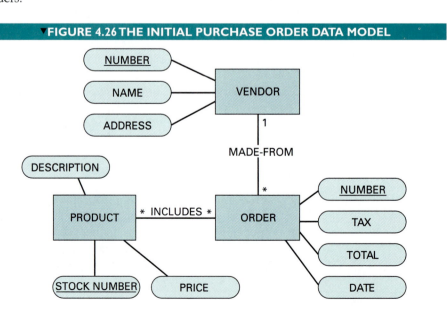

Eventually, a payment will be made for the order. To record this information, we enlarge the model to that shown in Figure 4.27. The PAYMENT object set has been added, with attributes CHECK NUMBER and DATE. The one–one cardinality indicates that each order will be paid for with one check, and each check will pay for one order.

▼FIGURE 4.27 THE EXPANDED PURCHASE ORDER DATA MODEL

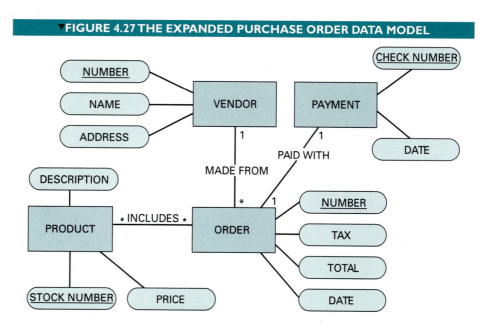

A Data Model for Project Billing

When a project is complete, Manwaring often sends an invoice for services rendered and for supplies used on the project. A sample invoice is shown in Figure 4.28. This invoice includes date, invoice number, and project title, as well as an itemization of the services and supplies being charged for.

From this form, we can identify CLIENT, PROJECT, and CHARGE object sets with their attributes. These are shown with the relationships between the object sets in Figure 4.29. Note that there are two different *types* of charges: consulting service charges and supply charges. Since the consulting service charge includes an identification of the consultant, we must divide the CHARGE object set into two subsets: SERVICE and SUPPLY CHARGE. The CHARGE object set has two attributes, AMOUNT and DESCRIPTION, which both of these subsets inherit. In addition, the SERVICE specialization of CHARGE has the CONSULTANT attribute.

The purchase order and invoice forms illustrate the process of using existing reports to define a conceptual data model. The database analyst gathering the data needed for database design uses a wide variety of existing reports to contribute to the conceptual data model. In addition, the analyst uses the interviewing process to determine additional information requirements by identifying the types of questions that management needs to be able to answer. The data obtained from reports and from interviews are combined in the design of a comprehensive conceptual data model. This model will eventually be implemented as a database schema and will be the basis for both data processing and management information systems.

▼FIGURE 4.28 AN INVOICE FOR MANWARING CONSULTING SERVICES

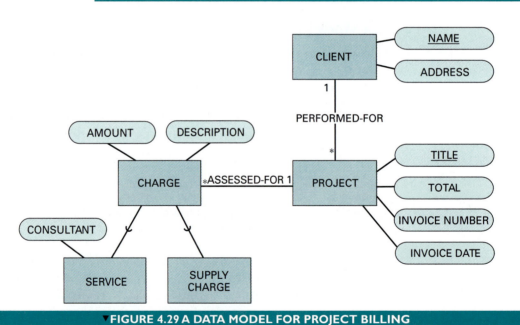

▼FIGURE 4.29 A DATA MODEL FOR PROJECT BILLING

▼Aggregation

The conceptual data models developed previously apply the basic concepts of conceptual data modeling. In the remainder of the chapter, we expand these relatively simple techniques to encompass the more complex situations which arise naturally in business. We will focus on aggregate object sets in this section and conceptual object sets in the next. These two concepts occur often in practical situations. By understanding these techniques, you will increase your skill in carrying out the requirements definition and conceptual design steps of the database development life cycle.

Although the models we have created with basic modeling concepts are relatively simple, it is easy to see their power and usefulness. However, most problems we actually encounter in business are considerably more complex and often involve the use of an **aggregate**, a relationship viewed as an object set, or a **higher-level relationship**, which involves three or more object sets.

aggregate A relationship viewed as an object set.

We saw earlier that a relationship can be used as an object set. For example, when we initially defined and discussed relationships, we noted that each man and woman who are related by the IS-MARRIED-TO relationship constitute a *married couple*, which is itself an object. As such, the married couple can have its own attributes, such as anniversary date, total earnings, and address. Moreover, it can participate in other relationships, such as OWN-AUTOMOBILE and ARE-PARENTS-OF. Thus, the IS-MARRIED-TO relationship can be viewed as an object set whose elements are married couples.

higher-level relationship A relationship between three or more object sets.

This is true of any relationship. Relationships can be viewed as objects and can have attributes and participate in other relationships. As we noted, such relationships are called aggregates. Graphically, we will represent an aggregate by drawing a box around the relationship and its participating object sets (Figure 4.30). Sometimes, for convenience, we will give the aggregate an objectlike name—a noun—in addition to its relationship name. In Figure 4.30, for example, MARRIED-COUPLE is the object set name given to the IS-MARRIED-TO relationship. This is reasonable if a relationship is to be used as an object set.

binary relationship A relationship between two object sets.

All of the relationships we have considered to this point involve two object sets. Such relationships are called **binary**. However, relationships can also involve three or more object sets. These *higher-level* relationships are denoted as **n-ary relationships**, where *n* stands for the number of object sets being related. A 3-ary relationship is called *ternary*. To use more understandable terminology, however, we will often refer to 3-ary or 4-ary relationships as three-way or four-way relationships.

n-ary relationship A relationship between *n* object sets.

Let's illustrate these concepts with an example. Suppose Dick Greenberg of International Product Distribution (IPD) wants to track sales of a line of products by country. To help him we create an object set PRODUCT and an object set COUNTRY and establish a relationship (IS-SOLD-IN) between them (Figure 4.31(a)). An instance in PRODUCT, say "dishwasher soap #5," is related to an instance in COUNTRY, say England, if dishwasher soap #5 is sold in England. If we treat the IS-SOLD-IN relationship as an object set, then we can give it the attribute QUANTITY to indicate how many of each product were sold in each country.

Notice that the QUANTITY attribute depends on *both* product *and* country. That is, we cannot determine the value of quantity from product alone nor from country alone—we need both of them. This is why QUANTITY is an attribute of the *relationship* between product and country rather than an attribute of either product or country alone. For this reason, the models of Figures 4.31(b) and 4.31(c) are both

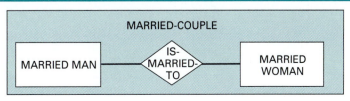

FIGURE 4.30 A RELATIONSHIP VIEWED AS AN OBJECT SET

incorrect. In case (b), the model does not distinguish between quantities sold in different *countries*, and in case (c), the model does not distinguish between quantities sold of different *products*.

The model of Figure 4.31(a) gives Dick the ability to track sales of products by country. Suppose, however, that he wants a finer breakdown of sales than this model can give. In particular, he would like to record the quantity of each product sold in each country *on each day*. Then we relate IS-SOLD-IN to DATE and give this new relationship the attribute QUANTITY (Figure 4.32(a)). Once again, the attribute applies to the outer relationship because instances from all three object sets—PRODUCT, COUNTRY, DATE—are needed to determine quantity.

Figure 4.32(a) gives the solution to this problem as two binary relationships, the first of which (IS-SOLD-IN) is an object set in the second relationship (SOLD-ON). We may find it more convenient to express this model as a single, three-way relationship as in Figure 4.32(b). Again we see that QUANTITY is an attribute of the relationship among the three object sets.

Any higher-level relationship can be broken down into a series of nested binary relationships. However, some of these binary relationships may not make sense to us when we try to relate them to something in the real world. Thus, we will sometimes use higher-level relationships to express concepts that we are trying to capture in a particular data model, since these relationships may be easier to relate to our problem.

▼FIGURE 4.31 MODELS FOR TRACKING SALES

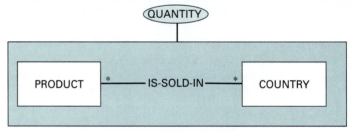

(a) A Correct Model for Tracking Sales

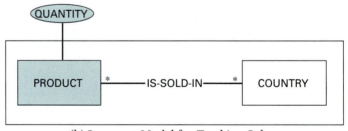

(b) Incorrect Model for Tracking Sales

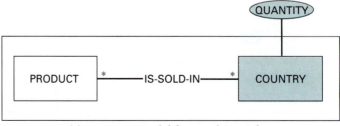

(c) Incorrect Model for Tracking Sales

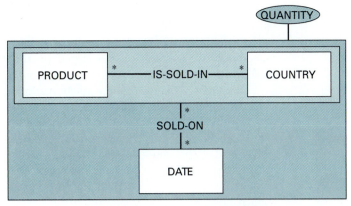

(a) Using Two Binary Relationships

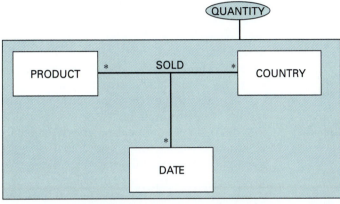

(b) Using a Three-Way Relationship

▼FIGURE 4.32 DIFFERENT WAYS TO TRACK SALES BY COUNTRY AND DATE

With respect to maximum cardinalities in higher-level relationships, we will assume that all the binary relationships that make up the higher-level relationship are many–many binary relationships. This assumption will almost always hold in practice.

We will now illustrate the power of these concepts by considering a number of other examples, all of them somewhat more complex than those we have previously considered.

Example 4: Premier Construction Company

Premier Construction erects buildings at a variety of locations. Each building requires a number of different types of materials in quantities that vary by building. Different crews carry out different portions of the project. For example, there may be a crew for framing, a crew for drywall, a crew for plumbing, a crew for masonry, and so on. In scheduling the construction of a building, Premier assigns different crews to different dates. Workers are assigned to different crews, depending on their skills. Thus, Hank Brigman can do both carpentry and masonry work and so is assigned at various times to framing, drywall, and masonry crews. The size of a crew varies according to the size and requirements of the building. Consequently, crews are made up as needed for a particular building. Also, a foreman is assigned to a particular crew for a particular building. A worker can be a foreman on one crew and simply a worker on another crew. Marcus Brown, owner of Premier, wants to know which of his workers are assigned to crews for various buildings, what materials are being used on the buildings, and when work on each building is scheduled. We will now design a conceptual data model that can provide the information Brown is seeking.

Figure 4.33(a) models the relationship between buildings and materials. The BUILDING object set contains an instance for each building in the database. The MATERIAL TYPE object set represents types of material such as "2 × 4 × 10' lumber," "#10 nails," and so on. The cardinalities of the relationship between BUILDING and MATERIAL TYPE state that each building requires many types of material and each type of material is used on many buildings. Note that the ADDRESS attribute applies only to BUILDING. The ADDRESS can be used as a key to uniquely identify a particular building.

The box around the REQUIRES relationship indicates that we wish to consider that relationship as an aggregate object set. We will then give this object set the attribute QUANTITY. The instances of this aggregate object set consist of pairs: a building and a type of material. Thus, for example, the pair made up of the building at 610 Fifth St. and 2 × 4 × 10' lumber may be an instance in the REQUIRES relationship. This pair is then assigned a quantity—say, 500 pieces—which is the quantity of 2 × 4 × 10' lumber required for this building (see Figure 4.33(b)).

It is important to note that the MATERIAL TYPE object set in this example represents a **conceptual** rather than a **physical** object. That is, each instance in MATERIAL TYPE represents a *type* of material rather than a specific, physical piece of material. This notion of conceptual as opposed to physical objects has frequent application in conceptual data modeling. In some cases, separate object sets for physical objects need to be modeled.

conceptual object An object representing a type of thing.

physical object An object representing a specific physical thing.

▼FIGURE 4.33 MODELING THE RELATIONSHIP OF BUILDINGS AND MATERIALS

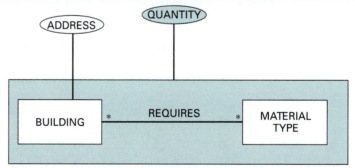

(a) The Relationship of Buildings and Materials

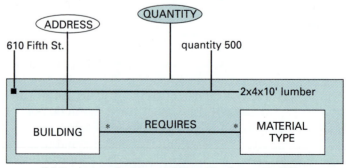

(b) Quantity of a Material Type Used on a Building

We now show how to represent the formation of crews and the assignment of workers and foremen to crews. Figure 4.34 shows a relationship between CREW TYPE and BUILDING object sets. CREW TYPE is another example of a conceptual object set. That is, the instances of CREW TYPE do not represent *particular* crews; rather, they represent *types* of crews, such as masonry or drywall. The relationship of a crew type and a building represents a particular crew—the crew assigned for that building to perform the task associated with its crew type. Therefore, we can view this relationship as an object and give it the name CREW.

Each crew, as an instance in the object set CREW, is scheduled to work on a number of different dates. For example, the plumbers will require a number of days to complete the plumbing in a given building. Thus, we have a many–many relationship, SCHEDULED-ON, between CREW and DATE.

Figure 4.35 shows the assignment of workers and foremen to crews. Note that the IS-FOREMAN-OF relationship is one–many. This is because a crew will have only one foreman. However, a worker can be foreman of many different crews. Figure 4.36 gives the composite diagram showing the complete data model for Premier Construction Company.

Example 5: Stratton's Fruit Orchards Continued

Example 2 gave some information on Vern Stratton's fruit-growing business. We now add some information and use it to derive the corresponding data model, which is somewhat more complex than the earlier model. This model will be more powerful and will be able to provide information needed for scheduling workers, for planting new trees, and for other management decisions needed in running the business.

Trees in Vern's orchards are planted in rows and columns. Each pair of consecutive rows is 20 feet apart, and each pair of consecutive columns is 20 feet apart. When a tree dies, it is pulled out, and eventually another tree is planted in its place.

Recall that species represent broad categories of fruit such as apple, peach, or cherry, and varieties represent subcategories, like Jonathan and Red Delicious (apples). Depending on weather conditions during the early months of the year, varieties blossom at different times. Harvest begins a set number of days from full blossom for a given variety.

In addition to handling this new information, our data model must be constructed so that questions such as the following can be answered:

How many bushels of Red Delicious apples did we get out of the Paynesville orchard last year? What was the average harvest date in all orchards for cling (variety) peaches in the last

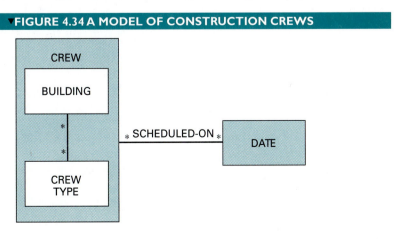

▼**FIGURE 4.34 A MODEL OF CONSTRUCTION CREWS**

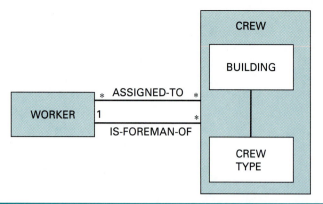

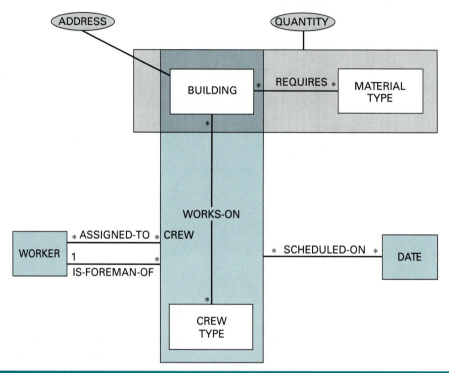

▼FIGURE 4.36 DATA MODEL FOR PREMIER CONSTRUCTION COMPANY

ten years? When will the Jonathans in the Lee's Valley orchard be ready for harvest this year? How many spaces are there in each orchard for new trees? How many would there be if we tore out trees whose average production the last five years is under one bushel?

Figure 4.37 gives the enhanced version of Figure 4.22. The LOCATION object set is another example of a conceptual object. It does not represent a specific location, but it is rather a row and column number that could occur in any orchard. Thus, an instance in LOCATION might be (10, 17), meaning the tenth row and the seventeenth column of *no* specific orchard. When this instance is related to a specific orchard—say, the Springtown orchard—then the *triple* (Springtown, 10, 17) stands for row 10, column 17 in the Springtown orchard.

In Figure 4.22, we merely related the trees to their orchards. Now we can identify both the orchard and the specific location (row and column) within the or-

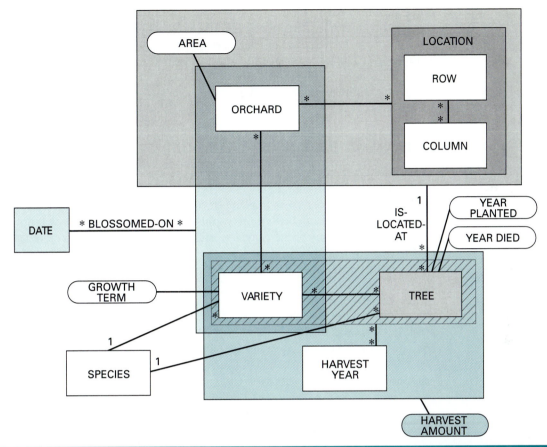

▼FIGURE 4.37 STRATTON FRUIT ORCHARDS DATA MODEL

chard where the tree is planted. This lets us answer the questions about the number of empty spaces in each orchard as follows:

The relationship that ties trees to their specific locations within an orchard is named IS-LOCATED-AT. Why is this relationship one–many? Clearly, a tree can have only one location, but why can a location have many trees? If we recall that we maintain the year that a tree died, we can see that the database keeps track of all the trees that have been at a specific location over the years. Now we merely identify all the trees associated with a particular space in the orchard. If they have all died, then we may assume that the space is available for a new tree.

This information can also be used to determine where the more fertile areas within each orchard are to be found. This is because we are also keeping track of the number of bushels of fruit each tree is producing each year. Over the years, the trees in the more fertile areas will consistently produce more fruit.

To determine when harvest time is for a given variety in a given orchard, we must record when full blossom took place for the variety in that orchard. Therefore, we connect ORCHARD and VARIETY in a relationship and further connect these two to DATE in the BLOSSOMED-ON relationship. This tells us when full blossom occurred for each variety in each orchard. The GROWTH TERM attribute of VARIETY tells us the number of days from full blossom until the beginning of harvest. By using the GROWTH TERM attribute in combination with the BLOSSOMED-ON relationship, we can tell when harvest time will be for each variety in each orchard. This information is essential for scheduling workers during the harvest season.

To record the amount of each variety harvested each year from each tree, we must relate each instance of the (TREE, VARIETY) relationship to the HARVEST YEAR. This three-way relationship will have the HARVEST AMOUNT attribute, which will tell us how many bushels were harvested of each variety from each tree each harvest year.

Example 6: Manwaring Consulting Services Continued

Earlier in the chapter, we created data models for a purchase order and an invoice from Manwaring Consulting Services. The forms used there were simplified to fit the basic modeling concepts available to us then. Using more advanced concepts, we can create data models for more sophisticated report forms. We will now examine enhanced versions of the purchase order and the invoice and create data models for them.

Figure 4.38 shows an enhanced purchase order for Manwaring Consulting Services. As you compare this form with that of Figure 4.25, please note that the new form includes columns for *Product Description*, *Quantity*, *Unit Price*, and *Extended Price*, whereas the original had only *Product Description* and *Price*. In the original form, the quantity being ordered was embedded in *Product Description*, while in the new form it is broken out separately. *Unit Price* did not appear at all on the original form. *Price* on the original form is the same thing as *Extended Price* on the new form.

There are two advantages to the new form: (1) Since *Unit Price* is a function of the product being ordered, *Extended Price* can automatically be calculated from *Quantity* and *Unit Price*. The old form required this calculation to be done by hand.

▼FIGURE 4.38 AN ENHANCED PURCHASE ORDER FOR MANWARING CONSULTING SERVICES

MANWARING CONSULTING
SERVICES
950 MAIN
EASTON, PA 11111

PURCHASE ORDER

Date	Order Number	Vendor Number
3/29	388	23

Stock #	Product Description	Quantity	Unit Price	Extended Price
3821	#2 Pencils	3	4.00	12.00
4919	Legal Pads	4	8.90	35.60
	Tax			2.86
			Total	50.46

Consolidated Office Supplies
414 S. Choctaw Drive
Flagship, PA 12345

(2) Since *Quantity* is listed separately, it is possible to perform calculations with it, both on the purchase order form itself and in determining the total quantity of any product ordered over an extended period of time. Such calculations can be used to answer questions like:

How many pads of legal paper did we use last year?

Figure 4.39 shows the data model derived from the new purchase order form. Note that we have aggregated the relationship between PRODUCT and ORDER. QUANTITY and EXTENDED PRICE are attributes of the *aggregate* because they depend on both PRODUCT and ORDER. That is, the *quantity* is the number of the *product* being ordered on that particular *order*. EXTENDED PRICE is a calculated attribute that applies to both PRODUCT and ORDER in the same way as QUANTITY. Notice also that DESCRIPTION, STOCK NUMBER, and UNIT PRICE are all attributes of PRODUCT, since they depend only on PRODUCT and not on ORDER. DESCRIPTION in the new model has a different meaning than it did in the model of Figure 4.26, since in the earlier model DESCRIPTION included the quantity being ordered.

Figure 4.40 shows an enhanced version of the Manwaring invoice. In comparing this invoice with that of Figure 4.28, note that charges have been separated into *Consulting Charges* and *Other Charges*. In the enhanced invoice, we show *Activity* and *Hours* rather than *Charge Description* as in the original. *Charge Description* was a free-form field in which the user could write whatever descriptive information seemed appropriate. *Activity* and *Hours*, on the other hand, are much more precise. *Activity* includes only a specified number of predefined activities, such as systems analysis, system design, programming, and user training, which the consultants could be engaged in. *Hours*, of course, must be numeric. This approach makes it much easier for an automated system to calculate the number of hours each consultant has been involved in each type of activity for each client.

The data model for this invoice is shown in Figure 4.41. We have aggregated the relationship between CONSULTANT and ACTIVITY, as well as the relationship between this aggregate and PROJECT. The larger aggregate, therefore, has attributes

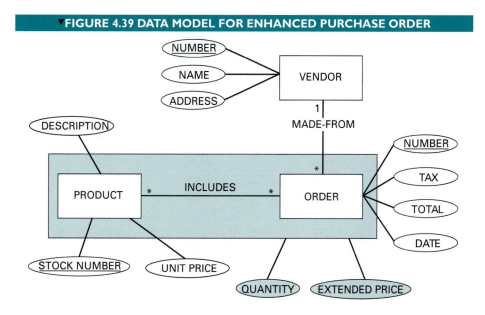

▼FIGURE 4.39 DATA MODEL FOR ENHANCED PURCHASE ORDER

MANWARING CONSULTING
SERVICES
950 MAIN
EASTON, PA 11111

INVOICE

Date	Invoice Number	Project
12/27	349	Cost Accounting System

Consultant	Activity	Hours	Rate	Amount
Rodriguez	System Analysis	30	$60/hr.	1800.00
Rodriguez	System Design	30	$60/hr.	1800.00
Rodriguez	Programming	20	$60/hr.	1200.00
Chatman	Programming	60	$40/hr.	2400.00
			Consulting Total	7200.00

OTHER CHARGES

Description	Amount
Supplies (Paper, Photocopying, etc.)	35.00
Other Total	35.00
Invoice total	7235.00

Client: Robespierre Manufacturing
1793 Bonaparte Road
Bastille, PA 10000

▼**FIGURE 4.40 ENHANCED INVOICE FOR MANWARING CONSULTING SERVICES**

of HOURS and AMOUNT. This is because the value of the HOURS attribute depends on the three factors of consultant, activity, and project. That is, the HOURS attribute tells us how long a given *consultant* engaged in a given *activity* on a given *project*.

Notice that the RATE attribute is attached directly to the CONSULTANT object set, since it depends only on the consultant. That is, Manwaring charges the same hourly rate for a given consultant regardless of the activity the consultant is engaged in. This is shown in Figure 4.40, the enhanced invoice, where we can see that the rate for Rodriguez is always $60 per hour.

AMOUNT indicates the charge for the consultant's work on an activity for a project. This is calculated by multiplying the *rate* from the consultant's RATE attribute by the *hours* from the HOURS attribute for the appropriate *consultant, activity*, and *project*.

At the beginning of the chapter, we saw that Joan Manwaring was interested in a system that would relate consultants, activities, and clients so that she could obtain information about their relationships. Figure 4.41 provides the data model needed. The data supported by this data model can be manipulated to create a large number of reports, two of which are shown in Figures 4.42(a) and 4.42(b).

The consultant activity report of Figure 4.42(a) shows how many hours each consultant spent in each activity during the past year. For example, Chatman spent

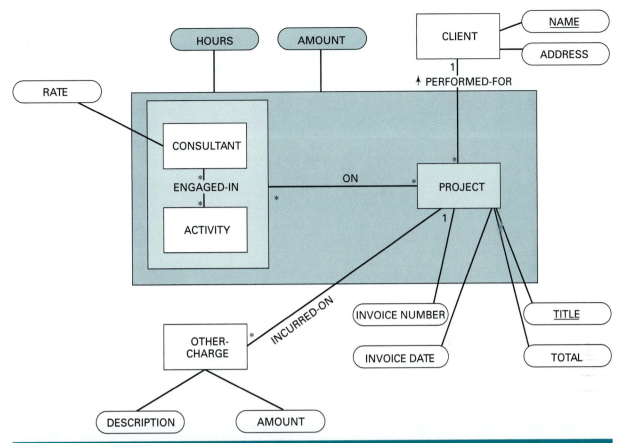

MANWARING CONSULTING
SERVICES

CONSULTANT ACTIVITY REPORT
For Year Ending December 31, 19__

CONSULTANT	ACTIVITY	HOURS
Chatman	Programming	950
	User Training	600
	Office Analysis	450
Farasopoulos	Data Entry	30
	File Conversion	1400
	User Training	350
	Office Analysis	220
Harris	File Conversion	1140
	Programming	500
	System Design	120
	Office Analysis	240
Rodriguez	Programming	150
	System Design	800
	Systems Analysis	750
	User Training	100
	Office Analysis	200

(a) A Report Relating Consultants to Activities

```
        MANWARING CONSULTING
              SERVICES

        CONSULTANT-CLIENT REPORT
        For Year Ending December 31, 19__


CONSULTANT              CLIENT                HOURS

Chatman             Robespierre                60
                    Statten                   400
                    Sunderman                 950
                    Universal                 140
Farasopoulos        Storehouse                 30
                    Sunderman                1100
                    Watanabe                  650
Harris              Goldman                   950
                    Martino                   425
                    Storehouse                200
                    Universal                 185
Rodriguez           Goldman                   800
                    Martino                   840
                    Robespierre                80
                    Storehouse                 80
```

(b) A Report Relating Consultant to Clients

▼FIGURE 4.42 TYPICAL REPORTS USED AT MANWARING

950 hours programming, 600 hours training users, and 450 hours in the office in activities that could not be billed to clients. The consultant-client report of Figure 4.42(b) shows how many hours each consultant spent in billable activity for each client.

The data model of Figure 4.41 could be used to obtain a number of other similar reports. For example, a report could be generated showing precisely which activities each consultant performed for each client and on which project. Of course, the number of hours they spent on each activity could also be shown. Another report could be the average percent of each project's billable hours spent in each activity. For example, if the report showed that on average, systems analysis took only 5 percent of the project time, additional training could be scheduled to teach consultants better systems analysis skills.

Aggregation and higher-level relationships are powerful tools that have frequent application in modeling complex business problems. Indeed, nearly every business problem has sufficient complexity to require the application of this concept. The examples given in this chapter illustrate the power of aggregation and the rich variety of situations to which it can be applied.

▼ Modeling Conceptual Objects Versus Physical Objects

Although aggregation and higher-level relationships are very useful tools for solving a large variety of data modeling problems, there are certain problems whose more difficult aspects can be solved with more basic tools. In this section, we look at problems that arise because of ambiguities in our daily language. As you will see, once we understand and separate the concepts involved in these ambiguities, we can solve the data modeling problems simply by defining the appropriate object

conceptual object set
An object set whose instances are conceptual objects.

sets. Aggregates and other concepts can then be used to build additional constructs into the data models as needed.

In the previous section, we noted several instances of **conceptual object sets**. For example, MATERIAL TYPE and CREW TYPE in the Premier Construction Company data model were conceptual object sets, since their instances represented *types* of things rather than specific, concrete examples of those types. A material type might be "2 × 4 × 10' lumber" rather than a specific piece of lumber. A *crew type* could be "roofing" or "electrical," whereas a specific *crew* might be "roofing for the 320 Main Street building."

physical object set An object set whose instances are physical objects.

It is often necessary to distinguish between conceptual object sets and the **physical object sets** that correspond to them because both types of object sets need to be represented in the same data model. This is illustrated in the following example.

The Library Problem

A student calls a library and asks:

STUDENT: Do you have *The Pickwick Papers* by Charles Dickens?

LIBRARIAN: (Enters query of on-line catalog) No, we don't.

S: How about *Bleak House*?

L: (Enters second query) No.

S: How many books *do* you have by Dickens?

L: (Enters a third query) We have twelve.

S: Really? What are they?

L: We have *A Tale of Two Cities*, Copy 1; *A Tale of Two Cities*, Copy 2; *A Tale of Two Cities*, Copy 3; and so forth, through Copy 12.

S: Those are all the same book! You don't have twelve books by Dickens, you only have one.

L: No, they aren't all the same. One is the Signet Classic Edition, one is a German translation, one a French translation, one is a condensed version, and so on.

S: But the fact remains that they are all *really* the same book. No matter what may be done to put it into a different edition, it is still *A Tale of Two Cities*. You really only have one book by Dickens.

This conversation, based on Kent (1978), would never happen since no librarian would make the kind of argument our librarian is making. However, it serves to point up a significant problem we have with the natural language that we as humans use in normal conversation. In this example, what do we mean by *book*? Without giving it further thought, and outside the context of this conversation, we might think that "a book is a book," and there should not be any ambiguity in our use of the word. Yet the student and the librarian are using book in two very different senses. One sense—the student's—is that a book is something conceptual that can have many different physical versions. Thus, *A Tale of Two Cities* is "really" the same book whether it is copy 1 or copy 8, whether it is in English or French, or whether it is the full, unabridged version or a condensed version. The librarian, on the other hand, is using (at least initially) the other sense: A book is something physical that we can hold, leaf through, and put up on a shelf. The library needs to account for every *physical* book it has, regardless of whether it is the first or the twelfth copy of a given *conceptual* book.

Sometimes we distinguish between these two usages by insisting that physical books be referred to as *copies* or *volumes*. Thus, we may say, "How many volumes does the library contain?" But as analysts interviewing users, we need to recognize that people frequently don't observe such conventions. They simply say "book," and sometimes they mean "conceptual book" and sometimes "physical book." In designing a database, we need to be able to detect the differences in intended meanings. In some cases, users will be referring to a *conceptual object*, which is an abstract or generalized version of an object. In other cases, users will be referring to a *physical object*, or a specific instance of a conceptual object. If we are to meet the needs of all database users, however, our data models must capture the conceptual-physical distinction.

There may be other subtle distinctions to capture as well. In the discussion between student and librarian, the librarian eventually concedes that there is a difference between a physical and conceptual book but insists that books are conceptually different if their editions are different. That is, the Signet Classic edition of *A Tale of Two Cities* is a different conceptual book than a condensed version. The student insists, however, that the edition is irrelevant and that, conceptually, the book remains the same through all its various editions.

Certainly both parties have a legitimate viewpoint. Since we are interested in database design, we don't have to determine which party is "right." We only need to decide what kind of questions the users want the system to answer. Once we have identified the type of information needed, we can make decisions about the data design. Ideally, we would like to satisfy all points of view, including *both* the student's and the librarian's.

Creating the Library Data Model

During the requirements definition phase of the DDLC, we as analysts are involved in interviewing users to determine their needs and expectations from a database system. During this phase, it is very important that we correctly identify the objects and relationships that make up the normal part of the users' day-to-day activity. Thus, if there are subtle distinctions in the meanings of different terms that occur naturally in business transactions, we need to be able to identify them so that we will model business relationships accurately.

As we create a model for the library problem, let us consider the following sample questions:

How many books does the library have by Charles Dickens? How many different books does the library have in the Signet Classic edition? How many books does the library have that are in their second edition? How many copies does the library have of *Pride and Prejudice*?

From these questions we can identify three different types of "books":

A conceptual book
An edition of a conceptual book
A physical book

From the first two of these, we can construct two object sets and a relationship (Figure 4.43). Notice the minimum and maximum cardinalities for CONCEPTUAL-BOOK. These cardinalities show that the CONCEPTUAL-BOOK-EDITION object set

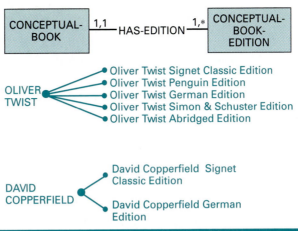

▼FIGURE 4.43 A PRELIMINARY SOLUTION TO THE LIBRARY PROBLEM

dependent object set
An object set whose instances *must* be related to at least one other instance of another object set.

is **dependent** on the CONCEPTUAL-BOOK object set. That is, each conceptual book edition is an edition of one and only one conceptual book.

Although this solution answers some of the questions, it ultimately fails because it is unable to answer questions like:

How many different books does the library have in the Signet Classic edition?

The problem lies with the CONCEPTUAL-BOOK-EDITION object set. Since each instance is an edition of a particular book, we cannot match identical editions of different books. An additional problem with this solution is that it requires CONCEPTUAL-BOOK-EDITION to contain considerably more object instances than are actually necessary.

Figure 4.44 gives a better solution. In this case, EDITION is an independent object set that stands on its own. Since a conceptual book can have many editions, EDITION cannot be an attribute of CONCEPTUAL-BOOK. Thus, the relationship between CONCEPTUAL-BOOK and EDITION is many–many. With this model, the questions about editions can be answered, and there is no unnecessary duplication of conceptual editions. For example, Signet Classic Edition appears only once in the EDITION object set, whereas it appeared twice, embedded in "Oliver Twist Signet Classic Edition" and "David Copperfield Signet Classic Edition," in the CONCEPTUAL-BOOK-EDITION object set of Figure 4.43. Since there could be many books in the

▼FIGURE 4.44 A BETTER SOLUTION TO THE LIBRARY PROBLEM

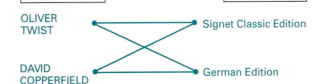

Signet Classic Edition, our new approach eliminates a great deal of potential duplication.

Using Figure 4.44, we can add the notion of "physical books" to our model (Figure 4.45). An instance of PHYSICAL-BOOK represents an actual volume which can be marked with a call number and which can be checked out to only one library patron at a time. For this example, we assume that the call number includes *all* the information needed to uniquely identify a particular physical book. Therefore, the *external key* for each physical book is the call number, or *physical identification number*, by which it can be tracked for inventory control purposes. The call number may include information such as *copy number* that distinguishes one copy of a given conceptual book from another copy of the same book.

Notice the one–many cardinality of the IS-CONTAINED-IN relationship of Figure 4.45. Such cardinality asserts that a given book-edition combination can be contained in many different physical books. This corresponds to our understanding of reality. But the cardinality also asserts that a given physical book can contain only one book-edition. Is this accurate?

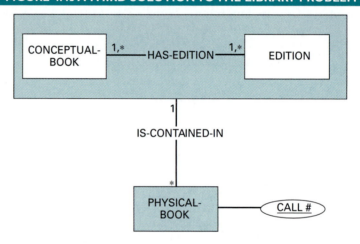

▼FIGURE 4.45 A THIRD SOLUTION TO THE LIBRARY PROBLEM

Consider a book containing the collected works of Jane Austen. Such a book contains a number of different conceptual books, although we might say they all have the same edition. All of these conceptual books are contained in the same physical book, as shown in Figure 4.46. Since this situation is not unusual, for the sake of accuracy we must amend the cardinality of Figure 4.45 from one–many to many–many (Figure 4.47). That is, a single physical book can be related to multiple conceptual books.

Our data model still may not go far enough. If library users need to identify books by the language in which they are published, we will need to break out language as a separate object. Language might be an attribute of a book-edition combination (assuming that an edition of a book can be in only one language), or it might be a separate object set, which has a many–many relationship with book-edition. That is, a given edition of a book might contain portions in Italian, French, Spanish, English, and so on. Figure 4.48 shows LANGUAGE as an object set related through the IS-IN-LANGUAGE relationship to the aggregate of HAS-EDITION. A physical book then would map to an object instance consisting of conceptual book, edition, and language, which is in the aggregate of IS-IN-LANGUAGE.

The distinction between conceptual books and physical books is crucial to the solution of this problem. More importantly, this conceptual-physical distinction is

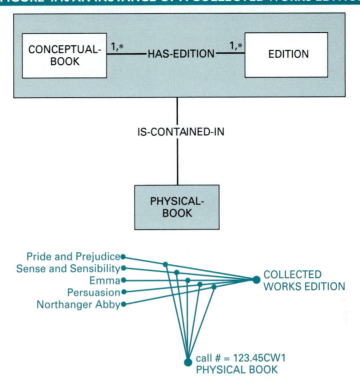

▼FIGURE 4.46 AN INSTANCE OF A COLLECTED WORKS EDITION

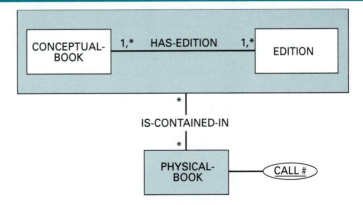

▼FIGURE 4.47 AN AMENDED SOLUTION TO THE LIBRARY PROBLEM

useful in solving many similar data modeling problems. You will encounter it in many types of business situations. Any time a word is used ambiguously, the potential for the problem exists. As we have shown, however, the solution is quite simple. By defining separate object sets, one for each distinct meaning of the ambiguous term, and by defining appropriate relationships between these object sets, a data model can be constructed that will provide all the information the users require. Additional examples will help to clarify this.

Tracking Manufactured Parts

Robespierre Manufacturing ("Products on the Cutting Edge") has design facilities, manufacturing facilities, and warehouses. These facilities design, produce, and store

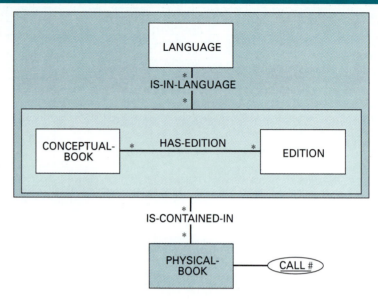

parts. A part is designed in only one facility but may be manufactured and stored in several facilities. After interviewing the owners, Louis and Marie Blades, and several other officers and managers of Robespierre, the database analysts determined that the following questions were typical:

Which parts were designed in which facility? If a particular part fails, can we trace it back to the facility that designed it and the facility that manufactured it? What quantity of part A235 is stored in the Lexington warehouse?

It is clear that most of these questions have to do with tracking specific parts, which are designed at one facility, manufactured at another, and then stored in a warehouse. Figure 4.49 is the result of our first attempt at a data model for this problem. Note the cardinalities. We can answer the first question—"Which parts were designed in which facility?"—because each part is designed in only one facility. Moreover, if a part fails, we can use the part number to identify the part and determine where it was designed. But we cannot tell where the part was

▼FIGURE 4.49 A PRELIMINARY SOLUTION TO THE MANUFACTURING PROBLEM

manufactured, since a given part can be manufactured in many different facilities. The third question—"What quantity of part A235 is stored in the Lexington warehouse?"—can be answered since our model captures the quantity of the part stored in the warehouse for each part/warehouse combination. Thus, the data model of Figure 4.49 provides most of the information needed to answer the questions.

A better data model that answers all these questions is shown in Figure 4.50. Here we have distinguished between conceptual parts and physical parts. A conceptual part represents a *type* of part and has a part number, which is assigned when the part is designed. It is precisely what was meant by PART in Figure 4.49. A physical part is a particular instance of its corresponding conceptual part. Therefore, the relationship between CONCEPTUAL PART and PHYSICAL PART is one–many: A physical part corresponds to only one conceptual part, but a conceptual part corresponds to many physical parts. A physical part has a serial number that uniquely identifies it. Moreover, it was manufactured in only one facility and, at any given time, is stored in only one warehouse.

This data model answers all the questions listed earlier. Note that we have omitted QUANTITY as an attribute in this data model. The quantity of parts in a warehouse can be determined by finding the desired warehouse instance in the WAREHOUSE object set and then counting the number of physical parts related to the warehouse by the IS-STORED-AT relationship. Since the computer can easily count the number of such instances, it is unnecessary for us to create a superfluous QUANTITY attribute.

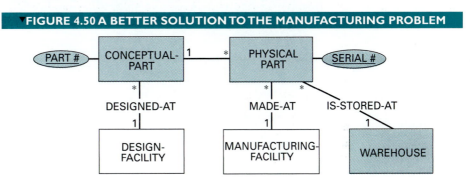

▼**FIGURE 4.50 A BETTER SOLUTION TO THE MANUFACTURING PROBLEM**

Conceptual Objects for Manwaring Consulting Services

Over a period of several years, Manwaring has developed a number of computer applications systems for its clients. After working with many different clients, the Manwaring staff has found that clients often have similar needs and the same basic software can be used for these needs. For example, Statten needs an accounts receivable system, an accounts payable system, and a cost accounting system. Sunderman needs an accounts payable system, a cost accounting system, and a payroll system. By creating generalized systems for accounts receivable, accounts payable, cost accounting, payroll, inventory control, and so forth, Manwaring can satisfy many clients' needs at reduced cost. From this experience came the decision to create base systems in each of these areas.

Figure 4.51(a) shows a data model that gives the relationship between the base systems and the client systems that use them. The base systems have *version numbers* to indicate different versions of the system. For example, the first version of the accounts payable system may have had version number 1.0. The second and third versions may have had numbers 1.1 and 2.0, respectively. Since each base system can have many version numbers, and since each version number can apply to many base systems, the relationship between BASE SYSTEM and VERSION NUMBER is many–many.

Each client system is related to the base system(s) from which it is constituted. However, since the client will always receive a specific *version* of the base system, the client system is related to *both* the base system and the version number. That is, the IS-INCLUDED-IN relationship is between CLIENT SYSTEM and the *aggregate* of BASE SYSTEM and VERSION NUMBER. The IS-INCLUDED-IN relationship is many–many because a given client system will include many base-system/version-number combinations, and a given base-system/version-number combination will be included in many different client systems.

Figure 4.51(b) shows instances from this data model. The system for client Statten is shown as a dot beneath the CLIENT SYSTEM box. This system includes accounts payable, version 2.0, and so in the diagram it is connected to the (accounts payable, 2.0) pair. If the Statten system included other base-system versions, there could be other such instances illustrated.

This data model further illustrates the conceptual-physical distinction. The BASE SYSTEM object set is a conceptual object set, and the CLIENT SYSTEM object set is a physical object set. In fact, this example is very similar to the library example given earlier. If you compare Figure 4.51(a) with Figure 4.47, you can see the following correspondence:

▼FIGURE 4.51 DATA MODELS OF CONCEPTUAL AND PHYSICAL SYSTEMS

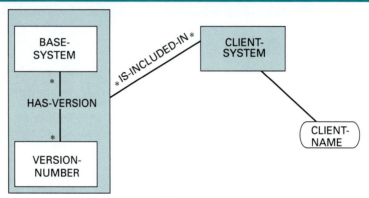

(a) Data Model for Installed Systems

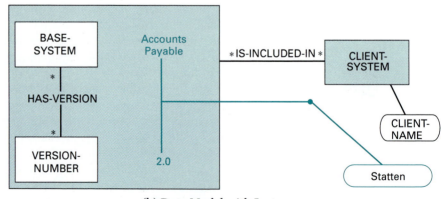

(b) Data Model with Instances

```
CONCEPTUAL BOOK ──────────── BASE SYSTEM
EDITION ──────────────── VERSION NUMBER
PHYSICAL BOOK ──────────── CLIENT SYSTEM
```

The purpose of this example, as well as those that precede it in this section, is to illustrate the ambiguities lurking in the natural language used to describe the requirements of database users. To make sure our data models are accurate and complete, we must carefully analyze the circumstances of the application and the kind of information desired by the users of the database system.

▼ View Integration: An Example

The examples we have been using in the last three chapters tend to be unified in that we create a single model to satisfy all the requirements of the users with whom we are working. In a large organization, such a simple approach is impossible, and a database development project would require the creation of a number of different data models by analyst teams working with users in different areas. These separate models are called **views**, since each of them represents the way a given user group looks at the database. To create a single, integrated database, these different views must be integrated into a single data model.

view A definition of a restricted portion of the database.

As an example, let's take two of the data models for Manwaring Consulting Services and see how they can be integrated into a single data model. The approach will be to preserve each view in its original state, to the extent possible, and to connect object sets in different views by creating new relationships between them.

Consider Figures 4.41 and 4.51(a). Figure 4.41 contains a CLIENT object set with a NAME attribute, and Figure 4.51(a) contains a CLIENT SYSTEM object set with a CLIENT NAME attribute. Since the CLIENT NAME attribute of Figure 4.51(a) and the NAME attribute of Figure 4.41 represent the same attribute, an integrated model would drop one of them as redundant. A possible solution would be to relate CLIENT SYSTEM to CLIENT and drop CLIENT NAME as an attribute of CLIENT SYSTEM, as in Figure 4.52(a).

However, this solution fails to consider other portions of Figure 4.41. Client systems, for example, are developed during projects. Thus, it seems more reasonable to relate the CLIENT SYSTEM object set to the PROJECT object set, as shown in Figure 4.52(b). The INSTALLED-DURING relationship indicates that a given client system was created during a series of projects, all of them for the same client. Thus, we can trace from a *client system*, through the *projects* used to install it, to the *client* for whom the projects were performed. This solution integrates the two views and gives the single, unified data model we are seeking.

View integration for a large organization's database is a complex problem requiring analysis of the object sets, attributes, and relationships of the views by the analysts and users most familiar with them. We have shown here a simple example which illustrates some of the basic concepts involved. In an actual business situation, the process of view integration may work in some cases but not in others. As indicated earlier, because of the complexity of the database development project, some organizations have chosen *not* to have a single corporate database for all information needs. By choosing this approach, they have avoided some of the more difficult aspects of view integration. Of course, the smaller databases will still represent a variety of user views, and each of these databases will require the view integration process for their successful design.

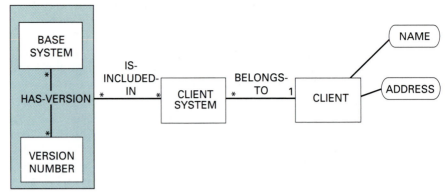

(a) A First Attempt at View Integration

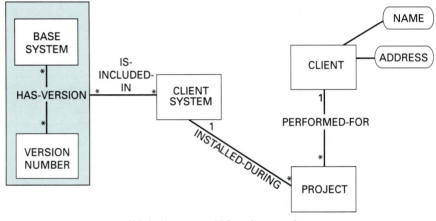

(b) An Improved View Integration

▼**FIGURE 4.52 EXAMPLES OF VIEW INTEGRATION**

Summary

In this chapter, we have studied the fundamentals of conceptual data modeling. We have defined the general concept of a data model, have described a modeling methodology, and have shown how this methodology can be used on sets of user queries and existing reports.

The word *model* is often used on three different levels: as a methodology for creating second-level models, as a database schema which defines the types of data to be captured for a particular application, and as an implemented database which contains specific facts structured according to the second-level schema.

A conceptual data model is also called *semantic*, since it captures the meanings of things in the real world. Conceptual data models consist of object sets, relationships and their aggregates, attributes, specialization sets, cardinality indicators, and keys. Object sets can be lexical, containing instances which can be printed, or abstract, containing instances which cannot be printed. Instances in abstract object sets are represented by surrogate keys, which are internal identifiers with no external meaning. Relationships establish connections between instances in two object sets. Attributes are relationships between two object sets which are functional in the direction of one of the object sets. Specialization object sets, as subsets of another object set, provide a means for defining attributes for some instances without the need for defining them for others.

A relationship's cardinalities indicate how many of one set are related under the relationship to a single element in the other set. Cardinalities are one–one, one–many, and many–many. Keys uniquely identify objects. Surrogate keys are internal identifiers. External keys are sets of lexical attributes which together identify an element in an object set. An aggregate is a relationship viewed as an object set. By using aggregates, it is possible to address more complex modeling problems. Aggregates can have attributes and participate in other relationships. These new relationships can also be aggregated and can be used as object sets in other relationships.

Conceptual object sets represent entities that are types of things. For example, a book in a conceptual object set is not a specific, physical book, but rather represents a complex, conceptual entity developed by the author. The conceptual book can have many different editions, and each edition can result in the printing of many physical copies of the book. The physical copies are physical books which would be represented in their own object set. Many other examples of the conceptual-physical distinction exist. By understanding how a single word such as *book* is used in ambiguous ways, the analyst is better prepared to create modeling structures to handle different possible meanings.

By analyzing questions users want to answer and reports the organization needs, conceptual data models can be constructed. In a large database development project, different analysts will work with different user groups to create data models or views, which must be integrated. The process involves removing only those object sets, relationships, and attributes which are redundant between views and then connecting the views by defining new relationships. This process requires analysts and users working in different areas to communicate to understand how the views can be accurately integrated.

Review Questions

1. Define each of the following terms in your own words:
   a. model
   b. object-oriented model
   c. object set
   d. lexical object set
   e. surrogate key
   f. generalization
   g. aggregate object set
   h. functional relationship
   i. cardinality
   j. one-many
   k. attribute
   l. *n*-ary relationship

2. Identify and describe six constructs used in conceptual data modeling.

3. Discuss how interviewing and report analysis are used with conceptual data modeling in the process of conceptual database design.

4. Discuss how a series of potential user queries is analyzed to determine the following constructs in a conceptual data model:
   a. object sets
   b. attributes
   c. relationships
   d. specializations

5. Discuss how a report is analyzed to determine the following constructs in a conceptual data model:

    a. object sets

    b. attributes

    c. relationships

    d. specializations

6. In what situations are aggregates needed in data modeling? When are higher-level relationships appropriate? Give examples from business situations.

Problems and Exercises

Part A

  1. Match each term with its definition:

__*many–many*	a. Value used to uniquely identify an object instance
__*binary relationship*	b. Relationship between three or more object sets
__*aggregate*	c. Lexical attributes whose values identify a single instance
__*semantic model*	d. Object set consisting of instances that cannot be printed
__*abstract object set*	e. A linking between instances of two object sets
__*specialization*	f. Particular member of an object set
__*relationship*	g. Relationship cardinalities of many in both directions
__*one–one*	h. Object set that is a subset of another object set
__*map*	i. Property of having all the attributes of the generalization set it specializes
__*object instance*	j. To associate elements in one sphere with elements in another sphere
__*external key*	k. Relationship viewed as an object set
__*null value*	l. Relationship cardinalities of one in both directions
__*key*	m. Captures the meanings of real-world entities and relationships
__*inheritance*	n. Attribute value that does not exist for a specific object instance
__*higher-level relationship*	o. Relationship between two object sets

Part B. For each of the following problems, create a conceptual data model, consisting of object sets, relationships, attributes, and so on, that can be used to answer questions similar to the questions given. Indicate cardinalities.

Assume these models are for a university environment.

  2. How many faculty members are assigned to the math department? What are their names? Who is assigned to the music department?

(Note: "Math" and "music" are just examples of departments. Your model should also be able to answer these questions if, say, sociology, political science, or mechanical engineering were substituted for math or music.)

  3. Which students are majoring in history? In English?

  4. Which faculty members are teaching courses in sociology? Which courses are they teaching?

5. How many students are taking Physics 201? Which section is Andrea Edens taking?

6. How many German majors are formally registered in the honors program? For those who are, who is their honors program advisor?

Assume these models are for a retailer.

7. Which products are priced above $200? Which of these have a cost under $150? Which come from manufacturers in the Midwest? What are the names of these manufacturers?

8. Which salespeople have sold products priced above $200? What were the dates of these sales? What is the base salary for these salespeople?

Assume the following models are for a bank. Derive these models by adding to the model in Figure 4.21.

9. What percentage of the bank's checking account holders are bank employees?

10. How many tellers have savings accounts with the bank? How many managers do? How many tellers do not?

11. Which managers having savings accounts with the bank manage employees having savings accounts with the bank?

Part C. Indicate which questions *cannot* be answered by the indicated data model and explain why they cannot.
(Figure 4.21)

12. What is the average savings account balance for manufacturers having over 500 employees?

13. How many women opened checking accounts on December 5, 1988?
(Figure 4.22)

14. How many spaces are available for new trees in the Heber City orchard?

15. What is the average life span of Jonathan apple trees in the Pleasantville orchard? (Jonathan is a variety, apple is a species.)

16. How many peach trees in the Springtown orchard bear more than two varieties?

Part D.

17. Derive a conceptual data model by analyzing the report shown in Figure 4.1E.

▼FIGURE 4.1E A SAMPLE CONSULTANT PROFILE REPORT

MANWARING CONSULTING
SERVICES

CONSULTANT PROFILE REPORT

Name	SSN	Date Hired	Skill Code	Skill Description
Farasopoulas	539-88-4242	11/22/84	A	User Training
			B	Data Entry
			D	File Conversion
Harris	560-43-1111	8/11/86	C	Programming
			D	File Conversion
			F	System Design
Rodriguez	524-33-8119	7/3/85	A	User Training
			C	Programming
			E	Systems Analysis
			F	System Design

Part E. Aggregation.

18. For each of the following statements, draw a data model showing a relationship between object sets, an aggregation of the relationship, and attributes of the aggregate.

    a. Students take classes and get grades in the classes.

    b. Sections of courses are offered at specified times and in specified rooms and buildings.

    c. Each school term can be represented as a season (fall, winter, spring, summer) and a year and begins and ends on specified dates.

    d. Each day employees work a certain number of hours.

    e. People subscribe to magazines and their subscriptions have beginning and ending dates.

    f. Pilots have a certain number of hours of training on each type of aircraft.

For each of the following problems, create a conceptual data model, consisting of object sets, relationships, attributes, and so on, that can be used to answer questions similar to the questions given. Use aggregates and higher-level relationships as needed. Indicate cardinalities.

19. How many students are taking Physics 201? Which section is Andrea Edens taking? How many times has Jim Hardy taken Accounting 201, when, who were his instructors, and what grades did he receive?

Dustin Tomes, history professor, wants to use a database to get answers to questions about European history. Create a separate data model for each problem.

20. How many of the kings of Prussia were named Fredrick? When did they live and when did they reign? Did they rule over any other countries during their lifetimes? Were any of the countries in Europe ruled by women in the seventeenth century? If so, which ones?

21. Was Marie Antoinette's grandfather the ruler of any country? Which one and when? Who was her mother? Were rulers of two different countries ever married to each other? How many of Henry VIII's children became monarchs of England? Who were their mothers?

Brick Wall Communications owns a group of television stations. These stations televise syndicated programs, commercial messages, and live sporting events. Create a separate data model for each problem.

22. Which stations have broadcast *Batman* syndicated programs? Did Brick Wall rebroadcast any of the episodes from the 1988 season of *The Cosby Show* last year? Did they show the fifth episode? When and on which stations?

23. How many baseball games did Brick Wall broadcast last year? On what dates did they broadcast games between the Dodgers and the Mets? Which teams were featured the most often? What about football games? Basketball games? Tennis matches? Golf tournaments? Other types of sports? Did Steffi Graf play tennis on any Brick Wall stations? Which station and when?

24. Which commercial messages has Brick Wall shown more than three times during an hour on a single station? When did this happen? During which hour, on which date, and station? How much did Brick Wall charge for each of these commercial message broadcasts?

Frank Howe, managing partner of the law firm of Dewey, Kleenem, Outt, and Howe, has decided that the firm's attorneys would be helped substantially by having a database directly applicable to legal questions. For each problem, create a separate data model.

25. In what cases have opinions been offered on Section 411.3c of the federal code? Which courts were involved? When were these opinions handed down? What sections of the federal code were interpreted by the *Black* v. *Williams* case?

26. Which law firms have represented General Continental in court during the last ten years? What were the cases; which party did the verdict favor; and what was the size of the award? What were the opposing law firms? What other large companies were these law firms representing in cases at the same time?

Part F.

27. As part of a project for Acme Insurance Company, one of Manwaring's analysts created a report to measure the productivity of Acme's data entry personnel. This report gives a tally for each day of the month of the number of transactions of each type entered by each clerk. Derive a conceptual data model which could be used as the basis for the report shown in Figure 4.2E.

Part G. Use conceptual and physical object sets in creating data models for the following problems:

28. An airline wants to answer questions like the following about its airplanes:

What is the seating capacity of the Boeing 727? How many engines does it have? What is the average age of the 727s in the fleet? Who is the chief mechanic responsible for servicing aircraft number 1388? What company manufactured that aircraft?

▼FIGURE 4.2E REPORT GIVING DAILY TALLY OF TRANSACTION TYPES ENTERED BY EACH CLERK

ACME INSURANCE COMPANY

MONTHLY CLERICAL PRODUCTIVITY REPORT
For Month Ending March 31

Employee No.	Name	Date	Transaction Type	Number Completed
3855	J. Perkins	3/1	New Policy	15
			Payment	75
			Claim	22
		3/2	New Policy	18
			Policy Change	53
			Claim	25
		• • •		
3921	S. Stallone	3/1	Payment	45
			Policy Change	83
			Claim	10
		3/2	New Policy	8
			Payment	63
			Policy Change	35
		• • •		

29. The Administrative Services Division of a large city must keep track of its computer equipment. It also wants to answer questions about the computer models it has. Create a data model for the following questions:

What is the maximum memory the IBM PC can have? How about the PC-XT and PC-AT? What is the maximum possible memory size for the Macintosh II? Which of our employees have IBM PCs in their offices? Who has the computer with serial number 4538842? How much main memory does it have?

Part H. View Integration.

30. Create integrated data models from the views (or data models) you created in:
   a. Problems 2, 3, 4, 5, and 6.
   b. Problems 7 and 8.
   c. Problems 20 and 21.
   d. Problems 22, 23, and 24.
   e. Problems 25 and 26.

Projects and Professional Issues

1. Create a conceptual data model for a portion of an organization. Your model should have at least five object sets with their attributes and relationships. Try to determine conditions when specialization sets are required.

2. Read papers on each of the following data models and determine how these models handle aggregation. Determine whether the papers provide enough information to answer these questions: Can an aggregate have attributes in the model? Can it participate in relationships? Can these relationships also be aggregated?
   a. The entity-relationship Model (Chen, 1976).
   b. The semantic data model (Hammer and McLeod, 1981).
   c. The functional data model (Shipman, 1981).

C H A P T E R

5

THE RELATIONAL DATA MODEL

Marcus Brown, *owner of Premier Construction Company, is discussing database implementation with Tony Melton, Premier's information systems manager. Conceptual design for the database system has been completed, and the project team is now ready to move into implementation design for a relational database management system.*

"It's not clear to me, Tony, why we went through the conceptual design step to produce a conceptual database model if we knew from the start that we would have to convert to a relational model anyway."

"Conceptual design is essential for creating a database schema that is logically sound, Marcus, but at present there are few systems that can actually run a conceptual model database. Now that we've created a good logical model for our business, we need to implement *it on a system suited to our application needs. We've chosen a relational database management system because for our purposes it is the most advanced available."*

"That's fine, but I understand it is necessary to normalize *a relational database before it is ready for implementation. I'm not exactly sure what that means, but won't it require you to do additional database design?"*

"The process used to convert a conceptual data model to a relational model is one of the powerful aspects of conceptual data modeling. By following a straightforward, mechanical conversion process, we will create a relational implementation design that is completely normalized. In essence, we have the best of both worlds."

The focus of this chapter is the relational data model and its use as a database implementation design model. We will define the model constructs, discuss the normalization process, and show how any conceptual model can be easily converted to an equivalent relational model. After reading this chapter, you should be able to:

▼ Explain the fundamental concepts of the relational model, including relations, attributes, domains, keys, foreign keys, entity integrity, and referential integrity.

▼ Demonstrate how relations can be normalized. The normalization process requires an understanding of first through fourth normal forms, functional dependencies, and multivalued dependencies.

▼ Transform a conceptual data model to a relational data model in fourth normal form.

▼ The Relational Data Model and System Development

In 1970, the way people viewed databases was permanently changed when E. F. Codd introduced the relational data model (Codd, 1970). At that time, the existing approaches to database structure used physical pointers, or disk addresses, to relate records in different files. Suppose, for example, we need to relate record *A* to record *B* in one of these early systems. To do this, we would add to record *A* a field containing the disk address of record *B*. This added field, or physical pointer, would always point from record *A* to record *B*. Codd demonstrated that these databases significantly limited the types of data manipulation that could easily be done by the end user. Moreover, they were highly vulnerable to changes in the physical environment. Whenever new disk drives were added to the computer system configuration and data were moved from one physical location to another, extensive data file conversion was required. If fields were added to a record format in a file, all the existing records in the file would have new physical locations, requiring additional data conversion. Thus, users and software were restricted by physical considerations from using data in the large variety of ways that the logical structure would have allowed.

The relational model, based on logical relationships in data, overcame these problems. It allowed the user to be totally unconcerned with, even unaware of, the physical structure of data. In addition, Codd proposed two logically based data manipulation languages that promised more power in accessing and processing data. These languages, relational algebra and relational calculus, are discussed in Chapter 6. Today these languages provide the basis for the commercial relational database languages used in many of the most popular commercial database management systems (DBMSs). We will describe these DBMSs in more detail in Part III.

In this chapter, we will review two approaches to relational database design. The first approach is more traditional. In this approach, conceptual design does not include conceptual data modeling but proceeds directly to the creation of a relational database schema consisting of relational table definitions. Design is then completed by normalizing these table definitions according to a well-defined process.

The second approach assumes the creation of a conceptual data model during conceptual design. This model is then mechanically converted to a relational model. The conversion process will automatically guarantee normalization of the resulting relational model.

The first approach was traditionally used before conceptual models became known and established. It is still useful today in situations requiring a relatively simple database schema. In such cases, the analyst may find it easier to create and normalize relational table definitions directly from user information. The second approach using conceptual models is valuable in the design of large, complex database schemas needed for corporate database systems.

After we introduce the concepts of the relational model, we will discuss the normalization process and the process of converting a conceptual model.

▼ The Relational Data Model: Fundamental Concepts

Relations

relational data model A data model representing data in the form of tables.

relation A two-dimensional table containing rows and columns of data.

The **relational data model** organizes and represents data in the form of tables or **relations**. *Relation* is a term that comes from mathematics and represents a simple two-dimensional table, consisting of rows and columns of data. Examples of relations are found in the database developed for Premier Construction Company, a company we encountered earlier.

Figure 5.1 gives a revised conceptual data model that provides the basis for Premier's relational database. Note that this data model contains three object sets, WORKER, BUILDING, and SKILL, and one aggregate object set, ASSIGNMENT. Although the WORKER object set appears twice in the model, it is the same object set both times. Thus, both copies of WORKER have the same attributes and participate

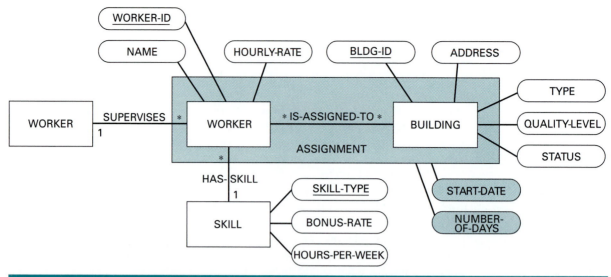

in the same relationships. The ASSIGNMENT object set is the aggregation of the IS-ASSIGNED-TO relationship between WORKER and BUILDING. That is, each assignment consists of a pair—a worker and a building—and means that the worker is assigned to work on the building. Each of these assignments has two attributes: START-DATE, or the date on which the worker is assigned to start work on the building; and NUMBER-OF-DAYS, meaning the anticipated number of days required for the worker to complete work on the building. Thus, the ASSIGNMENT aggregate object set has the two attributes, START-DATE and NUMBER-OF-DAYS.

Besides the IS-ASSIGNED-TO relationship, the model contains the HAS-SKILL relationship and the SUPERVISES relationship. The HAS-SKILL relationship associates a skill, such as plumbing, roofing, or framing, with each worker. The skill has a description, a bonus rate, and the number of hours per week that a worker of that skill type can work before the bonus becomes effective. Since workers are supervised by other workers, the SUPERVISES relationship assigns to each worker a supervisor from the WORKER object set. A relationship like SUPERVISES, which relates an object set to itself, is **recursive**.

recursive relationship A relationship that relates an object set to itself.

relation attribute A column in a relation.

By using a process discussed later in the chapter, this data model can be converted into a relational data model. Figure 5.2 shows a relation with sample data values, which represents the WORKER object set, its attributes, and two of its relationships. Each column in the relation is an **attribute** of the relation. The name of the column is called the *attribute name*. We use the terms *attribute* and *attribute name* rather than *column* and *column name* to be consistent with relational database conventions. The attribute names of WORKER are WORKER-ID, NAME, HOURLY-RATE, SKILL-TYPE, and SUPV-ID. These attributes correspond to attributes and relationships in the conceptual data model as follows:

Conceptual Model	Relation Attribute
WORKER-ID (Attribute)	WORKER-ID
NAME (Attribute)	NAME
HOURLY-RATE (Attribute)	HOURLY-RATE
HAS-SKILL (Relationship)	SKILL-TYPE
SUPERVISES (Relationship)	SUPV-ID

```
WORKER
WORKER-ID          NAME          HOURLY-RATE     SKILL-TYPE      SUPV-ID
1235          M. Faraday            12.50         Electric        1311  ◄─┐
1412          C. Nemo               13.75         Plumbing        1520  ◄─┤
2920          R. Garret             10.00         Roofing               ◄─┤  rows
3231          P. Mason              17.40         Framing               ◄─┤  or
1520          H. Rickover           11.75         Plumbing              ◄─┤  tuples
1311          C. Coulomb            15.50         Electric              ◄─┤
3001          J. Barrister           8.20         Framing        3231  ◄─┘
                 ▲             ▲             ▲             ▲             ▲
                 └─────────────┴─────────────┴─────────────┴─────────────┘
                                    attributes
```

A relational database equivalent to the entire conceptual data model for Premier is shown, together with sample values, in Figure 5.3. As noted, we will explain the process of converting such a conceptual data model to a relational model later in the chapter.

degree of a relation
The number of attributes in a relation.

The number of attributes in a relation is called the **degree of the relation**. The degree of WORKER is five. So that the user does not have to remember the order of attributes in a relation, it is assumed that the order in which the attributes are listed is immaterial. From this, it follows that no two attributes in a relation can have the same name.

tuple A row in a relation.

The rows of a relation are also called **tuples**. It is assumed that there is no prespecified order to the rows, or tuples, of a relation and that no two tuples have identical sets of values.

A common notation used to represent relations such as the one in Figure 5.2 is

```
WORKER (WORKER-ID, NAME, HOURLY-RATE, SKILL-TYPE, SUPV-ID)
```

That is, the name of the relation is followed by the names of its attributes in parentheses.

attribute domain The set from which an attribute takes its values.

The set of all possible values that an attribute may have is the **domain** of the attribute. Two domains are the same only if they have the same meaning. Thus, NAME and SKILL-TYPE reference different domains, even though each consists of strings of characters. It is not necessary for two attributes with the same domain to have the same name. SUPV-ID, for example, has the same domain as WORKER-ID. In both cases, the domain consists of worker identification numbers.

Null Values

Suppose an attribute is not applicable in a specific case. For example, some employees in the WORKER relation do not have supervisors. Consequently, no value exists for SUPV-ID for these employees. In addition, when we are entering data for a row in a relation, we might not know the values of one or more of the attributes for that row. In either case, we enter nothing, and that row is recorded in the database with **null values** for those attributes. A null value is not blank or zero; it is simply unknown or inapplicable and may be supplied at a later time.

null value The value given an attribute in a tuple if the attribute is inapplicable or its value is unknown.

Keys

It is clear that the rows of WORKER contain information about individual employees. In fact, we would expect each employee to be represented by one and only one row in WORKER. Thus, if some attribute uniquely identifies an employee, we

```
WORKER
WORKER-ID     NAME                HOURLY-RATE      SKILL-TYPE      SUPV-ID
1235          M. Faraday          12.50            Electric        1311
1412          C. Nemo             13.75            Plumbing        1520
2920          R. Garret           10.00            Roofing
3231          P. Mason            17.40            Framing
1520          H. Rickover         11.75            Plumbing
1311          C. Coulomb          15.50            Electric
3001          J. Barrister         8.20            Framing         3231

ASSIGNMENT
WORKER-ID     BLDG-ID      START-DATE      NUM-DAYS
1235          312          10/10              5
1412          312          10/01             10
1235          515          10/17             22
1412          460          12/08             18
1412          435          10/15             15
1412          515          11/05              8
1311          435          10/08             12

BUILDING
BLDG-ID       BLDG-ADDRESS        TYPE            QLTY-LEVEL      STATUS
312           123 Elm             Office               2            2
435           456 Maple           Retail               1            1
515           789 Oak             Residence            3            1
210           1011 Birch          Office               3            1
111           1213 Aspen          Office               4            1
460           1415 Beech          Warehouse            3            3

SKILL
SKILL-TYPE       BONUS-RATE      HRS-PER-WEEK
Plumbing         3.00            35
Electric         3.50            37
Roofing          2.00            40
Framing          5.00            35
```

▼FIGURE 5.3 SAMPLE RELATIONS IN THE PREMIER CONSTRUCTION COMPANY DATABASE

superkey A set of attributes that uniquely identifies each row in a relation.

key A minimal set of attributes that uniquely identifies each row in a relation.

functionally determine To uniquely determine a value.

should expect the same attribute to uniquely identify the row for that employee in WORKER. Let us assume that the WORKER-ID attribute uniquely identifies an employee. Then the value of the WORKER-ID attribute uniquely identifies a row in WORKER, and we say that WORKER-ID is a key in the WORKER relation.

Any set of attributes that uniquely identifies each tuple in a relation is termed a **superkey**. A **key** of a relation is a *minimal* set of such attributes. That is, a key is a minimal superkey. By *minimal*, we mean that no subset of the set of key attributes will uniquely identify tuples in a relation. A key can also be described as a minimal set of attributes that uniquely determines, or **functionally determines**, each attribute value in a tuple.

In our discussion of the conceptual model in Chapter 4, we referred to *surrogate keys*, which are internal object identifiers that have no meaning outside a computer system, and *external keys*, which are lexical attributes that do have meaning outside the system. *Keys* in the relational model are external keys in the sense explained in Chapter 4. That is, they are externally meaningful attributes and their values are assigned by users.

To illustrate the relational model concepts of keys and superkeys, let us consider the database of Figure 5.3. In the WORKER relation, the values of the attribute set

```
{WORKER-ID, NAME}
```

uniquely identify any tuple in the relation. Therefore, this set is a superkey for WORKER. However, this set of attributes is not minimal and is therefore not a key. In this example, WORKER-ID by itself is a key, since any row in the relation is uniquely identified by WORKER-ID.

In the ASSIGNMENT relation, the key consists of the WORKER-ID and the BLDG-ID attributes. Neither WORKER-ID alone nor BLDG-ID alone uniquely identifies every row, but the two attributes together *do* provide the unique identification required for a key. A key consisting of more than one attribute is called a **composite key**.

In any given relation, there may be more than one set of attributes that could be chosen as a key. These are called **candidate keys**. It may appear, for example, that NAME is a candidate key in the WORKER relation. This would be so if we could assume that NAME will *always* be unique. If we cannot make that assumption, then NAME is not a candidate key. When one of the candidate keys is selected as the relation key, it may be called the **primary key**. The candidate key that is the easiest to use in day-to-day data entry work is normally selected as the primary key. We will ordinarily use the term *key* to mean primary key.

Having introduced the concept of a key, we can augment the notation used to identify a relation by underlining the key attributes. The relations of Figure 5.3 are designated as follows:

```
WORKER (WORKER-ID, NAME, HOURLY-RATE, SKILL-TYPE, SUPV-ID)
ASSIGNMENT (WORKER-ID, BLDG-ID, START-DATE, NUM-DAYS)
BUILDING (BLDG-ID, BLDG-ADDRESS, TYPE, QLTY-LEVEL, STATUS)
SKILL (SKILL-TYPE, BONUS-RATE, HOURS-PER-WEEK)
```

Note that since ASSIGNMENT has two key attributes, both of them are underlined. This means that WORKER-ID and BLDG-ID *together* are a key for ASSIGNMENT. It does *not* mean that each of them is, by itself, a key.

Foreign Keys

The database schema given previously has instances of the same attribute name being used in different relations. Examples of this are SKILL-TYPE in the WORKER and SKILL relations, and BLDG-ID in the ASSIGNMENT and BUILDING relations. Both of these attributes provide instances of the concept of a *foreign key*.

A **foreign key** is a set of attributes in one relation that is a key in another (or possibly the same) relation. SKILL-TYPE in the WORKER relation and BLDG-ID in the ASSIGNMENT relation are examples of foreign keys, since SKILL-TYPE is the key of the SKILL relation, and BLDG-ID is the key of the BUILDING relation. Foreign keys are the essential links between relations. They are used to tie data in one relation to data in another relation. Thus, SKILL-TYPE links the WORKER relation to the SKILL relation, and WORKER-ID and BLDG-ID in the ASSIGNMENT relation show the link between WORKER and BUILDING.

Foreign key attributes need not have the same names as the key attributes to which they correspond. For example, WORKER-ID and SUPV-ID in the WORKER

composite key A key consisting of more than one attribute.

candidate key Any set of attributes that could be chosen as a key of a relation.

primary key The candidate key designated for principal use in uniquely identifying rows in a relation.

foreign key A set of attributes in one relation that constitutes a key in some other (or possibly the same) relation; used to indicate logical links between relations.

relation have different names but both take their values from the domain of worker identification numbers. Thus, SUPV-ID is a foreign key in the WORKER relation that references the key of its own relation. For any worker, the SUPV-ID attribute indicates the worker's supervisor—who is another worker. Consequently, SUPV-ID must contain a value that is a key of some other tuple in the WORKER relation. For example, in Figure 5.3, the supervisor of worker 1235 is worker 1311. In other words, M. Faraday's supervisor is C. Coulomb. SUPV-ID is an example of a **recursive foreign key**, a foreign key that references its own relation.

Because of the vital importance of foreign key information in the definition of a relational database schema, we will now revise the previously defined schema to show foreign key definitions:

```
WORKER (WORKER-ID, NAME, HOURLY-RATE, SKILL-TYPE, SUPV-ID)
Foreign Keys:  SKILL-TYPE REFERENCES SKILL
               SUPV-ID REFERENCES WORKER
ASSIGNMENT (WORKER-ID, BLDG-ID, START-DATE, NUM-DAYS)
Foreign Keys:  WORKER-ID REFERENCES WORKER
               BLDG-ID REFERENCES BUILDING
BUILDING (BLDG-ID, BLDG-ADDRESS, TYPE, QLTY-LEVEL, STATUS)
SKILL (SKILL-TYPE, BONUS-RATE, HOURS-PER-WEEK)
```

Note that a relation's foreign keys are defined immediately after the definition of the relation name, attribute, and keys. The statement

```
SKILL-TYPE REFERENCES SKILL
```

is a foreign key definition for the WORKER relation and indicates that the SKILL-TYPE attribute in WORKER is a foreign key that references the key attribute (which also happens to be named SKILL-TYPE) in the SKILL relation.

A listing such as this one that gives relation names followed by their attribute names with key attributes underlined and with foreign keys designated is called a **relational database schema**. It is the primary output of implementation design in a DDLC that implements a relational database. Moreover, it corresponds to the conceptual level of the ANSI/SPARC model.

Integrity Constraints

A **constraint** is a rule that restricts the values that may be present in the database. Codd's relational data model includes several constraints that are used to verify the validity of data in a database as well as to add meaningful structure to the data. We will consider the following constraints:

Entity integrity

Referential integrity

Functional dependencies

We will consider entity integrity and referential integrity now and discuss functional dependencies later in the chapter. The integrity constraints provide a logical basis for maintaining the validity of data values in the database, thus preventing errors in database updating and in information processing. Such capability has obvious value, since a principal purpose of database processing is to provide accurate information for management and executive decisions.

Entity Integrity. The rows in a relation represent instances in the database of specific real-world objects or *entities* (as we will call them here to be consistent with relational terminology). For example, a row in WORKER represents a specific employee, a row in BUILDING represents a specific building, a row in ASSIGNMENT represents a specific assignment of an employee to a building, and so on. The key of the relation uniquely identifies each row and, hence, each entity instance. Thus, if users want to retrieve or manipulate the data stored in a specific row, they must know the value for the key of that row. That means we do not want any entity to be represented in the database unless we have a complete identification of the entity's key attributes. Thus, we cannot allow the key, or any part of the key, to be a null value. This is summed up in the **entity integrity rule**:

entity integrity rule
No key attribute of a row may be null.

No key attribute of any row in a relation may have a null value.

Referential Integrity. In constructing relations, foreign keys are used to tie rows in one relation to rows in another. For example, SKILL-TYPE is used in the WORKER relation to tell us the principal skill of each employee so that bonus pay rates may be calculated. Therefore, it is extremely important that the value of SKILL-TYPE in any employee's row correspond to an actual SKILL-TYPE value in the SKILL relation. Otherwise, the employee's SKILL-TYPE would point nowhere. A database in which all non-null foreign keys reference actual key values in other relations observes referential integrity. Thus, we have the **referential integrity rule**:

referential integrity rule The value of a non-null foreign key must be an actual key value in some relation.

Every foreign key must either be null, or its value must be the actual value of a key in another relation.

▼ The Normalization Process

Consider the relation of Figure 5.4 which partially combines the data of WORKER and ASSIGNMENT. Let us assume for this section that the relational database schema was not transformed from a conceptual model but was designed directly from information collected from potential database users. We assume also that the original design of the database did not include the relations of Figure 5.3 but *did* include the relation of Figure 5.4. We want to see how problems can arise through careless database design, and how such problems can be avoided by following a set of well-defined principles called **normalization**.

normalization The process of converting a relation to a standard form.

With a little analysis, we can see that the relation of Figure 5.4 is not well designed. For example, the four tuples for worker 1412 repeat the same name and skill type information. This **data redundancy**, or repetition, not only wastes space;

data redundancy Repetition of data in a database.

| ▼ FIGURE 5.4 A DIFFERENT VERSION OF THE RELATION WORKER |

```
WORKER
WORKER-ID    NAME          SKILL-TYPE    SUPV-ID    BLDG-ID
1235         M. Faraday    Electric      1311       312
1235         M. Faraday    Electric      1311       515
1412         C. Nemo       Plumbing                 312
1412         C. Nemo       Plumbing                 460
1412         C. Nemo       Plumbing                 435
1412         C. Nemo       Plumbing                 515
1311         C. Coulomb    Electric                 435
```

it can lead to loss of **data integrity** (loss of consistency) in the database. The problem is brought about by the fact that one individual may be working on more than one building at a time. Suppose C. Nemo's skill type is in error, but only the first tuple is corrected. We would then have an inconsistency among the tuples containing information about C. Nemo. This is called an **update anomaly**.

Alternatively, suppose that Nemo has been on sick leave for three months and all the buildings to which he was assigned are completed. If it is decided to delete all the rows containing information about completed buildings from the relation, then the information about C. Nemo's worker ID, name, and skill type will be lost. This is termed a **deletion anomaly**. Conversely, we might have hired a new employee named Spandolf, who has not yet been assigned to a building. If we assume null entries are not allowed, then we cannot enter information regarding Spandolf until he has been assigned to a building. This is termed an **insertion anomaly**.

Update, deletion, and insertion anomalies are obviously undesirable. How can we prevent, or at least minimize, such problems? Clearly, dividing the WORKER relation of Figure 5.4 into the two relations, WORKER and ASSIGNMENT, of Figure 5.3 appears to do away with the anomalies. This is an intuitive solution. We will now show a more formal method called decomposition for achieving the same result. **Decomposition** is the process of splitting relations into multiple relations to eliminate anomalies and maintain data integrity. To do this, we use **normal forms** or rules for structuring relations.

First Normal Form

A relation is in **first normal form (1NF)** if the values in the relation are **atomic** for every attribute in the relation. By this we mean simply that no attribute value can be a set of values or, as it is sometimes expressed, a *repeating group*. Codd's definition of a relation includes the condition that the relation be in first normal form. Therefore, all the relation schemes we will encounter will be 1NF. However, to clarify the concept, let's look at an example of a table that is not a 1NF relation.

In Figure 5.5, consider the values entered for the attribute BLDG-ID. Here we have combined each worker's building assignments into a single set. The value of the attribute BLDG-ID is the set of buildings on which the person is working. Suppose we are interested in only one of the worker's buildings. This information may be difficult to extract, since the identifier for the building of interest is buried within a set within a tuple.

The relation in Figure 5.5 is not 1NF because BLDG-ID is not atomic. That is, in any given tuple, BLDG-ID can have multiple values. The relation shown in Figure 5.4 would be 1NF, however, because the value in which we are interested, that of an individual building, can be identified merely by referencing an attribute name, BLDG-ID.

▼FIGURE 5.5 A VERSION OF THE RELATION WORKER THAT IS NOT IN FIRST NORMAL FORM				

WORKER				
WORKER-ID	NAME	SKILL-TYPE	SUPV-ID	BLDG-ID
1235	M. Faraday	Electric	1311	{312, 515}
1412	C. Nemo	Plumbing		{312, 460, 435, 515}
1311	C. Coulomb	Electric		435

Since Codd's original definition of the relational model required *all* relations to be 1NF, Figure 5.5 is not even a legitimate relation. We will follow Codd's definition and assume that all relations must be 1NF.

The next two normal forms, second normal form and third normal form, apply to relations that are constrained by functional dependencies. Before proceeding to these normal forms, we must first explain functional dependencies.

Functional Dependencies

Earlier in the chapter, we discussed the entity and referential integrity constraints. Functional dependencies (FDs) provide a means for defining additional constraints on a relational schema. The essential idea is that a tuple's value in one attribute uniquely determines the tuple's value in another attribute. For example, in every tuple in Figure 5.4, WORKER-ID uniquely determines NAME, and WORKER-ID uniquely determines SKILL-TYPE. We write these two functional dependencies as:

```
FD: WORKER-ID → NAME
FD: WORKER-ID → SKILL-TYPE
```

functional dependency The value of an attribute in a tuple determines the value of another attribute in the tuple.

More formally, we can define a **functional dependency** as follows: if A and B are attributes in a relation R, then

```
FD: A → B
```

means that if any two tuples in R have the same value for their A attribute, they *must* have the same value for their B attribute. This definition also applies if A and B are sets of columns rather than just single columns.

The notation "→" is read "functionally determines." Thus, in these examples, WORKER-ID functionally determines NAME, WORKER-ID functionally determines SKILL-TYPE, and A functionally determines B.

determinant The attribute(s) on the left side of a functional dependency; determine(s) the value of other attributes in the tuple.

The attribute on the left-hand side of an FD is called a **determinant** because its value determines the value of the attribute on the right-hand side. A relation's key is a determinant, since its value uniquely determines the value of every attribute in a tuple.

Second Normal Form

second normal form (2NF) No nonkey attribute may be functionally dependent on just a part of the key.

Second and third normal forms deal with the relationship between key and nonkey attributes. A relation is in **second normal form (2NF)** if no nonkey attribute is functionally dependent on just a part of the key. Thus, 2NF can be violated only when a key is a composite key or, in other words, one that consists of more than one attribute.

Examine the relation scheme of Figure 5.6. Here the key consists of WORKER-ID and BLDG-ID together. NAME is determined by WORKER-ID and so is functionally dependent on a part of the key. That is, knowing WORKER-ID for the worker is sufficient to identify the worker's name. Thus, the relation is not 2NF. Leaving this relation in its present non-2NF form can lead to the following problems:

1. The worker name is repeated in every row that refers to an assignment for that worker.

2. If the name of the worker changes, every row recording an assignment of that worker must be updated. This, as you may remember, is an update anomaly.

FACULTY	FNAME	COMMITTEE	COURSE
	Jones	Admissions	IM101
	Jones	Scholarship	IM101
	Jones	Admissions	IM102
	Jones	Scholarship	IM102
	Jones	Admissions	IM103
	Jones	Scholarship	IM103

▼FIGURE 5.10 THE RELATION FACULTY WITH A MULTIVALUED DEPENDENCY

multivalued dependency (MVD) A constraint that guarantees the mutual independence of multivalued attributes.

fourth normal form (4NF) A relation that is in third normal form and has no multivalued dependencies.

A condition that enforces attribute independence by requiring this duplication of values is called a **multivalued dependency (MVD)**. MVDs are constraints on relations just as FDs are constraints. Clearly, since they require an enormous duplication of data values, an important aspect of the normalization process should be to eliminate multivalued dependencies. This is done with fourth normal form.

A relation is in **fourth normal form (4NF)** if it is 3NF and has no multivalued dependencies. Since the problem of multivalued dependencies arises from multivalued attributes, we can reach a solution by placing all multivalued attributes in relations by themselves, together with the key to which the attribute values apply. Figure 5.11 illustrates this. FNAME is a key value in some other relation that identifies the faculty member to which the information applies. We list the committees Jones is assigned to by including one row for each committee. Jones's name is repeated each time. The same is true of the courses that Jones teaches. The relations in Figure 5.11 are in fourth normal form (4NF) because all multivalued attributes (in this case, COMMITTEE and COURSE) have been placed in relations by themselves. Moreover, this approach overcomes the problems of the various approaches shown in Figure 5.9. As a final note, we point out that the keys of these 4NF relations are *both* the attributes in the relation. That is, the key of FAC-COMM is (FNAME, COMMITTEE) and the key of FAC-COURSE is (FNAME, COURSE).

Other Normal Forms

Several other norms have been proposed to eliminate additional anomalies. We will briefly discuss two of these: fifth normal form (5NF) and domain/key normal form (DKNF).

fifth normal form (5NF) A normal form that eliminates join dependencies.

Fifth Normal Form.   Functional dependency and multivalued dependency constraints result in the need for second, third, and fourth Normal Forms. **Fifth normal form (5NF)** eliminates anomalies that result from a special type of constraint

▼FIGURE 5.11 THE RELATIONS FAC-COMM AND FAC-COURSE ARE BOTH 4NF

FAC-COMM	FNAME	COMMITTEE
	Jones	Admissions
	Jones	Scholarship

FAC-COURSE	FNAME	COURSE
	Jones	IM101
	Jones	IM102
	Jones	IM103

called *join dependencies*. These dependencies are principally of theoretical interest and are of highly dubious practical value. Consequently, fifth normal form has virtually no practical application.

Domain/Key Normal Form.   Fagin (1981) proposed a normal form based on the definitions of keys and attribute domains. He showed that a relation is in **domain/key normal form (DKNF)** if and only if every constraint on the relation is a consequence of the definitions of domains and keys. This is an important result. However, he did not provide a general method for converting a non-DKNF relation into a DKNF relation.

▼ Transforming a Conceptual Model to a Relational Model

It is generally agreed that conceptual models provide a more accurate representation of the complexities of an application problem than do the relational and other early data models. Thus, in Chapter 4 we discussed conceptual modeling and demonstrated how a large variety of applications problems could be solved with conceptual models. However, few systems exist at present on which conceptual models are implemented. Thus, we need some method for translating conceptual models to models that can be implemented. Since we are studying the relational model in this chapter, we will focus on methods of transforming any conceptual model into a relational model.

A conceptual data model consists of objects, relationships, attributes, specializations, aggregates, and so forth. We will now show methods of transforming each of these constructs to relations. An important characteristic of the process we will describe is that it results in the creation of relations normalized to fourth normal form. Consequently, following conversion of a conceptual model to a relational model, further normalization is unnecessary.

Transforming Object Sets and Attributes

Consider the simple conceptual model of Figure 5.12. We see an object set with two attributes. PERSON is an abstract (that is, nonlexical) object set, but SS# and BIRTHDATE are lexical attributes. Since attributes in the relational model must be lexical, SS# and BIRTHDATE can both be attributes in a relation. Therefore, we can transform this diagram into a relation with attributes as follows:

```
PERSON (SS#, BIRTHDATE)
```

What is the key? Since we can (and will) assume that SS# uniquely identifies a person, we conclude that SS# is the key. We have, therefore

---

▼FIGURE 5.12 A CONCEPTUAL MODEL OF PERSON

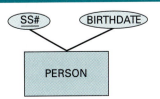

Note also that only the key columns from CUSTOMER and CHECKING-ACCOUNT are used in HAS-CHKG-ACCOUNT. That is, even if CUSTOMER and CHECKING-ACCOUNT had other columns, HAS-CHKG-ACCOUNT would only use the key columns from these two relations. The following schema illustrates this:

```
CUSTOMER(CUSTOMER-#, NAME, ADDRESS, PHONE-#)
CHECKING-ACCOUNT(CH-ACCOUNT-#, BALANCE, DATE-OPENED)
HAS-CHKG-ACCOUNT(CUSTOMER-#, CH-ACCOUNT-#)
Foreign Keys: CUSTOMER-# REFERENCES CUSTOMER
              CH-ACCOUNT-# REFERENCES CHECKING-ACCOUNT
```

The foreign key descriptions indicate that both of the key attributes of HAS-CHKG-ACCOUNT are also foreign keys. We call HAS-CHKG-ACCOUNT an *intersection relation* because it represents the instances where CUSTOMER and CHECKING-ACCOUNT meet, or intersect. As we will see in the next section, it is possible for an intersection relation, such as HAS-CHKG-ACCOUNT, to have additional nonkey attributes that apply only to it.

Transforming Aggregate Object Sets

Consider Figure 5.18, which shows a conceptual model for tracking sales of International Product Distribution. IS-SOLD-IN, a relationship aggregated to be considered an object set, has a QUANTITY attribute. We transform this model in accordance with the rules given previously. Since the relationship is many–many, we create three relations:

```
PRODUCT (PRODUCT-#)
COUNTRY (COUNTRY-NAME)
IS-SOLD-IN (PRODUCT-#, COUNTRY-NAME, QUANTITY)
Foreign Keys: PRODUCT-# REFERENCES PRODUCT
              COUNTRY-NAME REFERENCES COUNTRY
```

We have created key attributes of PRODUCT-# and COUNTRY-NAME to distinguish them from the names of their respective relations. We have also placed QUANTITY in the IS-SOLD-IN relation because it is an attribute that applies to that relation. If IS-SOLD-IN had other attributes that applied to it, they would be added to the relation in a similar manner. The PRODUCT and COUNTRY relations are shown with only one attribute, but of course they could have other attributes as well. If no other attributes are needed for these relations in the database, then they can be eliminated from the schema; and the schema will consist of the IS-SOLD-IN relation only.

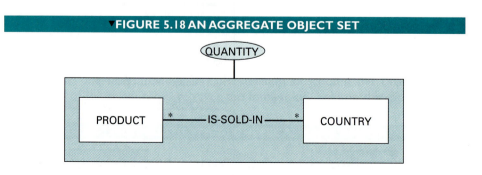

▼FIGURE 5.18 AN AGGREGATE OBJECT SET

Figure 5.19 shows IS-SOLD-IN related to DATE. In this case, the QUANTITY attribute applies to those products sold in a particular country on a particular date. We can transform this model to a relational model as:

```
IS-SOLD-IN (PRODUCT-#, COUNTRY-NAME)
SOLD-ON (PRODUCT-#, COUNTRY-NAME, DATE, QUANTITY)
```

(We have omitted the one-column relations that define the object sets.) Notice, however, that all of the information contained in IS-SOLD-IN is also contained in SOLD-ON. Thus, we can eliminate IS-SOLD-IN from the schema. If IS-SOLD-IN had nonkey attributes, then it could not be eliminated. By eliminating IS-SOLD-IN from the schema, we are saying that the model of Figure 5.19 is essentially a three-way relationship with an attribute. Thus, it is equivalent to Figure 5.20. The relational model for Figure 5.20 would be

```
SOLD (PRODUCT-#, COUNTRY-NAME, DATE, QUANTITY)
```

which is the same as the preceding SOLD-ON except for the name of the relation.

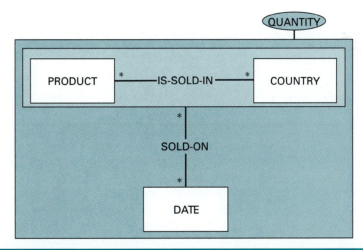

▼FIGURE 5.19 NESTED AGGREGATE

▼FIGURE 5.20 A THREE-WAY RELATIONSHIP

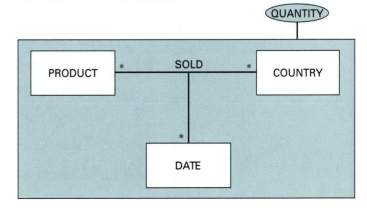

Transforming Recursive Relationships

Figure 5.21 shows a portion of the model of Figure 5.1. It is important to realize that the WORKER object set, which appears twice in the diagram, is the *same object set* both times. Both copies of WORKER have the same attributes, even though they are only shown attached to the copy on the right. The model uses two copies of WORKER for convenience in showing the SUPERVISES relationship which exists between WORKER and WORKER. This relationship is called *recursive* because it exists between an object set and itself. In this case, the relationship with its one–many cardinality means that one worker supervises many workers.

How do we transform the WORKER object set together with its attributes and the SUPERVISES relationship into a relation? Using the approaches we have already studied, we would arrive at the following:

```
WORKER (WORKER-ID, NAME, HOURLY-RATE, WORKER-ID)
```

This solution is incorrect because the WORKER relation has two attributes named WORKER-ID, and no two attributes within a relation are allowed to have the same name. The solution is to change the name of the second WORKER-ID attribute to a name that reflects the SUPERVISES relationship it represents. Thus, we change it to SUPV-ID:

```
WORKER (WORKER-ID, NAME, HOURLY-RATE, SUPV-ID)
Foreign Key: SUPV-ID REFERENCES WORKER
```

Notice that SUPV-ID is a recursive foreign key, since it references WORKER-ID, which is the key of the relation SUPV-ID is in. That is, recursive foreign keys will result from the transformation of recursive relationships. Sample data for the WORKER relation are shown in Figure 5.22.

In summary, we have shown ways of translating conceptual model constructs—objects, attributes, relationships, specializations, and aggregates—to relations. After all translation of specific constructs is complete, then the resulting schema should be reviewed for redundancy. Any redundant relations—that is, relations whose information is entirely contained in other relations in the schema—should be eliminated from the schema.

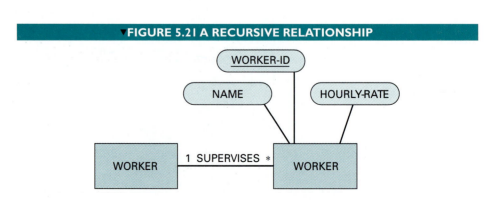

▼FIGURE 5.21 A RECURSIVE RELATIONSHIP

```
WORKER
WORKER-ID      NAME             HOURLY-RATE      SUPV-ID
1235           M. Faraday       12.50            1311
1412           C. Nemo          13.75            1520
2920           R. Garret        10.00
3231           P. Mason         17.40
1520           H. Rickover      11.75
1311           C. Coulomb       15.50
3001           J. Barrister      8.20            3231
```

▼**FIGURE 5.22 A RELATION WITH A RECURSIVE FOREIGN KEY (SUPV-ID)**

In addition, note that all of the relations are normalized to fourth normal form. The reason for this is as follows: Functional dependencies, as defined for the relational model, are attributes, one–one relationships, or one–many relationships. The process we described for converting each of these to attributes in a relation guaranteed that they would only be dependent on key attributes. Thus, each relation will be 3NF. The multivalued attributes of the relational model occur only in many–many relationships. Since these are converted to relations whose composite keys consist of the keys of the individual object sets, they are guaranteed to be 4NF.

Transformation Examples: Manwaring Consulting Services

In Chapter 4, we created a conceptual model for Manwaring Consulting Service's project billing. This model is shown in Figure 5.23. Applying the principles of this chapter, we will now convert this model to a relational schema.

The relations for the PROJECT and CLIENT object sets are as follows:

▼**FIGURE 5.23 A DATA MODEL FOR PROJECT BILLING**

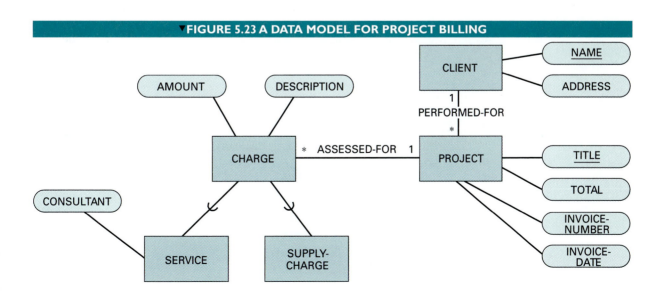

```
CLIENT (CLIENT-NAME, CLIENT-ADDRESS)
PROJECT (PROJECT-#, CLIENT-NAME, PROJECT-TITLE,
         TOTAL-CHARGE, INVOICE-#, INVOICE-DATE)
Foreign Key: CLIENT-NAME REFERENCES CLIENT
```

PROJECT-# was added as an attribute because we needed an external key for PRO-JECT. PROJECT-TITLE does not uniquely identify a project. INVOICE-# is unique but is not an appropriate key for a relation describing projects. For the sake of clarity, we have also changed some of the attribute names—for example, CLIENT-NAME and PROJECT-TITLE. The change to CLIENT-NAME was essential, since it is used as a foreign key in PROJECT.

In addition to these two relations, we need relations for CHARGE and SER-VICE:

```
CHARGE (CHARGE-#, PROJECT-#, AMOUNT, DESCRIPTION)
Foreign Key: PROJECT-# REFERENCES PROJECT
SERVICE (CHARGE-#, PROJECT-#, CONSULTANT)
Foreign Key: CHARGE-#, PROJECT-# REFERENCE CHARGE
```

In converting the CHARGE object set to a relation, we had to make a decision about its key. In this case, we decided that the project to which a specific charge applies partially identifies the charge. Therefore, we used PROJECT-# as a part of the key. We then added CHARGE-# as the remaining part of the key. This means that different charges can have the same CHARGE-# if they are not related to the same project.

The SERVICE object set is a specialization of the CHARGE object set. For this reason, the SERVICE relation must have the same key as the CHARGE relation. Of course, this means that this two-column key is a foreign key that references CHARGE. In addition, the SERVICE relation has the CONSULTANT attribute, which indicates the consultant who performed the service. Even though SUPPLY CHARGE is also a specialization of CHARGE, it does not merit its own relation because it has no attributes of its own. All the information needed about supply charges can be found in the CHARGE relation.

Figure 5.24 shows the data model we developed for Manwaring's project billing in Chapter 4. We will now convert it to a relational model. The CLIENT and PROJECT object sets are converted as before:

```
CLIENT (CLIENT-NAME, CLIENT-ADDRESS)
PROJECT (PROJECT-#, CLIENT-NAME, PROJECT-TITLE,
        TOTAL-CHARGE, INVOICE-#, INVOICE-DATE)
Foreign Key: CLIENT-NAME REFERENCES CLIENT
```

The object set OTHER-CHARGE in this model corresponds to CHARGE in the previous model:

```
OTHER-CHARGE (CHARGE-#, PROJECT-#, AMOUNT, DESCRIPTION)
Foreign Key: PROJECT-# REFERENCES PROJECT
```

We also need a relation for CONSULTANT:

```
CONSULTANT (CONSULTANT-NAME, RATE)
```

Finally, we need to represent the relationships in the large box. Since the ENGAGED-IN relationship has no attributes of its own, we can embed it in the rela-

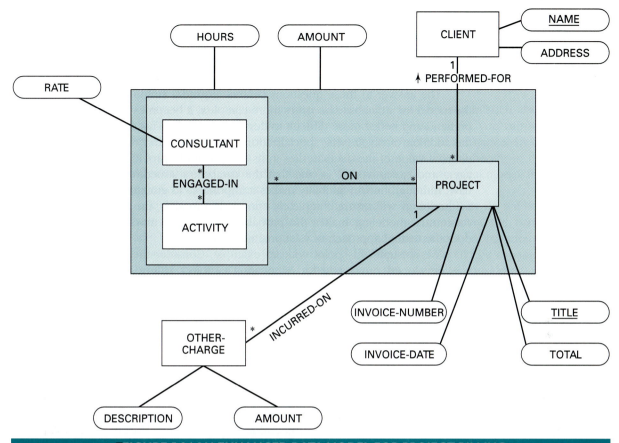

tion representing the ON relationship. This relation is equivalent to a three-way relationship, so its key will consist of three attributes. It also has two nonkey attributes, HOURS and AMOUNT.

```
ENGAGED-IN-ACTIVITY-ON (CONSULTANT-NAME, ACTIVITY, PROJECT-#,
                       HOURS, AMOUNT)
    Foreign Keys: CONSULTANT-NAME REFERENCES CONSULTANT
                  PROJECT-# REFERENCES PROJECT
```

Since "ON" does not give a very good description of the meaning of the relation, we have given it a new name that we feel is more descriptive.

While the process of converting a conceptual model to a relational model is mechanical and straightforward, it does require some human intelligence. We have illustrated this in the previous two examples, where we selected keys in various ways and changed the names of attributes and relations as needed. Nevertheless, the process is comparatively simple, and all resulting relations are in fourth normal form.

▼ Comparison of Conceptual and Relational Data Modeling

Students, particularly those who have previously had experience with relational DBMSs, sometimes wonder why we bother with conceptual modeling when we're going to eventually be implementing the database system in the relational model

The process of transforming a conceptual model to a relational model involves creating a relation for each object set in the model. The attributes of the object set are attributes of the relation. If an external key attribute exists, it can be used as the relation's key. Otherwise, a key attribute may be created by the analyst. However, it is best if such an attribute arises naturally in the application being modeled. One–one and one–many relationships are converted to the relational model by making them attributes of the appropriate relation. Many–many relationships correspond to multivalued attributes and are converted to fourth normal form by creating a relation whose two-column key is taken from the keys of the two object sets participating in the relationship. Specialization sets are converted by creating separate relations, which take their key from the relation corresponding to the generalization set. Recursive relationships may also be modeled by creating a new attribute name, which is descriptive of the relationship.

Conceptual data models are inherently easier to comprehend than relational models, because they conform more to the way we naturally look at things, as mirrored in our language through the use of nouns and verbs. This shows that the process of developing a conceptual model and then converting it to a normalized relational model is worth the effort because in complex modeling situations we would be too likely to make critical errors. Since implementation must normally be carried out in the relational model, the step of converting from conceptual to relational continues to be essential.

Review Questions

1. Define each of the following terms in your own words:
   a. relational data model
   b. recursive relationship
   c. degree of a relation
   d. attribute domain
   e. superkey
   f. functionally determine
   g. candidate key
   h. foreign key
   i. relational database schema
   j. entity integrity rule
   k. normalization
   l. data redundancy
   m. update anomaly
   n. insertion anomaly
   o. normal forms
   p. atomic value
   q. determinant
   r. projection of a relation
   s. Boyce-Codd normal form
   t. multivalued dependency
   u. fifth normal form
   v. intersection relation

2. Compare and contrast:
- **a.** Keys and superkeys
- **b.** Foreign keys and keys
- **c.** Foreign keys and recursive foreign keys
- **d.** Attributes and domains
- **e.** Attributes and columns
- **f.** Tuples and rows
- **g.** Entity integrity and referential integrity
- **h.** Candidate keys and primary keys

3. React to the following statement, paraphrased from Kent (1983): A relation is in third normal form if every nonkey attribute is dependent on the key, the whole key, and nothing but the key. Which part of the statement applies to second normal form, and which applies to third normal form?

4. Explain why it is undesirable to have relations that are not in second or third normal form.

5. Describe the process of transforming a conceptual model to a relational model for each of the following:
- **a.** Object set and attributes with and without an external key
- **b.** One–one relationship
- **c.** One–many relationship
- **d.** Many–many relationship
- **e.** Specialization relationship
- **f.** Aggregate
- **g.** Recursive relationship

6. Compare and contrast these two approaches to data modeling: (1) First develop a conceptual model and then mechanically convert it to a normalized relational schema. (2) Skip the conceptual model step and develop a relational model, using normalization theory to remove anomalies. What advantages and disadvantages does each approach have?

Problems and Exercises

1. Match each term with its definition:

__*domain/key normal form*	a. A nonkey attribute is functionally dependent on one or more other nonkey attributes
__*second normal form*	b. Every determinant is a key
__*relation attribute*	c. Value of an attribute if the attribute is inapplicable or its value is unknown
__*referential integrity*	d. Consistency of data in a database
__*tuple*	e. Two-dimensional table containing rows and columns of data
__*null value*	f. Minimal set of attributes that uniquely identifies each row
__*third normal form*	g. In third normal form with no multivalued dependencies

__primary key	h Foreign key that references its own relation
__relation	i. A column in a relation
__recursive foreign key	j. The value of a non-null foreign key must be an actual key value in some relation
__constraint	k. Key consisting of more than one attribute
__data integrity	l. Splitting a relation into multiple relations
__composite key	m. Row in a relation
__decomposition of relations	n. No nonkey attribute may be functionally dependent on just a part of the key
__first normal form	o. All attribute values must be atomic
__functional dependency	p. Unintended loss of data due to deletion of other data
__deletion anomaly	q. Rule that restricts the values in a database
__fourth normal form	r. Requires every constraint to result from definitions of domains and keys
__key	s. Candidate key designated for principal use in identifying rows
__transitive dependency	t. The value of an attribute in a tuple determines the value of another attribute in the tuple

2. Consider the following relation (capitalized letters are attribute names, lower-case letters and numbers are values):

X

A	B	C	D	E
a1	b2	c1	d3	e2
a3	b2	c3	d2	e4
a1	b3	c1	d1	e2
a2	b4	c1	d4	e2

Circle the functional dependencies that seem to apply to X.

a. $A \rightarrow C$ b. $D \rightarrow E$ c. $C \rightarrow A$ d. $E \rightarrow B$
e. $E \rightarrow A$ f. $C \rightarrow B$ g. $B \rightarrow D$ h. $B \rightarrow A$

Identify a possible key for X.

3. Consider the following relation (capitalized letters are attribute names, lower-case letters and numbers are values):

Y

A	B	C	D	E
a1	b2	c1	d3	e2
a2	b2	c3	d3	e4
a1	b3	c2	d1	e2
a2	b4	c5	d1	e5

Circle the functional dependencies that do *not* apply to Y.

a. $A \rightarrow C$ b. $D \rightarrow E$ c. $C \rightarrow A$ d. $E \rightarrow B$
e. $E \rightarrow A$ f. $C \rightarrow B$ g. $B \rightarrow D$ h. $B \rightarrow A$

Identify a possible key for Y.

4. Consider the following relation (capitalized letters are attribute names, lower-case letters and numbers are values):

Z

A	B	C	D	E
a1	b2	c2	d3	e2
a1	b2	c2	d1	e4
a2	b3	c2	d1	e5
a2	b4	c5	d1	e5

Circle the functional dependencies that seem to apply to Z.

a. $E \rightarrow D$ b. $D \rightarrow E$ c. $C \rightarrow A$ d. $E \rightarrow B$

e. $E \rightarrow A$ f. $B \rightarrow C$ g. $B \rightarrow D$ h. $B \rightarrow A$

Identify a possible key for Z.

5. For each of the following relations, indicate which normal forms the relations conform to (if any) and show how the relation can be decomposed into multiple relations each of which conforms to the highest normal form.

A. EMPLOYEE (<u>SS#</u>, NAME, ADDRESS, PHONE, FATHER, SKILLS)
FD: ADDRESS → PHONE

B. WORKER (<u>W-ID</u>, W-NAME, SPOUSE-SS#, SPOUSE-NAME)
FD: SPOUSE-SS# → SPOUSE-NAME

C. SALE (<u>DATE</u>, <u>CUSTOMER</u>, <u>PRODUCT</u>, VENDOR, VENDOR-CITY, SALESREP)
FD: CUSTOMER → SALESREP

D. EMPLOYEE (<u>SS#</u>, NAME, ADDRESS, PHONE, FATHER, FATHERS-ADDRESS)
FD: FATHER → FATHERS-ADDRESS

E. WORKER (<u>W-ID</u>, W-NAME, SPOUSE-NAME, CHILDREN)

F. SALE (<u>DATE</u>, <u>CUSTOMER</u>, <u>PRODUCT</u>, VENDOR, VENDOR-CITY, SALESREP)
FD: VENDOR → VENDOR-CITY, FD: PRODUCT → VENDOR

G. STUDENT (<u>STUDENT-#</u>, NAME, BLDG, FLOOR, SENIOR-RESIDENT)
FD: BLDG, FLOOR → SENIOR-RESIDENT

H. ENROLLMENT (<u>COURSE-#</u>, <u>STUDENT-#</u>, GRADE, INSTRUCTOR, ROOM-#)
FD: COURSE-# → INSTRUCTOR, FD: COURSE-# → ROOM-#

I. ACTIVITY (<u>STUDENT-#</u>, <u>DESCRIPTION</u>, DATE, BLDG, ROOM, COST)
FD: DESCRIPTION → BLDG, FD: DESCRIPTION → ROOM,
FD: BLDG → COST

6. Create a relational schema, with all relations 4NF, for the following information about a life insurance company:

The company has a large number of policies. For each policy, we want to know the policyholder's social security number, name, address, and birthdate. We also need to know the policy number, annual premium, and death benefit amount. Moreover, we want to know the agent number, name, and state of residence of the agent who wrote the policy. A policyholder can have many policies, and an agent will write many policies.

7. Convert the following conceptual models to relational schemas that show relation names, attributes, keys, and foreign keys.

    a. Figure 5.1E
    b. Figure 5.2E

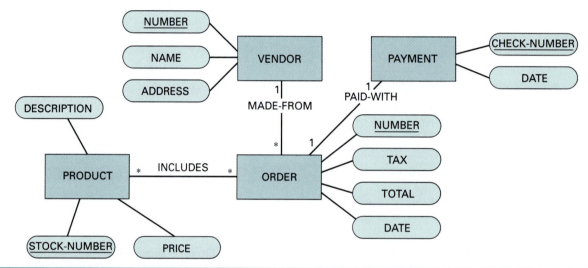

▼**FIGURE 5.1E PURCHASE ORDER DATA MODEL FOR MANWARING CONSULTING SERVICES**

▼**FIGURE 5.2E DATA MODEL FOR ENHANCED PURCHASE ORDER**

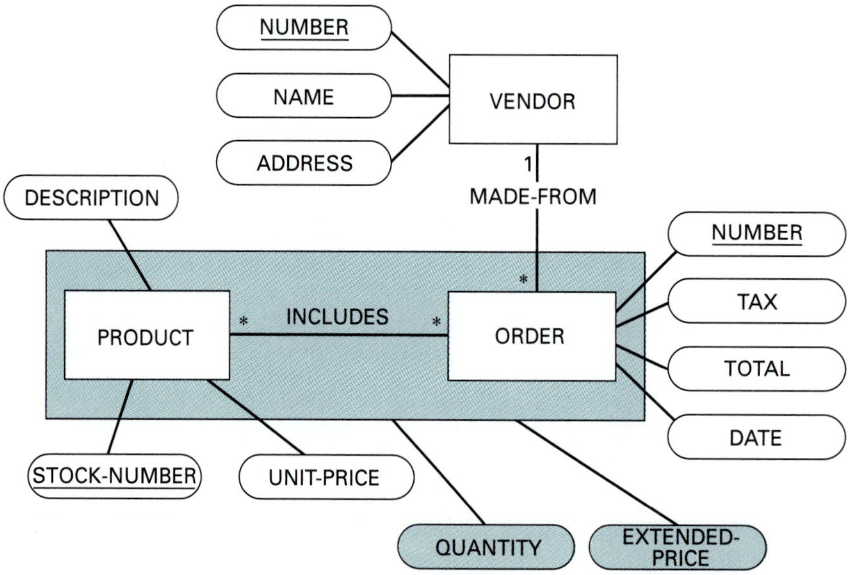

Projects and Professional Issues

1. Without using a conceptual model for conceptual design, create a relational database schema for an organization that you have contact or experience with. Create at least eight relations that are normalized to fourth normal form.

2. Carry out project 1 again, this time by first designing a conceptual model and converting it to a relational model using the methods of this chapter. Compare your experience in the two projects.

3

RELATIONAL DATABASE IMPLEMENTATION

▼

I n Part III we explore the languages and systems used for database system implementation in the relational model. These include relational algebra and calculus, as well as the commercial languages of SQL and Query-by-Example. We also examine principles related to physical implementation problems.

Our discussion of relational algebra and calculus in Chapter 6 thoroughly examines these languages, which form the basis for all other relational languages. Numerous examples are used to clarify both languages.

Chapter 7 examines SQL, the ANSI standard relational language. In addition to presenting its essential features as given in the SQL-89 standard, we also discuss a number of the important features provided by the 1992 standard.

Chapter 8 presents Query-by-Example, a graphical relational language which has several commercial implementations. Our discussion examines one of these commercial implementations, PARADOX.

In chapter 9 we approach the new area of client/server systems. We look at two server database systems, SQL Server and Oracle. We also discuss a client application development environment, PowerBuilder.

Chapter 10 discusses physical implementation techniques. We examine direct-access storage devices, data formats, and traditional file organizations. Moreover, we define techniques of mapping by using pointers, chains, rings, inverted lists, and B+-trees and show how these may be used to map logical data structures. We also discuss secondary key structure and query optimization techniques.

C H A P T E R

RELATIONAL ALGEBRA
AND CALCULUS

Cordelia Molini and Reggie Townsend, information systems practitioners at International Product Distribution (IPD), are discussing the differences in relational database languages. Reggie has recently been introduced to relational databases and is striving to comprehend their conceptual basis. However, he does not understand the significant structural differences between some of the commercial languages. Cordelia explains: "When Codd originally proposed the relational data model, he recommended a procedural language, relational algebra, and a nonprocedural language, relational calculus."

"I'm afraid I don't understand those terms, Cordelia. What do you mean by procedural and nonprocedural?"

"In a nonprocedural language, we tell the computer what has to be done, not how to do it. In a procedural language, we tell the computer how each step is to be executed. Traditional computer languages are procedural. The relational model has made the development of nonprocedural languages more practical."

"It would appear, then, that nonprocedural languages are superior to procedural languages. So why aren't all relational languages modeled after relational calculus?"

"The more popular ones, such as SQL, QBE, and QUEL, tend to be. Relational algebra does have definite advantages, however, and some languages, such as those in the R·base systems, are modeled after it. To fully understand the relational model and the languages used to manipulate it, it's important to completely grasp both approaches."

This chapter provides a comprehensive introduction to relational algebra and relational calculus, which form the basis for the commercial languages used with relational databases. After becoming acquainted with these two languages, you will be prepared to learn and use any of the many database languages that are based on them. After reading this chapter, you should be able to:

▼ List the operations of relational algebra and show how they can be used to create new relations from existing relations.

▼ Demonstrate the structure of query solutions in relational calculus, most especially the conditional statements that must be formed to define a query solution.

▼ Formulate solutions to specific types of queries in both languages.

▼ A Revolutionary Advance in Data Manipulation

In 1970–1971, E. F. Codd published two papers introducing the relational data model and the relational data manipulation languages, relational algebra and relational calculus. Although the relational data model itself was important, the relational languages were more significant in touching off the relational database revolution. After all, the relational model, in which data are represented in tables, is very similar to the file-oriented models that already existed. Admittedly, the changes in terminology—from *file* to *relation,* from *field* to *attribute,* and so on—were important, since they emphasized the logical meaning of data rather than their physical structure. But, in retrospect, it appears that the most important aspect of the new model was its concrete data languages, which allow the manipulation of data solely on the basis of their logical characteristics. In this chapter, we will study the two languages Codd proposed, relational algebra and relational calculus.

In his original paper, Codd introduced the relational data model and relational algebra (Codd, 1970). **Relational algebra** is a **procedural** language for manipulating relations. That is, relational algebra uses a step-by-step approach to create a relation containing the data that answer the query. In subsequent papers, Codd introduced relational calculus (Codd, 1971a, 1971b). **Relational calculus** is **non-procedural**. In relational calculus, a query is solved by defining a solution relation in a single step.

Codd showed that relational algebra and relational calculus are logically equivalent—a fact of considerable importance. It meant that any query that could be formulated in relational calculus could be formulated in relational algebra, and vice versa. This provided a means of measuring the logical power of a query language. If a language was at least as powerful as relational algebra, it was called **relationally complete**. This means that any query that can be formulated in relational algebra must be formulable in the "relationally complete" language. Thus, as commercial relational languages are developed, their logical power can be tested by comparing them with relational algebra or relational calculus. If a language is less powerful than either of these, then there will be certain queries which cannot be formulated in the commercial language.

Relational algebra is also important because it contributes much of the vocabulary and many of the basic relational data manipulation concepts that are commonly found in commercial database languages. Such terms as *select, project, join,* and *union compatible* all originate in relational algebra. In addition, some commercial database languages are based on relational algebra.

Relational calculus is important for two reasons: (1) It is based on the predicate calculus of formal logic, which is a powerful method of determining the truth of a statement from the truth of its components. Consequently, relational calculus has as firm a logical foundation as any programming language in existence. (2) Several commercial relational languages are conceptually close to it. We will be studying some of these languages in later chapters.

Both relational algebra and calculus, as formulated by Codd and as discussed in this chapter, are theoretical languages. That is, here we are interested only in the conceptual aspects of algebra and calculus, not in specific implementations of them. Therefore, we will be rather free and informal in our definition and use of syntax. If these were actual commercial languages—such as those we will study later in the book—we would need to be more precise. Throughout this chapter, we will use the database of Figure 6.1 to illustrate our examples. This database is taken from the International Product Distribution case introduced in Chapter 1.

▼ Relational Algebra

Relational algebra operations manipulate relations. That is, these operations use one or two existing relations to create a new relation. This new relation may then be used as input to a new operation. This powerful concept—the creation of new relations from old ones—makes possible an infinite variety of data manipulations. It also makes the solution of queries considerably easier, since we can experiment with partial solutions until we find an approach that will work.

relational algebra A procedural language for manipulating relations.

procedural Language that provides a step-by-step method for solving problems.

relational calculus A nonprocedural language for defining query solutions.

nonprocedural Language that provides a means for stating *what* is desired rather than *how* to get it.

relationally complete Having the same logical power as relational algebra or calculus.

```
CUSTOMER
                                                        BEGINNING    CURRENT
CUST ID    CUST NAME     ADDRESS           COUNTRY      BALANCE      BALANCE
100        Watabe Bros   Box 241, Tokyo    Japan        45,551       52,113
101        Maltzl        Salzburg          Austria      75,314       77,200
105        Jefferson     B 918, Chicago    USA          49,333       57,811
110        Gomez         Santiago          Chile        27,400       35,414

SALESPERSON

SALPERS ID     SALPERS NAME      MANAGER ID     OFFICE        COMM %
10             Rodney Jones      27             Chicago       10
14             Masaji Matsu      44             Tokyo         11
23             Francois Moire    35             Brussels       9
37             Elena Hermana     12             B. A.         13
39             Goro Azuma        44             Tokyo         10
27             Terry Cardon                     Chicago       15
44             Albert Ige        27             Tokyo         12
35             Brigit Bovary     27             Brussels      11
12             Buster Sanchez    27             B. A.         10

PRODUCT

PROD ID     PROD DESC          MANUFACTR ID      COST      PRICE
1035        Sweater            210               1.25      2.00
2241        Table Lamp         317               2.25      3.25
2249        Table Lamp         317               3.55      4.80
2518        Brass Sculpture    253                .60      1.20

SALE

DATE      CUST ID     SALPERS ID     PROD ID     QTY
02/28     100         10             2241        200
02/12     101         23             2518        300
02/15     101         23             1035        150
02/19     100         39             2518        200
02/02     101         23             1035        200
02/05     105         10             2241        100
02/22     110         37             2518        150
02/14     105         10             2249         50
02/01     101         23             2249         75
02/04     101         23             2241        250

MANUFACTURER

MANUFACTR ID      MANUFACTR NAME      ADDRESS       COUNTRY
210               Kiwi Klothes        Auckland      New Zealand
253               Brass Works         Lagos         Nigeria
317               Llama Llamps        Lima          Peru
```

▼FIGURE 6.1 SAMPLE DATA FROM THE IPD DATABASE

Relational algebra consists of the following nine operations: union, intersection, difference, product, select, project, join, divide, and assignment. The first four of these operations are taken from mathematical set theory and are largely the same as the operations found there. This is reasonable, since relations are themselves sets, so set operations can be applied to them. The next four are new operations that apply specifically to the relational data model. The last operation—assignment—

Query: Who are the salespeople in Tokyo getting more than 10% commission?

    Solution: SELECT(SALESPERSON: OFFICE = 'Tokyo' and COMM_% > 10)

Result:

SALPERS ID	SALPERS NAME	MANAGER ID	OFFICE	COMM %
14	Masaji Matsu	44	Tokyo	11
44	Albert Ige	27	Tokyo	12

Query: Who is reporting to manager 27 or getting over 10% commission?

    Solution: SELECT(SALESPERSON: MANAGER_ID = 27 or COMM_% > 10)

Result:

SALPERS ID	SALPERS NAME	MANAGER ID	OFFICE	COMM %
10	Rodney Jones	27	Chicago	10
14	Masaji Matsu	44	Tokyo	11
37	Elena Hermana	12	B. A.	13
27	Terry Cardon		Chicago	15
44	Albert Ige	27	Tokyo	12
35	Brigit Bovary	27	Brussels	11
12	Buster Sanchez	27	B. A.	10

Project

Several of the queries used to illustrate the select operation asked "Who . . .," which suggests that users wanted just the names of the salespeople satisfying the query condition. Yet the answer to each query included entire rows of data taken from the SALESPERSON relation, since the select operation always selects entire rows. Clearly we need some way to eliminate unwanted columns. If the select operation may be thought of as eliminating unwanted rows, the **project** operation can be thought of as eliminating unwanted columns. The relation resulting from a project operation is called a **projection** of the original relation.

    Unlike the other relational algebra operations, the project operation does not require any special keyword or symbol. Rather, to create a projection—a relation consisting of only certain identified columns of another relation—we merely list the original relation followed by brackets enclosing the columns that we want to keep. For example, if we wish to identify the salespeople in the Tokyo office, we could project the name column from the SP_TOKYO relation shown on p. 182.

```
SP_TOKYO [SALPERS_NAME]
```

This gives the following relation:

SALPERS NAME
Masaji Matsu
Goro Azuma
Albert Ige

We could have chosen more than one column. Thus, if we want the ID, the Name, and the Manager of these salespeople we enter:

project Relational algebra operation that creates a relation by deleting columns from an existing relation.

projection Relation resulting from a project operation.

```
SP_TOKYO [SALPERS_ID, SALPERS_NAME, MANAGER_ID]
```

The result would be:

SALPERS ID	SALPERS NAME	MANAGER ID
14	Masaji Matsu	44
39	Goro Azuma	44
44	Albert Ige	27

Suppose we are interested in knowing all the different commission percentages being paid to salespeople. We can obtain these by merely projecting on the COMM_% column of the SALESPERSON relation:

```
SALESPERSON [COMM_%]
```

This gives the following result:

COMM %
10
11
9
13
15
12

Notice that each commission rate appears only one time, even though several different salespeople have the same commission rate. Because a relation is a set, a given rate appears only once. This is an important feature of the project operation. It automatically eliminates duplicate rows from the resulting relation. This also happens when the resulting relation consists of more than one column. If any two entire rows in a relation are identical column for column, the row appears only once in the relation.

The project operation presents a convenient opportunity for showing the nesting of operations in relational algebra. By *nesting*, we mean the execution of more than one operation without explicitly assigning a name to the intermediate result relations. For example, let's add a project operation to one of the queries used to illustrate the select operation:

Query: Which salespeople are getting less than 11% commission?

Solution: SELECT(SALESPERSON: COMM_% < 11) [SALPERS_NAME]

Result:

SALPERS NAME
Rodney Jones
Francois Moire
Goro Azuma
Buster Sanchez

In this example, the select operation is performed first, followed by the projection of the resulting relation on the SALPERS_NAME column. It is permissible to nest relational algebra operations as desired, using parentheses where needed to show the order of operations.

work, since it applies to only one row at a time. However, the theta join does allow at least a two-row comparison. We will use it in joining a relation to itself:

```
A := SALESPERSON[COMM_%]
B := A
C := JOIN(A, B: A.COMM_% > B.COMM_%)
```

The result of this join follows:

```
C

A.COMM_%        B.COMM_%
10                 9
11                10
11                 9
13                10
13                11
13                 9
13                12
15                10
15                11
15                 9
15                12
15                13
12                10
12                11
12                 9
```

How can we use this relation to solve the problem? If we examine the columns separately, we discover an important fact. The left column, *A*.COMM_%, contains all the commission rates *except* the lowest one, and the right column, *B*.COMM_%, contains all the commission rates *except* the highest. This leads us to the solution to the problem. By *subtracting* the set of commission rates in the right column from the set of *all* commission rates, we are left with the highest commission rate, as requested by the query.

```
D := C [B.COMM_%]
E := A - D
```

D is the right column of *C* and so contains all the commission rates except the highest, and *A* contains all the commission rates. Their difference, *E*, contains only the highest commission rate and is therefore the solution to the query.

It should be clear that to obtain the *minimum* commission rate, it is only necessary to substitute the *A*.COMM_% column for the *B*.COMM_% column in the definition of *D*. The rest of the solution remains the same.

The solution to this query involves two "tricks": (1) joining a relation to itself, using the theta join, and (2) subtracting a relation containing everything *except* what the query asks for from the set of all possible values. This second point is important and often necessary for solving the more difficult queries in relational algebra.

▼ Relational Calculus

Relational calculus uses an entirely different approach than relational algebra. Nevertheless, the two languages are logically equivalent. This means that any query that can be solved in one language can be solved in the other. We will be more brief in our coverage of relational calculus, since the language itself has fewer constructs.

Query: `Who are the salespeople in the Tokyo office?`

This query is solved in relational calculus as follows:

`{r.SALPERS_NAME : r IN SALESPERSON and r.OFFICE = 'Tokyo'}`

The braces ({ }) enclosing the statement indicate that the solution to the query is a set of data values. Precisely what is in this set is described by the statement. The solution given here illustrates most of the features of relational calculus. We list the parts of the solution and explain their meanings:

1. r

2. r.SALPERS_NAME

3. the colon (:)

4. r IN SALESPERSON

5. r.OFFICE = 'Tokyo'

1. r is a variable that stands for an arbitrary row. The relation from which r comes is defined by "r IN SALESPERSON," which means that r is a row in SALESPERSON. We will use lower-case letters near r in the alphabet, such as s, t, p, and q, as row variables.

2. r.SALPERS_NAME is the value of the SALPERS_NAME attribute in row r.

3. The colon (:) separates the target list from the qualifying statement. The target list in this case is

`r.SALPERS_NAME`

and the qualifying statement is

`r IN SALESPERSON and r.OFFICE = 'Tokyo'`

We will explain the meanings of these shortly. The colon can be read as "such that."

4. "r IN SALESPERSON" was explained in point 1.

5. "r.OFFICE = 'Tokyo'" means that the value of the OFFICE attribute in row r is 'Tokyo'.

Target List and Qualifying Statement

target list A list in a relational calculus statement that defines the attributes of the solution relation.

qualifying statement A condition in a relational calculus statement that restricts membership in a solution relation.

The solution to every query in relational calculus is a relation which is defined by a target list and a qualifying statement. The **target list** defines the attributes of the solution relation. The **qualifying statement** is a condition used to determine which values from the database actually go into the solution relation. We now explain how this works.

In the preceding example, the target list was r.SALPERS_NAME. In other words, the solution relation has only one attribute, the name of the salesperson. The actual values that go into the solution relation are those taken from the rows that satisfy the qualifying statement. In this example, a salesperson's name is taken from a row r and placed in the solution relation if the row r satisfies the condition

```
r IN SALESPERSON and r.OFFICE = 'Tokyo'
```

The system examines the rows of SALESPERSON, as shown in Figure 6.1, one by one. The first row is temporarily given the name *r*, and the qualifying statement is tested for truth or falsity. In this case, since *r*.OFFICE = 'Chicago', the qualifying statement is false, so *r*.SALPERS_NAME (Rodney Jones) is *not* placed in the solution relation. The system then moves on to the second row, gives it the name *r*, and tests the qualifying statement again. This time the statement is true, so Masaji Matsu is placed in the solution relation. This process is repeated for every row in SALESPERSON. The result is shown as follows:

```
SALPERS NAME
Masaji Matsu
Goro Azuma
Albert Ige
```

For most queries, the target list will consist of a single attribute. However, the target list can consist of multiple attributes. For example, consider the query:

Query: Give all attributes for salespeople in the Tokyo office.

    Solution: {r : r IN SALESPERSON and r.OFFICE = 'Tokyo'}

Here we have indicated that all attributes are to be included by merely listing *r*. This means that the entire row should be included. We also could have listed all of the attributes separated by commas:

```
{(r.SALPERS_ID, r.SALPERS_NAME, r.MANAGER_ID, r.OFFICE,
r.COMM_%) : r IN SALESPERSON and r.OFFICE = 'Tokyo'}
```

In addition, we may choose to list any subset of these attributes we desire.

From our explanation so far, it should be easy to see how the select and project operations of relational algebra are supported in relational calculus. Union, intersection, difference, and product operations can also be readily derived from the constructs of relational calculus we have discussed to this point. Since calculus does not use the step-by-step procedure of algebra, the assignment statement is not needed. Thus, the only relational algebra operations for which we have not yet shown relational calculus equivalents are join and divide. These require the *quantifiers*: existential for join and universal for divide.

The Existential Quantifier

existential quantifier
Relational calculus expression affirming the existence of at least one row to which a condition applies.

A quantifier *quantifies,* or indicates the quantity of something. The **existential quantifier** states that at least one instance of a particular type of thing exists. In relational calculus, the existential quantifier is used to state that a particular type of row in a relation exists.

Let's consider an example to clarify this concept:

Query: List names of customers who have purchased product 2518.

Obviously, the solution to this query is a relation containing the names of certain customers. This is a single-column relation so the target list is clearly

```
r.CUST_NAME
```

where *r* is a row in CUSTOMER.

So we have the target list, but what is the qualifying statement? To be in the solution, the customer must meet the condition of having purchased product 2518. In other words, if a given customer's ID is found in a row of SALE with PROD_ID = 2518, then that customer is in the solution. Thus, the condition must be that there exists at least one row in SALE that contains the customer's ID and a PROD_ID of 2518. We state this as follows:

```
there exists s IN SALE
 (s.CUST_ID = r.CUST_ID and s.PROD_ID = 2518)
```

This is read as: "There exists a row *s* in SALE, such that *s*.CUST_ID = *r*.CUST_ID, and *s*.PROD_ID = 2518." (The words *there exists* constitute the existential quantifier.)

Notice that this is a statement about the row *r*. If it is true that for a given *r* such a row *s* exists, then *r*.CUST_NAME is placed in the solution relation. If the statement is false—that is, if no such *s* exists for this *r*—then *r*.CUST_NAME is not placed in the solution relation.

The complete relational calculus solution for this query is:

```
{r.CUST_NAME : r IN CUSTOMER and there exists s IN SALE
                  (s.CUST_ID = r.CUST_ID
                  and s.PROD_ID = 2518)}
```

This solution describes a relation consisting of a single column and containing customer names taken from the rows of the relation CUSTOMER. A given name is placed in the solution relation if its row (*r*) satisfies the condition following the colon. Let's look at a few of the rows in CUSTOMER to see how the condition would be applied.

Consider Figure 6.10. The first row of CUSTOMER (which we have marked *r*) has CUST_ID = 100. The CUST_NAME (Watabe Bros) will be placed in the solution relation if a row exists in SALE having CUST_ID = 100 and PROD_ID = 2518. Such a row does in fact exist, and we have marked it *s*. Thus, *r* satisfies the qualifying statement, and *r*.CUST_NAME is placed in the solution. We repeat this process for each row of CUSTOMER. When the second row is designated *r*, we must find a corresponding *s* in SALE. In this case, the corresponding *s* is the second row of SALE. So Maltzl is placed in the solution. As we proceed further, we see that customer 105 (Jefferson) is *not* placed in the solution, but customer 110 (Gomez) is. The solution set would be:

```
CUST NAME
Watabe Bros
Maltzl
Gomez
```

In relational algebra, the solution to this query would involve the join. Thus, we have shown how the existential quantifier is used in relational calculus to accomplish the function of the join. As a final example, we look at a more complex query that requires two joins.

```
CUSTOMER
CUST                                                      BEGINNING      CURRENT
ID        CUST NAME      ADDRESS            COUNTRY       BALANCE        BALANCE
100       Watabe Bros    Box 241, Tokyo     Japan         45,551         52,113      r
101       Maltzl         Salzburg           Austria       75,314         77,200
105       Jefferson      B 918, Chicago     USA           49,333         57,811
110       Gomez          Santiago           Chile         27,400         35,414

SALE
DATE          CUST ID        SALPERS ID       PROD ID        QTY
02/28          100              10             2241          200
02/12          101              23             2518          300
02/15          101              23             1035          150
02/19          100              39             2518          200        s
02/02          101              23             1035          200
02/05          105              10             2241          100
02/22          110              37             2518          150
02/14          105              10             2249           50
02/01          101              23             2249           75
02/04          101              23             2241          250
```

▼FIGURE 6.10 THE EXISTENTIAL QUANTIFIER APPLIED TO THE CUSTOMER AND SALE RELATIONS

Query: Who has bought table lamps?

This query was used to illustrate the join in our discussion of relational algebra. The solution relation is given on page 189. The solution in relational calculus is:

```
{r.CUST_NAME : r IN CUSTOMER and there exists s IN SALE and there
                        exists t IN PRODUCT
          (r.CUST_ID = s.CUST_ID and
          s.PROD_ID = t.PROD_ID and
          t.PROD_DESC = 'Table Lamp')}
```

Note that just as the relational algebra solution required two joins, the relational calculus solution requires two existentially quantified row variables, s and t. A sample set of values for r, s, and t is shown in Figure 6.11. This sample set shows that Jefferson is included in the solution relation because there exist rows in SALE and in PRODUCT that prove that Jefferson has bought table lamps.

The Universal Quantifier*

universal quantifier
Relational calculus expression stating that some condition applies to *every* row of some type.

The **universal quantifier** states that some condition applies to *all* or to *every* row of some type. It is used to provide the same capability as relational algebra's divide operation. We illustrate it using the same query we used for the divide.

Query: List salespeople who have sold every product.

Note that the condition for selecting a salesperson includes the word *every*. Only salespeople who have sold *every* product are included in the solution relation. If you skip ahead to the following result, you can easily see that only one salesperson satisfies the condition of the query.

---

*This section may be omitted without loss of continuity.

```
CUSTOMER

CUST
ID      CUST NAME       ADDRESS                         BEGINNING   CURRENT
100     Watabe Bros     Box 241, Tokyo    COUNTRY       BALANCE     BALANCE
101     Maltzl          Salzburg          Japan         45,551      52,113
105     Jefferson       B 918, Chicago    Austria       75,314      77,200
110     Gomez           Santiago          USA           49,333      57,811     r
                                          Chile         27,400      35,414

SALE

DATE        CUST ID       SALPERS ID      PROD ID      QTY
02/28         100            10            2241        200
02/12         101            23            2518        300
02/15         101            23            1035        150
02/19         100            39            2518        200
02/02         101            23            1035        200
02/05         105            10            2241        100        s
02/22         110            37            2518        150
02/14         105            10            2249         50
02/01         101            23            2249         75
02/04         101            23            2241        250

PRODUCT

PROD ID     PROD DESC              MANUFACTR ID     COST      PRICE
1035        Sweater                    210          1.25      2.00
2241        Table Lamp                 317          2.25      3.25        t
2249        Table Lamp                 317          3.55      4.80
2518        Brass Sculpture            253           .60      1.20
```

▼FIGURE 6.11 THE EXISTENTIAL QUANTIFIER APPLIED TO CUSTOMER, SALE, AND PRODUCT

The calculus solution to this query follows:

```
{r.SALPERS_NAME : r IN SALESPERSON and for every p IN PRODUCT
                  there exists s IN SALE
                  (r.SALPERS_ID = s.SALPERS_ID and
                  s.PROD_ID = p.PROD_ID)}
```
The result is:
SALPERS NAME
Francois Moire

A salesperson's name from a row *r* in SALESPERSON is placed in the solution relation if the qualifying statement is true about that row *r*. Figure 6.12 shows how the qualifying statement is true when *r* is the row containing data about Francois Moire. For each row *p* in PRODUCT, there must be a row *s* in SALE satisfying the condition. The figure shows the correspondence between rows of PRODUCT and rows of SALE in satisfying the condition. That is,

```
s(1)      corresponds to      p(1)
s(2)      corresponds to      p(2)
s(3)      corresponds to      p(3)
s(4)      corresponds to      p(4)
```

SALESPERSON

SALPERS ID	SALPERS NAME	MANAGER ID	OFFICE	COMM %	
10	Rodney Jones	27	Chicago	10	
14	Masaji Matsu	44	Tokyo	11	
23	Francois Moire	35	Brussels	9	r
37	Elena Hermana	12	B. A.	13	
39	Goro Azuma	44	Tokyo	10	
27	Terry Cardon		Chicago	15	
44	Albert Ige	27	Tokyo	12	
35	Brigit Bovary	27	Brussels	11	
12	Buster Sanchez	27	B. A.	10	

PRODUCT

PROD ID	PROD DESC	MANUFACTR ID	COST	PRICE	
1035	Sweater	210	1.25	2.00	p(1)
2241	Table Lamp	317	2.25	3.25	p(2)
2249	Table Lamp	317	3.55	4.80	p(3)
2518	Brass Sculpture	253	.60	1.20	p(4)

SALE

DATE	CUST ID	SALPERS ID	PROD ID	QTY	
02/28	100	10	2241	200	
02/12	101	23	2518	300	s(4)
02/15	101	23	1035	150	s(1)
02/19	100	39	2518	200	
02/02	101	23	1035	200	
02/05	105	10	2241	100	
02/22	110	37	2518	150	
02/14	105	10	2249	50	
02/01	101	23	2249	75	s(3)
02/04	101	23	2241	250	s(2)

▼FIGURE 6.12 THE UNIVERSAL QUANTIFIER APPLIED TO SALESPERSON, PRODUCT, AND SALE

In each of these rows of SALE, the SALPERS_ID is Francois Moire's (23), and each of the four sale rows corresponds to one of the four possible products. Therefore, Moire has sold *every* product.

▼ Relative Difficulty of Relational Algebra and Relational Calculus

The conventional wisdom in database languages holds that nonprocedural languages should be easier to use than procedural languages. This has not been borne out by experiment, however. The results of a number of experiments (Welty and Stemple, 1981; Hansen and Hansen, 1987, 1988) indicate that people generally perform better in solving problems with a procedural language than they do with a nonprocedural language. This is particularly true when the problems are logically more complex. In the specific case of relational algebra versus relational calculus, users tend to find the universal quantifier of calculus difficult to comprehend. Consequently, they are often unable to solve queries requiring this quantifier. Although the corresponding operation in relational algebra—division—is difficult to grasp, the percentage of people who do so successfully is far larger than the percentage of people who learn to use the universal quantifier successfully.

Our own view on this subject is that no good alternative has yet been developed for solving the more difficult queries that involve "every" in the condition. As will be discussed in Chapter 7, the approach used by SQL, the NOT EXISTS predicate, seems no better than the alternatives provided by algebra and calculus. Hopefully, additional research will strengthen database languages in this area.

Summary

In this chapter, we have presented Codd's relational algebra and relational calculus. Both of these theoretical languages manipulate relations in a relational database on the basis of their logical characteristics and without regard to the physical structures used for implementation. Relational algebra is a procedural language that uses step-by-step solutions to query problems. Relational calculus, however, is nonprocedural, meaning that the solution to a query is formulated as a definition of the desired result rather than as a process that will produce the desired result. Codd showed that relational algebra and calculus are logically equivalent or, in other words, that any query that can be solved in one language can also be solved in the other.

Relational algebra consists of nine operations: union, intersection, subtraction, product, select, project, join, divide, and assignment. Union, intersection, subtraction, and product are very similar to the set operations of the same names. Select is used to apply a condition to a relation and produce a new relation consisting of those rows satisfying the condition. Project creates a new relation by removing columns from an existing relation. Join connects relations on columns containing comparable information. Divide identifies the rows in a relation that match every row in another relation. Assignment gives a name to a relation.

Relational calculus defines the solution to a query as a relational set. The relation definition consists of a target list, defining the attributes in the solution relation, and a qualifying statement, which is a condition that the elements in the target list must satisfy. Relational calculus takes its name from predicate calculus in symbolic logic and uses the Boolean connectives (and, or, not) to link conditions which may be true or false. It also uses the existential and universal quantifiers which state, respectively, that an instance of some type *exists*, or that a condition is true for *every* instance of a specified type.

Although conventional wisdom holds that a nonprocedural language is easier for people to use than is a procedural language, research suggests that in the case of relational languages this may not always be true. For some difficult queries, the step-by-step approach of a procedural language like relational algebra provides the flexibility people need for formulating query solutions. Further research in this area will perhaps result in the development of languages that users can easily apply to the solution of queries having a wide range of complexity.

Review Questions

Questions marked with an asterisk (*) pertain to the chapter's optional material.

1. Define each of the following terms in your own words:
   a. relational algebra
   b. nonprocedural

c. relationally complete

d. union compatible

e. intersection

f. subtraction

g. project

h. natural join

i. theta join

j. qualifying statement

k. divide

a. universal quantifier

2. Describe the circumstances when you would use each of the following relational algebra operations:

a. Select

b. Project

c. Join

d. Assignment

e. Subtraction

f. Intersection

g. Divide

3. Explain the function of each of the following in a relational calculus query solution:

a. Target list

b. Qualifying statement

c. Boolean connective (and, or, not)

d. Existential quantifier

e. Universal quantifier

4. Why doesn't relational calculus need something similar to the assignment statement of relational algebra?

5. Consider the following statement: "Nonprocedural languages are easier to use for naive users." Using your experience, discuss this statement.

6. Discuss the significance of saying that relational algebra and relational calculus are relationally complete and what that means for evaluating commercial DBMSs.

Problems and Exercises

1. Match each term to its definition.

__*difference*	a. Gives a name to a relation
__*union*	b. Theta join based on equality of specified columns
__*procedural*	c. List that defines the attributes of the solution relation
__*existential quantifier*	d. Language that provides a step-by-step method for solving problems
__*select*	e. Operation that connects relations
__*join*	f. Relation resulting from a project operation
__*product*	g. Expansion of the natural join that includes *all* rows from both relations

__equijoin_   h. Creates the Cartesian product of two relations

_outer join   i. Creates the set difference of two union-compatible relations

_relational calculus   j. Affirms the existence of at least one row to which a condition applies

_assignment   k. Creates the set union of two union-compatible relations

_projection   l. Relational algebra operation that uses a condition to choose rows from a relation

_target list   m. A nonprocedural language for defining query solutions

2. Using the following relational schema, indicate which relational algebra operation(s) might be used to answer the given query:

```
CUSTOMER (CUST_ID, CUST_NAME, ANNUAL_REVENUE)
SHIPMENT (SHIPMENT_#, CUST_ID, WEIGHT, TRUCK_#, DESTINATION)
```

  a. Which customers have annual revenue exceeding $5 million?
  b. What is the name of customer 433?
  c. What is the destination city of shipment #3244?
  d. Which trucks have carried packages weighing over 100 pounds?
  e. What are the names of customers who have sent packages to Sioux City, Iowa?
  f. To what destinations have companies with revenue less than $1 million sent packages?

Use this relational schema for the following set of queries:

```
CUSTOMER (CUST_ID, CUST_NAME, ANNUAL_REVENUE)
SHIPMENT (SHIPMENT_#, CUST_ID, WEIGHT, TRUCK_#, DESTINATION)
Foreign Key: DESTINATION REFERENCES CITY_NAME IN CITY
TRUCK (TRUCK_#, DRIVER_NAME)
CITY (CITY_NAME, POPULATION)
```

3. Give relational algebra solutions to the following queries:
  a. A list of shipment numbers for shipments weighing over 20 pounds.
  b. Names of customers with more than $10 million in annual revenue.
  c. The driver of truck #45.
  d. The names of cities which have received shipments weighing over 100 pounds.
  e. The name and annual revenue of customers who have sent shipments weighing over 100 pounds.
  f. The truck numbers of trucks which have carried shipments weighing over 100 pounds.
  g. The names of drivers who have delivered shipments weighing over 100 pounds.
  h. Cities which have received shipments from customers having over $15 million in annual revenue.
  i. Customers having over $5 million in annual revenue who have sent shipments weighing less than 1 pound.
  j. Customers having over $5 million in annual revenue who have sent shipments weighing less than 1 pound or have sent a shipment to San Francisco.

k. Customers whose shipments have been delivered by truck driver Jensen.

l. Drivers who have delivered shipments for customers with annual revenue over $20 million to cities with population over 1 million.

m. Customers who have had shipments delivered by every driver.

n. Cities which have received shipments from every customer.

o. Drivers who have delivered shipments to every city.

p. Customers who have sent shipments to every city with population over 500,000. (Hint: First create the set of cities with population over 500,000.)

q. Give a list of customers and annual revenue for those customers whose annual revenue is the maximum for the customers in the database.

r. Give a list of customers, all of whose shipments weigh over 25 pounds. (Hint: First find customers who have at least one shipment less than 25 pounds.)

s. Give a list of customers that send all their shipments to a single city. (Note: The city may or may not be the same for each of these customers.) (Hint: First find customers that send shipments to more than one city.)

4. Give relational calculus solutions for the queries of problem 3.

Projects and Professional Issues

1. Compare your solutions to the queries in problems 3 and 4 of the preceding section. Which queries seemed easier to solve in relational algebra and which in relational calculus? In each case why do you suppose the one language was easier to use than the other? Which of the two languages do you prefer? Why?

2. Read Codd's papers on relational algebra and calculus (Codd 1970, 1971a, 1971b). Write an essay comparing the two languages and discuss how Codd showed their logical equivalence.

3. Write sketches of programs in a language like COBOL or Pascal to solve the queries 3 a, e, m, and r. Compare the complexity of these programs with that of the query solutions in relational algebra and calculus.

C H A P T E R

RELATIONAL IMPLEMENTATION WITH SQL

Tony Melton and Annette Chang, information systems practitioners at Premier Construction Company, are discussing their recently installed relational database management system.

"Tony, what advantages are there in having SQL as the language of our system, rather than one of the other available relational database languages?"

"Probably the chief advantage, Annette, is that SQL is both the ANSI standard relational language as well as the de facto standard for business. This means that it is widely supported and that we can feel confident of minimizing our risk if we change hardware or software vendors."

"But what about the language itself? How does SQL stack up as a relational language in its own right?"

"SQL is a powerful language. It has all the logical power of Codd's relational calculus, as well as the additional capability of handling groupings of rows and applying statistical functions to them. Moreover, we can define our database schemas, identify keys and non-null columns with default values, and embed SQL statements in programs written in other languages. In addition to all that, in our system the information schema that contains defining information for all schemas in a database is itself a relational database which we can query with SQL. Perhaps most important of all, the SQL-92 standard adds a number of valuable enhancements to the language which vendors will likely be anxious to implement. Through SQL, we can truly take advantage of the power of the 'relational revolution.'"

In this chapter, we study the parts of relational database management systems having to do with the SQL language, including topics from the SQL-92 ANSI standard. After reading this chapter, you should be able to:

▼ Explain basic facts about the historical development of relational database management systems.

▼ Define a relational database schema in SQL.

▼ Formulate SQL queries of varying complexity.

▼ Insert, update, and delete data in a relational database through SQL commands.

▼ Discuss some aspects of embedding SQL statements in a traditional or "host" programming language.

▼ Define and query data views in SQL.

▼ Explain some basic elements in the structure of an SQL information schema.

▼ Relational Implementations: An Overview

The aftermath of the publication of Codd's papers introducing the relational model and relational languages (algebra and calculus) was a great deal of activity in the commercial and research communities to develop implemented versions of relational languages. The three most important languages to come out of this effort are probably SQL (Structured Query Language, and pronounced either "ess-cue-ell" or "sequel"), QBE (Query-by-Example), and QUEL (Query Language). SQL and QBE both originated at IBM during the seventies and perform many similar functions, although SQL is a textual language while QBE is graphical. QUEL is the original language of INGRES, a relational database management system developed during the seventies at the University of California, Berkeley.

SQL was the outgrowth of IBM's System R research project. This project included the development of a relational database system and the language SEQUEL (for Structured English Query Language). In the late seventies, SQL (changed from SEQUEL) became part of the public domain and was first available as a language for a commercial system from Oracle Corporation. In 1981, IBM released SQL/DS, which is a commercial database management system (DBMS) that supports SQL. In 1983, IBM released SQL as part of the DB2 DBMS.

In 1986, the first ANSI standard for SQL was approved. This standard was later revised (modestly) in 1989 and (significantly) in 1992. SQL is, and seems likely to remain, the only ANSI standard relational database language. Moreover, SQL is the de facto standard in business, since it is by far the relational language of choice in commercial systems. Numerous vendors have released implementations of SQL since 1980.

In addition to the mainframe versions of SQL listed previously, many client/server and personal computer versions of SQL are available. These include Sybase SQL Server, Microsoft SQL Server, IBM OS/2 Extended Edition Database Manager, DEC Rdb/VMS, and Oracle Server for OS/2 (Khoshafian et al.) for client/server systems, and XDB and SQLBase, as well as versions of R:Base and dBASE, for the personal computer.

The INGRES system was originally developed as a database management system with its own data language, QUEL, which like SQL is modeled on relational calculus. In the last few years, commercial INGRES has been expanded to support SQL as well as QUEL. This is important since SQL has been adopted as the ANSI standard.

Relational database management systems support a wide variety of features in addition to their language capability. These features include security, integrity, high-performance data access and update, and data dictionary or information schema control. While some of these features are covered in this chapter, others are discussed elsewhere (see, for example, Chapters 11 and 12). In this chapter, we will discuss the SQL language and the information schema features of a relational DBMS. In Chapter 9 we discuss language features of two client/server relational DBMSs.

Although the name SQL suggests that it is a "query" language, it includes table definition, database update, view definition, and privilege granting, in addition to query facilities. In this chapter, we will study the table definition, query, update, and view definition capabilities of SQL—in that order. Our coverage of SQL will include aspects of the 1992 ANSI standard, known as SQL-92. SQL-92 is a significant enhancement to the earlier versions of standard SQL and is too large for us to cover in this chapter, or even in this book. (For more complete coverage see Melton and Simon, 1993 or Date and Darwen, 1994). Nevertheless, we do provide coverage of several of its features, concentrating on those which we deem most important. We will also examine its information schema features. To illustrate our examples, we will use a relational database taken from a simple version of the case of the Premier Construction Company. The sample database is shown in Figure 7.1.

```
WORKER

WORKER_ID    WORKER_NAME    HRLY_RATE    SKILL_TYPE    SUPV_ID
1235         M. Faraday     12.50        Electric      1311
1412         C. Nemo        13.75        Plumbing      1520
2920         R. Garret      10.00        Roofing       2920
3231         P. Mason       17.40        Framing       3231
1520         H. Rickover    11.75        Plumbing      1520
1311         C. Coulomb     15.50        Electric      1311
3001         J. Barrister    8.20        Framing       3231

ASSIGNMENT

WORKER_ID    BLDG_ID    START_DATE    NUM_DAYS
1235         312        10/10           5
1412         312        10/01          10
1235         515        10/17          22
2920         460        10/05          18
1412         460        12/08          18
2920         435        10/28          10
2920         210        11/10          15
3231         111        10/10           8
1412         435        10/15          15
1412         515        11/05           8
3231         312        10/24          20
1520         515        10/09          14
1311         435        10/08          12
1412         210        11/15          12
1412         111        12/01           4
3001         111        10/08          14
1311         460        10/23          24
1520         312        10/30          17
3001         210        10/27          14

BUILDING

BLDG_ID    BLDG_ADDRESS    TYPE         QLTY_LEVEL    STATUS
312        123 Elm         Office            2           2
435        456 Maple       Retail            1           1
515        789 Oak         Residence         3           1
210        1011 Birch      Office            3           1
111        1213 Aspen      Office            4           1
460        1415 Beech      Warehouse         3           3
```

▼FIGURE 7.1 PREMIER CONSTRUCTION COMPANY DATABASE

▼ Schema and Table Definition

catalog In SQL-92 a named collection of schemas.

SQL-92, unlike earlier versions, allows a user to define multiple schemas. Multiple schemas can be grouped together in **catalogs,** which in SQL-92 are named collections of schemas. Each catalog contains a special schema, named INFORMA-TION_SCHEMA, which contains metadata and which we will discuss later in the chapter. All other schemas in a catalog are user defined. As a point of clarification, we should note that the term *catalog* as used in SQL-92 is a departure from the standard and traditional use of the term with databases. A catalog is normally thought of as containing the metadata that define the database. In SQL-92 the information schema performs this function.

Schema Definition

SQL-92 defines a catalog as a named collection of schemas but does not indicate how a catalog should be defined. That is left to the DBMS implementation. Schema definition, however, is defined in SQL-92. Defining a database schema in SQL is straightforward. It is only necessary to identify the start of a schema definition, with a CREATE SCHEMA statement and optional AUTHORIZATION clause, and then define each domain, table, view, and so forth in the schema. A sample schema definition statement is as follows:

```
CREATE SCHEMA PREMIER_CONSTRUCTION
   AUTHORIZATION TONY_MELTON
      domain definitions
      table definitions
      view definitions
      etc.
```

schema owner Person who has authority and responsibility for granting access to tables, columns, and views in a database schema.

Each CREATE SCHEMA statement indicates to the DBMS that what follows is a database schema. The schema's name—PREMIER_CONSTRUCTION in our example—is also indicated in this statement. The AUTHORIZATION clause indicates the name of the **owner** of the schema. This person is known to the system and can grant to other users access and update privileges for the database defined in the schema. Obviously, this structure implies that many database schemas can exist in the same installation. These can be owned by different individuals, but under the control of the DBMS each schema can be accessed by users other than their owner.

Data Types and Domains

Before showing how tables are defined we should look first at how the domains from which columns take their values are defined or predefined.

In the sense of the relational model, as discussed in Chapter 5, a domain is a set from which a column in a relation takes its values. In that sense, predefined data types are domains. However, SQL defines domains in a slightly different way, which we shall discuss shortly. In any case, SQL provides predefined data types and allows for user-defined domains. By the SQL definition both predefined datatypes and user-defined domains are domains in the relational model sense. We now consider these.

Data Types.   SQL-92 defines the following data types:

Exact numerics:

▼ Integer

▼ Small integer

▼ Numeric (p,s)

▼ Decimal (p,s)

For both of the last two data types (numeric and decimal) you indicate a precision (p) and scale (s). The precision indicates the total number of digits in the number, and the scale indicates how many of these are to the right of the decimal point.

Approximate numerics:

- ▼ Real
- ▼ Double precision
- ▼ Float

These data types are normally used for scientific and engineering calculations.

Character strings:

- ▼ Character (n)
- ▼ Character varying (n)

Character fields always store n characters, even if the value entered must be padded with blanks on the right. Character varying fields only store the number of characters entered up to a maximum of n.

Bit strings:

- ▼ Bit (n)
- ▼ Bit varying (n)

These fields are used for flags and other bit-controlled masks.

Datetimes:

- ▼ Date
- ▼ Time
- ▼ Timestamp
- ▼ Time with time zone
- ▼ Timestamp with time zone

Date is in the order, year, month, day, with the year having four digits. The time is hours (0–23), minutes, seconds, and decimal fractions of a second. Timestamp is date plus time.

Intervals:

- ▼ Year-month
- ▼ Day-time

An interval is the difference between two dates (year-month) or between two times (day-time). For example, between December 1994 and January 1996 the interval is one year and one month.

constraint A rule that restricts the values in a database.

default value A value which is automatically inserted if the user fails to specify a value.

domain definition A specialized data type defined within a schema and used in column definitions.

Domain Definition. Data types with defined **constraints** and **default values** can be combined into domain definitions. A **domain definition** is a specialized data type which can be defined within a schema and used as desired in column definitions. For example, suppose we wished to define a domain of item identifiers to be used in the definitions of such columns as WORKER_ID and BLDG_ID. We anticipate this definition will be complex, involving a data type, a default value, and a non-null constraint, and since we will be using it over and over again in the database schema, we would like to simplify our work. Thus, we create a domain as follows:

```
CREATE DOMAIN ITEM_IDENTIFIER NUMERIC (4) DEFAULT 0
   CHECK (VALUE IS NOT NULL)
```

This definition says that a domain named ITEM_IDENTIFIER has the following properties: Its data type is four-digit numeric, its default value is zero, and it can never be null. Any column defined with this domain as its data type will have all these properties. Note that we could not simply say "NOT NULL" in the definition. Rather, SQL requires us to use what is called a CHECK constraint to accomplish the same thing. Having done this we can define columns in our schema with ITEM_IDENTIFIER as their data type.

Defining Tables

Tables are defined in three steps:

1. The name of the table is given.
2. Each column is defined, possibly including column constraints.
3. Table constraints are defined.

The following is a schema definition for the database of Figure 7.1.

```
CREATE SCHEMA PREMIER_CONSTRUCTION
   AUTHORIZATION TONY_MELTON
   domain definitions
CREATE TABLE WORKER (
   WORKER_ID       ITEM_IDENTIFIER     PRIMARY KEY,
   WORKER_NAME     CHARACTER (12),
   HRLY_RATE       NUMERIC (5,2),
   SKILL_TYPE      CHARACTER (8),
   SUPV_ID         NUMERIC (4),
   FOREIGN KEY SUPV_ID REFERENCES WORKER
                       ON DELETE SET NULL)
CREATE TABLE ASSIGNMENT (
   WORKER_ID       ITEM_IDENTIFIER,
   BLDG_ID         ITEM_IDENTIFIER,
   START_DATE      DATE,
   NUM_DAYS        INTERVAL DAY (3),
   PRIMARY KEY (WORKER_ID, BLDG_ID),
   FOREIGN KEY WORKER_ID REFERENCES WORKER
                       ON DELETE CASCADE,
   FOREIGN KEY BLDG_ID REFERENCES BUILDING
                       ON DELETE CASCADE)
CREATE TABLE BUILDING (
   BLDG_ID         ITEM_IDENTIFIER     PRIMARY KEY,
   BLDG_ADDRESS    CHAR (12),
   TYPE            CHAR (9) DEFAULT 'Office'
      CHECK (TYPE IN
        ('OFFICE', 'Warehouse', 'Retail', 'Residence')),
   QLTY_LEVEL      NUMERIC (1),
   STATUS          NUMERIC (1) DEFAULT 1
      CHECK (STATUS > 0 AND STATUS < 4))
```

Following the CREATE SCHEMA statement, and possibly other statements like CREATE DOMAIN statements, are CREATE TABLE statements—one for each table to be defined. The CREATE TABLE statement itself identifies the name of the table, which must be unique within the schema. The statements following CREATE TABLE, enclosed in parentheses and separated by commas, either (1) define columns or (2) define table constraints.

Column Definition. Let's look at the definitions of the first three columns of WORKER:

```
WORKER_ID        ITEM_IDENTIFIER     PRIMARY KEY
WORKER_NAME      CHARACTER (12)
HRLY_RATE        NUMERIC (5,2)
```

as well as two from ASSIGNMENT:

```
START_DATE    DATE
NUM_DAYS      INTERVAL DAY (3)
```

and two from BUILDING:

```
TYPE        CHAR (9)    DEFAULT 'Office'
   CHECK (TYPE IN
     ('Office', 'Warehouse', 'Retail', 'Residence'))
   STATUS   NUMERIC (1)    DEFAULT 1
     CHECK (STATUS > 0 AND STATUS < 4)
```

Each column is defined by giving its name, its data type, which may be a pre-defined data type or a user-defined domain, what its default value is to be, and whether specific constraints (for example, NOT NULL, PRIMARY KEY, and CHECK constraints) apply to it. The first three columns in our example are named, respectively, WORKER_ID, WORKER_NAME, and HRLY_RATE. Their data types are ITEM_IDENTIFIER, character, and numeric. The two columns from ASSIGNMENT (START_DATE and NUM_DAYS) illustrate two other data types: date and interval.

A numeric data type means that the column's data values must be numbers, possibly with a decimal point. WORKER_ID's data type is ITEM_IDENTIFIER, a user-defined domain, which was defined as NUMERIC (4), meaning that it has four significant digits and *no* digits to the right of the decimal point. HRLY_RATE has a data type of NUMERIC (5,2), meaning that it has five significant digits, two of which are to the right of the decimal.

A character data type means that the column's data values consist of character strings, made up of alphanumeric characters, possibly in combination with special characters. The maximum length of the character string is indicated in parentheses. Thus, WORKER_NAME may have character string values no more than 12 characters in length.

A date data type (such as that for START_DATE) means that the column's data values will be dates, in year (four digits), month (two digits), day (two digits) format. An interval data type (like that for NUM_DAYS) is given either in years and/or months or in days, minutes, hours, and/or seconds. We have chosen the interval data type of DAY (3), which means that NUM_DAYS can be any number of days from 0 to 999. Date and interval data types have the advantage that they can be added and subtracted. Thus, we could add NUM_DAYS to START_DATE and obtain the ending date of the worker's assignment (assuming that after starting work on a building the worker takes no weekends or holidays off and doesn't work on any other building).

WORKER_ID is also subject to two constraints: NOT NULL and PRIMARY KEY. The NOT NULL constraint is inherited from its domain definition and means that WORKER_ID is not allowed to have a null value. PRIMARY KEY means that no two rows in the WORKER table may have the same value for WORKER_ID and that for purposes of foreign key references WORKER_ID is considered to be the primary key. The NOT NULL constraint enforces the entity integrity rule, which states that no key column can be null.

The TYPE and STATUS columns in the BUILDING table have DEFAULT values defined. If a tuple is added to the BUILDING table and, for example, a value for the STATUS column is not entered, the system will automatically set the value of STATUS for that tuple to 1. Similarly, the TYPE is automatically set to 'Office,' if no value is entered. Every column has a default value which, if not defined in the schema, is null. Notice that we have not defined a default value for WORKER_ID, since it inherits its default value (0) from the domain definition.

TYPE and STATUS columns also have CHECK constraints defined. These constraints limit the possible values which may be entered in these columns. In particular TYPE must have one of the values in the set ('Office', 'Warehouse', 'Retail', 'Residence'), and STATUS must be between 1 and 3.

We have now explained the column definition section of the schema. It remains to discuss the table constraints. In this schema table constraints are:

```
FOREIGN KEY SUPV_ID REFERENCES WORKER
            ON DELETE SET NULL)
```

which constrains the WORKER table, and:

```
PRIMARY KEY (WORKER_ID, BLDG_ID),
FOREIGN KEY WORKER_ID REFERENCES WORKER
                        ON DELETE CASCADE,
FOREIGN KEY BLDG_ID REFERENCES BUILDING
                        ON DELETE CASCADE
```

which constrain the ASSIGNMENT table. Let's look at each of these. The foreign key constraint on the WORKER table:

```
FOREIGN KEY SUPV_ID REFERENCES WORKER
                    ON DELETE SET NULL
```

recursive foreign key
A foreign key that references its own relation.

indicates that SUPV_ID is a **recursive foreign key** (see Chapter 5). That is, it is a foreign key which references its own relation. Note that the syntax used in this statement, up to the words "ON DELETE . . ." is identical to that used for defining foreign keys in Chapter 5. It simply identifies the foreign key column(s) in the present relation and states which relation these columns point to. In this case the foreign key column is in WORKER, and it points to the WORKER relation. The ON DELETE SET NULL clause tells the system that if the tuple to which the foreign key points is deleted, then the foreign key value should be set to null. For example, suppose we deleted the tuple with WORKER_ID 1311 in the WORKER relation of Figure 7.1. Then the SUPV_ID of the first tuple (with WORKER_ID 1235) would point to a nonexistent worker, that is, to a worker tuple no longer in the database. This would violate referential integrity. To prevent this the ON DELETE SET NULL clause instructs the DBMS to set the foreign key value (SUPV_ID in tuple 1235) to null if the tuple it is pointing to (tuple 1311) is deleted. Thus, before deletion the table looks like this:

```
WORKER
WORKER_ID     WORKER_NAME      HRLY_RATE      SKILL_TYPE      SUPV_ID
  1235        M. Faraday         12.50         Electric         1311
  . . .
  1311        C. Coulomb         15.50         Electric         1311
```

and after deletion it looks like this:

```
WORKER
WORKER_ID     WORKER_NAME      HRLY_RATE      SKILL_TYPE      SUPV_ID
  1235        M. Faraday         12.50         Electric        [null]
```

The table constraints on the ASSIGNMENT table are:

```
PRIMARY KEY (WORKER_ID, BLDG_ID),
FOREIGN KEY WORKER_ID REFERENCES WORKER
                    ON DELETE CASCADE,
FOREIGN KEY BLDG_ID REFERENCES BUILDING
                    ON DELETE CASCADE
```

With the exception of the ON DELETE CASCADE clause in the two foreign key constraints, which we will discuss shortly, these constraints are straightforward. The PRIMARY KEY (WORKER_ID, BLDG_ID) constraint tells the system that WORKER_ID and BLDG_ID constitute a composite foreign key for the table. Therefore, the combined value of these two columns must be unique for every tuple in the table.

ON DELETE CASCADE is similar to ON DELETE SET NULL in that action is taken whenever the tuple referenced by the foreign key is deleted. Consider, for example, the following tuples in the database of Figure 7.1:

```
ASSIGNMENT
WORKER_ID     BLDG_ID      START_DATE      NUM_DAYS
  1235          312          10/10            5
  1235          515          10/17           22
WORKER
WORKER_ID     WORKER_NAME      HRLY_RATE      SKILL_TYPE      SUPV_ID
  1235        M. Faraday         12.50         Electric         1311
```

WORKER_ID in the ASSIGNMENT table is a foreign key that points to the WORKER table. ON DELETE CASCADE means that if the referenced tuple in the WORKER relation (1235 in this example) is deleted, then that deletion should "cascade" to all referencing tuples in the ASSIGNMENT table. In this example, WORKER_ID 1235 in the WORKER table is referenced by two tuples in the assignment table, as shown in the preceding example. If the WORKER tuple 1235 is deleted, then the system will automatically delete the two corresponding tuples in the ASSIGNMENT table. This is the correct handling of this foreign key because if the WORKER tuple is deleted, then the ASSIGNMENT tuples are meaningless, so they should be deleted.

The ON DELETE clause is similar to an ON UPDATE clause, and both these clauses have the following options:

▼ CASCADE

▼ SET NULL

▼ SET DEFAULT

If the option is SET DEFAULT, then the system sets the foreign key's value to the column's default value. Naturally, as is noted in Date and Darwen (1994), the foreign key will now point to a tuple in the referenced relation having this default value as its key value, so such a tuple must exist. If either the ON DELETE or ON UPDATE clause is omitted, then delete and update actions will be disallowed by the system if such actions would violate referential integrity.

Before we leave this schema definition, we should mention that unlike relations in the relational model, it is not required that every SQL table have a primary key. In other words, if no key is identified, then two rows in a table may have identical values. A table in SQL is called a **multiset,** meaning that it may have duplicate entries. In this way, SQL makes a minor departure from the relational model. Of course, any table that does not have a primary key may not be referenced via a foreign key from another table (Date and Darwen, 1994).

This **schema definition** *describes* the database to the DBMS, but it does not cause any actual data values to be entered. Data values are entered and manipulated by the SQL data manipulation language, which we describe in detail in the next section.

multiset A set that may have duplicate entries.

schema definition Description of a database to the DBMS.

Other Schema Manipulation Statements. Besides the CREATE TABLE statement, which defines a new table, SQL-92 provides other statements for changing the definitions of tables (ALTER TABLE) or for deleting tables from the schema (DROP TABLE). ALTER TABLE can be used to add a column to a table, change the definition of an existing column, or drop a column from a table. DROP TABLE will delete all rows currently in the named table and will remove the entire definition of the table from the schema. Entire schemas can be dropped via the DROP SCHEMA statement. However, since this can be a rather dangerous operation, either CASCADE or RESTRICT must be specified with it.

```
DROP SCHEMA schema-name CASCADE
```

means to drop the schema named as well as all tables, data, and other schema objects which still exist.

```
DROP SCHEMA schema-name RESTRICT
```

means to drop the schema only if all other schema objects have already been deleted.

▼ Data Manipulation

SQL contains a wide variety of data manipulation capabilities, both for querying and for updating a database. These capabilities depend only on the logical structure of the database, not on its physical structure, consistent with the requirements of the relational model. Initially, SQL's syntactic structure was modeled on (or at a minimum *appeared* to be modeled on) Codd's relational calculus. The only operation from relational algebra which was supported was union. SQL-92, however, directly implements union, intersection, difference, and join, in addition to supporting the syntax, similar to relational calculus, which it supported before. The operations of select, project, and product were, and continue to be, supported in a rather straightforward fashion, while divide and assignment are supported, although perhaps more awkwardly.

We will describe SQL's query language first, followed by its operations for entering and changing data. The data change operations are described last because their structure depends to some extent on the structure of the query language.

Simple Queries

simple query A query involving only one database table.

For us, a **simple query** is one involving only a single database table. Simple queries help to illustrate the basic structure of SQL.

Query: Who are the plumbers?
```
SELECT WORKER_NAME
FROM WORKER
WHERE SKILL_TYPE = 'Plumbing'
```

Result:
```
WORKER_NAME
C. Nemo
H. Rickover
```

This query illustrates the three most often used clauses of SQL: the SELECT clause, the FROM clause, and the WHERE clause. Although we have placed them on separate lines in this example, they could all appear on the same line. They may also be indented, and terms within clauses may be separated by an arbitrary number of blank spaces. Let's discuss the features of each clause.

SELECT clause Identifies the columns desired in the query.

Select. The **SELECT clause** lists the *columns* desired in the result of the query. They are always the columns of a relational table. In our example, the resulting table has a single column (WORKER_NAME), but it could have several columns, or it could include computed values and literal values. We will show examples of each of these. If the desired result contains more than one column, the columns are all listed in the SELECT clause and separated by commas. For example, SELECT WORKER_ID, WORKER_NAME would cause both WORKER_ID and WORKER_NAME to be listed as columns in the resulting table.

FROM clause Lists the existing tables referenced by the query.

From. The **FROM clause** lists one or more *tables* to be referenced by the query. All columns listed in the SELECT or WHERE clauses must be found in one of the tables of the FROM clause. In SQL-92 these tables may be directly defined in the database schema as base tables or views, or they may themselves be unnamed tables which are the results of SQL queries. If the latter, then the query is explicitly given in the FROM clause.

WHERE clause Gives the condition for selecting rows from identified tables.

Where. The **WHERE clause** contains a *condition* for selecting rows from the table(s) listed in the FROM clause. In our example, the condition is that the SKILL_TYPE column must have the literal value 'Plumbing,' placed in single quotes, as is customary for alphanumeric literals in SQL. The WHERE clause is the most versatile clause of SQL and can contain a wide variety of conditions. Much of our discussion will illustrate the different constructions allowed in the WHERE clause.

The SQL query given previously is processed by the system in the order FROM, WHERE, SELECT. That is, the rows of the table referenced in the FROM clause (WORKER) are set up in a work area for processing. Then the WHERE clause is applied to each row, one by one. Any row not satisfying the WHERE clause is eliminated from consideration. Those rows that satisfy the WHERE clause are then processed by the SELECT clause. In our example, the WORKER_NAME from each of these rows is selected, and all of these selected values are displayed as the result of the query.

Query: List all data about office buildings.
```
SELECT *
FROM BUILDING
WHERE TYPE = 'Office'
```

Result:

BLDG_ID	BLDG_ADDRESS	TYPE	QLTY_LEVEL	STATUS
312	123 Elm	Office	2	2
210	1011 Birch	Office	3	1
111	1213 Aspen	Office	4	1

The "*" in the SELECT clause means "the entire row." This is a convenient shorthand we will employ often.

Query: What is the weekly wage rate for each electrician?
```
SELECT WORKER_NAME, 'Weekly Wage Rate = ', 40 * HRLY_RATE
FROM WORKER
WHERE SKILL_TYPE = 'Electric'
ORDER BY WORKER_NAME
```

Result:
```
WORKER_NAME
C. Coulomb   Weekly Wage Rate = 620.00
M. Faraday   Weekly Wage Rate = 500.00
```

character string literals Literals formed from alphanumeric and "special" characters.

This query illustrates the use of both alphanumeric literals, or **character string literals** (in this example, 'Weekly Wage Rate = '), and of computations in the SELECT clause. Computations involving numeric columns and numeric literals in combination with the standard arithmetical operations (+, -, *, /), grouped as needed with parentheses, can be defined in the SELECT clause. We have also included a new clause, the ORDER BY clause, that is used to sort the result of the query in ascending alphanumeric order of the indicated column. If descending order is desired, it must be specified by adding "DESC" to the command. Multiple columns may be specified in the ORDER BY clause, and some may be in ascending order and some in descending order. The primary sort key column is specified first.

Query: Who gets an hourly rate between $10 and $12?
```
SELECT *
FROM WORKER
WHERE HRLY_RATE > = 10 AND HRLY_RATE < = 12
```

Result:

WORKER_ID	WORKER_NAME	HRLY_RATE	SKILL_TYPE	SUPV_ID
2920	R. Garret	10.00	Roofing	2920
1520	H. Rickover	11.75	Plumbing	1520

comparison operators =, <>, <, >, <=, >=.

Boolean connectives AND, OR, NOT.

This query illustrates some additional features of the WHERE clause: comparison operators and the Boolean connective AND. The six **comparison operators** (=, <> [not equals], <, >, <=, >=) may be used to compare columns with other columns or with literals. The **Boolean connectives** AND, OR, and NOT may be used to create compound conditions or to negate a condition. Parentheses may also be used as they ordinarily are in programming languages to group conditions.

This query could also be solved using the BETWEEN operator:

```
SELECT *
FROM WORKER
WHERE HRLY_RATE BETWEEN 10 AND 12
```

BETWEEN can be used in a comparison of some value with two other values, the first smaller than the second, if the comparison value can be equal to either the smaller or the larger, or can be equal to any value in between.

Query: List the plumbers, roofers, and electricians.
```
SELECT *
FROM WORKER
WHERE SKILL_TYPE IN ('PLUMBING', 'ROOFING', 'ELECTRIC')
```

Result:

WORKER_ID	WORKER_NAME	HRLY_RATE	SKILL_TYPE	SUPV_ID
1235	M. Faraday	12.50	Electric	1311
1412	C. Nemo	13.75	Plumbing	1520
2920	R. Garret	10.00	Roofing	2920
1520	H. Rickover	11.75	Plumbing	1520
1311	C. Coulomb	15.50	Electric	1311

This query introduces and illustrates the use of the IN comparison operator. The WHERE clause evaluates to 'true' if the skill type for the row is found *in the set* contained in parentheses—that is, if the skill type is plumbing, roofing, or electric. We will have more occasion to use the IN operator with subqueries.

Suppose we can't remember the exact spelling of a skill type. Is it "Electric," or "Electrical," or "Electrician"? **Wild card characters,** special symbols that stand for unspecified strings of characters, make it easier to use inexact spelling in a query.

wild card characters
Special symbols that stand for unspecified strings of characters.

Query: Find all workers whose skill type begins with "Elec".
```
SELECT*
FROM WORKER
WHERE SKILL_TYPE LIKE 'Elec%'
```

Result:

WORKER_ID	WORKER_NAME	HRLY_RATE	SKILL_TYPE	SUPV_ID
1235	M. Faraday	12.50	Electric	1311
1311	C. Coulomb	15.50	Electric	1311

SQL has two wild card characters, % (percent) and _ (underscore). The underscore stands for exactly one unspecified character. The percent stands for zero or more unspecified characters. The LIKE operator is used to compare character variables and literals when wild card characters are used. Other examples:

```
WORKER_NAME LIKE '___Coulomb'
WORKER_NAME LIKE '___C%'
```

The first example evaluates to true if WORKER_NAME consists of three characters followed by 'Coulomb.' In the WORKER relation, for example, all worker names begin with a first initial, a period, and a space. So this sample condition would find all workers whose last name is "Coulomb." In the second example the condition would identify all workers whose last name begins with "C."

Query: Find all work assignments which will start in the next two weeks.

```
SELECT *
FROM ASSIGNMENT
WHERE START_DATE BETWEEN CURRENT_DATE AND
               CURRENT_DATE + INTERVAL '14' DAY
```

Result: (Assuming CURRENT_DATE = 10/10)

WORKER_ID	BLDG_ID	START_DATE	NUM_DAYS
1235	312	10/10	5
1235	515	10/17	22
3231	111	10/10	8
1412	435	10/15	15
3231	312	10/24	20
1311	460	10/23	24

This query illustrates the use of the BETWEEN operator with values of date and interval data types. CURRENT_DATE is a function which always returns today's date. The expression

```
CURRENT_DATE + INTERVAL '14' DAY
```

adds an interval of two weeks to the current date. Thus, an assignment tuple is selected (assuming the current date is 10/10) if its START_DATE column is in the range 10/10 to 10/24. You can see from this that we can combine date fields with interval fields by addition. We can also subtract them. Moreover, we can multiply interval fields by integral values. For example, suppose we want to identify a date that is some number of weeks (which we identify by the variable NUM_WEEKS) in the future. Then we can identify it by

```
CURRENT_DATE + INTERVAL '7' DAY * NUM_WEEKS
```

Multiple-Table Queries

The ability to connect data items across table boundaries is essential in any database language. In relational algebra, this is accomplished through the *join*. Although a large portion of SQL is modeled primarily after relational calculus, it connects data between tables in a manner similar to the join of relational algebra. We will now show how this is done. Consider this query:

Query: What are the skill types of workers assigned to building 435?

The data needed to solve this query are found in two relations: WORKER and ASSIGNMENT. The SQL solution requires the listing of both of these relations in the FROM clause, together with a particular type of WHERE clause condition:

```
SELECT SKILL_TYPE
FROM WORKER, ASSIGNMENT
WHERE WORKER.WORKER_ID = ASSIGNMENT.WORKER_ID AND BLDG_ID = 435
```

What is happening here? We must consider two steps in the system's processing of the query.

1. As usual, the FROM clause is processed first. In this case, however, since there are two tables in the clause, the system creates the **Cartesian product** of the rows in these tables. This means that one huge table is (logically) created, consisting of all the *columns* from both tables, and pairing up every *row* in one table with every *row* in the other table in the clause. In our example, since there are five columns in WORKER and four columns in ASSIGNMENT, there will be nine columns in the Cartesian product created by the FROM clause. The total number of rows in this Cartesian product relation is $m \times n$, where m is the number of rows in WORKER and n is the number of rows in ASSIGNMENT: Since WORKER has 7 rows and AS-SIGNMENT has 19 rows, the Cartesian product will have 7×19 or 133 rows. An illustration of this is given in Chapter 6, Figures 6.6(a) and 6.6(b). If there are more than two tables in the FROM clause, the Cartesian product is created from *all* the tables in the clause.

Cartesian product Result of pairing each row in one table with *every* row in another table.

2. After creating this giant relation, the system applies the WHERE clause as before. Each row of the relation created by the FROM clause is examined for conformity to the WHERE clause. Those not satisfying the WHERE condition are eliminated from consideration. The SELECT clause is then applied to the remaining rows.

The WHERE clause in this query contains two conditions:

1. WORKER.WORKER_ID = ASSIGNMENT.WORKER_ID
2. BLDG_ID = 435

The first of these is the join condition. Note that since both the WORKER and ASSIGNMENT relations contain a column named WORKER_ID, the product relation will contain *two* columns with this name. To distinguish between them, we prefix to the column name the name of the relation from which the column originated.

The first condition states that for any given row to be selected, the value of the WORKER_ID column that came from the WORKER relation must be equal to the value of the WORKER_ID column that came from the ASSIGNMENT relation. In

▼FIGURE 7.2 JOINING WORKER AND ASSIGNMENT

WORKER.WORKER_ID	WORKER_NAME	HRLY_RATE	SKILL_TYPE	SUPV_ID
1412	C. Nemo	13.75	Plumbing	1520
2920	R. Garret	10.00	Roofing	2920
1311	C. Coulomb	15.50	Electric	1311

ASSIGNMENT.WORKER_ID	BLDG_ID	START_DATE	NUM_DAYS
1412	435	10/15	15
2920	435	10/28	10
1311	435	10/08	12

effect, we are joining the two relations on WORKER_ID. All rows for which these two columns are not equal are eliminated from the product relation. This is precisely what happens in the natural join of relational algebra. (This differs from the natural join, however, in that the redundant WORKER_ID column is *not* automatically eliminated in SQL.) The complete join of these two relations, with the additional condition that BLDG_ID = 435, is shown in Figure 7.2. The application of the SELECT clause produces the final result of the query:

```
SKILL_TYPE
Plumbing
Roofing
Electric
```

We now show how a relation can be joined to itself in SQL.

Query: List workers with the names of their supervisors.
```
SELECT A.WORKER_NAME, B.WORKER_NAME
FROM WORKER A, WORKER B
WHERE B.WORKER_ID = A.SUPV_ID
```

alias Alternate name given to a relation.

The FROM clause in this example defines two "copies" of the WORKER relation, given the alias names *A* and *B*. An **alias** is an alternate name given to a relation. The *A* and *B* copies of WORKER are joined in the WHERE clause by setting the WORKER_ID in *B* equal to the SUPV_ID in *A*. Thus, each row in *A* has attached to it the row from *B* containing the information about the *A* row's supervisor (Figure 7.3). By selecting the two worker names from each row, we obtain the required list of workers paired with their supervisors:

```
A.WORKER_NAME      B.WORKER_NAME
M. Faraday         C. Coulomb
C. Nemo            H. Rickover
```

▼**FIGURE 7.3 JOINING TWO COPIES OF WORKER**

A.WORKER_ID	A.WORKER_NAME	A.HRLY_RATE	A.SKILL_TYPE	A.SUPV_ID
1235	M. Faraday	12.50	Electric	1311
1412	C. Nemo	13.75	Plumbing	1520
2920	R. Garret	10.00	Roofing	2920
3231	P. Mason	17.40	Framing	3231
1520	H. Rickover	11.75	Plumbing	1520
1311	C. Coulomb	15.50	Electric	1311
3001	J. Barrister	8.20	Framing	3231

B.WORKER_ID	B.WORKER_NAME	B.HRLY_RATE	B.SKILL_TYPE	B.SUPV_ID
1311	C. Coulomb	15.50	Electric	1311
1520	H. Rickover	11.75	Plumbing	1520
2920	R. Garret	10.00	Roofing	2920
3231	P. Mason	17.40	Framing	3231
1520	H. Rickover	11.75	Plumbing	1520
1311	C. Coulomb	15.50	Electric	1311
3231	P. Mason	17.40	Framing	3231

```
R. Garret          R. Garret
P. Mason           P. Mason
H. Rickover        H. Rickover
C. Coulomb         C. Coulomb
J. Barrister       P. Mason
```

A. WORKER_NAME represents the worker, and B.WORKER_NAME represents the supervisor. Notice that some workers supervise themselves, as indicated by the fact that SUPV_ID = WORKER_ID for those workers.

More than two relations can be joined at once in SQL:

Query: List the names of workers assigned to office buildings.

We need to join all three relations to get the required data in one place. This is done in the following query:

```
SELECT WORKER_NAME
FROM WORKER, ASSIGNMENT, BUILDING
WHERE WORKER.WORKER_ID = ASSIGNMENT.WORKER_ID AND
    ASSIGNMENT.BLDG_ID = BUILDING.BLDG_ID        AND
    TYPE = 'Office'
```

Result:

WORKER_NAME
M. Faraday
C. Nemo
R. Garret
P. Mason
H. Rickover
J. Barrister

Notice that if a column name (for example, WORKER_ID or BLDG_ID) appears in more than one relation, we must prefix the column name by the originating relation name to eliminate ambiguity. But if the column name appears in only one relation, as does TYPE in this example, then there is no ambiguity, so the relation name need not be prefixed.

This SQL statement causes the creation of a single relation from the three relations in the database. The first two relations are joined on WORKER_ID, after which the resulting relation is joined with the third relation on BLDG_ID. The condition

```
TYPE = 'Office'
```

in the WHERE clause causes all rows to be eliminated except those that apply to office buildings. This satisfies the requirement of the query.

Subqueries

subquery A query within a query.

A **subquery,** or query within a query, can be placed within the WHERE clause of a query, resulting in the expansion of the WHERE clause's capability. Let's consider an example.

Query: What are the skill types of workers assigned to building 435?

We used this example to illustrate the join. Thus, subqueries give us at least a partial equivalent to the join.

```
SELECT SKILL_TYPE
FROM WORKER
WHERE WORKER_ID IN
    (SELECT WORKER_ID
     FROM ASSIGNMENT
     WHERE BLDG_ID = 435)
```

The subquery in this example is

```
(SELECT WORKER_ID
 FROM ASSIGNMENT
 WHERE BLDG_ID = 435)
```

outer query The main query that contains all the subqueries.

The query that contains this subquery is called the **outer query** or the main query. The subquery causes the following set of worker IDs to be generated:

```
WORKER_ID
2920
1412
1311
```

This set of IDs then takes the place of the subquery in the outer query. At this point, the outer query is executed using the set generated by the subquery. The outer query causes each row in WORKER to be evaluated with respect to the WHERE clause. If the row's WORKER_ID is *IN* the set generated by the subquery, then the SKILL_TYPE of the row is selected and displayed as part of the result of the query:

```
SKILL_TYPE
Plumbing
Roofing
Electric
```

It is very important that the SELECT clause of the subquery contain WORKER_ID and *only* WORKER_ID. Otherwise, the WHERE clause of the outer query, which states that WORKER_ID is *IN* a set of worker IDs, would not make sense.

Note that the subquery may logically be executed before *any* row is examined by the main query. In a sense, the subquery is independent of the main query. It could be executed as a query in its own right. We say that this kind of subquery is **noncorrelated** or not correlated to the main query. As will see shortly, subqueries may also be correlated.

noncorrelated sub-query A subquery whose value does not depend on any outer query.

Here is an example of a subquery within a subquery.

Query: List the names of workers assigned to office buildings.

Again, we are looking at a query we used to study the join.

```
SELECT WORKER_NAME
FROM WORKER
WHERE WORKER_ID IN
   (SELECT WORKER_ID
    FROM ASSIGNMENT
    WHERE BLDG_ID IN
      (SELECT BLDG_ID
       FROM BUILDING
       WHERE TYPE = 'Office'))
```

Result:

WORKER_NAME
M. Faraday
C. Nemo
R. Garret
P. Mason
H. Rickover
J. Barrister

Observe that we did not have to prefix any column names with relation names. This is so because each subquery deals with one and only one relation, so no ambiguity can result.

The evaluation of this query proceeds from the inside out. Thus, the innermost (or "bottom-most") subquery is evaluated first, then the subquery that contains it, followed by the outer query.

Correlated Subqueries. The subqueries we have studied so far are independent of the main queries that use them. By this we mean that the subqueries could exist as queries in their own right. We are now going to look at a class of subqueries whose value upon execution depends on the row being examined by the main query. Such subqueries are called **correlated subqueries**.

correlated subquery
A subquery whose result depends on the row being examined by an outer query.

Query: List workers who receive a higher hourly wage than their supervisors.

The pivotal word in this query is their. That is, the supervisor row to examine depends directly on the worker row being examined. This query can be solved by using a correlated subquery.

```
SELECT WORKER_NAME
FROM WORKER A
WHERE A.HRLY_RATE >
   (SELECT B.HRLY_RATE
    FROM WORKER B
    WHERE B.WORKER_ID = A.SUPV_ID)
```

Result:

WORKER_NAME
C. Nemo

The logical steps involved in executing this query are as follows:

1. The system makes two copies of the WORKER relation, copy *A* and copy *B*. As we have defined them, *A* refers to the worker, and *B* refers to the supervisor.

2. The system then examines each row of *A*. A given row is selected if it satisfies the condition in the WHERE clause. This condition states that the row will be selected if its HRLY_RATE is *greater than* the HRLY_RATE generated by the subquery.

3. The subquery selects the HRLY_RATE from the row of *B* whose WORKER_ID is equal to that of the SUPV_ID of the row of *A* currently being examined by the main query. This is the HRLY_RATE of *A*'s supervisor.

Note that since *A*.HRLY_RATE can only be compared to a single value, the subquery must of necessity generate only one value. This value *changes depending on the row of A being examined*. Thus, the subquery is correlated to the main query. We will see other applications for correlated subqueries later when we study built-in functions.

EXISTS and NOT EXISTS

Suppose we want to identify all the workers who are *not* assigned to a particular building. On the face of it, a query like this would seem easily solved by the simple negation of the affirmative version of the query. Suppose, for example, that the building of interest has the BLDG_ID 435. Then consider this "solution":

```
SELECT WORKER_ID
FROM ASSIGNMENT
WHERE BLDG_ID <> 435
```

Unfortunately, this is a misformulation of the solution. This solution merely gives the IDs of the workers who are working on buildings other than building 435. Obviously, some of these workers may be assigned to building 435 as well.

A correct solution could utilize the NOT EXISTS operator:

```
SELECT WORKER_ID
FROM WORKER
WHERE NOT EXISTS
   (SELECT *
    FROM ASSIGNMENT
    WHERE ASSIGNMENT.WORKER_ID = WORKER.WORKER_ID AND
      BLDG_ID = 435)
```
Result:

WORKER_ID
1235
3231
1520
3001

EXISTS operator Evaluates to true if resulting set is not empty.

NOT EXISTS operator Evaluates to true if resulting set is empty.

The **EXISTS** and **NOT EXISTS operators** always precede a subquery. EXISTS evaluates to true if the set resulting from the subquery is not empty. If the resulting set is empty, then the EXISTS operator evaluates to false. The NOT EXISTS operator, naturally, works in precisely the opposite manner. It evaluates to true if the resulting set is empty and false otherwise.

In this example, we have used NOT EXISTS. The subquery selects all those rows in ASSIGNMENT that have the same WORKER_ID as the row currently being examined by the main query and a BLDG_ID equal to 435. If that set is empty, then the worker row being examined by the main query is selected, since that means that the worker in question does *not* work on building 435.

The solution we gave here involves a correlated subquery. If we use IN instead of NOT EXISTS, we can use a noncorrelated subquery:

```
SELECT WORKER_ID
FROM WORKER
WHERE WORKER_ID NOT IN
   (SELECT WORKER_ID
    FROM ASSIGNMENT
    WHERE BLDG_ID = 435)
```

This solution is also simpler than the solution using NOT EXISTS. It is natural to ask, therefore, why we should use EXISTS or NOT EXISTS at all. The answer is simply that NOT EXISTS provides the only means available to solve queries containing the "every" quantifier in their condition. In Chapter 6, we saw that such queries are solved with division in relational algebra and with the universal quantifier in relational calculus. The following is an example of a query containing "every" in its condition:

Query: List workers who are assigned to every building.

This query may be solved in SQL by using a double negative. We restate the query with such a double negative as follows:

Query: List workers such that there is *no* building to which they are *not* assigned.

We have emphasized the two negatives. It should be clear that this query is logically equivalent to the previous one.

Now we wish to formulate a solution in SQL. To make the final solution clearer, we first give a solution to a preliminary problem: the problem of identifying the buildings to which a hypothetical worker, "1234," is *not* assigned.

```
(I) SELECT BLDG_ID
    FROM BUILDING
    WHERE NOT EXISTS
      (SELECT *
       FROM ASSIGNMENT
       WHERE ASSIGNMENT.BLDG_ID = BUILDING.BLDG_ID AND
          ASSIGNMENT.WORKER_ID = 1234)
```

We have labeled this query (I) because we will refer to it later. If there are no buildings that satisfy this query, then worker 1234 must be assigned to *every* building and so would satisfy the original query. To obtain a solution to the original query then, our second step is to generalize query (I) from the specific worker 1234 to the variable WORKER_ID and to make this modified query a subquery in a larger query. The following accomplishes this:

```
(II) SELECT WORKER_ID
     FROM WORKER
     WHERE NOT EXISTS
       (SELECT BLDG_ID
        FROM BUILDING
```

```
WHERE NOT EXISTS
  (SELECT *
   FROM ASSIGNMENT
   WHERE ASSIGNMENT.BLDG_ID = BUILDING.BLDG_ID AND
     ASSIGNMENT.WORKER_ID = WORKER.WORKER_ID))
```

Result:
WORKER_ID
1412

Observe that the subquery that starts on the fourth line of query (II) is identical to query (I), except that we have replaced "1234" with WORKER.WORKER_ID. Query (II) may be read as follows:

```
Select WORKER_ID from WORKER if there does not exist a building
to which WORKER_ID is not assigned.
```

This satisfies the requirement of the original query.

We see then that NOT EXISTS can be used to formulate answers to the types of queries for which the division operation of relational algebra and the universal quantifier of relational calculus (Chapter 6) were needed. In terms of ease of use, however, the NOT EXISTS operator doesn't seem to offer any particular advantages. That is, it does not appear that SQL queries using NOT EXISTS twice are any easier to understand than solutions using division in relational algebra or universal quantifiers in relational calculus. Additional research needs to be done to develop language constructs that allow a more natural solution to these types of queries.

Built-In Functions

Consider questions like these:

What are the highest and lowest hourly wages? What is the average number of days that workers are assigned to building 435? What is the total number of days allocated for plumbing on building 312? How many different skill types are there?

built-in function Statistical function that operates on a set of rows—SUM, AVG, COUNT, MAX, MIN.

set function A built-in function.

These questions require statistical functions that examine a set of rows in a relation and produce a single value. SQL provides five such functions called **built-in** or **set functions.** The five functions are SUM, AVG, COUNT, MAX, and MIN.

```
Query: What are the highest and lowest hourly wages?
SELECT MAX(HRLY_RATE), MIN(HRLY_RATE)
FROM WORKER
```

Result: 17.40, 8.20

The MAX and MIN functions operate on a single column in a relation. They select the largest or the smallest value, respectively, to be found in that column. The solution for this query does not include a WHERE clause. For most queries, this need not be the case, as our next example shows.

```
Query: What is the average number of days that workers are as-
signed to building 435?
```

```
SELECT AVG(NUM_DAYS)
FROM ASSIGNMENT
WHERE BLDG_ID = 435
```

Result: 12.33

To calculate the average, only rows in ASSIGNMENT for building 435 are considered. As is normally the case in SQL, the WHERE clause restricts consideration to these rows.

Query: What is the total number of days allocated for plumbing on building 312?
```
SELECT SUM(NUM_DAYS)
FROM ASSIGNMENT, WORKER
WHERE WORKER.WORKER_ID = ASSIGNMENT.WORKER_ID AND
   SKILL_TYPE = 'Plumbing' AND
   BLDG_ID = 312
```

Result: 27

This solution used the join of ASSIGNMENT and WORKER. This was necessary since SKILL_TYPE is in WORKER, and BLDG_ID is in ASSIGNMENT.

Query: How many different skill types are there?
```
SELECT COUNT (DISTINCT SKILL_TYPE)
FROM WORKER
```

Result: 4

Since the same skill type is repeated in several different rows, it is necessary to use the keyword "DISTINCT" in this query, so that the system will not count the same skill type more than once. **DISTINCT** may be used with any of the built-in functions, although naturally it is a redundant operator with the MAX and MIN functions.

DISTINCT Operator that eliminates duplicate rows.

SUM and AVG must be used with columns that are numeric. The other functions can be used either with numeric or with character string data. All the functions except COUNT may be used with computed expressions. For example:

Query: What is the average weekly wage?
```
SELECT AVG(40 * HRLY_RATE)
FROM WORKER
```

Result: 509.14

COUNT may refer to entire rows rather than just a single column:

Query: How many buildings have quality level 3?
```
SELECT COUNT (*)
FROM BUILDING
WHERE QLTY_LEVEL = 3
```

Result: 3

As all these examples show that if a built-in function appears in the SELECT clause, then nothing but built-in functions may appear in that SELECT clause. The only exception to this occurs in conjunction with the GROUP BY clause, which we now examine.

GROUP BY and HAVING

Management is often interested in knowing statistical information as it applies to each group in a set of groups. For example, consider the following query:

Query: For each supervisor, what is the highest hourly wage paid to a worker reporting to that supervisor?

To solve this query, we must divide the workers into groups, each reporting to a single supervisor. Then we determine the maximum wage paid in each group. We do this in SQL in this manner:

```
SELECT SUPV_ID, MAX(HRLY_RATE)
FROM WORKER
GROUP BY SUPV_ID
```

Result:

SUPV_ID	MAX(HRLY_RATE)
1311	15.50
1520	13.75
2920	10.00
3231	17.40

In processing this query, the system proceeds by first dividing the rows of WORKER into groups, using the following rule: Rows are placed in the same group if and only if they have the same SUPV_ID. Now the SELECT clause is applied to each group. Since a given group can have only one value for SUPV_ID, there is no ambiguity as to the value of SUPV_ID for that group. The SELECT clause calls for the SUPV_ID to be displayed and for the MAX(HRLY_RATE) to be calculated and displayed *for each group*. The result is as shown.

Only column names appearing in a GROUP BY clause may appear in a SELECT clause with a built-in function. Note that SUPV_ID can appear in the SELECT clause, since it appeared in the GROUP BY clause.

GROUP BY clause Indicates that rows should be grouped on a common value of specified column(s).

The **GROUP BY** clause suggests the possibility of doing some sophisticated computations. For example, we may want to know the average of all these maximum hourly rates. Computations within built-in functions are restricted, however, in that no built-in function may contain another built-in function. Thus, an expression like

```
AVG(MAX(HRLY_RATE))
```

is illegal. Solving such a query would require two steps. The first step would place the maximum hourly rates in a new relation, and the second step would calculate the average of these.

It is permissible to use the WHERE clause with GROUP BY:

Query: For each type of building, what is the average quality level for buildings of status 1?

```
SELECT TYPE, AVG(QLTY_LEVEL)
FROM BUILDING
WHERE STATUS = 1
GROUP BY TYPE
```

Result:

TYPE	AVG(QLTY LEVEL)
Retail	1
Residence	3
Office	3.5

The WHERE clause is executed before the GROUP BY clause. Thus, no group may contain a row with a status other than 1. The rows of status 1 are grouped by TYPE and the SELECT clause is applied to each group.

We can also apply a condition to the groups formed by the GROUP BY clause. This is done with the **HAVING clause.** Suppose, for example, we wish to make one of the previous queries more specific.

HAVING clause Places conditions on groups.

Query: For each supervisor *managing more than one worker*, what is the highest hourly wage paid to a worker reporting to that supervisor?

We could indicate this by the proper use of the HAVING clause:

```
SELECT SUPV_ID, MAX(HRLY_RATE)
FROM WORKER
GROUP BY SUPV_ID
HAVING COUNT(*) > 1
```

Result:

SUPV_ID	MAX(HRLY_RATE)
1311	15.50
1520	13.75
3231	17.40

The difference between the WHERE clause and the HAVING clause is that the WHERE clause is applied to *rows* while the HAVING clause is applied to *groups*.

A query may contain both a WHERE clause and a HAVING clause. In that case, the WHERE clause is applied first, since it applies before the groups are formed. For example, consider the following revision to a query given previously:

Query: For each type of building, what is the average quality level for buildings of status 1? Consider only those types of buildings having a maximum quality level no higher than 3.

```
SELECT TYPE, AVG(QLTY_LEVEL)
FROM BUILDING
WHERE STATUS = 1
GROUP BY TYPE
HAVING MAX(QLTY_LEVEL) <= 3
```

Result:

<u>TYPE</u>
Retail   1
Residence   3

Observe that starting with the FROM clause, the clauses in SQL statements are applied in order, and then the SELECT clause is applied last. Thus, the WHERE clause is applied to the BUILDING relation, and all rows having a STATUS other than 1 are eliminated. The rows remaining are grouped by TYPE, with all rows of the same TYPE being in the same group. This creates a number of groups—one for each value of TYPE. The HAVING clause is then applied to each of the groups, and those having a maximum quality level over 3 are eliminated. Finally, the SELECT clause is applied to the groups that remain.

Built-In Functions with Subqueries

A built-in function may appear only in a SELECT clause or a HAVING clause. However, a SELECT clause containing a built-in function may be part of a subquery. In the following, we see an example of such a subquery:

Query: Which workers receive a higher-than-average hourly wage?

```
SELECT WORKER_NAME
FROM WORKER
WHERE HRLY_RATE >
   (SELECT AVG(HRLY_RATE)
    FROM WORKER)
```

Result:

<u>WORKER_NAME</u>
C. Nemo
P. Mason
C. Coulomb

Note that this subquery is a noncorrelated subquery, which produces precisely one value—the average hourly wage. The main query selects a worker only if the hourly wage for that worker is above this calculated average.

Correlated subqueries may also be used with built-in functions:

Query: Which workers receive an hourly wage higher than the average of those workers reporting to the worker's supervisor?

In this case, instead of calculating a single average for all workers, we must calculate an average for each group of workers reporting to the same supervisor. Moreover, this calculation must be performed anew for each worker being examined by the main query.

```
SELECT A.WORKER_NAME
FROM WORKER A
WHERE A.HRLY_RATE >
   (SELECT AVG(B.HRLY_RATE)
    FROM WORKER B
    WHERE B.SUPV_ID = A.SUPV_ID)
```

```
Result:

A.WORKER_NAME
C. Nemo
P. Mason
C. Coulomb
```

The WHERE clause of the subquery contains the crucial correlation condition. This condition guarantees that the average will only be calculated for those workers having the same supervisor as the worker being examined by the main query.

Relational Algebra Operations

As noted earlier and as you have probably observed, SQL seems to have a flavor of relational calculus with a target list (the SELECT clause) and a qualifying statement (the WHERE clause). SQL-92, however, has implemented a number of the relational algebra operations, which we will now discuss. Specifically, union, intersect, difference, and join are available as explicit operators in SQL-92. We examine each of these in turn.

union compatible
Two or more relations that have equivalent columns as to number and domains.

The UNION, INTERSECT, and EXCEPT Operators.   As in relational algebra the union, intersect, and difference operations apply to two relations at a time, which must be **union compatible.** This term has a slightly different meeting in SQL. Two relations are union compatible if they have the same number of columns, and corresponding columns have compatible data types, that is, data types which can be readily converted from one to the other. Two numeric data types, for example, need not be identical, but one should be convertible to the other.

For our discussion of union, intersect, and difference, we use the same example we used in Chapter 6 for these relational algebra operations (Figure 7.4). This figure shows two relations of salespeople, one consisting of salespeople who are managed by someone, and one of salespeople who manage someone.

▼ FIGURE 7.4 TWO SALESPERSON RELATIONS SP_SUBORD

SALPERS_ID	SALPERS_NAME	MANAGER_ID	OFFICE	COMM %
10	Rodney Jones	27	Chicago	10
14	Masaji Matsu	44	Tokyo	11
23	Francois Moire	35	Brussels	9
37	Elena Hermana	12	B. A.	13
39	Goro Azuma	44	Tokyo	10
44	Albert Ige	27	Toyko	12
35	Brigit Bovary	27	Brussels	11
12	Buster Sanchez	27	B. A.	10

SP_MGR

SALPERS_ID	SALPERS_NAME	MANAGER_ID	OFFICE	COMM %
27	Terry Cardon		Chicago	15
44	Albert Ige	27	Tokyo	12
35	Brigit Bovary	27	Brussels	11
12	Buster Sanchez	27	B. A.	10

```
SALESPERSON
SALPERS_ID      SALPERS_NAME        MANAGER_ID      OFFICE         COMM %
10              Rodney Jones        27              Chicago        10
14              Masaji Matsu        44              Tokyo          11
23              Francois Moire      35              Brussels        9
37              Elena Hermana       12              B. A.          13
39              Goro Azuma          44              Tokyo          10
27              Terry Cardon                        Chicago        15
44              Albert Ige          27              Tokyo          12
35              Brigit Bovary       27              Brussels       11
12              Buster Sanchez      27              B. A.          10
```

▼FIGURE 7.5 THE UNION OF SP_SUBORD AND SP_MGR

UNION Operation that creates the set union of two relations.

UNION.   Suppose we wish to obtain a single relation of all salespeople. We use the SQL statement

```
(SELECT * FROM SP_SUBORD)
UNION
(SELECT * FROM SP_MGR)
```

or the alternate form

```
SELECT *
FROM (TABLE SP_SUBORD UNION TABLE SP_MGR)
```

The result is shown in Figure 7.5. As with relational algebra, the union of two relations is a relation containing every row that is in one relation or the other.

In our example no row appears more than once, even if it appears in both relations. However, if we use the form

```
(SELECT * FROM SP_SUBORD)
UNION ALL
(SELECT * FROM SP_MGR)
```

or the form

```
SELECT *
FROM (TABLE SP_SUBORD UNION ALL TABLE SP_MGR)
```

then those rows that appear in both relations will appear twice in the union.

INTERSECT Operation that creates the set intersection of two relations.

INTERSECT.   Suppose we want to identify those salespeople who are managers but who in turn are managed by someone else. In other words, we want the inter-

▼FIGURE 7.6 THE INTERSECTION OF SP_SUBORD AND SP_MGR

```
SP_SUBORD_MGR

SALPERS_ID      SALPERS_NAME        MANAGER_ID      OFFICE         COMM %
44              Albert Ige          27              Tokyo          12
35              Brigit Bovary       27              Brussels       11
12              Buster Sanchez      27              B.A.           10
```

section of the two relations to get all rows that are in both relations. We use the SQL statement

```
(SELECT * FROM SP_SUBORD)
INTERSECT
(SELECT * FROM SP_MGR)
```

or the alternate form

```
SELECT *
FROM (TABLE SP_SUBORD INTERSECT TABLE SP_MGR)
```

The result is given in Figure 7.6.

As with the UNION no row in the result of this INTERSECT appears more than once. However, if there are m copies of a row in one relation and n copies of the same row in the other relation, and $m < n$, then the INTERSECT of the two relations will yield m copies of that row if this syntax is used:

```
(SELECT * FROM SP_SUBORD)
INTERSECT ALL
(SELECT * FROM SP_MGR)
```

As with the UNION the keyword ALL indicates that duplicates of rows should be considered as if they are unique rows in and of themselves.

EXCEPT Operation that creates the set difference of two relations.

EXCEPT. Suppose we wish to identify those salespeople who are managed by no one. We want to subtract the SP_SUBORD relation from the SP_MGR relation. In SQL-92 set difference is accomplished through the EXCEPT operation. For this example we use the statement

```
(SELECT * FROM SP_MGR)
EXCEPT
(SELECT * FROM SP_SUBORD)
```

or the alternate form

```
SELECT *
FROM (TABLE SP_MGR EXCEPT TABLE SP_SUBORD)
```

The result is shown in Figure 7.7.

If we use the syntax

```
(SELECT * FROM SP_MGR)
EXCEPT ALL
(SELECT * FROM SP_SUBORD)
```

▼**FIGURE 7.7 THE RESULT OF SP_MGR − SP_SUBORD**

SP_MGR_MGR

SALPERS_ID	SALPERS_NAME	MANAGER_ID	OFFICE	COMM %
27	Terry Cardon		Chicago	15

and there are m copies of a given row in SP_MGR and n copies of the same row in SP_SUBORD, where $m > n$, then there will be $m - n$ copies of the row in the result. If $m <= n$, there will be no copies of the row in the result.

Now that we have introduced the basic ideas of the UNION, INTERSECT, and EXCEPT SQL operators, we want to look at them a little more closely. The restriction that the two operand relations be union compatible seems a little strong. After all, how often do we deal with two relations that have exactly the same columns? Let's look at some modified syntax and examples where this restriction does not get in the way. Consider the following query:

Query: Which plumbers start jobs on October 9?

```
(SELECT * FROM WORKER
WHERE SKILL_TYPE = 'Plumbing')
INTERSECT CORRESPONDING BY (WORKER_ID)
(SELECT * FROM ASSIGNMENT
 WHERE START_DATE = '10/09')
```

Result:

```
WORKER_ID
1520
```

We have highlighted the portion of the SQL statement which is significant for our discussion. The two SELECT statements have defined two result relations which are definitely not union compatible. However, we can take the intersection of these two, provided we consider only columns which are in *both* relations. We identify the columns to consider in the CORRESPONDING BY clause. In this case, we consider only the WORKER_ID column. The system will then reduce the result of both the SELECT statements to the values in the WORKER_ID column. Then it will take the intersection of these two sets, and this will be the result of the query. That is, the result will be the WORKER_IDs of those workers who are plumbers and who have a work assignment starting on October 9—exactly as required.

The same approach is used for the UNION and EXCEPT operators. The CORRESPONDING BY clause follows the operator and indicates the columns, which are common to both relations, that are to be considered. Let's look at some more examples.

Query: Which buildings are office buildings or have worker 1412 assigned to them?

```
(SELECT * FROM BUILDING
 WHERE TYPE = 'Office')
UNION CORRESPONDING BY (BLDG_ID)
(SELECT * FROM ASSIGNMENT
 WHERE WORKER_ID = 1412)
```

Result:

```
BLDG_ID
312
210
111
460
435
515
```

Query: Which office buildings do not have worker 1235 assigned to them?

```
(SELECT *FROM BUILDING
 WHERE TYPE = 'Office')
EXCEPT CORRESPONDING BY (BLDG_ID)
(SELECT * FROM ASSIGNMENT
 WHERE WORKER_ID = 1235)
```

Result:
<u>BLDG_ID</u>
210
111

You have probably noticed that these queries are relatively easy to formulate. We simply identify the appropriate subsets of tuples from the two relations and then apply the relevant operator, UNION, INTERSECT, or EXCEPT. This adds considerable practical power to the language, since many people will find such queries easier to formulate using this approach. For example, consider the last query using the "old" SQL approach:

```
SELECT BLDG_ID
FROM BUILDING
WHERE TYPE = 'Office' AND
   NOT EXISTS
      (SELECT *
       FROM ASSIGNMENT
       WHERE BUILDING.BLDG_ID = ASSIGNMENT.BLDG_ID
         AND WORKER_ID = 1235)
```

This solution uses a correlated subquery with the NOT EXISTS operator. It isn't far-fetched to suggest that most people would have considerably more difficulty formulating this solution than the one that uses EXCEPT. Note that the query *could* be solved in the old SQL syntax. It's just not as easy.

The JOIN Operator. SQL-92 contains a number of explicit join operations—the natural join, the inner join, various outer joins, the union join, and the cross join. We will consider only the natural and inner joins.

NATURAL JOIN Operation that connects relations when common columns have equal values.

Natural Join. Semantically, the natural join has the same meaning in SQL as it does in relational algebra. Suppose we wish to join the WORKER and ASSIGNMENT tables. We can use the syntax

```
WORKER NATURAL JOIN ASSIGNMENT
```

The result of this statement will be the same table as would result from the statement

```
SELECT W.WORKER_ID, WORKER_NAME, HRLY_RATE, SKILL_TYPE,
   SUPV_ID, WORKER_ID, BLDG_ID, START_DATE, NUM_DAYS
FROM WORKER W, ASSIGNMENT
WHERE W.WORKER_ID = ASSIGNMENT.WORKER_ID
```

except that the first column would be named WORKER_ID rather than W.WORKER_ID. In general, the natural join causes two tables to join on all their common columns, but those columns are included in the result only once. In the resulting relation the common columns appear first, followed by the remaining columns of the first relation, followed by the remaining columns of the second relation.

Join USING.   Suppose we have two relations, *A* and *B*, and they have common columns *K*, *L*, *M*, and *N*. Suppose though that we don't want to join on all the common columns, but rather only on columns *L* and *N*. Then we can use the statement

```
A JOIN  B USING (L, N)
```

This statement will have the same effect as a SELECT statement that in the SELECT clause lists *L* and *N* first followed by the remaining columns of *A* and the remaining columns of *B*. The WHERE clause of this statement will have the form

```
WHERE A.L = B.L AND A.N = B.N
```

Join ON.   If we wish to use a more generalized condition for joining two relations, we can use this form. For example, suppose we want to join WORKER to itself by connecting the SUPV_ID to the WORKER_ID to obtain information about each worker's supervisor. We use the following

```
WORKER W JOIN WORKER SUPV
    ON W.SUPV_ID = SUPV.WORKER_ID
```

In this example we have created two copies of the WORKER relation and given them the aliases W and SUPV, respectively. The ON clause contains a condition stating that the SUPV_ID from the W copy must be equal to the WORKER_ID from the SUPV copy of the WORKER relation.

Now let's look at some variations of the preceding example. Instead of using actual table or view names in a join statement, we can use tables derived from other operations. We illustrate this approach with several queries.

```
Query: Give assignment and worker data for plumbers who start
jobs on October 9.
(SELECT * FROM WORKER WHERE SKILL_TYPE = 'Plumbing')
NATURAL JOIN
(SELECT * FROM ASSIGNMENT WHERE START_DATE = '10/09')
```

You may have noticed that this query is nearly identical to that used to illustrate the INTERSECT operator earlier. The difference here is that instead of only getting a list of WORKER_IDs we get all relevant information because WORKER tuples are joined with ASSIGNMENT tuples.

```
Query: Give assignment, worker, and building data for plumbers
who start jobs on October 9 to work on residence buildings.
(SELECT * FROM WORKER WHERE SKILL_TYPE = 'Plumbing')
NATURAL JOIN
(SELECT * FROM ASSIGNMENT WHERE START_DATE = '10/09')
NATURAL JOIN
(SELECT * FROM BUILDING WHERE TYPE = 'Residence')
```

In this case the WORKER_ID and BLDG_ID, the join columns, will appear first in the result, followed by the remaining columns from the WORKER, ASSIGNMENT, and BUILDING relations, in that order. If that gives us more information than we want, we can embed this entire statement in the FROM clause of a SELECT statement that specifies the desired columns:

```
SELECT WORKER_NAME, START_DATE, BLDG_ID, BLDG_ADDRESS
FROM (SELECT * FROM WORKER WHERE SKILL_TYPE = 'Plumbing')
NATURAL JOIN
(SELECT * FROM ASSIGNMENT WHERE START_DATE = '10/09')
NATURAL JOIN
(SELECT * FROM BUILDING WHERE TYPE = 'Residence')
```

Database Change Operations

SQL provides three database change operations, INSERT, UPDATE, and DELETE, to allow the addition of rows, the changing of values in rows, and the deletion of rows, respectively, to or from a specified relation in the database. We will discuss each of these separately.

INSERT Operation that causes rows to be added to a relation.

INSERT. INSERT operations allow either a single row to be inserted into a relation, by the specification of values for columns in the row, or a set of rows to be inserted by the specification of a query defining the rows to be inserted.

```
INSERT INTO ASSIGNMENT (WORKER_ID, BLDG_ID, START_DATE)
VALUES (1284, 485, 05/13)
```

This statement inserts a single row into ASSIGNMENT. The names of the columns to which the respective values are to be given are shown in parentheses following the name of the table to be updated. Since we have omitted NUM_DAYS, a null value will be placed in that column of the inserted row.

Suppose we created a new relation named BUILDING_2 consisting of BLDG_ID, TYPE, and QLTY_LEVEL columns, and we wished to populate it with rows from BUILDING have status 2. Then we would use the second form of the INSERT statement.

```
INSERT INTO BUILDING_2
    SELECT BLDG_ID, TYPE, QLTY_LEVEL
    FROM BUILDING
    WHERE STATUS = 2
```

UPDATE Operation that changes column values in rows.

UPDATE. UPDATE operations always apply to all the rows that satisfy the WHERE clause in the UPDATE statement. If we wanted to give everybody working for supervisor 1520 a 5 percent wage increase, the following statement would be needed:

```
UPDATE WORKER
SET HRLY_RATE = 1.05 * HRLY_RATE
WHERE SUPV_ID = 1520
```

If there is no WHERE clause, then the operation applies to every row in the relation. For example, if we wanted to give *every* worker a 5 percent increase, we would merely omit the WHERE clause from the UPDATE statement.

DELETE Operation that removes rows from a relation.

DELETE. DELETE operations also apply to all rows that satisfy the WHERE clause in the DELETE statement. If there is no WHERE clause, then all rows in the relation are deleted. Suppose everybody working for supervisor 1520 has been laid off, and we wish to delete them from the database. Then this statement will do the job:

```
DELETE FROM WORKER
WHERE SUPV_ID = 1520
```

Using SQL With Data Processing Languages

The relational approach of using single statements to manipulate sets of rows in a relation is an advancement over the one-record-at-a-time data manipulation methods of traditional languages. Since SQL is intended to be used in large organizations which use traditional languages, however, a method is needed to allow the integration of SQL statements into programs of traditional languages. This is provided with embedded SQL.

embedded SQL A set of statements that allows SQL to be used with traditional programming languages.

host language Language of programs in which SQL statements can be embedded.

Embedded SQL provides a set of statements used to embed SQL statements in programs of languages like COBOL, C, and Pascal (called the **host language**). These statements include flag statements, which notify a preprocessor that what follows should be replaced by CALLs to DBMS routines. They also include special facilities, called cursors, which allow single-record processing on the results of SQL queries.

The following is an example of embedded SQL code:

```
EXEC SQL
    DECLARE WORK_ASGNMNT CURSOR
    FOR
        SELECT *
        FROM ASSIGNMENT
        WHERE WORKER_ID = REQUESTED-WORKER-ID
END-EXEC
```

flag statements SQL statements embedded in an application program to signal the beginning or end of a set of SQL statements.

This code should be embedded in a program written in COBOL as the host language. The first line (EXEC SQL) and the last line (END-EXEC) are **flag statements** and indicate that the lines contained between them are SQL code. The COBOL program containing this SQL code would be processed by a precompiler before it is compiled. The precompiler recognizes the flag statements and replaces them with CALL statements to DBMS subprograms which at execution time will handle the SQL code. When the COBOL program is compiled, the compiler ignores the SQL CALL statements and compiles the remainder of the program.

cursor Embedded SQL facility where the result of an SQL query is stored for subsequent processing.

The rest of our example contains an SQL declare cursor statement, which defines a cursor. A **cursor** is like a file, whose contents are generated at execution time. Notice that the definition of the cursor includes a SELECT statement. The WHERE clause references a column in ASSIGNMENT (WORKER_ID) and states that a row should be selected if WORKER_ID is equal to a variable in the (COBOL) program (REQUESTED-WORKER-ID). No data are selected until the cursor is *opened* by a separate statement. The **OPEN cursor statement**

OPEN cursor statement Embedded SQL statement that causes the DBMS to process a cursor's query and store its result in the cursor.

```
OPEN WORK_ASGNMNT
```

will cause the DBMS to execute the SELECT statement. Individual rows placed in the cursor during execution of the OPEN can be retrieved by the execution of a **FETCH statement**, which is analogous to a READ statement. Other statements are provided to allow the updating and deletion of data from database tables. A CLOSE statement removes the data from the cursor, so that it can be OPENed again with new data reflecting the current contents of the database.

FETCH statement A statement that retrieves a single row from an opened cursor.

Embedded SQL provides the interface needed for the successful use of SQL in the large-scale batch and on-line programs of large processing organizations. With time, this need will probably decrease, as new languages emerge which are capable of making full use of the relation-at-a-time processing capability of SQL.

▼ View Definition

base table A table that contains basic or real data.

view A definition of a restricted portion of the database.

Early in the chapter, we showed how tables are defined in a database schema. These tables are called **base tables** because they contain the basic data of the database. Portions of these base tables as well as information derived from them can be defined in database views, which are also defined as part of the database schema.

A **view** is a window into a portion of the database. Views are useful for maintaining confidentiality by restricting access to selected parts of the database and for simplifying frequently used query types. For example, to preserve confidentiality, we may wish to create a view showing all information about workers except their hourly wage rate.

```
CREATE VIEW B_WORKER
AS SELECT WORKER_ID, WORKER_NAME, SKILL_TYPE, SUPV_ID
   FROM WORKER
```

B_WORKER in this example is the name of the newly created view. The view name may be followed by the names of the columns in the view enclosed in parentheses. In this case, we have omitted column names, so the view columns simply inherit their names from the relation they are taken from. The portion of this statement following the word "AS" is called a **query specification**. Any legal query specification may appear in a view definition.

query specification Definition of a query used in a view definition, cursor declaration, or other statement.

The system does not actually generate the data values for B_WORKER until it is accessed. At that time the query specification defining B_WORKER is executed, creating B_WORKER from the data that exist in WORKER at the time of execution. Thus, the data in views change dynamically as the data in the underlying base tables change.

Suppose we are often interested in information about electricians, the buildings they are assigned to, and the starting date of the assignment. This view definition will work:

```
CREATE VIEW ELEC_ASSIGNMENT AS
   SELECT WORKER_NAME, BLDG_ID, START_DATE
   FROM WORKER, ASSIGNMENT
   WHERE SKILL_TYPE = 'Electric' AND
      WORKER.WORKER_ID = ASSIGNMENT.WORKER_ID
```

If ELEC_ASSIGNMENT were accessed, the system would first generate its data values. Using our database, ELEC_ASSIGNMENT would appear as follows:

```
ELEC_ASSIGNMENT
WORKER_NAME      BLDG_ID      START_DATE
M. Faraday       312          10/10
M. Faraday       515          10/17
C. Coulomb       435          10/08
C. Coulomb       460          10/23
```

Views may be queried. Suppose we are interested in the electricians assigned to building 435.

Query: Who are the electricians assigned to building 435 and when do they start work?

```
SELECT WORKER_NAME, START_DATE
FROM ELEC_ASSIGNMENT
WHERE BLDG_ID = 435
```

Result: C. Coulomb 10/08

The system first created the relation as shown, and then the query was applied to that relation.

We may also use the result of a grouping operation to define a view. Let's take another look at a query given earlier that derived supervisors together with the maximum hourly rate of workers reporting to them:

```
CREATE VIEW MAX_WAGE (SUPV_ID, MAX_HRLY_RATE) AS
      SELECT SUPV_ID, MAX(HRLY_RATE)
      FROM WORKER
      GROUP BY SUPV_ID
```

Notice that in this example we have included names for the columns in the view. These immediately follow the name of the view (MAX_WAGE). It was necessary to include column names in this case because one of the columns is a computation from a built-in function and has no name it can inherit.

We can query this view to determine, for example, which supervisors have workers receiving an hourly rate over a given amount.

Query: Which supervisors have workers receiving an hourly rate above $12?

```
SELECT SUPV_ID
FROM MAX_WAGE
WHERE MAX_HRLY_RATE > 12
```

In processing the query, the system first creates the result of executing the view's query specification:

```
MAX_WAGE
SUPV_ID      MAX_HRLY_RATE
1311         15.50
1520         13.75
2920         10.00
3231         17.40
```

It then applies the query itself to this result:

```
SUPV_ID
1311
1520
3231
```

Restrictions on View Queries and Updates

A view that is defined with a GROUP BY clause in the query specification is called a *grouped view*. In ANSI standard SQL, there are severe limitations on queries on grouped views. These limitations are (Melton and Simon, 1993, p. 196).

Summary

In this chapter, we studied aspects of relational database implementations with the SQL query language. We briefly reviewed the historical development of SQL systems; we showed how SQL database schemas can be defined; we studied the SQL data manipulation language in detail; we outlined view definition; and we gave a brief introduction to the system information schema.

SQL originated at IBM during the seventies as part of the System R project. Since that time, it has been implemented by a large variety of commercial vendors as the language of their relational DBMS. It is available in both the mainframe and microcomputer environment, and it has become the ANSI standard for relational languages.

SQL catalogs are named collections of schemas, each including a number of user-created schemas as well as an information schema which contains metadata defining all schemas in the catalog. SQL database schemas are defined through CREATE SCHEMA, CREATE DOMAIN, and CREATE TABLE commands. These define specific schemas and their owners, domains, tables, and columns. Domains are used as data types in column definitions. Constraints can also be defined for individual columns as well as for tables. Constraints include primary key and foreign key constraints. Also more generalized CHECK constraints can be defined.

SQL data manipulation includes all of the relational algebra capability defined by Codd, yet its original formulation is based on a relational calculus structure. SQL-92, however, includes more direct implementations of relational algebra operations such as the join, union, intersect, and difference. In addition, SQL provides the capability of grouping rows on a common value for a specified column and of calculating statistical functions for these groups. Data manipulation also allows the insertion, update, and deletion of single rows as well as groups of rows. Finally, SQL statements can be embedded in traditional programs written in languages such as COBOL, C, or Pascal. Through cursors, SQL statements can generate query results which can be processed one row at a time by the program written in the host language.

Views are defined in the database schema by using the SQL query language. Views can be queried and, under certain conditions, they can be updated.

The system information schema in a truly relational system should be structured as a relational database. We saw how the SQL-92 information schema satisfies this requirement. Distinct advantages are found in systems that have information schemas with this structure. In particular, the information schema can be queried using the same language as is used for normal database queries.

Review Questions

1. Define each of the following terms in your own words:
   a. catalog
   b. schema owner
   c. domain definition
   d. character string literals
   e. comparison operators
   f. Boolean connectives
   g. outer query
   h. correlated subquery

i. built-in function
j. DISTINCT
k. GROUP BY clause
l. INSERT
m. DELETE
n. embedded SQL
o. host language
p. cursor
q. FETCH
r. view
s. query specification
t. information schema
u. default value
v. recursive foreign key
w. union compatible
x. UNION
y. EXCEPT
z. NATURAL JOIN

2. Briefly describe the early development of SQL. Which vendor was the first to offer a commercial release of SQL? Describe the variety of systems on which SQL is now available.

3. a. What are the SQL-92 commands used to define a database schema?
   b. How can a single column or a multicolumn key be defined? How is a foreign key defined? A default value? What is the difference between a column constraint and a table constraint? How can more generalized constraints be defined?
   c. List ten different data types available in SQL-92.

4. Describe the kinds of things that can be found in each of these SQL clauses:
   a. SELECT
   b. FROM
   c. WHERE
   d. GROUP BY
   e. HAVING
   f. ORDER BY

5. Describe the action of each of the operations:
   a. UNION
   b. INTERSECT
   c. EXCEPT
   d. NATURAL JOIN
   e. JOIN USING
   f. JOIN ON

6. How are query specifications used in each data change operation?

7. Describe how a cursor works.

8. What is a database view and how can it be used?

9. Describe how SQL can be used with the information schema to obtain information about a database.

e. Who are the customers having over $5 million in annual revenue who have sent shipments weighing less than 1 pound or have sent a shipment to San Francisco?

f. Who are the drivers who have delivered shipments for customers with annual revenue over $20 million to cities with populations over 1 million?

Subqueries

6. a. List the cities that have received shipments from customers having over $15 million in annual revenue.

b. List the names of drivers who have delivered shipments weighing over 100 pounds.

c. List the name and annual revenue of customers who have sent shipments weighing over 100 pounds.

d. List the name and annual revenue of customers whose shipments have been delivered by truck driver Jensen.

NOT EXISTS

7. a. List customers who have had shipments delivered by every truck.

b. List cities that have received shipments from every customer.

c. List drivers who have delivered shipments to every city.

Built-In Functions

8. a. What is the average weight of a shipment?

b. What is the average weight of a shipment going to Atlanta?

c. How many shipments has customer 433 sent?

d. Which cities in the database have the largest and smallest populations?

e. What is the total weight of packages (shipments) carried in truck 82?

f. Give a list of customers and annual revenue for those customers in the database. (Hint: Use a subquery.)

g. Give a list of customers, all of whose shipments weigh over 25 pounds. (Hint: Use a correlated subquery.)

h. Give a list of customers who send all their shipments to a single city. (Note: The city may or may not be the same for each of these customers.)

GROUP BY and HAVING

9. a. For each customer, what is the average weight of a package (shipment) sent by that customer?

b. For each city, what is the maximum weight of a package sent to that city?

c. For each city with population over 1 million, what is the minimum weight of a package sent to that city?

d. For each city that has received at least ten packages, what is the average weight of a package sent to that city?

Relational Algebra Operations

10. a. Customers who are manufacturers or have sent a package to St. Louis.

b. Cities of population over 1 million which have received a 100-pound package from customer 311.

c. Trucks driven by Jake Stinson which have never delivered a shipment to Denver.

d. Customers with annual revenue over $10 million which have sent packages under 1 pound to cities with population less than 10,000.

Database Change Operations

11. Write database change operations to accomplish each of the following:
   a. Add truck 95 with driver Winston.
   b. Delete all cities from the database with population under 5,000. Don't forget to update the SHIPMENT relation.
   c. Convert the weight of every shipment to kilograms by dividing the weight by 2.2.

Cursors

12. Create a cursor declaration which will identify all information about customers who have sent a shipment to a city with more than 500,000 population.

Views

13. Create views for each of the following:
   a. Customers with annual revenue under $1 million.
   b. Customers with annual revenue between $1 million and $5 million.
   c. Customers with annual revenue over $5 million.

14. Use these views to answer the following queries:
   a. Which drivers have taken shipments to Los Angeles for customers with revenue over $5 million?
   b. What are the populations of cities which have received shipments from customers with revenue between $1 million and $5 million?
   c. Which drivers have taken shipments to cities for customers with revenue under $1 million, and what are the populations of those cities?

Projects and Professional Issues

1. Write a research paper on the development of SQL from its earliest stages at IBM. Discuss its first commercial releases from Oracle and IBM, its status as the ANSI standard, and recent mainframe and microcomputer releases.

2. Write a research paper that critiques the 1992 ANSI standard of SQL. Compare this standard with two or three commercial products.

3. Study embedded SQL in detail. Determine how it interfaces with one or two host languages.

4. Study the information schemas of two different relational database management systems. How can they be used with SQL to provide information to users?

*"**H**ow do you like working with the system now that we've added Query-by-Example, Irv?"*

Annette Chang is interested in users' reactions to the new relational database query language that Premier Construction Company has recently installed. She's talking with Irv Bernstein, company controller.

"Annette, I can honestly say that I never thought any computer language would be so easy to use. Once I understood how the data tables were laid out, it was easy to see how to construct queries. Of course, I'm only using simple queries now, and I might not find it so easy to use as my needs grow more sophisticated."

"I think you'll find that for most of the things you want to do, the language is easy to understand. I will be glad to help you with any queries that you feel you can't solve; but I think that in any case, you'll be on your own in a very short time."

Query-by-Example is a graphical version of the SQL relational data language. It is particularly well suited to the needs of the typical user. In this chapter, you will become familiar with many of the features of this language, as well as a microcomputer implementation, PARADOX FOR WINDOWS. After reading this chapter, you should be able to:

▼ Discuss some of the background and historical facts relating to the theoretical and commercial implementation of Query-by-Example (QBE).

▼ Develop solutions to a large variety of queries in QBE.

▼ Make changes to the database in QBE.

▼ Evaluate the strengths and weaknesses of QBE as a relational language.

▼ Be able to develop your own applications using PARADOX FOR WINDOWS.

▼ Introduction

Query-by-Example (QBE) was developed during the seventies at IBM's Thomas J. Watson Research Center (Zloof, 1975; Date, 1986). The time of its development roughly parallels that of SQL, and the two languages are logically similar. QBE has been released as a commercial product for some time now and is commonly used as a query tool by end users. Typically, QBE is supported when SQL is also supported, and the tables accessed by QBE are defined through the SQL table definition facility.

Both languages are supported in the Query Management Facility (QMF) offered by IBM. QMF is a shell program that provides a user interface to QBE and SQL. Users interact with QMF through on-line terminals using menu screens and function keys. The user selects either of the two languages and formats and executes queries in the selected language. QMF then provides means for printing the results of these queries in reports with formatting that includes headings and other standard features.

QBE is also supported by other vendors. Borland, for example, offers PARADOX as a full-functioned version of QBE which includes table definition. Although the syntax is slightly different from IBM's, the language is basically the same. Lotus 1-2-3 also provides a simple database query language which uses an approach similar to that of QBE. Because QBE allows nontechnical users to formulate queries so easily, it is likely to remain an important part of commercial database systems for some time.

In this chapter, we will study the data manipulation features of QBE in some detail. We will use the IBM commercial implementation as our standard. We shall also cover PARADOX FOR WINDOWS, which is an implementation of QBE concepts that is widely used on microcomputer systems.

▼ Data Manipulation

textual language A computer language whose statements consist of character string symbols.

Traditional computer languages are **textual,** providing for the formulation of problem solutions in textual character string symbols. QBE, however, is a **graphical** language that structures query solutions by means of pictorial representations of database tables. By placing symbols in the proper places in table columns, the user can specify query selection conditions, grouping, data display, and database update operations.

graphical language A computer language that uses pictorial representations to solve problems.

Although QBE is a graphical language, it has many structural similarities with SQL. Both languages support a similar array of conditional expressions, built-in functions, grouping, multiple-table queries, and the like. There are also areas of difference between the two languages. In particular, some SQL features do not appear in QBE. We will point out the most important similarities and differences as our discussion proceeds. Except as noted, we will use the same queries to illustrate QBE features as we used for SQL. The resulting data values will therefore be the same.

Since most QBE systems use databases that have been defined using SQL data definition commands, we will not discuss data definition in QBE.

Simple Queries

simple query A query involving only one database table.

As with SQL, we will first investigate **simple queries** involving only one database table.

example table In QBE, a skeleton table showing the table name and the column names above blank spaces used for entry of query conditions.

As a graphical language, QBE must provide some means for the user to interact graphically with the database. This is done through the display of skeleton tables or, in QBE terminology, **example tables.** By executing a system command, the user can cause the display of an example table for any table in the database. A sample database is shown in Figure 8.1, and Figure 8.2 shows example tables for each of the three tables in the database. In each case, the name of the table appears in the first column, followed in order by the names of each of the table's columns. A blank space is left below each of these table and column names, allowing user query input. We will now illustrate the use of example tables through sample queries.

Query: Who are the plumbers?

The QBE solution appears in Figure 8.3. We have placed "P." below the WORKER_NAME column to indicate that we want the value in that column displayed (or printed). This is equivalent to placing WORKER_NAME in the SELECT clause of an SQL statement. By placing the literal value "Plumbing" in the SKILL_TYPE column, we are stating the condition that only those rows having SKILL_TYPE equal to "Plumbing" should be selected.

```
WORKER

WORKER_ID    WORKER_NAME      HRLY_RATE      SKILL_TYPE      SUPV_ID
1235         M. Faraday       12.50          Electric        1311
1412         C. Nemo          13.75          Plumbing        1520
2920         R. Garret        10.00          Roofing         2920
3231         P. Mason         17.40          Framing         3231
1520         H. Rickover      11.75          Plumbing        1520
1311         C. Coulomb       15.50          Electric        1311
3001         J. Barrister      8.20          Framing         3231

ASSIGNMENT

WORKER_ID    BLDG_ID      START_DATE     NUM_DAYS
1235         312          10/10           5
1412         312          10/01          10
1235         515          10/17          22
2920         460          10/05          18
1412         460          12/08          18
2920         435          10/28          10
2920         210          11/10          15
3231         111          10/10           8
1412         435          10/15          15
1412         515          11/05           8
3231         312          10/24          20
1520         515          10/09          14
1311         435          10/08          12
1412         210          11/15          12
1412         111          12/01           4
3001         111          10/08          14
1311         460          10/23          24
1520         312          10/30          17
3001         210          10/27          14

BUILDING

BLDG_ID      BLDG_ADDRESS     TYPE           QLTY_LEVEL      STATUS
312          123 Elm          Office         2               2
435          456 Maple        Retail         1               1
515          789 Oak          Residence      3               1
210          1011 Birch       Office         3               1
111          1213 Aspen       Office         4               1
460          1415 Beech       Warehouse      3               3
```

▼FIGURE 8.1 PREMIER CONSTRUCTION COMPANY DATABASE

▼FIGURE 8.2 EXAMPLE TABLES

WORKER	WORKER_ID	WORKER_NAME	HRLY_RATE	SKILL_TYPE	SUPV_ID
ASSIGNMENT	WORKER_ID	BLDG_ID	START_DATE	NUM_DAYS	
BUILDING	BLDG_ID	BLDG_ADDRESS	TYPE	QLTY_LEVEL	STATUS

WORKER	WORKER_ID	WORKER_NAME	HRLY_RATE	SKILL_TYPE	SUPV_ID
		P.		Plumbing	

▼FIGURE 8.3

▼FIGURE 8.4

```
WORKER_NAME
C. Nemo
H. Rickover
```

Notice that the QBE command in this example is followed by a period. Thus, "P." is the display command. The literal value "Plumbing" indicates a data selection condition. QBE commands always end with a period, and literal values appear exactly as they are normally written. The result of the query is shown in Figure 8.4. Notice that the result is a relational table, as is always the case with relational languages.

Query: List all data about office buildings.

In the QBE solution (Figure 8.5), the "P." appears below the table name, indicating that the entire row for each office building should be displayed. "Office" appears under TYPE as the qualifying condition for selecting rows.

```
Result:
BLDG_ID        BLDG_ADDRESS     TYPE        QLTY_LEVEL      STATUS

  312            123 Elm        Office          2             2
  210            1011 Birch     Office          3             1
  111            1213 Aspen     Office          4             1
```

Query: What is the weekly wage rate for each electrician?

In this QBE solution (Figure 8.6), we have introduced a second table having no column headings. Such a table is called a **target table** because it contains information about the final result, or the target, of the query. In this query, it is the equivalent of the SELECT clause of SQL. Note that "P." appears in the first column of the target table. This means that every column in the target table is to be displayed. The second and fourth columns contain the example elements _WN and _HR. An **example element** is a variable that represents a typical, unspecified value of a column in a table. In this case, the example elements are defined in columns 3 and 4

target table In QBE, a table without column headings that is used to define query output.

example element In QBE, a variable representing an unspecified value in a column of a table.

BUILDING	BLDG_ID	BLDG_ADDRESS	TYPE	QLTY_LEVEL	STATUS
P.			Office		

▼FIGURE 8.5

▼FIGURE 8.6

WORKER	WORKER_ID	WORKER_NAME	HRLY_RATE	SKILL_TYPE	SUPV_ID
		_WN	_HR	Electric	
P.	_WN	'Weekly Wage Rate = '	40 * _HR		

of the example table shown above the target table. Note that QBE variables begin with an underscore (_). Since _WN is in the WORKER_NAME column, it stands for any possible value in this column of the WORKER relation. Similarly, _HR stands for the corresponding HRLY_RATE. In this query, we have shown both a computation (column 4 of the target table) and a literal value (column 3 of the target table).

```
Result:  WORKER_NAME
         C. Coulomb    Weekly Wage Rate = 620.00
         M. Faraday    Weekly Wage Rate = 500.00
```

Query: Who gets an hourly rate less than $10?

We have given this new query to illustrate the specification of simple comparison conditions in QBE (Figure 8.7). Note that the condition

```
< 10
```

can be placed right in the example table.

```
Result: WORKER_NAME
        J. Barrister
```

Query: Who are the plumbers receiving over $12 per hour?

The solution (Figure 8.8) to this new query shows that a compound condition can be expressed in an example table. The conditions in this table are equivalent to:

```
HRLY_RATE > 12  AND  SKILL_TYPE = 'Plumbing'
```

That is, when two conditions appear on the same line in an example table, *both* conditions must hold for a row to be selected. In this case, we chose to display all data from the selected rows, so we placed "P." in the first column.

```
Result:
WORKER_ID    WORKER_NAME    HRLY_RATE    SKILL_TYPE    SUPV_ID
1412         C. Nemo        13.75        Plumbing      1520
```

Query: List workers who are plumbers or who are receiving over $12 per hour.

WORKER	WORKER_ID	WORKER_NAME	HRLY_RATE	SKILL_TYPE	SUPV_ID
		P.	<10		

▼**FIGURE 8.7**

▼**FIGURE 8.8**

WORKER	WORKER_ID	WORKER_NAME	HRLY_RATE	SKILL_TYPE	SUPV_ID
P.			>12	Plumbing	

The solution (Figure 8.9) to this new query illustrates that conditions specified on two different lines of a QBE query are equivalent to conditions connected by a Boolean OR. Note the placement of the "P." command. It appears on both lines and in every column that is to be displayed.

```
Result:
WORKER_NAME        HRLY_RATE        SKILL_TYPE
M. Faraday           12.50          Electric
C. Nemo              13.75          Plumbing
P. Mason             17.40          Framing
H. Rickover          11.75          Plumbing
C. Coulomb           15.50          Electric
```

Query: Who gets an hourly rate between $10 and $12?

The solution appears in Figure 8.10.

```
Result:
WORKER_ID     WORKER_NAME     HRLY_RATE     SKILL_TYPE     SUPV_ID
2920          R. Garret         10.00        Roofing        2920
1520          H. Rickover       11.75        Plumbing       1520
```

condition box In QBE, a box in which a complex query condition can be expressed.

To solve this query, we have introduced a **condition box.** This box, labeled CONDITIONS, contains any constraints on data values that the user desires. In this example, since two conditions apply simultaneously to values in the same column, it is convenient to create a single condition, using a Boolean AND, and place it in the condition box.

Multiple-Table Queries

multiple-table query A query involving more than one table.

The most important aspect of **multiple-table queries** involves connecting data *across* tables or, in other words, joining tables. We now see how to perform a join in QBE.

Query: What are the skill types of workers assigned to building 435?

WORKER	WORKER_ID	WORKER_NAME	HRLY_RATE	SKILL_TYPE	SUPV_ID
		P.	P. > 12	P.	
		P.	P.	P. Plumbing	

▼**FIGURE 8.9**

▼**FIGURE 8.10**

WORKER	WORKER_ID	WORKER_NAME	HRLY_RATE	SKILL_TYPE	SUPV_ID
P.			_HR		

CONDITIONS
_HR >= 10 AND _HR <= 12

The important thing to notice in the QBE solution (Figure 8.11) to this query is that the same example element, _WI, appears in both example tables, WORKER and AS-SIGNMENT. This is how a join condition is expressed in QBE. It means that a selected *pair* of rows from the two tables must have the *same value* for the two respective columns. We chose _WI as the example element since it is an appropriate abbreviation of the column name, WORKER_ID. We could have chosen another example element, such as _X, but that would not have been meaningful in this context. Additionally, the literal 435 is placed in the BLDG_ID column of ASSIGNMENT to indicate that only rows for building 435 should be considered. Finally, the "P." in the SKILL_TYPE column means the value in that column will be displayed.

Result:

SKILL_TYPE
Plumbing
Roofing
Electric

Query: List workers with the names of their supervisors.

The solution (Figure 8.12) to this query illustrates the ease with which a relation can be joined to itself in QBE. Observe that by using the example element _SI in both example tables, we have required that SUPV_ID in the first copy of WORKER be equal to WORKER_ID in the second copy of WORKER. The WORKER_NAME column from both tables is then displayed as shown in the target table. The second column represents the supervisor's name. It is assumed in the database that workers having no supervisors are their own supervisors.

Result:

WORKER_NAME	WORKER_NAME
M. Faraday	C. Coulomb
C. Nemo	H. Rickover
R. Garret	R. Garret
P. Mason	P. Mason
H. Rickover	H. Rickover
C. Coulomb	C. Coulomb
J. Barrister	P. Mason

WORKER	WORKER_ID	WORKER_NAME	HRLY_RATE	SKILL_TYPE	SUPV_ID
	_WI			P.	
ASSIGNMENT	WORKER_ID	BLDG_ID	START_DATE	NUM_DAYS	
	_WI	435			

▼**FIGURE 8.11**

▼**FIGURE 8.12**

WORKER	WORKER_ID	WORKER_NAME	HRLY_RATE	SKILL_TYPE	SUPV_ID
		_WN			_SI
WORKER	WORKER_ID	WORKER_NAME	HRLY_RATE	SKILL_TYPE	SUPV_ID
	_SI	_SN			
P.	_WN	_SN			

Query: List the names of workers assigned to office buildings.

The solution (Figure 8.13) to this query illustrates the joining of three tables. It is hard to imagine such a join being more easily or clearly accomplished than it is here in QBE. The power of graphical programming should be obvious from this example.

Result:
WORKER_NAME
M. Faraday
C. Nemo
R. Garret
P. Mason
H. Rickover
J. Barrister

Query: List workers who receive a higher hourly wage than their supervisors.

We have once again joined WORKER to itself (Figure 8.14). This time, however, we needed a condition box to select only those workers who receive a higher wage than their supervisors. The condition box is the only means available for comparing values in two different columns. Note that this query was solved with a correlated subquery in our SQL discussion.

Result:
WORKER_NAME
C. Nemo

Built-In Functions

built-in function Statistical function that operates on a set of rows—SUM, AVG, MAX, MIN, CNT.

QBE also supports **built-in** (or statistical) **functions,** as does SQL. These are used to find the largest and smallest elements in a column, to calculate the average or total value of a column, and to count the total number of elements in a column. The

WORKER	WORKER_ID	WORKER_NAME	HRLY_RATE	SKILL_TYPE	SUPV_ID
	_WI	P.			
ASSIGNMENT	WORKER_ID	BLDG_ID	START_DATE	NUM_DAYS	
	_WI	_BI			
BUILDING	BLDG_ID	BLDG_ADDRESS	TYPE	QLTY_LEVEL	STATUS
	_BI		Office		

▼**FIGURE 8.13**

▼**FIGURE 8.14**

WORKER	WORKER_ID	WORKER_NAME	HRLY_RATE	SKILL_TYPE	SUPV_ID
		_WN P.	_WR		_SI
WORKER	WORKER_ID	WORKER_NAME	HRLY_RATE	SKILL_TYPE	SUPV_ID
	_SI		_SR		
CONDITIONS					
_WR > _SR					

built-in functions have the names MAX, MIN, AVG, SUM, and CNT (count) in QBE. They may appear in target tables or condition boxes.

Query: What are the highest and lowest hourly wages?

The solution appears in Figure 8.15.

Result: 18.40, 8.20

This result, consisting of two values, can be thought of as a two-column table with one row. The column headings could be MAX_RATE and MIN_RATE. Thus, the result of every query is still a relational table.

Query: What is the average number of days that workers are assigned to building 435?

The solution appears in Figure 8.16.

Result: 12.33

Query: What is the total number of days allocated for plumbing on building 312?

The solution appears in Figure 8.17.

Result: 27

Query: How many different skill types are there?

The UNQ. operator (Figure 8.18) guarantees that only unique occurrences of skill type will be counted. That is, duplicates will be discarded in figuring the count.

WORKER	WORKER_ID	WORKER_NAME	HRLY_RATE	SKILL_TYPE	SUPV_ID
			_HR		
P.	MAX._HR	MIN._HR			

▼**FIGURE 8.15**

ASSIGNMENT	WORKER_ID	BLDG_ID	START_DATE	NUM_DAYS
		435		_ND
P.	AVG._ND			

▼**FIGURE 8.16**

▼**FIGURE 8.17**

WORKER	WORKER_ID	WORKER_NAME	HRLY_RATE	SKILL_TYPE	SUPV_ID
	_WI			Plumbing	

ASSIGNMENT	WORKER_ID	BLDG_ID	START_DATE	NUM_DAYS
	_WI	312		_ND
P.	SUM._ND			

WORKER	WORKER_ID	WORKER_NAME	HRLY_RATE	SKILL_TYPE	SUPV_ID
				_CT	
P.	CNT.UNQ._CT				

▼FIGURE 8.18

Result: 4

Query: What is the average weekly wage?

The solution appears in Figure 8.19.

Result: 509.14

Query: How many buildings have quality level 3?

The solution appears in Figure 8.20.

Result: 3

GROUP BY

Just as in SQL, we can group rows having a common value in one or more columns. This means that the rows of a relation are split into groups, one group for each value of a designated column. Statistical functions can then be applied to each group.

Query: For each supervisor, what is the highest hourly wage paid to a worker reporting to that supervisor?

"G." indicates the grouping column (Figure 8.21). In this case, we are grouping by SUPV_ID, since we want the maximum wage of workers by supervisor. The target table is then used to indicate the display of the grouping column together with any built-in functions that apply to the groups.

WORKER	WORKER_ID	WORKER_NAME	HRLY_RATE	SKILL_TYPE	SUPV_ID
			_HR		
P.	AVG.(40 * _HR)				

▼FIGURE 8.19

BUILDING	BLDG_ID	BLDG_ADDRESS	TYPE	QLTY_LEVEL	STATUS
	_BI			3	
P.	CNT._BI				

▼FIGURE 8.20

▼FIGURE 8.21

WORKER	WORKER_ID	WORKER_NAME	HRLY_RATE	SKILL_TYPE	SUPV_ID
			_HR		G. _SI
P.	_SI	MAX._HR			

ASSIGNMENT	WORKER_ID	BLDG_ID	START_DATE	NUM_DAYS
I.	1284	485	05/13	

▼**FIGURE 8.26**

The next query (Figure 8.27) will add rows to a relation named BUILDING_2, which consists of BLDG_ID, TYPE, and QLTY_LEVEL columns. The rows added are those in BUILDING having status 2.

Observe that we have placed a condition (STATUS = 2) on the rows of *BUILD-ING*, while the insert command (I.) is in the *BUILDING_2* table. Thus, we are performing a query on *BUILDING*, and the rows selected are inserted into *BUILDING_2*. A table such as BUILDING_2 could be used, for example, as a temporary table on which a large variety of queries would be carried out.

Update. The QBE query shown in Figure 8.28 gives everybody working for supervisor 1520 a 5 percent wage increase.

We needed to show the HRLY_RATE column twice: once to define the variable _H, and once to indicate the update command (U.) and formula (_H * 1.05). Incidentally, this facility of displaying multiple copies of the same column in an example table may also be used in queries (e.g., if multiple conditions apply to the same column under the AND relationship).

Delete. If we want to delete everybody working for supervisor 1520, then we may use the query shown in Figure 8.29, where D. indicates the delete command.

BUILDING	BLDG_ID	BLDG_ADDRESS	TYPE	QLTY_LEVEL	STATUS
	_BI		_T	_QL	2

BUILDING_2	BLDG_ID	TYPE	QLTY_LEVEL	
I.	_BI	_T	_QL	

▼**FIGURE 8.27**

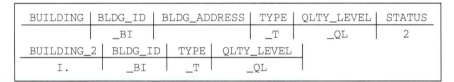

WORKER	WORKER_ID	WORKER_NAME	HRLY_RATE	HRLY_RATE	SKILL_TYPE	SUPV_ID
			_H	U. _H*1.05		1520

▼**FIGURE 8.28**

▼**FIGURE 8.29**

WORKER	WORKER_ID	WORKER_NAME	HRLY_RATE	SKILL_TYPE	SUPV_ID
D.					1520

▼ Paradox for Windows

PARADOX FOR WINDOWS A microcomputer DBMS whose query language is like QBE.

A powerful DBMS for microcomputing environments that incorporates the concepts of QBE is **PARADOX FOR WINDOWS.** Since many users of this book may rely on personal or laboratory microcomputers, we devote the remainder of this chapter to covering some of the important features and capabilities of PARADOX FOR WINDOWS.

Data Definition and Entry

The PARADOX data definition language is very simple to learn. Clicking on the *File* menu produces the choices shown in Figure 8.30 (Note: There are keyboard counterparts for all choices. These can be referenced in any PARADOX FOR WINDOWS manual.) Choose *N*ew from the File menu and *T*able from the submenu. This produces the window shown in Figure 8.31. You should choose PARADOX FOR WINDOWS by clicking on the OK button. You will see a screen similar to Figure 8.32.

Let's suppose that we wish to create a manufacturing database comprised of the relations shown in Figure 8.33. We'll walk you through the creation of the PERSNEL relation—you can then do the rest as an exercise. Type **Empno** in the Field

▼**FIGURE 8.30**

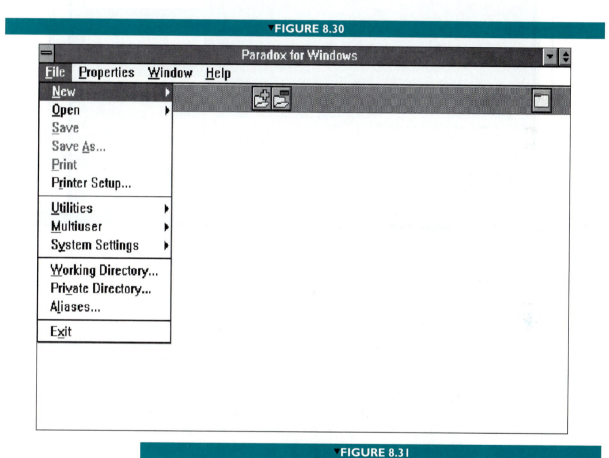

▼**FIGURE 8.31**

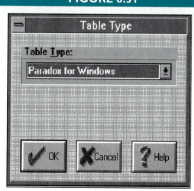

Data Manipulation

The PARADOX data manipulation language can be accessed by choosing the following menu options: *File | New | Query*. Since the query language is visual in the manner of QBE, the user does not need to memorize complex query commands. All that is necessary is to bring up the query window. The tables to be queried and examples of the required data can then be specified.

Selecting Attributes and Rows

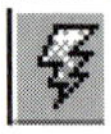

To select attributes on the query form, the user first selects *File | New | Query*, clicks on the table name and then on OK. This causes a blank sample table to appear (see Figure 8.36). The user then clicks the check box next to the desired attribute which places a "√" in that attribute's column. After the **Run Query button** (on the Speedbar) is pressed, PARADOX produces an answer table containing all of the values of the checked attributes as they currently exist in the table.

To rename an attribute during a query so that the field name in the answer table is different from the attribute name in the query table, the user simply enters "as" after the selection criterion, followed by the new attribute name. An example is given in Figure 8.37. Here we are seeking the names of all employees in Department 100. Note that we are changing the attribute name "Empname" to "Name" for the purpose of output only. As you can see, attributes are chosen by use of the "√", whereas rows are selected based upon supplied criteria—in this case "Deptno = 100".

Conjunctive and Disjunctive Queries

conjunctive query A query whose conditions are connected by "and," or an equivalent symbol.

Figure 8.38 extends the query of Figure 8.37 to request the names of all employees in Department 100 who are making more than $30,000 per year. This is a **conjunctive** ("and") query in that we are asking for a list of all employees who are in Department 100 *and* who are earning over $30,000 per year. Conjunction is readily extended to more than two conditions by simply entering all the "and" conditions on one line of the query. Conjunctions may involve several attributes, as well as several values for a single attribute.

Suppose that we require a conjunction on the values of a single attribute, such as requiring the salary to be greater than $30,000 *and* less than $50,000. This is done as shown in Figure 8.39. The comma between the desired values establishes the required conjunction.

disjunctive query A query whose conditions are connected by "or," or an equivalent symbol.

The **disjunctive** ("or") condition can be indicated in two ways. Two or more rows in a query form serve to indicate an "or" connective between each row, as shown in Figure 8.40. We have requested here a list of all employee names who are in Department 100, *or* who are earning more than $30,000 a year. A second way is

---

▼**FIGURE 8.36**

Query : <Untitled>

PERSNEL.DB — Empno — Empname — Deptno — Projno — Salary

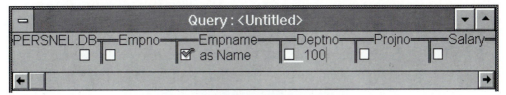

(a) The Query

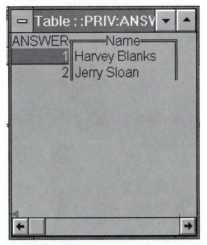

(b) The Answer

▼**FIGURE 8.37**

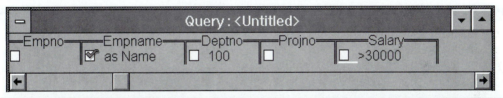

▼**FIGURE 8.38**

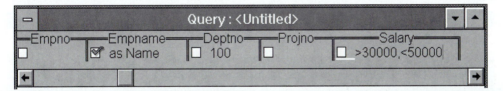

▼**FIGURE 8.39**

▼**FIGURE 8.40**

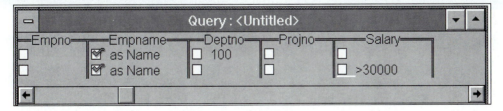

illustrated in Figure 8.41 where "or" is simply inserted between the conditions. This method can be used only where the "or" condition applies to the contents of a single attribute. In Figure 8.41 we have requested the names of employees who are assigned to Department 100, *or* who are assigned to Department 200.

As with any query language, "or" and "and" conditions can be combined within one query. An example is given in Figure 8.42. Here we have requested the names of employees who are assigned to departments 100 *or* 200 *and* who earn more than $30,000 per year.

Calculations. Calculations may be performed within the query form. All calculations must be preceded with the CALC operator. An example is seen in Figure 8.43. We have requested a calculation of the average of all salaries. In Figure 8.44, we see a similar example, only here we have requested the average salary by department. Putting a check mark in the Department column will perform the indicated calculation for groups of records having the same value in the Department attribute. In these two examples we have used the CALC operator in conjunction with the summary operator AVERAGE. Other summary operators include SUM, COUNT, MAX, and MIN. Specialized calculations may also be performed.

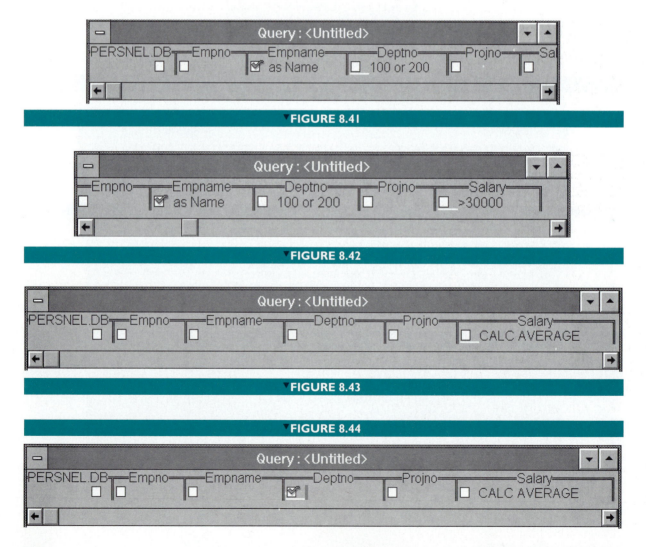

▼**FIGURE 8.41**

▼**FIGURE 8.42**

▼**FIGURE 8.43**

▼**FIGURE 8.44**

Linking Tables.   Queries involving single tables are quite simple since they only require identifying the attributes desired in the output and the conditions that must be satisfied. More complex queries generally involve linking the data in one table with that of another (or several others). This is accomplished in a straightforward way in PARADOX.

An example is shown in Figure 8.45. Here we wish to produce a list of employee names for those individuals assigned to the marketing department. The "√" denotes the attribute whose values we wish to have printed. By clicking the **Join Tables button** on the Speedbar and then clicking the attributes from the two tables that will be used as a link, PARADOX places a unique "EG" variable showing that the link has been successful. (EG comes from the Latin, *exempli gratia,* which means "for example.") The "EG01" entered into the DEPTNO columns of both the DEPTS and PERSNEL tables acts as a variable by which the tables are linked (we could just as well use "x" or "y"). However, notice that the "EG01" in the DEPTS table is restricted to that value of DEPTNO associated with the name "Marketing." Thus, if we suppose that the marketing department's number is 300, then the only allowable "EG01" in DEPTS is 300. When an employee who is associated with DEPTNO 300 is found in the PERSNEL Table, the name is retrieved as part of the query solution.

A slightly more complicated example is shown in Figure 8.46. Here we have requested a list of all vendors who supply parts for projects located in "Outland." We see that the PRPARTS and PARTS tables are linked by the variable named "EG02." Whenever a match is found on PARTNO, the two related rows are linked. Looking further at the PRPARTS table, we see that those parts are then linked to those projects in "Outland" through the variable "EG01." This variable connects the rows in the PRPARTS table to the appropriate rows in the PROJECTS table.

Join Tables button

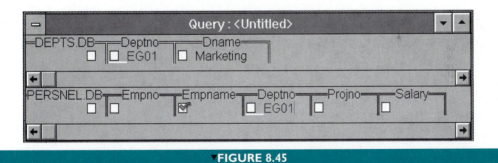

▼FIGURE 8.45

▼FIGURE 8.46

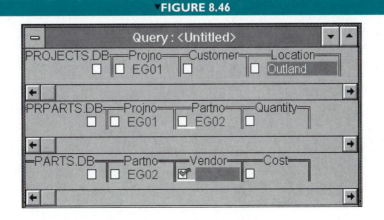

Application Language

The PARADOX Application Language (*OBJECTPAL*) is a high-level, object-oriented, and structured database programming language. It provides the user with a method of integrating PARADOX's interactive commands into an application. The writing of programs is usually viewed as a series of statements composed of simple assertions, conditional statements, and iterative statements. We briefly present the general syntax for the latter two structures.

conditional statement
A statement that tests for the presence of a condition and directs further processing accordingly.

Conditional Statements. The general syntax for IF-THEN-ELSE statements is as follows:

```
IF <condition>
    THEN <statements>
    ELSE <statements>
ENDIF
```

SWITCH statement A statement that enables testing for a series of conditions.

CASE statement Used with SWITCH statement to direct processing when a condition is found to be true.

SWITCH statements are similar to multiple IF-THEN-ELSE statements. Whereas each IF-THEN-ELSE statement contains just two branches, the SWITCH statement contains one CASE statement for each possible branch. The **CASE** statement contains a condition followed by a colon and a set of commands. Only one of the CASE statements is performed each time the SWITCH statement is executed. Here is one example:

```
SWITCH
    CASE choice = "Customer Data": <list-of-commands-A>
    CASE choice = "Transactions":  <list-of-commands-B>
    .
    .
    .
    OTHERWISE: <list-of-commands-K>
ENDSWITCH
```

The first CASE statement having a true condition is performed. If none of the CASE statement conditions is true, then the OTHERWISE statement is performed.

iteration statement A statement that may be repeated a specified number of times.

Iteration Statements. The general syntax for an **iteration statement** is as follows:

```
WHILE <condition>
    <list of statements to be executed>
ENDWHILE
```

The WHILE condition is checked and, if it is true, the list of statements is executed. Each time the condition is satisfied the list is executed. The ENDWHILE statement causes execution to be transferred again to the WHILE statement. When the WHILE condition fails, program control is passed to the first statement following the ENDWHILE.

Summary

In this chapter, we have studied the data manipulation features of Query-by-Example (QBE). We looked briefly at the history and commercial implementations of the language, and then we studied simple, single-table queries, multiple-table queries, queries with built-in functions, queries involving grouping of rows, and database change operations. At the end of our discussion, we briefly compared QBE with SQL.

QBE was developed during the seventies by IBM as a graphical, relational database language. It was later implemented and released as a commercial package, which runs together with SQL under IBM's Query Management Facility. Other vendors, such as Borland with PARADOX, have released commercial products using QBE.

QBE provides the display of example tables, which are skeletons of tables in the database. Example tables show the name of the table as well as the names of all the table's columns. Users formulate queries by entering conditions into the example tables in the columns to which the conditions apply. Variables, called example elements, can also be used to state conditions; that is, example elements can be used to connect two tables and to state more complex conditions in condition boxes. Target tables can also be used to formulate definitions of complex output.

Statistical functions applying to sets of rows in tables are also available. These functions can be used to calculate the average of a set of values, the total of a set of values, the maximum and minimum, and the total number of a set of values. Rows can also be grouped, and statistical functions can be applied to each of the individual groups. In addition, queries can be formulated to add rows, change rows, and delete rows from selected tables in the database.

QBE is used primarily as an end-user query and update language. It is logically weaker than SQL, since it cannot be embedded in the programs of a traditional language. Still, it is much easier to use than a purely textual language and will probably have substantial importance for a number of years.

We also explored a microcomputer implementation of QBE concepts called PARADOX FOR WINDOWS.

Review Questions

1. Define each of the following terms in your own words.
   a. graphical language
   b. example table
   c. target table
   d. example element
   e. condition box

2. Discuss the relationship between SQL and QBE.

3. When should each of the following be used in a QBE query?
   a. Condition box
   b. Target table
   c. Example element
   d. Multiple example tables

4. Discuss the strengths and weaknesses of QBE as a relational language.

C H A P T E R

CLIENT/SERVER DATABASE SYSTEMS

*"**S**o what exactly is client/server?"*

Susan Broadbent and Sanford Mallon are discussing the possibilities of changing their home office operation from a traditional mainframe to a client/server platform. Susan is reluctant to proceed until she can see a clear advantage to making a change.

Sanford replies, "Instead of having a single, powerful, mainframe computer which handles all of our main applications, a client/server platform is a network which links personal desktop computers with powerful computers called servers. Our database management system will run on the server and the other computers will access the database over the network through the server."

"Then what advantages does this approach offer?"

"All of our people already have desktop machines they use for stand-alone applications like word processing and spreadsheets. By linking them we have all the advantages of a network, such as software sharing and electronic mail, but in addition we can get distinct client/server advantages."

"Such as?"

"The server will run a powerful, dedicated DBMS while the client machines will each have their own Graphical User Interfaces (GUIs) to give much more powerful and easy-to-use presentations of data, reports, and so on. In addition, our systems staff will have powerful tools to develop systems on the client machines and at the same time they can use all the tools available for the DBMS. We'll get a lot more function out of the computers we already own, thus leveraging our capital investment."

"Now, that's interesting. Let's look into it further."

We have discussed some initial aspects of client/server systems in earlier chapters. In this chapter we will expand on that discussion, illustrating the functions that are available in client/server systems both at the DBMS or server end and at the application development or client end. After reading this chapter you will be able to:

▼ Understand the division of labor made possible by the client/server approach and see how that division benefits organizations by allowing full use of their systems' capacity.

▼ Define database schemas in the language of a server DBMS, utilizing many powerful capabilities.

▼ Utilize the data manipulation language of a server DBMS to write programs that take advantage of the unique power of relational database concepts.

▼ Understand the modern application development environment by which client systems are produced that can interact with server DBMSs.

Obviously, if we specify a default value for a column, then a null value will *not* be automatically entered if the user fails to enter a value. The default value will be entered instead. Thus, if we enter a value in the *Default* box, it doesn't matter what we've specified with regard to null values. The entry in the *Nulls* box is made obsolete by any entry in the *Default* box. We will normally make an entry in the *Nulls* box as if no default were going to be specified, since if a default is ever dropped we want the *Nulls* box to have the appropriate entry.

Now let's define a default for the skill_type column. By default we want a worker's skill type to be "Framing." We define the default by accessing the *Manage Defaults* box, which is virtually identical to the *Manage Rules* box (Figure 9.4) and works in the same way. We enter:

```
CREATE DEFAULT skill_deflt AS
'Framing'
```

and create this default definition. Now it can be used in any table in which we wish to define 'Framing' as a default. In the table definition screen we enter "skill_deflt" in the *Default* box for the skill_type column. In general, a default value must be a constant expression. That is, it cannot include variable values or table or column names, but only constant values, possibly connected by arithmetic operators.

Now we are ready to define a rule for this column to restrict the possible values the user can enter. We want skill type to be limited to the values Electric, Plumbing, Framing, and Roofing, so we will construct a rule to that effect:

```
CREATE RULE valid_skill_type AS
@skill_type in ('Electric', 'Plumbing', 'Framing', 'Roofing')
```

After creating this rule, we enter its name, valid_skill_type, in the *Rule* box, and the definition of the skill_type column is now complete.

The last column in the table is supv_id. This will also have a datatype of id_type. However, we also want to specify a default value. We leave it as an exercise for you to specify a default value of 3231 for supv_id (see Problem 3). The table can now be created. The other tables, assignment and building, can be created in a similar manner (see Problem 5).

Defining Primary and Foreign Keys.   In order to use the DBMS's automatic enforcement of the relational models entity and referential integrity rules, we must define primary and foreign keys. This is a rather simple process, which we discuss now. We will be using portions of Oracle's command language. Before we begin, we remark that primary and foreign keys are defined as **constraints** in Oracle. That is, they are restrictions on the possible values of tuples and attributes in the database tables. For our discussion, we assume the following schema.

constraint A restriction on the possible values of tuples and attributes in a database.

```
worker (worker_id, name, hourly_rate, skill_type, supv_id)
Foreign Key:      supv_id references worker
assignment (worker_id, bldg_id, start_date, num_days)
Foreign Keys:     worker_id references worker
                  bldg_id references building
building (bldg_id, bldg_address, type, qlty_level, status)
assignment_tool (worker_id, bldg_id, tool, start_date, end_date)
Foreign Key:      worker_id, bldg_id reference assignment
```

First, we need to define primary keys. In the command language of Oracle, primary keys are defined within the context of a table definition. For example, suppose we wished to define the worker table:

```
CREATE TABLE worker
   (worker_id id_type CONSTRAINT pk_wid PRIMARY KEY,
    ...
```

We have shown the beginning of the definition of the worker table, defining the first column, worker_id, with datatype, id_type. We have highlighted the definition of worker_id as a primary key. The keyword, CONSTRAINT, indicates that what follows is a constraint on that column. "pk_wid" is the name we have given to the constraint. If there are attempts to violate this constraint, the system will send an error message, identifying the constraint by name. After the constraint name, the keywords, PRIMARY KEY, indicate that this column, worker_id, is to be a primary key. This means that its values must be unique within the worker relation and that it can never be null. This constraint is called a **column constraint** because it is stated as part of the definition of a column.

column constraint A constraint that is stated in the definition of a column in a table.

Now let's define the primary key of the assignment table. This key consists of two columns, worker_id and bldg_id, and therefore cannot be defined as a column constraint. Instead, it must be defined as a table constraint, as part of the table definition, but not as part of the definition of any column. We define it within the context of a table definition:

```
CREATE TABLE assignment
   (worker_id id_type,
    bldg_id id_type,
    ... ,
    CONSTRAINT pk_wkblid PRIMARY KEY (worker_id, bldg_id))
```

As in the preceding example, we have highlighted the primary key constraint definition. The name of the constraint is "pk_wkblid." The keywords, PRIMARY KEY, indicate that what follows in parentheses (worker_id, bldg_id) together constitute a primary key for this table. Note that this definition does not apply to any single column and, therefore, is not a column constraint. Rather it is a **table constraint** because it constrains the values of these columns seen as a unit within this table. The columns worker_id and bldg_id, taken together, must have unique values in the table, and neither column can be null.

table constraint A constraint that applies to multiple columns in a table simultaneously.

If we assume that all primary keys in our schema have been defined, we can now turn to the definitions of foreign keys. As with primary keys, these can be defined through column constraints, if they are single-column foreign keys, or table constraints, if they are multicolumn foreign keys. For an example of single-column foreign keys, let's look again at the definition of the assignment table:

```
CREATE TABLE assignment
   (worker_id id_type REFERENCES worker,
    bldg_id id_type REFERENCES building,
    ...
```

Note that we did not use the CONSTRAINT keyword this time. We could have used it, but since it is optional we don't have to. The keyword, REFERENCES, indicates a foreign key definition. The column is a foreign key referencing the table indicated

perform updates on those tuples. But now we have the additional capability of using calculations on relations to make decisions.

The conditional expression which controls the execution of an IF statement can include constants, local variables, and subqueries. It can include column names only as part of subqueries. Any other reference to a column name will be ambiguous, since it would not be clear which tuple is being referred to. A subquery can only be used if it follows an EXISTS keyword or if it produces a single value (as in the preceding example) and can, therefore, be compared with a constant or local variable value.

A second example shows that we can use more than one select statement in a single conditional expression. Suppose we want to increase the wage of the plumbers if their current average wage is more than a dollar under the average wage of the roofers:

```
IF (select avg(hrly_rate) from worker
      where skill_type = 'Plumbing') <
    (select avg(hrly_rate) from worker
      where skill_type = 'Roofing') + 1.00
  update worker
    set hrly_rate = hrly_rate + .50
    where skill_type = 'Plumbing'
```

Again, we have highlighted the conditional expression. As you can see, it contains two queries, each of which produces an average wage. A comparison is made between these, and if the comparison holds, the update statement is executed.

As a third example, to illustrate the EXISTS operator, suppose we want to give everyone a raise if H. Rickover is anyone's supervisor:

```
IF EXISTS (select * from worker where supv_id in
        (select worker_id from worker
          where worker_name = 'H. Rickover'))
  BEGIN
    update worker
      set hrly_rate = hrly_rate + .50
    print 'Let''s all celebrate!!!'
  END
ELSE
  BEGIN
    update worker
      set hrly_rate = hrly_rate - .50
    print 'Sorry, guys, that''s the way it goes!!'
  END
```

This example is a little complex, so we will pause to give some additional explanation. The condition contains a query with a subquery:

```
select * from worker where supv_id in
        (select worker_id from worker
          where worker_name = 'H. Rickover')
```

The subquery

```
(select worker_id from worker
        where worker_name = 'H. Rickover')
```

will give us H. Rickover's worker_id. The main query then will select all tuples that have H. Rickover as their supervisor. Finally, the complete condition

```
EXISTS (select * from worker where supv_id in
        (select worker_id from worker
          where worker_name = 'H. Rickover'))
```

will be true only if there are any workers who have H. Rickover as their supervisor. This corresponds with the condition stated at the beginning. Now, if any such workers exist, we want to give everyone a $0.50 raise. Otherwise, we decrease everyone's wage by $0.50.

In this example then we also illustrated the ELSE in the IF statement, the print command, and the use of BEGIN...END to create statement blocks. The ELSE is operative whenever the conditional expression is false. In this case, we reduce everyone's wage by $0.50. The print command sends a message to the user. Its message is delimited by single quotes. If an apostrophe is part of the message, it is indicated through the use of two apostrophes.

IF statements can be nested within other IF statements, following the IF or the ELSE. The number of nesting levels is not limited.

SQL statements work on relations as a whole, so it's only logical that IF statements controlling their execution should use conditions that apply to relations as a whole as well. The examples given previously illustrate their application.

WHILE statement A statement which uses a condition to control the iterative execution of a statement block.

WHILE Statements: Iterative Execution.   The syntax of the **WHILE statement** is as follows:

```
WHILE <conditional expression>
  <statement block>
```

The WHILE statement causes the statement block to be repeatedly executed, as long as the conditional expression evaluates to true. The conditional expression in this statement has the same definition as in the IF statement. Let's look at an example.

Suppose we want to double everyone's pay until the average pay for plumbers is above $20.00. If the plumbers' average pay is already above $20.00, we do nothing, otherwise we double everyone's pay:

```
WHILE (select avg(hrly_rate) from worker
       where skill_type = 'Plumbing') < 20.00
  BEGIN
    print 'We''re doubling your pay!!!'
    update worker
      set hrly_rate = 2 * hrly_rate
  END
```

Again, as with the IF statement, the condition controlling execution of the WHILE loop contains a query which performs a calculation on the worker relation as a whole. As long as this condition is true, the statements within the WHILE loop will execute. Thus, suppose the average wage for plumbers is $4.50. Then everybody's wage will be doubled, and the message "We're doubling your pay!!!" will be printed. Now the average wage for plumbers will be $9.00. Since that is still less than $20.00, everybody's wage will be doubled again, and the message will appear a second time. Now the average wage for plumbers is $18.00. Again, it is less than

$20.00, so everybody's wage will be doubled a third and final time. And, of course, the message will be printed a third time as well. (Nice program, *nicht wahr*? Don't you wish *your* boss had it?)

Once a statement block begins executing in a WHILE loop, it will ordinarily continue executing until it is complete. Even if the value of the conditional expression changes to false before the end of the statement block, execution continues. After the statement block has been executed entirely, the conditional expression is evaluated again, and, if it is true, execution of the statement block is repeated. If the expression is false, execution starts at the statement after the WHILE loop's statement block. Under some circumstances, however, we would prefer to break out of the WHILE loop or to start it over again before the statement block is finished. In the next section we see how this can be done.

Using BREAK and CONTINUE.   The keyword **BREAK** tells the system to immediately exit from the WHILE loop and begin execution with the first statement after the WHILE's statement block. **CONTINUE** tells it to ignore the remainder of the statement block, to evaluate the conditional expression, and, if true, to execute the statement block again. This will be clarified with a detailed example. Assume we want to repeat a block of code as long as everybody's wage is below $40.00:

```
(I)    WHILE (select max(hrly_rate) from worker) < 40.00
       BEGIN
(II)      update worker
             set hrly_rate = 1.1 * hrly_rate
(III)     IF (select avg(hrly_rate) from worker) < 20.00
             CONTINUE
(IV)      IF (select min(hrly_rate) from worker) > 15.00
             BREAK
(V)       update worker
             set hrly_rate = hrly_rate + 1.00
             where skill_type = 'Plumbing'
       END
(VI) .....
```

For ease of reference we have labeled the significant statements in this example with Roman numerals. This WHILE loop will be executed as long as the maximum wage paid any worker is under $40.00 (statement (I)). Statement (II) shows that we wish to give every worker a 10 percent raise each time through the loop. Statement (III) checks to see if the average wage for all workers is below $20.00. If so, CONTINUE is executed, meaning that all the rest of the statements in the loop are skipped and control returns again to statement (I). Once the average wage reaches $20.00, statement (IV) is executed. If the minimum wage is larger than $15.00, BREAK is executed, and statement (VI) (which is not specified) is given control. If the minimum wage does not exceed $15.00, statement (V) is executed, and $1.00 is added to the wage of plumbers. After statement (V), control returns again to statement (I) where the system checks again whether the maximum wage is less than $40.00. If it is, the loop executes again. Otherwise, control goes to statement (VI).

DECLARE and Local Variables.   No programming language would be complete without **local variables** in which to place temporary working values. In SQL Server's language such variables are declared, given a system or user-defined datatype, assigned a value via a select statement, and used within the same procedure.

Let's look at an example that uses a local variable to determine execution of a WHILE loop.

We declare the local variable by giving it a name beginning with @:

```
declare @index int   /* "int" means integer */
select @index = 3
WHILE @index > 0
   BEGIN
      delete worker where hrly_rate > 20.00
      update worker set hrly_rate = hrly_rate * 1.1
      select @index = @index - 1
   END
```

This example executes the WHILE loop exactly three times. Each time we delete all workers making over $20.00/hour and then increase everyone else's wage by 10 percent. The first line also illustrates how comments can be added to programs.

Stored Procedures

Stored procedures are SQL programs that are compiled the first time they're executed and then stored for later use. They provide a number of advantages over programs that are written, immediately executed, then never used again: (1) Procedures that have already been compiled execute very fast. (2) They can receive and return **parameters**—variables used to pass data into and out of stored procedures—making it possible to create utility modules or to otherwise modularize a large and complex program. Let's look at an example.

Suppose we frequently want a count of the number of workers in the worker relation. After defining a local variable, @worker_count, we *could* write the query:

```
select @worker_count = count(*) from worker
```

Or, instead, we could create a procedure:

```
create procedure count_workers @wo_count int output
```

as

```
select @wo_count = count(*) from worker
```

The first line of this statement

```
create procedure count_workers @wo_count int output
```

names the procedure, "count_workers," and immediately afterward defines any parameters with their datatypes and states whether they are input or output. In our example, @wo_count is a parameter of type integer ("int"), which is used for output. Now let's see how this procedure will work.

When the procedure is called, its query part

```
select @wo_count = count(*) from worker
```

is executed, and the result is placed in the output variable @wo_count and returned to the calling program. Output parameters are identified by placing "output" or

parameter A variable used to pass data into and out of a stored procedure.

"out" after their datatype definition. Input parameters are any parameters that are not identified as output parameters. The keyword "as" signals the end of the parameter definitions and the beginning of the procedure definition. Everything after "as" constitutes the executable part of the procedure.

Now let's see how this procedure, count_workers, is executed. First, we define the local variable, @worker_count, as an integer variable which will receive the output value of the procedure. Then we execute the procedure:

```
declare @worker_count int
execute count_workers @worker_count output
```

This execute statement will cause the count_workers procedure defined previously to be executed, and the result of the procedure will be placed in the local variable, @worker_count.

You can see that this approach is slightly simpler than writing out the query

```
select @wo_count = count(*) from worker
```

every time. The advantage of using stored procedures is significantly greater, of course, if the procedure itself is larger and more complex.

As a second, more complex example, suppose we would like a stored procedure to calculate the average wage of workers by an identified skill type. That is, the calling program passes a skill type to the stored procedure, and the stored procedure returns the average wage for workers having that skill type. We would create the procedure, calc_avg_wage, as follows:

```
create procedure calc_avg_wage @avg_hrly_rate money output,
   @skill_type char(8)
as
select @avg_hrly_rate = avg(hrly_rate)
from worker
where skill_type = @skill_type
```

This stored procedure has an output parameter, @avg_hrly_rate, and an input parameter, @skill_type. The calling program must indicate a local variable of type money to hold the output parameter value and a value for skill type. Moreover, it must give these parameters in the same order as they were listed when the procedure was created. Here is an example of the execution of calc_avg_wage that does all this:

```
declare @avg_wage money
exec calc_avg_wage @avg_wage output, Plumbing
```

Note that "exec" can be used as shorthand for "execute." Although the input value, "Plumbing," is character data, it does not need to be in quotes unless it has an embedded blank, punctuation, or begins with a numeral. The calc_avg_wage procedure will use "Plumbing" as its value for @skill_type and so will execute as:

```
select @avg_hrly_rate = avg(hrly_rate)
from worker
where skill_type = 'Plumbing'
```

It will calculate the average hourly rate for plumbers, and when it returns to the calling program, this result will be placed in the variable @avg_wage.

default parameter value The value of a parameter supplied by the system if the calling program omits the value.

Default Values.   In defining a stored procedure, it's possible to specify **default parameter values.** If the calling program omits a value for an input parameter, then the default value is used by the program. The default value can be any valid value for the datatype, including null. Let's look at an example that uses null. We shall merely modify the previous example. This way, if the calling program only specifies the output parameter but no skill type, we will calculate the average wage for *all* workers. The modified procedure looks like this:

```
create procedure calc_avg_wage @avg_hrly_rate money output,
    @skill_type char(8) = null
as
if @skill_type = null
    select @avg_hrly_rate = avg(hrly_rate)
    from worker
else
    select @avg_hrly_rate = avg(hrly_rate)
    from worker
    where skill_type = @skill_type
```

If you compare this version of the procedure with the previous version, you will see that the default is defined immediately after the datatype definition of the parameter:

```
@skill_type char(8) = null
```

By placing "= null" after the parameter definition, we are saying that if no value is passed for this parameter, the parameter assumes the value of null. The executable part of the procedure then is modified to handle the possibility that the calling program did not pass a skill type.

Using RETURN.   When the last statement of a procedure is executed, the procedure is finished and returns control to the calling procedure. What if the logic of the procedure is such that we want to exit early? The RETURN statement causes the stored procedure to terminate and immediately return control to the calling program. Suppose we want to combine a variety of functions in a single stored procedure. For example, we want to allow the user to request the maximum, minimum, or average wage from worker. A procedure to do this would be:

```
create procedure calc_wage_fcns @fcn_type char(3),
        @ret_value money output
as
    if fcn_type = 'max'
        begin
            select @ret_value = max(hrly_rate) from worker
            return
        end
    if fcn_type = 'min'
        begin
            select @ret_value = min(hrly_rate) from worker
            return
        end
    if fcn_type = 'avg'
        begin
            select @ret_value = avg(hrly_rate) from worker
            return
        end
```

or the deleted table is empty, then the update statement using it will simply have no effect on the worker relation. Thus, this trigger will work as we wished it to work.

Using Triggers in SQL Server and Oracle.   Triggers fire whenever the specified type of update (insert, delete, update) occurs to the table. It doesn't matter which user or which program makes the update. If a trigger is defined for that update, then it will fire. Consequently, it is important to reserve the use of triggers to those operations that must *always* be performed following the specified update. In the examples we gave previously, you can see situations in which triggers would be appropriately used. But there are many others.

One very important use of triggers is in enforcing business and other integrity rules. For example, SQL Server uses triggers to enforce primary key uniqueness and referential integrity. In Oracle, on the other hand, these features are built into the data definition language. That is, in Oracle we merely declare certain attributes to be primary or foreign keys and the uniqueness and referential integrity are automatically maintained. But in SQL Server triggers must be defined to enforce these constraints. Triggers, then, are essential tools for database integrity in SQL Server.

However, Oracle databases require triggers for similar reasons as well. Although primary and foreign keys are enforced automatically, any business rule that requires reference to other database tables can only be enforced in Oracle through a trigger. You will recall that as part of database schema definition Oracle allows the definition of CHECK constraints to enforce rules on the database. Recall also, however, that CHECK constraints may not include queries that reference other tables or even other tuples in the same table. That is, CHECK constraints can only look at one tuple at a time. Thus, consider a rule like

"No worker may be scheduled for more than 100 days of work at a time"

which requires a query on the assignment table to calculate the total number of days (num_days) a given worker has in assignments. It is impossible to declare a CHECK constraint to enforce this rule. However, a trigger can enforce it very nicely.

▼ Developing Client Applications

The preceding section described the database or server side of client/server applications. In this section we will look at an application development environment, PowerBuilder, which is used to build client-side applications that can interface over networks with database systems. PowerBuilder is a graphical application development environment which runs in Windows. It can be used to create application programs that interface with a large number of different commercial relational database management systems (DBMSs). To help in the creation of application programs, PowerBuilder provides a number of **painters,** which are interactive subprograms that accomplish specific types of functions needed for full application development. Both PowerBuilder and the applications developed using it will run on either a stand-alone or client/server platform.

painter An interactive subprogram that performs a specific type of functionality needed for full application development.

PowerBuilder's Approach

Logically, the process of developing applications in PowerBuilder is as follows:

1. First, a database must be defined. This involves giving the database a name, defining tables with their columns, datatypes, keys, foreign keys, and so on. We addressed this step in the first part of the chapter and assume it has already been accomplished.

2. After the database has been defined, we can start developing applications. This is done using PowerBuilder's painters. Normally, for each application we must perform three major steps:

    a. Define the application. This is done with the Application painter.

    b. Define the application's windows. This is done with the Window painter. Windows are the means whereby users can interact with the application. To give users the capabilities needed, we define windows with buttons, various list boxes and data input boxes, and menus. Various other painters are used to accomplish all these functions.

    c. The application will act on data in the database. Therefore, we must identify the data needed for input, the data to be changed, and the data which will be output. This data identification is done through DataWindows, which are defined in the DataWindow painter. DataWindows must be defined in the DataWindow painter before they can be placed in a window. That is, this step must be done before the previous step can be completed.

Using PowerBuilder

The main screen of the PowerBuilder application development environment is shown in Figure 9.8. This screen contains a title bar at the top, with a menu bar on the next line, and the "PowerBar" on the third line. The PowerBar shows the icons

▼FIGURE 9.11 PREMIER CONSTRUCTION COMPANY DATABASE

WORKER

WORKER_ID	WORKER_NAME	HRLY_RATE	SKILL_TYPE	SUPV_ID
1235	M. Faraday	12.50	Electric	1311
1412	C. Nemo	13.75	Plumbing	1520
2920	R. Garret	10.00	Roofing	2920
3231	P. Mason	17.40	Framing	3231
1520	H. Rickover	11.75	Plumbing	1520
1311	C. Coulomb	15.50	Electric	1311
3001	J. Barrister	8.20	Framing	3231

ASSIGNMENT

WORKER_ID	BLDG_ID	START_DATE	NUM_DAYS
1235	312	10/10	5
1412	312	10/01	10
1235	515	10/17	22
2920	460	10/05	18
1412	460	12/08	18
2920	435	10/28	10
2920	210	11/10	15
3231	111	10/10	8
1412	435	10/15	15
1412	515	11/05	8
3231	312	10/24	20
1520	515	10/09	14
1311	435	10/08	12
1412	210	11/15	12
1412	111	12/01	4
3001	111	10/08	14
1311	460	10/23	24
1520	312	10/30	17
3001	210	10/27	14

BUILDING

BLDG_ID	BLDG_ADDRESS	TYPE	QLTY_LEVEL	STATUS
312	123 Elm	Office	2	2
435	456 Maple	Retail	1	1
515	789 Oak	Residence	3	1
210	1011 Birch	Office	3	1
111	1213 Aspen	Office	4	1
460	1415 Beech	Warehouse	3	3

DataWindow A SQL query which can be placed in a window.

placed in our application's window, as shown in Figure 9.10. A **DataWindow** is actually a SQL query which can be placed in a window. So, before we can create the application's window, we must create the DataWindows.

After we have completed our application, it will work as follows. When the application starts, it will query the worker table and will list all workers in the top data window. Then, as the user clicks on the line of some selected worker, the second window containing all the worker's building assignments will fill. Finally, a click on any assignment tuple in the second window will cause the third window containing complete information about the building to be displayed.

To create the completed application, we must proceed as follows:

1. First, we define the application, using the Application painter.
2. Next, we define the three DataWindows, using the DataWindow painter.
3. Finally, we define the application's window, using the Window painter.

Application painter A painter used to define the general aspects of an application, such as the application's name and library.

So, let us begin with step 1. If we were using PowerBuilder, we would enter the **Application painter** by clicking on the **Appl** button in the PowerBar. After we obtain the Save Application box (Figure 9.12), we name the application by typing "a_worker_assignment_building" in the first box. This application will display data from the worker, assignment, and building tables, and so we indicate this by using these table names. We prefix them with "a_" as a convention to indicate that this is an application for these tables. In the **Comments:** box we enter, "This application displays all workers, and assignment and building information for a selected worker." We place in the **Libraries:** box the file name a_wab.pbl to indicate this is where we want all objects having to do with this application to be placed. The suffix ".pbl" stands for "PowerBuilder library" and is a standard suffix in PowerBuilder for this purpose. PowerBuilder will automatically control this library and will place in and retrieve from it all objects we create or update for use in our application.

We have now defined the general aspects of our application. A summary description of what we have done so far in our application is shown in Figure 9.13. Our next step is to create the DataWindows we will use in it.

▼FIGURE 9.12 THE SAVE APPLICATION BOX

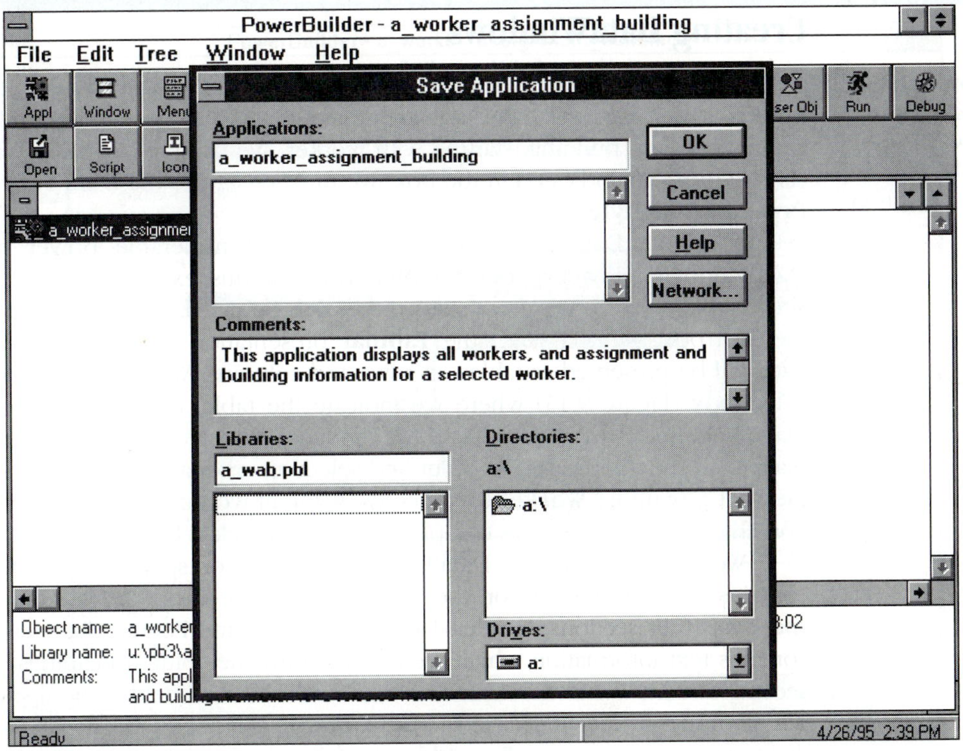

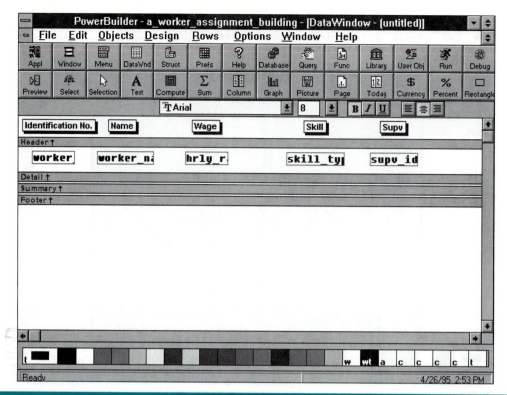

▼**FIGURE 9.16 DATAWINDOW PAINTER WORKSPACE**

Preview A feature that allows the developer to see how a DataWindow will appear when placed in a window.

now, we can use PowerBuilder's **Preview** feature to see how the DataWindow will look (Figure 9.17). Note that the Header information shows in the DataWindow just as we saw it on the previous screen. However, the Detail information lists the actual data contained in the worker table—one line for each tuple. We could use the scroll bar on the right to display all the tuples of the table. If some of the data fields are not long enough or are not properly aligned, we can return to the DataWindow workspace to change them. When we're finished with this, we will have completed our definition of the DataWindow for the worker table. We name it d_worker and store it in the library for this application.

Our second DataWindow will be for the assignment table. We will again designate **Quick Select** for the data source and **Tabular** as the presentation style. In the Quick Select box we indicate the assignment table with all its columns and mark **Worker Id** and **Bldg Id** as **Ascending** in the Sort order. Before we are finished with this Quick Select, however, we must do something different from what we did with the first DataWindow.

Recall how we want to use this DataWindow. Unlike the previous DataWindow which displays a list of *all* workers, we will only display assignment tuples for one worker at a time. The user will look at the list of workers in the first DataWindow and will click on a particular worker row. We now want to display in the second DataWindow all assignment tuples for the indicated worker. Thus, we want this window to retrieve only those tuples that apply to a user-selected worker. We must therefore modify the data query for the assignment table's DataWindow by giving it a Where clause that will cause it to display only the assignment tuples of the selected worker. We do this by placing in the Where clause a variable which will con-

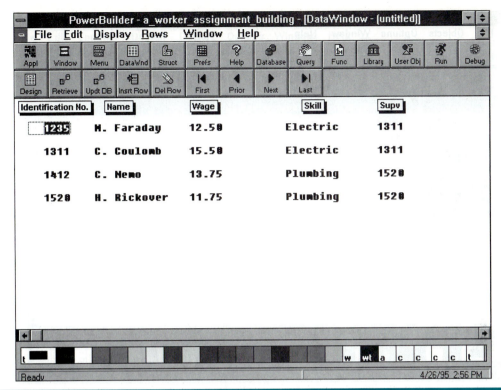

▼FIGURE 9.17 USING THE PREVIEW FEATURE TO SEE HOW THE DATAWINDOW WILL LOOK

tain the selected Worker_Id as an argument value. This value will be placed in the variable at execution time when the user clicks on the worker tuple. To make the needed modification to the assignment table's DataWindow, we now access a new window showing the assignment table with all its columns and a new set of buttons that allows us to build more complex queries (Figure 9.18).

First, we define the retrieval argument variable we indicated previously. This retrieval argument variable, named ra_worker_id, will contain the Worker_Id for the worker whose assignment tuples we want to retrieve. Now we use the functions of this screen to construct a Where clause that looks like

```
WHERE worker_id = :ra_worker_id
```

(The colon in :ra_worker_id indicates that ra_worker_id is a variable rather than a column in the database.) After defining the Where clause, we return to the DataWindow painter workspace (see Figure 9.16) and make any necessary modifications as we did with the first DataWindow. We have now completed the definition of the second DataWindow. We name it d_assignment and store it in the library.

To define the third DataWindow, we essentially repeat the process we used for the second DataWindow. Define data source and presentation style as before and choose the building table with all its columns to be displayed. Again we must define a retrieval argument because we are only interested in seeing information for the building in the assignment tuple the user clicks on. This time we define the retrieval argument as ra_bldg_id and build the following Where clause:

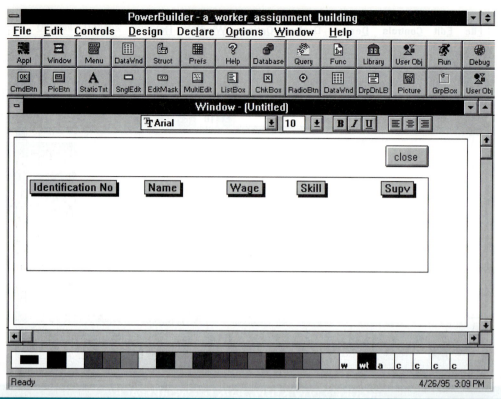

▼FIGURE 9.20 PLACING A DATAWINDOW CONTROL IN A WINDOW

▼FIGURE 9.21 THE FINAL DESIGN OF THE WINDOW FOR WORKER_ASSIGNMENT_BUILDING

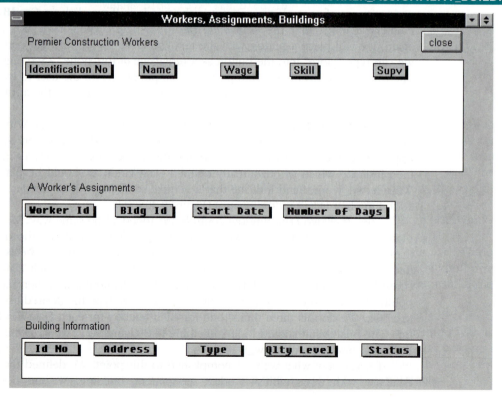

process of creating an application that will access that database, list the tuples of all the workers in it, and list the assignment tuples for a selected worker as well as the building tuple for a selected assignment tuple. In creating that application we used the Application painter to define it and give it a name, we used the DataWindow painter to define three DataWindow objects (d_worker, d_assignment, and d_building), and we used the Window painter to create a simple window containing controls for the three DataWindows and a command button to close the application. To outward appearances we have done everything necessary for our application.

But something is missing. We have all the pieces we need—the database, the application, the DataWindows, and the window with its controls—but we haven't tied them all together completely. To do that we must write scripts for the controls as well as for the window and application themselves. These scripts, containing commands with appropriate parameters, will make sure that the right thing happens at the right time.

Unfortunately, the script language for PowerBuilder is quite large and complicated and is, therefore, beyond the scope of this book. However, before ending this section we will indicate the tasks for which scripts must be written to make our application function properly. We will also describe the logic behind the structure of the application and its scripts. Though we will not cover the script language's specific syntax, you will see more clearly the philosophy embodied in it.

event-driven Application feature that means scripts are written to respond to events that take place.

PowerBuilder applications are **event-driven.** This means that the scripts are written to respond to events that take place. Examples of events include the beginning of an application, the opening of a window, and the clicking on a button or a line in a DataWindow. Each time an event occurs the script for that event executes. Thus, to write the correct script for each event we need to know what the event is supposed to accomplish in the application. To do this we need to understand the overall structure of the application and how each piece fits into that structure.

Applications are structured hierarchically. The first event in any application is the execution of the application itself. When the user initiates the application, the script for the "open" event for the application executes. One of the main duties of this script will normally be to open the initial window of the application. This triggers a new event: the open event for the initial window. This in turn causes a new script to be executed. After the window displays, the user has a series of options—buttons that may be pushed, DataWindows that can be scrolled or lines to be clicked on, and so on. These are additional events for which scripts may be written. Altogether the scripts will determine what processing takes place in response to which events.

Now let's look at the processing and events that logically need to take place in our application, and by so doing we will identify which scripts need to be written.

Event 1: **Application Open Event.** This event will set up a transaction communication area, which is needed to identify the DBMS the application will be communicating with, and will open the initial window (w_wab). Opening the initial window is itself an event for which a script must be written.

Event 2: **Window Open Event.** When the initial window (w_wab) opens, we want the window to display and the list of workers from the worker table to display in the topmost DataWindow. Therefore, a script needs to be written to make sure this happens.

Event 3: **Click on a Worker Line Event.** The user viewing the list of workers in the topmost DataWindow can scroll the list up and down and see all workers. If the list of the worker's building assignments is desired, the user need merely click on the worker's data line. This triggers an event for which a script must be written. This script will cause all assignment tuples for the indicated worker to display in the second DataWindow.

Event 4: **Click on an Assignment Line Event.** The user may obtain information about the building of a particular assignment by clicking on that assignment's line in the DataWindow. This triggers an event for which a script must retrieve the indicated building tuple and display it in the third DataWindow.

Event 5: **Click on the Close Command Button.** The user can end the application by simply clicking on this button.

These are all the events of our application. The next step for the developer then would be to develop the scripts for each of these. After this has been done, our application is finished, and we can test it by running it. Initially, it will show all the workers listed in the topmost DataWindow with a vertical scroll bar on the right. If we click on a worker tuple, then all the assignment tuples for that worker will be listed. If we then click on an assignment tuple, the building information will be displayed.

▼ Some Final Comments

We have given some detailed coverage of client application development systems (PowerBuilder) and server DBMSs (Oracle and SQL Server). You will note that both types of systems include programming languages that allow extensive manipulation of data for computation, update, and presentation. One advantage of the open-systems concept mentioned in Chapter 1 is that we can have "the best of both worlds" provided a good interface between the two worlds exists.

In the present example experience shows that there are certain operations that are better performed at the database level and certain that are better at the client level. In particular, if we find that one of the systems (say the client system) lacks a certain capability, we can turn to the database management system and develop the capability there. For example, it may be difficult to perform manipulation of sets of tuples at the client level, but the DBMS is optimized to provide precisely such manipulation. Thus, the system developer has multiple tools available for solving problems. If a problem can't be handled easily by the DBMS language, perhaps it can be by the client-oriented language, and vice versa. By having multiple tools available, we have more means at our disposal for delivering powerful, timely systems.

An additional advantage of the client/server approach and the system development software found at the client and the server nodes is that the principle of modularization is enforced by the separation of hardware. Thus, we have no choice but to split some of the functions into logically and physically separated pieces. The interfaces between these pieces must be clearly defined and precisely implemented, so that all the advantages of modularization that have been traditionally identified are now required of the system developer.

Hopefully, this chapter has given you some feeling for the significant potential of client/server systems to greatly expand the power of applications systems in business applications. A review of the current trade literature leaves little doubt that client/server systems are here to stay and that they will have an increasingly important impact on all of our professional lives for some time into the future.

Summary

In this chapter we expanded on the ideas associated with client/server database systems that were introduced in earlier chapters. We explained that a client/server platform is a network of computers, some of which act as servers in providing services of varying types to the other client computers. By separating function we can specialize our hardware systems, optimizing client machines and server machines so that each can do its assigned task better. We looked at software systems, both for server computers and client computers. We examined the SQL Server and Oracle DBMSs in some detail, looking at their data definition and data manipulation features. Then we reviewed PowerBuilder, an environment for developing applications on client computers.

The data definition languages of SQL Server and Oracle allow us to define database tables by creating user-defined datatypes, tables, columns, and constraints on all of these. User-defined datatypes are developed from basic system-supplied datatypes by adding extra restrictions to these. These datatypes can then be used in the definition of specific columns within tables. In defining tables we define columns with their datatypes and constraints. Constraints can be rules that restrict the values that can be in columns, they can indicate whether null values are allowed, and they can also enforce uniqueness of the column's value within the table. They also define single-column or multicolumn primary keys and foreign keys. Finally, constraints can be more general by using the concept of a CHECK constraint, which indicates a rule that each tuple must adhere to.

The data manipulation languages of these two DBMSs are very powerful, allowing for blocks of statements, IF statements, WHILE loops, local variables, and stored procedures with passed input and output parameters. The condition used with the IF and WHILE statements, unlike typical conditions in programming languages, can use values computed from whole relations rather than merely from single tuples within relations. These systems also support triggers, which are programs written in the data manipulation language, and which execute every time a database change of a specified type (either insert, delete, or update) occurs to a specified relation. They allow for the centralized enforcement of a wide range of types of business rules and the calculation of important derived values.

Application development of client systems can take place in an environment that provides the capabilities long established in graphical user interfaces. Using PowerBuilder as an example, we studied the definition of applications, DataWindows which define queries and presentation of query results, and windows into which DataWindows and other user-oriented controls are placed. We also described the types of events that the user could cause to happen in a window and for which we would write program scripts that would respond properly to these events.

Finally, we noted that client and server system development environments provide us with the opportunity of using multiple tools in creating modularized systems of considerable power and flexibility.

Review Questions

1. Define each of the following terms in your own words:
  a. Graphical User Interface (GUI)
  b. rule
  c. default value

d. column constraint

e. CHECK constraint

f. control-of-flow language

g. stored procedure

h. statement block

i. BREAK

j. local variable

k. default parameter value

l. trigger test tables

m. DataWindow

n. Application painter

o. Window painter

p. control

2. Describe how user-defined datatypes can be used in defining database tables. Why are they valuable?

3. Describe the relationship between a null value constraint and a default value. If a default value is defined, should the null value constraint be defined? Why?

4. What is the difference between a rule and a CHECK constraint?

5. What is the difference between a CHECK constraint and a trigger?

6. What is the difference between column constraints and table constraints?

7. What happens when ON DELETE RESTRICT is in effect? What happens when ON DELETE CASCADE is in effect?

8. What is the difference between the UNIQUE constraint, the PRIMARY KEY constraint, and the NOT NULL constraint?

9. List the different constructs in control-of-flow language.

10. What is a statement block and how is it indicated?

11. In what way do IF and WHILE statements in control-of-flow language differ fundamentally from corresponding statements in conventional languages?

12. How are BREAK and CONTINUE used?

13. Through what statement are local variables defined in control-of-flow language?

14. What aspect of stored procedures makes it possible for them to be used in creating program modules that can communicate with each other?

15. Discuss the advantages of stored procedures.

16. What can triggers do that declared constraints cannot do?

17. What function do painters perform in PowerBuilder?

18. List the PowerBuilder painters.

19. What is the difference between a window and a DataWindow?

20. Discuss the procedure by which queries are defined for DataWindows.

21. Discuss the procedure by which controls are placed in windows.

22. What examples of events that occur on a window are discussed in the chapter?

Problems and Exercises

For all problems, answers should be developed using the facilities of SQL Server, Oracle, or PowerBuilder as discussed in this chapter.

1. Match each term with its definition.

__client/server platform	a. Performs type of functionality needed for full application development
__user-defined datatype	b. Oracle's data manipulation language
__constraint	c. Guarantees no two tuples will have identical values for column(s)
__table constraint	d. Means scripts are written to respond to occurrences
__UNIQUE constraint	e. Local area network of computers which give and receive services
__PL/SQL	f. Causes execution control to return to first statement in a WHILE loop
__IF statement	g. Customized subtype of a system-supplied datatype
__WHILE statement	h. Restriction on possible values of tuples and attributes
__CONTINUE	i. Constructs objects that access database and place results in windows
__parameter	j. Used to pass data into and out of a stored procedure
__trigger	k. Statement whose execution depends on truth value of a condition
__painter	l. Applies to multiple columns simultaneously
__DataWindow painter	m. Statement that uses a condition to control iterative execution
__Preview	n. Executes when a specified update is attempted on a specified table
__event-driven	o. Allows developer to see how a DataWindow will appear when placed in a window

2. Identify appropriate default values in a college database for the following:
  a. A new student's year in school.
  b. A new professor's rank.
  c. A new student's expected year of graduation.

3. Define a default of 3231 for use with the supv_id column in the worker table.

4. Specify name, type, length, default, and rule as needed in user-defined datatypes for each of the following:
  a. A datatype to define age, between 0 and 80, set to 18 if no value is entered.
  b. A datatype to define hourly wage, between $5.00 and $20.00, set to $5.00 if no wage is entered.
  c. A datatype to define gender, must be male or female.
  d. A datatype to define marital status, must be single or married, and is single if nothing is entered.

5. Define these tables where the basic column information is as follows:

```
building
    bldg_id         id_type
    bldg_address    character 12  nulls
    type            character 9   nulls, no default, value must be
                                  Office, Retail, Residence, or
                                  Warehouse
    qlty_level      integer       nulls, default = 1, value must be
                                  between 1 and 4, inclusive
    status          integer       nulls, default = 1, value must be
                                  between 1 and 3, inclusive
assignment
    worker_id       id_type
    bldg_id         id_type
    start_date      datetime      nulls
    num_days        integer       nulls, value must be greater than
                                  0
```

6. Define a database schema, including table names, columns, and primary and foreign keys for the schema in Figure 9.1E.

▼**FIGURE 9.1E PURCHASE ORDER DATA MODEL FOR MANAGING CONSULTING SERVICE**

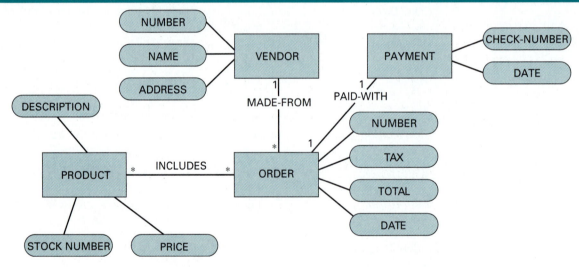

7. Define CHECK constraints for each of the following:
  a. In the building relation, if type is Office, then qlty_level must be above 2.
  b. In the worker relation, if skill_type is Plumbing, the hrly_rate must be above 10.00.
  c. In the worker relation, if supv_id is not null, the hrly_rate must be under 20.00.

8. Create control-of-flow statements to do each of the following:
  a. If the average status of buildings is over 1, increase the hourly wage of all framing workers by 1.00/hour.
  b. If supervisor 3335 is assigned to work more than a total of 30 days on various buildings, repeatedly decrease his assigned number of days on each building by 1 day until he is working less than 25 total days.

9. Create a stored procedure which will take skill_type as a parameter and will calculate and return the average number of days in the assignment tuples of all workers of that skill type.

10. Assume there is a column in the building relation, tot_num_days, which contains the total number of days workers are assigned to work on the building. Create a trigger which will update this column every time there is an update to the assignment table.

11. Describe the windows, DataWindows, and other controls you would use to create the following PowerBuilder applications:

    a. An application which allows the user to view and update tuples in the worker relation by skill_type. The user would choose a skill_type, and the system would show all workers having that skill type. The user could then change data values in selected worker tuples and indicate that the database should be updated.

    b. This application is the same as the preceding one except it applies to buildings. The user selects buildings based on type.

Professional Issues

1. Obtain working copies of several server DBMSs (such as SQL Server or Oracle) and examine their data definition and data manipulation features. Specifically, identify which DBMSs allow the data definition features of user-defined datatypes, rules, defaults, primary keys, and foreign keys, with automatic enforcement of the latter two. Identify which DBMSs support IF and WHILE statements as well as other control-of-flow language features discussed in this chapter, with conditions that apply to entire relations rather than just single tuples at a time. Write a report comparing these DBMSs.

2. Obtain working copies of several client application development environment packages (such as PowerBuilder or SQLWindows) and examine their capabilities with respect to window, DataWindow, and other control definition, as well as their data manipulation languages. Write a report comparing these facilities.

C H A P T E R

PHYSICAL DATABASE SYSTEMS

Billie Tollefson, currently the manager of computing services at the Zeus Corporation, is finding the attitude of one of her fellow workers unsettling. Archie Krepsbach, who is in charge of materials requirements planning (MRP) in the manufacturing division, had complained to the vice president of manufacturing about the questionable performance of computing services in satisfying MRP's information needs. "Here we have this new database system, which is touted as moving us into the forefront of information management, but I can't always get the information I need when I need it. I am frustrated with the response times I am getting from our DBMS."

Upon hearing this from her boss, Billie responded: "I can appreciate Archie's frustration with our response time, but what he apparently doesn't understand is that the types of reports he needs are particularly difficult to produce in a timely fashion. If he had a better understanding of the complexities of physical database organization, he might find it easier to be patient with our turnaround time. He would also see the need to identify reports that require rapid turnaround and those that can wait a little longer. Then we could fine-tune the database to provide better response on the high-priority information." After contemplating the matter for a day or two, Billie decided to recommend to her boss that in-house training seminars be offered to acquaint users with the fundamentals of physical database design and operation.

This chapter deals with the physical structures that are used to implement databases. After reading this chapter, you should be able to:

▼ Describe the structures for physically accessing the database.

▼ Explain the fundamentals of disk storage, retrieval, and performance.

▼ Understand basic types of file organization and how they function.

▼ Describe the use of pointers to create linked lists, inverted lists, and B+-trees.

▼ Understand how logical data models are mapped to physical data structures.

▼ Define and understand secondary keys.

▼ Understand basic principles of query optimization.

▼ Introduction

Physical database organization is a vast topic, and its detail is primarily of interest to technical specialists involved with hardware and systems software design. Yet the overall performance of a database system is determined in large part by the physical data structures used and the efficiency with which the system operates on those structures. Although users should not have to master physical database design details, these details do affect performance, a major consideration in a user's satisfaction with a database system. Can the user get the information desired—in the appropriate format—and in timely fashion? This last factor, "timely fashion," can be generally expressed as acceptable response time. The "information desired" and the "appropriate format" are not greatly affected by the physical database organization—but response time *is*. Response time is the elapsed time between the initiation of a database operation and the availability of the result. Slow response time is the most frequently expressed complaint by users of database systems, possibly because it is the most easily observed.

A good physical database design will store data in such a way that they can be retrieved, updated, and manipulated in as short a time as possible. In this chapter, we are concerned with those aspects of physical database organization that foster efficient database system operation. Although you, as a business system analyst, will very likely not be involved directly in the details of physical design and implementation, it is important for you to understand physical implementation problems and their typical solutions, since they will affect your systems at the user level.

▼ Physical Access of the Database

The system for physically accessing the database is shown in Figure 10.1. We see the *user* interacting with the database system by initiating a request. The **strategy selector** translates the user's command into its most efficient form for execution. The translated request then activates the **buffer manager** that controls the movement of data between main memory and disk storage. The **file manager** supports the buffer manager by managing the allocation of storage locations on disk and the associated data structures. In addition to the user data, the disk contains the **data dictionary,** which defines the structure of the user data and how they may be used.

The user data are stored as a physical database or collection of records. For example, one row in a relation may be stored as a physical record, with each attribute value of the row being stored in its own data field. Similarly, a logical record of a network or hierarchical model may be stored as a physical record with the logical data items becoming physical data items of the stored physical record.

▼ Physical Storage Media

Main memory is the storage medium used for data that are available for user operations. This is where the executing program resides. As data are required for the program to execute its functions, those data are transmitted from secondary storage to

strategy selector Software that translates a user request into an effective form for execution.

buffer manager Software that controls the movement of data between main memory and disk storage.

file manager Software that manages the allocation of storage locations and data structures.

data dictionary That part of the DBMS that defines the structure of user data and how they are to be used.

main memory Storage located in the central processing unit; used for data made available for user operations.

▼FIGURE 10.1

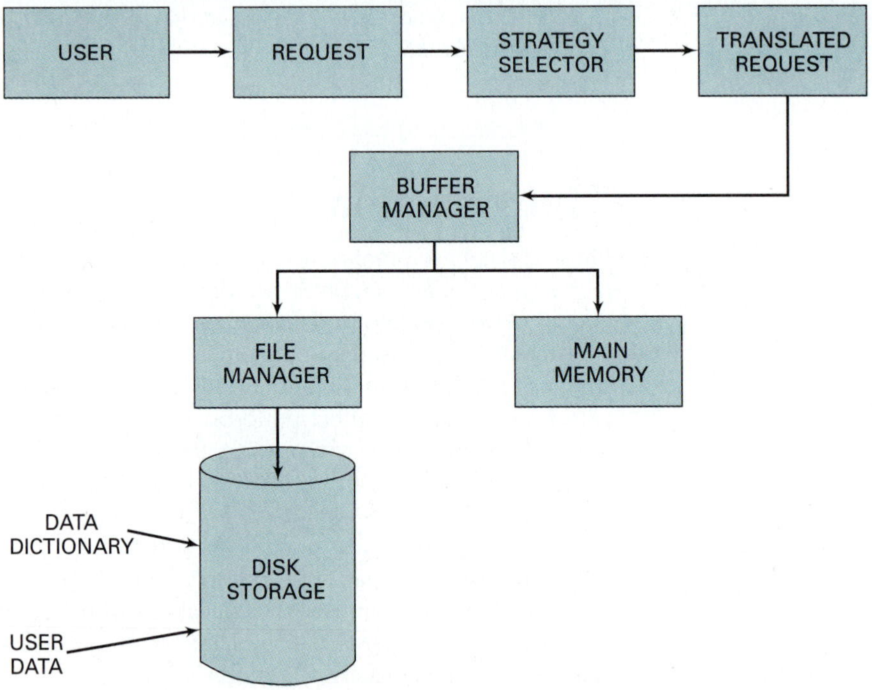

main memory. Although main memory may be able to store several megabytes of data, it is usually too small to store the entire database, and secondary storage is required.

Secondary Storage

Secondary storage for database systems is usually comprised of disk storage and magnetic tape storage. Typically, the entire database is stored on disk, and portions are transferred from disk to primary memory as needed. Disk storage is the principal form of direct-access storage, since individual records can be accessed directly or sequentially. Although magnetic tape storage is less expensive than disk storage, records can only be accessed sequentially (and more slowly than with disk). Its role in database systems is basically limited to archiving data.

The physical unit in which the disk recording medium is contained is called a **disk drive.** Each disk drive contains one disk pack or volume. Figures 10.2 and 10.3 show the principal components of the disk pack and the read/write mechanism required for data transmission. The disk pack is made up of a set of recording surfaces (disks) mounted on a shaft. In operation, the shaft and the disks rotate at a high rate of speed. Data are recorded on tracks, which are circular recording positions found on each surface (Figure 10.2). There may be several hundred tracks on a single surface. A common metaphor for the disk pack is a stack of phonograph records on a spindle, except that here the tracks are concentric and therefore do not spiral inward to the center.

As shown in Figure 10.3, a set of read/write heads, roughly like the teeth of a comb, moves as a group so that the read/write heads at the end of an arm can be positioned over all those tracks having the same radius. The set of such tracks is termed a **cylinder.** That is, a set of tracks of the same diameter rotating at high speed forms a conceptual cylinder. This is a useful definition since any positioning

disk drive Physical unit that contains the disk storage unit.

cylinder The same track extending through all surfaces of the disk storage unit.

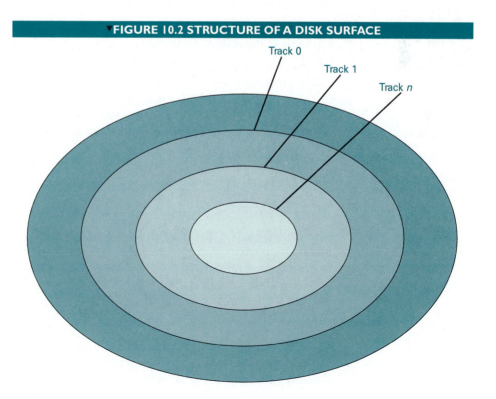

▼**FIGURE 10.2 STRUCTURE OF A DISK SURFACE**

Track 0

Track 1

Track n

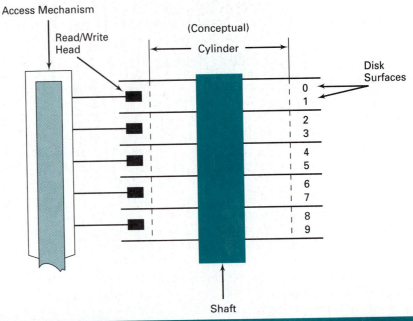

Access Mechanism

Read/Write Head

(Conceptual)
Cylinder

Disk Surfaces

0
1
2
3
4
5
6
7
8
9

Shaft

▾FIGURE 10.3 MAGNETIC DISK SYSTEM

of the set of read/write heads can be described by the cylinder location (for example, cylinder 199). Thus, all tracks in a given cylinder can be written to, or read from, without further movement of the read/write heads. The address of a record on disk usually requires specification of a cylinder number, a surface number, and a block number (discussed next).

Physical Storage Blocks

The physical record, or block, is the smallest physically addressable unit of data on a disk. Each track on a surface is made up of a number of blocks. A block may contain one or more logical records. Suppose that we have a blocking factor of 3, meaning that three logical records are stored in each block. We wish to retrieve the record of John Jones, stored at the following address:

Cylinder number: 5

Surface number: 2

Block number: 1

Refer to Figure 10.4. To retrieve John Jones's record, the read/write heads move into position over cylinder 5 (track 5 on all surfaces). The read/write head for surface number 2 is then activated and block numbers are read as the track rotates under the read/write head. When block 1 is detected, the entire block of three logical records is read into main memory, where John Jones's record is selected.

In our example, we have assumed the most general disk pack nomenclature where the read/write heads are attached to a movable access arm. Not all disk units are configured this way. A few have read/write heads that are permanently fixed for each cylinder. These units are typically more expensive but are faster, since there is no delay in moving the read/write heads into position over a new cylinder.

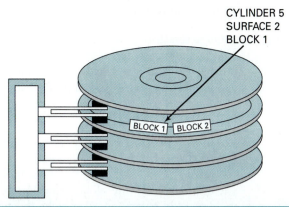

CYLINDER 5
SURFACE 2
BLOCK 1

BLOCK 1 | BLOCK 2

Generally, the time required to perform computations on a block is much less than the time required to transfer the data between secondary storage and primary storage. Therefore, a good design strategy is to identify, where possible, logical records that are likely to be required for the same operations and to group them in blocks. For example, suppose that a firm stocks three kinds of wire, *A, B,* and *C,* and that they are usually delivered in the same shipment. If blocks contain three records each, and the *A, B,* and *C* records are contained in separate blocks, three input/output (I/O) operations are required to update their records. However, if they are blocked together, then only one I/O operation is required. Since disk access is often a bottleneck in database operations, careful assignment of records to blocks can significantly enhance response time.

▼ Disk Performance Factors

In general, there are four factors that directly affect the speed with which data are transferred to and from disk storage: access motion time, head activation time, rotational delay, and data transfer rate.

Access Motion Time

access motion time
The time required to position the read/write heads of the disk drive over the desired cylinder.

Access motion time (*A*), sometimes termed *seek time,* is the time required to move the read/write heads from their current position to a new cylinder address. Obviously, a move to an adjacent cylinder will not take the same amount of time as a move across the entire disk surface (innermost track to outermost track, or vice versa). As a compromise in calculations, the average access motion time may be used—roughly the time required to move across one-half of the cylinders, although more sophisticated methods may be used. A standard assumption is that the likelihood of access for every record is the same, giving a uniform probability distribution. The average for a uniform distribution is halfway between the extreme values. For access motion time, the extreme values would be (1) stay positioned over the current cylinder, or (2) move from the innermost cylinder to the outermost (or vice versa). Given the uniform distribution assumption, the average will be the time to move across one-half of the cylinders. Twelve to twenty milliseconds are typical average access motion times, varying with the make and model of the disk drive.

Head Activation Time

head activation time
The time required to activate a read/write head.

Head activation time is the time required to electronically activate the head that is over the surface where data transfer is to take place. Relative to other performance factors, this time is generally regarded as being negligible. Consequently, head activation time is seldom used in performance calculations.

Rotational Delay

rotational delay The time required for the disk to rotate the sought-for record under the read/write head.

Rotational delay, or latency, is the third timing factor. It denotes the amount of time required for the desired block to rotate to the head, so that data transfer may commence. Rotational delay depends upon two factors: how fast the disk is rotating and the location of the block being sought in relationship to the read/write head at the time of its activation. Physically, this time could range from zero to the time required to complete one complete revolution of the disk (R). As an analogy, suppose you wanted to ride on the purple horse on the merry-go-round (assuming there is just one such horse). If you bought a ticket and ran to get on the merry-go-round, the likelihood that the purple horse would be just where you stepped on would be the same as that of any of the other horses. If you were a fanatic and attempted this a large number of times, you might eventually step on at precisely the point where the purple horse was located. You might also find that on occasion you just missed it and had to wait for a complete revolution of the merry-go-round. Over time, you would find that you were waiting about one-half revolution on average to get the purple horse. The implication of this story is that performance computations usually assume an average rotational delay of $R/2$.

Data Transfer Rate

data transfer rate The rate at which data can be read from the disk to main memory, or equivalently, the rate at which data are written from main memory to disk.

Data transfer rate (D) refers to the amount of time required to transfer data from the disk to (or from) primary memory. It is a function of the rotational speed and the density of the recorded data. Data transfer time is usually expressed in thousands of bytes per second.

Data Transfer Time

The expected time (T) to access a disk address and transfer a block of data is estimated as

$$T = A + \frac{R}{2} + \frac{L}{D}$$

where A is the access motion time, R is the rotational delay, L is the length of the block in bytes, and D is the data transfer rate.

Example of a Randomly Accessed Record. Suppose that claim records for an insurance company are stored three per block on disk (a blocking factor of 3), and that each claim record is 200 bytes long. The data transfer rate is 806,000 bytes per second. The average access motion time is 30 milliseconds. The disk unit rotates at a speed of 3,600 revolutions per minute. Suppose that a policyholder calls to inquire about the status of a claim. What is the data transfer time for the requisite block of data? In order to answer this question, we assign appropriate values to the preceding variables as follows:

$$A = .030 \text{ seconds}$$

$$\text{Revolutions per second} = \frac{7{,}200}{60} = 120$$

$$R = \frac{1}{120} \text{ second} = 0.0083 \text{ second}$$

$$\frac{R}{2} = 0.0083 \times \frac{1}{2} \ (\text{average wait is } \tfrac{1}{2} \text{ revolution}) = 0.00415$$

$$\frac{L}{D} = 600/806000 = 0.00074$$

Thus,

$$T = 0.030 + 0.00415 + 0.00074 = 0.03489 \text{ seconds}$$

Example of a Sequentially Accessed Record.   We now look at the problem of calculating average access time for a record on a sequentially accessed file. Suppose that instead of responding to a random access of a data block, as in the preceding example, we are now updating an insurance company's policyholder file with payments received at the beginning of the month. It makes sense that such files be organized sequentially by, say, policy number and that they are in sequential blocks by cylinder. That is, first, cylinder N is filled with sequential blocks, then cylinder $N + 1$, and so forth. In this way, we minimize head movement time. In particular, if the read/write heads are positioned at the starting cylinder, then all records on that cylinder may be transferred without further access motion time. Thus, in calculating the average access time for each record in a sequentially processed file, access motion time is neglibile and can be ignored.

There will be a slight delay each time the read/write function switches from one track of the cylinder to another. This is necessary in order to accommodate small differences in the alignment of tracks on different surfaces. For our purposes, this delay can be approximated by the time required for one-half rotation of the disk pack. Once the beginning record on a new track has been found, all remaining blocks from the track can be transmitted. Thus, if the policyholder file occupies eight tracks on a given cylinder, the number of one-half rotational delays will be 8.

Suppose further that each track contains 1,000 blocks. Then we have a total of 8,000 blocks and, with a blocking factor of 3, 24,000 policy records. We assume as before that each record is 200 bytes long, so our blocks are 600 bytes long. If we are processing the entire file sequentially, the average time to access a record can be computed as follows:

$$\text{Total time to read all blocks} =$$
$$0.00415(8) + 0.00074(8000) = 0.0664 + 5.92 = 5.9532$$

$$T = \frac{5.9532}{8000} = 0.00074415 \text{ seconds}$$

T represents the average transfer time for a sequentially accessed record in the policyholder file.

▼Data Storage Formats on Disk

In this section, we examine the physical aspects of data management on disk media. We look at formats on tracks and in physical records and at input/output management.

Track Formats

count-key format A data format for tracks that uses external keys.

count-data format A data format for tracks that uses no external keys.

Records can be stored on disk in either a **count-key format** or a **count-data format,** as shown in Figures 10.5 and 10.6. The fundamental difference is that the count-key format includes a key that is external to the data record itself. This key is used by the operating system to access a particular record. We use the term *record* here in the general sense of a physical record, which is another name for a block. Both the count-data and the count-key formats can be described by the definitions that follow.

Each track has an index point, which is a special mark to identify the beginning of each track. Since the track is circular, it also identifies the end of the track.

The home address (HA) identifies the cylinder and the number of the read/write head that services the track, as well as the condition of the track (flag)—whether it is operative or defective. If the track is defective, an alternative track to

---

▼FIGURE 10.5 THE COUNT-KEY FORMAT

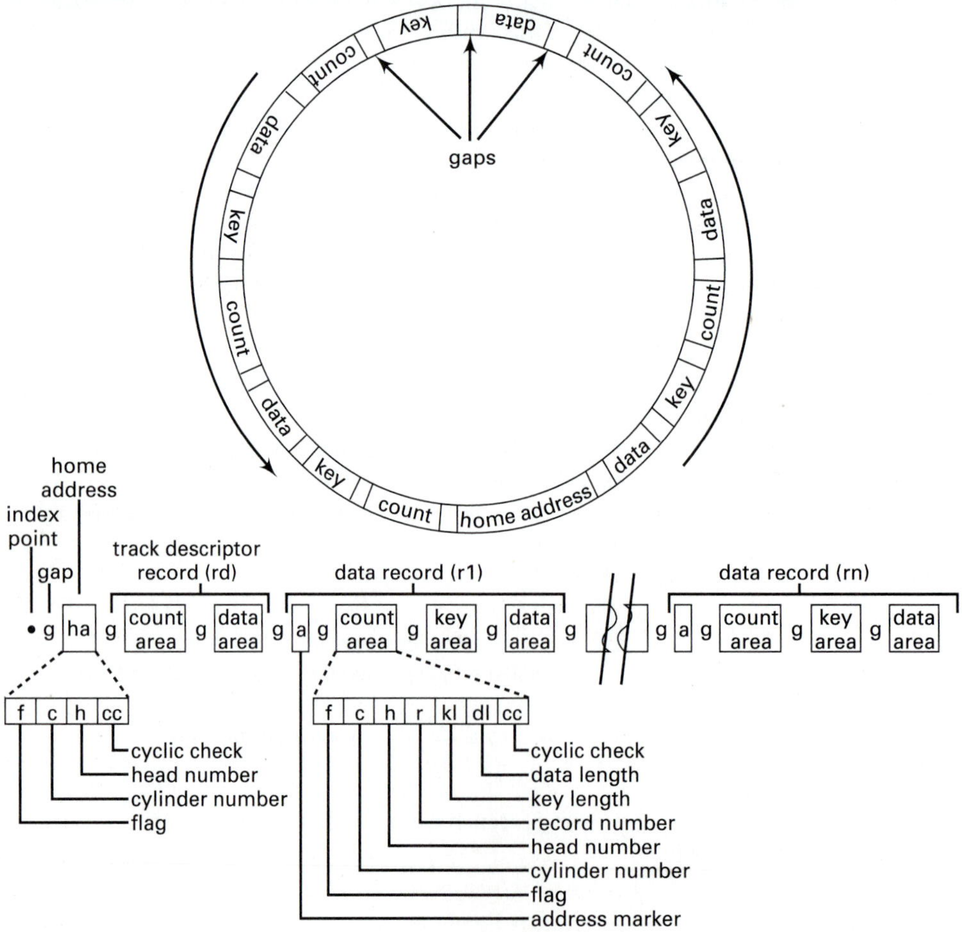

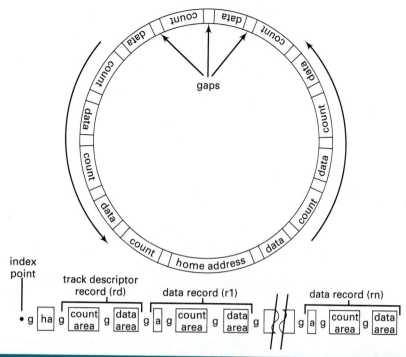

be used is indicated. A two-byte cyclic check is included as a means of error detection in input/output operations.

Gaps (G) separate the different areas on the track. The length of the gap may vary with the device, the location of the gap, and the length of the preceding area. The gap that follows the index point is different in length from the gap that follows the home address, and the length of the gap that follows a record depends on the length of that record. The reason for this is to provide adequate time for required equipment functions that are necessary as the gap rotates past the read/write head. These functions may vary with the type of area that has just preceded the gap.

The address marker (A) is a two-byte segment supplied by the control unit (the hardware that controls the disk drive) as the record is written. It enables the control unit to locate the beginning of the record at a later time.

The count area is detailed in Figure 10.5. The flag field repeats the information about the track condition and adds information used by the control unit. The cylinder number, head number, and record number fields collectively provide a unique identification for the record. The key-length field is a one-byte field. It always contains a 0 for a record of the count-data format. The data-length field supplies two bytes, which specify the number of bytes in the data area of the record, excluding the cyclic check. The cyclic check provides two bytes for error detection.

Record Formats

physical record A physical block of data.

Physical records, or blocks, can be stored on tracks in any of the four formats illustrated in Figure 10.7.

Fixed-length records. In this case, all records are of the same length. If the physical records are *unblocked,* there will be one logical record (for example, one payroll record) for each physical record (the data that are actually stored in the

(a) FIXED, UNBLOCKED

| | AAA | Record aaa |
| Count | Key | Data |

(b) FIXED, BLOCKED

| | FFF | AAA | Record aaa | CCC | Record ccc | | FFF | Record fff |
| Count | Key | | | | Data | | | |

A Block

(c) VARIABLE, UNBLOCKED

| | AAA | BL | RL | Record aaa |
| Count | Key | | Data | |

(d) VARIABLE, BLOCKED

| | FFF | BL | RL | AAA | Record aaa | | RL | CCC | Record ccc | | RL | FFF | Record fff |
| Count | Key | | | | | | Data | | | | | | |

▼**FIGURE 10.7 RECORD FORMATS**

record area of the track). If the records are blocked, more than one logical record will comprise each physical record. For instance, if there are three payroll records comprising every physical record, we then have blocked records with a blocking factor of three. In this case, the Key Area is typically assigned the key of the *highest* record in the block. This facilitates locating records of interest. Suppose that we have two succeeding blocks containing records 10,12,14, and 15,19,24, respectively. If the operating system is seeking logical record 15, the key for the first block will read 14, so record 15 cannot be in that block. The key for the next block will read 24. Since 24 is greater than 15, record 15 must be in that block. The entire block is then read into main memory where it is searched for record 15.

Variable-length records. The variable-length format, as the name implies, allows records to be of varying length. If database users need a logical customer record that stores data on outstanding invoices, this format would be appropriate, since the number of invoices will vary among customers. Because the record length is not uniform, a method of indicating where the record ends is required. This information is provided by the BL (block-length) and RL (record-length) areas. As with fixed-length formats, unblocked indicates that each block contains exactly one logical record. The blocked format allows several logical records to be stored in one block.

Input/Output Management

Based on the data formatting concepts of this section, we now briefly consider DBMS input/output operations. Suppose that an I/O instruction received from a user or application program is to be executed. The DBMS first checks to determine if the subschema associated with that I/O statement is defined in its data dictionary, as well as whether the user or program that is the source of that command is allowed to access that subschema. Assuming that all is well, the DBMS issues relevant I/O commands to the host operating system to access the specific physical records required. The operating system then searches the secondary storage devices and accesses the appropriate physical records. The operating system transfers those records to main memory where the DBMS extracts from the physical records those logical records requested and passes them to the user or application program for further disposition.

▼ File Organization and Addressing Methods

So far, you have learned something about the devices used to store data and the I/O operations used to transmit data to and from those devices. We now consider the methods of arranging data on those devices and addressing them in a way that facilitates storage and I/O operations.

There are three basic ways of physically organizing files on storage devices: sequential organization, indexed-sequential organization, and direct organization. This is not an entire set of all organization options available, but those that are omitted are modifications of these basic organizational types. Therefore, it is not necessary to be exhaustive in order to cover the essential concepts.

In discussing the topic at hand, the terms *organization* and *access* are often used loosely, if not interchangeably. The reason is that the way in which data are stored is closely intertwined with the method of access. We will attempt to clarify this in the discussion that follows.

Sequential File Organization

Sequential file organization means that records are stored adjacent to one another according to a key such as employee number, account number, and so forth. A conventional implementation arranges the records in ascending order of key values. This is an efficient method of organizing records when an application, such as a payroll program, will be updating a significant number of the stored records.

If a sequential file is maintained on magnetic tape, its records can only be accessed in a sequential manner. That is, if access to the tenth record in sequence is desired, generally the preceding nine records must be read. Direct access of a particular record is impossible. Consequently, magnetic tapes are not well suited for database operations and are usually relegated to producing log files and recording archival information.

Indexed-Sequential File Organization

When files are sequentially organized on a disk pack, however, direct access of records is possible. Indexed-sequential file organization provides facilities for accessing records both sequentially and directly. Records are stored in the usual physical sequence by primary key. In addition, an index of record locations is stored on the disk. This allows records to be accessed sequentially for applications requiring the updating of large numbers of records, as well as providing the ability to access records directly in response to user queries.

A simplified version of how indexed-sequential access operates is shown in Figure 10.8. The indexes and the records are both stored on disk. We have greatly limited the number of cylinders and tracks for purposes of our example. First notice that the records are organized sequentially on the three tracks shown for cylinder 1. Sequential processing is facilitated by simply beginning at the first record of the file, then proceeding through the file from first record to last. Direct access of records is also facilitated. Suppose that we wished to retrieve record 31. A search of the cylinder index reveals that record 31 is on cylinder 1. That is, the highest record key on cylinder 1 is 52, and since records are ordered sequentially by key, record 31 must be on cylinder 1. A search of the track index for cylinder 1 shows that record 31 is

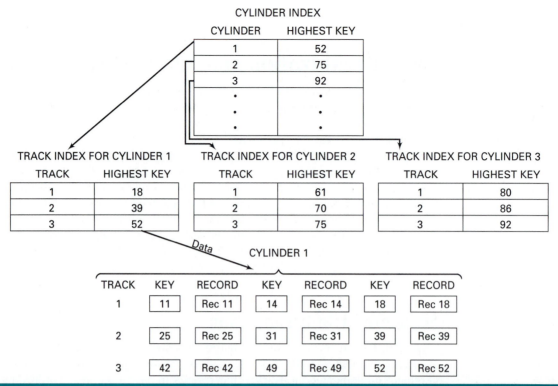

CYLINDER INDEX

CYLINDER	HIGHEST KEY
1	52
2	75
3	92
•	•
•	•
•	•

TRACK INDEX FOR CYLINDER 1

TRACK	HIGHEST KEY
1	18
2	39
3	52

TRACK INDEX FOR CYLINDER 2

TRACK	HIGHEST KEY
1	61
2	70
3	75

TRACK INDEX FOR CYLINDER 3

TRACK	HIGHEST KEY
1	80
2	86
3	92

Data   CYLINDER 1

TRACK	KEY	RECORD	KEY	RECORD	KEY	RECORD
1	11	Rec 11	14	Rec 14	18	Rec 18
2	25	Rec 25	31	Rec 31	39	Rec 39
3	42	Rec 42	49	Rec 49	52	Rec 52

▼FIGURE 10.8 EXAMPLE OF INDEXED-SEQUENTIAL ORGANIZATION AND ACCESS

on track 2. Thus, the read/write heads are moved to cylinder 1, and the read/write head for track 2 is activated. Track 2 is then searched sequentially to locate record 31. While sequential searching has not been completely eliminated, its scope has been reduced sufficiently to justify the term *direct access*.

Our example uses unblocked records, but it can easily be extended to blocked records. Think of the data area as containing, say, three records and the key area as now denoting the highest record key in the block. The search procedure would proceed in similar fashion.

Direct File Organization

Thus far, we have discussed two forms of file organization: sequential and indexed sequential. We have concurrently outlined the two associated methods of file access: sequential access and direct access. Records in a simple sequential file organization can only be accessed sequentially. Records in an indexed-sequential file organization can be accessed directly, as well as sequentially. We now turn to a discussion of a third type of file organization called direct or hashed. Only direct access methods are applicable to this type of file organization.

Static Hash Functions

One disadvantage of index schemes is that an index must be accessed and read to locate records. The use of *hashing* is a method of record addressing that eliminates the need for maintaining and searching indexes. Elimination of the index avoids the need to make two trips to secondary storage to access a record: one to read the index, and one to access the file.

There are important applications whose predominant need is for direct access of records, whose services could be encumbered by the use of indexing methods. Examples include reservation systems for airlines, hotels, and car rentals, as well as electronic funds transfer.

The basic idea is that of trading the time and effort associated with storing, maintaining, and searching an index for the time required for the central processing unit (CPU) to execute a hashing algorithm, which generates the record address. The hashing algorithm is a procedure for calculating a record address from some field in the record, usually the key. We turn to an example to help illustrate the method.

Suppose that 500 payroll records, each 100 bytes long, are to be stored on a magnetic disk having a 2,000-byte per block capacity. Exactly 25 blocks would be required if the records were addressed in a way that assigned exactly one record to each possible location in each of the 25 blocks. Since no hashing algorithm, $h(k_i)$ (where k_i is the record key), devised to date can be guaranteed to accomplish this, additional storage space, say 20 percent, is usually added to reduce the number of instances when the algorithm calculates the same address for more than one record (a collision). The ratio of the space actually required by the records in a file to the actual space allocated for the file is termed the *load factor*. In our example, the records require 25 blocks of storage space, but we are allocating $(25) \times (1.2) = 30$ blocks to reduce the number of collisions. The load factor is $(25/30 =) 83$ percent.

Effective strategies for direct storage of records will result in low search times and few collisions. This can be best accomplished by selecting low load factors, using large blocking factors, and by using a hashing algorithm that distributes records uniformly over the storage area. The best method of accomplishing the latter objective is by the use of a division remainder method, which we will illustrate.

Since we have allocated 30 blocks for storing our file, a uniform distribution of records to blocks will mean that roughly four out of every five possible storage addresses will be assigned to a record. Suppose the first record to be stored has a key (upon which the algorithm will operate) of 1562. We do the following (Figure 10.9):

▼FIGURE 10.9 USING A COMMON HASHING ALGORITHM TO DETERMINE A RECORD STORAGE LOCATION

Step 1:   Divide key by allocated file size in blocks

$$
\begin{array}{r}
52 \\
30\overline{)1562} \\
-150 \\
\hline
62 \\
-60 \\
\hline
2 \quad \text{the remainder}
\end{array}
$$

Step 2:   Add result of Step 1 to beginning address to obtain actual address of record with key value 1562

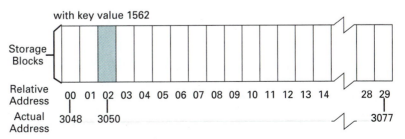

1. Divide the key by the number of storage blocks allocated. The remainder gives the relative storage location.

Remainder of (1562/30) = 2

Relative storage block = 2

Keeping the remainder is in effect guaranteeing that an address is always computed that is in the range 0 to 29 inclusive.

2. Add the result of (1) to the beginning block address to obtain the address at which the record is to be stored.

Suppose that our series of 30 blocks begins at address 3048 and runs through address 3077. Then record 1562 will be located at block location (2 + 3048 =) 3050. If there is to be just one record stored in each block, then no more records can be stored at address 3050. If several records are to be stored in each block, then records can continue to be stored at that address until the block is filled.

Let's assume that only one record is to be stored in each block, and that in the process of hashing, a second record is encountered that has key value 1592. It also computes to relative record address 2, and we have a collision. One method of dealing with collisions is to use the division hashing function with a refinement termed the *quadratic quotient method*. When no collisions occur, the resulting address is exactly the same as before, but if a collision does occur we now have a method of continuing on.

With the quadratic quotient method, when the key is divided by the table size, both the quotient, Q, and the remainder, R, are saved. Using Q and R, we can generate a sequence of relative record addresses by the formula

$$(R + Q_i^2 + i)(\text{modulo the number of blocks})$$

where i runs through the integers beginning with 0 until no collision results. Continuing with our example, for record 1562 we have,

$$(2 + 52 \times 0^2 + 0)\text{modulo } 30 = 2$$

as before. (Modulo 30 means divide by 30 and keep the remainder.) But the new record 1592 yields

$$(2 + 53 \times 0^2 + 0)\text{modulo } 30 = 2$$

Record 1562 is already at that relative address, so we iterate using the next value for i until we find an unoccupied address. For this example, we next compute

$$(2 + 53 \times 1^2 + 1)\text{modulo } 30 = 26$$

and we have an unoccupied address where this record can be stored.

When record 1592 must be found, the algorithm is computed in the usual way, first yielding a location where record 1562 is located. Since this is not the record being sought, the algorithm will be repeated until the desired record is found.

Another method of dealing with collisions is to simply store a pointer at the location computed by the algorithm. This pointer would indicate the address where the next record is located whose key also hashed to this location. If there are several such records, a pointer would be maintained at each storage location. In this way, there is a chain of pointers that can be followed until the desired record is found.

Dynamic Hash Functions

As you have seen, the static hash function is fairly simple. As the database grows, however, the static hash function loses its appeal. A growing number of collisions is assured, resulting in increased overhead to access records. One strategy for dealing with this problem is to allocate estimated space for future requirements at the outset; but this wastes storage space. Another scheme is to allocate additional storage and reorganize the file as it grows. This, too, involves considerable overhead in order to recompute the hash function for each record in the file and to generate new block assignments.

A better approach is provided by the *dynamic hash function*. In particular, the method we demonstrate here is called *extendable hashing*. Extendable hashing splits and combines blocks as the database grows or shrinks. This ensures efficient space utilization. Moreover, since reorganization involves only one block at a time, the associated overhead is minimal.

Extendable hashing uses a hash function, h, that has the useful characteristics of randomness and uniformity. It also (typically) uses a 32-bit binary string in order to create and identify block indexes. (Since we have already discussed one hashing algorithm at length, the reader should understand the basic ideas that underlay hashing. Thus, for economy of expression, we shall not specifically define h.)

Most algorithms use i bits at any time, where $0 \le i \le 32$. To begin, we set $i = 0$. The value of i will grow and shrink as the size of the database grows and shrinks. A schematic of the extendable hashing method is illustrated in Figure 10.10. To determine the block containing key, k_i, we do the following:

1. Compute $h(k_i) = x$ (represented as a binary string)

2. Take the first i high-order bits of x.

3. Use the i bits as a displacement into the block-address table, then follow the pointer to the related block.

To illustrate, consider a collection of inventory records having keys k_1, k_2, k_3, k_4, k_5, k_6, and k_7. Suppose that the high-order bits of $h(k_i)$, where k_i is a key, are those shown in Figure 10.10. Initially, we have the empty file shown in Figure 10.11(a). The 0 shown above the table holding block addresses indicates that 0 bits of $h(k_i)$ are required to compute the address block for a given key, k_i.

Suppose we first enter records having keys, k_2 and k_7. (To keep matters simple to follow, we assume that each memory block can contain a maximum of two records.)

▼FIGURE 10.10 HIGH-ORDER BITS RESULTING FROM HASHING

$h(k_1) = 0010\ldots$
$h(k_2) = 1101\ldots$
$h(k_3) = 1011\ldots$
$h(k_4) = 1000\ldots$
$h(k_5) = 1110\ldots$
$h(k_6) = 1010\ldots$
$h(k_7) = 0100\ldots$

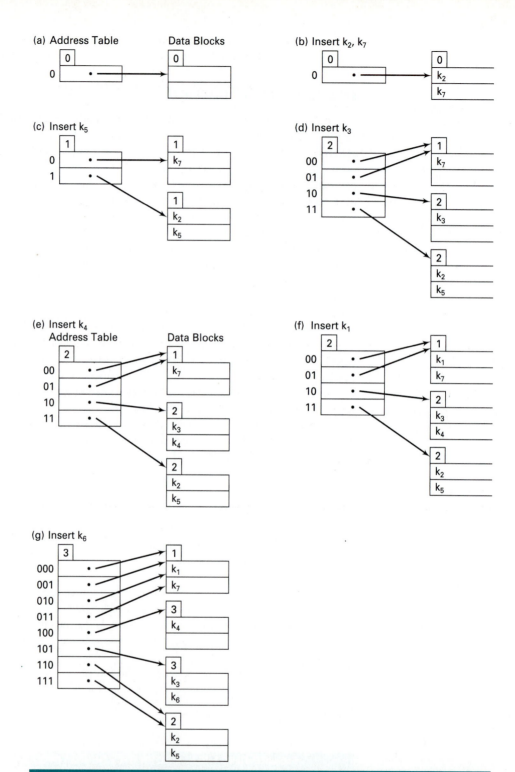

(a) Address Table   Data Blocks

(b) Insert k_2, k_7

(c) Insert k_5

(d) Insert k_3

(e) Insert k_4
Address Table   Data Blocks

(f) Insert k_1

(g) Insert k_6

▼**FIGURE 10.11 ILLUSTRATION OF DYNAMIC HASHING**

The address table points to a block of memory which is vacant, and the records are inserted as shown in Figure 10.11(b). If we next attempt to enter record k_5, we find that the block that is pointed to by the address table is full. We now need to increase the number of bits to use from the hash value. That is, we previously used 0 bits when we had just one memory block. Now we must use 1 bit, allowing $2^1 = 2$ memory blocks. This requires that we enlarge the address table to allow two entries, one for each data block.

Consequently, we split the memory block, placing those records having "0" as the high-order bit of the hash value in one block, and those records having "1" as the high-order bit in the other block. For our example, record k_7 is placed in the 0-block because the leftmost bit in $h(k_7)$ is 0, and records k_2 and k_5 are placed in the 1-block because the leftmost bit of both $h(k_2)$ and $h(k_5)$ is 1 (Figure 10.11(c)).

We next insert record k_3, which has "1" as its high-order value—but the 1-block is filled. Again, we must increase the number of bits to use from the hashed values. We now use 2 bits, allowing $2^2 = 4$ blocks, as shown in Figure 10.11(d). The former 1-block is split into the two blocks showing "2" for the i value. Only record 7 has a high-order value of "0," so both pointers from positions "00" and "01" point to the 1-block.

Records k_2, k_3, and k_5 all contain "1" in the high-order position, so they are allocated storage based on the value of the next-highest-order value, as shown.

Suppose record k_4 is next inserted. Record $h(k_4)$ has "10" in its two highest-order positions and is inserted in the block containing record k_3. This is shown in Figure 10.11(e).

Let's now insert record k_1. Its two highest-order bits are "00." The pointer from the "00" row of the index table points to a block that has a vacant slot, so record 1 is inserted with record 7, as shown in Figure 10.11(f).

Last, when record k_6 is considered, every available storage block is filled. We now adjust the index table to use the three highest-order bits, allowing $2^3 = 8$ blocks to be used. The two highest-ordered bits of record k_6 are "10." This is the same as records k_3 and k_4 that are currently stored in the second block. Therefore, this block is split. Records k_3 and k_6 both have "1" in the third-highest-ordered bit, so they are stored together, with record k_4 being inserted into the remaining block (Figure 10-11(g)). Note that if all three records had the same value in the third-highest-order bit, a fourth bit value would have been necessary, and so on.

If the file shrinks, the process is reversed.

Notice that overhead is reduced because memory is only reserved when it is required—for both the address table and the memory blocks. Wasted space is minimized. Moreover, reorganization is simplified since only one block is involved at a time.

▼ Implementing Logical Relationships

Next we outline the fundamentals of physical data structures, which are the underlying molecular structures that enable the universe of the database system to perform its functions. These physical data structures can be characterized in two ways: first by the way in which one database record is linked to another, and second by the way in which these linkages are used to support database operations.

Linked Lists

pointer A data item containing a physical address.

A fundamental concept in linking one physical database record with another is the use of **pointers.** A pointer is a field associated with one data record that is used to find a related data record. What does this mean?

Suppose that Zeus Corporation stores personnel information in the form of the logical records shown in Figure 10.12. One field of interest is SKILL. Suppose that a new position opens for an engineer. It may be desirable to retrieve for evaluation all

HEAD LIST

Accountant = 1	Seattle = 1
Draftsman = 2	Los Angeles = 2
Engineer = 3	Portland = 6

RECORD NUMBER	EMPLOYEE ID	NAME	LOCATION	SKILL	SKILL POINTER	LOCATION POINTER
1	0123	James	Seattle	Accountant	4	3
2	0211	Poirot	Los Angeles	Draftsman	6	4
3	0223	Smith	Seattle	Engineer	5	7
4	0245	Cubic	Los Angeles	Accountant	7	5
5	0301	Black	Los Angeles	Engineer	9	0
6	0401	Iwerks	Portland	Draftsman	10	8
7	0601	Ivans	Seattle	Accountant	8	9
8	0711	Nell	Portland	Accountant	0	10
9	0908	Steel	Seattle	Engineer	0	0
10	1067	Schwartz	Portland	Draftsman	0	0

head list A list of pointers, each of which points to the first record in a file.

linked list A set of physical records linked by pointers that are maintained in the records themselves.

the records of personnel who are engineers. Notice that for each of the personnel records, the SKILL POINTER data item contains the address of the next record that contains the same value for SKILL as does the current record. A **head list,** maintained separately on the disk, points to the first record in the database that contains the value "engineer" in the SKILL field. In our example, this would be Smith's record. This record points to Black, which in turn points to Steel. Such chains of pointers provide a means of linking records containing common values for attributes of interest. A list of records linked by such pointer chains is called a **linked list.** In our example, it facilitates rapid retrieval of the set of records for engineers. Linked lists obviously require some type of direct-access file organization in order to perform their function.

We could have accomplished the same goal if the personnel records were physically arranged on the disk so that all the engineers were in sequence beginning with the first record. There would be no need for pointers to retrieve all the records for engineers. The first record would be retrieved, then the second, and so on until the first record was encountered having another skill. So far, so good. If at a later time, however, there were a need to retrieve all the employees assigned to the Seattle office, this scheme would no longer work. We would have to have a copy of the file maintained elsewhere on disk that was physically ordered by location. This is obviously a storage inefficiency, and we have only considered one alternative query. Imagine the difficulty of anticipating all the query needs in advance and creating physical files to service each one.

What we have here is a conflict between physical ordering of records and logical ordering as required by the user. The use of pointers resolves this dilemma by allowing any finite number of logical lists to be represented, without requiring a reorganization of the physical sequence of the file.

In the example of Figure 10.12, note that the value contained in the SKILL POINTER field for Steel's record is "0." This is our notation to indicate a null pointer, or the end of the list. It communicates to the operating system that there are no more records in the linked list for engineers. Alternatively, the last record in a linked list may contain a pointer to the first record in the list, thus completing a ring structure. Ring structures can be useful for network DBMS systems where entry can occur at locations other than at the top of the linked list.

Inverted Lists

While linked lists are a useful way of implementing logical relationships among records, they do have limitations. If the list is extremely long, traversing the chain of records can be time-consuming. List maintenance can be cumbersome, particularly if there are frequent additions or deletions. Long lists are also subject to becoming disconnected due to operating system malfunction.

inverted list A directory wherein each entry contains pointers to all physical records containing a specified value.

An alternative method of accessing records according to logical order is through the use of inverted lists. An **inverted list** is a separate file, or index, that generally contains just two data items: a value of interest, such as "engineer," and all the addresses where records are located having that value. Figure 10.13 shows two inverted lists for the data of Figure 10.12. The use of the inverted list would eliminate the need for SKILL POINTER and LOCATION POINTER fields in the records themselves. In practice, both the inverted list and the file it references are maintained on direct-access files.

Again, the linked list requires that pointers be stored with the data records, whereas the inverted list eliminates that need by storing the pointers separately from the data. Both methods are supported by many DBMS products.

Balanced-Tree Index (B+-Tree)

A refinement of the inverted-list strategy is the B+-tree. B+-trees were developed in an effort to provide an efficient method for maintaining a hierarchy of indexes. A question raised by many observers on seeing the B+-tree for the first time is how it compares to the indexed-sequential file organization. The answer is that the B+-tree is more efficient. The performance of an indexed-sequential method degrades as the size of the file grows. While performance can be upgraded by reorganizing the file periodically, such reorganizations can become time-consuming and expensive. A B+-tree retains its efficiency as the file grows or shrinks.

The B+-tree provides multilevel indexing that is efficient for both sequential and direct processing of data records. A B+-tree consists of a hierarchy of index

▼FIGURE 10.13 EXAMPLES OF INVERTED LISTS

SKILL	ADDRESSES			
Accountant	1	4	7	8
Draftsman	2	6	10	
Engineer	3	5	9	

(a) Inverted List of Skills

LOCATION	ADDRESSES			
Los Angeles	2	4	5	
Portland	6	8	10	
Seattle	1	3	7	9

(b) Inverted List of Locations

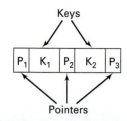

Keys

Pointers

▼**FIGURE 10.14**
B⁺-TREE INDEX
RECORD (IR) (n = 3)

rooted tree A hierarchy of index records that has a single index record at the highest level; that record is called the root.

leaf The lowest-level index record in a rooted tree.

path A set of pointers leading from one index record to another.

records together with a file of data records. The index records contain keys and pointers that are used to locate the data records. A typical index record (IR) in the B⁺-tree is shown in Figure 10.14. In this example, we have three pointers and two keys. In general, we may have a maximum of n pointers and $n-1$ keys, in an IR, n being determined by the designer of the B⁺-tree.

In order to describe the B⁺-tree, we need to define certain terms. A **rooted tree** is a hierarchy of IRs that has a single IR at the highest level. This IR is termed the *root*. An IR is a **leaf** if it is at the lowest level in the rooted tree. (These trees are upside down— root at the top, leaves at the bottom.) The pointers in all nonleaf IRs point to other IRs. The pointers in leaf IRs, however, point to the data records and other leaf IRs.

A B⁺-tree is balanced in the sense that all the leaf IRs are the same distance from the root IR. Distance is measured by the number of IRs that must be examined to reach a leaf IR. The sequence of IRs to be examined is called a **path.** This concept of balance guarantees access to all database records with the same degree of efficiency. In the discussion that follows, we will further establish the conventions for the B⁺-tree and clarify their use with some examples.

Formally, a B⁺-tree is a rooted tree satisfying the following requirements:

1. All paths from the root IR to a leaf IR are of the same length.
2. Each IR that is not a leaf contains at least $\lceil n/2 \rceil$ and at most n pointers to lower-level IRs. ($\lceil ./. \rceil$ denotes the arithmetic operation of rounding up to the next integer value. Thus, if n is 3, then $\lceil n/2 \rceil$ is 2. If n is 4, then $\lceil n/2 \rceil$ is 2.)
3. A leaf IR contains at least $\lceil (n-1)/2 \rceil$ and at most $n-1$ pointers to records in the data file.
4. The keys in an IR are ordered by value, $k_1 < k_2 \ldots < k_{n-1}$.
5. All keys in the subtree to which pointer p_1 points are strictly less than k_1.
6. For $2 <= i <= n-1$, all the keys in the subtree to which p_i points have values greater than or equal to k_{i-1} and less than k_i.
7. All the keys in the subtree to which pn points are greater than or equal to k_{n-1}. Therefore, for $i > 1$, k_{i-1} will always be the *lowest* key in the subtree pointed to by p_i.

Let's clarify these conventions by working through an example. (For brevity, in the discussion that follows, we will refer to the preceding seven requirements as rules.) The general procedure that is used is to find the leaf IR where the key value to be inserted should appear, then insert it if there is room. If the IR is full, we split it into two leaf IRs, order the existing keys plus the new one in ascending order, place the first $\lceil n/2 \rceil$ keys in the leftmost of the two IRs, and place the remaining keys in the other IR. After splitting a leaf IR, we adjust the keys and pointers in the IRs on the path leading to the leaf IR we've split.

Figure 10.15 shows an example of a B⁺-tree for $n = 3$ that indexes records having the following keys added in the order given:

31, 3, 18, 35, 29, 1, 33

The dashed lines in some positions indicate that no key is present. If no key is present, then there will be no pointer to its right either. The way in which pointers are used in the leaf IRs will be explained shortly.

We will now show how this tree was constructed by adding records to an empty tree. Refer to Figure 10.16. The first record to be added has the key "31." It is

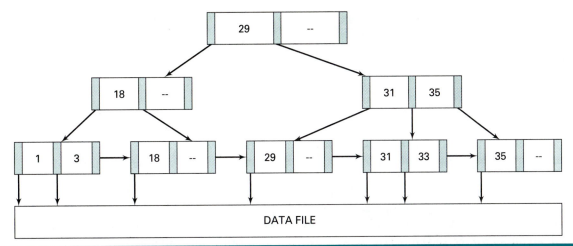

▾FIGURE 10.15 EXAMPLE B⁺-TREE (n = 3)

simply inserted into an IR as shown in Figure 10.16(a). Since our tree has only one IR, it is both a leaf and the root IR. In Figure 10.16(b), we find that there is space for indexing record 3 with no additional IRs being required. (Sorting within the IR is required by rule 4.) To keep matters straightforward, we have illustrated the data file only in Figure 10.16(a).

Things change when we index record 18. Inserting key 18 in the existing IR is not possible, since it is filled. Recall that a leaf IR can have at most $n - 1$ pointers to records in the data file (rule 3); in this case, only two are allowed. Consequently, we must split the existing IR, order the keys to be assigned, and per convention place the first $\lceil n/2 \rceil = 2$ of the ordered keys in the leftmost IR. The other key(s) are placed in the remaining IR. This is shown in the bottom-level IRs of Figure 10.16(c).

Since we now have more than one leaf IR, we need to add a higher-level IR in the tree to index the leaf IRs, as shown in the top level of Figure 10.16(c). (Otherwise, we no longer have a rooted tree.) This higher-level IR is now the root.

Note that there are $n = 3$ pointers in each IR. In each leaf IR, the leftmost pointer (p_1) points to the storage location where the complete record is stored for key k_1. p_2 performs the same function for k_2. However, p_3, points to the next leaf node in sequence, so that the file can be processed sequentially when needed.

Note also that in the newly created nonleaf IR shown in Figure 10.16(c), p_1 and p_2 are the only pointers needed and they satisfy the necessary rules (5–7). The pointer to the left of key value 31 points to a subtree whose key values are strictly less than 31. The pointer to the right of key value 31 points to those keys that are greater than or equal to 31.

Figure 10.16(d) shows the addition of record key 35. We search the tree for the location where key 35 should be placed. In this case we follow the right pointer in the root IR and find that key 35, which is greater than 31, should be located in the leaf node containing key 31. Since there is a vacant slot, we simply enter key 35 as shown. No other changes are required.

Figure 10.16(e) shows the addition of record 29. Since 29 is less than 31, we follow the left pointer in the root IR. The IR pointed to is where key 29 should go, but that IR is filled. Therefore, we split the existing IR, sort the competing keys, and enter the first $\lceil n/2 \rceil = 2$ keys in the leftmost IR, with the remaining key entered in the other IR as shown.

Adding record 1 (Figure 10.16(f)) follows a similar procedure. The IR containing keys 3 and 18 is split, and keys 1, 3, and 18 are allocated in the usual way. In

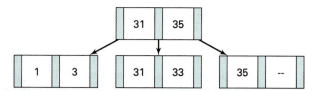

▼FIGURE 10.18 RESULT OF DELETING RECORD 29

Let's consider one more example of constructing a B$^+$-tree, only this time, we use $n = 4$ and the following set of record keys:

14, 95, 56, 22, 64, 29, 35, 43, 25

As shown in Figure 10.19(a), we fill the initial IR with record keys 14, 95, and 56. When we add record 22, we must split that node, order the set of keys, place the first $[n/2]$ (=2) keys in the first IR and the remaining keys (two in this case) in the second IR. This necessitates creating a root node with key 56 being entered (Figure 10-19 (b)).

Records 64 and 29 can now be entered with no change in the configuration of the tree (Figure 10.19(c)). The addition of record 35 causes a split in the leftmost node, with the four competing record keys being ordered and entered according to our previous rules. Records 43 and 25 can then be entered with no change in tree configuration. This result is shown in Figure 10.19(d).

The reader has no doubt surmised that larger values of n result in fewer splits being required for a given set of records, but on average more vacant space would appear in the B$^+$-tree.

The B$^+$-tree is the most widely used strategy for maintaining efficiency in the face of insertions and deletions. Similar concepts exist for an indexing method called a *B-tree* (without the "+"). A B-tree only allows a key to occur once in the

▼FIGURE 10.19 EXAMPLE OF B$^+$-TREE CONSTRUCTION ($n = 4$)

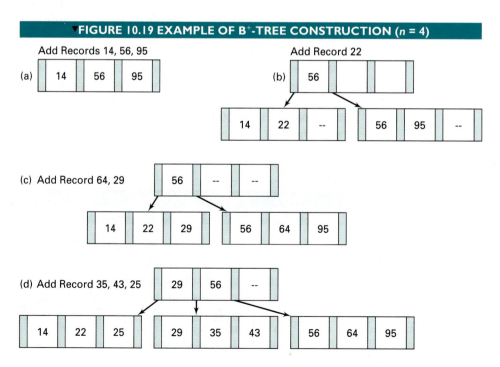

tree, thus reducing space requirements but complicating IR maintenance. Consequently, the B-tree has not realized the usage level of the B+-tree.

▼ Client/Server Implementation of Balanced-Tree Indexing

The use of balanced-tree indexes has enabled high levels of performance in client/server database systems. While the mechanics vary slightly in some instances, the basic objectives and methods remain consistent with our prior discussion.

Consider the example shown in Figure 10.20. The architecture is very similar to that discussed in the previous section, with a few adjustments necessary that we will discuss. The most important modification is *pages,* which are blocks of records. Notice in Figure 10.20 that the root page is at address 100 and contains two index records. The top index record indicates that the page *beginning with* data record 1 is found by next accessing the IR at address 200. Similarly, the page beginning with record 22 is found by next accessing the IR found at address 300.

Suppose that we wanted to access record 10. A search of the root page indicates that record 10 will be found by next accessing the index page located at address 200 (since 10 is less than 22). A search of that page indicates that record 10 will be found at the index page located at address 90 (since 10 is greater than 9). A search of this page (a leaf) indicates that the data for record 10 will be found in the data page located at address 400.

Similar mechanisms apply to the addition and deletion of records.

▼FIGURE 10.20 EXAMPLE OF BALANCE-TREE INDEXING IN A CLIENT/SERVER DATABASE SYSTEM

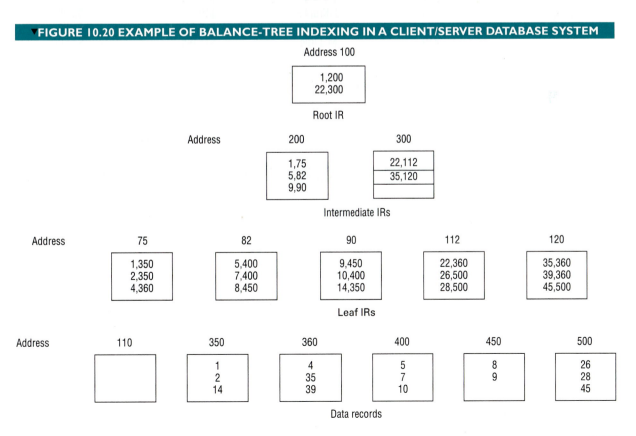

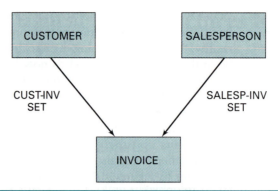

▼FIGURE 10.23 EXAMPLE OF A SIMPLE NETWORK STRUCTURE

This simple network can be represented by linked lists by creating pointers for each set. One group of pointers is necessary to connect CUSTOMER records to their INVOICE records, and another group of pointers is needed to connect SALESPERSON records to their INVOICE records. An instance of the logical relationship is shown in Figure 10.24. As a physical implementation method, however, this is awkward because the number of pointers required is variable: If there are three invoice records owned by a customer, three pointers are required; if there are five invoice records owned by a customer, then five pointers are required. As a practical matter, maintaining a variable number of pointer fields in an owner record is difficult. However, the linked list provides a way of avoiding that difficulty.

The way in which this is done is illustrated in Figure 10.25. Each customer record contains a pointer to the record number of the first invoice it owns. That invoice record will contain a record number pointer to the next invoice owned by the same customer. This process continues until the last invoice for a customer is linked. For example, CUSTOMER Smith's record points to Invoice #1 (record number 6), which points to Invoice #2 (record number 7), which is the last of Smith's invoices. The end of the list of invoices is indicated by a record number of 0 in the pointer field.

A more practical method of implementation is shown in Figure 10.26. Comparing Figure 10.26 to Figure 10.25, you can see that the only change is that the last

▼FIGURE 10.24 INSTANCE OF EXAMPLE IN FIGURE 10.20

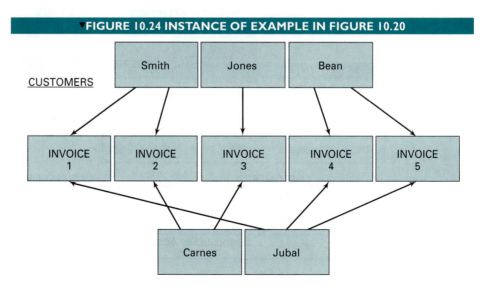

RELATIVE RECORD NUMBER	DATA RECORD	CUSTOMER INVOICE POINTER	SALESPERSON INVOICE POINTER
1	Smith	6	
2	Jones	8	
3	Bean	9	
4	Carnes		7
5	Jubal		6
6	Inv #1	7	9
7	Inv #2	0	8
8	Inv #3	0	0
9	Inv #4	10	10
10	Inv #5	0	0

CUSTOMER RECORDS: 1–3
SALESPERSON RECORDS: 4–5
INVOICE RECORDS: 6–10

▼FIGURE 10.25 SIMPLE NETWORK MAPPED TO LINKED LIST

▼FIGURE 10.26 SIMPLE NETWORK MAPPED TO RING STRUCTURE

RELATIVE ADDRESS	DATA RECORD	CUSTOMER INVOICE POINTER	SALESPERSON INVOICE POINTER
1	Smith	6	
2	Jones	8	
3	Bean	9	
4	Carnes		7
5	Jubal		6
6	Inv #1	7	9
7	Inv #2	1	8
8	Inv #3	2	4
9	Inv #4	10	10
10	Inv #5	3	5

CUSTOMER RECORDS: 1–3
SALESPERSON RECORDS: 4–5
INVOICE RECORDS: 6–10

record in each list contains a pointer back to the owner record. This ring structure facilitates the execution of the FIND OWNER, FIND FIRST, and FIND NEXT queries of common network data manipulation languages. Following the ring of pointers facilitates locating the desired record. (Network data manipulation languages are discussed in Chapter 15.)

Mapping Hierarchical Databases

As with network data structures, multiple pointers in parent records may be used to represent the relationships of a hierarchy or tree, as suggested in Figure 10.27. While the method of multiple pointers within a record provides connections be-

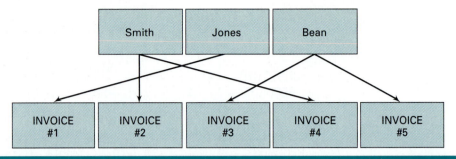

▼FIGURE 10.27 EXAMPLE OF HIERARCHICAL RELATIONSHIPS

tween parent and child records, it is not often used because of the variable number of pointers that may be necessary in each parent record. Variable-length records are particularly cumbersome when additions and deletions must be made.

The use of child-and-twin pointers reduces the complexity of maintaining multiple pointers and the restriction of child-to-parent mapping. Examine Figure 10.28. Here you see that the first pointer of each record contains the address of one child record, and the second pointer indicates the location of a twin record. In this fashion, each record contains exactly two pointer fields, which is much easier to maintain. As with any linked list, the pointers may be removed from the record itself and placed in an inverted list directory. For our example, this is shown in Figure 10.29.

▼ Secondary-Key Access

primary key A data item value that uniquely identifies a record.

secondary key A data item value that identifies a set of records.

To this point, we have been using the word *key* rather freely to mean a data item whose value uniquely identifies a record. Technically, this definition defines a **primary key.** There are also secondary keys that can be unique but are not required to be. A **secondary key** is one that identifies a *set* of records having the same value for the secondary key. Secondary keys play an important role in supporting the information requirements of DBMS users.

We illustrate the fundamental concepts by way of an example. The Cosmos Credit Union has several types of users of its database system. The tellers need to access customer account records in order to answer customer questions and to update records as transactions take place. Some customers may have only checking accounts. Others may have in addition, savings accounts, credit card accounts, or long-term loans.

▼FIGURE 10.28 HIERARCHY MAPPED TO LINKED LIST

RELATIVE ADDRESS	PARENT RECORD	CHILD POINTER	TWIN POINTER
1	Smith	5	2
2	Jones	4	3
3	Bean	6	0
4	Inv #1	0	0
5	Inv #2	0	7
6	Inv #3	0	8
7	Inv #4	0	0
8	Inv #5	0	0

0 = End of Invoice List

▼FIGURE 10.29 HIERARCHY MAPPED TO INVERTED LIST

CUSTOMER RECORD ID	INVOICE RECORD POINTER
Smith	5
Smith	7
Jones	4
Bean	6
Bean	8

The teller can probably get by using a primary key such as customer identification number to access all needed records. A loan officer, however, may at times need to retrieve those records having a certain credit card account limit (say $2,000), or those loans outstanding that have balances of over $50,000. A branch manager of the credit union may be interested in knowing the total loans outstanding of a particular type: auto, home improvement, personal, and so forth. These needs can all be serviced through use of secondary-key access methods.

Secondary-key access is accomplished by establishing indexes that traverse desired paths through the physical data records. Consider the following query:

Identify names of customers having 48-month loans.

Using Figure 10.30 as a sample instance, we show how this information would be provided through the use of linked lists. The primary key is CUSTOMER-NAME, and the secondary key is LOAN-PERIOD. There are three financing periods for loans: 24 months, 36 months, and 48 months. Thus, the secondary key allows the retrieval of sets of records associated with each of the three financing periods. Three pointers are thus required to identify the beginning record in each set (the head list). These pointers are stored separately from the data records themselves.

To compute the answer to the query, the list of head pointers is accessed, and the address 1 is found for the head of the list of records having financing period values of 48. The record located at address 1 contains a pointer to the next record having that value, and so on until the complete set is found.

The discerning reader will have noticed that secondary-key access was used earlier in the chapter when we introduced the idea of linked lists. You will recall that in that case we were retrieving records on the secondary keys SKILL and LOCATION.

Linked lists of secondary keys are particularly useful when physical files are very large. If in an extended version of the file used in Figure 10.30 we had 50,000 records of which only 100 had loan periods of 48 months, the use of the secondary key Loan-Period saves having to search the entire file of 50,000, a factor of (50,000/100 =) 500.

As you may have surmised, whenever we can represent lists with pointers embedded in the records, we also have the alternative of removing the pointers and maintaining them in an inverted list. Figure 10.31 shows the inverted list for the example of Figure 10.30.

▼FIGURE 10.30 USE OF EMBEDDED POINTERS ON SECONDARY KEY

HEAD LIST

24 = 3
36 = 2
48 = 1

RELATIVE ADDRESS	CUSTOMER-NAME	LOAN-TYPE	LOAN-PERIOD	LOAN-PERIOD POINTER
1	Nixon	Auto	48	6
2	Patton	Auto	36	4
3	Fortius	Boat	24	0
4	Wood	Auto	36	5
5	Cayman	Home	36	7
6	Vance	Auto	48	8
7	Costas	Home	36	0
8	Ubu	Auto	48	0

LOAN-PERIOD

24	3			
36	2	4	5	7
48	1	6	8	

▼FIGURE 10.31 USE OF INVERTED LIST ON SECONDARY KEY

▼ Query Optimization

Query optimization is an important consideration in a database system, since the difference in execution time between a good strategy and a poor strategy may be substantial. With the network and hierarchical data structures, optimization is left to the application programmer, since the data manipulation commands are embedded in a host programming language and are at the level of individual record manipulation. Relational queries, however, can be completely expressed in the relational query language and manipulate entire sets of records at a time. It is, therefore, possible and desirable to optimize queries automatically.

Our purpose in this section is to acquaint the reader with the fundamental ideas of query optimization without exploring all the details of this large field of study. We focus on the general question of how to efficiently compute an answer to a query in relational algebra. We will focus on the following three operators:

Select

Project

Join

We will use the following sample database:

```
EMPLOYEE(EMP-NAME, STREET, EMP-CITY)
ASSIGNMENT(PROJ-NAME, EMP-NAME, SKILL, HOURS)
PROJECT(PROJ-NAME, BUDGET, PROJ-CITY)
```

Combining Selection and Join Operations

Consider the following query:

Find the budgets and names of all projects that have employees living in Pasadena.

One way this query might be written and interpreted is as follows:

```
A := Join(EMPLOYEE, ASSIGNMENT, PROJECT)
B := Select(A: EMP-CITY = "Pasadena")
C := B[PROJ-NAME, BUDGET]
```

Since the Join operates on the three relations in their entirety, all tuples in all three relations must be examined. Thus, if there are n tuples in EMPLOYEE, m tuples in ASSIGNMENT, and k tuples in PROJECT, then $n \times m \times k$ inspections must be made. Contrast this with the following strategy.

```
A:= Select(EMPLOYEE: City = "Pasadena")
B:= Join(A,ASSIGNMENT,PROJECT)
C:= B[PROJ-NAME,BUDGET]
```

Suppose that there are t employees who live in Pasadena ($t <= n$). Then there are $t \times m \times k$ inspections that must be made, where

$$(t \times m \times k) <= (n \times m \times k)$$

If t is significantly smaller than n, this latter strategy will require considerably fewer inspections. Consequently, efficient execution suggests that selections be performed as early as possible.

Combining Projection, Selection, and Join Operations

In the preceding example, even the second query formulation carried unnecessary information with its operations. The desired relation requires only the values for two attributes: PROJ-NAME and BUDGET. All that is really needed then are the attributes necessary for the desired result and the attributes needed for the join. Appropriate use of the projection operator makes the query even more efficient, as follows:

```
A:= Select(EMPLOYEE: EMP-CITY = 'Pasadena') [EMP-NAME]
B:= ASSIGNMENT[PROJ-NAME, EMP-NAME]
C:= PROJECT[PROJ-NAME, BUDGET]
D:= Join(A,B,C) [PROJ-NAME,BUDGET]
```

In each step of this solution, we have projected out all unnecessary attributes, leaving only those required for the solution. The guideline then is to perform selections and projections as early as possible. Joins, being very time-consuming, should be performed as late as possible.

Summary

In this chapter, basic concepts of file organization and access which can be of value to both users and systems designers were introduced. Both groups should be conversant with the terminology and basic concepts of physical file organization and access in order to communicate better with technical personnel, to ask relevant questions of vendors, to be aware of alternatives, and to otherwise be able to contribute to the effective implementation of database systems.

We first discussed the physical storage media that support database system operations. We examined the way in which data are stored on disk and outlined the process of accessing data on disk. We further showed how access times are computed.

We outlined three basic methods of physical file organization: sequential, indexed sequential, and direct. Sequential organization is efficient when applications involve only the processing of significant numbers of records each time the file is accessed. Indexed-sequential organization is effective when there are significant applications that require sequential processing and there are significant applications that require direct processing. Direct organization is necessary when most critical applications require direct access to records. We demonstrated both static and dynamic approaches to direct file organization.

We also surveyed fundamental physical data structures that enable logical data relationships to be implemented. The most basic tool is the pointer. The pointer is a data item that contains a physical address of a stored record. Pointers may be embedded in the records themselves, thus chaining together a list of related records. Alternatively, an index of values, along with pointers to records containing those values, can be maintained separate from the records themselves. This is called an inverted list. An indexing scheme that maintains its efficiency regardless of the number of insertions and deletions is called the B$^+$-tree. We presented the concepts of the B$^+$-tree and showed how one would be constructed and used.

An outline was given of the methods by which logical data models are mapped to physical representations. In this way, we completed the journey from conceptual model to logical implementation model to physical implementation.

We then showed how pointers can be used in concert with secondary keys to facilitate retrieval of data.

Finally, we briefly discussed the topic of query optimization. While good relational DBMSs provide the necessary optimization, knowledge of the motivation and methods can provide insight to users of database systems.

Review Questions

1. Define each of the following terms in your own words:
   a. strategy selector
   b. file manager
   c. main memory
   d. cylinder
   e. physical record
   f. data transfer rate
   g. count-key format
   h. head list
   i. inverted list
   j. rooted tree
   k. leaf
   l. rotational delay
   m. disk drive
   n. clustering
   o. primary key

2. Why is the allocation of records to blocks a factor in database system performance?

3. Compare sequential, indexed-sequential, and direct file organization.

4. What are the desired features of a good hashing algorithm?

5. What is the purpose of the gap in a record format?

6. Distinguish between the count-data format and the count-key format.

7. What is latency?

8. Describe the principal operations involved in input/output management.

9. What efficiency is accomplished by using pointers?

10. Distinguish between a simple linked list and a ring.

11. What is a null pointer, and what does it signify?

12. What does the term B^+-*tree* stand for? What is the purpose of a B^+-tree?

13. Distinguish between a primary key and a secondary key.

Exercises and Problems

1. Match each term with its definition.

__*buffer manager*   a. A data item containing a physical address

__*data dictionary*   b. The time required to position the read/write heads
                               over a given cylinder

__*access motion time*   c. The time required to activate the read/write heads

__*head activation time*   d. Defines the structure of user data and how they
                               are to be used

__*pointer*   e. Software that controls the movement of data be-
                               tween main memory and disk storage

__*linked list*   f. A sequence of pointers connecting index records

__*path*   g. Physical records that are linked by embedded
                               pointers

__*secondary key*   h. A data item value that identifies a set of records

2. Suppose that we store records on a disk device having the following characteristics:

average access motion time: 0.02 seconds

disk rotation speed: 3,600 revolutions per minute

data transfer rate: 312,000 bytes per second

What is the expected data transfer time for a randomly accessed physical record that is 500 bytes in length?

3. How would your answer to (2) be changed if you were using a disk device with fixed read/write heads—that is, each track in each cylinder has its own read/write head?

4. Using the same parameters as given in (2), suppose that ten physical records are stored on a track. What would be the comparative data transfer times for (a) 30 records stored sequentially on the same cylinder, and (b) 30 records stored on three tracks not in the same cylinder?

5. If blocking facilitates efficient storage and retrieval of records, why not store entire files in one very large block?

6. Suppose that logical records are stored in blocks of four and that two succeeding blocks contain logical records 11, 13, 14, 19, and 21, 23, 24, 26. Describe how the operating system will locate record 23.

7. Why would sequential file organization be efficient for processing the weekly payroll? Why would it not be efficient for responding to user queries?

8. Since indexed-sequential file organization provides for both sequential and direct access of records, why do we need any other methods of file organization?

9. Use the quadratic quotient hashing algorithm to compute the relative addresses at which the following records are to be stored. Assume a loading factor of 80 percent. How many blocks are needed if this is the entire file? (Assume one record per block.)

Key	Name
14	Smith
24	Bean
28	Harris
23	Scott

10. Suppose that a dynamic hashing algorithm produces the following high-order bits for the specified record keys. Show how these records would be indexed and stored. Follow the example shown in the text, and assume that they are entered in the same order shown in that example.

$$h(k_1) = 0011...$$
$$h(k_2) = 1100...$$
$$h(k_3) = 1001...$$
$$h(k_4) = 1110...$$
$$h(k_5) = 1011...$$
$$h(k_6) = 0010...$$
$$h(k_7) = 1010...$$

11. Which do you think would be easier to maintain: an inverted list or a simple linked list? If your answer is that "it depends," give an example illustrating your point.

12. Create a B$^+$-tree for the following records: 20, 63, 34, 56, 43, 89, 45, 68, 52, 54, 14, 19, 7, 70, and 82. Let $n = 3$.

13. Show how the network of Figure 10.1E could be physically represented by:
   a. Using child-and-twin pointers
   b. Using address pointers maintained in an index
   c. A ring structure

▼**FIGURE 10.1E NETWORK FOR PROBLEM 13**

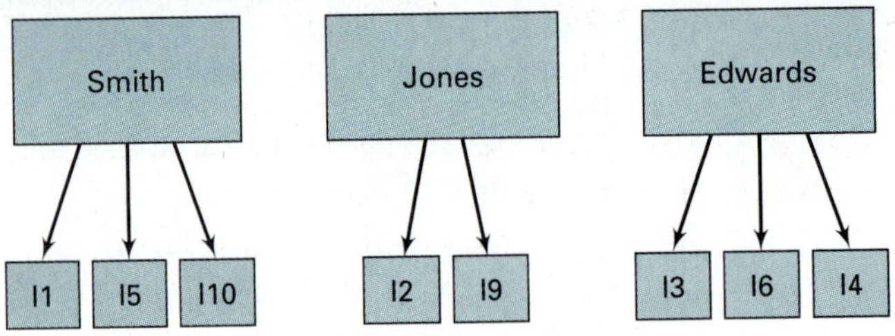

14. Construct a diagram of a hierarchical data model and show how it could be mapped to a physical representation.

15. Construct a diagram of a simple network and show how it could be mapped to a physical representation.

16. Construct a diagram of a complex network and show how it could be mapped to a physical representation.

17. Construct two relations which may need to be joined to satisfy a user query. Show how clustering might be used to make that query formulation more efficient.

18. Give an example of a personnel file that is physically ordered by Employee Number and includes linked lists to provide secondary keys on Insurance Plan (there are three types: *A*, *B*, and *C*), Employee Type (Hourly or Salaried), and Retirement Plan (*X* or *Y*).

19. Repeat problem 17 using an inverted list.

20. Consider the following database:

```
CUSTOMER(CUST#,NAME,CUSTCITY)
ACCOUNT(ACCT#,TYPE,CUST#,BALANCE,OFFICE#)
LOCATION(OFFICE#,ASSETS,CITY)
```

Show how the following queries could be written to execute more efficiently:

a. Query—Find the assets and office numbers of all locations that have customers living in Midway.

```
A:=JOIN(CUSTOMER,ACCOUNT,LOCATION)
B:=SELECT(A:CUSTCITY = "Midway")[OFFICE#,ASSETS]
```

b. Query—Find the assets and office numbers of all locations that have customers living in Midway with deposit balances over $1,500.

```
A:=JOIN(CUSTOMER,ACCOUNT,LOCATION)
B:=SELECT(A: CUSTCITY = "Midway" and BALANCE >
      1500)[OFFICE#,ASSETS]
```

Projects and Professional Issues

1. For each of the following, discuss which might be the appropriate method of file organization:
   a. A hospital database system to support its business operations
   b. An order-entry system for a manufacturing firm
   c. A car rental agency
   d. A distributor of pharmaceuticals
   e. A student records system at a university
   f. A hotel reservation system

2. Since physical data structures are determined by neither the systems analyst nor the user, is there any advantage to making either one literate on the topic?

3. Effective clustering of records to facilitate relational language operations may depend on the type and frequency of various types of queries. Can you think of a way of providing information that would aid in determining how to cluster records?

4. If you have access to information on commercial DBMSs, see if you can determine what types of physical data structures are supported.

C H A P T E R

DATABASE ADMINISTRATION AND CONTROL

At the weekly staff meeting of Manwaring Consulting Services, the main business was reporting on the status of the various projects under contract. Most of the projects involved database design and development; however, Elmer Nordland was directing a project whose main focus was on administrative and control issues. Joan Manwaring thought it might be instructive for the other project managers to learn about these issues and how Elmer's team was dealing with them.

Joan asked, "Elmer, are the technical problems of database systems separate from administrative and control issues? I've heard people say that good management is good management—that effective management principles do not vary with technology."

Elmer nodded. "There is some justification for that point of view, but as I see things, the two cannot really be considered separately. In fact, we are finding that some problems cannot be easily categorized in one camp or the other. It appears to me that successful database systems implementations are always accompanied by a sound understanding of administrative and control issues."

Information systems are increasingly viewed as resources that require good management as well as good technical features. Because database systems often form the nucleus of an organization's information system, they are the focus of many administrative issues, which we will address in this chapter. After reading this chapter, you should be able to:

▼ Explain the importance of database administration.

▼ List and describe the functions of the database administrator.

▼ Discuss how data integrity can be maintained.

▼ Describe how data security can be implemented.

▼ List the sources of database failures and compare the various recovery methods.

▼ Database Administration: An Overview

Database administration is basically concerned with ensuring that accurate and consistent information is available to users and applications when needed and in the form required. Thus, DBA interacts with both the system and users (Figure 11.1). Some organizations have split the responsibility for managing information system resources between a **data administrator (DA)** and a **database administrator (DBA)**. In such instances, the DA's responsibilities are usually concerned with developing general policies and procedures for the information system, while the DBA's responsibilities tend to be more technical, as suggested by Figure 11.1. The DBA will be concerned with such matters as establishing data definitions; developing programs to generate needed information; adding data to, and deleting data from, the database; implementing security and integrity controls; and managing database operations.

In addition to these primary responsibilities, the DBA should play a lead role in database planning and development and in educating users. This education includes such areas as:

1. How database technology can assist the various levels of management (important to winning and maintaining management support for the database system).

data administrator
Manager whose responsibilities are focused on establishing policies and procedures for the organization's information system.

database administrator Manager whose responsibilities are focused on management of the technical aspects of the database system.

implementation of a database system is hard to overemphasize. Certain aspects of their current work may be "taken over" by the database system, and standard design frameworks for systems and programs may change significantly. Accomplishing the desired preparation may include presentations to managers, training sessions for key personnel, and possibly the use of outside consultants. Training is usually the most important facet of preparation for change.

Training should give personnel a broad view of the function of a database system as an integral part of the firm's information system, as well as giving specific guidance as to how it can be used in the user's daily activities. To be successful, training should be regarded as a continuing process prompted by new hires, new releases of software, and the development of new or improved applications.

Establishing Standards and Procedures

Effective database administration requires the establishment of uniform standards and procedures. Their purpose is to maintain control of data security and data integrity in an efficient way. Standards are particularly applicable to controlling the development and use of database programming and operations.

In the programming area, standards are established to ensure that programs are adequately reviewed and tested before being put into production. These standards may require a review by a competent second party, as well as the use of test data to evaluate how a program handles both correct and erroneous data. The usual procedure includes documenting these test results.

In the area of operations, standards may be established for maintaining transaction logs, and procedures created for error correction, checkpoints, and backup and recovery.

Organizations having few standards and procedures may encounter difficulty in converting to the database environment, since the record shows that the integrated data management facilitated by database systems requires good, comprehensive standards and procedures. An organization that is beginning to implement a database system may find it useful to examine the standards in use at other organizations that are already using database systems. For example, the following functions form the nucleus of standards and procedures at Zeus Corporation.

1. *Analysis and Routing of Trouble Reports.*   At Zeus, a formal trouble-reporting system was established in order to report all errors to the DBA. Trouble reports are analyzed to determine the likely cause of each reported problem. The reports are then routed to the appropriate manager or user group for disposition. Each trouble report contains a complete log (time and location of problem) and descriptive information. Each report requires a formal response to the report's initiator specifying how the problem has been resolved.

2. *Monitoring of Hardware and Software.*   The status of all hardware and software is regularly monitored, and reports of failures and consequent action are made to appropriate managers and user groups. Periodic analysis of hardware and software requirements is made, forming the basis for decisions on replacement and upgrading, including needs for additional database storage media.

3. *Testing.*   Performance acceptance testing is conducted to evaluate all new procedures, software, and hardware. Structural and consistency checks of the database are conducted on a regular basis.

4. *Security.* In consultation with Zeus management, security classifications are implemented that identify which user groups are authorized to access specific data elements in the database and what actions may be performed thereon. Computer operations are frequently monitored to assure that these access controls are functioning in the intended way.

5. *Backup and Recovery.* Backup and recovery procedures are tested regularly to assure their effectiveness in restoring the database after any disruption of service. A disaster plan (to respond to natural disasters such as flooding or electrical outages) has been drawn up and is tested periodically to make sure it works.

6. *Performance Evaluation.* Priorities have been assigned to activities that compete for database resources, such as processing transactions, generating reports, and processing queries. System performance is monitored by collecting statistics on transaction volume, response time, error rates, and hardware utilization. Input is elicited from system users to monitor their satisfaction with the system's performance. Database size and growth is also tracked. File expansion programs are run and database reorganizations are performed as necessary. Activity logs and abnormal termination logs are reviewed and summaries prepared for management evaluation.

7. *Integrity Checking.* Schedules have been developed at Zeus for testing the integrity of the data stored in the database.

▼ DBA Goals

As you can see, much of the effort involved in database administration is concerned with ensuring the quality and the availability of the database system. This is in keeping with the basic DBA goals: maintaining the integrity, security, and availability of data.

A database must be protected from accidents, such as input or programming errors, from malicious use of the database, and from hardware or software failures that corrupt data. Protection from accidents that cause data inaccuracies is part of the goal of maintaining data integrity. These accidents include failures during transaction processing, logical errors that violate the assumption that transactions preserve database consistency constraints, and anomalies due to concurrent access to the database **(concurrent processing)**.

Protecting the database from unauthorized or malicious use is termed data security. Although the dividing line between data integrity and data security is not precise, a working definition is as follows:

1. **Integrity** is concerned with making certain that operations performed by users are correct and maintain database consistency.

2. **Security** is concerned with limiting users to performing only those operations that are allowed.

The possibility of hardware or software failure requires that **database recovery procedures** be implemented as well. That is, means must be provided to restore databases that have been corrupted by system malfunctions to a consistent state.

These facets of database management are examined in the sections that follow.

---

concurrent processing (concurrency) Occurs when two or more transactions concurrently request access to the same database record at about the same time.

data integrity The accuracy and consistency of data stored in the database system.

data security Refers to protecting the database system from unauthorized or malicious use.

database recovery procedures The means by which a database that has been corrupted by malfunctions can be restored to a correct and consistent state.

---

1. Change the customer record by reducing the balance of the account by $500.

2. Change the cash record by increasing its balance by $500.

Perhaps the second step fails. Then the accounts will be out of balance. Figure 11.5 shows what happens when these actions are performed as a series of independent steps (a) and when they are performed as a single atomic transaction (b). The key point is that when the actions are performed atomically and one fails, then no changes are applied to the database. Such transactions are said to be **aborted**.

To support transaction processing, a DBMS must maintain a transaction record of *every change* made to the database. One way in which this is done is to use a **log**. When a customer makes a $500 payment on account, the transaction actions include (1) crediting the customer account and (2) debiting the cash account. During the execution of the transaction, all write operations may be deferred until the last action of the transaction has been executed. The resulting updates are recorded on the transaction log. When all actions have been executed, the update information on the log is used to write the updated information to the appropriate database records. If the system fails before the transaction completes its entire execution, the information on the log is never written to those records. We will have more to say about this log when we discuss recovery techniques.

aborted transaction
Transaction that is canceled before changes are applied to the database.

log A record of all transactions and the corresponding changes to the database.

Concurrency Control

Suppose that the League of Women Voters (LWV) in Smithville decides to have a Ham and Turkey Dinner. The Chamber of Commerce (CC) in nearby Johnstown decides that it is also time to reward its members with a Ham and Beans Dinner. Both organizations contact their town's distribution center for Bounty Foods. The LWV wants 25 hams; the CC wants 35 hams. Both orders are transmitted to the database

---

▼FIGURE 11.5 INDEPENDENT AND ATOMIC TRANSACTIONS

Action		
CUSTOMER A/R ACCOUNT		Result
CUST # BALANCE	1. Credit payment of 500.	CUSTOMER A/R ACCOUNT
123 ...... 1000		CUST # BALANCE
CASH ACCOUNT		...... 500 ....
BALANCE	2. System fails.	CASH ACCOUNT
.... 1500		BALANCE
		.... 1500 ....

(a) Result of Applying Actions Independently

Transaction	Result
CUSTOMER A/R ACCOUNT	
CUST # BALANCE	
123 ...... 1000	1. Credit payment of 500. No change to CUSTOMER A/R ACCOUNT
CASH ACCOUNT	
BALANCE	
.... 1500	2. System fails No change to CASH ACCOUNT

No changes made because entire transaction was not successful.

(b) Result of Applying Actions Atomically

system at the regional warehouse at the same time (Figure 11.6). The LWV order arrives a fraction of a second before the order from the CC. An image of the inventory record for ham is placed into the computer's working area. The inventory record shows that 100 hams are in stock. But before the LWV transaction can be completed and the inventory record updated, the CC transaction also gets a copy of the same inventory record showing 100 hams in stock, which is placed in its working area. Both records show that the order in question can be filled.

Suppose the LWV transaction is completed first. The rewritten inventory record shows 100 − 25 = 75 hams left in stock. Upon completion of the CC transaction, the inventory record is overwritten with 100 − 35 = 65 hams in stock. What has really happened is that 60 hams have been sold from a stock of 100, leaving only *40* hams in the warehouse, but the system's inventory balance shows *65* hams on hand. Problems galore! This example illustrates the fundamental nature of concurrent processing:

If two or more users are accessing the database at the same time and transactions are interleaved (as in the Bounty Foods example), undesirable results may occur.

A common way of preventing the concurrency problem is through a simple locking policy. In the preceding example, the first transaction to arrive would **lock** (prevent access by any other transactions) the ham inventory record (Figure 11.7) until the first transaction's processing was complete. When a record is locked by

lock Prevents access to a database record by a second transaction until the first transaction has completed all of its actions.

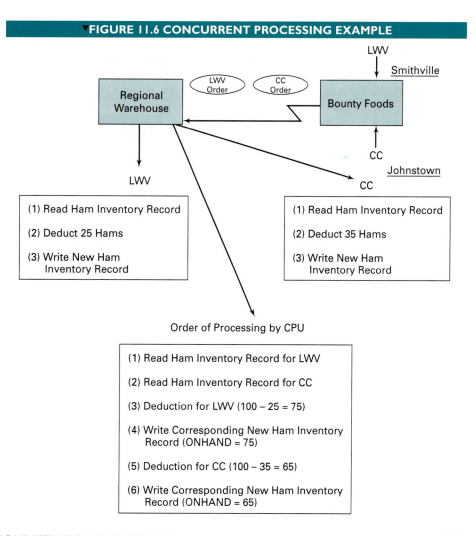

▼FIGURE 11.6 CONCURRENT PROCESSING EXAMPLE

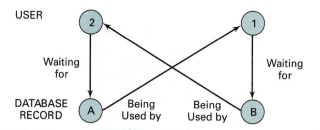

USER

Waiting for

Waiting for

DATABASE RECORD

Being Used by Being Used by

▼**FIGURE 11.9 DEADLOCK DETECTED BY IDENTIFYING CYCLES**

changed by a write operation performed by the other transaction. The concurrent holder of the read_lock would then be reading an incorrect value.

The use of two-phase locking with a deadlock-prevention protocol is shown in Figure 11.10(b). We have added the requirement that every transaction lock all of the data items it needs in advance. If any of the data items cannot be obtained, then none of the items is locked, and the transaction is placed on hold until all of the needed items are available. In Figure 11.10(b), we assume that T_1's request has begun momentarily prior to that of T_2. T_2 cannot lock all of its required data items until H and T are unlocked by T_1. In this way, the deadlock of Figure 11.10(a) is avoided; however, in this example the result has simply been the processing of transactions in serial fashion. This is specific to our example and would always occur when two transactions were competing for the exact same set of records.

An instance demonstrating parallel operations that are serializable is shown in Figure 11.11. In this case T_2 need only wait for T_1 to unlock item H. At that time, T_2 can

▼**FIGURE 11.10(a) EXAMPLE OF TWO-PHASE LOCKING LEADING TO DEADLOCK**

T_1	Turkey (T) and Ham (H) Inventory Values	T_2	Turkey (T) and Ham (H) Inventory Values
Read_lock (H)	DISALLOWED	Read_lock (T)	
Read_item (H)	H = 100	Read_item (T)	T = 30
Write_lock (T) ← DISALLOWED		Write_lock (H)	
Unlock (H)	T = 30	Unlock (T)	
Read_item (T)		Read_item (H)	
T = T – 25		H = H – 25	
Write_item (T)	T = 5	Write_item (H)	
Unlock (T)		Unlock (H)	

▼**FIGURE 11.10(b) EXAMPLE OF TWO-PHASE LOCKING WITH DEADLOCK-AVOIDANCE PROTOCOL RESULTING IN SERIAL PROCESSING**

T_1	Turkey (T) and Ham (H) Inventory Values	T_2	Turkey (T) and Ham (H) Inventory Values
Read_lock (H)			
Write_lock (T)		(waiting)	
Read_item (H)	H = 100		
Unlock (H)			
Read_item (T)	T = 30		
T = T – 25			
Write_item (T)	T = 5		
Unlock (T)			
		Write_lock (H)	
		Read_lock (T)	
		Read_item (H)	H = 100
		H = H – 25	
		Write_item (H)	H = 75
		Unlock (H)	
		Read_item (T)	T = 5
		Unlock (T)	

T₁	T and H Inventory Values	T₂	H and Beef (B) Inventory Values
Read_lock (H)			
Write_lock (T)		(waiting)	
Read_item (H)	H = 100		
Unlock (H)		Write_lock (H)	
Read_item (T)	T = 30	Read_lock (B)	
T = T − 25		Read_item (H)	H = 100
Write_item (T)	T = 5	H = H − 25	
Unlock (T)		Write_item (H)	H = 75
		Unlock (H)	
		Read_item (B)	B = 60
		Unlock (B)	

▼ FIGURE 11.11 EXAMPLE OF TWO-PHASE LOCKING WITH DEADLOCK-AVOIDANCE PROTOCOL RESULTING IN PARALLEL PROCESSING

lock all of the records needed for its processing, and both T_1 and T_2 can proceed in parallel. The results of both T_1 and T_2 are as if they were processed in serial fashion.

▼ Database Security

Database integrity problems can be challenging, but they are generally easier to cope with than malicious access to the database, which includes the following:

1. Theft of information.
2. Unauthorized modification of data.
3. Unauthorized destruction of data.

Thus, database security methods focus on preventing unauthorized users from accessing the database. Because DBMS features that make the database easy to access and manipulate also open doors to intruders, most DBMSs include security features that allow only authorized persons or programs to access data and then restrict the types of processing that can be accomplished once access is made.

Authentication

Database access usually requires user authentication and authorization. For user authentication, the first level of security establishes that the person seeking system entry is an authorized user. His or her identity may be established by (1) something the user knows, such as a log-on number and password, (2) something the user possesses, such as a plastic ID card, or (3) a physical representation of the user, such as a fingerprint or voiceprint.

Passwords, by far the most common and often the least expensive security method, are adequate for many applications. However, once a potential intruder knows the password length and the alphabet from which it is derived, passwords can be repeatedly generated and tried over a period of time until access is eventually gained. For some password schemes, the average time required to do this may be long enough to discourage casual intruders. If the potential payoff is large enough, however, the DBA should devise a password scheme that does not leave intrusion to chance.

The ideal password scheme limits unauthorized systems access by creating a password that is difficult to guess but still easy for the user to remember. For some applications, it may be quite sufficient to specify password parameters such as password length and alphabet to be used; then let the user devise the password. If this approach is used, it may be advisable to appoint a password supervisor to ensure that password parameters are satisfied and that duplications are avoided.

Whether users select their own passwords or whether passwords are issued from a central authority, it can be useful to have a supervisor who maintains an encrypted list of all passwords on a disk that is accessible only to that supervisor. Also, when an employee terminates or transfers to a new functional area, all passwords to which that employee had access should be changed. This is important, since disgruntled ex-employees have been known to sabotage systems.

For extremely sensitive systems, more sophisticated schemes may be considered. One such scheme programs the computer to conduct a question-and-answer session with the user, drawing on questions and answers the user has previously stored in the system. The questions are usually personal in nature, so only a valid user is likely to answer them correctly. Question sequences might occur as follows:

▼ What is your grandfather's middle name?

▼ When is your daughter's birthday?

▼ What is special about September 18?

When the user signs on and enters a personal identification number, the computer asks questions randomly selected from the stored data. The selection can also be varied from one time to another to limit the possibility that other persons may observe the answers to all the questions.

Still another method of protecting against unauthorized access is through the use of a prearranged algorithm. That is, the computer gives the prospective user an authentication number chosen at random and asks for a response. The user applies a prearranged transformation on the number and transmits the result. The computer compares the received value with what it has computed. If they match, then access is granted. This is particularly useful if a would-be intruder has tapped into a communication line. All that can be observed is the result of the algorithm applied to the number. The difficulty of figuring out the algorithm from this information is enormous.

Access control is enhanced if all denied-access attempts produce a log entry and a time delay (the latter increases the time required to gain unauthorized access). The system should automatically log off users who are unable to supply a valid password within a set time or number of trials. It is also desirable that passwords not be displayed on the screen and that users not leave the system unattended after sign-on has been accomplished.

An important aspect of database security is determining when user authentication alone is sufficient and when it should be combined with specific identification of the terminal. With the increasing incidence of illegal intrusion by so-called "hackers," there have been cases where user authorization was satisfied by someone who was not communicating from any of the legitimate system terminals. In addition, switching mechanisms sometimes misconnect. Noise in a communication line can cause a polling mechanism to connect an incorrect device due to address modification. Such errors are often undetected, which degrades reliability and can compromise security. Thus, automatic terminal identification is recommended whenever telecommunication switching equipment is used.

Undesirable outside intrusion may alternatively be prevented by implementing dial-up/call-back procedures. With this strategy, anyone attempting to gain system access supplies the necessary authentication information. The system then hangs up and calls back to a legitimate terminal location—assuming one was given. This way, if intrusion does occur, it has to emanate from a legitimate network microcomputer. Dial-up/call-back capabilities can, however, represent a significant additional expense.

Unauthorized system access can be further controlled by allowing only certain types of transactions to be transmitted from a given terminal. Restricting certain terminals to performing a narrow range of tasks can be an effective and easy-to-apply control. For example, terminals in relatively public areas can be limited to read-only functions.

Authorization and Views

view A restricted subset of a stored relation.

A **view** is a means of providing a user with a personalized model of the database. It is also a useful way of limiting a user's access to various portions of the database: Data a user does not need to see are simply hidden from view. This simplifies system usage while promoting security. Views can be represented by executing selects, projections, and joins on existing relations. The user might also be restricted from seeing any part of an existing relation, or from executing joins on certain relations.

By creating different views for different classes of users, a high degree of access control is automatically attained. Although a user may be denied direct access to a base relation, the user may be able to access *part* of that relation through a view. Consequently, a combination of relational-level security and view-level security can be used to limit a user's access to precisely the data that the user needs.

Types of View Access Different types of access authorization may be allowed for a particular view, such as the following:

1. Read authorization: allows reading, but not modification of data.
2. Insert authorization: allows insertion of new data, but no modification of existing data.
3. Update authorization: allows modification of data, but not deletion.
4. Delete authorization: allows deletion of data.

These types of authorizations are typically made by assigning different passwords to a view. For example, suppose that in a PROJECTS relation (Figure 11.12), we wanted to restrict a particular user, Harry Bean, to having read-authorization access to just the PROJNO and LOCATION attributes. This could be realized by creating a view that includes only the PROJNO and LOCATION attributes, as shown in Figure 11.13. A password with read access may then be defined for PROJNO_LOC, as follows:

```
GRANT READ ACCESS ON PROJNO_LOC TO HARRY BEAN
```

▼FIGURE 11.12 PROJECTS RELATION

PROJECTS PROJNO	CUSTOMER	LOCATION
1	BURGER, W.	VAUDEVILLE
2	DOWNING, B.	SERIES CITY
3	MCENROE, J.	OUTLAND
4	DEXTER, M.	MARTINSVILLE
5	JOINER, W.	ALPENHAGEN
6	NIXON, R.	SAN CLEMENTE
7	MARX, K.	OUTLAND
8	BOND, J.	MARTINSVILLE
9	ELWAY, J.	ALPENHAGEN
10	LETTERMAN, D.	OUTLAND

```
PROJNO_LOC
PROJNO          LOCATION
   1            VAUDEVILLE
   2            SERIES CITY
   3            OUTLAND
   4            MARTINSVILE
   5            ALPENHAGEN
   6            SAN CLEMENTE
   7            OUTLAND
   8            MARTINSVILLE
   9            ALPENHAGEN
  10            OUTLAND
```

▼FIGURE 11.13 PROJNO_LOC RELATION

The general form for such SQL authorization is given using the GRANT statement:

```
GRANT <privilege list> ON <relation or view name> TO <user list>
```

The privilege list allows several privileges (e.g., read, delete, and/or update) to be granted in a single statement.

Views and Security in SQL. Because SQL has become the de facto standard for relational database languages and provides several facilities for using views for security, we will focus on SQL as our model for this section. The general syntax of SQL statements that create views is this:

```
CREATE VIEW viewname (list of attributes desired, if different
from base table)
        AS query
```

Let's consider a concrete example using the PERSNEL base relation that has the schema PERSNEL(ID,NAME,ADDRESS,HWAGE,DEPTNO). Suppose we want to limit access to the PERSNEL table for user U_1 to just those employees in Department 35. We would express this view as

```
CREATE VIEW DEPT_35
    AS SELECT ID, NAME, ADDRESS, HWAGE, DEPTNO
           FROM PERSNEL
           WHERE DEPTNO = 35
```

Read privileges are granted to U_1 in the usual way, and U_1 can now access the DEPT_35 view to see the needed subset of the base table, PERSNEL. Although the values of PERSNEL are actually stored on disk, any views derived from PERSNEL (e.g., DEPT_35) are created at the time they are used. This is unseen by U_1, however, and is generally of no concern to the user.

Suppose that U_1 is to be limited to a view of PERSNEL that excludes salary information (HWAGE). This view would be created in the following way:

```
CREATE VIEW PERS_NO_SAL
    AS SELECT ID, NAME, ADDRESS, DEPTNO
           FROM PERSNEL
```

These two examples demonstrate the creation of views that are, respectively, row and column subsets of the base relation PERSNEL. The next example shows how a view is created that is both a row and column subset of the base relation PERSNEL.

```
CREATE VIEW DEPT_35
AS SELECT ID, NAME, ADDRESS, DEPTNO
    FROM PERSNEL
    WHERE DEPTNO = 35
```

U_1 can now access a view of PERSNEL that includes ID, NAME, and ADDRESS (but not HWAGE) for those employees who are assigned to Department 35.

Some users may be assigned responsibility for maintaining data elements and are thereby permitted to access the SYSTABLES for which they have responsibility. Since the SYSTABLES are themselves relations, views can be created for them as well. An example follows:

```
CREATE VIEW MY-TABLES
AS SELECT *
    FROM SYSTABLES
    WHERE CREATOR = USER
```

USER is a keyword that requires a value assignment at time of execution. Thus, if user U_1 enters the statement

```
SELECT *
FROM MY_TABLES
```

the system will execute the query as if it were written

```
SELECT *
FROM SYSTABLES
WHERE CREATOR = U₁
```

Views like this are *context dependent,* since the result that is produced is dependent on the context (U_1) being used.

Views can also be constructed from more than one base relation. Consider the PERSNEL and PLANT base relations with the following schemas:

```
PERSNEL(ID,NAME,ADDRESS,HWAGE,DEPTNO,PLANT_ID)
PLANT(PLANT_ID,CITY,DEPTNO).
```

We create a view that identifies each employee with the city in which he or she works as follows:

```
CREATE VIEW EMPLOYEE_LOCATION
    AS SELECT ID, NAME, CITY
        FROM PERSNEL, PLANT
        WHERE PERSNEL.PID = PLANT.PID
```

Sometimes a user may be allowed access to summary data maintained in a base relation but not allowed access to individual values. For example, a user may be allowed access only to the average hourly-wage rate from the PERSNEL relation. This constraint could be established by creating the following view:

```
CREATE VIEW AVG_HRATE (ID, NAME, AVRATE, DEPTNO)
    AS SELECT ID, NAME, AVG(HWAGE), DEPTNO    FROM PERSNEL
    GROUP BY DEPTNO
```

Note what is happening here. An attribute is being created in the view (AVRATE) that does not exist in the base table, PERSNEL. Its values are created in the SELECT statement by specifying that the values in the attribute HWAGE be averaged by department number.

Although the use of views can be an effective means of ensuring security, the system must be able to adapt to changing requirements over time. SQL provides this capability through the use of GRANT and REVOKE privileges. Here are some examples:

```
GRANT SELECT ON TABLE PERSNEL TO JOHN, SYLVIA
```

This means that John and Sylvia are authorized to perform any SELECT operations on the PERSNEL table.

```
GRANT SELECT, UPDATE (HWAGE) ON TABLE PERSNEL TO HARVEY
```

This means that Harvey has the right to perform SELECT operations on the table PERSNEL as well as the right to update the HWAGE attribute.

```
REVOKE SELECT ON TABLE PERSNEL FROM JOHN
```

This means that John is no longer authorized to perform SELECT operations on the PERSNEL table.

These examples illustrate a few of the possibilities for granting or revoking authorization privileges. The list of privileges for both base relations and views includes SELECT, UPDATE, DELETE, and INSERT.

The GRANT option may cascade among users. For example, if John has the right to grant authority A to another user Sylvia, then Sylvia has the right to grant authority A to another user Dale, and so on. Consider the following example.

```
John:
GRANT SELECT ON TABLE PERSNEL TO SYLVIA WITH GRANT OPTION
Sylvia:
GRANT SELECT ON TABLE PERSNEL TO DALE WITH GRANT OPTION
```

As long as a user has received a GRANT OPTION, he or she can confer the same authority to others.

If John later wishes to revoke a GRANT OPTION, he could do so in the following way:

```
REVOKE SELECT ON TABLE PERSNEL FROM SYLVIA
```

This revocation would apply to Sylvia as well as to anyone to whom she had conferred authority, and so on.

Encryption

The various authentication and authorization measures that are standard for protecting access to databases may not be adequate for highly sensitive data. In such instances, it may be desirable to **encrypt** the data. Encrypted data cannot be read by an intruder unless that party knows the method of encryption. Considerable research has been devoted to developing encryption methods. Some are so simple that they are easy to decipher. Others are very difficult to decipher and provide a high level of protection.

encrypt To convert readable text to unreadable text by use of an algorithm; used to protect sensitive data.

We first demonstrate a simple encryption scheme. We then demonstrate a more complex, but more secure, method. A good source of material for the interested reader is contained in Hoffman (1979).

plaintext Readable text.

Simple Substitution Method. Suppose we wish to encrypt the message **(plaintext)**

Think snow.

ciphertext Encrypted plaintext.

A simple substitution method would be to shift each letter to its immediate successor in the alphabet. We assume that the *blank* appears immediately before the letter *a* and that it follows the letter *z*. "Think snow" is encrypted **(ciphertext)** to

uijolatopx.

If an intruder sees only the message "uijolatopx," there is probably insufficient information to break the code. However, if a large number of words are examined, it is possible to statistically examine the frequency with which characters occur, and, thereby, easily break the code. Better encryption schemes use an encryption key, as demonstrated in the next section.

Polyalphabetic Substitution Method. Suppose that we want to encrypt the same message, but we are now given the encryption key, say, "security." We proceed as follows:

1. Align the key beneath the plaintext, repeating it as many times as necessary for the plaintext to be completely "covered." In this example, we would have

```
Think snow
securityse.
```

2. Let *blank* occupy the twenty-seventh, and last, position in our alphabet. For each character, add the alphabetic position of the plaintext character and that of the key character, divide by 27, and keep the remainder. Replace the plaintext character with the character found in the position computed by the remainder. For our example, *T* is found in the twentieth place in the alphabet, while *s* is found in the nineteenth position. Thus,

   (20 + 19) = 39. The remainder on division by 27 is 12. (This process is called *division modulus 27*.)

L is the letter in the twelfth position in the alphabet. Thus, the letter *T* in the plaintext is encrypted as the letter *L* in the ciphertext.

This method is still too simple to be of wide use, but it does serve to illustrate the general strategy used in applications.

▼ Database Recovery

Because information stored on computer media is subject to loss or corruption caused by a wide range of events, it is important to provide means for restoring correct data to the database. Restoring the database to precisely the same state that existed at the time of system failure is not always possible, but database recovery procedures can restore the database to the state that existed shortly before the failure and identify the status of transaction processing at the time of the failure. With this capability, unprocessed transactions can be processed against the restored database to bring it back to a fully current status.

Sources of Failure

A useful classification of failure types includes the following:

1. System errors.   The system has entered an undesirable state, such as deadlock, which prevents the program from continuing with normal processing. This type of failure may or may not result in corruption of data files.
2. Hardware failures.   Two of the most common types of hardware failures are disk failure and loss of transmission capability over a transmission link. In the former case, the cause usually results from the disk read/write head coming in physical contact with the disk surface (a "head crash").
3. Logical errors.   Bad data or missing data are common conditions that may preclude a program's continuing with normal execution.

In the next section, we will discuss recovery procedures that are appropriate to different types of failures.

Recovery Procedures

To maintain data integrity, a transaction must be in one of the two following states:

1. *Aborted*.   A transaction may not always complete its process successfully. To be sure the incomplete transaction will not affect the consistent state of the database, such transactions must be aborted, restoring the database to the state it was in before the transaction in question began execution. Such restoration is achieved by *rollback* (to be discussed shortly).
2. *Committed*.   A transaction that successfully completes its processing is said to be *committed*. A **committed transaction** always leaves the database in a new consistent state.

committed transaction A transaction that successfully completes all its actions.

The log plays a key role in failure recovery. The log is a history of all the changes made to the database as well as the status of each transaction. It is obviously important that the data on the log not be lost or destroyed. Consequently, log information is stored on a mythical "stable storage" that survives all failures. In practice, this is approximated by maintaining multiple copies on disk.

A recovery strategy can be pursued by one of two approaches, logging with deferred updates or logging with immediate updates. Checkpointing provides additional efficiencies.

Log with deferred updates. Logging with deferred updates proceeds as follows:

1. When a transaction T begins, a record "$<T,>$", or equivalently, "$<T,START>$", is written to the log.

2. During the execution of transaction T, any writing of a new value, a_i, for attribute A, denoted "WRITE(A,a_i)," results in the writing of a new record to the log.

3. Each record of the type described in (2) will consist of the following fields:

   a. The transaction name, T.

   b. The attribute name, A.

   c. The new value of the attribute, a_i.

4. If all actions comprising T are successfully executed, we say that T partially commits, and write the record "$<T,COMMIT>$" to the log. After transaction T partially commits, the records associated with T in the log are used in executing the writes to the appropriate records in the database.

We illustrate this using our customer payment example once again. Recall that a $500 payment is being made on account.

The actions comprising this transaction are shown in Figure 11.14. The corresponding log entries are shown in Figure 11.15. Using the log, the DBMS can handle any failure that does not result in the loss of the log information itself. Prevention of loss of the log is addressed by replicating it on more than one disk. Since the corresponding probability of loss of the log is very small, this method is usually referred to as *stable storage*.

T: READ (A,a$_1$)	Read the current customer balance
a$_1$: = a$_1$ − 500	Reduce the balance owed by $500
WRITE (A,a$_1$)	Write the new balance
READ (B,b$_1$)	Read the current cash balance
b$_1$: = b$_1$ + 500	Increase the account balance by $500
WRITE (B,b$_1$)	Write the new balance

▼**FIGURE 11.14 TRANSACTION STEPS FOR RECORDING A CUSTOMER PAYMENT OF $500**

▼**FIGURE 11.15 DEFERRED UPDATE LOG ENTRIES FOR COMPLETE EXECUTION OF T (CUSTOMER PAYMENT OF $500)**

Time	Log Entries	Database Values
		A = 1000
		B = 1500
	<T,BEGIN>	
	<T,A,500>	
	<T,B,2000>	
	<T,COMMIT>	
		A = 500
		B = 2000

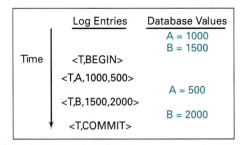

	Log Entries	Database Values
		A = 1000
		B = 1500
Time	<T,BEGIN>	
	<T,A,1000,500>	
		A = 500
	<T,B,1500,2000>	
		B = 2000
	<T,COMMIT>	

▼FIGURE 11-20 IMMEDIATE UPDATE LOG ENTRIES WHEN FAILURE OCCURS JUST AFTER THE ACTION, "<T,COMMIT>" IS EXECUTED

Checkpointing. From the preceding procedures, one might conclude that recovery only requires scanning the log for entries made by the most recent transaction or by a few of the recent transactions. In principle, there may be no limit on how far back in the log the system must look, since errors may have commenced with the first transaction. This can be very time-consuming and wasteful. A better way is to find a point that is sufficiently far back to ensure that any item written before that point has been done correctly and stored safely. The method by which this is done is called **checkpointing**.

During execution, the DBMS maintains the log as we have described but periodically performs checkpoints consisting of the following actions:

checkpointing Saving copies of the database at predetermined times during processing; database recovery begins or ends at the most recent checkpoint.

1. Temporarily halting the initiation of any new transactions until all active transactions are either committed or aborted.
2. Making a backup copy of the database.
3. Writing all log records currently residing in primary memory to stable storage.
4. Appending to the end of the log a record indicating that a checkpoint has occurred; then writing it to disk storage.

Assume that we are using a log with immediate updates, and consider the timeline for transactions $T_1 - T_4$ shown in Figure 11.21. When the system fails (t_f), the log need only be scanned as far back as the most recent checkpoint (t_c). T_1 is okay, unless there has been a disk failure that destroyed it (and possibly) other records prior to the last checkpoint. In that case, the database is reloaded from the backup copy that was made at the last checkpoint. In either case, T_2 and T_3 are redone from the log, and T_4 is undone from the log.

▼FIGURE 11.21 CHECKPOINTING EXAMPLE

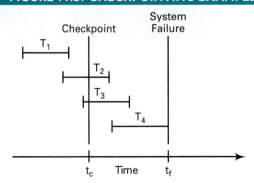

PART 4 ◆ MANAGING THE DATABASE ENVIRONMENT

Summary

A knowledge of administrative and control issues is necessary to the effective management of a database system. Because of multiple and concurrent user access of database systems, maintenance of database security and integrity is at once complex and essential.

In this chapter we first addressed the difference between data administration and database administration, focusing on database administration and its goals of maintaining the integrity, security, and availability of the database. Data integrity, which is the maintenance of accurate, reliable data, is ensured by implementing data integrity controls. Security is obtained by implementing data security controls. Data availability is enhanced by implementing backup and recovery procedures, which may include a disaster plan.

We then demonstrated some integrity capabilities of commercial query languages such as SQL and QBE. These capabilities do not yet provide all desired features, but this situation is expected to improve in the near future.

Another useful way to maintain database consistency is the atomic transaction, which requires that all transaction processing be completed or the transaction is aborted. When used with a log, this ensures that operating failures do not result in the recording of erroneous data.

Concurrent processing can corrupt the database. Simple locking procedures can preclude concurrent processing, but they may greatly restrict the operating efficiency of the database system. Methods such as two-phase locking are available to limit the problems associated with simple locking, while maintaining database integrity.

Database security is primarily concerned with determining who has legitimate access to what data, and then being sure that legitimacy is enforced. Authentication refers to methods of restricting access to the system. Authorization refers to methods of controlling what resources are accessible once system access is gained, and what can be done with those resources.

In relational database systems, the use of views can be an effective way of restricting what the user sees and manipulates, without having to alter stored relations. Using SQL, we demonstrated a number of ways in which views can be applied.

Encryption allows sensitive data to be stored and transmitted in a form which is unintelligible to other than legitimate users.

All database systems must have sound backup and recovery procedures to avoid inefficiencies and even catastrophic loss. These methods should be tested periodically to make certain that they are operable, complete, and reliable. Transaction logs with either deferred or immediate updates, checkpointing, and backup copies of the database are essential elements to backup and recovery.

Review Questions

1. Define each of the following terms in your own words:
  a. data administrator
  b. data integrity
  c. data security
  d. integrity control
  e. atomic transaction

f. log
g. deadlock
h. two-phase locking
i. write_lock
j. encrypt
k. ciphertext
l. checkpointing

2. What are the DBA's main functions? The DBA's goals?

3. What is the difference between a read_lock and a write_lock?

4. Compare and contrast the meaning of the terms *security* and *integrity*. Give an example of how the database could be affected by a breach of integrity and a breach of security.

5. Describe the role of the database administrator in implementing standards and procedures.

6. What is meant by backup and recovery?

7. Explain how concurrency can lead to an inconsistency in the database.

8. Develop an example, other than the one in the text, showing how a simple locking control could lead to deadlock.

9. Discuss two ways in which deadlock might be detected. What are their advantages and disadvantages?

10. Explain how two-phase locking works.

11. Distinguish between authorization and authentication.

Problems and Exercises

1. Match the following terms with their definitions:

__*database administrator*	a. The means by which a database that has been corrupted by system malfunctions can be restored to a consistent state
__*plaintext*	b. Manager whose responsibilities are focused on managing the technical aspects of the database system
__*concurrent processing*	c. Occurs when two or more transactions concurrently request access to the same database record at about the same time
__*database recovery procedures*	d. A restricted subset of a stored relation
__*transaction*	e. The user has the right to read a given record
__*aborted transaction*	f. A program unit whose execution preserves the consistency of the database
__*lock*	g. Readable text
__*read_lock*	h. Transaction that is canceled before changes are applied to the database
__*deadlock detection*	i. In transaction processing, prevents access to a database record by a second transaction

until the first transaction has completed all of its actions

___*view*

j. A periodic check by the DBMS to determine if the waiting line for some resource exceeds a predetermined limit

2. Using an example, demonstrate a data integrity problem that could be caused by a concurrent update process.

3. Using an example, illustrate how two-phase locking works.

4. Two transactions are said to be serializable if they can be executed in parallel (interleaved) in such a way that their results are identical to that achieved if one transaction was processed completely before the other was initiated. Consider the following two interleaved transactions, and suppose a consistency condition requires that A or B must always be equal to 1. Assume that $A = B = 1$ before these transactions execute.

```
    T₁                          T₂
Read_item(A)
                        Read_item(B)
                        Read_item(A)
Read_item(B)
If A = 1
   then B := B + 1
                        If B = 1
                           then A := A + 1
                        Write-item(A)
Write_item(B)
```

Will the consistency requirement be satisfied? Justify your answer. Is there an interleaved processing schedule that will guarantee serializability? If so, demonstrate it. If not, explain why.

5. Using the polyalphabetic substitution method and the encryption key, SECURITY, encrypt the plaintext message, "SELL ALL STOCKS."

6. Assuming a log with immediate updates, create the log entries corresponding to the following transaction actions:

```
T: read (A, a₁)        Read the current customer balance
a₁: = a₁ + 800         Debit the account by $800
write (A, a₁)          Write the new balance
read (B, b₁)           Read the current accounts payable balance
b₁: = b₁ + 800         Credit the account balance by $800
write (B, b₁)          Write the new balance
```

7. Suppose that in (6) a failure occurs just after the log record for the action

write (B, b_1)

has been written.
   a. Show the contents of the log at the time of failure.
   b. What action is necessary, and why? What are the resulting values of A and B?

8. Suppose that in (6) a failure occurs just after the "<T,COMMIT>" record is written to the log.

a. Show the contents of the log at the time of failure.

b. What action is necessary, and why? What are the resulting values of A and B?

9. Consider the following entries at the time of database system failure in the recovery log:

$<T_1, \text{BEGIN}>$	$<T_1, \text{BEGIN}>$	$<T_1, \text{BEGIN}>$
$<T_1, A, 500, 395>$	$<T_1, A, 500, 395>$	$<T_1, A, 500, 395>$
$<T_1, B, 800, 950>$	$<T_1, B, 800, 950>$	$<T_1, B, 800, 950>$
	$<T_1, \text{COMMIT}>$	$<T_1, \text{COMMIT}>$
	$<T_2, \text{BEGIN}>$	$<T_2, \text{BEGIN}>$
	$<T_2, C, 320, 419>$	$<T_2, C, 320, 419>$
		$<T_2, \text{COMMIT}>$
(A)	(B)	(C)

a. Assume a deferred-update log. Describe for each case (A, B, C) what recovery actions are necessary and why. Indicate what the values are for the given attributes after the recovery actions are completed.

b. Repeat the requirement of (a) assuming an immediate-update log.

Professional Issues

1. Do a short research study of what methods the major accounting firms use to audit database systems.

2. Compare and contrast the integrity controls available in SQL and QBE.

3. Compare and contrast the data security controls available in SQL and QBE.

DISTRIBUTED
DATABASE SYSTEMS

▼

Cordelia Molini and Reggie Townsend were sitting at lunch discussing the progress that had been made in implementing information systems at IPD.

Reggie commented, "I think that we are doing a good job. We have the latest relational technology in house, we have educated users in every functional area of the business, and there is evidence that our information systems are increasingly being used to support decision making throughout the company."

"Generally, I agree with you," responded Cordelia. "But I feel that there is still much to be done. Many of our managers are located at remote sites throughout the country, and I have heard rumors here and there that they would like to have control over that portion of the database system that applies to their operations. In fact, one manager commented to me that she didn't understand why data should be maintained in the corporate database when it was mainly updated and used by her."

"Sounds like we ought to be looking at distributing our database," suggested Reggie. "What kinds of changes would we be looking at if we moved in that direction?"

"Well," said Cordelia, "for one thing, we'd have to decide what data could be maintained locally and what data should be maintained centrally. And we'd still want to make certain corporate data available to remote sites. Our system for controlling data access would have to be more sophisticated in order to allow queries to be executed that required data from more than one site. There are other issues as well, but with our track record of success I believe that we are well positioned to begin thinking about a distributed database system."

This chapter provides an introduction to the exciting area of distributed database systems (DDS). While DDS is still a developing area, it is already playing a major role in some business operations. In the future, DDS may become a necessary technology for all organizations. With the dramatic advances in communications technology that are occurring, the potential is impressive. In this chapter you will learn:

- ▼ Why DDS is of value to an organization.
- ▼ The fundamental technologies and the terminology of a distributed database system (DDS).
- ▼ Elements of DDS design.
- ▼ Strategies and objectives that are important to DDSs.
- ▼ Optional configurations that are available for DDS, along with some of their advantages and disadvantages.
- ▼ The fundamental control problems associated with DDS and methods for dealing with them.
- ▼ The fundamentals of client/server systems.

▼ Why Distributed Databases?

distributed database A database that is distributed among a network of geographically separated locations.

With the widely prevalent centralized database system, users and application programs access the database from local sites as well as from remote locations. In contrast, a **distributed database** is not entirely stored in one central location but is distributed among a network of locations that are geographically separated and connected by communication links. Each location has its own database and is also able to access data maintained at other locations.

distributed database system A collection of locations, each of which operates a local database system, which can participate in the execution of transactions which access data at several locations.

The reasons for the development and use of **distributed database systems** are several and include the following:

1. Often organizations have branches or divisions in different locations. For a given location, L, there may be a set of data that is used frequently, perhaps exclusively, at L. In addition, L may sometimes need data that are used more frequently at another location, L'.

In a retail franchise business, for example, each store may benefit from its own database of inventory, sales, customer accounts, and employees. During business operations, transactions are conveniently processed against the local database. At the end of daily operations, summary results may be transmitted to corporate headquarters, where a franchisewide database is maintained. Periodically, each store may benefit by being able to access from the franchisewide database comparative sales and profit information of other stores as a measure of performance.

In a centralized database system, each site would need to use a communication link to the database for both types of information, and communications could become a significant bottleneck.

2. Allowing each site to store and maintain its own database allows immediate and efficient access to data that are used most frequently. Such data may be used at other sites as well, but usually with less frequency. Similarly, data stored at other locations can be accessed as required.

3. Distributed databases can upgrade reliability. If one site's computer fails, or if a communication link goes down, the rest of the network can possibly continue functioning. Moreover, when data are replicated at two or more sites, required data may still be available from a site which is still operable.

4. Allowing local control over the data used most frequently at a site can improve user satisfaction with the database system. That is to say, local databases can more nearly reflect an organization's administrative structure and thereby better service its managers' needs.

These are some of the advantages that are commonly held for distributed database systems. There are, however, instances when a distributed database system can be a disadvantage. Under circumstances where a great deal of intersite communication takes place, the overhead incurred by the associated coordination and control tasks can severely degrade performance. This may be especially likely when replicated data are maintained at several sites, thereby requiring extra resources to ensure that concurrent updates are consistent. We elaborate briefly.

The advantage of data replication is the speed gained in processing at sites where the duplicate data are maintained, as well as providing backup copies of data in case of a system failure at another location. Such duplication implies the use of extra storage space, and transaction processing and recovery become more difficult. When a transaction is processed, it may invoke a requirement to read and update data at different sites and to transmit related messages among sites. Before a transaction can be committed, the distributed database management system (DDBMS) must ensure that all the relevant sites have completed their processing. Only if processing has terminated normally at each site should the transaction be committed. Otherwise, the transaction must be undone at each participating site.

Finally, making data available to users throughout a network makes security inherently more complex for distributed databases than with its centralized counterpart.

While these limitations suggest caution in planning and implementing DDSs, the technology for mitigating such limitations is rapidly improving. In order for firms to be responsive, productive, and competitive, DDSs will increasingly be selected as the central component of an effective information systems strategy.

▼ A General DDS Model

local data Data that are maintained in a network site's own database.

global data Data that are maintained in a database whose location is different from at least one of its users.

link Communications channel between two network sites, which provides for data-transfer capability.

distributed database management system (DDBMS) The software which manages the distributed database system.

System for Distributed Databases (SSD) DDBMS marketed by Computer Corporation of America.

R* DDBMS marketed by IBM Corporation.

Distributed INGRESS DDBMS marketed by Relational Technology.

transaction The execution of a user program which interacts with the DDBMS.

agent A process which cooperates in completing a transaction.

local transaction A transaction requiring a unique agent.

global transaction A transaction requiring several agents.

A DDS is comprised of a collection of sites, each of which operates a local database system for processing activities that require only **local data**. Additionally, each site can process transactions requiring data that are stored at other sites **(global data)**. This requires that the various database sites be able to communicate data among themselves. The communications connections that provide the necessary data-transfer capabilities are called **links**. The link structure provides the basic architecture of a **distributed database management system (DDBMS)**, which is the systems software that manages the distributed databases.

Several commercial DDBMSs are implemented or are under development. These include **System for Distributed Databases (SDD)** (Computer Corporation of America), **R*** (IBM), and **Distributed INGRESS** (Relational Technology). IBM's popular DB2 includes some distributed support, as does INGRESS/STAR and Oracle7.

A DDBMS is a system composed of several DBMSs running at local sites, which are connected by a message-handling facility. The DDBMS data dictionary includes the usual information necessary for data management in addition to information concerning the location, replication, and fragmentation of data in the various relations. As queries are processed for retrieval or update of data, the DDBMS data dictionary can provide the required information on location and replication, while assuring that updates are propagated to the correct locations. The DDBMS data dictionary can be maintained at a central site, or subsets can be distributed among the various sites according to their needs. A full copy of the data dictionary can be obtained by taking the union of all the distributed subsets.

Users interact with the DDBMS by executing programs called **transactions**. Transactions in such systems are no longer restricted to single processes controlled by one software module, but they may invoke a set of cooperating processes running at several sites and controlled by independent software modules.

Each of the processes cooperating in the transaction is called an **agent**. A transaction requiring a unique agent is called a **local transaction**. A transaction requiring several agents is termed a **global transaction**.

A given agent can only access the data controlled by its local data management software. Access to data at another site requires cooperation with agents at those sites. An agent that initiates a transaction is called the initiating agent. The initiating agent can request the activation of agents at other sites in order to access needed data. Once activated, two or more agents can communicate by message exchange.

Transactions access records by issuing *read* and *write* operations. Read(x) returns the current value of x. Write (x,new value) updates the current value of x to a new value. A transaction issues read and write commands to the DDBMS and executes terminal input and output.

Each site participating in the DDBMS typically runs one or more of the following software modules: a transaction manager (TM), a data manager (DM), or a scheduler. Figure 12.1 illustrates their interrelationships. Transactions communicate with TMs; TMs talk to schedulers; schedulers communicate among themselves and

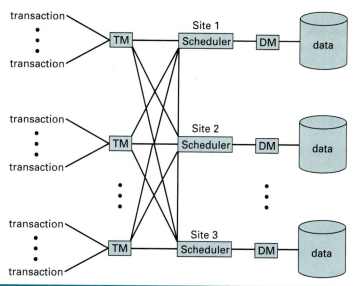

▼FIGURE 12.1 DDBMS ARCHITECTURE

also with DMs; and the DMs manage the data. These concepts are further illustrated in Figure 12.2.

Each transaction communicates all of its reads and writes to a single TM. A transaction also issues a *begin* operation to its TM when it begins executing and an *end* operation when it is finished. The TM communicates each read and write to a scheduler. Scheduler selection is determined by a concurrency-control algorithm, although the chosen scheduler is most often at the same site as the data being operated on.

The scheduler contols the sequence in which DMs process read commands and write commands, and maintains concurrency control. When a scheduler receives a read or write instruction, the scheduler can process the instruction immediately, delay processing by holding the instruction for later action, or reject the instruction in the case of a transmission error, access violation, or similar problem.

The DM executes each read and write it receives. For a read, the DM scans its local database and returns the requested value. For a write, the DM modifies its local database and returns an acknowledgment to the scheduler, which relays it back to the TM, which relays it back to the transaction.

▼FIGURE 12.2 PROCESSING OPERATIONS

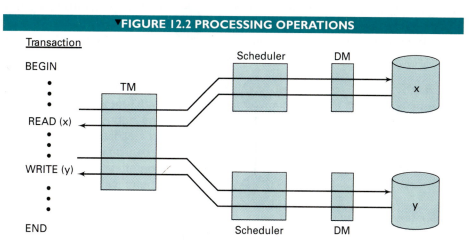

replication is introduced to increase the availability of the system: When a copy is unavailable due to site failure(s), it should be possible to access another copy.

Replication can also improve performance under routine conditions, since transactions have a greater probability of finding a copy locally. The trade-off is in the extra cost of the added storage and in the maintenance of mutual consistency among copies. The update of a local copy imposes the added overhead of transmitting that update to all the copies.

Formally, the advantages of replication are:

1. If one of the stations containing relation R fails, the relation can be retrieved from another site, and the system may continue any processing involving R. Thus, database availability is enhanced.

2. If most accesses to R only involve a read of the relation, then several sites can process queries involving R concurrently. The more copies of R there are throughout the network, the better the chance that a query can be executed without requiring data transmission between stations. There is a corresponding cost and time savings.

The principal offsetting disadvantage is that the system must ensure that all copies of R are identical. Thus, when an update of R occurs, that update must be propagated to all locations with the corresponding incurrence of overhead.

For replicated databases, at least two implementation alternatives are available. In one of these a centralized database is maintained, and copies of portions of the database are extracted for local use. This redundancy may be offset by the reduced communications costs due to the data being stored locally. Reliability is also improved, since loss of data at one location may be restored by the data copy which is maintained at another location.

The second alternative is to omit the centralized database but to replicate segments of the database at sites that are the most frequent users. The costs of maintaining the centralized database are thereby avoided, although communications costs may be increased.

Database Partitioning. Efficiency may result from a strategy that implements a partitioned database. With this approach, the database is distributed such that there is no overlapping, or replication, of data maintained at the various locations. Since there is no duplication of data, the costs associated with storing and maintaining redundant data are avoided. Data availability may be limited, however, if the same segment of data is used at more than one location. Reliability may also be affected, since a failure of one computer system means that the data which are stored at that location are not available to users anywhere in the system.

Because the distributed environment of the DDBMS allows the database to be physically partitioned, data security may also be improved, particularly when the partitioned segments have different security needs.

The most straightforward way of implementing a partitioned database is to treat it as a series of independently operated database systems with remote-access capability. An alternative, which is somewhat more complex, is one in which the database systems are integrated such that a single query by the user may require access to more than one of the database systems. While the underlying complexities should be transparent to the user, the actual operations may be quite involved. Think, for example, of a relational JOIN operation whose result requires tables which are maintained in two distinct database locations. We'll look at this problem in more detail shortly.

data fragmentation The partitioning of relations in a DDS.

Data Fragmentation. Data fragmentation applies to relational database systems. It refers to ways in which relations can be subdivided and distributed among network sites. This is an extension of the data-partioning stategy, which is generally concerned with locating entire relations (or files) from the database at various sites.

If a relation *R* is fragmented, it is divided into subsets (fragments) $R_1, R_2, \ldots, R_n$. The union of these fragments reconstruct the original relation *R*. This fragmentation can be *horizontal,* which assigns tuples to the various fragments; or it can be *vertical,* where selected attributes are projected onto the various fragments.

Why is fragmentation a consideration? As Maier (1983) observes, a database of airline reservations might be more effectively used if database subsets are stored at the location of their respective flight origins. Similarly, for a banking database, it may be useful to store database subsets at the location of the branch where the respective accounts are located.

If fragmentation is allowed, a given relation is not necessarily stored in its entirety at any single site. Its subsets may be distributed among several sites for performance considerations. Moreover, these subsets may be replicated.

horizontal fragmentation Partitioning a relation into subsets of its tuples.

Horizontal fragmentation is the division of tuples of a given relation into fragments. Usually fragments are disjoint and may be replicated. In this way replication is managed at the fragmentation level and not at the level of individual tuples.

To illustrate horizontal fragmentation, suppose that the relation *R* is the FLIGHT relation of Figure 12.5. This relation can be divided into two fragments, each of which consists of tuples identifying a common flight origination location (SF and Den). Such fragmentation is formally defined as a SELECTION on the relation *R*; that is,

```
Ri = SELECT (R: <condition on one or more attributes.>)
```

For our example, we might have

```
FLIGHT-ORIGDEN = SELECT (FLIGHT: ORIGIN = 'Den')
FLIGHT-ORIGSF = SELECT (FLIGHT: ORIGIN = 'SF')
```

The resulting fragments are shown in Figure 12.6. The fragment FLIGHT-ORIGINSF is stored at the San Franscisco airport and fragment FLIGHT-ORIGIND is stored at the Denver airport. The original relation can be restored by performing a UNION operation on FLIGHT-ORIGDEN and FLIGHT-ORIGINSF.

The preceding fragments are horizontally disjoint. That is, no tuple instance occurs in more than one fragment. We could, however, have a particular tuple of *R* appear in more than one R_i. For example, at San Francisco we might want to store tuples whose flights originate in San Francisco as well as those that arrive from LA.

FIGURE 12.5 FLIGHT RELATION

FLIGHT

Origin	Destination	Departure Time	Arrival Time
Den	SF	9A	10A
Den	SLC	7A	8A
Den	SF	1P	2P
Den	SF	6P	7P
SF	Den	8A	11A
SF	Den	12P	3P
SF	Den	5P	8P
SF	SLC	9A	11P

```
FLIGHT_ORIGINSF
Origin    Destination    Departure Time    Arrival Time
  SF          Den              8A               11A
  SF          Den             12P                3P
  SF          Den              5P                8P
  SF          SLC              9A               11P
FLIGHT_ORIGIND
Origin    Destination    Departure Time    Arrival Time
  Den          SF               9A               10A
  Den          SLC              7A                8A
  Den          SF               1P                2P
  Den          SF               6P                7P
```

▼FIGURE 12.6 HORIZONTAL FRAGMENTATION OF FLIGHT RELATION

vertical fragmentation
Partitioning a relation by projection of subsets of its attributes.

Vertical fragmentation is the division of the set of attributes of an object into possibly overlapping subsets. Fragments are obtained by projecting the original relation over each set of attributes. To ensure that the projections are a lossless decomposition of the relation, each vertical fragment will usually contain a key for the relation.

Vertical fragmentation is defined as

```
Rᵢ = R [<list of attribute names>]
```

$R_i = R$ [<list of attribute names>]

R can be reconstructed from the fragments by taking the natural join:

```
R = JOIN (R₁, R₂, . . . , Rₙ)
```

$R = JOIN (R_1, R_2, \ldots, R_n)$

Vertical fragmentation requires the addition of a special attribute to identify the tuple. The tuple identification attribute (TIA) is an address for a tuple. Since the addresses are unique, the TIA functions as a key for the augmented scheme for R. In Figure 12.7, we show the addition of a TIA attribute. In Figure 12.8, we show the FLIGHT relation decomposed vertically into the schemes FLIGHT1 and FLIGHT2. These relations result from computing:

```
FLIGHT1 = FLIGHT [ORIGIN,DEPARTURE-TIME,TIA]
FLIGHT2 = FLIGHT [DESTINATION,ARRIVAL-TIME,TIA]
```

To reconstruct the original FLIGHT relation from the fragments, we compute:

```
FLIGHT = JOIN (FLIGHT1, FLIGHT2)
```

▼FIGURE 12.7 AUGMENTED FLIGHT RELATION SHOWING TIA

```
FLIGHT
Origin    Destination    Departure Time    Arrival Time    TIA
  Den          SF               9A               10A         1
  Den          SLC              7A                8A         2
  Den          SF               1P                2P         3
  Den          SF               6P                7P         4
  SF           Den              8A               11A         5
  SF           Den             12P                3P         6
  SF           Den              5P                8P         7
  SF           SLC              9A               11P         8
```

```
FLIGHT1
Origin    Departure Time    TIA
  Den          9A            1
  Den          7A            2
  Den          1P            3
  Den          6P            4
  SF           8A            5
  SF          12P            6
  SF           5P            7
  SF           9A            8

FLIGHT2
Destination   Arrival Time   TIA
    SF           10A          1
    SLC           8A          2
    SF            2P          3
    SF            7P          4
    Den          11A          5
    Den           3P          6
    Den           8P          7
    SLC        11:30P         8
```

▼FIGURE 12.8 VERTICAL FRAGMENTATION OF FLIGHT RELATION

▼ Distribution of Nonfragmented Files*

In the preceding section, we have discussed ways of partitioning relations among network sites. In this section, we consider the case where complete relations are to be allocated among sites. This is always a central issue in the design and implementation of distributed database systems. The main reason is that most files are not fragmented because many important accesses need to retrieve all records in the files.

The method we outline for determining file allocation is adapted from Bell and Grimson (1991). The objective function of this method is that of maximizing local access, subject to storage constraints. This is realistic, since adding a relation to a site does not incur significant marginal cost so long as storage capacity is not exceeded. Conversely, the cost of accommodating the additional storage requirements is considered to be excessive over the short run. That is to say, increasing storage capacity may be necessary for a growing business over the longer horizon. This does no harm to our motivation and the analysis.

We begin by defining the notation to be used, as follows:

N = the number of sites, indexed by j

c_j = disk capacity at site j (Mbytes)

F = the number files, indexed by i

s_i = storage requirement of file i (Mbytes)

T = number of transactions, indexed by k

f_{jk} = frequency of transaction k emanating from site j

n_{ki} = number of accesses (for update and retrieval) required by transaction k to file i

d_{ij} = a decision variable that is assigned 1 if file i is allocated to station j; 0 otherwise.

---

*This section may be omitted without loss of continuity.

It follows that $\sum_j d_{ij} = 1$ for every i such that $1 \le i \le F$. Constraints on storage space can be expressed as $\sum_i d_{ij} \cdot s_i \le c_j$ for every j such that $1 \le j \le N$. That is to say, the storage requirements of all files assigned to a given station cannot exceed the storage capacity at that station. Moreover, j must be one of the N stations in the network.

The objective function is to maximize $(\sum_{ij} D_{ik}V_{ij})$ where $V_{ik} = \sum_k f_{ki}(n_{ki})$. Note that V_{ik} is a measure of the total accesses associated with a given file and transaction. The objective function attempts to place files at those locations having the highest V_{ij} values. Since remote accesses are more costly than local accesses, we wish to maximize local accesses. This is clarified by an example.

Suppose that we wish to allocate eight files among five sites, each site having 20-Mbyte disk storage. Figure 12.9 shows the access rates of transactions to files (n_{ki}). For example, each time transaction 1 is initiated, it requires 10 accesses to file 1, 10 accesses to file 2, 10 accesses to file 5, and 22 accesses to file 8.

Figure 12.10 shows the frequency at which the various transactions are generated from the five network sites—per uniform time period. For example, consider site 1. It generates 12 type-2 transactions, 20 of type 6, 2 of type 7, 13 of type 8, and 4 of type 9.

Figure 12.11 shows the result of multiplying the number of file accesses per transaction times the number of transactions generated at each site, V_{ij}.

We then step through the following procedure:

Step 1: Compute $J(i) = \{j' | V_{ij}, = \max V_{ij}\}$. In words, for each file identify the site requiring the largest number of accesses. These are the bold figures in Fig-

	File (Size)							
	1	2	3	4	5	6	7	8
Transactions	(5)*	(10)	(15)	(10)	(10)	(7)	(4)	(5)
1	10	10			10			22
2					21			8
3			70	70	145	14		
4			5	5	11	9		
5			4	4			10	10
6	3	9	5	1				12
7	9	2	2	4				
8	6	5	2	4				
9	1	2						
10								

▼FIGURE 12.9 RATES OF TRANSACTIONS TO FILES

▼FIGURE 12.10 FREQUENCY OF TRANSACTIONS IN SITES (f_{kj})

	Site				
Transactions	1	2	3	4	5
1		25			
2	12	30			
3		3	5	4	5
4			10	10	10
5			12	8	4
6	20	150	100	2	2
7	2	100		30	40
8	18	32	10	12	10
9	4	2			
10		4			

Sites	File (Size)							
	1 (5)	2 (10)	3 (15)	4 (10)	5 (10)	6 (7)	7 (4)	8 (5)
1	190	282	140	100	234	0	0	240
2	**1,800**	**1,964**	924	**888**	**1,315**	42	0	**1,800**
3	572	950	**972**	596	835	**160**	**120**	1,320
4	348	138	456	532	690	146	80	64
5	426	148	526	618	835	160	50	64

▼FIGURE 12.11 V_{ij} TABLE

ure 12.11. In this way, we identify the site having the maximum number of accesses to each file.

Step 2: Assign $d_{ij} = 1$ for all the bold entries, and $d_{ij} = 0$, otherwise.

Step 3: Check to see that site storage capacity has not been exceeded. Site 2 has been allocated files requiring 40 Mbytes of memory—but only 20 Mbytes are available.

Step 4: The maximum V_{ij} to be achieved from storing any files at site 2 is obtained by storing files 1, 2, and 8 there.

Step 5: The new V_{ij} table (Figure 12.12) is obtained by eliminating row 2 and columns 1, 2, and 8 from Figure 12.11 and recomputing $J(i)$. These are the bold entries in Figure 12.12.

Step 2': Assign $d_{ij} = 1$ to the bold entries; $d_{ij} = 0$, otherwise.

Step 3': Site 3 has been allocated files 3, 5, 6, and 7 requiring total storage capacity of 36 Mbytes. The site is overloaded.

Step 4': The maximum V_{ij} to be obtained from storing any files at site 3 is achieved by storing files 3 and 7 there.

Step 5': The new V_{ij} table (Figure 12.13) is obtained by eliminating row 2 and columns 1 and 5 from Figure 12.12. The new $J(i)$ are indicated by the bold values in Figure 12.13.

Step 2": Assign 1 to d_{ij} for those entries, 0 for the rest.

Step 3": Site 5 is allocated files requiring 27 MBytes. The site is overloaded.

Step 4": The maximum V_{ij} to be obtained at site 5 is from allocating files 4 and 5 there.

Sites	File Size				
	3 (15)	4 (10)	5 (10)	6 (7)	7 (4)
1	140	100	234	0	0
3	**972**	596	**835**	**160**	**120**
4	456	532	690	146	80
5	526	**618**	835	160	50

▼FIGURE 12.12 REDUCED V_{ij} TABLE

▼FIGURE 12.13 REDUCED V_{ij} TABLE

Sites	File (Size)		
	4 (10)	5 (10)	6 (7)
1	100	234	0
4	532	690	146
5	**618**	**835**	**160**

▼ Data Integrity in Distributed Database Systems

A distributed database system differs from a centralized database system in that its database resides at a set of sites *S*. As might be expected, control data integrity becomes a harder problem in the network environment. Transactions are no longer linearly ordered sequences of actions on data. That is to say, since data are distributed, the transaction activities may take place at a number of sites, and it can be difficult to maintain a time ordering among actions.

The most common problem is when two (or more) transactions are executing at the same time, and both require access to the same data record in order to complete their processing. We examined this concurrency problem for centralized database systems in Chapter 17. The problem is somewhat exacerbated in a distributed system, since there may be multiple copies of the same record. All copies must have the same value at all times, or else transactions may operate on inaccurate data.

Most concurrency control algorithms for distributed database systems use some form of check to see that the result of a transaction is the same as if its actions were executed serially. To implement concurrency control, the following must be known:

1. The type of scheduling algorithm used.
2. The location of the scheduler.
3. How replicated data are controlled.

serializability theory
States that a concurrency control algorithm is correct when its results are the same as if processes were executed serially.

serial execution Actions are executed one after another—no parallel actions.

These factors provide the basis for constructing rules that determine when a concurrency control algorithm is correct. The rules are based upon **serializability theory**. When transactions are performed sequentially, all the actions of one transaction are performed, and then all the actions of the next transaction are executed. There is no concurrency, and this is called a **serial execution**. When transactions are executed serially, they cannot interfere with one another since only one transaction is active at a time. We saw in an earlier example (Chapter 11) with concurrent requests to the database by the League of Women Voters and the Chamber of Commerce that transactions are not usually executed serially but are interleaved. An interleaved execution of transactions is said to be serializable if it produces the same result that some serial execution of those same transactions would produce.

To enforce serializability, the TMs located at each site must cooperate to provide concurrency control by use of locking mechanisms or by timestamping. As before, we are attempting to provide a means for preventing anomalies that may arise when transactions are executed in parallel against the database.

We extend our consideration of these issues by examining some of the principal methods of maintaining data integrity in a distributed database system.

Two-Phase Commit Protocol

Earlier we learned that maintenance of data integrity in database systems requires atomic processing of transactions. In the centralized systems of Chapter 11 this is accomplished by delaying changes to the database until the transaction is committed. In a distributed database system things are somewhat more involved. Before committing a transaction's updates, each subtransaction (that part of a transaction that is executed at a given site) must show that it is prepared to commit. Otherwise the transaction and all of its changes are entirely aborted. The existence of subtransactions at various sites necessitates this rule.

For a subtransaction to be ready to commit, all of its actions must have been completed successfully. If any subtransaction indicates that its actions cannot be completed, then all the subtransactions are aborted, and none of the changes are committed. This idea is illustrated in Figure 12.17.

Formally, the **two-phase commit protocol** executes as follows:

Phase 1. Consider a transaction T, which is initiated at one site and invokes subtransactions at other sites, as well as at the home site (where T was initiated). T consists entirely of subtransactions, each executing at a different site. The subtransaction at the home site we denote as the coordinator, C_i. The other subtransactions are designated as participants. Each subtransaction T_i of T decides whether to commit or abort. C_i sends a *prepare-to-commit* message to all sites where a T_i is being executed. T_i responds with a *vote-commit* or a *vote-abort* message to C_i.

Phase 2. Based on the information received in phase 1, C_i determines whether or not T can be committed. C_i then sends either a commit T or an abort T message to all T_i sites. Since a consensus vote-commit is required for T to be committed, T will not be committed if just one site responds vote-abort.

A major limitation of the two-phase commit protocol is that a failure of the coordinator can result in the transaction being blocked from completion until the coordinator is restored. A three-phase protocol has been proposed, which avoids this limitation but adds to overhead and cost. As a practical matter, the likelihood of blocking is often sufficiently low that the cost of the three-phase protocol is unwarranted.

Distributed Locking

Global transactions may involve a number of local subtransactions which are executed at different sites. The DDBMS must ensure that these transactions are executed in proper sequence.

Example 1. Suppose that transaction T_1 subtracts 25 turkeys from inventory, and that transaction T_2 subtracts 35 turkeys from inventory. Furthermore, suppose that T_1 is initiated at site 1, T_2 is initiated at site 2, and that copies of the Turkey Inventory Record (TIR) are maintained at sites 3 and 4. The global transactions T_1 and T_2 consist of local transactions at sites 1, 2, 3, and 4. T_1 must initiate two subtransactions

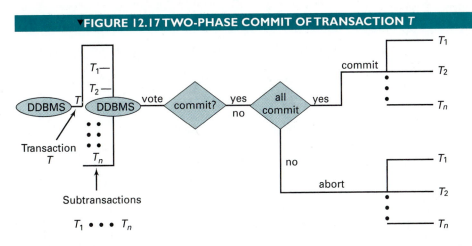

▼FIGURE 12.17 TWO-PHASE COMMIT OF TRANSACTION T

that deduct 25 from TIR at sites 3 and 4, as must T_2. The effects of these transactions must be coordinated such that the change to one copy of the TIR must not be made unless the same change to the other copy of the TIR is guaranteed.

The DDBMS at each location maintains a local lock manager, which administers the lock and unlock requests for data items stored at that site. Locks may be applied in two modes: shared and exclusive. If a transaction locks a record in shared mode, it can read that record but cannot update the record. If a transaction locks a record in exclusive mode, it can both read and update the record, and no other record can access the record while it is exclusively locked. At no time can two transactions hold exclusive locks on the same record. However, any number of transactions should be able to achieve shared locks on the same record at the same time.

If there is only a single copy of a record, then the logical record is identical to its only physical copy. Appropriate locks are maintained by sending lock-request messages to the site at which the copy resides. The TM at that site can grant or deny the lock, returning that result to the user.

When there are several copies of a record, however, the translation from physical locks to logical locks can be executed in a number of ways.

Distributed Two-Phase Locking

Recall that two-phase locking (2PL) synchronizes reads and writes by explicitly detecting and preventing conflicts between concurrent operations. Before reading data item *x*, a transaction must have a *readlock* on *x*. Before writing into *x*, it must have a *writelock* on *x*. The ownership of locks is generally governed by two rules:

1. Different transactions cannot simultaneously own conflicting locks.
2. Once a transaction surrenders ownership of a lock, it may never obtain additional locks.

The basis for this method is that a step can always proceed unless it conflicts with a previous step of an active transaction other than its own. In a distributed database system the test is exactly the same; the question is how to best carry it out. One way is for the DDBMS to check whether the record accessed by the step in question has been accessed by an active transaction. Using this approach, the TM is required to obtain locks before reading and writing data. That is, the TM must have received a readlock by the local DBMS from which the data are read. Similarly, before updating a record, a TM must have been provided a writelock from every database that stores the record in question.

Let's illustrate these ideas with an example.

Example 2. Suppose that a transaction *T* is composed of two actions, as follows:

1. $T_{1.1}$, which runs at site 1 and writes a new value for copy R_1 of record *R*, and
2. $T_{1.2}$, which runs at site 2 and writes the same new value as in (1) for copy R_2 of *R*.

Furthermore, consider a transaction T_2, which has two subtransactions $T_{2.1}$ running at site 1 and writing a new value to R_1, and $T_{2.2}$ running at site 2 and writing the same value into R_2. Two-phase locking is illustrated in Figure 12.18. Note that pairs of events on each line could occur simultaneously. The events at site 1 suggest that $T_{1.1}$ must precede $T_{2.1}$. At site 2, $T_{1.2}$ must precede $T_{2.2}$.

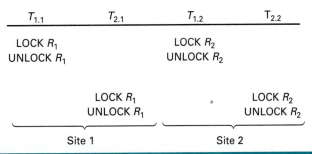

$T_{1.1}$	$T_{2.1}$	$T_{1.2}$	$T_{2.2}$
LOCK R_1 UNLOCK R_1		LOCK R_2 UNLOCK R_2	
	LOCK R_1 UNLOCK R_1		LOCK R_2 UNLOCK R_2

Site 1   Site 2

▼FIGURE 12.18 TWO-PHASE LOCKING EXAMPLE

A two-phase locking technique first goes through a phase of acquiring all the locks for a transaction, then a phase of releasing them: No lock may be acquired after any lock has been released. Papadimitriou (1988) proved that readlocks and writelocks will generate consistent schedules if and only if transactions process in two phases. This requires that the TM evaluate and rearrange, if necessary, the stream of steps arriving at each site. The TM must be a distributed program with a subprogram called a module, executing at each site. The computation of a module is a series of actions such as:

1. Receiving an action and granting its execution.

2. Sending a message to another site.

3. Receiving a message.

To show that this strategy always generates consistent schedules, it is necessary to show the order of locks remains the same as for a serial schedule.

Timestamping

timestamping A method of identifying messages with their time of transmission.

With a **timestamp** protocol, each transaction T_i is issued a timestamp $TS(T_i)$ when it enters the system. If T_i enters the system before T_j, then $TS(T_i) < TS(T_j)$. Timestamps are drawn from an increasing sequence of integers. The protocol manages concurrent execution so that it will be equivalent to a predetermined serial execution. That serial execution is defined by the increasing order of timestamps.

How do timestamps enforce the serialization of transaction processing? With each record (or data item) X in the database, two times are identified: read time (R-TS(X)), which is the highest timestamp possessed by any transaction to have read the record; and write-time (W-TS(X)), which is the the highest timestamp possessed by any transaction to have written to the record. Serialization is enforced in the following ways:

1. A transaction T_i, having a timestamp $TS(T_i)$, cannot read or write X if $TS(T_i) <$ W-TS(X).

2. A transaction T_i, with timestamp $TS(T_i)$, cannot write a record X with a read-time R-TS(X), if $TS(T_i) <$ R-TS(X).

To clarify, for any transaction T_i, if $TS(T_i) <$ W-TS(X), then any read operations by T_i, if allowed, will result in T_i reading a value that has been overwritten by the later transaction. Any write operation attempted by T_i, if allowed, results in writing an obsolete value of X. Both cases violate serializability, and all such requests should be rejected. In such instances, T_i should be aborted, issued a new timestamp, and restarted.

Similarly, if $TS(T_i) < R\text{-}TS(X)$, then any write operations by T_i, if allowed, means that the value that T_i is attempting to write was previously needed. As before, T_i should be aborted, issued a new timestamp, and restarted.

There are two principal methods of assigning unique timestamps. One is centralized, the other decentralized. In the centralized method, a single site is given responsibility for assigning the timestamps to transactions. With the decentralized scheme, each site is allowed to generate a unique local timestamp. A globally unique timestamp is derived by concatenating the unique local timestamp with (followed by) a unique site identifier. If the concatenation were reversed, the site with the highest identifier would consistently generate higher timestamps than all other sites.

Transaction timestamps may be created by having the TM keep a count of the number of transactions it has ever scheduled and assign the next number to each new transaction in turn. In this way, no two transactions can receive the same timestamp, and the relative order of the timestamps is consistent with the order in which the transactions are initiated. A second approach is to use the value of the machine's internal clock at the time a process initiates.

We illustrate with an example.

Example 3. Examine Figure 12.19. T_1 is given a timestamp of 25 and T_2 is given a timestamp of 30. (The initial read-time and write-time of records X and Y are assumed to be 0.) When T_1 reads X, it is given a read timestamp of 25 ($R\text{-}TS(X) = 25$). When T_2 writes to X, it is given $W\text{-}TS(X) = 30$. When T_2 writes to Y, we have $W\text{-}TS(Y) = 30$. When T_1 attempts to read Y, we have $TS(T^1) = 25 < W\text{-}TS(Y) = 30$. T_1 must be aborted, otherwise it would be reading a value that was written after the value that T_1 should read.

To implement this scheme in the distributed database environment, the following steps need to be followed:

1. Transactions may execute at any site. As they read and write any copy of the record, their timestamp is captured on the site copy of the record.

2. If a transaction writes a new value for the site copy of the record, the same value must be written into all copies of the record.

```
Timestamp      T₁                        T₂
             (25)                      (30)

        1. READ R (25)            READ R (30)
        2. WRITE R (25 < 30       WRITE R (30)
                  => abort)
```

▼ Database Recovery

In Chapter 11, recovery strategies were outlined which had as their foundation a transaction log. In a distributed system, a log must be maintained at each site. In addition to the previously specified information, the site log must record each message that it sends and receives. In the distributed database environment, there must be a means of detecting failure and reestablishing the system status at time of failure when the system comes back up. The site log indicates which subtransactions were started but did not commit at that site.

▼ Client/Server Systems

Client/server (CS) systems were explored in some detail in Chapter 9. We discuss CS briefly in this chapter for two reasons: (1) They are a special type of distributed database system, and (2) to provide an introduction for those who may have skipped the earlier chapter. Here our discussion of CS systems is on three levels. We first outline the general concepts underlying CS, then briefly relate these concepts to database systems. We then discuss a particular type of CS: SQL Server for Windows NT. Together, this should give you a general understanding of CS and its potential for supporting database systems, as well as a few of the features of a particular implementation.

General Concepts

The term *client/server* (*CS*) is not new, since CS systems involving multiple computers connected in a network is a concept that has been around for some time. A distinguishing concept of CS systems is that one or more of these computers may function as a provider of services to the remaining computers, which function as *clients* that process applications. Client and server have more formally been defined as follows (Ullman, 1993, p. xx):

Client: A computer or workstation attached to a network that is used to access network resources.

Server: A computer that furnishes clients with services such as databases, connections to a network, or large disk drives. Servers can be mainframes, minicomputers, large workstations, or LAN devices. More than one server can be involved in providing services to clients.

Arguably, the motivation for adopting CS technology is twofold. First, it may reduce costs over the long term. Second, CS technology facilitates the development of customized platforms for specific applications. The latter capability can enhance a firm's ability to respond to rapidly changing business conditions.

Figure 12.20 shows a CS system with two servers, a database server and a fax server. Suppose that Client A requires data contained in the database server. The user expresses the data request in the form of a query (e.g., SQL) and transmits it to the database server. The database server executes the query on its data and transmits the result to Client A. At the same time, Clients B and C may request data from the database server, and the database server may service several requests in parallel.

The fax server may supply fax numbers, as well as transmitting and receiving faxes for users.

CS systems are intended to be open systems in the sense that they allow the organization to choose from various vendor products as components of the CS.

4. Partitioned database implemented in an integrated fashion such that a single query requiring access to data at more than one site is handled by the DBMS, and its functioning is transparent to the user.

Several criteria were suggested to help determine the appropriate configuration.

The use of fragmentation of relations as a means of taking advantage of the capabilities of distributed database systems were discussed. Vertical and horizontal fragmentation were defined and their use was demonstrated. The use of semijoins as a means of limiting communications costs was also demonstrated. Many files are not subject to fragmentation, however. In such cases, a design issue is where to locate complete files. A practical method of analysis was presented.

Distributed concurrency control was discussed along with the use of a two-phase protocol for preventing data integrity problems. Timestamping and backup and recovery were also outlined.

Distributed database systems can be complex, but they offer capabilities which extend the advantages of database technology. We can expect to see their widespread use in organizations of many types.

Finally, we outlined the basic concepts of client/server systems. In terms of database systems, this is an important new concept because it facilitates application access to one or more database systems, offering considerable information retrieval power to the user.

Review Questions

1. Define each of the following terms in your own words:
   a. distributed database system
   b. global data
   c. distributed database management system
   d. R*
   e. transaction
   f. local transaction
   g. WAN
   h. serializability theory
   i. data fragmentation
   j. vertical fragmentation
   k. two-phase commit protocol
   l. timestamping

2. Describe how distributed database systems and centralized database systems differ.

3. Describe the software modules of a distributed database management system and how they operate to execute a transaction that requires data from more than one site.

4. Discuss several advantages of a distributed database system.

5. Under what conditions might a distributed database system not function as well as a centralized database system?

6. Describe six objectives/strategies of implementing a distributed database system.

7. Contrast the concepts of partitioned and replicated databases. When might each be preferred to the other?

8. Compare the semijoin to the natural join.

9. What is the purpose of the two-phase commit protocol? How does it work?

10. What is the purpose of timestamping? How does it work?

11. How is database recovery effected in a distributed database system?

Problems and Exercises

1. Match each term with its definition:

__local data	a. A process that cooperates in completing a transaction
__link	b. A transaction that requires data from more than one database location
__SSD	c. A communications channel between two sites in a computer network
__Distributed INGRESS	d. Data that are maintained in the database at one site in a distributed database system
__agent	e. The actions invoked by a transaction are executed in tandem
__global transaction	f. A computer network that is limited to a small geographic area
__LAN	g. A DDBMS supplied by Relational Technology
__serial execution	h. A DDBMS supplied by Computer Corporation of America
__horizontal fragmentation	i. Partitioning a relation into subsets of its tuples

2. Create a sample database for a firm having a database distributed at three locations. Choose a data distribution plan for this database, and justify your plan.

3. Show how vertical fragmentation may be applied to the plan developed in (2).

4. Show how horizontal fragmentation may be applied to the plan developed in (2).

5. Consider a relation

```
EMPLOYEE(ID, name, address, skill, projectno)
EQUIPMENT(IDNO, type, project)
```

Suppose that the EMPLOYEE relation is fragmented horizontally by projectno and each fragment is stored locally at its project site. Assume that the EQUIPMENT relation is stored in its entirety at the Seattle location. Describe a good strategy for processing the following queries:

    a. Find the join of employee and equipment.
    b. Get all employees for projects using R2 Trucks.
    c. Get all machines at the Parowan Project.
    d. Find all employees for the project using machine number 12.

6. Given the information in Figures 12.1E and 12.2E, determine the optimal distribution of the eight files among five sites, assuming a disk capacity of 25 Mbytes at each site.

Transactions	File (Size)							
	1 (8)	2 (8)	3 (16)	4 (9)	5 (10)	6 (7)	7 (5)	8 (4)
1	10	9				10		20
2						20		9
3				60	70	140	16	
4				6	5	15	10	
5				4	4			10
6	4	10		6	1			15
7	9	2		3	4			
8	6	5		2	4			
9	2	2						
10								

▼FIGURE 12.1E RATES OF TRANSACTIONS TO FILES

▼FIGURE 12.2E FREQUENCY OF TRANSACTIONS IN SITES (f_{kj})

Transactions	Site				
	1	2	3	4	5
1		25			
2	12	30			
3		3	5	4	5
4			10	10	10
5			12	8	4
6	20	150	100	2	2
7	2	100		30	40
8	18	32	12	12	10
9	4	2			
10		4			

7. Compute a semijoin for the following relations

$R_1 = X\ Y\ Z$ $R_2 = Z\ V\ W$
      $c\ b\ a$ $a\ d\ e$
      $d\ e\ f$ $a\ f\ h$
      $c\ b\ d$ $b\ a\ b$
      $e\ a\ b$ $c\ d\ c$
      $h\ j\ k$ $c\ b\ a$

8. Examine Figure 12.3E. Given the transaction history presented there, assume that a timestamping protocol was applied. Indicate where transactions would be aborted and explain why.

```
Timestamps are  T₁ = 1,  T₂ = 2,  and so on.

    T₁              T₂              T₃              T₄              T₅
                                                                read (Y)
                    read (X)
    read (X)
                                    write (X)
                                    write (Z)
                                                                read (Z)
                    read (Z)
                      abort
    read (Y)
                                                    write (Z)
                                                      abort
                                                                write (Y)
                                                                write (Z)
```

▼**FIGURE 12.3E TRANSACTION HISTORY FOR TIMESTAMPING**

Professional Issues

1. Write a short essay on the future of distributed database systems.

2. Do a library research project to gather examples of current implementations of distributed database systems. Can you find any material discussing performance issues?

3 Contact a professional accounting firm and inquire about the controls that should be present in a distributed processing system. Are there any areas where suitable controls are not in use?

4. One of the advantages of CS systems is that they can provide a means for a firm to change the way it operates—the way it does business. See if you can find an article or two that describe changes that have been facilitated by the implementation of a CS system.

▼ Analyzing Management Information Needs

management information Information to support company operations and decision makers.

We use the term **management information** in the general sense of information required to support a firm's operations and its decision makers in pursuit of company goals. The management information required by a firm providing a product that changes slowly in a stable market may be somewhat different from the information required by a firm that is in a volatile market, or that produces a variety of products subject to rapid obsolescence.

Consider the information needs of a manufacturing firm that uses material requirements planning (MRP) to manage its production processes. MRP requires an extensive database containing information on final product scheduling, inventories, bills of material, routing, and lead times to coordinate all phases of manufacture. If information on costs and resource needs for each manufacturing step is added, the MRP data can be used for cost accounting, shop floor control, and capacity planning and management. Such a database provides nearly all planning and control information needed for a manufacturing plant.

This database provides much of the management information required by the manufacturing firm. What kind of database system might best service such information needs? The database required for MRP provides a wealth of management information, but it is very difficult to build and maintain. Every manufacturing environment is dynamic—new products are added and old ones are deleted from the product line; designs and manufacturing methods change regularly; lead times vary; inventory problems and adjustments may occur frequently. Such requirements might favor a relational DBMS.

Contrast this with the manufacturing firm that operates a just-in-time (JIT) inventory system. The intent of a JIT system is that raw materials and subassemblies will move immediately from delivery through manufacturing to the consumption center. Parts are made in small batches, which are delivered frequently to the user. The information requirements for JIT are fairly simple. For example, when products are made in small batches, the production system makes only a few bad parts before errors are discovered, and the short lead times make it easy to trace problems back to their origins.

JIT systems function best when demand is high and production requirements result in nearly continuous production. A hierarchical or network DBMS (see Chapters 15 and 16) might be appropriate here.

Of course, it is inappropriate to make blanket recommendations based on these simplified scenarios. Our main point is that the management information needs of the firm should influence the choice of DBMS. Characteristics of management information needs that may affect the choice of DBMS could include the following:

1. The potential need for information that may require data from more than one application.

2. The number of applications where the relationships among data are well established and subject to little change.

3. The current and expected volume of insertions and deletions pertaining to existing and new data structures.

4. The way in which data need to be classified for decision making. For example, a manufacturer of packaged foods may make marketing promotion decisions based upon nationwide sales of its items. Another firm of the same type may

make the same decisions based upon sales in various locations within major cities. The former company requires a simpler set of data than the latter. If the latter wants to experiment with different views of the information in order to test several strategies, a good deal of flexibility is required.

Having introduced the problem of information needs at a general level, we now proceed to an examination of specific information requirements.

Determining Application Requirements

Determining the information requirements to be supported by a database system is a complex process that is essential in guiding the selection of a DBMS. The analysis process can be simplified, however, if you realize that users typically fall into two classes: regular, repetitive users and occasional users.

The repetitive user is the one whose applications may be described as production systems. The requirements for these transaction-driven systems are planned in advance and generally support routine company operations such as recording of sales, keeping track of inventory, and so forth. Ideally, the DBMS should be able to support these applications in an efficient way.

The occasional users may require the greatest flexibility, since their requirements are often unforeseen. Such users tend to require information for analysis and decision making as opposed to support of routine operations. This type of user needs powerful capabilities for classifying and combining data, as well as an easy-to-use query language.

Proponents of hierarchical and network data models have asserted that these models have superior capabilities for production-system applications (see the discussion in Chapters 15 and 16). Advocates of relational DBMSs claim these systems now provide improved performance in support of production systems in addition to more powerful capabilities for supporting ad hoc information needs than other models. The development of IDMS/R, which offers relational features on a network-based system, attempts to serve both needs.

Most firms are going to have a mix of needs and may go with a system that best supports their major type of need. Products such as IDMS/R are intended to minimize the sacrifice made on behalf of the less prominent need. At the same time, relational DBMSs are improving their efficiency in serving both types of information requirements.

Maintaining Data Consistency

The need to share data across multiple applications is the primary reason for implementing a database system. As discussed in Chapter 1, redundant data can result in a myriad of problems, most of which result from inconsistencies among duplicate copies of data records. Even in well-run installations, it is common for duplicate records to be updated on different time cycles. Thus, in such installations, data inconsistency is inevitable.

A good DBMS cannot guarantee that data inconsistencies will never occur, but it should provide capabilities for minimizing their occurrence. Consequently, any DBMS evaluation ought to include a consideration of the features that will ensure consistency between duplicate copies of the same data.

Response-Time Requirements

A DBMS has to perform at an expected level to be valuable to users. Unacceptable response time to user requests will lead to frustration; frustration will lead users to pursue other means of satisfying their information needs. Getting users to specify realistic response-time requirements can be a challenge, yet a dialogue with users focused on identifying ideal and minimum response-time requirements can be productive. The results can then be used in evaluating DBMS performance under varying application and volume requirements.

▼ DBMS Functions and Capabilities

To evaluate a DBMS's ability to service the firm's information requirements, we need to consider the functions provided and their underlying features.

The Data Dictionary/Directory

An effective database system will allow growth and modification in the database without compromising the integrity of its data. The data dictionary/directory (DD/D) aids the accomplishment of this objective by allowing the definitions of data to be maintained separately from the data itself. This allows changes to be made to the data definitions with no effect on the stored data. For example, the subschema used by a particular program could be modified without in any way affecting the stored data. Other benefits provided by the DD/D include these:

- ▼ Physical storage structures can be changed without affecting the programs that use the data.
- ▼ Passwords and other security measures can be stored in the DD/D to facilitate control over data access.
- ▼ Centralized data definition enables easy reporting on the status of the database: who is responsible for the various data items, what controls are applied to them, and what programs and users are accessing the data.

To yield these benefits, the DD/D usually includes the following features:

- ▼ A language for defining entries in the DD/D.
- ▼ A manipulation language for adding, deleting, and modifying entries in the DD/D.
- ▼ Methods for validating entries in the DD/D.
- ▼ Means for producing reports concerning the data contained in the DD/D.

An important development in relational DBMSs is the common practice of storing the directory itself as a set of relations. This enables the use of the DBMS data manipulation language for querying, updating, and maintaining the data dictionary. Figure 13.1 shows a fragment of a catalog (the name for a data dictionary used by DB2, IBM's relational DBMS). This catalog fragment contains information on the relations shown in Figure 13.2.

```
SYSTABLES      NAME        CREATOR      COLCOUNT
               PRODUCT     JHANSEN         3
               MFR         JHANSEN         4

SYSCOLUMNS     NAME        TBNAME       COLTYPE
               PRODID      PRODUCT      INTEGER
               PRODDESC    PRODUCT      CHAR
               MFRID       PRODUCT      INTEGER
               MFRID       MFR          INTEGER
               MRFNAME     MFR          CHAR
               ADDRESS     MFR          CHAR
               COUNTRY     MFR          CHAR
```

▼FIGURE 13.1 CATALOG FRAGMENT

```
PRODUCT
   PRODID        PRODDESC         MFRID
    1035          Sweater          210
    2241         Table Lamp        317
    2518       Brass Sculpture     253

MFR
   MFRID         MFRNAME        ADDRESS        COUNTRY
    210        Kiwi Klothes     Auckland     New Zealand
    253        Brass Works       Lagos         Nigeria
    317        Llama Llamps       Lima           Peru
```

▼FIGURE 13.2 BASE RELATIONS FOR CATALOG FRAGMENT OF FIGURE 13.1

Data Security and Integrity

Data security and integrity are essential to effective database operations and were covered in some depth in Chapter 11. They are also important considerations in selecting a DBMS. Specifically, you should be alert to the following capabilities:

access controls Controls that limit user access to programs and data.

▼ **Access controls** are an important factor because they are a means of preventing unauthorized access to data. In the data-sharing database environment, good access controls are essential.

concurrency controls Controls that maintain database integrity when two or more users simultaneously request a database record.

▼ **Concurrency controls** are a means of maintaining data integrity in the multiuser environment. Suppose user *A* and user *B* both access a given record at (essentially) the same time in order to process a transaction against that record. The DBMS must somehow limit access by one of the users until the other's transaction has been completed. Without this type of facility, the accuracy and consistency of the database can rapidly erode.

view controls Those controls that restrict access to views (subsets of base relations).

▼ **View controls** provide an automated means of limiting what a user is allowed to access from a given relation. This is a powerful feature that is commonly provided by relational DBMSs. The ease of creating views and the capability of the view facility can be a useful distinguishing factor among DBMSs. The DBMS purchaser may also be interested in whether views can be updated and what limitations may apply.

request for proposal (RFP) A formal document that outlines performance requirements and asks vendors to respond with a proposal for meeting those requirements.

The most common way of acquiring vendor information is to issue a **request for proposal (RFP)**. The RFP is useful in that it specifies the requirements the DBMSs must satisfy and requests information from the vendors to show how their DBMSs will satisfy those requirements. The response to the RFP can be a source of information to be compared to feedback received from users of a vendor's product. Discrepancies or inconsistencies can be referred to the vendor for clarification. This process may also suggest areas that should be directly tested. A suggested list of requirements in four categories is shown in Figure 13.3.

Benchmark Tests

benchmarking A method of comparing DBMS performance by testing its performance on actual applications.

Benchmarking is a conventional method for generating performance information to be used in the DBMS evaluation process. The intent is to simulate the application environment in order to generate realistic performance data. Modeling the real environment can be challenging, since it is difficult to keep all parameters of the operating environment constant: the operating system, the sequence of operations, multiprogramming, and so forth. The desired invariance can usually only be accomplished by the dedicated use of a computer for the benchmark. It can also be costly to train users to a desired level of knowledge concerning each DBMS.

Although the vendors of DBMSs often supply standard benchmark tests and demonstrate them as a service to the prospective buyer, it remains the purchaser's responsibility to determine the system features that are important and to ensure that those features are sufficiently demonstrated.

One useful approach is to include a requirement for benchmark specifications in the RFP in order to eliminate in advance those vendors whose product will not meet those specifications.

When the actual benchmark testing is done, the following elements should be considered:

▼ The test should be representative of the firm's application environment.

▼ The nature of the benchmark test should be established prior to the actual testing: requirements to be met, relative weights to be assigned to various components of the test, and the evaluation procedures to be followed.

▼FIGURE 13.3 EXAMPLES OF DBMS INFORMATION THAT MIGHT BE REQUESTED FROM VENDORS

FUNCTIONS	SECURITY AND INTEGRITY
Data Dictionary	Authentication
Data Manipulation Language	Authorization
Built-in Functions	Encryption
Access Control	Rollback Features
	Rollforward Features
	Transaction Processing
PERFORMANCE	VENDOR SUPPORT
Benchmark Results	Training
Memory Requirements	Documentation
Optimization Features	Responsiveness
	Upgrading

While the nature of benchmarking may vary from one firm to another, there are certain aspects of a DBMS that are necessary to every firm: main memory requirements, database storage requirements, service to multiple users who access the system concurrently, input/output requirements, and backup and recovery facilities.

▼ Evaluation Models

The acquisition of a DBMS reflects a major commitment by the firm. Methods of collecting and recording data may be affected. At a higher level, a commitment to providing better management information is implied. Most important, the acquisition of a DBMS represents a commitment to using information to improve the way in which the firm does business. These commitments require that the process of choosing a DBMS include consideration of important DBMS features in a rational and consistent manner. The attainment of these objectives can be aided by the use of a formal methodology. In the following discussion, we present two formal methods—a scoring model and a data envelopment model. The scoring model is easy to apply and has been widely used to aid in the DBMS selection process. The data envelopment model is more powerful, yet still easy to apply.

Scoring Model

The scoring model that we present has been widely used in practice. Many firms limit the recommended classification of requirements to just two: mandatory and desirable. As nearly as possible, the verification of mandatory requirements should not be subject to judgment or opinion. Desirable requirements may, and often do, include features that are harder to measure.

Conceptually, the scoring model is easy. Providing good input data is the hard part. We illustrate with a simple but representative example.

Example: Divide the required features into two categories, mandatory and desirable, as follows:

FEATURE \VENDOR   *A*   *B*   *C*
Mandatory
Views
Password Control
Backup Facility
Desirable
Relational Query Language
User Training

The selection of a weighting scheme is somewhat arbitrary, but it will work if it is consistent. One simple scheme is to assign a weight of 10 to each mandatory requirement and a weight of 1 to 9 to each desirable feature with the higher numbers indicating a higher degree of desirability. When this has been determined, a value between 1 and 10 can be assigned to each feature for each vendor, depending on how well the vendor's DBMS satisfies the requirement. A completed scoring table might look like this:

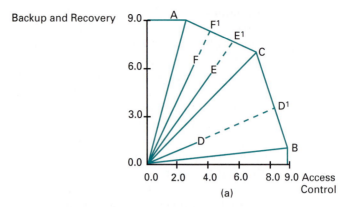

EFFICIENT FRONTIER AND EXPANSION PATHS FOR SIX DBMSs

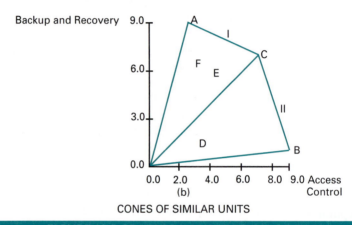

CONES OF SIMILAR UNITS

▼**FIGURE 13.5 GRAPHIC ILLUSTRATION OF DEA**

segment joining *B* and *C. D, B,* and *C* are all relatively strong in access-control capability compared to backup-and-recovery capability. However, *E* and *F* are relatively strong in backup-and-recovery capability, and their relative capability is computed by comparing them to *A* and *C.* Thus, the cone labeled I in Figure 13.5(b) contains the DBMSs that are strong in backup and recovery, while the cone labeled II contains those that are strong in access control. DBMS *C,* which is strong in both categories, is in both cones.

This graphical method of measuring relative capability is a valuable tool for illustrating DEA concepts, but it is limited to two criteria. To measure the relative capability of DBMSs characterized by more than two criteria, we must use linear programming (LP) models. The most realistic and practical formulation is based on assessing relative values of criteria.

Application.   The heart of making a decision about the choice of a DBMS is to be able to incorporate judgments about the relative importance of the criteria. Continuing with our example, *A* is best in backup and recovery but is weak in access control. *B* is best in access control but weak in backup and recovery. Both are on the frontier and have a relative capability of 1.0 as measured by DEA. However, to compare *A* and *B* in overall performance capability, we need to make some judgments about the relative importance of access control capability and backup and recovery capability.

A criterion-based LP model allows us to focus on the relative importance of the criteria. The decision variables are weights on the attributes, which express the relative importance of the attributes. The objective in using the LP model is to choose criterion weights that maximize the relative efficiency of the reference unit. Relative capability is measured as a ratio of the overall value of the reference unit compared to the overall value of the best in the set of DBMSs.

Figure 13.6 shows how the choice of criterion weights affects relative capability. When backup-and-recovery capability is assumed to be twice as important as access-control capability, A and C exhibit the best overall capability, each with an overall rating of 21 [= 1x(access-control rating) + 2x(backup-and-recovery rating)]. The relative capability of each DBMS is measured as the ratio of the overall rating to the highest overall rating. With these weights, B is considered to be 61.9 percent (=13/21) as good in terms of capability as A or C.

The last two columns lead to a much different result when access-control capability is assumed to be three times as important as backup-and-recovery capability. With these weights, B has the highest overall score of 29. A now has a relative capability of 62.1 percent (18/29), while C has dropped to 96.6 percent (28/29).

D, E, and F yield lesser overall capability ratings for both sets of weights. In fact, units off the frontier will never be the best for any set of weights and will always have a relative capability less than 1.0. In contrast, for any DBMS on the frontier, there will always be at least one set of weights for which the frontier DBMS will have the best overall score and, therefore, a relative efficiency of 1.0.

This observation leads directly to the criterion-based LP model to measure relative efficiency. The decision variables are the criteria weights and the objective is to maximize the relative capability of a given reference unit. The constraints are that each DBMS has a relative capability that does not exceed 100 percent. The verbal model is

MAXIMIZE THE VALUE OF THE REFERENCE UNIT
SUBJECT TO THE OVERALL VALUE OF EACH UNIT BEING LESS THAN OR EQUAL TO 1.

The full criterion-based model to measure D's relative capability is

MAX $3P + 2Q$ (D's overall rating; P = access-control rating; Q = backup-and-recovery rating)

ST $3P + 9Q <= 1$ (Limit on A's overall rating)

▼ FIGURE 13.6 EFFECT OF ATTRIBUTE WEIGHTS ON RELATIVE EFFICIENCY

			WEIGHT (ACCESS CONTROL) 1 (BACKUP AND RECOVERY) 2		WEIGHT (ACCESS CONTROL) 3 (BACKUP AND RECOVERY) 1	
DBMS	ACCESS CONTROL	BACKUP AND RECOVERY	OVERALL SCORE	RELATIVE EFFICIENCY	OVERALL SCORE	RELATIVE EFFICIENCY
A	3	9	21*	1.000	18	0.621
B	9	2	13	0.619	29*	1.000
C	7	7	21*	1.000	28	0.966
D	3	2	7	0.333	11	0.379
E	4	5	14	0.667	17	0.586
F	3	6	15	0.714	15	0.517
			MAX = 21		MAX = 29	

$$9P + 2Q <= 1 \quad \text{(Limit on } B\text{'s overall rating)}$$
$$7P + 7Q <= 1 \quad \text{(Limit on } C\text{'s overall rating)}$$
$$3P + 2Q <= 1 \quad \text{(Limit on } D\text{'s overall rating)}$$
$$4P + 5Q <= 1 \quad \text{(Limit on } E\text{'s overall rating)}$$
$$3P + 6Q <= 1 \quad \text{(Limit on } F\text{'s overall rating)}$$
$$P,Q >= 0 \quad \text{(nonnegativity)}$$

▼ Implementation Issues

Implementation planning and administration is as important to database systems as it is to the effective implementation of any new technology. In this section we outline some of the important considerations associated with DBMS implementation.

Database Administration

The responsibility for database administration is usually assigned to an individual called a database administrator (DBA). The DBA is charged with ensuring that the database system operates effectively and efficiently. In order to do this, the DBA's daily activities are concerned with the following tasks:

1. Servicing end-user requirements.
2. Ensuring database security and integrity.
3. Establishing backup-and-recovery procedures.

Servicing End-User Requirements.   The DBA is responsible for tracking the frequency of database use by end users and the response times needed by their database applications. This is done to be sure that user needs are being satisfied. The DBA is also involved with satisfying the training needs of users. This training includes providing appropriate tools to make the end users more productive. Examples might be special utilities or language capabilities.

Ensuring Database Security and Integrity.   By tracking the frequency of database use by users, the DBA obtains information that can help in determining needs for database controls. Unexpected user requests, for instance, may prompt an evaluation of the adequacy of access controls. For example, suppose that user U1 is not allowed to access individual records in the payroll file. Recently, U1 has been requesting aggregate data such as counts and sums of various fields in the table. U1 may be gathering data from which he or she is able to deduce individual attribute values that cannot be accessed directly. Additional access controls may be needed to prevent this.

In terms of database integrity, the DBA must make sure that there is a correct correspondence between the database and its definition as reflected in the data dictionary. The DBA must also maintain controls to restrict the updating of the database to authorized users. Maintaining the level of restriction put upon each user is the DBA's responsibility.

The DBA must further ensure that user-specified data controls are implemented and monitored. For example, users may have better knowledge than the DBA as to which data are sensitive and should be restricted and to what level. Cost data pertaining to manufacturing operations may be unrestricted from access by the cost accounting department, for example, but should not be accessed by other functional groups without prior permission.

Backup and Recovery. DBMSs provide facilities for maintaining data integrity during operations. However, they cannot otherwise guarantee database integrity. Corruption of data because of a disk failure, for example, may be outside the control of the DBMS. Such possibilities require that the DBA devise methods for restoring a complete and consistent database after a failure.

Restoration procedures typically involve utilities provided by the DBMS as part of a larger recovery plan designed by the DBA. This means that the DBA must be familiar with all DBMS functions and capabilities. The recovery plan would generally include the following procedures:

1. Identify backup-and-recovery utilities that are available to handle system failures.
2. Establish procedures to be followed by all who have a role in the recovery plan.
3. Create a plan for informing users who are affected by database failure concerning the potential impact the failure will have on their operations, as well as the estimated time to restore the database.
4. Create and conduct a schedule of tests for the recovery plan and standards by which to gauge the results. This ensures that the recovery plan will accomplish its objectives if a real disaster occurs.

Database Testing

Good testing procedures are needed to ensure that the database system fulfills user requirements and operates without major problems. In the development of new applications, testing runs second only to programming in terms of time required. Testing is normally focused on validating the following operations:

1. The loading of the database has been accomplished without violating the data integrity.
2. The applications interface correctly with the database.
3. The performance of the system satisfies the requirements for which the DBMS was acquired.

An objective of testing, which is sometimes overlooked, is finding out where the database system does not function as expected. Most problems arise when input values are unusual or erroneous, when combinations of conditions yield unexpected results, or when users take unanticipated actions. Consequently, test data should be generated to determine how the system handles the following types of inputs:

1. Values that have erroneous negative signs.
2. Invalid codes or keys.
3. Data that threaten referential integrity.
4. Null values.
5. An unauthorized user's attempts to change data.
6. Extreme values such as unusually large hours worked or unusually large receipts of goods.
7. Inappropriate units of measure.
8. Unauthorized attempts to change information contained in the data dictionary.

On the operational control level, the firm should be concerned with monitoring the use of computing resources. Management should be interested in the following information:

1. Who is using the database system, what data are being used, and how long are they being used?
2. What hardware resources are being used by the database system, when are they being used, and are there bottlenecks?
3. How much time is being used for routine processing versus ad hoc queries, and are there trends in such usage?

To make these ideas concrete, we illustrate some of the performance measures incorporated in IBM's relational DBMS DB2. The DB2 Performance Monitor is used in concert with the DB2 Instrumentation Facility to generate information on system performance. The DB2 Instrumentation Facility collects database system performance data, which can then be analyzed by the DB2 Performance Monitor in order to generate information of interest to the DBA and other management personnel. Examples of such information include the processing time for SQL queries, traces of SQL query execution, statistics on input and output data, and summary information on waiting times for execution of queries and programs.

Generation of test data that will check every possible undesired condition has been shown to be an intractable problem (Garey and Johnson, 1979). Consequently, sound testing of the database system requires thoughtful design of test data that are at once reasonably thorough and can be applied at reasonable cost and time.

Decision tables have been used with some success in generating test data. More sophisticated approaches are available to automatically generate test data.

Preparing Users for Change

Since user acceptance is essential to a successful database system implementation, preparing the users for the changes that will affect them is essential. How is this best accomplished?

Conceptually, the answer is simple: Involve the users in the development of the new systems, train them thoroughly, and include user-acceptance tests as part of the implementation effort. Carrying out these activities may be a bit more complex.

An important part of involving the users in the development of the database system is facilitated if users are convinced of the need for that system. Top management, in concert with functional analysts and systems analysts, should communicate clearly to users what the expected benefits might be, as well as any startup costs that might be borne by the user. This should be done at the earliest possible point in the development cycle.

Experience has shown that users develop feelings of support for a system when they have participated in its development and implementation. Key users may actually be selected as part of the development team; others should be consulted as the project progresses. Users need to participate and contribute. The objective here is not simply political. Often users may contribute ideas or observe considerations that have been overlooked and that would make the database system function better. We emphasize that user involvement is most effective when users participate throughout development and implementation. A courtesy consultation at the beginning and the end of the project will rarely work.

Involving users in the development and implementation of the database system provides another benefit: It prepares them for training in the use of the system. Users may subsequently receive training in system use by (1) reading operations and procedures manuals, (2) formal training sessions conducted by the vendor and the firm, and (3) informal training by an internal coordinator charged with assisting users as questions and problems arise. If the same types of questions are repeatedly encountered, the coordinator may arrange for a formal training session addressing the problem procedures.

Among other things, users will need to know how to process documents, present input, produce reports, correct errors, generate queries, and so on. As primary users become trained, they can be used as a resource to train other users in their functional area.

Loading the Database

Often the data to be stored in the database already exist on some computer-based medium such as magnetic tape. In the best cases, all the required data exist, and database loading may simply involve restructuring the existing data. That is to say, a program can be written that reads the old files and creates the structure needed for the new ones.

More often, the existing files do not contain all the data required by the new database. A commonly used approach for this case is to convert the existing files so that they contain the necessary data before the time comes to switch over to the database system. A noteworthy limitation of this approach is that the old system must continue to process daily transactions while this modification is being done.

Database Maintenance

Once the DBMS is installed and in operation, maintenance activities need to be organized and performed to ensure that effective service and operations are provided. In this section, we describe some of the necessary maintenance functions.

Managing Resources.   Over time, new data will be added to the database, some data may be deleted, and applications will be added or modified. Most firms will experience database growth. New requirements may change the mix of database applications, and it is important to monitor the effect of such changes. Database system resources such as storage devices, buffers, indexes, and tables need to be checked to determine their adequacy as system requirements change. This information is a help in making decisions about adding or upgrading resources, as well as forecasting future needs.

Backup and Recovery.   Saving a copy of the database at selected time intervals should be a standard backup practice. In this way, if the database being used is damaged or destroyed, it can be reconstructed by loading the backup copy and re-running all transactions that had been processed since the backup copy was made.

Database saves are usually made by using an operating system utility or a DBMS utility. The former backs up the entire disk file, including the physical data structures. Similar backup is available through use of the DBMS. However, the data structures are not actually represented in the saved data but are reconstructed during loading of the saved data. This process can be somewhat slow for large files.

Managing Changes to the Database System. Changes to the database system are inevitable as user needs change over time. Users may become more facile with the query language and extend the range and complexity of applications required of the system. As time passes, users often see new ways in which information from the database can be organized and retrieved to support the needs of their job. As these changes accumulate, enhancements to the database system may be needed.

Changes in user needs that amount to arranging data in more complex forms can degrade DBMS performance if they are widespread, but they may not require that the contents and structure of the database be changed. New applications, however, may require that attributes be added to tables, that new tables be created, that new views be formulated, that added indexes be constructed, and so on.

Changes such as these can be disruptive to operations and can degrade system performance. There is no pat solution to this possibility, but successful database implementations attempt to make the process of change orderly and subject to analysis and management involvement. Management may be called upon when one user's request for change degrades the availability and performance of the database system for other users.

Since decisions on change involve estimating effects, it is useful to monitor new implementations in order to assess the actual impact. Such monitoring can help to build expertise in forecasting the effects of changes requested in the future.

DBMS Monitoring Facilities. DBMSs offer differing capabilities. In this section, we give an overview of representative monitoring facilities that might be contained in a generic DBMS we call *G*.

G provides on-line capability for checking on current DBMS activities. A menu allows selection of monitoring functions such as these:

1. Input/output usage by user.
2. Number of read and write operations executed in a set time period.
3. Number of completed transactions per set time period.
4. Provision of an audit trail for activities of interest. For example, it might be desired to check on who is modifying the data in the PAYROLL TABLE. This could be accomplished with the following command:

```
AUDIT UPDATE ON PAYROLL BY SESSION;
```

The ON clause identifies the table to be audited, and the BY clause specifies how fine the level of auditing should be. BY SESSION, for example, writes an entry to the audit trail for each user *session* accessing the audited relation. As you can see, DBMSs need to have a reasonable range of monitoring capabilities.

Summary

In this chapter, we have addressed the tasks of DBMS selection and implementation. Our approach has been to begin with management information needs, proceeding to the types of system requirements those needs imply. We then characterized the basic DBMS functions that are available to service those system requirements and gave examples of how to subdivide them into their underlying features at a level that allows objective evaluation measurement. We then discussed a simple means of making an initial DBMS analysis by classifying features according to their importance. This was followed by a discussion of sources of information on commercial DBMSs.

Our discussion then considered two methods of overall DBMS evaluation: the multiattribute scoring model, which is simple and well known and data envelopment analysis, which is less well known but quite useful in that it is straightforward to use and provides powerful capabilities for handling decision-making input and yielding valuable comparative information as its output. It is particularly effective in categorizing DBMSs whose overall capabilities are similar.

We then discussed the principal factors that should be a part of a DBMS implementation strategy. Many of these factors carry over to long-term DBMS management as well. We saw that the database administration function plays an important role in implementation and that thorough testing is essential. We also discussed the need for preparing users for change through project participation as well as training.

The need for mechanisms for accommodating changing needs for database information was summarized, along with the requirement for backup and recovery. Finally, the role of performance monitoring was outlined.

Review Questions

1. Define each of the following terms in your own words:
   a. management information
   b. access controls
   c. encryption
   d. backup-and-recovery controls
   e. important feature
   f. optional feature
   g. unnecessary feature
   h. request for proposal (RFP)
   i. efficient frontier
   j. expansion point
   k. frontier point

2. Describe each of the following DBMS functions and capabilities:
   a. data dictionary/directory
   b. data security and integrity
   c. query, data manipulation, and reporting capabilities
   d. support of specialized programming requirements
   e. physical data organization options

3. Identify features that would be important for each of the functions in (2).

4. How should an analytical model's output be used in selecting a DBMS?

5. Describe how the scoring model can be used to assist in DBMS selection.

6. What value is there in including classifications such as UNNECESSARY and UNDESIRABLE?

7. Discuss the major issues of implementing a DBMS.

Problems and Exercises

1. Match the following terms with their definitions:

__*concurrency controls*

__*view controls*

__*mandatory feature*

__*undesirable feature*

__*benchmarking*
__*reference unit*

__*expansion path*

a. Controls that limit user access to a subset of a base table

b. Testing DBMS performance by running actual applications on it

c. In DEA analysis, the DBMS currently being evaluated

d. A DBMS feature that detracts from its value to the firm

e. The outer boundary in DEA analysis

f. Controls that maintain database integrity when two or more users simultaneously request a database record

g. In DEA analysis, the path from the origin through the reference unit

h. A DBMS feature that must be provided

2. Gather information on two network DBMSs. (This can usually be found in the library.) Do these DBMSs include the functions outlined in the chapter? Is there information on the features that enable those functions? Can you create a generic classification of features for firms in a particular industry?

3. Gather information on two relational DBMSs, and repeat the process described in exercise 2. Then see if you can find similar information on a hierarchical model or a network model and compare it to one of the relational systems. Is it easier or more difficult to find similar information. Why?

4. Using the data from two or three of the preceding DBMSs, create a scoring model. Justify your selection of criteria weights and DBMS ratings.

5. Linear programs (LPs) are widely available in business schools and computer science departments, often on a microcomputer. Use an LP to analyze the data for DBMSs *A–F* in the chapter. You might begin by using the exact data given, without weights. Then try the given weights. Finally experiment with some weights of your own.

6. After completing exercise 5, try applying DEA to the analysis you developed in exercise 4.

7. Based upon the chapter material, write a short procedural guide to be used in selecting a DBMS for a hypothetical company.

8. Write a brief guide to DBMS implementation procedures.

Projects and Professional Issues

1. Contact one or two local institutions that use DBMSs. Find out what approach they used in selecting their DBMS. Are they satisfied with the result?

2. Contact a vendor to acquire data on its DBMS. What information is contained in these data that would be useful input to the DBMS selection process?

5

ADVANCED TOPICS

▼

art 5 is composed of a single chapter that addresses recent advances in database system development. We cover object databases and knowledge-base systems, both of which offer important capabilities that may raise the level of database capability to higher echelons. Object databases are able to incorporate complexities that are beyond the capabilities of relational database systems. Knowledge-base systems apply predicate logic to relational database systems in order to infer additional, higher-level information from the data that is actually stored in the database.

This is exciting work, and will bring the reader to the state of the art in database system development.

C H A P T E R

14

ADVANCED SYSTEMS: OBJECT-ORIENTED DATABASE SYSTEMS AND KNOWLEDGE-BASE SYSTEMS

Sanford Mallon, CIO of International Product Distribution, was having lunch with Billy Clark, who had been a classmate of his at Obelisk University. Billy was now the database administrator at Simpson Technologies, a high-tech manufacturing firm. He had just returned from a visit to the headquarters of his DBMS vendor, Magicware, and was excited about some of the new developments he had seen. "You know, Sandy, we have been very happy with the improvements in management information we have realized from our current database system, and our management has been very receptive to its use. But now management is asking if we can do more."

Sanford replied, "What more could a database system do? We're using the same DBMS as you, and we think we are a state-of-the-art operation."

"Well," responded Billy, "we have one or two 'new hires' who are asking about object-oriented and knowledge-base systems. I had never heard of them, so I called Magicware to ask what they knew. It turns out they are developing a product—a knowledge-base system—that will perform the usual database management functions as well as incorporating object-oriented technology and 'expertise' in the form of rules that operate on the database. I didn't really understand it until I visited Magicware's offices and saw a demonstration. Now I'm pretty excited about presenting its capabilities to our management."

"Wait a minute," said Sanford. "You owe me. How about educating a buddy so that I can pursue this myself?"

object-oriented programming A powerful approach to complex programming that incorporates concepts of encapsulation, polymorphism, and inheritance.

Developments in **object-oriented programming** (OOP) are driving the current development of object DBMSs (ODBMSs) that will handle complex objects, inheritance, and other features that enable direct implementation of object-oriented conceptual models. At the same time relational database technology is being extended to combine data management capabilities with the application of logical rules to provide more refined information to management. Such systems are termed *knowledge-base systems* (KBS).

In this chapter, we will briefly survey some of the features that are motivating these developments and discuss some examples of how they extend the capabilities of existing database systems. After reading this chapter, you should be able to

▼ Understand the basic features of OOP and how they relate to ODBMS.

▼ Understand how the conceptual models of Chapter 4 relate to OOP and ODBMS.

▼ Discuss some of the principal ODBMS that are available commercially or are under development.

▼ Have a familiarity with a generic ODBMS query language.

▼ Explain how knowledge-base systems can extend the power of relational database systems to provide information for management.

▼ Identify the ways in which knowledge can be represented in the form of rules.

▼ Discuss languages such as PROLOG and LDL and explain how they are influencing the development of knowledge-base systems.

▼ An Evolution Toward Object-Oriented Database Systems

Attempts to Provide More Powerful Data Representation

With all of the power and success of relational database systems, there are some database applications whose complexity is not well handled by the relational model. Such applications typically involve data that are highly interrelated such as product definitions, multimedia, or bills of materials. The evolution of ODBMS is one effort to deal with these complexities. ODBMS developments are largely due to the genesis and refinement of OOP.

▼ The Contribution of Object-Oriented Programming (OOP)

The importance of OOP to the development of ODBMSs is considerable. OOP languages have greater expressability than typical database languages. However, OOP languages generally lack support for persistent objects—objects that need to exist beyond the scope of a particular user interface with the database. This has naturally led to developments, such as the ODBMS called Gemstone (Maier and Stein, 1992) that attempt to extend the capabilities of an OOP language to include the traditional data management capabilities of DBMS.

In Chapter 4 we have used certain fundamental ideas that derive from the development of object-oriented programming (OOP). In particular, our conceptual sets are analogous to the "classes" of OOP without the member functions. Conceptual set instances are like the objects of OOP. In OOP a class is defined by the following properties:

1. A set of variables (attributes) that contains the data for a class object.
2. Blocks of code called functions that perform operations on a class object's data.
3. A set of messages to which the class object responds.

In our conceptual modeling we have all the data structure of a class, but we define none of the functions or messages pertaining to those classes. Implementation requires addition of those features.

ODBMSs such as Gemstone combine OOP language capabilities with the storage management functions of a traditional DBMS. The following section outlines some of these basic features.

Class Abstraction

Refer to Figure 14.1. This is a reproduction of a fragment of Figure 4.21 that was studied earlier. We see that CUSTOMER is one class having the attribute CUSTOMER#. This is readily represented in the following way:

```
class CUSTOMER {
protected:
int CUSTOMER#;
      }
```

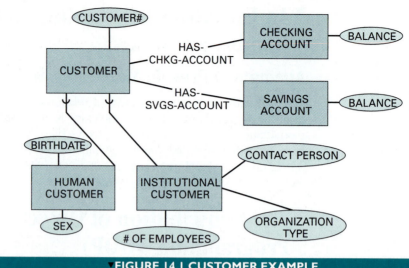

▼FIGURE 14.1 CUSTOMER EXAMPLE

We use C++ syntax (C++ is a widely used OOP language). The parts of the language we need here are quite easy to follow. For example, in the preceding code it is not hard to see that the term **class** denotes a class declaration. CUSTOMER is the label that is given to the class, and the code encompassed between braces defines the class members. In this case, the only member is CUSTOMER#, which requires a datatype—we have chosen integer (int). The ";" simply indicates the end of a statement.

class An abstract representation (template) of an object set.

Classes are abstractions in the same sense as sets in the conceptual model: They allow representation of those features of reality that are important to the problem at hand. These classes enable the definition of any finite number of objects of that class. The following code is illustrative:

```
class CUSTOMER {
      protected:
             int CUSTOMER#;
      }

main() {
      CUSTOMER cust1,cust2,cust3;
             }
```

We have added a function called "main" that enables three objects of the class CUSTOMER to be created: cust1, cust2, and cust3. While the class CUSTOMER has only one data element and no functions, it could easily be extended to encompass additional class members. Our point here is to illustrate the fact that once a class is defined, it is easy to create objects of that class. If you think about it for a moment, you may see that the class seems like a relational schema, and the objects seem like instances of that schema. This is true in a limited sense; however, a relation cannot contain a function, nor does it allow the features we discuss next.

There is a simple example of message passing at work here also. When an object is declared in a given class, a message is passed to the class to construct a template of the class in memory and give it the object name. (In this case, there are three messages.)

Derived Classes and Simple Inheritance

derived class A class that inherits features from another class.

From Figure 14.1, we have two additional objects, both specializations of the CUSTOMER object: HUMAN-CUSTOMER(HC) and INSTITUTIONAL-CUSTOMER(IC). These correspond to the following **derived classes**:

```
class HC:public CUSTOMER {
      protected:
      char sex;
      char birthdate[8];
      };

class IC:public CUSTOMER {
      protected:
      int NR_EMPLOYEES;
      char ORG_TYPE;
      char CONTACT_PERS[12];
      };
```

The notation, "class IC" declares a class labeled IC, as usual. The extension ":public CUSTOMER" declares HC(IC) as a derived class from the class CUSTOMER. The notation "public" means that the derived class is allowed access to all members of the CUSTOMER class—except those that may be declared "private." In the preceding examples, both HC and IC can access all members of CUSTOMER. For simplicity, we have omitted examples of class functions and message passing, but it is easy to think of functions that read data, write data, search for data, and execute logical and arithmetic operations on the class data.

We can now declare objects of the derived classes that not only have their own member data and functions but inherit all those from their base (parent) classes. For example, the C++ fragment

```
      .

      .
main() {
      IC instcust;
      HC humcust;
}
```

creates one object (instcust and humcust) for each of the derived classes (IC and HC). When each derived class object is declared, a message is passed that creates a template for the base class and then a template for the derived class.

The object "intcust" can accept and manipulate values for its own members labeled NR_EMPLOYEES, ORG_TYPE, and CONTACT_PERS; and also inherits the CUSTOMER# member from its base class.

Aggregation

complex object Corresponds to an aggregate or higher-level relationship as defined in Chapter 4.

What about aggregation? Consider the fragment of an object-oriented model shown in Figure 14.2. Here we have a relationship aggregated as a **complex object**. This would be represented as follows:

```
class PRODUCT {
      protected:
      int PROD_ID;
      };
```

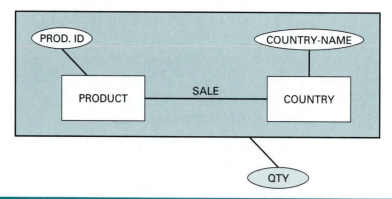

▼**FIGURE 14.2 AGGREGATION EXAMPLE**

```
class COUNTRY {
      protected:
      char COUNTRY_NAME[15];
      };

class SALE {
      protected:
      int QTY;
      COUNTRY cntry;
      PRODUCT prod;
      };
```

We see that COUNTRY and PRODUCT are described in the usual way. Those classes then become members of the SALE class. When a SALE object is declared, as follows:

```
SALE this_sale;
```

an instance of class SALE is created having the label this_sale. The object, this_sale, can then hold data for a particular sale, for example, "Germany", "Softsoap", "25". We thus have all the information aggregated that was desired.

An Extended Example Demonstrating Multiple Inheritance

We refer to Figures 14.3 and 14.4 for this section. Note that in the object-oriented model fragment of Figure 14.3 that we have three object sets: EMPLOYEE, MGT_TRAINEE, AND SALARIED_MGT_TRAINEE. EMPLOYEE and MGT_TRAINEE

▼**FIGURE 14.3 CONCEPTUAL MODEL WITH MULTIPLE INHERITANCE**

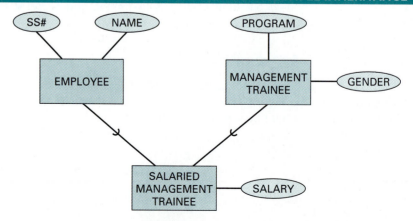

```
//This program demonstrates multiple inheritance.

//We first define the EMPLOYEE class
class employee
      {
            char   ss#[11];
            char   name[12];
            void   getData( )    //This is a member function for inputting
                                 //     data
                {
                cout  <<  "\nEnter employee social security number:  ";
                cin  >>  ss#;
                cout  <<  "Enter employee name:  ";
                cin  >>  name;
                }
      };
//We next define the MANAGEMENT TRAINEE class
class  mgt_trainee
      {
            char   gender;
            char   program[12];
            void   inData( )
                {
                cout  <<  "Enter trainee gender:  ";
                cin  >>  gender;
                cout  <<  "Enter trainee program type:  ";
                cin  >>  program;
                }
      };
//Next we define the derived class, SALARIED MANAGEMENT TRAINEE
class  sal_mgt_trainee:  public employee,  public mgt_trainee
      {
            float  salary;
            void  input( )
            {
             employee::getData( );
             mgt_trainee::inData( );
             cout  <<  "Enter the trainee's salary:  ";
             cin  >>  salary;
             }
      };
main( )
      {
       sal_mgt_trainee  smt1;
       smt1.input( );
       }
```

▼FIGURE 14.4 C++ IMPLEMENTATION OF THE OBJECT-ORIENTED MODEL OF FIGURE 14.3

are ordinary (base) object classes, whereas SALARIED_MGT_TRAINEE is a specialization of both EMPLOYEE and MGT_TRAINEE. That is, SALARIED_MGT_TRAINEE
inherits all the attributes of EMPLOYEE and MGT_TRAINEE, in addition to adding
the attribute SALARY. This is consistent with our earlier models of Chapter 4.

Having exposed the reader to some modest OOP representations, we now extend the presentation slightly to give a more complete picture. Consider now the C++
program of Figure 14.4, which converts the model fragment of Figure 14.3 into an OOP.

A number of comments (denoted by "//") have been included in the program. We clarify and extend those comments here. We first note the creation of the class called "employee". We previously made this label in capital letters to conform with the object-oriented model—but this was for ease of translation. It is not required. Observe that the class now contains not only the attributes from the EMPLOYEE object set, but contains a simple function, as well. This function is labeled "getData". Without delving further into syntax, it is easily seen that getData allows for data input.

We see a similar representation for the MGT_TRAINEE set. The SALARIED_MGT_TRAINEE set is declared as a class (with label "sal_mgt_trainee") in the usual way; but we also see the extension "public employee, public mgt_trainee" added. This extension means that the class "sal_mgt_trainee" inherits every attribute and function from the "employee" class and from the "mgt_trainee" class (unless they are declared to be "private," which none are in this example).

The "sal_mgt_trainee" class also has attributes and functions of its own. The attribute unique to "sal_mgt_trainee" is "salary." Notice that the "sal_mgt_trainee" class contains one function, "input". "void" simply means that no value is returned. "( )" means that this function receives no values. Observe that the "input" function utilizes functions from both its base classes.

"employee::getData( )" causes the getData function from the "employee" class to execute, securing the employee social security number and the employee name. "mgt_trainee::inData( )" causes the inData function from the "mgt_trainee" class to execute, obtaining the trainee gender and program identification. This is followed by instructions that obtain the mgt_trainee's salary.

None of these actions occur until they are invoked by an object. The "main" function is where operations begin. Here we see that an object of the "sal_mgt_-trainee" class is declared. This object is labeled "smt1". "smt1.input;" causes the "input" function of the "sal_mgt_trainee" class—of which smt1 is an object—to execute. Thus, all data that are input for that function call will be assigned to the object named "smt1".

While these are very simple examples, they serve to demonstrate the relationship between conceptual modeling and its implementation in object-oriented software. In particular, the following features are required for ODBMSs:

1. **The ability to handle complex objects**. The ODBMS should be able to store and manipulate higher-level objects—those that are composed of simpler objects and their relationships.

2. **The ability to incorporate methods that operate on the data of an object**. Functions that apply to an object should be encapsulated in the definition of that object.

3. **The ability to implement objects as members of classes**. The idea of a class as a set of object instances is the basis on which a query may be formulated. In relational databases, a query is issued against a relation or a collection of relations. In like manner, in **object-oriented databases,** a query must be issued against a class, or a set of classes.

4. **The ability to represent class hierarchy and inheritance**. ODBMSs allow the user to derive a new class from an existing class that inherits all the attributes and methods of one or more base (parent) classes. A class may have any number of derived classes, although some ODBMSs allow a class to have only one base class. In the first case, a class inherits attributes and methods from more than one base class. We saw this in the example of multiple inheritance.

In the second case, a derived class inherits attributes and methods from only one base class. We showed an example of this, as well.

object-oriented database systems Database systems that can implement conceptual models directly and can represent complexities that are beyond the capabilities of relational systems.

▼ Object-Oriented Database System Developments

In this section, we summarize some of the more well-known ODBMSs. We begin with GemStone (Meier and Stone, 1987).

GemStone

GemStone is based on the OOP language Smalltalk, with only a few extensions. It is a commercial product that provides OOP features, such as object identity and encapsulation, along with single inheritance and external interface as a set of messages. As a database management system, GemStone provides concurrency control and recovery, secondary storage management, and authorization. GemStone provides a query language that allows expressions to be formed over the instance variables of an object.

GemStone supports concurrent access and methods of maintaining database security and integrity.

Vbase

Vbase (Andrews and Harris, 1987) is also a commercial ODBMS. Vbase emphasizes OOP features such as strong typing and the use of abstract data types. Vbase uses a specification language, TDL, to define objects, to name database variables, and to declare constraints. Vbase uses an implementation language called COP.

Vbase allows objects to be created of some type (class), and their properties and operations are determined by this creation type. Vbase can also create aggregated objects and supports one–many, many–many relationships between objects. Vbase supports most of the expected functionality of a DBMS. Objects can be shared among multiple processes concurrently, backup-and-recovery facilities are provided, along with simple access control.

Orion

Orion is a prototype ODBMS being developed at MCC (Banerjee et al., 1987). As with GemStone, Orion is derived from the OOP language Smalltalk, but provides multiple inheritance capability. Additional database features include the capability to make a wide variety of changes to the database schema—such as class definitions and definition of the class hierarchy, as well as the ability to create and manipulate complex objects.

ORION is designed to support natural object-oriented needs such as CAD/CAM, as well as knowledge-base systems.

PDM

PDM (Manola and Dayal, 1986) is based on the DAPLEX functional data model. As a consequence, PDM's algebra is closely related to relational algebra with some important differences. Chief among these is the ability to apply multiargument functions to objects. PDM also includes an APPLY_APPEND operator that enables function composition to occur. In PDM, as in DAPLEX, everything is a function.

IRIS

IRIS (Fishman et al., 1987) is being developed by Hewlett-Packard. It bears close resemblance to the relational system. IRIS uses a relational storage manager similar to that used by System R, and it supports a query language based on SQL (OSQL). The

IRIS model allows representation of objects and collections of objects, as well as operations.

The DBMS consists of a query processor that implements the object-oriented data model that supports high-level structural abstractions, such as classification, generalization, and aggregation, as well as behavioral abstractions. The interfaces to IRIS include an object-oriented extension to SQL.

O₂

O_2 (Leeluse et al., 1988) supports object types, encapsulation, and inheritance. O_2 supports multiple languages, such as BASIC, C, and LISP. O_2 provides for encapsulation, inheritance, and operation overloading. In contrast to GemStone, in which everything is an object, O_2 does not define classes and methods as objects.

▼ A Generic Object Database Language

In this section we introduce a generic object database language called TEXTQUERY. As the name suggests, it is a text query language that operates on object databases. This language is not actually implemented, but it demonstrates many of the features common to object database languages.

The Data Model of Lerner College

A portion of a data model for Lerner College is shown in Figure 14.5. This model contains four object sets (FACULTY, STUDENT, COURSE, DEPARTMENT) and seven relationships. Each of the object sets has a number of attributes. To make our example more concrete, we have provided some sample data for the data model of

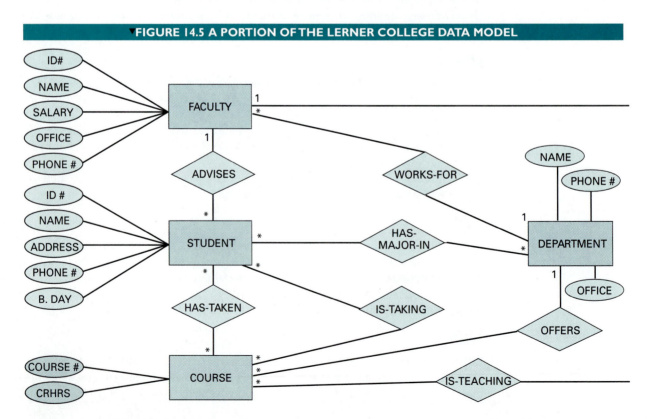

▼FIGURE 14.5 A PORTION OF THE LERNER COLLEGE DATA MODEL

Lerner College in Figure 14.6. This figure shows sample attribute values for instances in each of the object sets and one of the relationship sets (HAS-TAKEN). Figure 14.7 shows how instances in the object sets are related to each other via the given relationships.

Before we go on, it might be useful to review the distinction between an object instance and the values of its attributes. Thus, "John" is the name of a person, but the person we call "John" is not the same thing as his name. As an additional example, we may identify a person by a social security number, but the person is not a social security number. Therefore, Figure 14.5 represents object sets separately from their attributes. The advantage of this is that we can change attribute values, add attributes, and delete attributes without worrying about losing any of the

▼ FIGURE 14.6 REPRESENTATIVE VALUES FOR LERNER COLLEGE DATABASE

FACULTY

ID#	NAME	SALARY	OFFICE	PHONE#
821	Adams	38000	281 CB	4822
911	Clyde	27000	48 TMB	3085
237	Brown	38000	521 MCK	7324
113	Parker	33000	492 CB	6122
544	Hinman	42000	213 TMB	4188
145	Stevens	45000	312 CB	1203

DEPARTMENT

NAME	PHONE#	OFFICE#
MATH	8111	411 TMB
ENGLISH	4980	512 MCK
HISTORY	5233	313 CB

STUDENT

ID#	NAME	ADDR	PHONE#	BDAY
3825	Mary	214 HH	2112	12/3
4913	John	3A DG	3114	9/14
6255	Ann	4117 RCK	5311	3/5
4118	Kelly	311 ST	6622	4/24
3223	Roger	4214 RCK	1383	7/17

COURSE

COURSE#	CRHRS	COURSE#	CRHRS
H121	3	H250	2
E101	3	E372	3
E212	2	M336	3
M115	4	E456	3
M213	3	H312	3

HAS-TAKEN

NAME (STUDENT)	COURSE#	NAME (STUDENT)	COURSE
Mary	E101	Kelly	E456
John	H121	Roger	M115
John	E101	Roger	M213
Ann	E212	Roger	M336
Ann	H250	Roger	H312
Kelly	E372		

underlying object instances. We can also manipulate object instances without worrying about specific attributes or attribute values.

Figure 14.8 may help you understand the separation of object instance from object value. Figure 14.8(a) shows a typical representation of the STUDENT object set and the NAME attribute, while Figure 14.8(b) shows actual object instances and

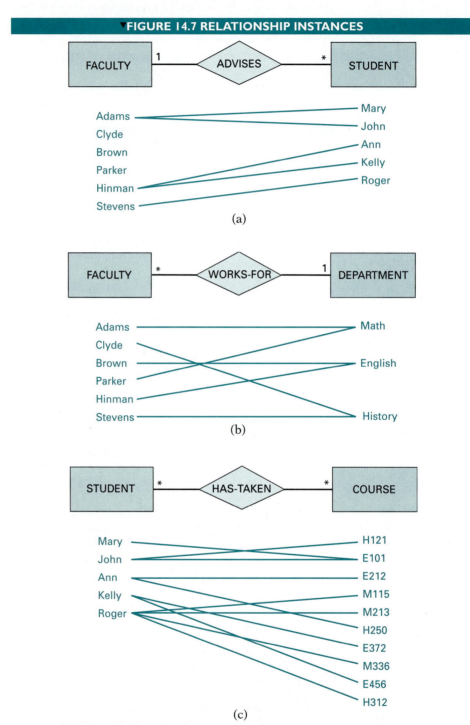

▼FIGURE 14.7 RELATIONSHIP INSTANCES

(a)

(b)

(c)

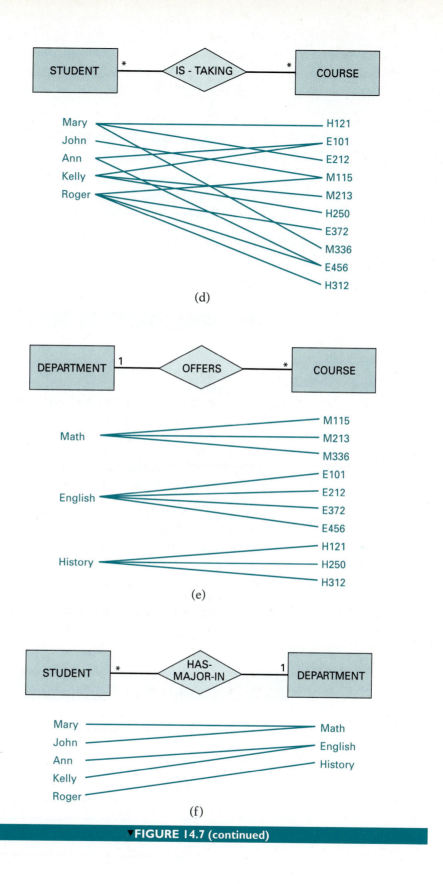

(d)

(e)

(f)

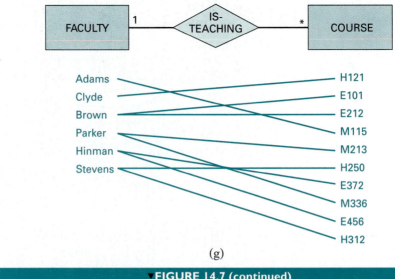

(g)

▼**FIGURE 14.7 (continued)**

attribute values. In this case, the STUDENT object set contains five instances, or students, represented by the five points shown in the STUDENT box. We have a value—a specific name—for the NAME attribute for each student. This value is indicated by a line drawn from the attribute value—the name—to the point representing the student. Thus, we have a line from "Mary" to the point that represents the student named "Mary" in the STUDENT object set.

Attributes are important because they identify and help us distinguish between object instances. In fact, a *key* is an attribute or set of attributes that uniquely identifies each object instance. However, for some purposes it is not necessary to use attribute values to distinguish between object instances. Thus, treating an object instance separately from its attribute values will make it easier to do certain types of data manipulation. This will be illustrated as we carry out various queries later in this chapter.

Note that we are using attributes—NAME and COURSE#—to identify object instances in our sample database (Figure 14.7 a–g rather than showing the instances as points that are connected to the attribute values. This is only done to simplify these diagrams.

▼**FIGURE 14.8 DISTINGUISHING BETWEEN ATTRIBUTES AND OBJECT INSTANCES**

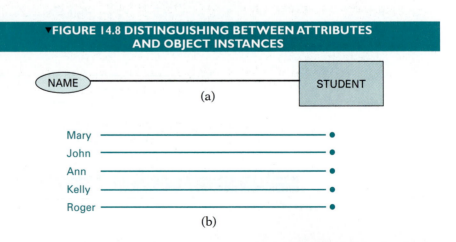

▼ Formulating Queries with Textquery

During their interviews with personnel in Administration, Records and Admissions, and elsewhere on campus, Roberta and Juan compiled a long list of questions that these potential database users would like to have answered. The following are a representative sample:

Who are the faculty members earning over $40,000? What are their names and salaries? Which faculty members work for the English department? What are the names of faculty from whom Kelly is taking classes? Which students have taken every course offered by the math department? Which students have taken every course offered by their major department? Which students are repeating classes? Which students have taken or are taking a history course?

The answers to these questions should be contained in the object and relationship sets of our database. If we can use a computer to access that database, we can answer these questions. The key is to formulate these queries in an object-oriented language, such as TextQuery, which could be translated into operations the computer can execute, allowing the computer to identify and access the appropriate data.

The Basic Format of Query Solutions in TextQuery

We begin our description of TextQuery with an example.

> *User Query:* What are the names and salaries of faculty members earning over $40,000?

From Figure 14.5 we can see that the data needed to answer this query are contained in the FACULTY object set and its attributes. We formulate the TextQuery solution to this query as follows:

```
{ (name, salary)  :  name IS-NAME-OF faculty AND
                     salary IS-SALARY-OF faculty AND
                     salary > 40000 }
```

This TextQuery solution defines a set whose definition is given within the braces. The definition should be read as: "The set of pairs of names and salaries such that the name is the name of some faculty member, the salary is the salary of the same faculty member, and the salary is greater than 40,000."

solution set A set of data values from the database that satisfies the conditions of a query.

If this TextQuery solution were applied to the database, it would yield a **solution set**—a set of data values from the database consisting of pairs of names and salaries that satisfies the conditions that the name and salary in the pair apply to the same faculty member and that the salary is greater than 40,000. Using the data of Figure 14.6, the solution set for this query is a set consisting of two pairs:

```
{ (HINMAN, 42000), (STEPHENS, 45000) }.
```

Let's now take the TextQuery solution apart and examine its pieces.

Terms. In the TextQuery solution, the words *name*, *salary*, and *faculty* represent instances of the object sets NAME, SALARY, and FACULTY, respectively. That is,

variable A symbolic name that represents an unspecified instance in an object set.

these words are **variables** that can take on any of the values in these three sets. IS-NAME-OF and IS-SALARY-OF are relationship names corresponding to the NAME and SALARY attributes that relate the faculty member to his or her name and salary. Thus, if the variable *faculty* represents the faculty member whose name is BROWN, then

```
name = BROWN, and
salary = 38000.
```

Set Definition Parts. The colon (:) separates the two main parts of the set definition—the target list and the qualification expression (Codd, 1971). The **target list**, a parenthesized list of variables, gives the desired format of a typical member of the solution set—in this case, a pair of elements consisting of a name and a salary. The **qualification expression** gives a condition that refers to the target list and must hold true for the elements in the solution set.

The target list in our example is

```
(name, salary)
```

and the qualification expression consists of three subexpressions:

```
name IS-NAME-OF faculty
salary IS-SALARY-OF faculty
salary > 40000
```

which are connected by logical ANDs.

By applying the TextQuery solution to the database, the solution set is generated. This is done by allowing the target list to assume, in turn, all possible combinations of values of name and salary. For each combination, the qualification expression is evaluated. If the expression is true, then the name-salary pair is placed in the solution set. If not, then the name-salary combination is discarded, and the next name-salary combination is examined.

For example, suppose

```
name = ADAMS
salary = 42,000.
```

Then the qualification expression will be true only if some instance of FACULTY exists whose name is ADAMS, whose salary is 42,000, and whose salary is greater than 40,000. In this case, the salary is greater than 40,000, but the qualification expression as a whole is false because there is no faculty member named Adams who has a salary of 42,000. (Look again at Figure 14.6.) Therefore, the (ADAMS, 42000) combination is not placed in the solution set.

Lets try this combination:

```
name = ADAMS
salary = 38,000.
```

There *is* a faculty member named ADAMS having a salary of 38,000, so the first two subexpressions of the qualification expression are true. But the last subexpression is false, since the salary is *not* greater than 40,000. Therefore, the qualification ex-

target list A parenthesized list of variables representing the desired format of a typical member of a query's solution set.

qualification expression A true-false condition that refers to the target list; must hold for the elements in the solution set.

pression is not true for the (ADAMS, 38000) combination, and this combination is not placed in the solution set either.

It is easy to see that (HINMAN, 42000) and (STEPHENS, 45000) are the only two combinations that do satisfy the qualification expression. Thus, these two pairs constitute the complete solution set for this query.

This query and its solution illustrate several rules of the TextQuery language. Before we go on, let's look at these rules and consider some enhancements that can be used in this and other queries.

1. Variables in TextQuery that represent instances of object sets are written in lower case. The lower-case name of an object set is considered a variable representing an instance of that object set.

2. Variables representing instances of an object set may also be defined by stating that the variable is IN the object set, as shown by the following examples:

```
f IN FACULTY
faculty2 IN FACULTY
faculty' IN FACULTY
```

These statements define *f, faculty2,* and *faculty'* as variables, each representing an instance in the object set FACULTY.

3. Attribute names of an object set can be transformed to relationship names by adding the prefix "IS-" and the suffix "-OF" to the attribute name. Thus,

```
IS-NAME-OF  and  IS-SALARY-OF
```

are relationship names created from the NAME and SALARY attributes, respectively.

4. A TextQuery solution is always a set definition, consisting of an expression—the target list—representing a typical element of the solution set, followed by a colon, followed by a condition—the qualification expression—that qualifies precisely the elements to be included in the solution set. The definition is enclosed in braces { } to indicate that we are defining a *set*—in particular, the set of all elements whose format is the target list and that satisfies the condition stated in the qualification expression.

5. Within a set definition, a variable retains its meaning from one occurrence to the next. Thus, in our example, *salary* is defined in the target list and occurs in the qualification expression. *It means the same thing every time it occurs.* If, during the computation of the solution set for the query, *salary* assumes the value 38,000 in the target list, then it has that same value each time it appears in the qualification expression.

6. If a variable does not appear in the target list but appears in the qualification expression, we say that that variable is *existentially quantified.* This means that some value *exists* in the object set for that variable. For example, in the expression

```
salary IS-SALARY-OF faculty
```

faculty is existentially quantified. The expression can be interpreted as: "There exists some faculty member such that *salary* is the salary of that faculty member."

Defining Relationship Directions

Our first example was a relatively simple one that involved just one object set and its attributes. The solution to other queries, however, will involve object sets that are linked by a series of relationships. Thus, we need to take a closer look at these relationships and what they mean intuitively. As we do so, we will develop the means of solving more complex queries. In this section, we will explore this concept further. We will be more precise in the next section where we will apply these ideas to formulating queries in TextQuery.

When we defined objects and relationships in Chapter 4, we compared objects to nouns and relationships to verbs. This suggests that a text language such as TextQuery resembles a natural language to some extent. You can see this if you look at Figure 14.5. The names of each of the relationships suggests a *direction* for reading the relationship. Thus, we would say

```
faculty ADVISES student
```

and not, as a matter of course,

```
student ADVISES faculty.
```

The relationship name suggests the relationship is to be read from FACULTY to STUDENT. Similarly, we have

```
faculty WORKS-FOR department
faculty IS-TEACHING course
student HAS-MAJOR-IN department
student HAS-TAKEN course
student IS-TAKING course
department OFFERS course
```

and none of these would make sense if the order were reversed. Each of these is an English-language sentence in the format

```
SUBJECT VERB OBJECT
```

that is in the active voice.

Now by changing the name of the relationship and using the passive voice, we can reverse the implied direction of most of these sentences. Thus, we have

```
student IS-ADVISED-BY faculty
course IS-TAUGHT-BY faculty
course HAS-BEEN-TAKEN-BY student
course IS-BEING-TAKEN-BY student
course IS-OFFERED-BY department
```

as sentences showing the *reverse* direction for reading these relationships. We can obtain the reverse direction of the other two relationships by appropriate renaming as follows:

```
department EMPLOYS faculty
(EMPLOYS reverses WORKS-FOR)
```

department HAS-MAJORING-STUDENT student
(HAS-MAJORING-STUDENT reverses HAS-MAJOR-IN)

The last relationship name (HAS-MAJORING-STUDENT) shows that we can always find some name that will reverse the direction of a relationship, even though the new name may be awkward and inconvenient.

Thus, the name chosen for a relationship suggests an intuitive direction that will allow the relationship to be stated as an English sentence in SUBJECT-VERB-OBJECT format. We can also create a substitute name for each relationship that makes it possible to read that relationship in the opposite direction. We can diagram this idea by updating Figure 14.5 to show the direction of relationship names. The arrow preceding or following each relationship name in Figure 14.9 indicates its direction.

The direction of relationship names is important for solving queries requiring navigation through a series of object sets and relationships. Depending on the needs of the query, we will sometimes navigate a relationship in one direction and other times navigate the same relationship in the opposite direction. Thus, the ability to go in either direction is very important. Since nearly every query will require this kind of navigation, we are establishing here the general framework for query solution.

We need to do the same thing for attributes as we have done for relationships. Recall that we can interpret attributes as relationships. As we saw earlier, we can create verb phrase names for them by embedding the attribute name between IS and OF. We can reverse the direction of attribute relationship names by prefixing the attribute name with HAS:

▼FIGURE 14.9 A PORTION OF THE LERNER COLLEGE DATA MODEL SHOWING RELATIONSHIP DIRECTIONS

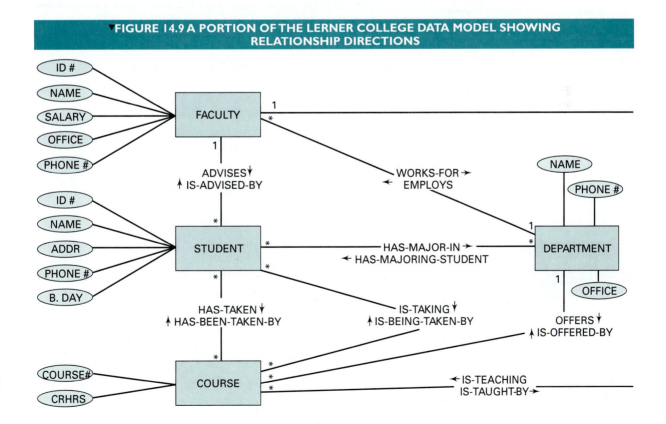

```
faculty HAS-NAME name
faculty HAS-SALARY salary
faculty HAS-OFFICE office
```

Finally, we need to derive names for specialization relationships. Suppose we have a set named MATH-COURSE that consists of all the courses offered by the math department. Then MATH-COURSE is a subset of COURSE. We name this specialization relationship IS-A, and this name holds in both directions. That is,

```
math-course IS-A course  and
course IS-A math-course
```

can both be true. The first is true for all instances of MATH-COURSE, while the second is true for only some of the instances of COURSE.

Navigating Over Attributes and Relationships

In the previous section, we saw that the names we use for objects, attributes, and relationships can be tailored to more readily allow their interpretation as English-language sentences. In this section, we will show how this idea will let us solve more complex queries in the TextQuery language.

User Query: What are the names of faculty members earning $38,000?

This query, just as the earlier query, requires data found only in the FACULTY object set and two of its attributes. In this case, however, salary only figures in the qualification expression, not the target list. The solution to this query illustrates the principle of navigating through relationships and object sets:

```
{name  :  name IS-NAME-OF faculty WHO HAS-SALARY 38000}
```

This solution may be read "the set of all names such that each name is the name of a faculty member who has a salary of 38000." It is equivalent to

```
{name  :  name IS-NAME-OF faculty AND
          faculty HAS-SALARY 38000}
```

Let's analyze the first solution by starting at the back and working our way forward:

```
faculty WHO HAS-SALARY 38000
```

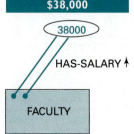

▼FIGURE 14.10
INSTANCES OF
FACULTY EARNING
$38,000

This is a statement about a faculty member that can be evaluated as true or false. It is true only for those in FACULTY who have a SALARY attribute of 38000. These faculty members constitute a subset of FACULTY (Figure 14.10). We see that there are two faculty members earning $38,000.

To explain the remainder of the query solution, we rewrite the qualification expression with parentheses:

```
name IS-NAME-OF (faculty WHO HAS-SALARY 38000)
```

This statement is true for a set of names: {ADAMS, BROWN}. The names in the set will be those that map under the IS-NAME-OF relationship to FACULTY instances who earn $38,000, the definition in the latter half of the query. This is shown in Figure 14.11.

Note how closely the format of the TextQuery solution matches the format of the original query, down to the position of the qualification expression, a salary of $38,000.

```
User Query: What are the names of faculty members earning
$38,000?

TextQuery Solution: name IS-NAME-OF faculty WHO HAS-SALARY 38000
```

Because they follow the format of the natural language queries, such solutions are said to be in the *interrogative format*. In using a data model to visualize this solution, however, we work *backwards*. You can see this in Figure 14.12. We start at the SALARY attribute and find 38000. Then we draw back to FACULTY to find those FACULTY instances who "HAS-SALARY" of 38000. Then we draw back one more step, using IS-NAME-OF, to NAME. If we put together our TextQuery solution after this visualization, we must retrace our steps going from NAME through IS-NAME-OF to FACULTY and then through HAS-SALARY to SALARY of 38000. This backtracking suggests there may be an alternate format that more closely echoes the solution we visualized on the diagram. We can formulate a solution in this alternate format as follows:

```
{name : 38000 IS-SALARY-OF faculty WHO HAS-NAME name}
```

▼FIGURE 14.11 NAMES OF FACULTY EARNING $38,000

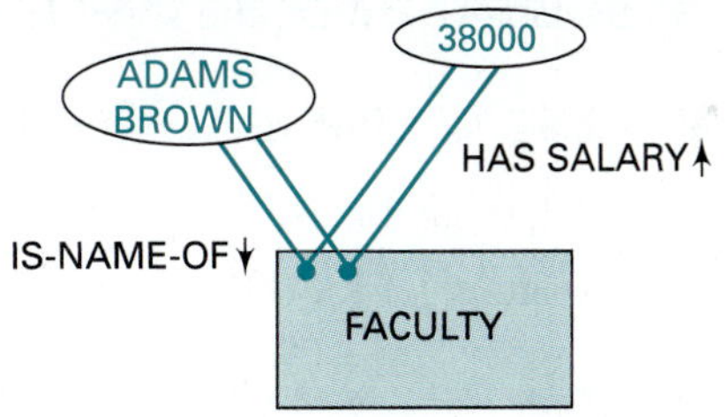

▼FIGURE 14.12 A VISUAL SOLUTION TO THE USER QUERY, "WHAT ARE THE NAMES OF FACULTY MEMBERS EARNING $38,000?"

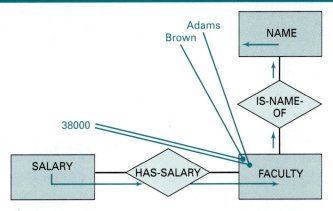

We see that the order of the qualification expression here is opposite to that of the interrogative format. Because this second format in more like a declarative sentence, it is called the *declarative format*. Either of these formats is permissible. Therefore, in developing TextQuery solutions to user queries you are encouraged to use whichever format you find more natural.

In both cases, we have simplified the target list to just a variable name, while the qualification expression we have developed traverses the object sets and their attributes via the relationships that link them. Relative pronouns such as WHO and WHICH are used in these expressions to increase their readability. They are *noise words* in the sense that they are present in the expression but have no effect on its meaning.

Let us now look at two more examples that provide further illustration of the concept of navigating over relationships.

```
User Query: Which faculty members work for the English depart-
ment?

TextQuery Solution: {faculty  :  faculty WORKS-FOR department
                                 WHICH HAS-NAME 'English'}
```

Although this solution answers the query, it is inadequate because the set of faculty members created cannot be displayed on an output device. If we want to produce a human-readable solution, we must create a set of attribute values that is human-readable. Therefore, we revise the solution to:

```
{name  :  name IS-NAME-OF faculty WHO WORKS-FOR department
                          WHICH HAS-NAME 'English'}
```

In declarative format, the solution is:

```
{name  :  'ENGLISH' IS-NAME-OF department WHICH EMPLOYS
                    faculty WHO HAS-NAME name}
```

The solution set for this query is shown in Figure 14.13.

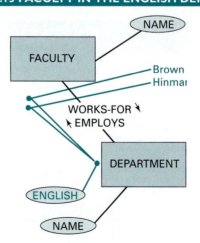

▼FIGURE 14.13 FACULTY IN THE ENGLISH DEPARTMENT

User Query: What are the names of faculty from whom Kelly is taking classes?

TextQuery Solution:

Interrogative format

```
{name  :  name IS-NAME-OF faculty WHO IS-TEACHING course
          WHICH IS-BEING-TAKEN-BY student
          WHO HAS-NAME 'KELLY'}
```

Declarative format

```
{name  :  'KELLY' IS-NAME-OF student WHO IS-TAKING course
          WHICH IS-BEING-TAKEN-BY faculty
          WHO HAS-NAME name}
```

The solution set is shown in Figure 14.14.

Figure 14.14 does *not* show the instances for the courses Kelly is taking, but from the previous examples it should be easy to visualize what is happening here. The name "KELLY" is connected to the student instance having that name. This student instance is in turn connected to the set of courses Kelly is taking. Each of these courses is connected to the faculty member teaching the course, and the faculty member is connected to his or her name.

Incidentally, this query provides an example of using an abstract object set (COURSE) without using any of its attributes. The solution to the query did not have to identify, for example, the precise course numbers of the courses Kelly is taking in order to identify which faculty members Kelly is taking courses from. It sufficed to use course instances in their abstract (attributeless) form.

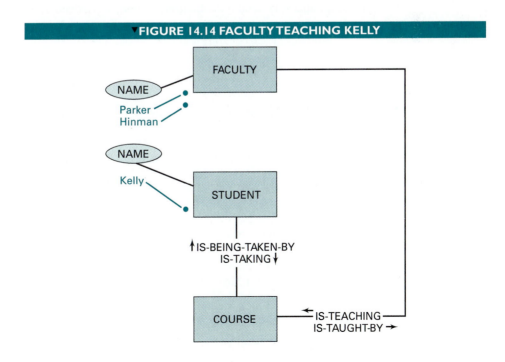

▼ **FIGURE 14.14 FACULTY TEACHING KELLY**

Assigning Names to Derived Sets

The solution sets resulting from the queries already illustrated were derived through the use of TextQuery. Often such sets are useful in their own right. We may, for example, find it convenient or faster to use these derived sets in other TextQuery queries without having to derive them again. We can do this if we simply assign a name to the derived set by which we can refer to it later. For example, if we want to identify the set of all math courses, we can assign the name MATH-COURSE to the appropriate set as follows:

```
MATH-COURSE  :=  {course  :  course IS-OFFERED BY department
                             WHICH HAS-NAME 'MATH'}
```

This example illustrates that names are assigned by stating the set's name, followed by the ":=" notation, and then the TextQuery definition of the set. The ":=" notation can be read "is the name assigned to."

Set Comparison Qualifications Expressions

Some queries can be solved best by using qualification expressions that involve set comparison. Consider the query:

User Query: Which students have taken every course offered by the math department?

We solve this query by generating the set of courses offered by the math department and then, for each student, comparing that set with the set of courses that the student has taken. If the set of all math courses *is contained in* the set of the student's courses, then the student has taken all the math courses and the student's name is placed in the query's solution set. Our TextQuery solution is in three steps and utilizes the facility of assigning names to derived sets:

```
TextQuery Solution:

    MATH-COURSE  :=  {course  :  course IS-OFFERED BY department
                                 WHICH HAS-NAME 'MATH'}

    STUDENT-ALL-MATH        :=

    {student  :  MATH-COURSE IS-CONTAINED-IN
              SET-OF (course WHICH HAS-BEEN-TAKEN-BY student)}

    NAME-STUDENT-ALL-MATH  :=  {name  :  name IS-NAME-OF student
                                AND student IN STUDENT-ALL-MATH}
```

These three steps may be explained as follows:

1. The first step defines MATH-COURSE, the set of all math courses, and is identical to the definition of MATH-COURSE given in the previous section.

2. The second step defines STUDENT-ALL-MATH, the set of students who have taken every math course, and includes some unfamiliar notation that we now explain.

Recall that for each student we wish to compare the set of math courses—MATH-COURSE—with the set of courses taken by that student. We defined the set of math courses in step 1. How do we define the set of courses taken by each particular student? This is done with the construct:

```
SET-OF (course WHICH HAS-BEEN-TAKEN-BY student)
```

This SET-OF construct is used to generate the set of courses that has been taken by the particular student being evaluated by the query. For example, if the student is Ann, then this construct is equivalent to:

```
{course  :  course HAS-BEEN-TAKEN-BY 'ANN'}
```

This is an example of a *dynamically generated set*. That is, a different set is generated for each value of the variable student. As the query is executed, the SET-OF construct will generate a set for Mary, a set for John, a set for Ann, a set for Kelly, and a set for Roger.

In step 2, the system evaluates each student in STUDENT by comparing the MATH-COURSE set with the set of courses taken by the student, using the IS-CONTAINED-IN comparison operator. If the entire set of math courses is contained in the student's set of courses, then the qualification expression using the IS-CONTAINED-IN operator evaluates to "true." In that case, the student is selected for inclusion in the set STUDENT-ALL-MATH.

3. NAME-STUDENT-ALL-MATH gives us the names of the students who have taken every math course. We could have avoided this step by expanding the qualification expression of step 2 to include this step's qualification expression, but that would have made step 2 more complicated and difficult to comprehend. We broke out step 1 as a separate step for the same reason. Thus, we see that the facility of assigning names to derived sets makes it possible to break query solutions down into a series of steps. This makes the process simpler and easier to grasp.

Applying this query to our sample database and using the information in Figure 14.7(c) and 14.7(e), we see that Roger is the only student who has taken all the math courses. Thus, the answer to the query is {ROGER}.

The converse of the IS-CONTAINED-IN operator is the CONTAINS operator. If we had used it in the preceding example, step 2 of our solution would have been:

```
STUDENT-ALL-MATH  :=

{student  :  SET-OF (course WHICH HAS-BEEN-TAKEN-BY student)
             CONTAINS MATH-COURSE}
```

Let's look at another example.

User Query: Which students have taken every course offered by their major department?

In the previous problem, we compared every student's set of courses taken with a single, fixed set (MATH-COURSE). In this problem we must compare each student's courses with a set of courses that varies with each student, since the major department varies from one student to the next.

```
TextQuery Solution:
   STUDENT-ALL-COURSE := {student :
                   SET-OF (course WHICH HAS-BEEN-TAKEN-BY student)
                   CONTAINS SET-OF (course WHICH IS-OFFERED-BY
             department WHICH HAS-MAJORING-STUDENT
                           student)}
```

This example shows that we can compare two dynamically generated sets. Of course, this only gives us the students, not their names. We obtain the set of names in the same way we did in the previous query.

Boolean Connectives

Our first TextQuery example used the *Boolean* (or logical) *connective* AND in the qualification expression. The qualification expressions for the other queries we have considered are *atomic* in the sense that they are made up of simple expressions not connected by AND, OR, or NOT. As with most computer languages, Text-Query lets us combine atomic qualification expressions by using the Boolean connectives. Furthermore, we can use parentheses to group expressions and thus eliminate ambiguities. These features give TextQuery increased power.

User Query: Which students are repeating classes?

```
TextQuery Solution:
   REPEATING-STUDENT := {student :  student IS-TAKING course
                              AND student HAS-TAKEN course}
```

Recall that the variable *course* in this qualification expression has the same value throughout the expression. That is, the meaning of *course* in

```
student IS-TAKING course
```

is the same as it is in

```
student HAS-TAKEN course.
```

The Boolean connective AND, which is being used here to join two atomic expressions, means that the qualification expression as a whole is true for a given student and course only if *both*

```
student IS-TAKING course
```

and

```
student HAS-TAKEN course
```

are true.

As before, another step is needed to obtain the students' names. To keep our presentation simple, we omit this step throughout this section.

User Query: Which students have taken or are taking a history course?

```
{student  :  student HAS-TAKEN course WHICH IS-OFFERED-BY
              department WHICH HAS-NAME 'HISTORY' OR
              student IS-TAKING course WHICH IS-OFFERED-BY
              department WHICH HAS-NAME 'HISTORY'}
```

A second simpler version creates the history subset of COURSE and uses the IN operator.

```
HISTORY-COURSE  :=  {course  :  course IS-OFFERED-BY
              department WHICH HAS-NAME 'HISTORY'}

STUDENT-HAS-TAKEN-HISTORY  :=
   {student  :  (student HAS-TAKEN course AND
              course IN HISTORY-COURSE) OR
          (student IS-TAKING course AND
              course IN HISTORY-COURSE)}
```

Here the Boolean OR is interpreted to make the qualification expression true when either the first half or the second half (or both halves) of the qualification expression is true. We also used AND in each half and grouped the halves with parentheses to prevent potential ambiguities.

User Query: Which students majoring in math have not yet taken a math course?

```
MATH-COURSE  :=  {course : course IS-OFFERED-BY department
                      WHICH HAS-NAME 'MATH'}

STUDENT-HAS-TAKEN-MATH  :=
      {student  :  (student HAS-TAKEN course AND
              course IN MATH-COURSE) OR
          (student IS-TAKING course AND
              course IN MATH-COURSE)}

NEW-MATH-STUDENT          :=
      {student  :  student HAS-MAJOR-IN department WHICH
                  HAS-NAME 'MATH'
              AND student NOT IN STUDENT-HAS-TAKEN-MATH}
```

The last line of the qualification expression could have been written:

```
AND NOT student IN STUDENT-HAS-TAKEN-MATH
```

That is, the NOT can be embedded in the atomic part of the expression to negate the effect of IN, or it can be part of the Boolean connective AND to negate the entire atomic expression. NOT can also be applied to the other comparison operators (CONTAINS, IS-CONTAINED-IN, <, >, =).

TextQuery provides a simple, elegant, and natural means of extracting data from an object-oriented database. It is similar to many traditional programming languages in that it uses textual representation of data, variables, and statements. It also has a nice connection with natural language, since the object sets and relationships on which it operates are themselves modeled as nouns and verbs.

extensional knowledge Facts that are stored in database relations.

intensional knowledge Knowledge that is deduced from extensional knowledge by the applications of rules.

extensional knowledge. Knowledge that is defined beyond the factual content of the database, usually by the use of logical mechanisms, is termed **intensional knowledge**. Most knowledge-base systems under development store the intensional knowledge in the form of logical rules.

Let's clarify these ideas with an example. Examine Figure 14.15. Our database consists of the single table, PARTS, which contains the attributes SUBPART and PART. We can retrieve the names of all parts of which part 250 is a subpart by the relational calculus query:

```
GET(X)  :- PARTS(250,X)
```

This syntax is only slightly different from what we have seen previously and is interpreted in a familiar way. In English, this would be read, "From the PARTS relation retrieve all the tuples having the value 250 in the SUBPART column, then assign the corresponding part value to the variable X. Store the value for X as a tuple in the GET relation."

In this example, the resulting values for X are 300 and 315.

PARTS	=	SUBPART	PART
		200	315
		250	300
		250	315
		300	324
		315	350

▼**FIGURE 14.15 PARTS TABLE**

Taking the information from this query a step further, we see that part 300, of which part 250 is a subpart, is itself a subpart of part 324. This can be seen by inspecting the PARTS relation. By transitivity, then, 250 is also a subpart of part 324 and so part 324 should probably be in the query solution. Logically, this transitivity of part and subpart could go on and on, but in this example of PARTS, there are only two levels of subparts. We see, however, that it would be convenient if we could write a query to find all the parts for which a given part is a primitive (second-level) subpart. (For example, part 250 is a primitive subpart for part 324.) One alternative is the addition of a table that lists parts and their primitive subparts, as illustrated in Figure 14.16. The query to find the parts for which part 250 is a primitive subpart is

```
GET(X)  :- PRIMITIVE_PARTS(250,X)
```

The result is 324 and 350.

▼**FIGURE 14.16 PRIMITIVE-PARTS TABLE**

PRIMITIVE_PARTS	=	PRIM PART	PART
		200	350
		250	324
		250	350

Unfortunately, the PRIMITIVE_PARTS table contains redundant data, that is, data already available in PARTS. It was derived from the PARTS table using our knowledge that a primitive subpart is a second-level subpart. Constructing special tables to answer every conceivable information need would be very inefficient. It would be better if we could just give the database a rule that establishes the desired relationships and operates directly on the original extensional database. This is roughly the type of capability that is sought by a KBS.

Returning to our example, let PARTS be the extensional database. We then define the intensional database as

```
PRIMITIVE_PARTS(X,Z) :- PARTS(X,Y) AND PARTS(Y,Z)
```

This may be read as

In the relation PRIMITIVE_PARTS, X is a primitive subpart of Z [PRIMITIVE_PARTS(X,Z)] if (:−), in the relation PARTS, X is a subpart of Y [PARTS(X,Y)] *and* Y is a subpart of Z [PARTS(Y,Z)].

We have simply defined a rule to operate on the PARTS table to retrieve primitive subpart information. We may now write a simple query to retrieve the desired information from PARTS:

```
GET(Z) :- PRIMITIVE_PARTS(250,Z)
```

The result is again 324 and 350, and the problem of maintaining redundant data has been eliminated.

One can imagine the clumsiness of a system where all such queries were satisfied by actually creating separate tables such as PRIMITIVE_PARTS. The intensional form allows specification of the same data in compact form: Redundancy is reduced, and storage space is saved.

To further illustrate fundamental concepts and to give you sufficient knowledge to perform hands-on exercises and projects, we introduce a logic implementation language. The language concepts we present are simple and provide an easy transition from the examples we have discussed to broader applications in a concrete way. We have chosen PROLOG, an implementation of the same relational calculus ideas we studied earlier, which also includes the capability for creating rules to operate on extensional databases. Moreover, PROLOG forms the basis for some of the KBS languages that are being developed, such as DATALOG and LDL.

Although most versions of PROLOG use more or less standard notation, a few minor differences may occur. We use a general form.

▼ Knowledge Representation with Rules

In this section, we elaborate on mechanisms for expressing logic with rules. We describe basic rule syntax and provide a general example of combining rules into backward-chaining and forward-chaining strategies of evaluation. We then discuss the expression of rules in PROLOG.

Rule Formation

Rules are a very intuitive method of representing knowledge. We have relied on your intuition in interpreting the rules that were illustrated in the previous discussion, and you could probably write some rules of your own just from studying those examples.

is TRUE.

Let's suppose that we want to know who the parents of Anne are. That is,

```
?parent(X,anne).
```

In words we are saying,

Look for any names that qualify as parents of Anne. Then assign them, one by one, to the variable *X*.

(Variable names in PROLOG must begin with a capital letter.)
A search of the database facts finds

```
mother(tami,anne), and
father(john,anne).
```

Thus, the result of the query will be

```
X = tami
X = john.
```

Logic-based languages provide the capability of computing answers to queries that cannot be easily accomplished by conventional database manipulation languages. Although view creation in conventional languages is similar to the use of rules to define intensional databases, the view definition capabilities of relational DBMSs are not as powerful as logical rules. In particular, relational languages cannot express recursive queries that are often useful for complex queries. (See Ullman, 1991 for details.) Transitive relationships such as hierarchies of parts, lists of ancestors, and management hierarchies are important examples.

Suppose that we have workers who are managed by department managers, and department managers who are managed by division managers. Both division and department managers may then be involved in evaluating worker performance. We can express this logical relationship recursively, as follows:

```
evaluates(X,Y) :- managerof(X,Y).  (1)
```

```
(read "X evaluates Y if X is manager of Y").
```

```
evaluates(X,Y) :- evaluates(Z,Y) & manager of(X,Z).(2)
```

```
(read "X evaluates Y if Z evaluates Y and X is manager of Z").
```

Suppose the following facts exist in the extensional database:

```
managerof(john,bob)
```

```
managerof(john,ray)
```

```
managerof(bob,frank).
```

We pose the following query:

```
    ?evaluates(john,bob).
```

The result is TRUE by rule (1), since

```
  managerof(john,bob)
```

is a fact. We pose another query

```
    ?evaluates(john,frank).
```

The result is TRUE by rule (2), since

```
  evaluates(bob,frank) and managerof(john,bob)
```

are both true.

Suppose we wished a list of all employees who are evaluated by John. This could be expressed as follows:

```
    ?evaluates(john,X).
```

The result would be

```
  X = Bob by rule (1)
  X = Ray by rule (1)
  X = Frank by rule (2).
```

We have presented an example where the evaluation (hierarchical) path is of length two—there are a maximum of two levels of evaluation. The use of a recursive rule easily extends to paths of any length. We provide a simple demonstration of its extension to a path of length three. Suppose that we add one fact to the preceding database, as follows:

```
  managerof(frank,carl).
```

We pose the following query:

```
    ?evaluates(john,carl).
```

The result is TRUE by the following train of logic:

1. Rule (2) establishes the truth of "evaluates(bob,carl)," since "evaluates-(frank,carl)" is true by rule (1), and "managerof(bob,frank)" is a database fact.
2. One more application of rule (2) yields the result, since "evaluates(bob,carl)" is established, and "managerof(john,bob)" is a database fact.

The basic concepts we have presented are these:

1. Rules can be expressed as clauses that take the form

```
  <conclusion> :- <list of hypotheses>.
```

The left-hand side of ":-" is true if the right-hand side of ":−" can be established through database facts or the truth of other rules.

2. Intensional (or deductive) databases can be developed from extensional databases by the addition of such rules.

We now take a closer look at PROLOG as a language for expressing rules.

▼A Simple PROLOG Database Application

In this section we outline the fundamental syntax of PROLOG and demonstrate a modest database application.

More PROLOG Fundamentals

first-order logic A logical structure that is characterized by a set of objects, a set of predicates (each of which evaluates to TRUE or FALSE), and a set of functions.

clause In PROLOG, the means by which facts and knowledge are expressed;
<conclusion> :− <list of hypotheses>

PROLOG (*Pro*gramming in *Log*ic) is a language whose statements are formulas of **first-order logic**, the basis for encoding knowledge as rules. PROLOG is the foundation language for the Fifth Generation Computer Systems Project, whose aim is to develop highly intelligent computer systems that can store vast amounts of information. PROLOG is also an important tool in artificial intelligence programming, particularly in the development of expert systems.

The fundamental component of PROLOG is the **clause**, the means by which facts and knowledge are expressed. For instance, Figure 14.17 shows two basic clauses: father(harry,jane) and father (X,jane). The first clause says, "harry is the father of jane." The second clause specifies that "X is the father of jane," where X specifies a variable.

We can also write conditional clauses that express rules in the manner we have seen. For instance, Figure 14.17 shows two rules: The first says that "X is the parent of Y" is true if "X is the mother of Y" is true (parent(X, Y) : - mother(X, Y)); the second says, "X is the parent of Y" is true if "X is the father of Y is true" (parent(X, Y): − father(X, Y.)

Conjunctions (ANDs) are denoted by using commas, and disjunctions (ORs) are denoted by semicolons. For example, we may have a basic rule such as X is the grandfather of Y, if X is the father of Z, *and* Z is a parent of Y.

```
grandfather(X,Y) : − father(X,Z),parent(Z,Y).
```

Finally, every clause in PROLOG must end with a period.

▼**FIGURE 14.17 SOME PROLOG CONVENTIONS**

```
(a) CLAUSES
    father      (harry, jane).
    father      (X, jane).

(b) CONDITIONAL CLAUSES
    parent      (X, Y):-    mother      (X, Y).
    parent      (X, Y):-    father      (X, Y).

(c) CONJUNCTIONS AND DISJUNCTIONS
    grandfather     (X, Y):-     father     (X, Z),    parent      (Z, Y).
    parent      (X, Y):-    mother      (X, Y);    father     (X, Y).
```

The Structure of a PROLOG Application

predicate symbols
Names applied to arguments in order to express a predicate.

PROLOG statements are composed of formulas that include **predicate symbols** (such as "parent," "father," or "grandfather") applied to arguments to produce "true" or "false" values. These arguments may include constants (such as "harry" and "jane") and variables (such as *X*, *Y*, and *Z*). (Constants may also be integers.) PROLOG convention specifies that predicate symbols and constants begin with a lower-case letter.

Let's clarify these notions. We first indicate the similarity between a relation name and its attributes and the logical notion of a predicate with its arguments. Refer again to Figure 14.15. This shows a relation named PARTS with the associated attributes, SUBPART and PART. In PROLOG, this relation is a predicate, PARTS, having the arguments SUBPART and PART. Thus, if we express the predicate

```
?parts(200,315),
```

the answer TRUE should be returned since the tuple <200,315> is one of the tuples of the corresponding relation.

A slightly more complex example can be constructed using Figure 14.18. The table names and attribute names have the following interpretation:

Attribute Name	Interpretation
v	vendor
vp	vendor parts
p	parts
vno	vendor numbers
vname	vendor name
location	location
pno	part number
q-rating	quality rating
pname	part name
ptype	part type
grade	grade

domain The PROLOG term for specification of datatype.

Notice that **domains** correspond to datatypes, **predicates** correspond to relational structures, and clauses represent tuples in relations. We define "laview" by the logical rule

predicate An expression that evaluates to TRUE or FALSE.

```
laview(12,Smith):- v(12,smith,la).
```

The rule says that (12,smith) is a fact of laview if (12,smith,la) is a fact of the v (vendor) predicate. A value such as "la" appearing on the right side of ":–", (but not on the left) may be interpreted as an existential condition. That is, for the preceding rule we may say that

```
laview(vno,vname) is true if there exists a tuple in v
such that v(vno,vname,la) is true.
```

We now illustrate the basic structure of a PROLOG implementation by using a simplified version of Figure 14.18.

```
/* Example */
```

```
domains
vname,location,pname,ptype, grade = string
vno,pno,q-rating = integer

predicates
v(vno,vname,location)
vp(vno,pno,q-rating)
p(pno,pname,ptype,grade)

clauses
v(1,james,1a).
v(2,cline,london).
v(3,marx,denver).
v(4,myers,sf).
vp(1,25,8).
vp(1,37,9).
vp(1,28,6).
vp(1,29,7).
vp(1,39,9).
vp(2,25,9).
vp(2,37,9).
vp(3,28,7).
vp(3,37,7).
vp(3,29,8).
vp(4,37,8).
vp(3,39,8).
vp(4,28,7).
vp(4,29,7).
p(25,flange,steel,a).
p(28,stirrup,brass,aa).
p(29,bolt,iron,a).
p(37,clip,brass,aa).
```

▾FIGURE 14.18 EXTENSIONAL DATABASE IN PROLOG

```
domains
vname, location = string
vno = integer

predicates
v(vno,vname,location)

clauses
v(1,james,1a).
v(2,cline,london).
v(3,marx,denver).
v(4,myers,sf).
```

The "domains" section allows the specification of the types of values (datatypes) that will be provided for the relational schema defined in the "predicates" section. The "clauses" section allows the entry of data, or values, for the respective relational attributes. The clauses section may be viewed as the instances of a relational database. This is the basic structure of all PROLOG implementations.

As it stands, with our simplified version of Figure 14.18, we have created an extensional database. It contains simple facts, and we execute ordinary queries in a

straightforward fashion. Suppose we wish to list the names of all vendors in Los Angeles ("la").
Our query is:

```
v(_,Vendor_name,la).
```

The result will be

```
Vendor_name = james,
```

How is the query interpreted? Essentially it goes this way:

1. Look in the relation v for tuples having "la" as the value for location. Retrieve the associated value for vname, and assign it to the variable name, Vendor_name.
2. Any word that begins with a capital letter is identified as a variable—in this case, Vendor_name.
3. Any word that begins with a lower-case letter is interpreted as an attribute value.
4. The use of "_" means that the corresponding attribute value has no bearing on the solution to the query and is ignored.

Database Application

We now demonstrate a database application using PROLOG. We represent our database as shown in Figure 14.18. The data that are entered are easily recognizable. Note that character strings are all lower-case letters. We have entered the database instances under the section of the PROLOG program identified as "clauses." As things stand, we have an extensional database. Recall that the "predicates" section requires a definition of the database in terms of relation names and the corresponding attributes, and that the "domains" section defines the types of data that comprise the attribute domains.

So far, so good. To implement an intensional database we need to do a bit more. Suppose we wish to know those vendors whose products are all rated 8 or above. One way of doing this is to find those vendors who supply parts whose rating is greater than or equal to 8; then find those vendors who supply parts that are rated less than 8. The desired information is found by finding those suppliers who are in the first group but not in the second. We illustrate as follows:

First Group: hrating(X) :- vp(X,_,Q) and Q>=8.

Interpretation: hrating(X) is the result we want for the first group. The relation name "hrating" (for high ratings) has been chosen arbitrarily. Relation names can be any combination of letters, digits, and underscore characters, but they must begin with a lower-case character. X is a variable, and the fact that we have it capitalized means that we want the result printed out. In English, our query could be stated as: If any tuple in the vp relation has a Q value greater than or equal to 8, then its X value (vendor number) is a solution and is a member of the relation hrating.

Second Group: lrating(X) : —vp(X,_,Q) and Q<8

Interpretation: Similar to that just described.

Solution: `bestquality(X):-hrating(X) and (not(lrating(X))`

Interpretation: A supplier is in the bestquality relation if it is in the group that supplies parts with quality ratings greater or equal to 8 but is not in the group that supplies parts having quality ratings less than 8.

A combined extensional and intensional database is shown in Figure 14.19. You should convince yourself that typea(X) yields a list of suppliers who provide grade-a parts.

▼FIGURE 14.19 COMBINED EXTENSIONAL AND INTENSIONAL DATABASES IN PROLOG

```
domains
vname,location,pname,ptype, grade = string
vno,pno,q-rating = integer

predicates
v(vno,vname,location)
vp(vno,pno,q-rating)
p(pno,pname,ptype,grade)

clauses
v(1,james,1a).
v(2,cline,london).
v(3,marx,denver).
v(4,myers,sf).
vp(1,25,8).
vp(1,37,9).
vp(1,28,6).
vp(1,29,7).
vp(1,39,9).
vp(2,25,9).
vp(2,37,9).
vp(3,28,7).
vp(3,37,7).
vp(3,29,8).
vp(4,37,8).
vp(3,39,8).
vp(4,28,7).
vp(4,29,7).
p(25,flange,steel,a).
p(28,stirrup,brass,aa).
p(29,bolt,iron,a).
p(37,clip,brass,aa).
p(39,clip,steel,aaa).
hrating(X):- vp(X,_,Q) and Q>=8.
lrating(X):- vp(X,_,Q) and Q<8.
bestquality(X):-hrating(X) and not (lrating(X)).
type1(X):- p(Y,_,_,a) and vp(X,_,_) and not (vp(X,Y)).
type2(X):- vp(X,_,_).
typea(X):- type2(X) and not (type1(X)).
```

▼ Datalog

While PROLOG is a useful implementation of logic programming, it does not provide the full functionality of a database system. This is not the purpose for which it was designed. Its powerful implementation of first-order logic, however, has led to attempts to couple it with traditional relational database systems. Most of these efforts have not produced ideal systems. DATALOG is an attempt to integrate concepts of logic with full database system capability.

DATALOG's foundations are in logic programming and automated theorem proving. DATALOG is in many ways a simplified version of logic programming. In particular, DATALOG does not allow function symbols in arguments as PROLOG does. DATALOG maintains the close relationship with relational databases by using predicate symbols to represent relations, as we did with PROLOG.

▼ Logic Data Language (LDL)

LDL represents an attempt to provide in one language the expressiveness of PROLOG combined with the capability to execute transactions (update, delete, and so on) in the relational database environment. The most important distinction between PROLOG and LDL is that LDL provides logical expressiveness as well as the full functionality of a DBMS. The following example is similar to one given by Chimenti et al. (1990). The record of an employee could have the following form:

```
employee(name(joe,smiley),admin, education(high_school, 1967)).
```

If one wanted to retain more information about the employee, each subargument could be refined into a more detailed description. This could lead to a complete educational record for a person, as follows:

```
employee(name(joe,smiley),admin,education({(highschool,
1967),(college(harvard,bs,math),1971) (college(harvard,ms,
engr),1973)})).
```

This nesting of sets provides significant flexibility and power. In addition, LDL has adapted PROLOG rule expression conventions into a language that has broader database management capability.

Summary

In this chapter, we have introduced the fundamental concepts of ODBMS and KBS.

We first illustrated how an OOP language implements the concepts presented in Chapter 4. We then briefly surveyed commercial and prototype ODBMSs and presented an object-oriented language. Knowledge-base systems attempt to extend the power of database systems beyond the data themselves to information that can be derived from the data. With this as a premise, we considered the role of knowledge in database systems and how rules enable the representation of knowledge. We elaborated on this theme by illustrating how a database might be constructed to include knowledge using PROLOG as an explanatory vehicle.

We then summarized LDL, which has extended the capabilities of PROLOG into database management functions as well as knowledge representation.

There is a growing need for extending database systems to incorporate features discussed in this chapter. It is expected that over the next decade interesting and useful developments will occur in these areas. Fortunately, the modeling methods developed earlier adapt readily to these advancements.

Review Questions

1. Define each of the following terms in your own words:
   a. class
   b. complex object
   c. expert system
   d. knowledge-base system
   e. extensional knowledge
   f. intensional knowledge

2. Why might an object-oriented database system be preferred to a relational database system?

3. Contrast predicate and clause in PROLOG. Give an example of each.

4. Why might a knowledge-base system be preferred to a database system?

Problems and Exercises

Part A

1. Match each term with its definition.

__*derived class*	a. A way of combining rules, proceeding from hypothesis to conclusion
__*object*	b. A logical structure made up of objects, predicates, and functions
__*object database system*	c. System software that manages data storage, and data and rule manipulation
__*backward chaining*	d. A class instance
__*forward chaining*	e. A way of combining rules, proceeding from conclusion to hypothesis
__*first-order logic*	f. A class that inherits features from another class
__*knowledge-base management system*	g. System software that manages data storage, and data and object manipulation

Part B

1. Draw a fragment of an object-oriented model that has two base object sets: STUDENT and EMPLOYEE. Then show respective specializations of those sets: ENGINEER and MANAGER. Let EMPLOYEE have attributes EMPNO and NAME. Let STUDENT have attributes SNO and NAME. ENGINEER has its own attribute TYPE (ME, EE, and so on), and MANAGER has its own attribute, DEPT.

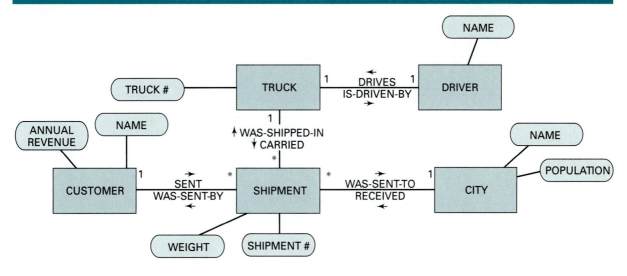

Following the example in the chapter, map your object-oriented model to classes in C++.

2. Using the model of Figure 14.1E, create solutions to each of the following user queries in TextQuery.

- **a.** A list of shipment numbers for shipments weighing over 20 pounds.
- **b.** Names of companies with more than $10 million in annual revenue.
- **c.** The population of Atlanta.
- **d.** The driver of Truck #45.
- **e.** The name and population of cities which have received shipments weighing over 100 pounds.
- **f.** The name and annual revenue of customers who have sent shipments weighing over 100 pounds.
- **g.** The truck numbers of trucks which have carried shipments weighing over 100 pounds.
- **h.** The names of drivers who have delivered shipments weighing over 100 pounds.
- **i.** Cities which have received shipments from customers having over $15 million in annual revenue.
- **j.** Customers having over $5 million in annual revenue who have sent shipments weighing less than 1 pound.
- **k.** Customers having over $5 million in annual revenue who either have sent shipments weighing less than 1 pound or have sent a shipment to San Francisco.
- **l.** Customers who have had shipments delivered by truck driver Jensen.
- **m.** Drivers who have delivered shipments for customers with annual revenue over $20 million to cities with population over 1 million.
- **n.** Customers who have had shipments delivered by every driver. (Hint: For the TextQuery solutions to exercises n–q, use the SET-OF construct with set comparison.)
- **o.** Cities which have received shipments from every customer.
- **p.** Drivers who have delivered shipments to every city.

```
mother(X,Y): - parent(X,Y), female(X).
father(X,Y): - parent(X,Y), male(X).
daughter(X,Y): - parent(Y,X), female(X).
son(X,Y): - parent(Y,X), male(X).
sibling(X,Y): - father(Z,X), father(Z,Y),
                  mother(W,X), mother(W,Y), (X≠Y).
brother(X,Y): - sibling(X,Y), male(X).
sister(X,Y): - sibling(X,Y), female(X).
uncle(X,Y): - brother(X,Z), parent(Z,Y).
uncle(X,Y): - parent(Z,Y), sibling(W,Z).
                married(W,X), male(X).

married(alan,belinda).      parent(felicia,john).
male(alan).                 parent(felicia,mary).
female(belinda).            parent(neva,darlene).
male(charles).
female(darlene).
male(edward).
parent(alan,charles).
parent(alan,darlene).
parent(alan,edward).
married(charles,felicia).
married(edward,grace).
female(grace).
female(felicia).
```

q. Customers who have sent shipments to every city with population over 500,000. (Hint: First create the set of cities with population over 500,000.)

r. Give a list of customers and annual revenue for those customers whose annual revenue is the maximum for the customers in the database.

s. Give a list of customers, all of whose shipments weigh over 25 pounds.

t. Give a list of customers that send all their shipments to a single city. (Note: The city may or may not be the same for each of these customers.)

3. For each of the following queries:

i. If the query can be answered using Figure 14.1E, provide the step-by-step procedures by which the result is found.

ii. If the query cannot be answered using Figure 14.1E, indicate the reasons why.
  a. Who are the siblings of Alan?
  b. Who are the children of Felicia?
  c. Who are the parents of Darlene?
  d. Who are the sons of Alan?
  e. Who are the brothers of Edward?
  f. Is Charles the brother of Darlene?
  g. Is Grace the sister of Charles?
  h. Does Belinda have any sisters?
  i. Who is the uncle of Belinda?
  j. Who are the uncles of Grace?

4. For any of the queries in (2) that could not be answered from Figure 14.1E, modify the database so that those queries can be satisfied.

5. Modify the rules of the database and add the facts needed to determine grand-parent relationships.

6. Write queries in PROLOG for the following problems. Use Figure 14.18.
   a. Which vendors supply parts having quality ratings greater than 8?
   b. Which vendors supply bolts?
   c. Which vendors supply brass clips?
   d. Which parts are made of steel?
   e. Where are vendors located who supply iron stirrups?
   f. Which vendors supply brass parts?
   g. Which vendors supply parts that are grade aa?
   h. What parts are supplied by James?
   i. For what quality levels does vendor w supply parts?
   j. What parts are supplied by vendors located in LA?

Projects and Professional Issues

1. Do some library research on ODBMS. Write an essay focusing on the similarities and differences in these products.

2. Do some library research on knowledge-base systems. Write an essay on which method of knowledge representation (logic, semantic networks, or frames) is most appropriate for building future KBSs. Explain the reasons for your conclusion.

3. Generate a small database for a hypothetical retail firm. Show how extending it to a knowledge base would enhance decision making in the firm.

6

LEGACY DATABASE SYSTEMS

▼

Legacy database systems represent the first database systems to have broad commercial use. While not as elegant as the relational, object, and knowledge-base systems, they remain in wide use, have powerful capabilities for many applications, and are worthy of study.

In Chapter 15, the definition of the network model is presented. Conceptual model mapping is defined and illustrated, and the network model data manipulation language is introduced and demonstrated.

Chapter 16 presents the hierarchical model. As with the network model, we examine conceptual model mapping. Additionally, the IMS data manipulation language is presented.

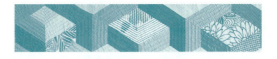

C H A P T E R

15

THE NETWORK
DATA MODEL

Rita Minkowski, the director of information systems for Zeus Corporation, was attending the monthly meeting of the local chapter of the Association for Computing Machinery (ACM). That evening's topic was "Relational Database Systems Versus Network and Hierarchical Database Systems."

John Stiller, regional sales manager for a popular network DBMS, began. "Relational systems can be expected to work well in satisfying user needs for ad hoc queries, but they can never achieve the performance needed for production systems. However, most database systems are going to be running a mixture of production transactions—such as updating inventory and sending out invoices—and ad hoc queries, with an emphasis on production systems. Unfortunately, highly efficient production systems and ad hoc queries are mutually disruptive activities. That is why we continue to support the network model. It supports the needs of most users with the greatest speed and efficiency."

The next speaker was Andrea Villa, an MIS professor at a local university. "Network and hierarchical systems are typically devoted almost entirely to production activities because that is what they do best. However," she continued, "they do not provide the flexibility needed to fully support ad hoc queries. With a network DBMS, you can churn out information on sales by region, but it may be more time-consuming to retrieve the type of summary data a marketing manager needs. Yet, we have a whole generation of managers who want—and expect—this kind of capability. That is why so many professionals have supported the relational model, which offers the flexibility needed to answer the sort of ad hoc queries managers have for summarized information."

In rebuttal, Stiller cited his own research, which showed that relational systems tend to be slower than network and hierarchical database systems, which have proven performance records. To get the same performance with a relational model, he indicated that users might have to undertake an expensive upgrade of their equipment and a redesign of their system.

Villa nodded her head. "Indeed, some of the newer relational systems may not yield the same performance statistics as some of the long-established network and hierarchical systems. And, in situations where the data structures and transaction patterns are very well understood in advance of design and implementation, the network and hierarchical systems can be customized to produce more impressive performance than some of the relational DBMSs. But what happens," she asked, "if the data structures change? Or the marketing manager wants summary data that were not a part of the original data structure or transaction patterns? To get the information, you may have to write a new application program or even redesign part of the database system. Either of these options are time-consuming and expensive. In a relational model, however, we can easily extract this information. This means that we can give managers the information they need to make sound strategic decisions. In the long run, this capability makes relational systems more efficient for more users."

The meeting was then opened up to questions and answers. What ensued was a lively debate that suggested that network and hierarchical databases are alive and well today, but perhaps not the models of the future.

I n this chapter, we present the fundamentals of the network data model. After reading this chapter, you should be able to:

▼ Describe the basic data structure from which the network data model is constructed.

▼ Explain the terminology used in describing the network data model.

▼ Use the fundamental methods of mapping from an object-oriented model to the network data model.

▼ Explain how the data description language is used to implement the network data structures.

▼ Describe how the DBTG data manipulation language operates to retrieve and update data.

▼ Evaluate the CODASYL DBTG model.

directed graph A mathematical structure in which points or nodes are connected by arrows or edges.

node Part of a network structure represented by a point.

edge Part of a network structure represented by an arrow.

network data model Represents data in network structures of record types connected in one–one or one–many relationships.

Conference on Data Systems Languages (CODASYL) An organization composed of representatives from hardware vendors, software vendors, and users; known principally for development of the COBOL language.

Database Task Group (DBTG) A subgroup of CODASYL given responsibility for developing standards for database management systems.

Integrated Data Store (IDS) One of the earliest database management systems; its architecture greatly influenced the DBTG recommendations for a network database model.

▼ Historical Background

Networks are a natural way of representing relationships among objects. They are widely used in mathematics, operations research, chemistry, physics, sociology, and other fields of inquiry. Since objects and their relationships are useful ways of modeling many of the business phenomena that concern us, it is not surprising that the network architecture applies to the organization of databases as well.

Networks can generally be represented by a mathematical structure called a **directed graph**. Directed graphs have a simple structure. They are constructed from points or **nodes** connected by arrows or **edges**. In the context of data models, the nodes can be thought of as data record types, and the edges can be thought of as representing one–one or one–many relationships. Thus, the **network data model** represents data in network structures of record types connected in one–one or one–many relationships. The graph structure enables simple representation of hierarchical relationships (such as genealogical data), membership relationships (such as department to which an employee is assigned), and many others. Moreover, once a relationship has been established between two objects, retrieval and manipulation of the related data can be efficiently executed.

As will be explained shortly, a hierarchy is a special case of a network. Correspondingly, the hierarchical data model, to be discussed in the next chapter, is a special case of the network data model. Even though the hierarchical data model historically precedes the network data model, it seems useful to discuss the more general graph structure of the network model first. Thus, we cover the network data model in this chapter and the hierarchical model in the next chapter.

The **Conference on Data Systems Languages (CODASYL),** an organization comprised of representatives from major hardware vendors, software vendors, and users, initially developed and standardized the COBOL language in the early 1960s. In the late 1960s, it appointed a subgroup named the **Database Task Group (DBTG)** to develop standards for database management systems. The DBTG was heavily influenced by the architecture used on the earliest DBMSs, the **Integrated Data Store (IDS),** developed earlier at General Electric. That influence led to recommendations for a network model in a preliminary report published in 1969.

This first report generated a number of suggestions for improvement, and a revised official report was published in 1971 and submitted to the American National Standards Institute (ANSI) for possible adoption as a national standard for DBMSs. ANSI took no action, and the 1971 report was followed by modified reports in 1978, 1981, and 1984.

Nonetheless, the 1971 document remains the fundamental statement of the network model, which came to be referred to as the CODASYL DBTG model. It has served as the basis for the development of network database management systems by several vendors. IDS (Honeywell) and IDMS (Computer Associates) are two of the better-known commercial implementations.

Although the network data model may in the future increasingly yield to the relational data model as the DBMS of choice, it is currently serving effectively in a number of database systems.

▼ Basic Concepts and Definitions
Three-Level Structure

The DBTG network model conforms to the ANSI/SPARC three-level database architecture (Chapter 3) as follows:

- ▼ The conceptual level (the logical view of all data and relationships in the database) is called the **schema**.
- ▼ The external level (the users' views of the data needed for various applications) is called the **subschema**.
- ▼ The internal level (the physical details of storage) is implicit in the implementation.

schema The logical view of all data and relationships in the database.

subschema Subsets of the schema which are defined by the user's view of the database.

Records and Sets

There are just two fundamental data structures in the network model, record types and sets. **Record types** are defined in the usual way as collections of logically related data items. For example, a customer record type might include the following data items: CustomerID, Name, Address, AmountOwed, and Date-of-Last-Payment. Note that we identified this collection as a *customer* record type, thus specifying by name the record type. All record types are given names such as CUSTOMER, INVOICE, SALESPERSON, and so forth.

A **set** in the DBTG model expresses a one–many (or one–one) relationship between two record types. (Note that this is not the usual mathematical definition of a set, which is just a collection of elements.) For example, one set might express the one–many relationship between customers and their outstanding invoice records. In every network set, one record type is the owner, and the other record type is the member. In the example just given, the customer record type is the owner and the invoice record type is the member. The one–many relationship incorporates the possibility that zero, one, or many invoice records may be related to a given customer record. That is, at a given time, a customer may have, say, ten, one, or zero outstanding invoices. The "many" really expresses capability rather than constraint.

Of course, there are situations where a relationship is strictly one–one, such as with truck and driver, but this is handled in the same way. Once the **owner record type** and the **member record type** are defined, all definitions apply as given.

record type A collection of logically related data items.

set In the DBTG model, a one–many relationship between two record types.

owner record type The record type on the "one" side of the one–many relationship of a DBTG set.

member record type The record type on the "many" side of the one–many relationship of a DBTG set.

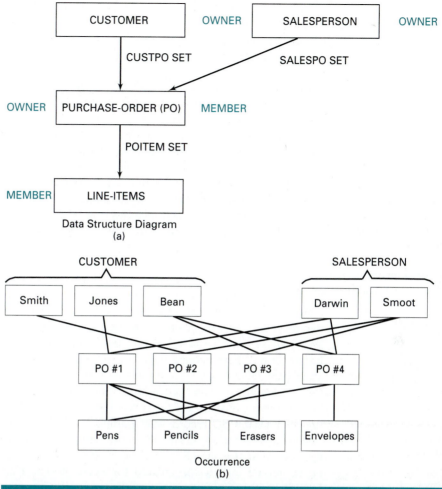

▼FIGURE 15.1 EXAMPLE OF NETWORK DATA STRUCTURE

These conventions are illustrated by the example shown in Figure 15.1. Figure 15.1(a) shows the general form of the data structure. This is called a Bachman diagram in honor of Charles Bachman, who was instrumental in the development of the IDS system at General Electric. Figure 15.1(b) shows actual values called **instances** or **occurrences**, which could occur in the structure of the Bachman diagram.

In Figure 15.1(a), we note certain conventions represented in the diagrams. First, sets are denoted by the arrow between record types, with the arrow pointing to the member record type (the "many" in the one–many relationship). Second, each set type is constructed of an owner record type, a member record type, and a name for the set type. The set name is the label given to the arrow. This corresponds to a graph in which the nodes are the record types and the edges are represented by the arrow-tipped lines connecting the record types. Third, the data structure is constructed from these simple set relationships. Figure 15.1(a) shows three sets: the CUSTPO set with owner CUSTOMER and member PURCHASE-ORDER; the SALESPO set with owner SALESPERSON and member PURCHASE-ORDER; and the POITEM set with owner PURCHASE-ORDER and member LINE-ITEMS.

instance Actual record values expressed in a data structure.

occurrence A synonym for instance.

Figure 15.1(a) provides an example of the difference between the network data model and the hierarchical data model. Notice that PURCHASE-ORDER is a member record type of two sets: CUSTPO and SALESPO. In the hierarchical data model, no record type can be a member of two different sets. However, this *is* allowed in the network data model. Thus, additional representational power is provided in the network data structure. This distinction is important because it is one of the principal differences between the network data model and the hierarchical data model to be discussed in the next chapter.

Since the network model allows only one–many relationships between record types, one might wonder how a many–many relationship is modeled. Figure 15.2 is a classic example of a relationship that is many–many. One student may be enrolled in many classes, and a given class can have many students. The DBTG model allows only **simple networks** in which all relationships are one–one or one–many. A **complex network,** which includes one or more many-many relationships, cannot be directly implemented in the DBTG model. There is, however, a method for transforming a complex network, such as the one in Figure 15.2, into the simple network form required for DBTG implementation.

The method is similar to the method by which conceptual models are mapped to relational tables. Recall that when the cardinality between two object sets is many–many, a relational table is created that contains the key attributes from the two related object sets. A similar method applies here. When two record types, such as STUDENT and CLASS, are connected in a many–many relationship, we create an intersection or **link record type** consisting of at least the keys from the STUDENT and CLASS records. Other attributes may be added at the discretion of the designer.

In Figure 15.3, this procedure is illustrated. A link record type named SC has been created, consisting of the fields STUDENT-ID and CLASS-ID. As shown in Figure 15.3(a), the SC record type partitions the many–many relationship into *two* one–many relationships. The SC record type accordingly becomes a member of two sets, the TAKINGCLASS SET and the ENROLLED SET. Figure 15.3(b) illustrates how an SC record instance is created for every student/class pair. For example, Rex Lupus owns three SC records, one for each class in which he is enrolled. Botany 500, in like manner, owns two SC records, one for each student enrolled. Additional storage and processing requirements are inherent in the creation of the artificial records, but the data model is now in simple network form and satisfies the DBTG requirements.

simple network A data structure in which all binary relationships are one–many.

complex network A data structure in which one or more binary relationships are many–many.

link record type A dummy record that is created in order to convert a complex network into an equivalent simple network; also called a link record type.

▼**FIGURE 15.2 EXAMPLE OF A COMPLEX NETWORK (MANY–MANY RELATIONSHIP)**

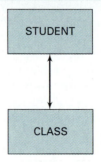

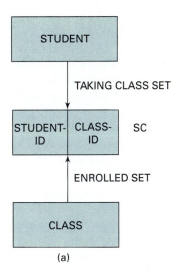

(a)

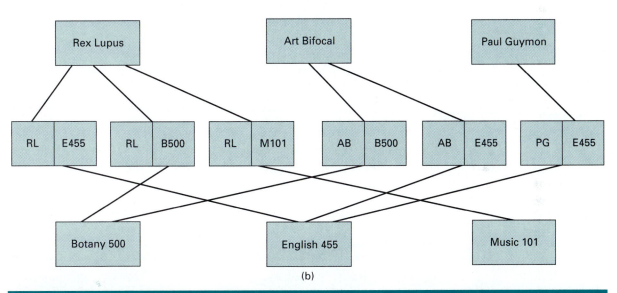

(b)

▼FIGURE 15.3 EXAMPLE OF USE OF INTERSECTION RECORDS TO CONVERT
A COMPLEX NETWORK TO A SIMPLE NETWORK

▼The Network Model's Relationship To Conceptual Modeling Semantics

As we have taken a conceptual data modeling approach to studying database systems, it is appropriate to examine the relationship between the network data model and the conceptual data model. In this section, we show how a conceptual data model can be transformed to a network model.

Transforming Object Sets and One–Many Relationships

logical record A record type as seen from the user's perspective.

physical link A means of connecting records by using the records' disk addresses.

The network model can be thought of as a conceptual data model with all the relationships limited to binary (two-object) sets and one–many or one–one relationships. This allows an uncomplicated graphical representation of data structures. Instead of the object sets of the conceptual data model, we have **logical records** which are connected with other logical records through **physical links** consisting of the records' addresses on disk. Each link represents a relationship between exactly two records. The relationship between two record types connected by the binary link is referred to as a set.

To clarify this, let's take another look at an example from International Product Distribution (IPD). We assume the same case facts as before and add that IPD is organized into the usual functional departments such as accounting, marketing, and so forth. Figure 15.4(a) is a fragment of a conceptual data model for IPD illustrating the relationship between customers and IPD accounts. Figure 15.4(b) shows how the model fragment is mapped to a network data structure.

The correspondence is quite direct. The names of the objects become the names of the records. The attributes of the objects become the fields of the records. The relationship between objects becomes the relationship between records. If the reality is that a customer may have many accounts, and that an account may belong to only one customer, as indicated in Figure 15.4(a), then an arrow would be added at the ACCOUNT end of the HAS-ACCOUNT link (Figures 15.4(b) and 15.5(a)). If a customer could only have one account, but that account could belong to several customers, then the arrow would be added at the customer end of the HAS-ACCOUNT link, as shown in Figure 15.5(b).

From the foregoing examples, we are led to the expression of these mapping rules:

> *Rule 1*: For each object set O in a conceptual schema, create a record type R in the network data structure. All attributes of O are represented as fields of R.

▼FIGURE 15.4 MAPPING OF CONCEPTUAL MODEL TO NETWORK STRUCTURE

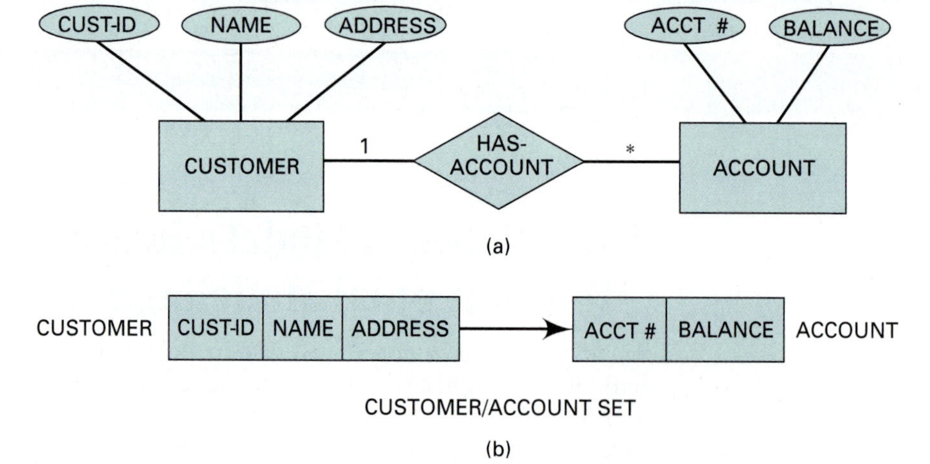

(a)

CUSTOMER/ACCOUNT SET

(b)

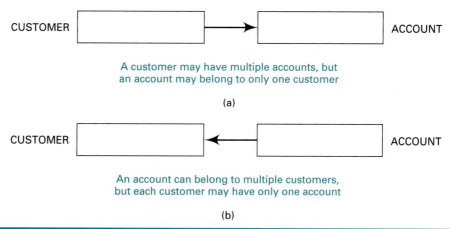

A customer may have multiple accounts, but
an account may belong to only one customer

(a)

An account can belong to multiple customers,
but each customer may have only one account

(b)

▼FIGURE 15.5 REPRESENTING ONE–MANY RELATIONSHIPS

Rule 2: For one–many relationships, the record type on the "one" side of the relationship becomes the owner, and the record type on the "many" side of the relationship becomes the member record type. If a relationship cardinality is strictly one–one, then the owner and member record types may be arbitrarily chosen.

Transforming *n*-ary Relationships

IPD also has some three-way relationships as shown in Figure 15.6(a), which do not satisfy the binary-relationship requirement. There is, however, an easy way of satisfying that requirement, as illustrated in Figure 15.6(b). A link record is created,

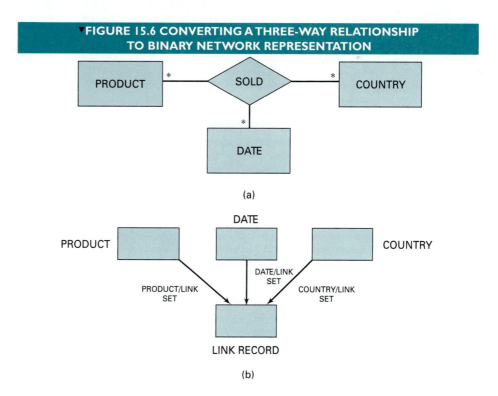

▼FIGURE 15.6 CONVERTING A THREE-WAY RELATIONSHIP
TO BINARY NETWORK REPRESENTATION

(a)

(b)

which must be comprised of at least a key field from each object set. The creation of this link record allows representation of the conceptual model structure in network form. All three relationships are now binary.

Note that the relationship between the existing records and the link record is one–many, with the link record always being the member record in the set. Occurrences are shown in Figure 15.7. The strategy of creating linking record types can be extended without modification to mapping n-ary relationships to the required form. We express our third mapping rule as:

> *Rule 3:* For each n-ary relationship, $n > 2$, create a linking record L, and make it the member record type in n set types. Designate the owner of each set type as the record type on the "one" side of the resulting one–many relationships.

Transforming Many–Many Relationships

As we saw with the earlier STUDENT-CLASS example, a similar situation could arise when many–many relationships are involved. As another example, consider a situation that exists at IPD. A manufacturer may produce many products, and any one of these products can be made by several manufacturers. A diagram of this situation is shown in Figure 15.8(a). Implementation requires that a link record be created, which we name LREC. This is shown in Figure 15.8(b). The relationship between PRODUCT and LREC is one–many, as is the relationship between MANUFACTURER and LREC. The requirements of the DBTG network model are satisfied.

An instance of this data model is given in Figure 15.9. Manufacturer Smith supplies products 115 and 116. Product 115 is supplied by Shirdlu, Inc. as well. Can you see what would happen if Joe Bean Mfg. also supplied product 116, or if Shirdlu began manufacturing product 120, or a new product—135?

Our final rule deals with this many–many situation.

> *Rule 4:* For each many–many relationship between object sets O_1 and O_2 create a link record type L and make it the member record type in two set types, of which the set type owners are the record types corresponding to O_1 and O_2.

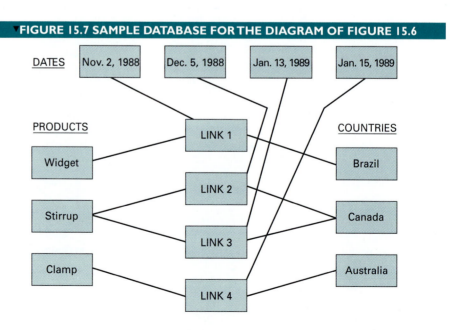

▼FIGURE 15.7 SAMPLE DATABASE FOR THE DIAGRAM OF FIGURE 15.6

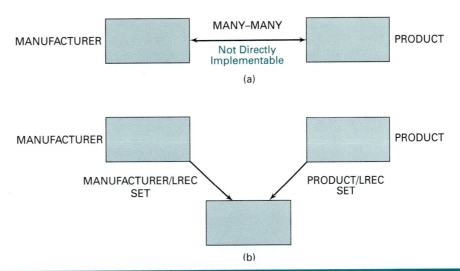

(a)

(b)

▼FIGURE 15.8 MAPPING OF MANY–MANY RELATIONSHIP TO CODASYL

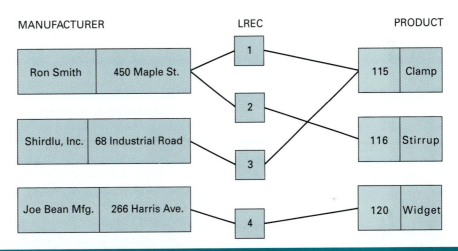

▼FIGURE 15.9 EXAMPLE OF THE USE OF A LINK RECORD TO CONVERT MANY–MANY RELATIONSHIPS TO ONE–ONE RELATIONSHIPS

▼ The DBTG Data Definition Language (DDL)

We now turn to the languages by which the network data model is implemented. These languages are the means by which the data structure or schema is specified and by which the data are stored and manipulated. The language used to specify the schema is called **data definition language (DDL)**, and the language used to store and manipulate data is called **data manipulation language (DML).** We cover the DBTG DDL in this section and DML in the next.

data definition language (DDL) The language used to specify a database schema.

data manipulation language (DML) The language used to store and manipulate data.

From Data Model to Schema

As noted earlier, the overall definition of a network database—its records and sets—is called a schema. In particular, the schema describes the relationships between record types, identifies the data items that make up each record type, and defines the owner-member record types that define the set types. A procedure for using the DDL in defining a schema is as follows:

- ▼ Create the conceptual data model.
- ▼ Map the conceptual data model to network data structure diagrams.
  - ▼ Check to see whether there are one–many relationships between record types. These can be implemented directly as DBTG sets.
  - ▼ If there are many–many relationships, transform them into two sets having one–many relationships by constructing the necessary link records.
  - ▼ If there are *n*-ary relationships, convert them to binary relationships by the method illustrated earlier.
- ▼ Use the DDL to implement the schema.

A schema is made up of the following components:

- ▼ A **schema section,** which names the schema.
- ▼ **Record sections,** which provide specifications of each record structure, its data items, and its location.
- ▼ **Set sections,** which specify all sets, including the owner and member record types.

schema section The section of the DBTG schema that names the schema.

record section The section of the DBTG schema that defines each record, its data items, and its location.

set section The section of the DBTG schema that defines sets and includes owner record types and member record types.

Consider the conceptual data model in Figure 15.10. IPD wishes to implement the related schema. The mapping to the network data structure is shown in Figure 15.11. The use of the DDL to implement the schema is shown in Figure 15.12. The lines of code are numbered for reference in our discussion.

The schema section is represented on line 1. This line identifies what follows as a schema description for a database named ACCOUNTSREC. This name is supplied by the user.

Lines 2 through 15 are devoted to the record section. Each record type is identified by name: CUSTOMER, INVOICE, and LINE-ITEM. For each record type, the component data items are defined. For CUSTOMER these are CUST-ID, NAME, AD-DRESS, and ACCOUNT-BALANCE. Each data item is given a datatype and a length specification. For example, ACCOUNT-BALANCE is assigned the NUMERIC

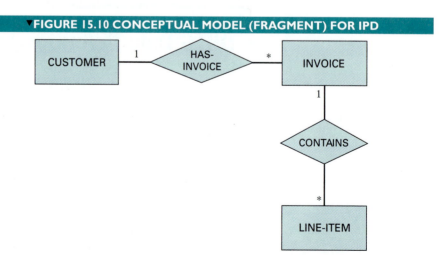

▼FIGURE 15.10 CONCEPTUAL MODEL (FRAGMENT) FOR IPD

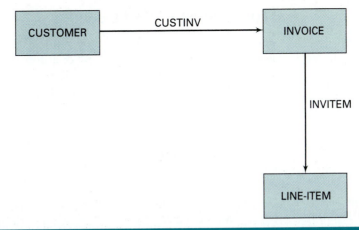

datatype and given a length of five characters, with two characters to the right of the decimal point. Those identified as INTEGER have an implied length.

When all records have been defined, sets can be specified. Lines 16 through 21 in Figure 15.12 show examples for the ACCOUNTSREC schema. Definition of a set requires at least the three lines shown. The first line is to name the set type, the second line is to name the owner record type, and the third line is to name the member record type. In Figure 15.12, one set is named CUSTINV, and has CUSTOMER as its owner record type and INVOICE as its member record type.

▼FIGURE 15.12 SCHEMA EXAMPLE

```
 1. SCHEMA NAME IS ACCOUNTSREC
 2. RECORD NAME IS CUSTOMER
 3. CUST-ID           TYPE IS   NUMERIC INTEGER
 4. NAME              TYPE IS   CHARACTER 15
 5. ADDRESS           TYPE IS   CHARACTER 20
 6. ACCOUNT-BALANCE TYPE IS     NUMERIC (5,2)

 7. RECORD NAME IS INVOICE
 8. INVNO     TYPE IS   NUMERIC INTEGER
 9. DATE      TYPE IS   CHARACTER 9
10. AMOUNT    TYPE IS   NUMERIC(5,2)
11. STATUS    TYPE IS   CHARACTER 2

12. RECORD NAME IS LINE-ITEM
13. STOCKNO         TYPE IS   NUMERIC INTEGER
14. DESCRIPTION     TYPE IS   CHARACTER 20
15. PRICE           TYPE IS   NUMERIC (4,2)

16. CUSTINV
17. OWNER IS CUSTOMER
18. MEMBER IS INVOICE

19. INVITEM
20. OWNER IS INVOICE
21. MEMBER IS LINE-ITEM
```

From Schema to Subschema

Whereas the schema defines the overall logical structure of the database, the subschema describes the external view of a user or application program. Subschemas are basically subsets of the schema. However, data independence (to allow for the variety of users' terminology) is provided by allowing some elements of the schema to differ. Data items can be grouped that were not grouped in the schema; data items, records, and sets can be renamed; and the order of the descriptions may be changed.

There is no accepted DBTG standard for the subschema; however, the following divisions are commonly used:

title division That portion of the DBTG subschema that provides for naming the subschema and its associated schema.

mapping division The portion of the DBTG subschema that provides for changing the names used in the schema to names chosen for the subschema.

structure division The division of the DBTG subschema where records, data items, and sets from the schema are defined.

subschema record section The section of the structure division that specifies subschema records, data items, and datatypes.

subschema set section The section of the structure division that defines the sets to be included.

- A **title division** that enables naming of the subschema and its associated schema.
- A **mapping division** that provides for changes in names from the schema to the subschema, if desired.
- A **structure division** that specifies the records, data items, and sets from the schema that are present in the subschema. This division is composed of record and set sections. The **subschema record section** defines the records and the data items from those records that are to be included, along with their datatypes. The **subschema set section** identifies the sets that are to be included.

We use as an example an application from IPD that computes the number of outstanding invoices by customer, as well as the amounts owed on those invoices. From the ACCOUNTSREC schema, the application requires only the CUSTOMER and INVOICE record types, and the CUSTINV set. The subschema is shown in Figure 15.13.

The name of the subschema (SS) is INVSTATUS. The mapping division shows that the CUSTOMER record of the schema has been renamed OWEDBY in the INVSTATUS subschema, and the CUST-INV set has been renamed OWEDBY-INV. This is done in the ALIAS section, where AD denotes "alias description." The CUSTOMER record from the schema has been renamed with the alias OWEDBY for the

FIGURE 15.13 SUBSCHEMA EXAMPLE

```
SS INVSTATUS WITHIN ACCOUNTSREC.
MAPPING DIVISION.
ALIAS SECTION.
AD RECORD CUSTOMER IS OWEDBY.
AD SET CUST-INV IS OWEDBY-INV.
STRUCTURE DIVISION.
RECORD SECTION.
01     OWEDBY.
       05     CUST-ID.
       05     NAME.
       05     ACCOUNT-BALANCE.
01     INVOICE ALL.
SET SECTION.
SD     OWEDBY-INV.
```

subschema, and just three of the four data items comprising CUSTOMER in the schema have been included. The INVOICE ALL statement indicates all data items from the record INVOICE in the schema have been included, so there is no need to specify them again.

As you can see, the subschema allows the user to use a predefined schema to tailor the schema to the requirements of a particular application.

▼ The DBTG Data Manipulation Language (DML)

The DBTG data manipulation language (DML) provides powerful commands for manipulating a network database system. It is the means by which the data contained in the database can be used to support organizational information requirements. Once the database is designed and created using the DDL, the DML allows users to execute operations on the database for purposes of providing information and reports, as well as updating and modifying record content.

As opposed to the DMLs of relational database systems, whose operators process entire relations at one time, the DBTG DML operators process records one at a time. Moreover, the DML must be embedded in a host language, such as COBOL. The basic commands used by the DML can be classified as **navigational commands, retrieval commands, update commands for records,** and **update commands for sets.** Commands from each of these groups are listed in Figure 15.14.

Before we illustrate the DBTG DML with examples, we need to define terms that will be necessary for our discussion.

The first concept is that of the **user working area (UWA).** Every user or application program has a UWA. The records in the subschema are stored in the UWA, along with **currency indicators** and **status flags.** The way in which the record is formatted in the UWA is called the **record template.**

Consider Figure 15.15. Here we show a possible working area related to the subschema defined in Figure 15.13. The OWEDBY currency pointer marks the location of the last processed record of that record type. The INVOICE currency pointer marks the location of the last processed record of that record type. The OWEDBY-INV currency pointer marks the location of the associated owner or member record of that set which was last accessed. The RUN-UNIT currency pointer marks the location of the last accessed record of any type.

We see that currency indicators function as placemarkers. When the user issues a FIND command (to be discussed), the record is found, and its place is

navigational commands DBTG DML commands used to find database records.

retrieval commands DBTG DML commands used to retrieve database records.

update commands for records DBTG DML commands used to change the values of records.

update commands for sets DBTG DML commands used to create, change, or delete set instances.

user working area (UWA) Portion of primary memory used to hold program variables that point to and hold the records of different record types while their contents are being operated upon by the host program.

currency indicators Placemarkers for records that have been found.

status flags Variables used to denote the success or failure of the last operation executed by the application program.

record templates Formats used for records that are read into the UWA.

▼ FIGURE 15.14 BASIC DBTG DML COMMANDS

Type	Command
Navigation	FIND
Retrieval	GET
Record Update	ERASE
	STORE
	MODIFY
Set Update	CONNECT
	DISCONNECT
	RECONNECT

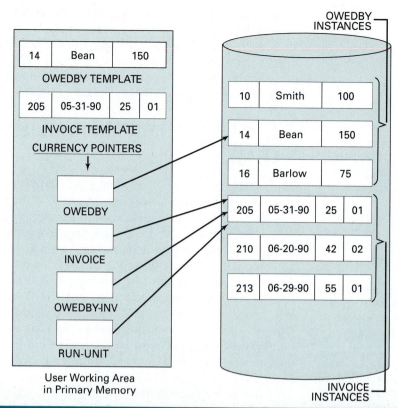

OWEDBY
INSTANCES

14	Bean	150

OWEDBY TEMPLATE

205	05-31-90	25	01

INVOICE TEMPLATE

CURRENCY POINTERS

OWEDBY

INVOICE

OWEDBY-INV

RUN-UNIT

User Working Area
in Primary Memory

10	Smith	100
14	Bean	150
16	Barlow	75
205	05-31-90	25	01
210	06-20-90	42	02
213	06-29-90	55	01

INVOICE
INSTANCES

▼FIGURE 15.15 RELATIONSHIP OF USER WORKING AREA
TO DATABASE INSTANCES

marked in the currency indicator. When a second command is issued, the DBMS refers to the currency indicator to determine which record is to be acted upon. Briefly, the type and function of the currency pointers are the following:

▼ *Current of Run Unit:* Run unit refers to the user's program. Current of the run unit contains the address of the record, or set instance, most recently accessed by the application program. In Figure 15.15, this is invoice 205.

▼ *Current of Record Type:* There is one currency indicator for each record type in the subschema. For each record type, the UWA contains the address of the record of that type most recently accessed by the program. In Figure 15.15, we have currency indicators for the OWEDBY and INVOICE record types, and they are pointing to the records for Bean and invoice 205, respectively.

▼ *Current of Set Type:* A currency pointer contains the address of the most recently accessed record of a given set type. A separate currency pointer is maintained for each set type. The pointer may point to a record of either the owner or member type depending on which was most recently accessed. Figure 15.15 shows the currency indicator for the only set type in this subschema, OWEDBY-INV, and it is pointing to the member record, invoice 205.

The preceding pointers are updated automatically as accesses take place in the database system. It is instructive to think of currency indicators as variables in a table. Figure 15.15 illustrates possible currency indicators for the INVSTATUS subschema.

Status flags are a set of variables used to communicate the outcome of the last operation applied in the application program. The flag used most frequently is *db-status*. Its value is set to "0" if the most recent operation succeeded; otherwise, it is set to an error code. The most common use of this flag is to signal the end of data. Other status flags include *db-set-name, db-record-name*, and *db-data-name*. These flags are set, as a means of identifying the source of a problem, when the last operation fails. We shall see examples of their use in the queries that follow.

DBTG Retrieval and Update Facilities

FIND commands select and locate a desired record or instance of a set. That is why they are called navigational commands. A GET command must then be used to actually retrieve the data. The FIND command could also be followed by an update command such as ERASE or MODIFY.

Syntactically, there are two forms of the FIND command as shown next. The optional parts of the commands are denoted by brackets ([...]) and names to be supplied by the user are indicated by the angle brackets (<...>).

```
FIND ANY <record name> [USING <field list>]
FIND DUPLICATE <record name> [USING <field list>]
```

We give several examples.

Example 1: A Simple Record Retrieval. Suppose that IPD wants the Customer information for Customer 105. The following commands apply:

```
MOVE 105 TO CUST-ID IN CUSTOMER
FIND ANY CUSTOMER USING CUST-ID
GET CUSTOMER
```

The FIND command sets the current of run-unit, current of CUSTOMER, and current of CUSTINV to point to the record of Customer 105. The GET command then brings the record into the CUSTOMER template in the UWA.

Example 2: Retrieval of All Records Having a Particular Characteristic. Suppose next that IPD wants all the records of customers having account balances of zero.

```
MOVE 0 TO ACCOUNT-BALANCE IN CUSTOMER
FIND ANY CUSTOMER USING ACCOUNT-BALANCE
DOWHILE DB-STATUS = 0
     GET CUSTOMER
     (process customer record)
     FIND DUPLICATE CUSTOMER USING ACCOUNT-BALANCE
END-DO
```

In this example, we have a loop that is controlled by DB-STATUS. That is, DB-STATUS will be set to a nonzero code when there are no more CUSTOMER accounts with zero balances. The first FIND locates the first CUSTOMER record having a zero balance. The next FIND looks for a DUPLICATE, meaning another record that has the same value of ACCOUNT-BALANCE that the current of CUSTOMER has.

Example 3: Deleting Records Using the ERASE Command.   IPD now wants to delete CUSTOMER accounts that have a zero ACCOUNT-BALANCE.

```
MOVE 0 TO ACCOUNT-BALANCE IN CUSTOMER
FIND FOR UPDATE ANY CUSTOMER USING ACCOUNT-BALANCE
DOWHILE DB-STATUS = 0
     ERASE CUSTOMER
     FIND FOR UPDATE DUPLICATE CUSTOMER USING ACCOUNT-BALANCE
END-DO
```

Comparing this query to that of Example 2, it may be seen that the ERASE command is used in place of GET. Additionally, the words FOR UPDATE are added to the FIND command, which communicates to the DBMS that an update is to occur and that the record must then be locked for the run-unit. Record locking prevents other users from updating this record while our run-unit is processing it. FOR UP-DATE is required when seeking records for operations other than GET.

We now turn to an example of modifying the content of stored records.

Example 4: Modifying the Contents of a Record.   As previously indicated, a special form of the FIND command—FIND FOR UPDATE—is used to modify record contents. FIND FOR UPDATE is used to locate the record; GET is used to move it to the UWA, where the changes are made. The MODIFY command is then used to re-place it in the database.

Suppose that IPD Customer 502 has just moved its offices and needs to have the address field of its record changed. The DML could be used in the following way:

```
MOVE 502 TO CUST-ID IN CUSTOMER
FIND FOR UPDATE ANY CUSTOMER USING CUST-ID
GET CUSTOMER
IF DB-STATUS = 0
     THEN MOVE '455 Cherry Lane, San Marino, CA' TO
ADDRESS IN CUSTOMER
          MODIFY ADDRESS
     ELSE (perform error routine)
END-IF
```

In this example, the MODIFY statement is used to identify the record field that is to be changed. If no record field identifier is supplied, the DBMS assumes that the entire record is to be changed.

Example 5: Adding a New Record to the Database.   The STORE command is used to insert new records into the database. The record is constructed in the UWA and then placed in the database by STORE.

IPD has a new customer record to add. The new customer's name is Harry Z. Smith, located at 201 S. Main, San Marino, California. Smith's company has just purchased $500.00 worth of goods. IPD has assigned a customer identification number of 503.

```
MOVE 503 TO CUST-ID IN CUSTOMER
MOVE 'HARRY Z SMITH' TO NAME IN CUSTOMER
MOVE '201 S. MAIN, SAN MARINO, CA' TO ADDRESS IN
```

```
CUSTOMER
        MOVE 500.00 TO ACCOUNT-BALANCE IN CUSTOMER
        STORE CUSTOMER
```

DBTG Set-Processing Facility

Sets are used to process records by relationship. The DBTG DML provides facilities for inserting records into set instances, removing records from set instances, and moving records around within set instances. Options are available to specify constraints on set membership as well. We explain this facility next.

Set Operations

The DBTG language provides three commands for processing sets. CONNECT adds a record to a set. DISCONNECT removes a record from a set. RECONNECT allows set membership to be changed. In order to add a new record to a particular set instance, the record must first be added to the database. Then the currency pointers of the record type and the set type must be set to point to the appropriate record and set instance. We give the following example.

Example 6: Placing a Record in a Set. Suppose that IPD Customer 431 has just made a $100.00 purchase on account, and the associated invoice (#231) has been prepared. Customer 431 is now the owner of a new invoice instance. The INVOICE record occurrence must be created, then connected to the CUSTINV set. This is done in the following way:

```
MOVE 231 to INVNO IN INVOICE
MOVE '7/7/90' TO DATE IN INVOICE
MOVE 100.00 TO INVOICE-AMOUNT IN INVOICE
STORE INVOICE
MOVE 431 TO CUST-ID IN CUSTOMER
FIND ANY CUSTOMER USING CUST-ID
CONNECT INVOICE TO CUSTOMER
```

The first four statements create the new invoice record and insert it into the database as in Example 5. At this point in processing, the new INVOICE record is the current of run-unit, the current of INVOICE, and the current of CUSTINV. The CONNECT command connects the current of the INVOICE record to the existing instance of the set. In this example, the new INVOICE record is connected to the CUSTINV occurrence owned by Customer 431.

Thus, after the STORE command, 431 is moved to the data item CUST-ID, and Customer 431's record becomes the current of CUSTINV. The CONNECT command then puts the new INVOICE record into this instance of the CUSTINV set.

A DISCONNECT command removes the run-unit's current record from one or more sets. This operation does not delete a record from the database, *it only removes a record from a set*. If deletion is desired, it is completed using the ERASE command as illustrated previously. We demonstrate the use of the DISCONNECT command in Example 7.

Example 7: Removing a Record from a Set. When an IPD invoice is paid, it is deleted from the set of outstanding invoices for that customer. Suppose, for example, that IPD Invoice 254 has just been paid in full.

```
MOVE 254 TO INVNO OF INVOICE
FIND ANY INVOICE USING INVNO
DISCONNECT INVOICE FROM CUSTINV
```

The first two statements locate the desired invoice. The final statement disconnects it from the set of which it is currently a member record. The record still remains in the database for audit and record-keeping purposes.

The RECONNECT command allows a record to have its set membership changed. For example, suppose that Invoice 510 is mistakenly assigned to the set owned by Customer 425, when it should have been connected to the set owned by Customer 431. The change to correct this situation would proceed as shown in the next example.

Example 8: Changing Set Membership.

```
MOVE 510 TO INVNO OF INVOICE
FIND ANY INVOICE USING INVNO
MOVE 431 TO CUST-ID IN CUSTOMER
FIND ANY CUSTOMER USING CUST-ID
RECONNECT INVOICE IN CUSTINV
```

The first two statements locate the desired INVOICE record. The third and fourth statements locate the desired CUSTOMER record. The last statement connects Invoice 510 to the set owned by Customer 431. This also effects removal of Invoice 510 from the set owned by Customer 425.

Set Membership Classification

set insertion class In DBTG, the way in which a member record gets placed in a set occurrence; can be manual or automatic.

set retention class In DBTG, determines how and when a member record can be removed from a set; can be fixed, mandatory, or optional.

manual insertion mode In DBTG, requires that the member record be placed in a set by using a CONNECT command to link it to the desired set occurrence.

automatic insertion mode In DBTG, when a new member record is created, the DBMS will automatically connect it to the correct set occurrence.

Two classes of set membership are **set insertion class** and **set retention class**. Set insertion is associated with the way in which a member gets placed in a set occurrence. Once a member record is assigned to a set, the set retention class determines how and when a member record can be removed from that set.

Set insertion modes are defined by the statement

```
INSERTION IS <insert mode>,
```

where the insert-mode options are manual or automatic.

▼ The **manual insertion mode** requires that the member record must be placed in a set by using a CONNECT command to link it to the desired set occurrence. Manual insertion is accomplished by the statement

```
CONNECT <record type> TO <set type>
```

Assume that we have the following subschema fragment:

```
SET NAME IS CUSTINV.
OWNER IS CUSTOMER
MEMBER IS INVOICE
INSERTION IS MANUAL
RETENTION IS OPTIONAL.
```

An example of its use was seen in Example 6.

▼ **Automatic insertion mode** means that when a new member record is created, the DBMS will automatically connect it to the correct set occurrence. This connection will occur whenever statements of the following type are executed:

```
STORE <record type>
```

Suppose in the preceding subschema fragment that MANUAL is replaced by AUTOMATIC. Example 6 would change in the following way:

```
MOVE 431 TO CUST-ID IN CUSTOMER
FIND ANY CUSTOMER USING CUST-ID
MOVE 231 to INVNO IN INVOICE
MOVE '7/7/90' TO DATE IN INVOICE
MOVE 100.00 TO INVOICE-AMOUNT IN INVOICE
STORE INVOICE
```

The first two lines make Customer 431 the current of the CUSTINV set. The next three statements create the new INVOICE record. The STORE command will insert the record into the desired CUSTINV set, since connection to this set is defined as AUTOMATIC.

Set retention options are

▼ Fixed, meaning that once a member record has been assigned to a set occurrence, it cannot be removed from that set occurrence unless the record is deleted from the database.

▼ Mandatory, meaning that once a member record has been placed in a set occurrence, it must always be in some occurrence of that set. It cannot be disconnected, or reconnected, to a set of another type.

▼ Optional, meaning that there are no restrictions imposed on connections or reconnections to set types. A record so designated need not be connected to any set whatsoever.

fixed retention In DBTG, once a member record has been assigned to a set occurrence, it cannot be removed from that set occurrence unless the record is deleted from the database.

The set retention mode also governs what is allowed when a record that is a set owner is erased. If the retention mode is **fixed**, the entire set will be erased. If the retention mode is **mandatory**, then the deletion operation is illegal since member records must belong to a set occurrence. If the retention mode is **optional**, then the record will be deleted and the member records of the set it owns will be disconnected and remain in the database without set membership.

mandatory retention In DBTG, once a member record has been placed in a set occurrence, it must always be in some occurrence of that set.

Example 9: Set Insertion and Retention Status. Consider the schema of Figure 15.12. We illustrate the use of set insertion and retention status specification by extending the definition of CUSTINV and INVITEM. Assume that we want to specify MANUAL insertion and OPTIONAL retention. The modified schema is shown in Figure 15.16.

optional retention In DBTG, there are no restrictions imposed on connections or reconnections to set types.

▼FIGURE 15.16 AN EXAMPLE OF THE USE OF SET INSERTION AND SET RETENTION STATUS

```
CUSTINV
OWNER IS CUSTOMER
MEMBER IS INVOICE
    INSERTION IS MANUAL
    RETENTION IS OPTIONAL

INVITEM
OWNER IS INVOICE
MEMBER IS LINE-ITEM
    INSERTION IS MANUAL
    RETENTION IS OPTIONAL
```

▼ IDMS/R—A DBTG DBMS

IDMS/R stands for Integrated Database Management System/Relational. It is based on the DBTG network model and is perhaps the most successful of the DBTG-based products. The R was added to indicate the addition of certain relational features to IDMS. The relational interface is primarily of interest to the user. The basic structure of IDMS remains closely aligned to DBTG network specifications.

IDMS applies the structural concepts of record and set as defined by DBTG. The IDMS schema is comprised of a SCHEMA DESCRIPTION section, RECORD DESCRIPTION sections, and SET DESCRIPTION sections according to DBTG design. In addition, it includes a FILE DESCRIPTION section which defines all internal files and assigns them to external files. IDMS also includes an AREA DESCRIPTION section, which assigns file partitions to specified areas. An **area** is a location in storage that contains one or more record types.

area In IDMS/R, location in storage that contains one or more record types.

The IDMS subschema contains no MAPPING division because aliases are not generally allowed for records, sets, or data items. When an entire record from the schema is used in the subschema, it is expressed by

```
ELEMENTS ARE ALL
```

If some subset of the record data items are required, it is denoted by

```
ELEMENTS ARE <data item 1> <data item 2> . . . <data item n>,
```

where data items can be permuted according to the needs of the application.

Sets are defined in a manner similar to that prescribed by DBTG, with some important differences. FIXED set retention is not available. Only MANDATORY and OPTIONAL retention capabilities are provided. There are also certain restrictions on which records are to be included in the subschema. IDMS/R mandates that sets that might be deleted by erasing an owner record be included in *any* subschema containing that record. This is to avoid propagating an ERASE to records that are not included in the set defined in this subschema. This could happen if the owner record were erased, causing the erasure of member records, which were, in turn, owners of another set not included in this schema.

Overall, IDMS structures are faithful to the recommendations of the DBTG report.

▼ CODASYL DBTG Evaluation

In this section, we compare the CODASYL DBTG model with the relational model to assess its comparative strengths and weaknesses.

Data Representation

A significant difference between the relational model and the network model is in the way in which relationships are represented. In the relational model, links between two relations are established by including in those two relations an attribute with the same domain of values—often with the same attribute name. Rows in each relation that are logically related will have the same values for that attribute. In the DBTG network model, one–many cardinalities between two record types are established by explicit definition of set type. The DBMS then connects records in each set type by physical pointers.

This means that records are physically connected when they participate in the same set occurrence. This explicit representation of set types has been asserted to be an advantage for the network model. A counter argument is that the network model uses two modeling concepts, the record type and the set type, whereas the relational model only uses one simple concept, the relation.

Data Manipulation Language

The DBTG DML navigational and retrieval operations are carried out on single records, in contrast to the relational model's operations which are carried out on entire relations. These DBTG operations must be embedded in a host programming language such as COBOL. Since the record-oriented manipulation operations are based on traditional file processing operations, the programmer needs to be intimately familiar with the currency indicators and their meanings to avoid error.

It would appear that the relational model may have the advantage when it comes to the DML. This is partially confirmed by the addition of relational user interfaces to IDMS, making it IDMS/R. The relational language systems provide high-level capabilities for operating on sets of tuples. Commercial implementations of these systems have incorporated complementary capability for grouping, sorting, and arithmetic. Additionally, the relational DMLs can be used directly or can be embedded in a host language.

Integrity Constraints

The DBTG network model provides a useful set of integrity constraints. It is particularly strong in its capability for protecting the integrity of sets. The set retention features allow the designer to determine how owner records may behave with respect to member records, and vice versa. MANDATORY and FIXED retention requires that every record must have an owner, for example, whereas OPTIONAL does not.

Semantic constraint capability, such as limiting the hours worked as recorded in an employee record to 60 or less, can only be implemented in the application program that operates on those records.

Implementation

The DBTG network model is especially well suited for database systems that are characterized by

▼ large size.
▼ well-defined repetitive queries.
▼ well-defined transactions.
▼ well-defined applications.

If these factors are all present, then the users and designers of the database system can focus efforts on ensuring that applications are programmed in the most efficient manner. The negative side is that unanticipated future applications may not work well, and may even require difficult database system reorganization.

Summary

In this chapter, we have presented the fundamentals of the DBTG network data model. This model has a rich history and is the basis for several successful DBMSs. We observed that a network forms a graph structure, which is a natural way of representing the relationships among data. We outlined the history of the DBTG recommendations for network standards, and we used those recommendations as a basis for the remainder of the chapter.

We found that the network data model utilizes two basic constructs: the record type and the set type. Records are defined as collections of logically related data items. Sets are defined by owner and member records that have a logical linkage. A data structure diagram for the network data model consists of boxes, which represent record types, and arrows, which establish relationships between record types. These named relationships form set types.

The way in which conceptual data models are mapped to network data structures was demonstrated, and rules were provided to guide that process. Methods of mapping one–one, one–many, and many–many relationships were demonstrated. It was also shown how to convert n-ary relationships to an equivalent set of binary relationships by creating a link record.

The DBTG languages were then presented. The DBTG DDL provides a means of creating and defining the database. Concepts used to define the database included the schema, which defines the logical structure of the network in terms of its record types and set types.

Once the schema is defined, external views of that structure needed by database users and applications are defined using a subschema for each such view. The subschema allows selection of only those data needed from the schema. Data items can be renamed or reordered to suit the needs of the application.

The DBTG DML was then discussed, and a number of examples were given. We saw that the DBTG DML is single-record oriented and provides a number of features to ensure maintenance of database integrity. DML commands can be classified as navigational commands, retrieval commands, and update commands. Update commands are used for updating records, as well as for updating set occurrences.

The most widely used commercial implementation of the DBTG network data model, IDMS/R was briefly outlined. While the R indicates that some relational user interface features have been added, IDMS/R basically follows the design recommendations of DBTG.

This was followed by a summary evaluation of the DBTG model. It is generally accepted that for predetermined transactions on the database, programs can be devised that make the network model very efficient. Its disadvantages seem to center on weak facilities for adapting to changed requirements and ad hoc queries.

Review Questions

1. Define each of the following terms in your own words:
   a. CODASYL
   b. DBTG
   c. IDS
   d. network data model

e. DML

f. logical record

g. physical link

h. DDL

i. title division

j. mapping division

k. structure division

l. record occurrence

m. subschema record section

n. set occurrence

o. owner record type

p. member record type

q. subschema set section

r. user working area

s. currency indicator

t. status flag

u. retrieval commands

v. navigational commands

2. Briefly define what function is performed by each of the following DBTG DML commands:

a. FIND

b. GET

c. STORE

d. ERASE

3. Briefly discuss the three-level architecture of the DBTG network model. Focus on the functions of each of the three levels and how they relate to one another.

4. How is the DBTG definition different from the mathematical definition of a set as a collection of objects?

5. Using an example, show how the use of a link record allows a complex network to be transformed into a simple network.

6. What would happen if an *n*-ary relationship ($n > 2$) were not transformed into equivalent binary relationships in the network data structure?

7. Compare the ways in which the relational data model and the DBTG model represent relationships.

8. How do relational data manipulation languages differ from the DBTG DML?

9. Suppose your boss asked you to explain the relative advantages and disadvantages of relational database systems versus the DBTG network model. What would you say?

Problems and Exercises

1. Match the following terms with their definitions:

___*schema*   a. A name given to the relationship between an owner record type and a member record type

__*subschema*

__*record type*

__*set type*

__*set retention class*
__*complex network*

__*simple network*

__*link record type*

b. The user's view of the logical data structure of a database

c. In DBTG, determines when a member record can be removed from a set

d. The logical structure of all data and relationships in the database

e. The name given to records of the same type

f. Occurs when there is at least one many–many relationship

g. A dummy record created in order to allow implementation on a DBTG system

h. A data structure in which all binary relationships are one–many

2. State any rules from the chapter that would be used in transforming the conceptual model of Figure 15.1E to a DBTG data structure. Show the resulting data structure.

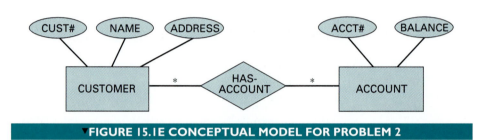

▼FIGURE 15.1E CONCEPTUAL MODEL FOR PROBLEM 2

3. Complete the requirements of Problem 2 using the conceptual data model of Figure 15.2E.

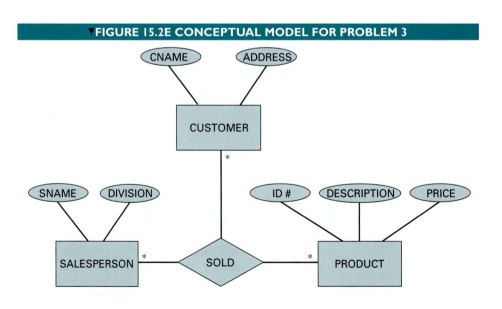

▼FIGURE 15.2E CONCEPTUAL MODEL FOR PROBLEM 3

4. Map the conceptual data model of Figure 15.3E to a DBTG data structure. From that structure create a DBTG schema. State any necessary assumptions.

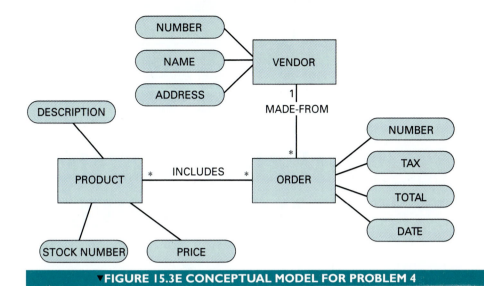

▼**FIGURE 15.3E CONCEPTUAL MODEL FOR PROBLEM 4**

5. For the schema of Problem 4, create a subschema for an application that views only the VENDOR and ORDER record types.

6. For the DBTG data structure created in Problem 4, write DML statements to do the following:
- **a.** Retrieve the record for Vendor 13.
- **b.** Retrieve all orders in the amount of $100.00.
- **c.** Delete order #256.
- **d.** Change the address for Vendor 13 to '912 Adams Street, Gainesville, FL'.
- **e.** Add Vendor 15 to the database. Vendor 15's name is 'Mike Otteson', and the address is 'Buster Building, Suite 95, Toronto, Canada'.
- **f.** Add Invoice #285 to the database; connect it to Vendor 15.
- **g.** Delete Invoice #842 from the database.

Projects and Professional Issues

1. Research the database literature to find discussions of the various database models. Based upon your findings, develop a report to help Rita Minkowski resolve the debate she heard at the ACM meeting.

2. Find more detailed descriptions of IDMS/R. What relational features have been added? Can you conclude that these features overcome any advantages that may have been claimed for relational database systems? Explain.

3. If you were charged with developing recommendations for improving the DBTG network model, what suggestions would you make? Be specific.

4. Can you develop any improvements in the method of transforming a conceptual data model to a DBTG data structure? What are they, and how do they improve the transformation method?

C H A P T E R

THE HIERARCHICAL DATA MODEL

William (Bill) Orange, the chairperson of the local chapter of the Association for Computing Machinery (ACM), was on the phone with Rita Minkowski. "Rita, our discussion of database systems at the last meeting was so well received that we've decided to devote the next three meetings to surveys of the hierarchical, network, and relational models. Do you think you could cover the hierarchical model in the next meeting?"

"Certainly, Bill. What would you like me to discuss?"

"The philosophy of the model and some of the more general aspects of database implementation. Perhaps you could indicate some of the reasons it might be chosen over the competing models. I believe you have had quite a bit of experience with IBM's IMS database system, and that alone should qualify you to describe the hierarchical model."

"Well, I have spent a lot of time with IMS, and I would be glad to represent that point of view at the next meeting. Thanks for the invitation."

I In this chapter, we present the fundamentals of the hierarchical data model. After reading this chapter, you should be able to:

▼ Describe the basic data structure from which the hierarchical data model is constructed.

▼ Explain the terminology used in describing the hierarchical data model.

▼ Use the fundamental methods of mapping from a conceptual data model to the hierarchical data model.

▼ Describe the terminology and structure of the IMS implementation.

▼ Explain how the IMS data description language is used to implement hierarchical data structures.

▼ Discuss how the IMS data manipulation language operates to retrieve and update data.

▼ Discuss the practical advantages and disadvantages of the hierarchical model.

IMS IBM's Information Management System; leading DBMS based on the hierarchical data model.

TDMS System Development Corporation's Time-Shared Data Management System; DBMS based on the hierarchical data model.

MARK IV Control Data Corporation's Multi-Access Retrieval System; DBMS based on the hierarchical data model.

System-2000 SAS Institute's hierarchical DBMS; DBMS based on the hierarchical data model.

▼ Introduction

Unlike the relational data model, which is firmly grounded in mathematics, and the network data model, which evolved from an effort to establish detailed standards, the hierarchical data model has developed from practice. There is no original document that delineates the hierarchical model, as there is with the other two models. Since the hierarchical data model has no standard, its study requires an examination of DBMSs used in practice. Fortunately for the student, the hierarchical database implementations are dominated by one system, **IMS** (IBM's Information Management System). In fact, IMS is currently the most widely used of all DBMSs. Expositions on the hierarchical model invariably incorporate the vocabulary and conventions of IMS. We will do the same.

Other hierarchical systems are in use, however, including **TDMS** (System Development Corporation's Time-Shared Data Management System), **MARK IV** (Control Data Corporation's Multi-Access Retrieval System), and **System-2000** (SAS Institute).

Both hierarchical and network DBMSs were developed in the early 1960s. IMS was developed in a joint effort between IBM and North American Aviation (later to become Rockwell) to develop a DBMS to support the Apollo moon project—one of the largest engineering projects undertaken to that time. A key factor in the development of IMS was the need to manage the millions of parts that were related to one another in a hierarchical manner. That is, smaller parts were used to construct larger subassemblies, which became the components of larger modules, and so forth.

Although the relational system, DB2, is rapidly gaining on IMS in terms of number of installations, for large planned transaction systems requiring rapid response, IMS remains a competitive system. A complementary reason for the durability of IMS is that many data structures are inherently hierarchical. For example, a company may contain departments (one level), departments have employees (a second level), and employees have skills (a third level). While this data structure could be implemented in the network model, that model's more robust representational capability may provide more system complexity (overhead) than needed. In fact, one reason that developers of IMS did not adopt the IDS approach used at General Electric (see Chapter 9) was that the IDS approach would require more disk storage than IMS.

parent The point at the tail of the arrow in a hierarchical data structure.

child The point at the head of the arrow in a hierarchical data structure.

tree A hierarchical data structure; that is, a network structure where a child segment type is linked to just one parent segment type.

hierarchical data model Data model in which all relationships are structured as trees.

segment type Corresponds to an object in the object-oriented data model; also called a segment.

parent-child relationship type (PCR type) Logical relationship between a parent segment type and a child segment type.

▼ Basic Concepts and Definitions

On the conceptual level, the hierarchical data model is simply a special case of the network data model. As described in the previous chapter, a network is a directed graph constructed of points connected by arrows. Applying this concept to data models, the points are data record types, and the arrows represent one–one or one–many relationships. An arrow in a network has a point at each end. The point at the tail of the arrow is called the **parent** in hierarchical model terminology, and the point at the head of the arrow is called the **child.** The principal difference between the network and hierarchical models is that the network model allows a child record type to have more than one parent record type, whereas the hierarchical model does not. The kind of network structure permitted by the hierarchical model is called a **tree**. Relationships in the **hierarchical data model** are organized as collections of trees rather than as arbitrary graphs.

While the vocabulary of the hierarchical model varies somewhat from that of the network data model, there are many natural architectural similarities. As with the network model, there are two basic concepts associated with the hierarchical data structure: **segment types,** or simply segments, and **parent-child relationship types** (PCR types). Segment is used analogously to the network record type. A PCR type is similar to the network set type, except that a segment type can only participate as a child in one PCR type.

As an example, consider Figure 16.1. Figure 16.1(a) shows a conceptual data model defining one–many relationships between DEPARTMENT and EMPLOYEE and between RETIREMENT PLAN and EMPLOYEE. The DEPARTMENT, EMPLOYEE, and RETIREMENT PLAN object sets each have their own attributes, although for the present example the attribute names are omitted. In addition, the relationships' cardinalities indicate that each department occurrence has many employees, while each employee is assigned to only one department. Also, each employee has only

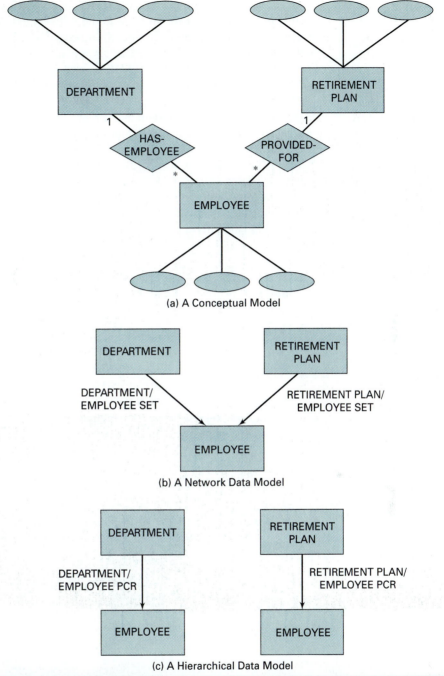

(a) A Conceptual Model

(b) A Network Data Model

(c) A Hierarchical Data Model

▼FIGURE 16.1 A CONCEPTUAL DATA MODEL AND ITS NETWORK AND HIERARCHICAL REPRESENTATIONS

one retirement plan, but a given retirement plan is provided for many employees. The representation of these object sets and relationships in the network and hierarchical models is shown in Figures 16.1(b) and 16.1(c).

Figure 16.1(b) illustrates a data structure where (in network terminology) the EMPLOYEE record type is a member of the DEPARTMENT/EMPLOYEE set, as well as a member of the RETIREMENT PLAN/EMPLOYEE set. While this data structure is directly implementable in the network model, it cannot be directly implemented in the hierarchical model. In order to be implemented in the hierarchical model, it must be modified as shown in Figure 16.1(c). Note that in Figure 16.1(c) the DEPARTMENT/EMPLOYEE and the RETIREMENT PLAN/EMPLOYEE sets of Figure 16.1(b) have been transformed to their hierarchical analogs: the DEPARMENT/EMPLOYEE and the RETIREMENT PLAN/EMPLOYEE PCR types. Also, the EMPLOYEE segment has been shown twice, since in the hierarchical model no segment can participate as a child in more than one PCR type. The EMPLOYEE segment can actually only participate in *one* of these PCRs. EMPLOYEE in the other PCR will consist of pointers to the original EMPLOYEE segment, as we will explain later.

The reason for the transformation of Figure 16.1(c) is that the hierarchical model uses the tree as its fundamental structure. A tree data structure is comprised of a hierarchy of segments conforming to the following conventions:

root segment In a tree, the segment type that does not participate as a child segment in any PCR.

1. There is a single segment, called the root, at the highest level. The **root segment** does not participate as the child segment in any PCR type.

2. With the exception of the root segment, every segment participates as a child segment in exactly one PCR type.

3. A segment can participate as a parent segment in more than one PCR type (for example, EMPLOYEE in Figure 16.2).

4. A parent segment occurrence may have any number of child segment occurrences (children), but each child segment may have only a single parent segment. This establishes a one–many constraint on the relationship between parent and child segments in a tree.

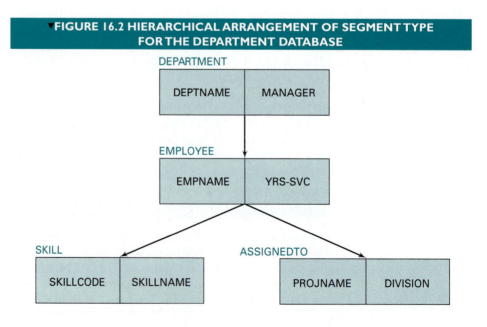

▼**FIGURE 16.2 HIERARCHICAL ARRANGEMENT OF SEGMENT TYPE FOR THE DEPARTMENT DATABASE**

5. A segment that has no children is termed a **leaf segment.**

6. For any segment type *A,* there is a single path in the tree from the root to *A.* The records along this path are called the **ancestors** of *A. A* is a **dependent segment** of all segments on that path, including the root.

7. A segment *A* may itself be the root of a subtree.

Figure 16.2 is an example of a three-level tree, in this case representing DEPARTMENT, EMPLOYEE, SKILL, and ASSIGNEDTO segment types and their relationships. A hierarchical database schema is a collection of rooted trees of this type. Each such tree is referred to as a **database tree**. The tree of Figure 16.2 has DEPARTMENT as its root segment and has two subtree types, rooted in the EMPLOYEE segment. One of these subtree types goes from EMPLOYEE to SKILL and the other from EMPLOYEE to ASSIGNEDTO. EMPLOYEE, in turn, has two subtree types, rooted in the SKILL and ASSIGNEDTO segment types. These last two subtree types are, in a sense, trivial, since they consist merely of SKILL alone and ASSIGNEDTO alone. An occurrence of a root and all its dependent segments is termed a **database record**. A database record for the model of Figure 16.2 would consist of an occurrence of a DEPARTMENT segment, together with all its associated EMPLOYEE segments, together with all their associated SKILL and ASSIGNEDTO segments.

Note that DEPARTMENT is the parent segment type of the DEPARTMENT-EMPLOYEE PCR type. All remaining segment types (that is, EMPLOYEE, SKILL, and ASSIGNEDTO) are *dependent* segment types. EMPLOYEE is the child segment type of the DEPARTMENT-EMPLOYEE PCR type. EMPLOYEE also functions as a parent segment type of the EMPLOYEE-SKILL PCR type, as well as a parent segment of the EMPLOYEE-ASSIGNEDTO PCR type. As with the network model, the arrowheads indicate the "many" side of the one–many relationships.

Figure 16.2 also gives us an opportunity to compare the hierarchical data model with the relational data model. Relationships that in a relational model would be represented by foreign keys are represented in the hierarchical data model by parent-child links. For instance, the link between DEPARTMENT and EMPLOYEE might be accomplished in the relational model by placing a DEPTNAME attribute in the EMPLOYEE record. In the hierarchical data model of Figure 16.2, this relationship is represented by the DEPARTMENT-EMPLOYEE link, which is implemented in hierarchical databases by placing a physical disk address (or *pointer*) in the DEPARTMENT segment.

We next turn to a consideration of occurrences of database trees. Figure 16.3 shows a sample segment occurrence for the model of Figure 16.2. For each database tree occurrence, there is by definition exactly one occurrence of DEPARTMENT. That is, each department will be the root of a distinct database tree occurrence. In this example, the Marketing Department is in a root segment that has two employee segments. Each employee segment owns one or more SKILL segments, and one or more ASSIGNEDTO segments. This database tree occurrence then includes the DEPARTMENT segment for Marketing as well as all its associated EMPLOYEE, SKILL, and ASSIGNEDTO segments.

We use Figure 16.3 to add a new definition to our vocabulary. Occurrences of the same segment type having the same parent are termed *twins.* For the Marketing Department segment, employees Bond and Jones are **twin segment** occurrences

▼Hierarchical Model's Relationship to Conceptual Modeling Semantics

Transforming a conceptual model to a hierarchical data structure is very similar to mapping to the network model but with some important variations due to the tree structure requirement of the hierarchical model. We examine various conceptual data modeling structures and show how they can be transformed into structures of the hierarchical model.

Transforming One–Many Relationships

Examine the conceptual model of Figure 16.6(a). The mapping of this model to a corresponding hierarchical data structure is shown in Figure 16.6(b). The example suggests that the mapping is identical to that applied to the network model. Each object set with its attributes becomes a logical segment. Each relationship becomes a binary link, and relationships are restricted to being one–many.

We remind the reader that in the network model, however, the employee record type could belong to more than one owner record, as suggested by the conceptual data model of Figure 16.7(a). In a network model version of this model, the EMPLOYEE record type would be owned by two record types: DEPARTMENT and RETIREMENT-PLAN. In the hierarchical model, this is not allowed. The corresponding data structure would require two trees, as suggested in Figure 16.7(b). Note that this introduces redundancy into the model since each EMPLOYEE **segment occurrence** is recorded twice.

segment occurrence
IMS terminology for record occurrence.

This redundancy can be limited, however. The first occurrence of a segment (in this case, EMPLOYEE) would be stored in the usual way. Subsequent occurrences would not store the actual segment but would store a pointer in the form of a physical disk address giving the location of the stored segment. Thus, there is no data redundancy, but there is additional storage space required for the pointer.

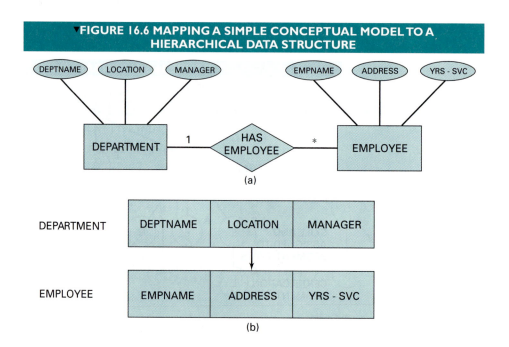

▼FIGURE 16.6 MAPPING A SIMPLE CONCEPTUAL MODEL TO A HIERARCHICAL DATA STRUCTURE

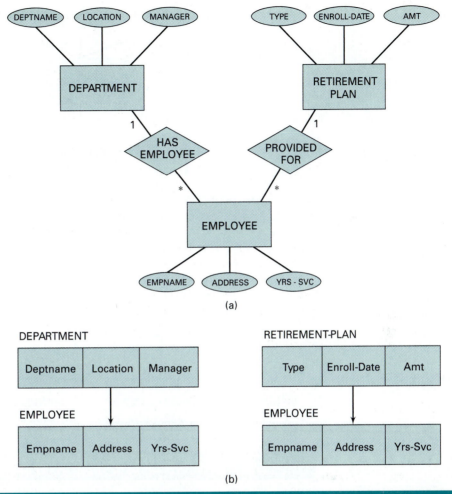

(a)

(b)

▼**FIGURE 16.7 MAPPING A CONCEPTUAL MODEL WITH TWO PCRs**

Our first rules for mapping follow.

Rule 1. For each object set O in a conceptual model, create a segment type S in the hierarchical model. All attributes of O are represented as fields of S.

Rule 2. For one–many relationships between two object sets, create corresponding tree structure diagrams, making each object set a segment and making the one–many relationship a parent-child relationship. The segment on the "many" side of the relationship becomes the child segment, and the segment on the "one" side of the relationship becomes the parent.

Transforming Many–Many Relationships

Rules 1 and 2 cover a large number of mapping requirements. We may, however, generate object-oriented models requiring the mapping of many–many binary relationships. Recall that we had similar situations in mapping from the object-oriented model to the network model.

Figure 16.8(a) illustrates an object-oriented model fragment of a manufacturer-product relationship. This relationship is many–many, since a given product may be supplied by many manufacturers, and a given manufacturer supplies a number of

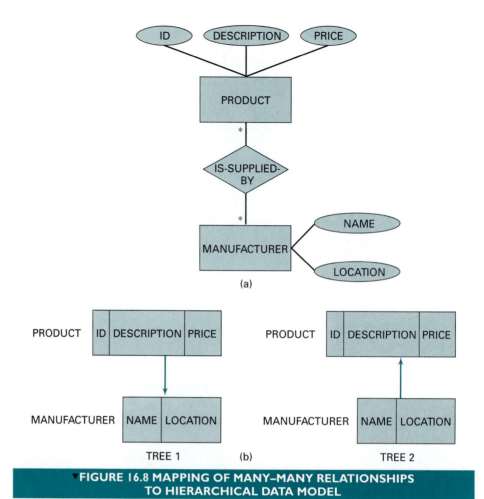

(a)

TREE 1   (b)   TREE 2

▼FIGURE 16.8 MAPPING OF MANY–MANY RELATIONSHIPS TO HIERARCHICAL DATA MODEL

products. The object-oriented fragment is mapped to the hierarchical data structure as shown in Figure 16.8(b). We have created two trees, one having PRODUCT as the root, and the other having MANUFACTURER as its root. This provides the desired one–many relationships in each tree. The rule we have followed is this:

> *Rule 3.*   For object sets, O_1 and O_2, that have a many–many binary relationship, and from which segments S_1 and S_2 have been defined, construct two different one–many PCRs: S_1 to S_2, and S_2 to S_1. In one of the PCRs, the actual data segments for both segment types will be replaced by pointers.

A somewhat more complex situation arises when the object-oriented relationship carries an attribute as shown in Figure 16.9. The attribute QUANTITY has been added to the aggregate of the IS-SUPPLIED-BY relationship to indicate the maximum quantity of a product that can be supplied in one shipment from a manufacturer. In cases like this, an additional segment type is created in mapping to the hierarchical data structure.

This is shown in Figure 16.10. Both of the object sets involved in the binary many–many relationship will function as the parent segment type in separate trees. A new segment type QUANTITY is inserted between the PRODUCT and MANUFACTURER segments to indicate the maximum quantity a particular manufacturer will ship of a particular product. In one tree, one–many links are established from

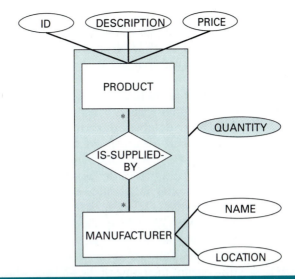

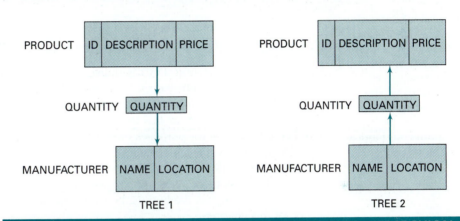

TREE 1   TREE 2

▼FIGURE 16.10 MAPPING A MANY–MANY RELATIONSHIP TO HIERARCHICAL DATA MODEL, WHERE THE RELATIONSHIP CARRIES AN ATTRIBUTE

PRODUCT to QUANTITY and from QUANTITY to MANUFACTURER. The process is reversed in the other tree. We have two parent-child relationships in each three-level tree structure. This procedure is captured in the following rule:

Rule 4.   If a binary many–many relationship has attribute data, create a new intersection segment *I*, which contains that data. Each of the segment types created from the object sets will function as the root of a distinct tree. Insert the new segment between the two object set segment types and establish the corresponding one–many relationships between parent-child segments. If any of those parent-child relationships are exactly one–one, the attribute data might be combined into the segments created from the object sets.

▼The IMS Architecture

Since the hierarchical data model has no standard, we continue to use its most widely used implementation, IMS, as a basis for exposition. In this way, IMS is presented as a baseline hierarchical model, if not a true standard.

IMS records must be hierarchically ordered as suggested by Figure 16.1(c). Here we see a pair of two-level trees. In Figure 16.2, we see a three-level tree. IMS allows at most 15 levels in a tree, although it is rare for an implementation to contain more than four levels in a tree. IMS also limits the number of segment types to 225.

DL/1 Data Language 1, the IMS data manipulation language.

database description (DBD) The way in which data are physically stored in IMS (internal database structure).

DL/1 (Data Language 1) is the component of IMS that provides for database storage and retrieval. A rough counterpart to the schema used in the network data model is the **database description (DBD)**. This provides the framework for the internal database structure. It establishes the way in which data are stored for use by IMS. The DBD defines the format, length, and location of each data item to be accessed by DL/I. It also defines the position of each segment in the tree structure.

external database The user view of the data in IMS.

program specification block (PSB) Specifies the names of each segment an application program will access; corresponds to a user view or subschema.

program communication block (PCB) A component of the PSB.

The **external database**, or user view, which was expressed by the subschema in the network model, is described in IMS by the **program specification block (PSB)**. The PSB specifies the names of each segment that a program will access. The PSB, in turn, is subdivided into **program communication blocks (PCBs)** that define the view of the database required for each user application. The PCB contains the name of the DBD of which it is a subset.

Examples of the DBD and the PCB will illustrate the fundamental IMS architecture.

Defining the Physical Database—The DBD

As observed previously, the DBD is similar to the network schema, and the PSB is similar to the network subschema. We first clarify the DBD functions with an example. Figure 16.2 depicts four segment types: DEPARTMENT, EMPLOYEE, SKILL, and ASSIGNEDTO. The DBD for this tree is presented in Figure 16.11. The statements have been numbered for purposes of explanation.

Statement 1 is the DBD statement. This statement identifies the name of the database, in this case NAME = DEPTPERS. The statement also specifies the method of database access to be used, in this case HISAM, which denotes the hierarchical index sequential access method. (IMS access methods will be discussed in a later section of this chapter.)

FIGURE 16.11 DBD FOR MODEL OF FIGURE 16.2

```
 1 DBD     NAME = DEPTPERS, ACCESS = HISAM

 2 SEGM    NAME = DEPARTMENT, PARENT = 0, BYTES = 20
 3 FIELD   NAME = (DEPTNAME,SEQ,U), BYTES = 10, START = 1, TYPE = C
 4 FIELD   NAME = MANAGER, BYTES = 10, START = 11, TYPE = C

 5 SEGM    NAME = EMPLOYEE, PARENT = DEPARTMENT, BYTES = 22
 6 FIELD   NAME = (EMPNAME,SEQ), BYTES = 20, START = 1, TYPE = C
 7 FIELD   NAME = YRS-SVC, BYTES = 2, START = 21, TYPE = P

 8 SEGM    NAME = SKILL, PARENT = EMPLOYEE, BYTES = 17
 9 FIELD   NAME = (SKILLCODE,SEQ), BYTES = 2, START = 1, TYPE = P
10 FIELD   NAME = SKILLNAME, BYTES = 15, START = 3, TYPE = C

11 SEGM    NAME = ASSIGNEDTO, PARENT = EMPLOYEE, BYTES = 4
12 FIELD   NAME = (PROJNO,SEQ), BYTES = 2, START = 1, TYPE = P
13 FIELD   NAME = DIVISION, BYTES = 2, START = 5, TYPE = C

14 DBGEN
```

SEGM An IMS statement that defines the fields to be included in a segment to be used by a program.

The DBD statement is followed by a series of segment (SEGM) statements. The **SEGM** statement defines the group of data items (fields in IMS) comprising that segment and how they are ordered. The first segment in Figure 16.11 is identified in statement 2. The segment is named DEPARTMENT. The assignment PARENT = 0 means that DEPARTMENT is a root segment, "0" meaning that it has no parent segment. BYTES = 20 establishes the length of the segment. In statement 3, DEPT-NAME is the first field in the DEPARTMENT segment. It is identified as a sequence field for the DEPARTMENT segment by the NAME = (DEPTNAME, SEQ, U) assignment. That is, as new occurrences of segments are stored, they will be arranged in sequence according to the value of this field in the segment. The "U" means that DEPTNAME must be unique—no two segments can have the same DEPTNAME. As can be seen, the remaining specifications establish the starting location of the field in the segment, the length of the field, and the datatype. The common datatypes are *P* (packed decimal) and *C* (character).

We need to describe at least one more segment in order to see how the parent-child relationships are established. Statement 5 begins the definition of the EMPLOYEE segment. After it is given a name, it is assigned a PARENT = DEPART-MENT parameter. This establishes the parent-child relationship between the DE-PARTMENT and EMPLOYEE segments. Segment occurrences will be added in sequence by employee name [NAME = (EMPNAME, SEQ)], but those names need not be unique as with DEPTNAME in the prior segment.

With these two descriptions, the remainder of Figure 16.11 is easily interpreted.

Defining the Logical Database—The PSB

Recall that the PSB is something like the network subschema, in that it specifies the view of the data to be used by an application program. The PSB contains one or more program communication blocks (PCBs). The PCB specifies the segments that an application program is allowed to access. Programs cannot access segments not defined in a PCB. Accordingly, the PCB identifies the relevant database and specifies any **sensitive segments** (SENSEG) to be included.

sensitive segment A segment that is accessible to a program; abbreviated SENSEG.

Consider the example shown in Figure 16.12. Suppose that Zeus Corporation has an application that requires just the DEPARTMENT names and EMPLOYEE names from those two segments. Beginning with line 1, TYPE = DB is required for each PCB to be defined. The database from which this PCB is drawn is called DEPTPERS (DBDNAME = DEPTPERS). PROCOPT is used to denote processing options, meaning the operations that the application program may execute on the PCB. These options include

G = GET
I = INSERT
R = REPLACE
D = DELETE
A = ALL

fully concatenated key Means of identifying the location of a segment in the database.

GET specifies read-only access to segments in the PCB. INSERT allows the addition of new segments to the PCB. REPLACE permits segments to be retrieved and modified. DELETE allows segments to be retrieved and deleted. PROCOPT = A, as shown in Figure 16.12, means that all these processing options are allowed for this application. When a segment is used by the program, IMS identifies its location in the database by recording a **fully concatenated key**. The KEYLEN = 18 establishes the longest concatenated key that the program can access. Roughly, this refers to the longest key that would be obtained by adjoining the key fields along any path through the hierarchy.

```
1 PCB      TYPE = DB, DBDNAME = DEPTPERS, PROCOPT = A, KEYLEN = 18
2 SENSEG   NAME = DEPARTMENT, PARENT = 0
3 SENFLD   NAME = DEPTNAME, START = 1
4 SENSEG   NAME = EMPLOYEE, PARENT = DEPARTMENT
5 SENFLD   NAME = EMPNAME, START = 1
```

▼FIGURE 16.12 PCB EXAMPLE

The SENSEG and SENFLD statements (lines 2–5) identify those segments and fields that are accessible to the application. In Figure 16.12, there are two sensitive (accessible to the program) segments: DEPARTMENT and EMPLOYEE. The sensitive fields for the respective segments are denoted by the SENFLD statements, with the same meaning (accessibility) applying. Note that dependent segments must explicitly identify their parent segments. For example, the parent of EMPLOYEE is DEPARTMENT, as indicated by the PARENT = DEPARTMENT clause on line 4. START = 1 means that the field starts in the first byte of the segment.

▼ IMS Access Methods

IMS provides for four access methods: HSAM, HISAM, HDAM, and HIDAM. Recall that this choice is reflected in the DBD by the entry "ACCESS = <choice of access method>". The following subsections summarize the four methods.

HSAM

HSAM IMS access method; very fast for sequential retrieval of segments.

HSAM denotes the *hierarchic sequential access method* of database access. Segments are physically adjacent on the storage media, so HSAM could be implemented on either tape or disk. Segments are ordered according to the preorder traversal scheme that allows the hierarchical data structure to be maintained.

HSAM is practical only for reading the data. That is to say, this structure is not flexible enough to support effective updating of the database. Updating segments requires that a new version of the database be created and stored.

HISAM

HISAM IMS access method; provides capability for both sequential and direct segment retrieval.

HISAM, *hierarchic indexed-sequential access method*, stores segments in hierarchic sequence, as in HSAM, but provides the ability to gain direct access to specific root segments according to an index. Thereafter, dependent segments of the accessed root segment are accessed sequentially, as with HSAM.

HDAM

HDAM IMS access method; provides rapid direct access of segments but no capability for sequential processing.

HDAM stands for *hierarchic direct-access method*. This method does not relate segments by an index or by physical proximity but through pointers (fields containing physical disk addresses). Access to roots is gained through use of a hashing algorithm (see Chapter 10). Examine the tree occurrence of Figure 16.13. The pointers that link segments of an occurrence can be *hierarchical* as shown in Figure 16.14, or *child and twin* as shown in Figure 16.15.

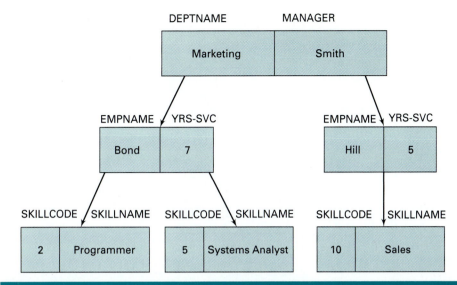

▼FIGURE 16.13 TREE OCCURRENCE EXAMPLE

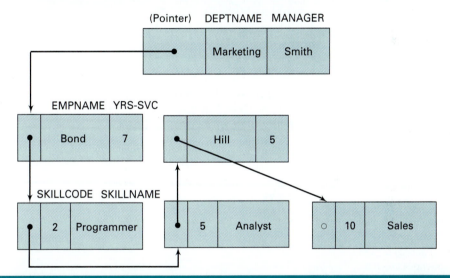

▼FIGURE 16.14 HIERARCHICAL POINTERS IN PREORDER
TRAVERSAL SEQUENCE

When hierarchical pointers are used, each segment points to its successor in preorder traversal sequence ("0" indicates no segment follows). For example, to access the record for employee Hill in Figure 16.14, we would start at the Marketing department record, use its pointer to get the record for employee Bond, then follow that record's pointer to the Programmer skill record, thence to the Analyst skill record, and finally to Hill's record.

When child-and-twin pointers are used, each segment contains a pointer to the next segment on the same level (twin) and a pointer to the next child segment. In Figure 16.15 the leftmost pointer in each segment is the child pointer, and the pointer to its right is the twin pointer. Twin pointers are simpler to implement since every segment contains exactly two pointers.

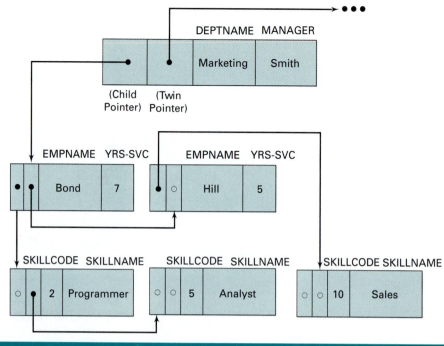

To access Hill's record in Figure 16.15, we start once more at the Marketing department record, follow the child pointer to the first employee record (Bond), and follow that record's *twin* pointer to Hill's record. To access Hill's Sales skill record, we merely follow the child pointer in Hill's record directly to the desired record.

HIDAM

HIDAM IMS access method; provides for direct access of root segments as well as sequential retrieval.

HIDAM, *hierarchic indexed direct-access method*, is basically the same as HDAM but permits indexed access to roots as well as pointer access to dependent segments.

▼ The IMS Data Manipulation Language

In this section we define and illustrate the features of the IMS data manipulation language, DL/1. The programmer accessing and manipulating an IMS database needs to understand these features to properly interact with them.

Program Work Area

segment template Program work area format for a segment.

currency pointer Contains the address of the segment in the tree that was accessed last.

In order for DL/1 (or any application program) to execute operations on an IMS database, the system maintains a program work area that contains the following variables:

▼ **Segment templates** giving the segment layout for each segment type in the database.

▼ **Currency pointers** for each database tree. These contain the address of the segment in the tree that has been most recently accessed.

status flag Field whose value indicates the result of the last database operation (for example, successful or not successful).

▼ **Status flags** that indicate the outcome of the last database operation. For example, a "0" might be assigned if the last operation was successful and another symbol if it was not. Following an operation, the program can refer to the status flag to determine what to do next.

DL/1: An Overview

The data manipulation language for IMS is termed *DL/1*, for Data Language 1. Below, we give examples of the most commonly used commands of *DL/1*:

Command	Meaning
GET UNIQUE (GU)	Retrieve the first segment that satisfies a given condition
GET NEXT (GN)	Retrieve the next segment
GET NEXT WITHIN PARENT (GNP)	Retrieves the next segment, but only within the current parent segment
<hold options> GHU, GHN, GHNP	Lock the database for GU, GN, GNP
INSERT (ISRT)	Add a new segment to the database
REPLACE (REPL)	Modify the value of a segment field
DELETE (DLET)	Delete a segment.

The common syntax for *DL/1* is

Command <WHERE qualification>.

Let's now look at some examples of the use of these commands.

Get Unique (GU)

The GET command is used to select a segment occurrence. GET UNIQUE selects a segment having a particular value into the working area. The segment desired is defined in parentheses by a qualifying condition called a segment search argument (SSA).

Example 1: A Simple Segment Retrieval

```
GU DEPARTMENT (DEPTNAME = 'Marketing')
```

In this example, the SSA is DEPTNAME = 'Marketing'. The GU command will retrieve the first segment that satisfies the SSA. In the next example, note the difference when we wish to retrieve the segment for employee Steve Smith who is assigned to the Marketing Department.

Example 2: Retrieval of a Dependent Segment

```
GU DEPARTMENT (DEPTNAME = 'Marketing')
   EMPLOYEE?  (EMPNAME = 'Steve Smith')
```

Since the EMPLOYEE segment is dependent, a hierarchical path is specified. The GU operator will retrieve only the segment at the bottom of the path. That is, no Marketing segment will be retrieved.

Now, suppose that we didn't know the department to which Steve Smith is assigned. The query could be handled as shown in the next example.

Example 3: Retrieval of Dependent Segment When Parent Occurrence Is Not Known

```
GU DEPARTMENT
   EMPLOYEE (EMPNAME = 'Steve Smith')
```

This query will result in a sequential scan of DEPARTMENT segments until the dependent segment for Steve Smith is found.

Get Next (GN)

If instead of merely retrieving the first occurrence of a segment having a specified value, we wish to retrieve all segments having that value, we may use GU in concert with the GET NEXT (GN) command. For example, suppose that we want to retrieve all the EMPLOYEE segments for the Marketing Department. This would be done in the following way.

Example 4: Retrieval of a Set of Segments

```
GU DEPARTMENT (DEPTNAME = 'Marketing')
   EMPLOYEE
GN EMPLOYEE
```

The GU operator will effect the retrieval of the first EMPLOYEE segment for the Marketing Department. The GN operator will then direct the retrieval of the next employee segment for the Marketing Department. As long as there is a second employee occurrence for the Marketing Department, this query does what we want. However, if there were no remaining employee segments when the GN command was executed, the system would go on to find the next EMPLOYEE segment regardless of the department to which he or she was assigned. This possibility can be prevented by using the GNP command, as we will demonstrate in Example 6, but first we show a simple modification to the query of Example 4 that allows retrieval of all employee segments in the database.

Example 5: Retrieving All Segments of a Particular Type

```
GU DEPARTMENT
   EMPLOYEE
MORE GN EMPLOYEE
   GOTO MORE
```

As long as there is another occurrence of an EMPLOYEE segment, the loop identified by the statement label MORE will be executed.

Get Next Within Parent (GNP)

GNP differs from GN in that IMS only retrieves the segments that are dependent on a single parent occurrence. Turning again to Example 4, that query could be modified to use GNP as in Example 6.

Example 6: Retrieving Segments for Just One Parent

```
GU DEPARTMENT (DEPTNAME = 'Marketing')
   EMPLOYEE
GNP EMPLOYEE
```

In this instance, if there was not another EMPLOYEE segment in the Marketing Department, execution would stop, and the user would have the desired restriction to employees in the Marketing Department.

As another example, suppose that we seek all the SKILLS segments for employee Steve Smith who works in the Marketing Department. The following commands would apply.

Example 7: Retrieving Segments for Just One Parent

```
GU DEPARTMENT (DEPTNAME = 'Marketing')
   EMPLOYEE (EMPNAME = 'Steve Smith')
   SKILLS
NEXT GNP SKILLS
   GOTO NEXT
```

The GU command retrieves the first SKILL segment for Steve Smith. The GNP command then sequentially retrieves the remaining SKILL segments for Steve Smith.

Get Hold

The GET HOLD command may occur in one of three forms: GET HOLD UNIQUE (GHU), GET HOLD NEXT (GHN), and GET HOLD NEXT WITHIN PARENT (GHNP). The programmer uses these commands in the same way as GU, GN, and GNP, except that the GET HOLD commands must be used to inform the DBMS that a change or deletion is to be performed on the retrieved segment. That is, GHU, GHN, and GHNP are used in conjunction with REPLACE or DELETE commands.

Replace (REPL)

To modify an existing segment, it must be transferred into the work area, where the desired changes to the segment fields are made. Using *DL/1* the target segment must first be retrieved using one of the GET HOLD commands. The segment is then modified, and the REPL command writes the updated segment. The following example illustrates how we would proceed if we desired to change the salary of Irving Schatz, who is an employee in the Marketing Department, from $20,000 to $25,000.

Example 8: Modifying Segment Field Values

```
GHU DEPARTMENT (DEPTNAME = 'Marketing')
   EMPLOYEE (EMPNAME = 'Irving Schatz')
   MOVE 25000 TO SALARY
   REPL
```

Delete (DLET)

A segment is deleted by first targeting the segment using a GET HOLD and then using the DLET statement. Suppose that Irving Schatz leaves the firm. Example 9 would apply.

Example 9: Deleting a Segment   The commands

```
GHU DEPARTMENT (DEPTNAME = 'Marketing')
  EMPLOYEE (EMPNAME = 'Irving Schatz')
DLET
```

will delete the EMPLOYEE segment for Irving Schatz from the database. When a segment is deleted, any dependent segments are also deleted, so Schatz's SKILL and ASSIGNEDTO segments would also be deleted.

Insert (INSRT)

New segments are added to the database using the INSRT command. The associated field values must first be moved into a work area. These are then linked to the relevant parent-segment names. Thus, if the segment to be inserted is a dependent segment, the parent segment must already exist.

Bob Lee has just completed the Engineering Drafting curriculum at a local junior college. We wish to add a new SKILL segment for Bob Lee to the database.

Example 10: Adding a Segment

```
MOVE 598 TO SKILLCODE
MOVE 'ENGINEERING DRAFTSMAN' TO SKILLNAME
MOVE 0 TO YRS-EXPERIENCE
ISRT DEPARTMENT (DEPTNAME = 'Engineering')
EMPLOYEE (EMPNAME = 'Bob Lee')
SKILL
```

This segment will be inserted as the last skill segment under Bob Lee's name.

▼ Hierarchical Data Model Evaluation

In this section, we examine the strengths and weaknesses of the hierarchical data model. We look at data representation and data manipulation.

Data Representation

There are three features that define the hierarchical data structure: trees, segments, and fields of segments. While any object-oriented model can be transformed to a hierarchical data structure, the requirement that all database records be trees may result in segment duplication. Any situation whose natural mapping results in a segment being a child segment of two distinct parent segments requires that those parent segments occur in separate trees.

While such duplication eliminates certain implementation difficulties, it has these negative results:

1. Storage space is used inefficiently since the segment is repeated.
2. The possibility of inconsistent data is created. If the data are changed in one segment copy but not the other, the database is inconsistent.

This problem has been dealt with by the use of *virtual segments* and pointers. A virtual segment contains no data but has a pointer to a physical data segment where data are stored. When a segment is required to be replicated in two or more database trees, the actual data are stored in just one of the trees. All other instances of that data segment will contain a pointer to the location where the actual data are stored. Refer to Figure 16.16. Notice that the pointer shown by the broken line addresses the root of the tree containing the actual data in a dependent segment.

A major limitation of the hierarchical model is that there are many applications for which a tree is not the natural data structure. We have seen this, for example, in the manipulations required to convert a situation where a child segment naturally belongs to two parents into two tree structures. These types of occurrences can generate many trees and an associated inefficiency in the use of storage space.

For applications that are inherently hierarchical in nature and for which the query transactions are stable, the hierarchical model may be quite satisfactory. The fact that there are about 7,000 IMS installations tends to support this conclusion, although some are switching to relational database systems.

Data Manipulation Language

The language interface provided for the hierarchical model generally differs with the vendor. This means that programmers need to be aware of which relationships must be predefined to the system and which do not. This programmer reliance is not entirely satisfactory, since the programmer may not be knowledgeable about all of the integrated requirements that have been built into the system. Additionally, if the hierarchical database is reorganized, it may have a negative effect on the performance of existing production programs, since the structure that supports application *A* may not be the best structure to support application *B*.

On the positive side, since IMS dominates the hierarchical implementations, a programmer who has worked with IMS may be quite familiar with the internal workings of the *DL/1* language. Moreover, for stable database use, the concern about reorganization may be minor.

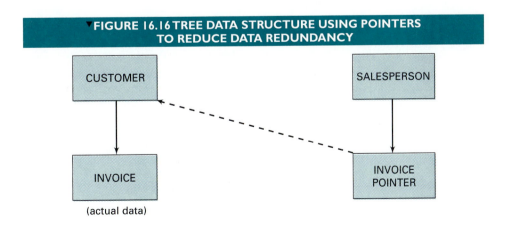

▼FIGURE 16.16 TREE DATA STRUCTURE USING POINTERS TO REDUCE DATA REDUNDANCY

Summary

The nomenclature of the hierarchical model can be summarized in the following way:

1. A hierarchical data structure is constructed from a group of segments.

2. Each hierarchical data structure must take the form of a tree. A tree is characterized by one or more parent-child relationships, where each such relationship is one–many. Every tree will have one segment that functions only as a parent segment. This segment is called the root.

3. All parent-child relationships in a tree extend from the root downward.

4. Any segment in a tree, excepting the root segment, is a child segment of some parent segment. If a path of parent-child relationships is traced from a higher-level segment, *H,* to a lower-level segment, *S,* all segments on that path, including *S,* are dependent (also descendant) segments of *H.*

5. No segment may appear on more than one path from the root segment. If the natural model results in more than one path, a separate tree must be created for each additional path.

The hierarchical data model continues to play an important role in practical database implementations. It is especially prevalent in large data processing centers that are supported by IBM mainframe computers.

A hierarchical database is constructed of collections of segments that are connected to one another by pointers. Each segment is a collection of fields, each of which contains only one data value. A pointer establishes the necessary logical links between two segments. In this sense, the hierarchical model is very similar to the network model where data and relationships are represented by record types and pointers.

The hierarchical model differs in that the segments are organized as collections of trees (only one parent segment allowed) rather than arbitrary graphs (where more than one parent record type is allowed).

Some limitations of the hierarchical data model are

1. The logical and physical characteristics of the model are not clearly separated.

2. Manipulations are required in order to represent nonhierarchical data relationships.

3. Ad hoc query requirements may require reorganizing the database.

From the standpoint of efficiently processing a database, the hierarchical data model is competitive. However, as business leaders look increasingly at using information as a strategic tool, the hierarchical data model is likely to fall short of providing the necessary capability.

Review Questions

(Questions marked with an asterisk (*) are optional.)

1. Define each of the following terms in your own words:
   a. IMS
   b. TDMS

  c. MARK IV
  d. System-2000
  e. hierarchical data model
  f. tree
  g. segment occurrence
  h. ancestor
  i. database record
  j. twin segments
  k. PCR type
  l. hierarchical occurrence tree
  m. preorder traversal
  n. HSAM
  o. HISAM
  p. HDAM
  q. HIDAM
  r. *DL/1*
  s. record template
  t. currency pointer
  u. status flag

 2. Define the function that is performed by each of the following DL/1 commands

GU

GN

GNP

GHU

GHN

GHNP

ISRT

REPL

DLET

 3. Briefly discuss the DBD, its structure and function.

 4. Describe the composition and function of the PSB.

 5. What is the purpose of creating an intersection record in mapping object-oriented models to hierarchical networks?

 6. In IMS, how many subtrees can there be in a tree?

* **7.** Compare the data representation methods of the relational data model, the network model, and the hierarchical data model.

* **8.** Do you think *DL/1* is simpler than the DBTG DML? Support your answer.

 9. What advantages does IMS offer as compared to the DBTG model and the relational model?

Problems and Exercises

1. Match the following terms with their definitions:

___*segment type*

___*parent-child relationship*

___*DBD*

___*PSB*

___*PCB*

___*sensitive segment*

___*root segment*

___*leaf segment*

a. The way in which data are physically stored in IMS

b. A component of the PSB

c. A collection of PCBs

d. A segment that can be accessed by an application program

e. A segment type that does not participate as a child segment in any PCR

f. A segment type that has no child segment types

g. Corresponds to an object in the object-oriented model

h. Logical relationship between a parent segment type and a child segment type

2. State any rules from the chapter that would be used in transforming the object-oriented diagram of Figure 16.1E to a hierarchical data structure. Show the resulting transformation.

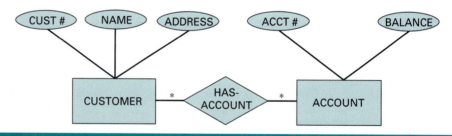

▾FIGURE 16.1E CONCEPTUAL MODEL FOR PROBLEM 2

3. Map the object-oriented diagram of Figure 16.2E to a hierarchical data structure.

▾FIGURE 16.2E CONCEPTUAL MODEL FOR PROBLEM 3

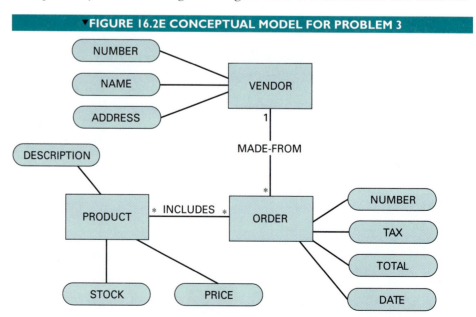

4. Write a DBD to match the data structure of problem 3.

5. Write a PSB to allow the DBD to be accessed by an application that uses only the VENDOR and ORDER segments (see problem 4).

6. For the hierarchical data structure of problem 3, write *DL/1* commands to do the following:
   a. Retrieve the record for Vendor 13.
   b. Retrieve all orders in the amount of $100.00.
   c. Delete order #256.
   d. Change the address for Vendor 13 to '912 Adams Street, Gainesville, FL'.
   e. Add Vendor 15 to the database. Vendor 15's name is 'Mike Otteson', and the address is, Buster Building, Suite 95, Toronto, Canada.
   f. Add Invoice #285 to the database.
   g. Delete Invoice #842.

Projects and Professional Issues

1. Write a short report comparing the advantages and disadvantages of the hierarchical data model. Compare and contrast it to the relational and network models.

2. Find a commercial firm that uses IMS. Are the users satisfied with its capabilities? How is it used? Is the firm planning to change?

3. If you were charged with developing recommendations for improving the hierarchical model, what suggestions would you include?

4. Can you refine and improve any of the suggested rules for transforming object-oriented models to hierarchical data structures? What are they? When do they apply? Give examples.

GLOSSARY

A

aborted transaction Transaction that is canceled before changes are applied to the database.

abstract object set An object set consisting of instances that cannot be printed.

access controls Controls that limit user access to programs and data.

access motion time The time required to position the read/write heads of the disk drive over the desired cylinder.

agent A process which cooperates in completing a transaction.

aggregate A relationship viewed as an object set.

aggregate object set A relationship viewed as an object set.

alias Alternate name given to a relation.

ancestor In a hierarchy, a segment type that is found on the same path but at a higher level in the tree.

application painter A painter used to define the general aspects of an application, such as the application's name and library.

application program A computer program that performs a specific task of practical value in a business situation.

application-specific knowledge Knowledge that is determined by the rules and conventions that apply to a specific problem domain.

area In IDMS/R, location in storage that contains one or more record types.

assignment Relational algebra operation that gives a name to a relation.

atomic transaction A transaction in which all actions associated with the transaction are executed to completion, or none is performed.

atomic value Value that is not a set of values or a repeating group.

attribute domain The set from which an attribute takes its values.

attribute Functional relationship from an object set to another set.

automatic insertion mode In DBTG, when a new member record is created, the DBMS will automatically connect it to the correct set occurrence.

B

backup-and-recovery controls Those controls that provide for restoring the database in case of system failure.

backward chaining A logical chain of rules proceeding from a conclusion to a hypothesis.

base table A table that contains basic or real data.

benchmarking A method of comparing DBMS performance by testing its performance on actual applications.

binary relationship A relationship between two object sets.

Boolean connectives AND, OR, NOT.

Boyce-Codd normal form (BCNF) Every determinant is a key.

BREAK A keyword which causes execution control to exit from an iterative WHILE loop.

buffer manager Software that controls the movement of data between main memory and disk storage.

built-in function Statistical function that operates on a set of rows—SUM, AVG, MAX, MIN, CNT.

C

candidate key Any set of attributes that could be chosen as a key of a relation.

cardinality The maximum number of instances of one object set related to a single instance of the other object set.

Cartesian product Result of pairing each row in one table with *every* row in another table.

CASE statement Used with SWITCH statement to direct processing when a condition is found to be true.

catalog In SQL-92 a named collection of schemas.

centralized database Database physically confined to a single location.

character string literals Literals formed from alphanumeric and "special" characters.

CHECK constraint A general constraint on either a column or a table, stated in a conditional expression.

checkpointing Saving copies of the database at predetermined times during processing; database recovery begins or ends at the most recent checkpoint.

child An "owned" record in a hierarchical relationship.

ciphertext Encrypted plaintext.

class An abstract representation (template) of an object set.

clause In PROLOG, the means by which facts and knowledge are expressed.

client/server platform A local area network consisting of client computers which receive services from a server computer.

clustering Placing in the same block the records of relations that are likely to be joined frequently.

column constraint A constraint that is stated in the definition of a column in a table.

committed transaction A transaction that successfully completes all its actions.

comparison operators =, <>, <, >, <=, >=.

complex network A data structure in which one or more binary relationships are many–many.

complex object Corresponds to an aggregate or higher-level relationship as defined in Chapter 4.

composite key A key consisting of more than one attribute.

conceptual database design Identification of data elements, relationships, and constraints for a database.

conceptual design Creation of conceptual-level schema for database.

conceptual level Database structural level defining logical schema of database.

conceptual object An object representing a type of thing.

conceptual object set An object set whose instances are conceptual objects.

concurrency controls Controls that maintain database integrity when two or more users simultaneously request a database record.

concurrent processing (concurrency) Occurs when two or more transactions concurrently request access to the same database record at about the same time.

condition box In QBE, a box in which a complex query condition can be expressed.

conditional statement A statement that tests for the presence of a condition and directs further processing accordingly.

Conference on Data Systems Languages (CODASYL) An organization composed of representatives from hardware vendors, software vendors, and users; known principally for development of the COBOL language.

conjunctive query A query whose conditions are connected by "and," or an equivalent symbol.

constraint A rule that restricts the values in a database.

CONTINUE A keyword which causes execution control to return to the first statement in a WHILE loop.

control A graphical device by which the user interacts with the system.

control-of-flow language SQL Server's data manipulation language.

correlated subquery A subquery whose result depends on the row being examined by an outer query.

count-data format A data format for tracks that uses no external keys.

count-key format A data format for tracks that uses external keys.

currency indicators Placemarkers for records that have been found.

currency pointer Contains the address of the segment in the tree that was accessed last.

cursor Embedded SQL facility where the result of an SQL query is stored for subsequent processing.

cylinder The same track extending through all surfaces of the disk storage unit.

D

data Isolated facts.

data administrator Manager whose responsibilities are focused on establishing policies and procedures for the organization's information system.

data definition language (DDL) The language used to specify a database schema.

data dictionary That part of the DBMS that defines the structure of user data and how they are to be used.

data fragmentation The partitioning of relations in a DDS.

data integration Combining data for common use.

data integrity Accuracy and consistency of data values in the database.

data integrity Consistency of data in a database.

data integrity The accuracy and consistency of data stored in the database system.

data manipulation language (DML) The language used to store and manipulate data.

data model A conceptual method of structuring data.

data processing system An automated system for processing the data for the records of an organization.

data redundancy Repetition of data in a database.

data security Refers to protecting the database system from unauthorized or malicious use.

data transfer rate The rate at which data can be read from the disk to main memory, or equivalently, the rate at which data are written from main memory to disk.

data view A definition of a restricted portion of the database; also called a view.

data-oriented approach Focuses on the analysis of data used by the functions.

Database Task Group (DBTG) A subgroup of CODASYL given responsibility for developing standards for database management systems.

database A collection of interrelated, shared, and controlled data.

database administration Personnel with responsibility for controlling and protecting the database.

database administrator Manager whose responsibilities are focused on management of the technical aspects of the database system.

database description (DBD) The way in which data are physically stored in IMS (internal database structure).

database development life cycle (DDLC) A process for designing, implementing, and maintaining a database system.

database implementation The steps required to change a conceptual design to a functioning database.

database management system (DBMS) Systems software that facilitates the management of a database.

database planning Strategic effort to determine information needs for an extended period.

database record An occurrence of a root and all its dependent segment types.

database recovery procedures The means by which a database that has been corrupted by malfunctions can be restored to a correct and consistent state.

database server A program running on server hardware to provide database services to client machines.

database system A database, a database management system, and appropriate hardware and personnel.

database tree A tree that has a root.

DataWindow painter A painter that constructs DataWindow objects that access the database and place the results in windows.

deadlock Two transactions are mutually excluded from accessing the next record required to complete their transactions; also called a "deadly embrace."

deadlock detection A periodic check by the DBMS to determine if the waiting line for some resource exceeds a predetermined limit.

decision support system Automated system providing strategic information to senior management.

decomposition of relations Splitting a relation into multiple relations.

default parameter value The value of a parameter supplied by the system if the calling program omits the value.

default value A value which is automatically inserted if the user fails to specify a value.

degree of a relation The number of attributes in a relation.

DELETE Operation that removes rows from a relation.

deletion anomaly Unintended loss of data due to deletion of other data.

dependent object set An object set whose instances *must* be related to at least one other instance of another object set.

dependent segment type All record types other than the root segment type.

derived class A class that inherits features from another class.

determinant The attribute(s) on the left side of a functional dependency; determine(s) the value of other attributes in the tuple.

difference Relational algebra operation that creates the set difference of two union-compatible relations.

directed graph A mathematical structure in which points or nodes are connected by arrows or edges.

disjunctive query A query whose conditions are connected by "or," or an equivalent symbol.

disk drive Physical unit that contains the disk storage unit.

DISTINCT Operator that eliminates duplicate rows.

Distributed INGRESS DDBMS marketed by Relational Technology.

distributed database A database that is distributed among a network of geographically separated locations.

distributed database management system (DDBMS) The software which manages the distributed database system.

distributed database system A database system made of several systems at local sites, connected by communication lines.

divide Relational algebra operation that creates a new relation by selecting the rows in one relation that match *every* row in another relation.

DL/1 Data Language 1, the IMS data manipulation language.

domain The PROLOG term for specification of datatype.

domain definition A specialized data type defined within a schema and used in column definitions.

domain/key normal form (DKNF) Requires every constraint to result from definitions of domains and keys.

E

economic feasibility Cost-benefit study of proposed database system.

edge Part of a network structure represented by an arrow.

efficient frontier The outer boundary in DEA analysis.

electronic data processing Computer automation of paperwork at the operational level of an organization.

embedded SQL A set of statements that allows SQL to be used with traditional programming languages.

encrypt To convert readable text to unreadable text by use of an algorithm; used to protect sensitive data.

encryption Encoding data to make them unintelligible to unauthorized persons.

enterprise-directing knowledge Knowledge that helps an enterprise to make decisions.

entity integrity rule No key attribute of a row may be null.

equijoin Theta join based on equality of specified columns.

event-driven Application feature that means scripts are written to respond to events that take place.

example element In QBE, a variable representing an unspecified value in a column of a table.

example table In QBE, a skeleton table showing the table name and the column names above blank spaces used for entry of query conditions.

EXCEPT Operation that creates the set difference of two relations.

existential quantifier Relational calculus expression affirming the existence of at least one row to which a condition applies.

EXISTS operator Evaluates to true if resulting set is not empty.

expansion path The path from the origin through the reference unit in DEA analysis.

expansion point Any point on the expansion path in DEA analysis.

expert systems Systems that model the decision-making processes of experts in various problem domains, such as medical diagnosis, audit decision making, and so forth; a special type of AI development.

extensional knowledge Facts that are stored in database relations.

external database The user view of the data in IMS.

external key A set of lexical attributes whose values always identify a single object instance.

external level Database structural level defining user views.

F

feasibility study Portion of the DDLC that determines technological, operational, and economic feasibility of database.

FETCH statement A statement that retrieves a single row from an opened cursor.

fifth normal form (5NF) A normal form that eliminates join dependencies.

file manager Software that manages the allocation of storage locations and data structures.

first normal form (1NF) All attribute values must be atomic.

first-order logic A logical structure that is characterized by a set of objects, a set of predicates (each of which evaluates to TRUE or FALSE), and a set of functions.

fixed retention In DBTG, once a member record has been assigned to a set occurrence, it cannot be removed from that set occurrence unless the record is deleted from the database.

flag statements SQL statements embedded in an application program to signal the beginning or end of a set of SQL statements.

foreign key A set of attributes in one relation that constitutes a key in some other (or possibly the same) relation; used to indicate logical links between relations.

forward chaining A logical chain of rules proceeding from a hypothesis to a conclusion.

fourth normal form (4NF) A relation that is in third normal form and has no multivalued dependencies.

FROM clause Lists the existing tables referenced by the query.

frontier point Any point on the frontier in DEA analysis.

fully concatenated key Means of identifying the location of a segment in the database.

function-oriented approach Views a system from the perspective of the functions it should perform.

functional dependency The value of an attribute in a tuple determines the value of another attribute in the tuple.

functional relationship A relationship having a maximum cardinality of one in at least one direction.

functionally determine To uniquely determine a value.

G

general procedural knowledge Knowledge that can only be described by a procedure.

generalization An object set that is a superset of (or contains) another object set.

global data Data that are maintained in a database whose location is different from at least one of its users.

global transaction A transaction requiring several agents.

Graphical User Interface (GUI) Screens and functions that provide a graphical means for an end user to access a computer system.

graphical language A computer language that uses pictorial representations to solve problems.

GROUP BY clause Indicates that rows should be grouped on a common value of specified column(s).

H

HAVING clause Places conditions on groups.

HDAM IMS access method; provides rapid direct access of segments but no capability for sequential processing.

head activation time The time required to activate a read/write head.

head list A list of pointers, each of which points to the first record in a file.

hierarchical data model Data model in which all relationships are structured as trees.

hierarchical model A data model that assumes all data relationships can be structured as hierarchies.

hierarchical occurrence tree Representation of segment occurrences in a tree structure that reflects all PCR types.

higher-level relationship A relationship between three or more object sets.

HISAM IMS access method; provides capability for both sequential and direct segment retrieval.

homonym A term that has different meanings in different contexts.

horizontal fragmentation Partitioning a relation into subsets of its tuples.

host language Language of programs in which SQL statements can be embedded.

HSAM IMS access method; very fast for **HIDAM** IMS access method; provides for direct access of root segments as well as sequential retrieval.

I

identifier An external key.

IF statement A statement whose execution depends on the truth value of a stated condition.

important feature A DBMS feature that is not mandatory but makes the DBMS more attractive.

IMS IBM's Information Management System; leading DBMS based on the hierarchical data model.

information Organized or summarized data.

information center An area where users have facilities to do their own computing.

information schema Schema in a catalog containing metadata.

information system An automated system which organizes data to produce information.

inherit The property of a specialization set that causes it to have all the attributes of its generalization set.

INSERT Operation that causes rows to be added to a relation.

insertion anomaly Inability to add data to the database due to absence of other data.

instance Actual record values expressed in a data structure.

Integrated Data Store (IDS) One of the earliest database management systems; its architecture greatly influenced the DBTG recommendations for a network database model.

integrity control (constraint) A restriction applied to a given set of data; used to minimize data entry error.

intensional knowledge Knowledge that is deduced from extensional knowledge by the applications of rules.

internal level Database structural level defining physical view of database.

interoperability The state of multiple heterogeneous systems communicating and contributing to completion of a common task.

INTERSECT Operation that creates the set intersection of two relations.

intersection Relational algebra operation that creates the set intersection of two union-compatible relations.

intersection relation A relation representing instances where two other relations meet in a many–many relationship.

inverted list A directory wherein each entry contains pointers to all physical records containing a specified value.

iteration statement A statement that may be repeated a specified number of times.

J

join Relational algebra operation that connects relations.

Join ON Operation that connects relations when a condition holds.

Join Tables button

Join USING Operation that connects relations when designated common columns have equal values.

K

key A minimal set of attributes that uniquely identifies each row in a relation.

knowledge-base management system System software that supports the usual range of DBMS functions, as well as managing the deductive process of the rule database operating on the fact database.

knowledge-base system A system that provides the full range of database system capabilities for data storage and manipulation, as well as a facility for creating, storing, and executing rules of inference on stored data tables.

knowledge-based system An alternative term for knowledge-base system.

L

leaf The lowest-level index record in a rooted tree.

leaf segment In a tree, any segment type that has no child segment types.

lexical object set An object set consisting of instances that can be printed.

link Communications channel between two network sites, which provides for data-transfer capability.

link record type A dummy record that is created in order to convert a complex network into an equivalent simple network; also called a link record type.

linked list A set of physical records linked by pointers that are maintained in the records themselves.

local data Data that are maintained in a network site's own database.

local transaction A transaction requiring a unique agent.

local variable A variable defined for use within a procedure to store temporary working values.

local-area network (LAN) A computer network with the sites located within a short distance (usually less than a mile) of one another.

lock Prevents access to a database record by a second transaction until the first transaction has completed all of its actions.

log A record of all transactions and the corresponding changes to the database.

logical record A record type as seen from the user's perspective.

M

main memory Storage located in the central processing unit; used for data made available for user operations.

management information Information to support company operations and decision makers.

management information system Automated system focused on information for middle management.

mandatory feature A DBMS feature that must be provided.

mandatory retention In DBTG, once a member record has been placed in a set occurrence, it must always be in some occurrence of that set.

manual insertion mode In DBTG, requires that the member record be placed in a set by using a CONNECT command to link it to the desired set occurrence.

many–many Relationship cardinalities of many in both directions.

map To associate elements in one sphere with elements in another sphere.

mapping division The portion of the DBTG subschema that provides for changing the names used in the schema to names chosen for the subschema.

MARK IV Control Data Corporation's Multi-Access Retrieval System; DBMS based on the hierarchical data model.

member record type The record type on the "many" side of the one–many relationship of a DBTG set.

metadata Data in the data dictionary which describe the database.

model A representation of reality that retains only selected details.

multiple-table query A query involving more than one table.

multiset A set that may have duplicate entries.

multivalued dependency (MVD) A constraint that guarantees the mutual independence of multivalued attributes.

n-ary relationship A relationship between *n* object sets.

natural join Join operation that connects relations when common columns have equal values.

navigational commands DBTG DML commands used to find database records.

network A data relationship in which a record can be owned by records from more than one file.

network data model Represents data in network structures of record types connected in one–one or one–many relationships.

node Part of a network structure represented by a point.

noncorrelated subquery A subquery whose value does not depend on any outer query.

nonprocedural Language that provides a means for stating *what* is desired rather than *how* to get it.

normal forms Rules for structuring relations that eliminate anomalies.

normalization The process of converting a relation to a standard form.

NOT EXISTS operator Evaluates to true if resulting set is empty.

null attribute value An attribute value that does not exist for a specific object instance.

null value The value given an attribute in a tuple if the attribute is inapplicable or its value is unknown.

object instance A particular member of an object set.

object set A set of things of the same kind.

object-oriented database systems Database systems that can implement conceptual models directly and can represent complexities that are beyond the capabilities of relational systems.

object-oriented model A model representing real-world entities as objects rather than records.

object-oriented programming A powerful approach to complex programming that incorporates concepts of encapsulation, polymorphism, and inheritance.

occurrence A synonym for instance.

one–many Relationship cardinalities of one in one direction and many in the other.

one–one Relationship cardinalities of one in both directions.

OPEN cursor statement Embedded SQL statement that causes the DBMS to process a cursor's query and store its result in the cursor.

Open Table button

open systems The concept of connecting a variety of computer hardware and software to work in concert to achieve user goals.

operational feasibility Determination of availability of expertise and personnel needed for the database system.

optional feature A DBMS feature that is of secondary importance; may help to distinguish among otherwise equally rated DBMSs.

optional retention In DBTG, there are no restrictions imposed on connections or reconnections to set types.

outer join Expansion of the natural join that includes *all* rows from both relations.

outer query The main query that contains all the subqueries.

owner record type The record type on the "one" side of the one–many relationship of a DBTG set.

painter An interactive subprogram that performs a specific type of functionality needed for full application development.

PARADOX FOR WINDOWS A microcomputer DBMS whose query language is like QBE.

parameter A variable used to pass data into and out of a stored procedure.

parent An "owner" record in a hierarchical relationship.

parent-child relationship type (PCR type) Logical relationship between a parent segment type and a child segment type.

path A set of pointers leading from one index record to another.

physical database design Determination of storage devices, access methods, and indexes for using a database.

physical link A means of connecting records by using the records' disk addresses.

physical object An object representing a specific physical thing.

physical object set An object set whose instances are physical objects.

physical record A physical block of data.

PL/SQL Oracle's data manipulation language.

plaintext Readable text.

pointer A physical address which identifies where a record can be found on disk.

practitioners People responsible for the database system and its associated application software.

predicate An expression that evaluates to TRUE or FALSE.

predicate symbols Names applied to arguments in order to express a predicate.

preliminary planning Planning for a database that occurs during the strategic database planning process.

preorder traversal A method of converting a tree structure to a flat file that retains the necessary information about the hierarchical relationships.

preview A feature that allows the developer to see how a DataWindow will appear when placed in a window.

primary key The candidate key designated for principal use in uniquely identifying rows in a relation.

procedural Language that provides a step-by-step method for solving problems.

procedure Written instructions describing the steps needed to accomplish a given task in a system.

product Relational algebra operation that creates the Cartesian product of two relations.

program communication block (PCB) A component of the PSB.

program specification block (PSB) Specifies the names of each segment an application program will access; corresponds to a user view or subschema.

project Relational algebra operation that creates a relation by deleting columns from an existing relation.

projection of a relation A relation consisting of selected attributes from another relation.

projection Relation resulting from a project operation.

Q

qualification expression A true-false condition that refers to the target list; must hold for the elements in the solution set.

qualifying statement A condition in a relational calculus statement that restricts membership in a solution relation.

query specification Definition of a query used in a view definition, cursor declaration, or other statement.

R

R* DDBMS marketed by IBM Corporation.

random access processing A file access method that provides direct access to a specific record.

read_lock The user has the right to read a given record.

record section The section of the DBTG schema that defines each record, its data items, and its location.

record templates Formats used for records that are read into the UWA.

record type A collection of logically related data items.

recursive foreign key A foreign key that references its own relation.

recursive relationship A relationship that relates an object set to itself.

reference unit The DBMS currently being evaluated in DEA analysis.

referential integrity rule The value of a non-null foreign key must be an actual key value in some relation.

relation A two-dimensional table containing rows and columns of data.

relation attribute A column in a relation.

relational algebra A procedural language for manipulating relations.

relational calculus A nonprocedural language for defining query solutions.

relational data model A data model representing data in the form of tables.

relational database schema A listing showing relation names, attribute names, key attributes, and foreign keys.

relationally complete Having the same logical power as relational algebra or calculus.

relationship A linking between instances of two object sets.

request for proposal (RFP) A formal document that outlines performance requirements and asks vendors to respond with a proposal for meeting those requirements.

requirements definition Determination of management and functional area information requirements.

retrieval commands DBTG DML commands used to retrieve database records.

retrieve only access Database access with no update allowed.

root segment In a tree, the segment type that does not participate as a child segment in any PCR.

rooted tree A hierarchy of index records that has a single index record at the highest level; that record is called the root.

rotational delay The time required for the disk to rotate the sought-for record under the read/write head.

rule A restriction on the value allowed in a column, stated in a conditional expression.

Run Query button

S

schema A definition of the logical structure of the entire database.

schema definition Description of a database to the DBMS.

schema owner Person who has authority and responsibility for granting access to tables, columns, and views in a database schema.

schema section The section of the DBTG schema that names the schema.

second normal form (2NF) No nonkey attribute may be functionally dependent on just a part of the key.

secondary key A data item value that identifies a set of records.

SEGM An IMS statement that defines the fields to be included in a segment to be used by a program.

segment occurrence IMS terminology for record occurrence.

segment template Program work area format for a segment.

segment type Corresponds to an object in the object-oriented data model; also called a segment.

select Relational algebra operation that uses a condition to select rows from a relation.

SELECT clause Identifies the columns desired in the query.

semantic model A model that captures the meanings of real-world entities and relationships.

sensitive segment A segment that is accessible to a program; abbreviated SENSEG.

serial execution Actions are executed one after another—no parallel actions.

serializability theory States that a concurrency control algorithm is correct when its results are the same as if processes were executed serially.

set In the DBTG model, a one-many relationship between two record types.

set function A built-in function.

set insertion class In DBTG, the way in which a member record gets placed in a set occurrence; can be manual or automatic.

set retention class In DBTG, determines how and when a member record can be removed from a set; can be fixed, mandatory, or optional.

set section The section of the DBTG schema that defines sets and includes owner record types and member record types.

simple network A data structure in which all binary relationships are one–many.

simple query A query involving only one database table.

solution set A set of data values from the database that satisfies the conditions of a query.

specialization An object set that is a subset of another object set.

statement block Either a single SQL statement without delimiters, or a set of two or more SQL statements delimited by BEGIN... END.

status flags Variables used to denote the success or failure of the last operation executed by the application program.

stored procedure A written program compiled into machine language and saved for repeated and more efficient execution.

strategy selector Software that translates a user request into an effective form for execution.

structural knowledge Knowledge about dependencies and constraints among data.

structure division The division of the DBTG subschema where records, data items, and sets from the schema are defined.

subquery A query within a query.

subschema Subsets of the schema which are defined by the user's view of the database.

subschema record section The section of the structure division that specifies subschema records, data items, and datatypes.

subschema set section The section of the structure division that defines the sets to be included.

subtraction The relational algebra difference operation.

superkey A set of attributes that uniquely identifies each row in a relation.

surrogate key A unique computer system identifier for an abstract object instance; it has no meaning outside the computer system.

SWITCH statement A statement that enables testing for a series of conditions.

synonyms Terms that mean the same thing.

System for Distributed Databases (SSD) DDBMS marketed by Computer Corporation of America.

system development life cycle (SDLC) A process for system development.

System-2000 SAS Institute's hierarchical DBMS; DBMS based on the hierarchical data model.

T

table constraint A constraint that applies to multiple columns in a table simultaneously.

target list A parenthesized list of variables representing the desired format of a typical member of a query's solution set.

target table In QBE, a table without column headings that is used to define query output.

TDMS System Development Corporation's Time-Shared Data Management System; DBMS based on the hierarchical data model.

technological feasibility Determination of hardware and software availability for database system.

textual language A computer language whose statements consist of character string symbols.

theta join Join operation that connects relations when values from specified columns have a specified relationship.

ABRIAL, J. "Data Semantics." In Klimbie and Koffeman, 1974.

AGRAWAL, R., GHOSH, S., IMIELINSKI, T., IYER, B., AND SWAMI, A. "An Interval Classifier for Database Mining Applications." In VLDB 1992.

AHO, A., BEERI, C., AND ULLMAN, J. "The Theory of Joins in Relational Databases." TODS, 4:3, September 1979.

AHO, A.V., HOPCROFT, E., & ULLMAN, J.D. *The Design and Analysis of Computer Programs*, Addison-Wesley, 1975.

ALASHQUR, A.M., SU, S.Y.W., AND LAM, H. "OQL: A Query Language for Manipulating Object-Oriented Databases." In VLDB 1989.

ALBANO, A., DE ANTONELLIS, V., AND DE LEVA, A. (editors). *Computer-Aided Database Design: The DATAID Project*, North-Holland, 1985.

ALBANO, A., BERGAMINI, R., GHELLI, G., AND ORSINI, R. "An Object Data Model with Roles." In VLDB 1993.

ALLEN, F., LOOMIS, M., AND MANNINO, M. "The Integrated Dictionary/Directory System." *Computing Surveys*, 14:2, June 1982.

ANDANY, J., LEONARD, M., AND PALISSER, C. "Management of Schema Evolution in Databases." In VLDB 1991.

ANDREWS, T. AND HARRIS, C. "Combining Language and Database Advances in an Object-Oriented Development Environment." In *OOPSLA 1987*.

ANDRIOLE, S. J., ED. 1985. *Applications in Artificial Intelligence*, Princeton, NJ: Petrocelli Books, 1985.

ANSI 1981. Proposed American National Standard for a Data Definition Language for Network Structured Databases. American National Standards Institute, Document ANSI X3H2, 1981.

ANSI 1986A. American National Standards Institute: The Database Language NDL, Document ANSI X3.133, 1986.

ANSI 1986B. American National Standards Institute: The Database Language SQL, Document ANSI X3.135, 1986.

ANSI 1989. American National Standards Institute: Information Resource Dictionary Systems, Document ANSI X3.138, 1989.

ASHTON-TATE CORPORATION. *dBASE IV Language Reference*, Ashton-Tate, 1988.

ASTRAHAN, M. ET AL. "System R: A Relational Approach to Data Base Management." TODS, 1:2, June 1976.

ASTRAHAN, M. ET AL. "A History and Evaluation of System R." *IBM Research Report RJ2843*, June 1980.

ATRE, S. *Data Base: Structured Techniques for Design, Performance, and Management*, New York: Wiley, 1980.

ATRE, S. *Data Base Management Systems for the Eighties*, QED Information Sciences, 1983.

BABAD, Y. M., AND J. A. HOFFER. "Even No Data Has a Value." CACM 27:8, August, 1984.

BACHMAN, C. "Data Structure Diagrams." *Data Base* (Bulletin of ACM SIGFIDET), 1:2, March 1969.

BACHMAN, C. "The Programmer as a Navigator." CACM, 16:11, November 1973.

BACHMAN, C. "The Data Structure Set Model." In Rustin 1974.

BANERJEE, J., CHOU, H., GARZA, J., KIM, W., WOELK, D., BALLOU, N., AND KIM, H. "Data Model Issues for Object-Oriented Applications." *ACM Transactions on Database Systems* 5, 197-208, 1987.

BAROODY, A. AND DEWITT, D. "An Object-Oriented Approach to Database System Implementation." TODS, 6:4, December 1981.

BATINI, C., LENZERINI, M., AND NAVATHE, S. "A Comparative Analysis of Methodologies for Database Schema Integration." *Computing Surveys*, 18:4, December 1986.

BATORY, D. ET AL. "GENESIS: An Extensible Database Management System." TSE, 14:11, November 1988.

BATRA, D., J. A. HOFFER, AND R. P. BOSTROM. "A Comparison of the Representations Developed Using the Relational and Entity-Relationship Data Models." CACM, 33:12, December 1990.

BAYER, R. AND MCCREIGHT, E. "Organization and Maintenance of Large Ordered Indexes." *Acta Informatica*, 1:3, February 1972.

BEECH, DAVID. "Collections of Objects in SQL3." In VLDB 1993.

BEERI, C. AND MILO, T. "A Model for Active Object Oriented Database." In VLDB 1991.

BELL, D. AND GRIMSON, J. *Distributed Database Systems*. Reading, MA: Addison-Wesley, 1992.

BERNSTEIN, P. AND GOODMAN, N. "The Power of Natural Semijoins." *SIAM Journal of Computing*, 10:4, December 1981.

BERNSTEIN, P. AND GOODMAN, N. "Concurrency Control in Distributed Database Systems." *Computing Surveys*, 13:2, June 1981.

BERNSTEIN, P., HADZILACOS, V., AND GOODMAN, N. *Concurrency Control and Recovery in Database Systems*, Reading, MA: Addison-Wesley, 1988.

BERNSTEIN, PHILIP A., GYLLSTROM, PER O., AND WIMBERG, TOM. "STDL-A Portable Language for Transaction Processing." In VLDB 1993.

BERNSTEIN, P. "Synthesizing Third Normal Form Relations from Functional Dependencies." TODS, 1:4, December 1976.

BETRA, D., J. A. HOFFER, AND R. B. BOSTROM. "A Comparison of User Performance Between the Relational and Extended Entity Relationship Model in the Discovery Phase of Database Design." In ICIS 1988.

BHARGAVA, B. (editor). *Concurrency and Reliability in Distributed Systems*, New York: Van Nostrand-Reinhold, 1987.

BILLER, H. "On the Equivalence of Data Base Schemas—A Semantic Approach to Data Translation." *Information Systems*, 4:1, 1979.

BJORNER, D. AND LOVENGREN, H. "Formalization of Database Systems and a Formal Definition of IMS." In VLDB 1982.

BLASGEN, M. AND ESWARAN, K. "On the Evaluation of Queries in a Relational Database System." *IBM Systems Journal*, 16:1, January 1976.

BLASGEN, M., ET AL. "System R: An Architectural Overview." *IBM Systems Journal*, 20:1, January 1981.

BLOOMBECKER, J. J. "Short-Circuiting Computer Crime." *Datamation*, October 1, 1989.

BOAR, B. H. *Application Prototyping*, New York: Wiley, 1984.

BOCCA, J. "EDUCE—A Marriage of Convenience: Prolog and a Relational DBMS." *Proceedings of the Third International Conference on Logic Programming*, New York: Springer-Verlag, 1986.

BOEHM, B.W. *Software Engineering Economics*, Englewood Cliffs, NJ: Prentice Hall, 1981.

BOHL, M. *Introduction to IBM Direct Access Storage Devices*, Chicago: Science Research Associates, 1981.

BORLAND INTERNATIONAL. *Paradox 3.0 User's Guide*, Scotts Valley, CA: Borland, 1988.

BOUZEGHOUB, M. AND METAIS, E. "Semantic Modeling of Object Oriented Databases." In VLDB 1991.

BRACCHI, G. AND PERNICI, B. "The Design Requirements of Office Systems." TOOIS, 2:2, April 1984.

BRACCHI, G. AND PERNICI, B. "Decision Support in Office Information Systems." In Holsapple and Whinston 1987.

BRACHMAN, R. AND LEVESQUE, H. "What Makes a Knowledge Base Knowledgeable? A View of Databases from the Knowledge Level." In EDS 1984.

BRADLEY, J. *File and Data Base Techniques*, New York: Holt, Rinehart & Winston, 1982.

BRANT, D.A., GROSE, T., LOFASO, B., AND MIRANKER, D.P. "Effects of Database Size on Rule System Performance: Five Case Studies." In VLDB 1991.

BRAY, O. *Distributed Database Management Systems*, Lexington, MA: Lexington Books, 1982.

BRODIE, M., MYLOPOULOS, J., AND SCHMIDT, J. (editors). *On Conceptual Modeling*, New York: Springer-Verlag, 1984.

BRODSKY, ALEXANDER, JAFFAR, JOXAN, AND MAHER, MICHAEL J. "Toward Practical Constraint Databases." In VLDB 1993.

BROSEY, M. AND SHNEIDERMAN, B. "Two Experimental Comparisons of Relational and Hierarchical Database Models." *International Journal of Man-Machine Studies*, 1978.

BROWN, R. "Data Integrity and SQL." *Database Programming and Design*, March 1988.

BROWNING, D. "Data Managers and LANs." *PC Tech Journal*, 5:5, May 1987.

BRUCE, T., J. FULLER, AND T. MORIARTY. "So You Want a Repository." *Database Programming and Design*, May 1989.

BUBENKO, J., BERILD, S., LINDERCRONA-OHLIN, E., AND NACHMENS, S. "From Information Requirements to DBTG Data Structures." *Proceedings of the ACM SIGMOD/SIGPLAN Conference on Data Abstraction*, 1976.

BUNEMAN, P. AND FRANKEL, R. "FQL: A Functional Query Language." In SIGMOD 1979.

CAMPBELL, D., EMBLEY, D., AND CZEJDO, B. "A Relationally Complete Query Language for the Entity-Relationship Model." In ER 1985.

CAMPBELL, D., EMBLEY, D., AND CZEJDO, B. "Graphical Query Formulation for an Entity-Relationship Model." *Data and Knowledge Engineering*, 2 (1987), 89-121.

CARDENAS, A. *Data Base Management Systems*, Second Edition, Newton, MA: Allyn and Bacon, 1985.

CAREY, M., DEWITT, D., AND VANDENBERG, S. "A Data Model and Query Language for Exodus." In SIGMOD 1988.

CAREY, M., DEWITT, D., RICHARDSON, J. AND SHEKITA, E. "Object and File Management in the EXODUS Extensible Database System." In VLDB 1986.

CAREY, M. ET AL. "The Architecture of the EXODUS Extensible DBMS." In Dittrich and Dayal 1986.

CARLIS, J. AND MARCH, S. "A Descriptive Model of Physical Database Design Problems and Solutions." In DE 1984.

CASANOVA, M. AND VIDAL, V. "Toward a Sound View Integration Method." PODS, 1982.

CERI, S. (editor). *Methodology and Tools for Database Design*, North-Holland, 1983.

CERI, S. AND PELAGATTI, G. *Distributed Databases: Principles and Systems*, New York: McGraw-Hill, 1984.

CERI, S., NAVATHE, S., AND WIEDERHOLD, G. "Distribution Design of Logical Database Schemas." TSE, 9:4, July 1983.

CHA, S.K. AND WIEDERHOLD, G. "Kaleidoscope Data Model for an English-like Query Language." In VLDB 1991.

CHAMBERLIN, D. AND BOYCE, R. "SEQUEL: A Structured English Query Language." In SIGMOD 1984.

CHAMBERLIN, D., ET AL. "SEQUEL 2: A Unified Approach to Data Definition, Manipulation, and Control." *IBM Journal of Research and Development*, 20:6, November 1976.

CHAMBERLIN, D., ET AL. "A History and Evaluation of System R." CACM, 24:10, October 1981.

CHAMPINE, G. A. "Six Approaches to Distributed Data Bases." *Datamation*, May 1977.

CHAN, A., AND H. K. T. WONG. "Serving Up dBASE." *Data Base Programming & Design*, February 1990.

CHANG, C. AND WALKER, A. "PROSQL: A Prolog Programming Interface with SQL/DS." In EDS 1984.

CHEN AND ASSOCIATES. *E-R Designer Reference Manual*, 1988.

CHEN, I.A., AND McLEOD, D. "Derived Data Update in Semantic Databases." In VLDB 1989.

CHEN, LING TONY AND ROTEM, DORON. "Declustering Objects for Visualization." In VLDB 1993.

CHEN, P. "The Entity Relationship Model—Toward a Unified View of Data." TODS, 1:1, March 1976.

CHEN, P. *The Entity-Relationship Approach to Logical Data Base Design*, Q.E.D. Information Sciences, Data Base Monograph Series no. 6, 1977.

CHIMENTI, D., GAMBOA, R., KRISHNAMURTHY, R., NAQVI, S., TSUR, S., AND ZANIOLO, C. "The LDL System Prototype." *IEEE Transactions on Knowledge and Data Engineering*, 2:1, March 1990.

CHOUINARD, P. "Supertypes, Subtypes, and DB2." *Database Programming and Design*, October 1989.

CHRISTODOULAKIS, S. ET AL. "Development of a Multimedia Information System for an Office Environment." In VLDB 1984.

CLAYBROOK, B. *File Management Techniques*, New York: Wiley, 1983.

CODASYL. Data Base Task Group April 71 Report, ACM, 1971.

CODASYL. Data Description Language Journal of Development, Canadian Government Publishing Centre, 1978.

CODD, E. "A Relational Model for Large Shared Data Banks." CACM, 13:6, June 1970.

CODD, E. "Relational completeness of data base sublanguages." *Courant Computer Science Symposium 6, Data Base Systems*, Englewood Cliffs, NJ: Prentice Hall, 1971.

CODD, E. "A Data Base Sublanguage Founded on the Relational Calculus." *Proceedings of the ACM SIGFIDET Workshop on Data Description, Access, and Control*, November 1971.

CODD, E. "Further Normalization of the Data Base Relational Model." In Rustin 1972.

CODD, E. "Recent Investigations in Relational Database Systems." *Proceedings of the IFIP Congress*, 1974.

CODD, E. "How About Recently? (English Dialog with Relational Data Bases Using Rendezvous Version 1)." In Shneiderman 1978.

CODD, E. "Extending the Database Relational Model to Capture More Meaning." TODS, 4:4, December 1979.

CODD, E. "Relational Database: A Practical Foundation for Productivity." CACM, 25:2, December 1982.

CODD, E. "Is Your DBMS Really Relational?" and "Does Your DBMS Run By the Rules." *Computerworld*, October 14 and October 21, 1985.

CODD, E. "An Evaluation Scheme for Database Management Systems That Are Claimed to be Relational." In DE 1986.

COMER, D. "The Ubiquitous B-tree." *Computing Surveys*, 11:2, June 1979.

CONTE, P. "In Search of Consistency." *Database Programming and Design*, August 1989.

CREASY, P.N. "ENIAM: A More Complete Conceptual Schema Language." In VLDB 1989.

CURTICE, R., AND CASEY, W. "Database: What's in Store." *Datamation*, December 1, 1985.

CURTICE, R. "Data Dictionaries: An Assessment of Current Practice and Problems." In VLDB 1981.

CZEJDO, B., ELMASRI, R., RUSINKIEWICZ, M., AND EMBLEY, D. "An Algebraic Language for Graphical Query Formulation Using an Extended Entity-Relationship Model." *Proceedings of the ACM Computer Science Conference*, 1987.

DATE, C. AND WHITE, C. *A Guide to SQL/DS*, Reading, MA: Addison-Wesley, 1988.

DATE, C. AND WHITE, C. *A Guide to DB2*, Second Edition, Reading, MA: Addison-Wesley, 1988.

DATE, C. *An Introduction to Database Systems, Volume 2*, Reading, MA: Addison-Wesley, 1983.

DATE, C. "The Outer Join." *Proceedings of the Second International Conference on Databases*, 1983.

DATE, C. "A Critique of the SQL Database Language." *ACM SIGMOD Record*, 14:3, November 1984.

DATE, C. *An Introduction to Database Systems, Vol. 1* (4th ed.), Reading, MA: Addison-Wesley, 1986.

DATE, C. "Where SQL Falls Short." *Datamation*, May 1, 1987.

DATE, C. AND DARWEN, H. *A Guide to the SQL Standard, 3rd Edition*, Reading, MA: Addison-Wesley, 1994.

DAVIES, C. "Recovery Semantics for a DB/DC System." *Proceedings of the ACM National Conference*, 1973.

DAYAL, U., HSU, M., AND LADIN, R. "A Transactional Model for Long-Running Activities." In VLDB 1991.

DBTG. Report of the CODASYL Data Base Task Group, ACM, April 1971.

DELIS, A. AND ROUSSOPOULOS, N. "Performance and Scalability of Client-Server Database Architectures." In VLDB 1992.

DEMARCO, T. *Structured Analysis and System Specification*, Prentice-Hall Yourdan, Inc., 1979.

DENNING, D. AND DENNING, P. "Data Security." *Computing Surveys*, 11:3, September 1979.

DIAZ, O., PATON, N. AND GRAY, P. "Rule Management in Object-Oriented Databases: A Uniform Approach." In VLDB 1991.

DI BATTISTA, G. AND LENZERINI, M. "A Deductive Method for Entity-Relationship Modeling." In VLDB 1989.

DIFFIE, W. AND HELLMAN, M. "Privacy and Authentication." *Proceedings of the IEEE*, 67:3, March 1979.

DITTRICH, K. AND DAYAL, U. (editors). *Proceedings of the International Workshop on Object-Oriented Database Systems*, IEEE CS, September 1986.

DITTRICH, K. "Object-Oriented Database Systems: The Notion and the Issues." In Dittrich and Dayal 1986.

DODD, G. "Elements of Data Management Systems." *Computing Surveys*, 1:2, June 1969.

DOS SANTOS, C., NEUHOLD, E., AND FURTADO, A. "A Data Type Approach to the Entity-Relationship Model." In ER 1979.

DUMPALA, S. AND ARORA, S. "Schema Translation Using the Entity-Relationship Approach." In ER 1983.

EICK, C.F. "A Methodology for the Design and Transformation of Conceptual Schemas." In VLDB 1991.

ELLIS, C. AND NUTT, G. "Office Information Systems and Computer Science." *Computing Surveys*, 12:1, March 1980.

ELLZEY, R.S. *Data Structures for Computer Information Systems*, Science Research Associates, 1982.

ELMASRI, R. AND LARSON, J. "A Graphical Query Facility for ER Databases." In ER 1985.

ELMASRI, R. AND NAVATHE, S. "Object Integration in Logical Database Design." In DE 1984.

ELMASRI, R. AND NAVATHE, S. *Fundamentals of Database Systems*, Menlo Park, CA: Benjamin/Cummings, 1989.

ELMASRI, R. AND WIEDERHOLD, G. "Data Model Integration Using the Structural Model." In SIGMOD 1979.

ELMASRI, R. AND WIEDERHOLD, G. "Structural Properties of Relationships and Their Representation." NCC, AFIPS, 49, 1980.

ELMASRI, R. AND WIEDERHOLD, G. "GORDAS: A Formal, High-Level Query Language for the Entity-Relationship Model." In ER 1981.

ELMASRI, R., WEELDREYER, J., AND HEVNER, A. "The Category Concept: An Extension to the Entity-Relationship Model." *International Journal on Data and Knowledge Engineering*, 1:1, May 1985.

FAGIN, R. "Multivalued Dependencies and a New Normal Form for Relational Databases." TODS, 2:3, September 1977.

FAGIN, R. "Normal Forms and Relational Database Operators." In SIGMOD 1979.

FAGIN, R. "A Normal Form for Relational Databases That is Based on Domains and Keys." TODS, 6:3, September 1981.

FERNANDEZ, E., SUMMERS, R., AND WOOD, C. *Database Security and Integrity*, Reading, MA: Addison-Wesley, 1981.

FISHMAN, D. ET AL. "IRIS: An Object-Oriented DBMS." TOOIS, 4:2, April 1986.

FISHMAN, D., BEECH, D., CATE, H., CHOW, E., CONNORS, T., DAVIS, J., DERRETT, N., HOCH, C., KENT, W., LYNGBAEK, P., MAHBOD, B., NEIMAT, M., RYAN, T., AND SHAN, M. IRIS: An Object-Oriented Database Management System. TOOIS 5: 216-226, 1987.

FLAVIN, M. *Fundamental Concepts of Information Modeling*, Englewood Cliffs, NJ: Yourdon Press, 1981.

FLEMING, C., AND VON HALLE, B. "An Overview of Logical Data Modeling." *Data Resource Management*, Winter 1990.

FRANKLIN, M.J., CAREY, M.J., AND LIVNY, M. "Global Memory Management in Client-Server DBMS Architectures." In VLDB 1992.

FRANKLIN, MICHAEL J., CAREY, MICHAEL J., AND LIVNY, MIRON. "Local Disk Caching for Client-Server Database Systems." In VLDB 1993.

FRY, J. AND SIBLEY, E. "Evolution of Data-Base Management Systems." *Computing Surveys*, 8:1, March 1976.

FURTADO, A. "Formal Aspects of the Relational Model." *Information Systems*, 3:2, 1978.

GABBAY, D. AND MCBRIEN, P. "Temporal Logic & Historical Databases." In VLDB 1991.

GADIA, S. "A Homogeneous Relational Model and Query Language for Temporal Databases." TODS, 13:4, December 1988.

GALLAIRE, H. AND MINKER, J. (editors). *Logic and Databases*, Plenum Press, 1978.

GALLAIRE, H., MINKER, J., AND NICOLAS, J. "Logic and Databases: A Deductive Approach." *Computing Surveys*, 16:2, June 1984.

GAL-OZ, NURITH, GUDES, EHUD, AND FERNANDEZ, EDUARDO B. "A Model of Methods Access Authorization in Object-Oriented Databases." In VLDB 1993.

GARDARIN, G., CHEINEY, J-P., KIERNAN, G., PASTRE, D., AND STORA, H. "Managing Complex Objects in an Extensible Relational DBMS." In VLDB 1989.

GARDARIN, G., AND VALDURIEZ, P. *Relational Databases and Knowledge Bases*, Reading, MA: Addison-Wesley, 1989.

GAREY, M. *Computers and Intractability: A Guide to the Theory of NP-Completeness*, W.H. Freeman and Company, 1979.

GEHANI, N.H., JAGADISH, H.V., AND SHMUELI, O. "Composite Event Specification in Active Databases: Model & Implementation." In VLDB 1992.

GEHANI, N.H. AND JAGADISH, H.V. "Ode as an Active Database: Constraints and Triggers." In VLDB 1991.

GHANDEHARIZADEH, SHAHRAM, HULL, RICHARD, JACOBS, DEAN, CASTILLO, JAIME, ESCOBAR-MOLANO, MARTHA, LU, SHIH-HUI, LUO, JUNHUI, TSANG, CHIU, AND ZHOU, GANG. "On Implementing a Language for Specifying Active Database Execution Models." In VLDB 1993.

GOLDFINE, A. AND KONIG, P. A Technical Overview of the Information Resource Dictionary System (IRDS), Second Edition, NBS IR 88-3700, National Bureau of Standards, 1988.

GORMAN, K., AND CHOOBINEH, J. "An Overview of the Object-Oriented Entity Relationship Model (OOERM)." *Proceedings of the Twenty-Third Annual Hawaii International Conference on Information Systems*, 1990.

GOTLIEB, L. "Computing Joins of Relations." In SIGMOD 1975.

GRAY, J., MCJONES, P., AND BLASGEN, M. "The Recovery Manager of the System R Database Manager." *Computing Surveys*, 13:2, June 1981.

GRAY, J. "The Transaction Concept: Virtues and Limitations." In VLDB 1981.

GREENBLATT, D., AND J. WAXMAN. "A Study of Three Database Query Languages." In Shneiderman 1978.

GREFEN, PAUL W.P.J. "Combining Theory and Practice in Integrity Control: A Declarative Approach to the Specification of a Transaction Modification Subsystem." In VLDB 1993.

GUIMARAES, T. "Information Resources Management: Improving the Focus." *Information Resources Management Journal*, Fall 1988.

GUPTA, A., WEYMOUTH, T.E., AND JAIN, R. "Semantic Queries with Pictures: the VIMSYS Model." In VLDB 1991.

HAMMER, M. AND MCLEOD, D. "Semantic Integrity in a Relational Data Base System." In VLDB 1975.

HAMMER, M., AND D. MCLEOD. "The Semantic Data Model: A Modelling Mechanism for Data Base Applications." In SIGMOD 1978.

HAMMER, M. AND MCLEOD, D. "Database Descriptions with SDM: A Semantic Data Model." TODS, 6:3, September 1980.

HAN, J., CAI, Y., AND CERCONE, N. "Knowledge Discovery in Databases: An Attribute-

Oriented Approach." In VLDB 1992.

HANSEN, G. *Database Processing with Fourth Generation Languages*, Cincinnati: South-Western, 1988.

HANSEN, G. AND HANSEN, J. "Procedural and Non-procedural Languages Revisited: A Comparison of Relational Algebra and Relational Calculus." *International Journal of Man-Machine Studies*, (1987), 26, 683-694.

HANSEN, G. AND HANSEN, J. "Human Performance in Relational Algebra, Tuple Calculus, and Domain Calculus." *International Journal of Man-Machine Studies*, (1988), 29, 503-516.

HARRINGTON, J. *Relational Database Management for Microcomputer: Design and Implementation*, New York: Holt, Rinehart, and Winston, 1987.

HARRIS, L. "The ROBOT System: Natural Language Processing Applied to Data Base Query." *Proceedings of the ACM National Conference*, December 1978.

HASKIN, R. AND LORIE, R. "On Extending the Functions of a Relational Database System." In SIGMOD 1982.

HAWRYSZKIEWYCA, I.T. *Database Analysis and Design, 2nd Ed.*, New York: Macmillan, 1991.

HAYES-ROTH, R., WATERMAN, D., AND LENAT, D. (editors). *Building Expert Systems*, Reading, MA: Addison-Wesley, 1983.

HEIMBIGNER, D. "Experiences With an Object Manager for a Process-Centered Environment." In VLDB 1992.

HELD, G. AND STONEBRAKER, M. "B-Trees Reexamined." CACM, 21:2, February 1978.

HIMMELSTEIN, M. "Cooperative Database Processing." *Database Programming and Design*, October 1989.

HOFFER, J., MICHAELE, S., AND CARROLL, J. "The Pitfalls of Strategic Data and Systems Planning: A Research Agenda." *Proceedings of the Twenty-Second Annual Hawaii International Conference on System Sciences. Vol. IV*, 1989.

HOFFER, J. "An Empirical Investigation with Individual Differences in Database Models." In ICIS 1982.

HOLLAND, R. H. "Data Base Planning Entails Return to Basics." *Computerworld*, October 27, 1980.

HOLSAPPLE, C. AND WHINSTON, A. (editors). *Decision Support Theory and Application*, New York: Springer-Verlag, 1987.

HUBBARD, G.U. *Computer-Assisted Data Base Design*, New York: Van Nostrand Reinhold, 1981.

HULL, R. AND KING, R. "Semantic Database Modeling: Survey, Applications, and Research Issues." *Computing Surveys*, 19:3, September 1987.

HULL, R. AND JACOBS, D. "Language Constructs for Programming Active Databases." In VLDB 1991.

IMIELINSKI, T. AND LIPSKI, W. "On Representing Incomplete Information in a Relational Database." In VLDB 1981.

ISHIKAWA, HIROSHI AND KUBOTA, KAZUMI. "An Active Object-Oriented Database: A Multi-Paradigm Approach to Constraint Management." In VLDB 1993.

JACKSON, M.A. *Principles of Program Design*, Orlando: Academic Press, 1975.

JAQUA, D. "SQL Database Security." *Database Programming and Design*, July 1988.

JARDINE, D. (editor). *The ANSI/SPARC DBMS Model*, North-Holland, 1977.

KAPP, D. AND LEBEN, J. *IMS Programming Techniques*, New York: Van Nostrand-Reinhold, 1978.

KENT, W. *Data and Reality*, North-Holland, 1978.

KENT, W. "Limitations of Record-Based Information Models." TODS, 4:1, March 1979.

KENT, W. "A Simple Guide to Five Normal Forms in Relational Database Theory." CACM, 26:2, February 1983.

KENT, W. "Solving Domain Mismatch and Schema Mismatch Problems with an Object-Oriented Database Programming Language." In VLDB 1991.

KHOSHAFIAN, S., CHAN, A., WONG, A., WONG, H.K.T. *Client/Server SQL Applications*, Morgan Kaufmann, 1992.

KIM, W. "Relational Database Systems." *Computing Surveys*, 11:3, September 1979.

KIM, W. "On Optimizing an SQL-like Nested Query." TODS, 3:3, September 1982.

KIM, W., REINER, D., AND BATORY, D. (editors). *Query Processing in Database Systems*, New York: Springer-Verlag, 1985.

KIM, W. "A Model of Queries for Object-Oriented Databases." In VLDB 1989.

KLIMBIE, J. AND KOFFEMAN, K. (editors). *Data Base Management*, North-Holland, 1974.

KNUTH, D. *The Art of Computer Programming, Volume 3: Sorting and Searching*, Reading, MA: Addison-Wesley, 1973.

KORTH, H. AND SILBERSCHATZ, A. *Database System Concepts*, New York: McGraw-Hill, 1986.

KORTH, H. AND SILBERSCHATZ, A. *Database System Concepts, 2nd Edition*, New York: McGraw-Hill, 1991.

KROENKE, D. AND DOLAN, K. *Database Processing, Third Edition*, Chicago: Science Research Associates, 1988.

KROENKE, D. "Developing Object-Oriented Database Applications on Microcomputers." *Proceedings of the Second International Conference on Computers and Applications*, Beijing, June 1987.

KULL, D. "Anatomy of a 4GL Disaster." *Computer Decisions*, February 11, 1986.

KUNTZ, M. AND MELCHERT, R. "Pasta-3's Graphical Query Language: Direct Manipulation, Cooperative Queries, Full Expressive Power." In VLDB 1989.

LAMPSON, BUTLER AND LOMET, DAVID. "A New Presumed Commit Optimization for Two Phase Commit." In VLDB 1993.

LARSON, P. "Dynamic Hashing." *BIT*, 18, 1978.

LARSON, P. "Analysis of Index-Sequential Files with Overflow Chaining." TODS, 6:4, December 1981.

LÉCLUSE, C., RICHAR, P., AND VELEZ, F. "O_2, An Object-Oriented Data Model." *ACM International Conference on the Management of Data*. Chicago, IL, 1988.

LÉCLUSE, C. AND RICHARD, P. "The O_2 Database Programming Language." In VLDB 1989.

LEDERER, A., AND SETHIK, V. "Pitfalls in Planning." *Datamation*, June 1, 1989.

LEE, S.K. "An Extended Relational Database Model for Uncertain and Imprecise Information." In VLDB 1992.

LEFKOVITZ, H. C. *Proposed American National Standards Information Resource Dictionary System*, QED Information Sciences, 1985.

LEISS, E. *Principles of Data Security*, New York: Plenum Press, 1982.

LENZERINI, M. AND SANTUCCI, C. "Cardinality Constraints in the Entity Relationship Model." In ER 1983.

LIEN, E. AND WEINGERGER, P. "Consistency, Concurrency, and Crash Recovery." In SIGMOD 1978.

LITWIN, P. "Faking Multi-Table Forms." *Data Based Advisor*, October 1989.

LITWIN, W. "Virtual Hashing: A Dynamically Changing Hashing." In VLDB 1978.

LITWIN, W. "Linear Hashing: A New Tool for File and Table Addressing." In VLDB 1980.

LIU, K. AND SUNDERRAMAN, R. "On Representing Indefinite and Maybe Information in Relational Databases." In DE 1988.

LIVADAS, P. *File Structures: Theory and Practice*, Englewood Cliffs, NJ: Prentice Hall, 1989.

LOCKEMANN, P. AND KNUTSEN, W. "Recovery of Disk Contents after System Failure." CACM, 11:8, August 1968.

LOMET, DAVID B. "Key Range Locking Strategies for Improved Concurrency." In VLDB 1993.

LOZINSKII, E. "A Problem-Oriented Inferential Database System." TODS, 11:3, September 1986.

LYON, L. "CASE and the Database." *Database Programming and Design*, May 1989.

MAIER, D., STEIN, J., OTIS, A., AND PURDY, A. "Development of an Object-Oriented DBMS." OOPSLA, 1986.

MAIER, D. AND STEIN, J. "Development and Implementation of an Object-Oriented

DBMS". In B. Shriver and P. Wegner, eds. *Research Directions in Object-Oriented Programming*, 355-392. Cambridge, MA: MIT Press, 1987.

MAIER, D. *The Theory of Relational Databases*, Rockville, MD: Computer Science Press, 1983.

MANOLA, F. AND DAYAL, U. "PDM: An Object-Orieinted Data Model." *International Workshop on Object-Orieinted Database Systems*. Pacific Grove, CA, 1986.

MARKOWITZ, V. AND RAZ, Y. "ERROL: An Entity-Relationship, Role Oriented, Query Language." In ER 1983.

MARTIN, E., DeHAYES, D., HOFFER, J., AND PERKINS, W. *Managing Information Technology: What Managers Need to Know*, New York: Macmillan, 1991.

MARTIN, J. *Computer Data Base Organization. 2nd ed.*, Englewood Cliffs, NJ: Prentice Hall, 1977.

MARTIN, J. *An End-User's Guide to Data Base*, Englewood Cliffs, NJ: Prentice Hall, 1981.

MARTIN, J. *Strategic Data Planning Methodologies*, Englewood Cliffs, NJ: Prentice Hall, 1982.

MARTIN, J. *Managing the Data-Base Environment*, Englewood Cliffs, NJ: Prentice Hall, 1983.

MCFADDEN, F. AND HOFFER, J. *Database Management, Third Edition*, Menlo Park, CA: Benjamin/Cummings, 1991.

MCGEE, W. "The Information Management System IMS/VS, Part I: General Structure and Operation." *IBM Systems Journal*, 16:2, June 1977.

MELTON, J. AND SIMON, A. *Understanding the New SQL: A Complete Guide*, Morgan Kaufmann, 1993.

MEYER, B. *Object-oriented Software Construction*, Englewood Cliffs, NJ: Prentice Hall, 1988.

MICRORIM, INC. *R:BASE for DOS User's Manual*. Redmond, WA: Microrim, 1987.

MILLER, R.J., IOANNIDIS, Y.E., AND RAMAKRISHNAN, R. "The Use of Information Capacity in Schema Integration and Translation." In VLDB 1993.

MISSIKOFF, M. AND WIEDERHOLD, G. "Toward a Unified Approach for Expert and Database Systems." In EDS 1984.

MITSCHANG, B. "Extending the Relational Algebra to Capture Complex Objects." In VLDB 1989.

MOTRO, A. "Using Integrity Constraints to Provide Intensional Answers to Relational Queries." In VLDB 1989.

NAFFAH, N. (editor). *Office Information Systems*, North-Holland, 1982.

NAVATHE, S. AND GADGIL, S. "A Methodology for View Integration in Logical Database Design." In VLDB 1982.

NAVATHE, S. AND KERSCHBERG, L. "Role of Data Dictionaries in Database Design." *Information and Management*, 10:1, January 1986.

NAVATHE, S. AND PILLALAMARRI, M. "Toward Making the ER Approach Object-Oriented." In ER 1988.

NAVATHE, S. AND SCHKOLNICK, M. "View Representation in Logical Database Design." In SIGMOD 1978.

NAVATHE, S., ELMASRI, R., AND LARSON, J. "Integrating User Views in Database Design." *IEEE Computer*, 19:1, January 1986.

NAVATHE, S. "An Intuitive View to Normalize Network-Structured Data." In VLDB 1980.

NG, P. "Further Analysis of the Entity-Relationship Approach to Database Design." TSE, 7:1, January 1981.

NIEVERGELT, J. "Binary Search Trees and File Organization." *Computing Surveys*, 6:3, September 1974.

NIJSSEN, G. (editor). *Modelling in Data Base Management Systems*, North-Holland, 1976.

OHSUGA, S. "Knowledge Based Systems as a New Interactive Computer System of the Next Generation." In *Computer Science and Technologies*, North-Holland, 1982.

OLIVE, A. "On the Design and Implementation of Information Systems from Deductive Conceptual Models." In VLDB, 1989.

OLLE, T. W. *The CODASYL Approach to Data Base Management*, Chichester, England: Wiley, 1980.

OZSOYOGLU, G., OZSOYOGLU, Z., AND MATROS, V. "Extending Relational Algebra and Relational Calculus with Set Valued Attributes and Aggregate Functions." TODS, 12:4, December 1985.

OZSOYOGLU, Z. AND YUAN, L. "A New Normal Form for Nested Relations." TODS, 12:1, March 1987.

PAPADIMITRIOU, C. *The Theory of Database Concurrency Control*, Rockville, MD: Computer Science Press, 1986.

PARENT, C. AND SPACCAPIETRA, S. "An Algebra for a General Entity-Relationship Model." TSE, 11:7, July 1985.

PARKER, D.S., SIMON, E., AND VALDURIEZ, P. "SVP: A Model Capturing Sets, Streams, and Parallelism." In VLDB 1992.

PERCY, T. "My Data, Right or Wrong." *Datamation*, June 1, 1986.

PONCELET, P., TESSEIRE, M., CICCHETTI, R., AND LAKHAL, L. "Towards a Formal Approach for Object Database Design." In VLDB 1993.

POULOVASSILIS, ALEXANDRA AND SMALL, CAROL. "A Domain-theoretic Approach to Integrating Functional and Logic Database Languages." In VLDB 1993.

RAMAKRISHNAN, R., SRIVASTAVA, D., AND SUDARSHAN, S. "CORAL: Control, Relations and Logic." In VLDB 1992.

RAZ, Y. "The Principle of Commitment Ordering, or Guaranteeing Serializability in a Heterogeneous Environment of Multiple Autonomous Resource Managers Using Atomic Commitment." In VLDB 1992.

READ, R.L., FUSSELL, D.S., AND SILBERSCHATZ, A. "A Multi-Resolution Relational Data Model." In VLDB 1992.

REISNER, P. "Use of Psychological Experimentation as an Aid to Development of a Query Language." TSE, 3:3, May 1977.

REISNER, P. "Human Factors Studies of Database Query Language: A Survey and Assessment." *Computing Surveys*, 13:1, March 1981.

RETTIG, M. "Gourmet Guide to the DB2 Catalog." *Data Base Programming and Design*, February 1989.

RICHARDSON, J. "Supporting Lists in a Data Model (A Timely Approach)." In VLDB 1992.

RISCH, T. "Monitoring Database Objects." In VLDB 1989.

ROSENTHAL, A., CHAKRAVARTHY, U.S., BLAUSTEIN, B., AND BLAKELY, J. "Situation Monitoring for Active Databases." In VLDB 1989.

ROTH, M. AND KORTH, H. "The Design of Non-1NF Relational Databases into Nested Normal Form." In SIGMOD 1987.

ROTHNIE, J. ET AL. "Introduction to a System for Distributed Databases (SDD-1)." TODS, 5:1, March 1980.

RUBEL, M. C. "Keeping The Garbage Out." *Data Based Advisor*, April 1989.

RUBEL, M. C. "Entering Data into Screen Forms." *Data Based Advisor*, May 1989.

RUBEL, M. C. "Creating a Report." *Data Based Advisor*, July 1989.

RUDENSTEINER, E.A. "Multiview: A Methodology for Supporting Multiple Views in Object-Oriented Databases." In VLDB 1992.

RUSTIN, R. (editor). *Data Base Systems*, Englewood Cliffs, NJ: Prentice Hall, 1972.

RUSTIN, R. (editor). *Proceedings of the ACM SIGMOD Debate on Data Models: Data Structure Set Versus Relational*, 1974.

SAYLES, J. S. "All in a row." *Data Based Advisor*, December 1989.

SCHAEFFER, H. *Data Center Operations*, Englewood Cliffs, NJ: Prentice Hall, 1981.

SCHEUERMANN, P. (editor). *Improving Database Usability and Responsiveness*, Orlando: Academic Press, 1982.

SCHKOLNICK, M. "A Survey of Physical Database Design Methodology and Techniques." In VLDB 1978.

SCHMIDT, J. AND SWENSON, J. "On the Semantics of the Relational Model." In SIGMOD 1975.

SCHREIER, U., PIRAHESH, H., AGRAWAL, R., AND MOHAN, C. "Alert: An Architecture for Transforming a Passive DBMS into an Active DBMS." In VLDB 1991.

SCHUR, S. G. "Building an Active Distributed Database." *Database Programming and Design*, April 1989.

SEGEV, A. AND ZHAO, J.L. "Data Management for Large Rule Systems." In VLDB 1991.

SHANK, M., BOYNTON, A. AND ZMUD, R. "Critical Success Factor Analysis as a Methodology for IS Planning." *MIS Quarterly*, 9:2, June 1985.

SHETH, A., LARSON, J., CORNELIO, A., AND NAVATHE, S. "A Tool for Integrating Conceptual Schemas and User Views." In DE 1988.

SHIPMAN, D. "The Functional Data Model and the Data Language DAPLEX." TODS, 6:1, March 1981.

SHNEIDERMAN, B. (editor). *Databases: Improving Usability and Responsiveness*, Orlando: Academic Press, 1978.

SHOENS, K., LUNIEWSKI, A., SCHWARZ, P., STAMOS, J., AND THOMAS, J. "The Rufus System: Information Organization for Semi-Structured Data." In VLDB 1993.

SIBLEY, E. "The Development of Database Technology." *Computing Surveys*, 8:1, March 1976.

SIEGEL, M. AND MADNICK, S.E. "A Metadata Approach to Resolving Semantic Conflicts." In VLDB 1991.

SIEGELMANN, H.T. AND BADRINATH, B.R. "Integrating Implicit Answers with Object-Oriented Queries." In VLDB 1991.

SIMON, E., KIERNAN, J., AND DE MAINDREVILLE, C. "Implementing High-Level Active Rules on Top of Relational Databases." In VLDB 1992.

SMITH, J. AND SMITH, D. "Database Abstractions: Aggregation and Generalization." TODS, 2:2, June 1977.

SMITH, P. AND BARNES, G. *Files & Databases: An Introduction*, Reading, MA: Addison-Wesley, 1987.

SMITH, K. AND WINSLETT, M. "Entity Modeling in the MLS Relational Model." In VLDB 1992.

SNODGRASS, R. AND AHN, I. "A Taxonomy of Time in Databases." In SIGMOD 1985.

SPRAGUE, R., AND MCNURLINK, B. *Information Systems in Practice*, Englewood Cliffs, NJ: Prentice Hall, 1986.

SPRAGUE, R. AND WATSON, H. *Decision Support Systems, 2nd Edition*, Englewood Cliffs, NJ: Prentice Hall, 1989.

SRIVASTAVA, DIVESH, RAMAKRISHNAN, RAGHU, SESHADRI, PRAVEEN, AND SUDARSHAN, S. "Coral++: Adding Object-Orientation to a Logic Database Language." In VLDB 1993.

STONEBRAKER, M., WONG, E., KREPS, P. AND HELD, G. "The Design and Implementation of INGRES." TODS, 1:3, September 1976.

STOREY, V. C., AND R. C. GOLDSTEIN. "A Methodology for Creating User Views in Database Design." TODS, 13:3, September 1988.

SU, S.Y.W. AND CHEN, H-H.M. "A Temporal Knowledge Representation Model OSAM*/T and its Query Language OQL/T." In VLDB 1991.

TALENS, G., OUSSALAH, C., AND COLINAS, M.F. "Versions of Simple and Composite Objects." In VLDB 1993.

TAYLOR, R. AND FRANK, R. "CODASYL Data Base Management Systems." *Computing Surveys*, 8:1, March 1976.

TEOREY, T. AND FRY, J. *Design of Database Structures*, Englewood Cliffs, NJ: Prentice Hall, 1982.

TEORY, T., YANG, D., AND FRY, J. "A Logical Design Methodology for Relational Databases Using the Extended Entity-Relationship Model." *Computing Surveys*, 18:2, June 1986.

THOMAS, J. AND GOULD, J. "A Psychological Study of Query By Example." NCC, AFIPS, 44, 1975.

THOMAS, J. AND DEBLOCH S. "A Plan-Operator Concept for Client-Based Knowledge Processing." In VLDB 1993.

TODD, S. "The Peterlee Relational Test Vehicle—A System Overview." *IBM Systems Journal*, 15:4, December 1976.

TSICHRITZIS, D. AND KLUG, A. (editors). *The ANSI/X3/SPARC DBMS Framework*, AFIPS Press, 1978.

TSICHRITZIS, D., AND LOCHOVSKY, F. "Hierarchical Data-base Management: A Survey." *Computing Surveys*, 8:1, March 1976.

TSICHRITZIS, D., AND LOCHOVSKY, F. *Data Base Management Systems*. New York: Academic Press, 1977.

TSICHRITZIS, D. AND LOCHOVSKY, F. *Data Models*, Englewood Cliffs: Prentice Hall, 1982.

TSICHRITZIS, D. "Forms Mangement." CACM, 25:7, July 1982.

UHROWCZIK, P. "Data Dictionary/Directories." *IBM Systems Journal*, 12:4, December 1973.

ULLMAN, J. *Principles of Database Systems, Second Edition*, Rockville, MD: Computer Science Press, 1982.

ULLMAN, J. *Principles of Database and Knowledge-Base Systems*, Rockville, MD: Computer Science Press, 1990.

UMBAUGH, R., (editor). *The Handbook of MIS Management*, Auerbach, 1985.

VALDURIEZ, P. AND GARDARIN, G. *Analysis and Comparison of Relational Database Systems*, Reading, MA: Addison-Wesley, 1989.

VETTER, M., AND MADDISON, R.N. *Database Design Methodology*, Englewood Cliffs, NJ: Prentice Hall, 1981.

VETTER, M. *Strategy for Data Modeling*, Wiley, 1987.

WELDON, J. *Data Base Administration*, New York: Plenum Press, 1981.

WELTY, C., AND STEMPLE, D. "Human Factors Comparison of a Procedural and a Nonprocedural Query Language." TODS, 6:4, December 1981.

WERTZ, C. *The Data Dictionary: Concepts and Uses*, QED Information Sciences, 1986.

WHITTEN, J., BENTLEY, L., AND HO, T. *Systems Analysis and Design Methods*, St. Louis: Times Mirror/Mosby, 1986.

WIEDERHOLD, G. *Database Design*, Second Edition, New York: McGraw-Hill, 1983.

WIEDERHOLD, G. "Knowledge and Database Management." *IEEE Software*, 8:1, January 1984.

WIEDERHOLD, G. "Views, Objects, and Databases." *Computer*, 19:12, December 1986.

WITKOWSKI, ANDREW, CARIÑO, FELIPE, AND KOSTAMAA, PEKKA. "NCR 3700 - The Next-Generation Industrial Database Computer." In VLDB 1993.

WYLIE, C. *101 Puzzles in Thought and Logic*, Mineola, NY: Dover Publications, Inc., 1957.

WINKLER-PARENTZ, H. B. "Can You Trust Your DBMS?" *Database Programming and Design*, July 1989.

WIORKOWSKI, G., AND D. KULL. "Distributed DB2." *Database Programming and Design*, April 1989.

WOOD, D. "A Primer of Features and Performance Issues of Relational DBMSs." *Data Resource Management*, 1:1, Winter 1990.

YAO, S. (editor). *Principles of Database Design, Volume 1: Logical Organizations*, Englewood Cliffs, NJ: Prentice Hall, 1985.

YOURDON, E., & CONSTANTINE, L. *Structured Design*, Englewood Cliffs, NJ: Prentice Hall, 1979.

ZANIOLO, C. ET AL. "Object-Oriented Database Systems and Knowledge Systems." In EDS 1984.

ZLOOF, M. "Query By Example." NCC, AFIPS, 44, 1975.

ZLOOF, M. M. "Query-by-Example: A Data Base Language." *IBM Systems Journal*, 16:4, 1977.

INDEX

C